CW00543012

Lucien Musset

The Bayeux Tapestry

New edition

Translated by Richard Rex

The Boydell Press

First published in 2002 as
La Tapisserie de Bayeux
Éditions Zodiaque, Paris

English translation 2005
The Boydell Press, Woodbridge

ISBN 1 84383 163 5

The Boydell Press is an imprint of Boydell & Brewer Ltd
PO Box 9, Woodbridge, Suffolk IP12 3DF, UK
and of Boydell & Brewer Inc.
668 Mt Hope Avenue, Rochester, NY 14620, USA
web site: www.boydellandbrewer.com

This publication is printed on acid-free paper
English edition designed by Tina Ranft
Printed in China by Compass Press

Contents

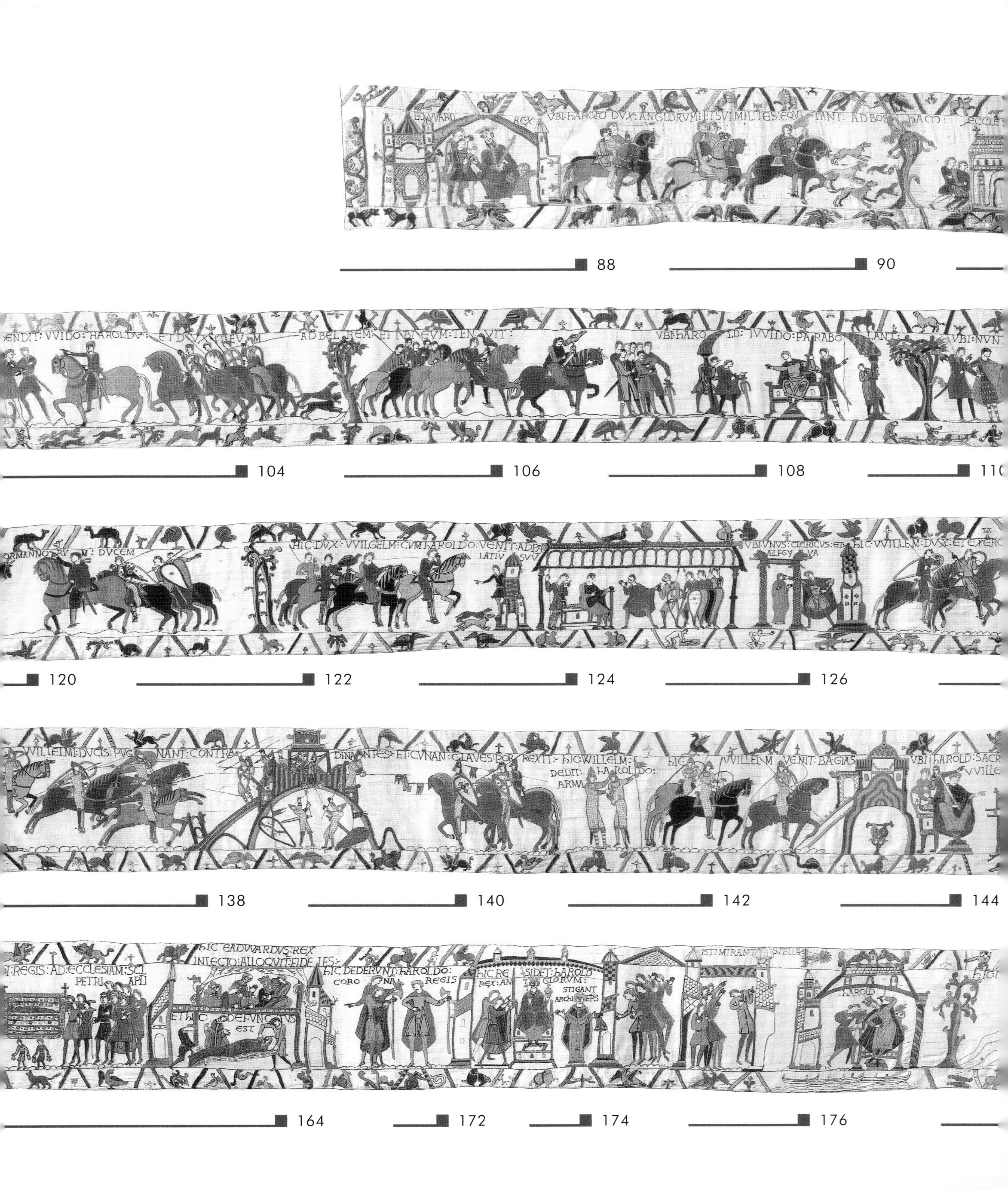

EDWARD REX
UBI HAROLD DUX ANGLORUM ET SUI MILITES EQUITANT AD BOSHAM
88
90
ADDUXIT EUM AD BELREM ET IBI EUM TENUIT
UBI HAROLD ET UUIDO PARABOLANT
104
106
108
HIC DUX UUILGELM CUM HAROLDO VENIT AD PALATIU SUU
UBI UNUS CLERICUS ET ÆLFGYVA
120
122
124
126
NANT CONTRA DINANTES ET CUNAN CLAVES PORREXIT
HIC WILLELM DEDIT HAROLDO ARMA
HIC WILLELM VENIT BAGIAS
138
140
142
144
PETRI APLI
HIC EADWARDUS REX IN LECTO ALLOQUIT FIDELES
ET HIC DEFUNCTUS EST
HIC DEDERUNT HAROLDO CORONA REGIS
HIC RESIDET HAROLD REX ANGLORUM
STIGANT ARCHIEPS
ISTI MIRANT STELLA
HAROLD
164
172
174
176

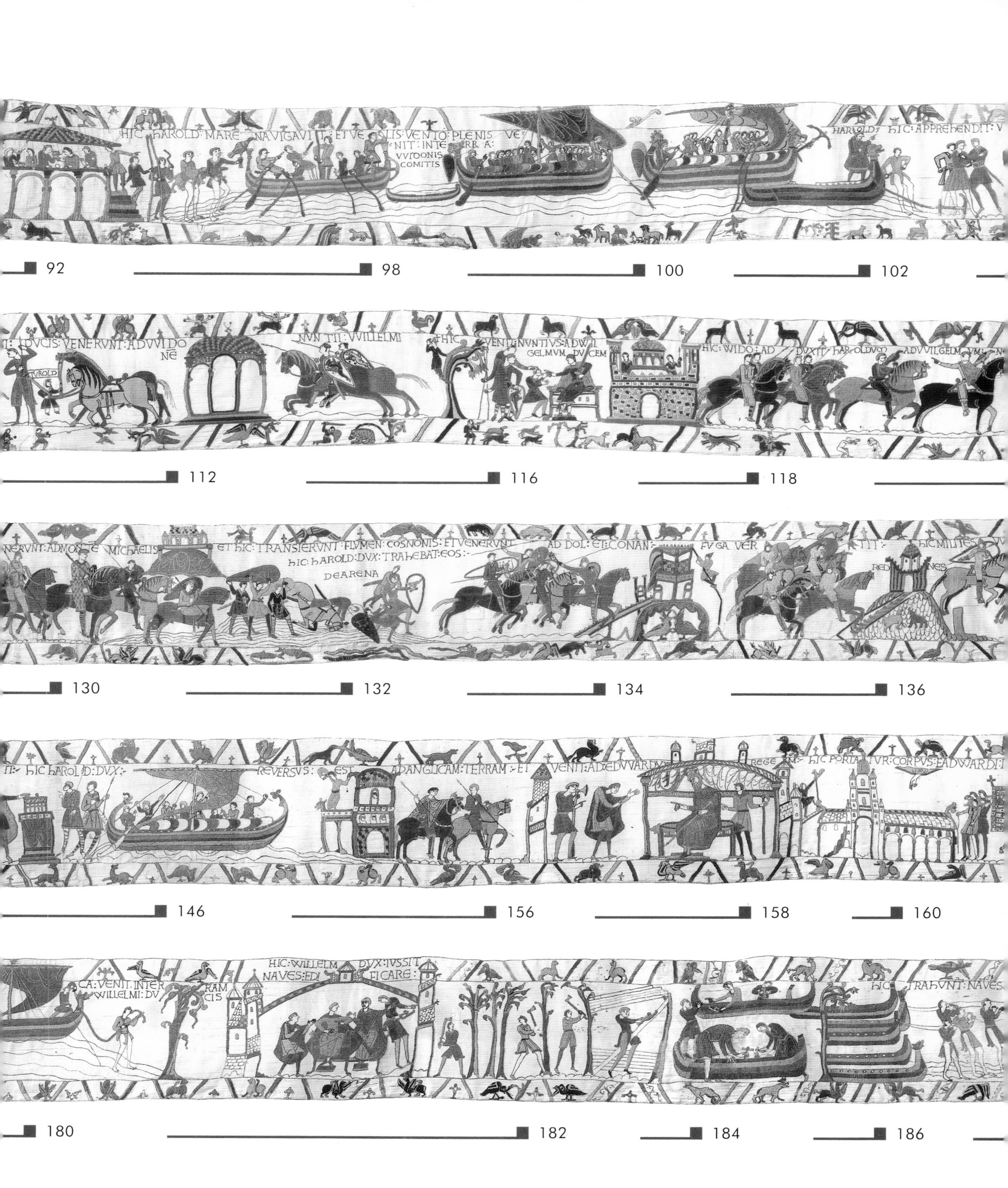
HIC HAROLD: MARE NAVIGAVIT: ET VE LIS VENTO PLENIS VE NIT: INTE RRA: VVIDONIS COMITIS
HAROLD: HIC: APPREHENDIT: V
92
98
100
102
II: DUCIS: VENERUNT: AD VVIDO NE
TUROLD
NUNTII: VVILLELMI
HIC VENIT NUNTIUS AD VVIL GELMUM DUCEM
HIC: WIDO: AD DUXIT: HAROLDUM AD VVILGELMUM: N
112
116
118
NERUNT: AD MONTE MICHAELIS
ET HIC: TRANSIERUNT: FLUMEN: COSNONIS: ET VENERUNT AD DOL: ET: CONAN: FUGA VER TIT:
HIC: HAROLD: DUX: TRAHEBAT: EOS: DE ARENA
HIC MILITES: VV
RED NES
130
132
134
136
IT: HIC HAROLD: DUX: REVERSUS: EST AD ANGLICAM: TERRAM: ET VENIT: AD: EDVVARDU REGEM: HIC PORTATUR: CORPUS: EADWARDI: I
146
156
158
160
CA: VENIT: INTER RAM CIS WILLELMI: DU
HIC: WILLELM DUX: IUSSIT NAVES: EDI FICARE:
HIC TRAHUNT: NAVES
180
182
184
186

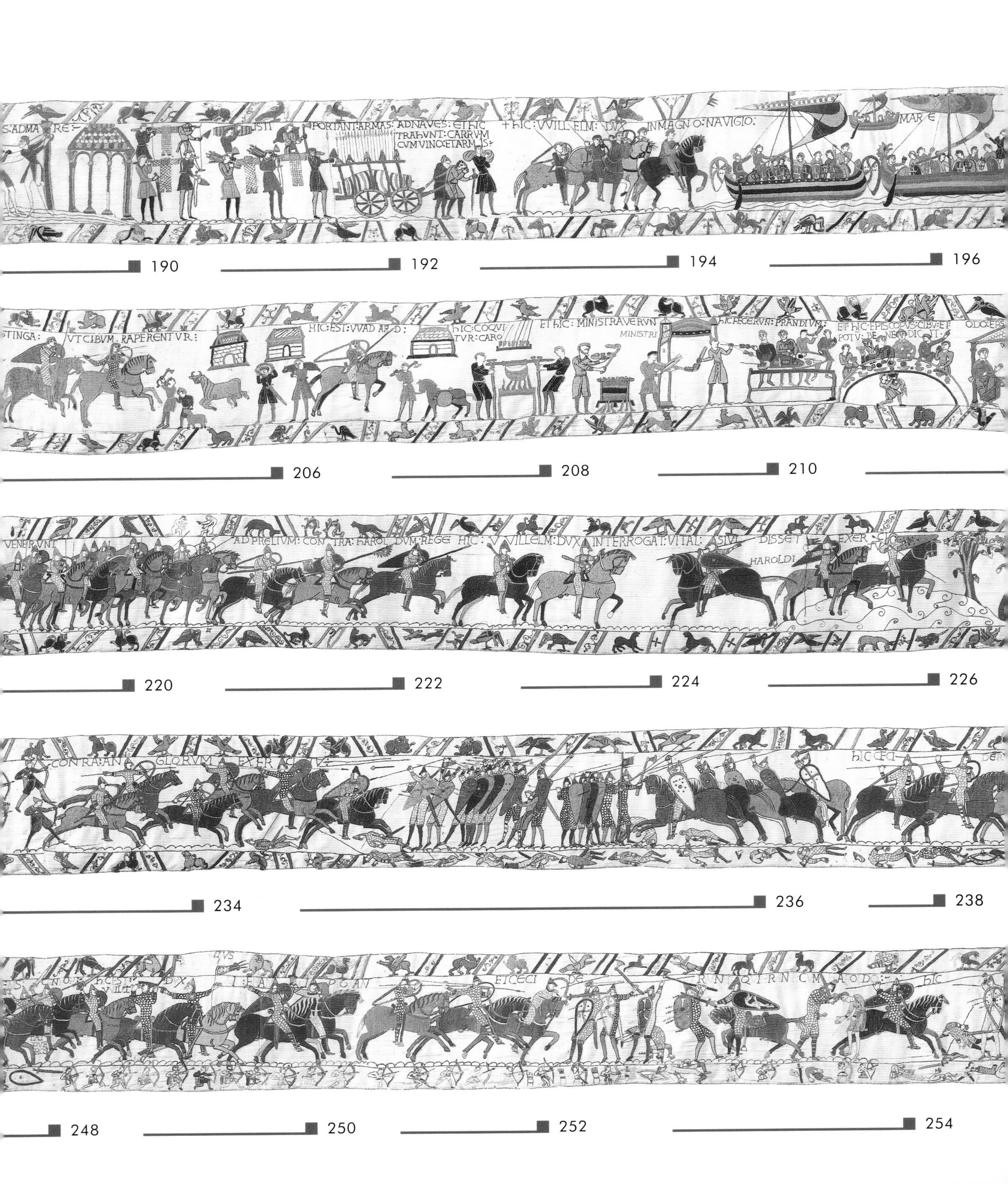
PORTANT:ARMAS: AD NAVES: ET HIC
TRAHVNT: CARRVM
CVM VINO: ET ARMIS:
+ HIC: VVILL ELM: DVX IN MAGNO: NAVIGIO:
MARE
190
192
194
196
VT CIBVM RAPERENTVR:
HIC: EST: VVADARD:
HIC: COQVITVR: CARO
ET HIC: MINISTRAVERVNT
MINISTRI
HIC FECERVNT: PRANDIVM:
ET HIC: EPISCOPVS: CIBV ET POTV BENEDICIT
ODO: EPS
206
208
210
VENERVNT
AD PRELIVM: CONTRA: HAROLDVM: REGE
HIC: VVILLELM: DVX INTERROGAT: VITAL: A
HAROLDI
220
222
224
226
CONTRA: ANGLORVM EXERCITVM:
HIC CECI
DER
234
236
238
248
250
252
254

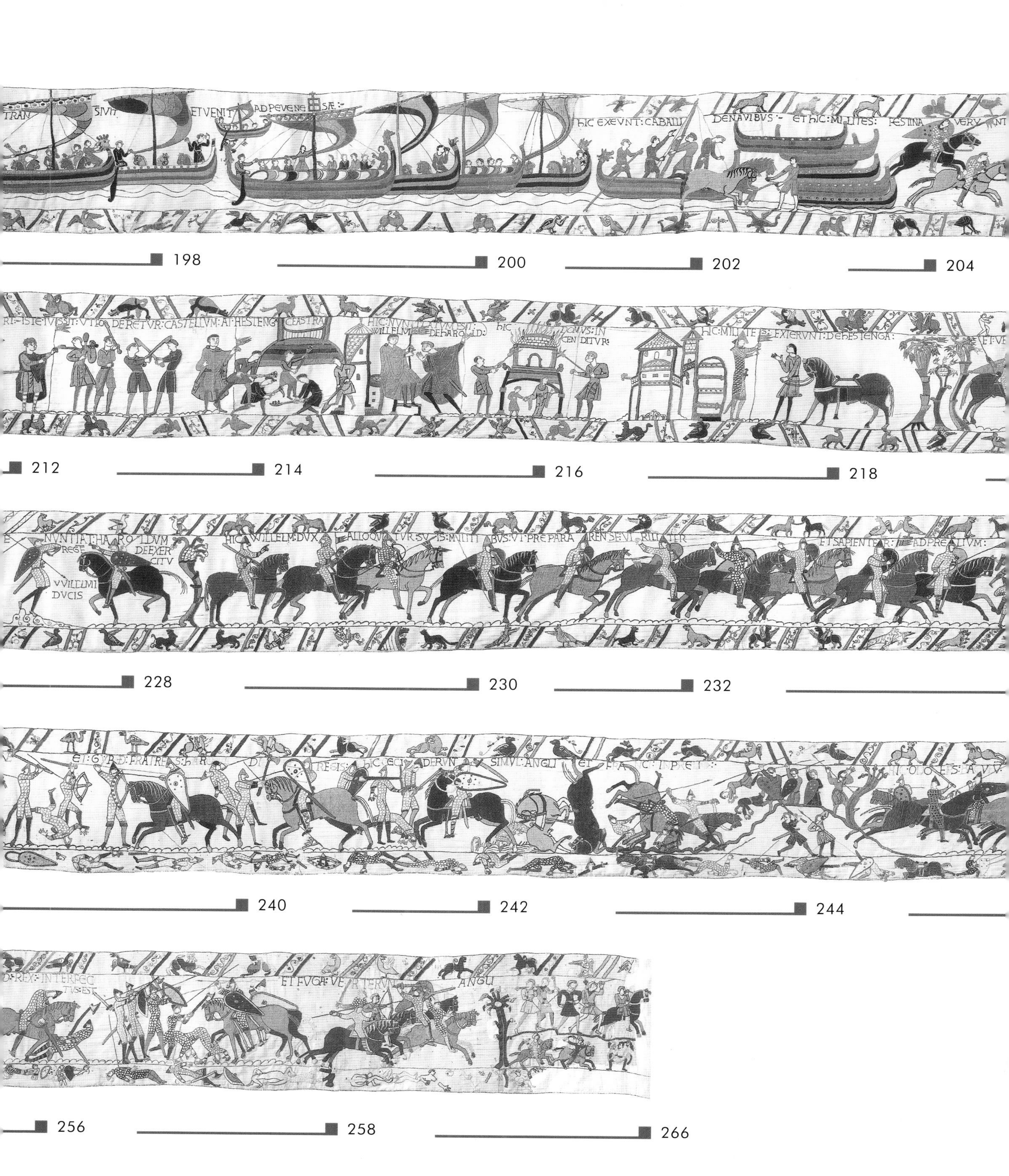

HIC EXEUNT: CABALLI DE NAVIBUS: ET HIC: MILITES: FESTINA
198
200
202
204
CASTELLUM
CEASTRA
HIC: MILITES: EXIERUNT: DE HESTENGA:
212
214
216
218
NUNTIAT: HAROLDUM
REGE
DE EXERCITU
VVILLELMI DUCIS
HIC WILLELM DUX
ET SAPIENTER
228
230
232
SIMUL: ANGLI ET FRANCI: IN PRELIO:
240
242
244
ET FUGA: VERTERUNT ANGLI
256
258
266

PREFACE.

The Bayeux Tapestry is one of the supreme achievements of the Norman Romanesque, the extraordinarily delicate product of the simplest of artistic techniques — an embroidery of woollen thread on linen backing. Its survival almost intact over nine centuries is little short of miraculous, given how many great stone buildings have been reduced to ruins in that time. Removed from Bayeux Cathedral in the 1790s, amidst the turmoil of the French Revolution, it was subsequently entrusted by Napoleon Bonaparte to the care of the citizens of Bayeux, where today it is displayed at the Centre Guillaume-le-Conquérant in a U-shaped gallery purpose-built to show it at its best. People of all ages and nationalities come each year in their hundreds of thousands to view it. No one leaves disappointed. Its exceptional length, the harmony and freshness of its colours, its exquisite workmanship, and the genius of its guiding spirit combine to make it endlessly fascinating.

This anonymous and undated artefact bears unique testimony to the intertwined history of eleventh-century England and Normandy, and has therefore held the attention of historians (and even at times of politicians) ever since it was rediscovered in the eighteenth century, giving rise to over 600 learned books and articles. It is endlessly informative, not only relating the events of the years 1064-66 which brought Duke William of Normandy to the English throne, but also affording us unparalleled insights into the everyday realities of life at that time. If, as I believe, it is impossible for us today to approach the Tapestry in exactly the same spirit as the contemporaries of those who commissioned and created it, we can nevertheless strive to enter into that spirit and bring it nearer to us through a close and careful scrutiny of its details. Professor Lucien Musset's learned and elegant study gives us the keys to unlock its secrets.

SYLVETTE LEMAGNEN
Conservator of the Bayeux Tapestry
March 2002

FOREWORD.

This book does not pretend to revolutionise the study of the Bayeux Tapestry. Unlike many recent books on the subject, whose wilder speculations tend to cancel each other out, it seeks merely to take stock of the more reliable findings of the last half century or so of scholarship. Many questions still remain open and cannot be given any definitive answer here. But from time to time I do emphasise some relatively new angles: the Tapestry's location in the cultural milieu of eleventh-century north-western Europe, and in particular its links with the Scandinavian world; its artistic significance, and the literary characteristics of its captions; its historical importance as a source which is independent of the chronicle tradition; and its tactful handling of such matters as were liable to divide the Normans and the English.

Nor does this account aspire to be comprehensive. It avoids issues of a narrowly technical nature and mostly refrains from advancing theories which cannot command some degree of consensus among specialists. Rather, it is intended as an introduction to the interpretation of a unique and almost unfathomably rewarding cultural artefact. If, as such, it can be of some value to its readers, be they professional historians or just interested amateurs, it will have served its purpose.

Long and close familiarity with the Tapestry, reaching back more than half a century, is my starting-point. In 1955 I had the particular privilege of being allowed to inspect it outside its case and under helpful lighting. Then, in 1984, I was fortunate enough to be able to examine its reverse side when it was being transferred to a new display case. Over the years, the curators have been unfailingly generous with their assistance. This seems the most appropriate place for me to put on record my gratitude to them and also to the municipal authorities of the Ville de Bayeux. But my greatest debts are to all my scholarly predecessors who, since the start of the eighteenth century, have grappled with and sought to solve the problems posed by this fascinating work of art.

The first part of the book analyses the Tapestry as a whole under a series of thematic headings. The second part is a step-by-step examination of the Tapestry which picks out a host of further details. I have taken the opportunity afforded by the preparation of this second edition to correct various errors that came to light in the earlier edition of 1989 and also to take account as far as possible of work published since then.

LUCIEN MUSSET

Emeritus Professor at the University of Caen

March 2002

Part One General Issues

I

A SHORT HISTORY OF THE TAPESTRY

ACCORDING TO A MYTH conjured out of thin air in the eighteenth century and popularised in the Romantic era, the Bayeux Tapestry was the work of Matilda, William the Conqueror's queen. But there is neither external nor internal evidence for this utterly gratuitous attribution. There should therefore be no more talk of 'Queen Matilda's Tapestry'.[1]

In fact, the documentary history of the Tapestry is strangely sketchy and disappointing. Its first appearance in the historical record is as late as 1476, when it is listed in an inventory of the treasury of Bayeux Cathedral, amongst a motley collection of altar cloths, liturgical vestments, banners, curtains, and the like:

> Item, a very long and narrow hanging, embroidered with images and writing depicting the conquest of England, which is hung around the nave of the church on the day and through the octaves of the relics.

The identification of this item with the Tapestry seems clear enough. It apparently escaped the iconoclastic attentions of the Huguenots during the sack of Bayeux in 1562, although they played havoc with other memorabilia of the Conqueror that were kept in the cathedral. And the custom persisted of hanging the Tapestry 'in the nave from St John's day [24 June, the feast of the Nativity of St John the Baptist] to the eve of the dedication day' — the words are those of an eighteenth-century canon of the cathedral.[2] It was not until the early years of the eighteenth century, when its existence was noted by the Intendant of Caen, N. J. Foucault, that the Tapestry would emerge from this long historical silence. It then came to the attention of Antoine Lancelot, who in 1724 submitted a preliminary report on it to the Academy of Inscriptions and Literature, though without having been able to ascertain precisely where or what it was. It was first properly identified and fully described by the great Benedictine scholar Dom Bernard du Montfaucon in 1729-30, in the first two volumes of his *Les Monuments de la Monarchie française*.[2a] The Tapestry soon became famous, and various drawings were made which show us exactly how it looked at that time. Soon the English began to take an interest, most notably Andrew Coltee Ducarel in 1752 and Charles Stothard in 1818-20. It is hardly worth tracing the subsequent evolution of the Tapestry's ever increasing celebrity.

Three episodes from its recent history, however, deserve some attention. Confiscated as public property in 1792, the Tapestry was to have been used to cover military wagons and would thus have perished, but for the intervention of a Bayeux lawyer, Léonard Leforestier. Saved from the vicissitudes of the French Revolution, the Tapestry was briefly removed to Paris to be displayed in the Louvre early in 1804, for obvious propaganda reasons in the context of Napoleon's projected invasion of England. After that it was 'entrusted to the inhabitants of the town of Bayeux', who made it available for scholarly study, initially on a contraption with a couple of spindles that could only just accommodate it. Preserved in the Municipal Library of Bayeux (which classified it, oddly enough, as a manuscript), it was relocated in 1913 along with that library in what had been the lodgings of the Dean of the Cathedral Chapter, facing the cathedral. During the Second World War it survived some extraordinary dangers and misadventures, and was briefly evacuated to the Louvre, where it was studied by German scholars (notably Professor Herbert Jankuhn, a specialist in the Viking era[3]). Since February 1983 it has been on display in satisfactorily secure conditions (questionable though they are from the point of view of understanding the work as a whole) in the seventeenth-century Old Seminary, itself now a part of the library.

An obvious starting-point for this exploration of the Tapestry is to ask how far we can regard it, in its present state, as authentic. Fortunately, numerous analyses, especially those conducted during its relocation in 1984, allow us to dispel any doubts. Of course, it has more than once been subject to restoration — not always sensitively executed — above all at the beginning of the nineteenth century. But the areas seriously affected are reasonably limited: the first scene; a few minor tears in the upper borders (one of them involving the almost complete loss of a name in the captions of scene 55, p. 251); and worst of all practically the whole of the final scene (scene 58, pp. 266–267), whose caption is a blatant forgery, perpetrated shortly before 1814 and motivated by the anti-English feeling then so prevalent. In fact, Montfaucon had already noted in the eighteenth century that this section was 'so damaged that practically nothing can be made out; the writing is completely erased; but in the less damaged places you can see the French following up their victory, and slaughtering any English they find'.

There is, however, no documentary evidence as to the origins of the Tapestry or the conditions under which it was manufactured. Only the internal evidence furnished by the Tapestry itself can shed light on these matters, with an inevitable (if gradually diminishing) degree of uncertainty. That said, there is now a good degree of consensus on several points.

For a start, specialists now mostly agree that the Tapestry is a product of the eleventh century, manufactured relatively soon after the Norman Conquest. The technical details of the shipping and weaponry, not to mention the artistic style, are simply too authentic to have been subsequent fabrications.[4] They do not belong to the twelfth century, as is still occasionally suggested. There is not even a hint of anachronism, especially not if the Tapestry is viewed in that North-West European context to which both Anglo-Saxon England and ducal Normandy belonged. Although some scholars have suggested that the story it tells is dependent on various chronicles written after 1077, their arguments are unconvincing. For the Tapestry itself represents, as we shall see, an entirely independent historical tradition about the Conquest.

The second point on which almost everyone agrees is that the Tapestry has an intrinsic connection with Bayeux itself, the only place in Normandy (apart from Mont-Saint-Michel) mentioned on it by name. Bishop Odo of Bayeux (1049-97), William the Conqueror's half-brother, also has a special place on it: he is twice mentioned by name and indubitably appears at two other points.[5] Moreover, the key scene of the whole story, Harold's oath to William, takes place, according to the captions, at Bayeux. We know that the cathedral there was being rebuilt at some point after 1049, and that its solemn dedication was celebrated on 14 July 1077 in the presence of Archbishop Lanfranc of Canterbury, King William and Queen Matilda, and a host of prelates and barons.[6] This would have been the perfect moment to present the Tapestry to the cathedral. This theory has been mooted often enough, and remains highly plausible even though there is documentary evidence only for the grants of land made on that occasion. In any case, given the connection between Odo and the Tapestry — for which, as we shall see, there is much circumstantial evidence, notably the identification of the otherwise insignificant individuals labelled Vital and Wadard — it could hardly have been commissioned after 1082. For in that year Odo fell out of favour with his brother and was imprisoned, losing all his lands and authority in Kent, a county to which numerous aspects of the commentary will turn our attention. Thus everything tends to confirm the conclusion reached by most recent authorities, namely that the Tapestry was produced around 1077, or at least before 1082, during the lifetimes of King William (d. 1087) and Bishop Odo (d. 1097).

That leaves the delicate questions of where and why it was created. There are no good reasons to doubt that the Tapestry was made in England — although not everyone is convinced. Saving the details for later, it is enough for now to note that there are some decisive arguments: the characteristically Anglo-Saxon spellings of certain names; the dispassionate attitude of the captions towards the defeated Harold, whose royal status is never disputed; the general tone, which is far from hostile to the English; the many stylistic parallels with illuminations in eleventh-century English manuscripts (especially those of Canterbury); and finally the high reputation of Kentish workshops in the field of embroidery.

The true purpose of the Tapestry has long been understood,[7] and is crucially bound up with the fact that, as attested in the fifteenth century, it was hung each year in the nave of the cathedral 'on the day and through the octaves of the relics', in other words, according to the liturgical calendar of Bayeux, during the second week in July, which included the anniversary of the dedication of the church. For upon closer examination it is clear that the central theme of the narrative is not the conquest of England, as fifteenth-century viewers imagined, but the oath taken in 1064 by Harold at Bayeux on the relics contained in two caskets — an oath whose causes and circumstances are explained in detail (even though its terms and conditions are left in obscurity) and whose eventual consequence was catastrophic defeat for the perjured Harold and his people at Hastings.

If the Tapestry had been entirely secular in character and purpose, there would have been no particular reason for it to start in 1064 rather than, say, 1042 (the accession of Edward the Confessor) or at least 1051, when William of Normandy began to take a serious interest in the English succession. Nor would more than a third of its length have been devoted to a preliminary storyline which does little to explain the political and military course of the Norman Conquest. Moreover, the ending of the story seems unduly abrupt except on the assumption that the death of the perjurer constitutes in itself a satisfactory conclusion. The divine chastisement which terminates an almost sacrilegious reign is an object lesson in the power of relics.

The Tapestry was thus perfectly suited to the context in which it was formerly displayed. Its purpose was to make the faithful reflect on the sanctity of oaths sworn in the presence of relics and on the risks incurred by those who breached them.

II

The Tapestry in Artistic Context

The Bayeux Tapestry is not, in the strict sense of the term, a tapestry at all, for it is not woven but embroidered. It is worth briefly considering its physical aspects even though a detailed technical examination is not one of the concerns of this book.[8]

The embroidery is stitched on a strip of greyish linen averaging about fifty centimetres in width, and composed of nine sections of uneven length, ranging from 6.60m to 13.75m for those that survive whole. The seams between the sections are skilfully sewn and exceedingly hard to make out. Nevertheless, it looks as though they were joined together after the embroidery had been done. The whole strip is in its turn sewn in an altogether cruder fashion onto a linen backing that was added in 1724. In the late eighteenth or early nineteenth century, large ink numerals were written on the linen backing, providing a reference-system for the Tapestry which is widely used (and followed in this book) even though its divisions are arbitrary and distinctly unequal. The last two numbers (57 and 58) were added still later.

The embroidery is done in woollen thread of eight different colours. The original dyes were of the highest quality and have not undergone any significant deterioration through the lengthy exposure to daylight resulting from the conditions in which the Tapestry was traditionally displayed. We shall not seek to identify them, although they must have been of vegetable extraction. The colours used are: red, two shades of yellow, two of green, and three of blue (one of them almost black). They are not always absolutely consistent in tone.

The embroidery uses two kinds of stitch: 'stem stitch' for the outlines; and laid or couched stitch to fill them in. (The so-called 'chain stitch' appears only in modern restoration work.) The captions are done in stem stitch, except where they have been restored — this task having been in general a matter of restoring lost threads between the fairly obvious needle-holes left by the original seamstresses. Similar repairs have been done on some of the features in the final section, such as the arrow which strikes a soldier in the eye in the scene which shows Harold's death. This is all quite clear on examination of the back of the embroidered strip (in contrast, the eventual repairs done in couched stitch are scarcely visible).

The Tapestry is now about 64.38m long, but has obviously lost at least a little material at the beginning, and rather more at the end. As it stands, the final section is a mere 5.25m — about 1.40m less than the next shortest section, and far less than the first two sections, which are both over 13m. A reasonable estimate might be that the wear and tear of centuries have eroded some 1.50m, which is consistent with what might be deduced about the story as it survives in its truncated state.

There is no discernible evidence today that any preliminary drawings were traced onto the cloth or that marks were made indicating which colours were to be used. But while the choice of colour could have been left to the discretion of the needlewomen (for there seems to be no intrinsic significance in the colours), it is hard to believe that there was no outline, or at least that there was nothing like the 'cartoons' used by tapestry weavers or the patterns used by modern embroiderers. Whatever they may in fact have been, in what follows they will be referred to for convenience as 'patterns'. Their general stylistic unity is apparent. Yet while many different hands must have been at work along the Tapestry, we cannot at present tell one from another.

The Tapestry is divided for most of its length into three horizontal zones, with a central zone some 33cm high carrying the historical narrative between the upper and lower borders, each about 7cm high. Except in a few minor episodes (e.g. scenes 7, pp. 104–105; 10, p. 112; 11, p. 116; 20, pp. 141–142; etc), the story unfolds continuously from left to right. As we shall see, the most important scenes (the Channel crossing and the final phase of the Battle of Hastings) sometimes encroach onto one or other of the borders.

Although the Tapestry seems today disconcertingly bereft of any artistic or cultural context, this is not in fact the case. However, the search for that context takes us far away from eleventh-century England and France, neither of which can offer anything remotely comparable to the Tapestry. The search leads us to the Scandinavian world, c. 800-1200 AD.

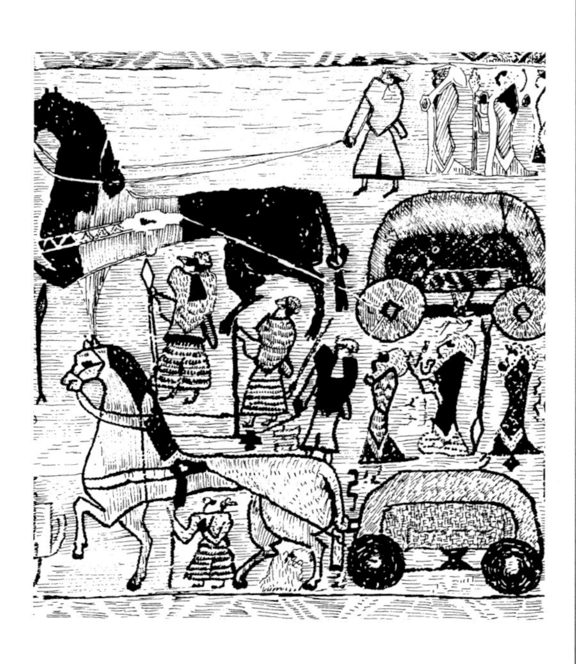

1. Fragment of the ninth-century Oseberg Tapestry from Norway, after Bjørn Hougen.

The trail starts in the mid-ninth century, with the fragmentary strips of narrative textile found in 1904 among the grave goods of what was probably a royal ship burial at Oseberg, south-west of Oslo (fig. 1). These tapestry fragments, woven in coloured wool which is today almost completely faded, are conserved in the Bygdøya Museum. Though rather small (between 16cm and 23cm high), they were presumably meant as wall-hangings. To the casual observer they offer little more than a blur of brown and grey, but their overall design has been reconstructed by Mary Storm. The pictures have no captions — at that time Scandinavian culture was not literate — and probably depict ritual or mythological scenes. Horsemen and horse-drawn carts with solid wheels march from right to left between narrow borders bearing geometrical motifs. The overall effect, though rather more crowded, is not markedly different from that of the Bayeux Tapestry, though here the empty spaces are filled with extra little patterns, mostly geometrical. The human figures are crudely executed: while they are differentiated by costume, their individual features are indistinguishable and they are almost all shown in profile. The meaning of this work eludes us, but the possibility that it is a historical narrative cannot be ruled out.

A closer relative to the Tapestry is another Norwegian fabric fragment, from around the year 900, found in 1876 in the tomb of Haugen at Rolsvøy. A mixture of woollen thread (still extant) and linen thread (now lost), it shows five men and two women on a shore with a ship alongside (fig. 2). In 1910, three strips of tapestry from around the year 1100 were found in the church of Överhogdal, in Härjedal in Sweden, and entrusted to the museum at Östersund. The first two may illustrate episodes from a mythological cycle, the *Völsungasaga*. The drawing is very crude: people, horses, and ships move from left to right between the familiar geometrical borders (fig. 3). Some thirteenth-century fragments, too damaged to be made out, were found at the church of Røn in Norway. And Trondheim Museum houses a late twelfth-century tapestry from Høylandet (in Mandal, Norway) with a distinctly Christian subject: the Adoration of the Magi, done in blue and white on a red background.[9] Finally, a tapestry from the first half of the thirteenth century, found at Baldishol in Hedmark and now preserved in Oslo's Museum of Applied Arts, shows images of April and May in front of an arcade (fig. 4). Once, no doubt, part of a cycle depicting the months of the year, it bespeaks an entirely different aesthetic: 1.18m high and executed in the international style, its format has nothing in common with the earlier narrative textiles.

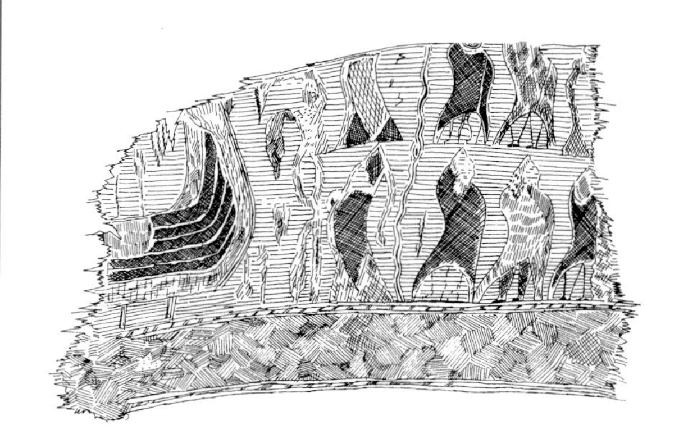

2. The Rolvsøy Tapestry (Norway, tenth century), after Sofie Krafft.

In Sweden, an illuminating comparison can be made with the Skog Tapestry from Hälsingland, discovered in 1912 and dating from about 1050-1150.[10] On the left stand some buildings (including a two-storey church) and three large crowned figures generally identified with the three gods worshipped at Uppsala; on the right gallop some badly drawn horses. The subject is generally thought to be linked to the Christian missionaries who converted the Swedes around 1100. Although there are the usual twin borders with geometrical designs, the general effect is rather different from that of the Bayeux Tapestry: the figures are stiff and angular and the spaces swarm with birds. This piece

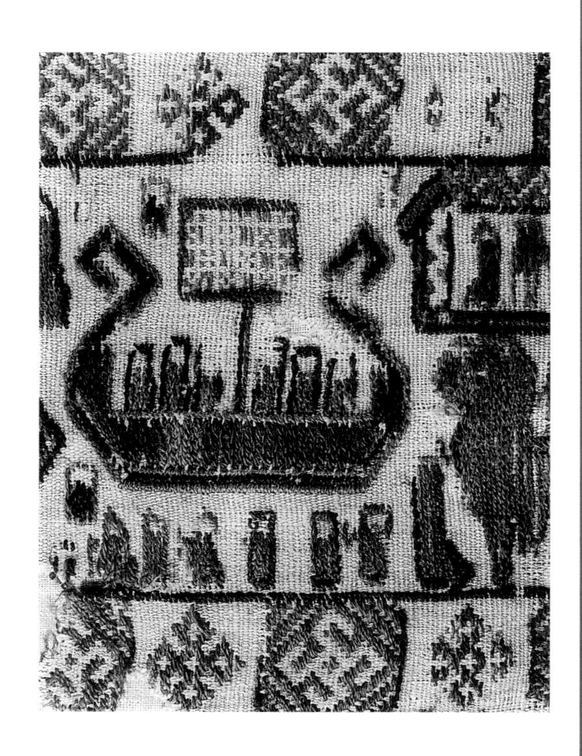

3. Detail from the Överhogdal Tapestry (Sweden, twelfth century), Östersund Museum, Sweden.

is probably closer to popular culture than to the courtly art of the Oseberg and Bayeux Tapestries.[11]

These similarities with Scandinavian tapestries were certainly no mere matter of chance. The Bayeux Tapestry originated in a cultural milieu close to and heavily influenced by the Nordic world. Anglo-Saxon England was profoundly affected by the Vikings and the Danes in the last century of its existence, and it is in this context that we find the most striking evidence of similar artefacts — not, this time, in archaeological finds but in historical documents.

The most remarkable reference is in the *Liber Eliensis*, a text compiled in the mid-twelfth century at the monastic cathedral of Ely. Having mentioned the ealdorman Brihtnoth, the Anglo-Saxon chieftain slain by the Danes in 991 at the Battle of Maldon and commemorated in the heroic poem of that name, the text reads:

> his wife, a lady named Aelfleda, at the time when her husband was killed and buried, gave to this church his domain of *Ratenduna* ... and a necklace of gold and a coloured woven wall-hanging showing his deeds, in memory of his greatness.[12]

Aelfleda's will is extant, but makes no mention of this wall-hanging, dealing only with bequests of land. Nevertheless, the chronicler's testimony is plausible. Thus a few months or at most a few years after it took place, one of the most momentous events of the late tenth century had already been commemorated in a coloured wall-hanging commissioned in memory of one of its most illustrious participants. This can hardly have been an isolated instance. Other aristocratic wills from the late tenth century mention decorative wall-hangings, though without specifying their subjects. They were used to adorn chambers and halls. Nor were they unknown in churches, albeit with less worldly subjects: in the mid-twelfth century, King Stephen's brother gave Winchester Cathedral 'a linen cloth on which were woven the miracles of Our Lady'.[13]

None of these English wall-hangings has survived. But their relationship with the Bayeux Tapestry and its martial images seems undeniable, given that so many texts bear witness to the skill of English seamstresses, notably one Aethelwynn, who was associated with the great monastic reformer Saint Dunstan. William of Poitiers extolled the talent of Englishwomen in needlework and cloth of gold. And English sources note that Queen Edith, Edward the Confessor's wife, excelled *in arte manuum*, in handicraft. Similar skills were attributed to several English ladies of the tenth and eleventh centuries.[14]

This taste for narrative textiles was no doubt found elsewhere, though firm evidence is hard to come by. Hangings of this kind are sometimes reproduced in mural paintings. The best known example of this, dating from the late twelfth or early thirteenth century, is found in the crypt of the cathedral at Aquileia in Venezia-Giulia (Italy). The lower register of the painting depicts cavalry battles (perhaps episodes from the crusades or else scenes from the Bible) as though on tapestries hanging at the base of the walls. They are not in a particularly good state of repair, but it is worth noting that wall-hangings of military scenes were apparently not considered inherently unsuitable decorations for a notable place of worship. On a more modest scale, similar imitation draperies are found in the lower register of the wall-paintings in the church of Cians (Alpes-Maritimes, France). Outside this ecclesiastical context, such imitation draperies were often painted on the walls of *châteaux*, as for example in the great chamber on the first floor of the *château* of the Counts of Carcassonne. At the level of the princely court it was common for battle scenes to be painted in honour of the master of the house. According to Liutprand of Cremona, Henry the Fowler had some made for his palace at Magdeburg to celebrate his victory over the Magyars in 934.[15]

It is sometimes argued that, notwithstanding the clear moral of the tale told on the Bayeux Tapestry, the worldly and even indecent character of some its scenes and images shows that it must originally have been designed for a secular building. But a single text is enough to refute this idea. In the eminently sacred milieu of the Benedictine Abbey of Saint-Florent de Saumur in Anjou, an eminently devout patron, Mathieu de Loudun (Abbot from 1128-55; then Bishop of Angers, 1156-62), commissioned a wall-hanging to be displayed 'in the nave of the church on solemn feasts'. It was to show 'archers, lions, and various other animals' – exactly the sort of thing so common on the borders of the Bayeux Tapestry.[16]

The most intriguing documentary testimony of all is that of Baudry de Bourgueil, an Angevin by birth who died as Bishop of Dol in 1130. According to him, a tapestry which sounds remarkably similar to that of Bayeux formed part of the décor of the chamber of Countess Adela of Blois, the daughter of William the Conqueror, a chamber which he describes in 1,368 lines of Latin verse written shortly before 1102. But Baudry was an eloquent writer with a fertile imagination, and it is hard for us to be sure just what in his description is fact, and what fiction. The tapestry he describes may in fact be a fictionalised version of the Bayeux Tapestry itself, which Baudry, who often visited Normandy, could easily have seen.[17] Minute scrutiny of the text by experts in both literature and the fine arts has inevitably given rise to diverse interpretations, but, without going into excessive detail, some observations can safely be offered. For a start, the poem can hardly be a faithful description of reality: to accommodate its decorative scheme, Adela's chamber would have had to be gigantic — and quite uninhabitable. As a recent critic has said, 'merely to read it ... is dizzying: the excess of ornament and the luxuriousness of the materials ... would seem to come straight out of poetic fancy'.[18] On the floor, we are told, was a map showing the three parts of the known world, Asia, Europe, and Africa, full of learned emblems and surrounded by the figures of the four winds — not unlike the floors in some medieval religious buildings (for example at Die and Turin).[19] The ceiling was adorned with astronomical figures. On the walls were draperies (and we know from Wace that the Conqueror himself had such hangings in his chamber) executed in precious materials: cloth of gold and silver, and silk: improbable perhaps, but not impossible, given the reputation of Englishwomen for such handiwork, though there is no extant precedent for the pearls and precious stones he says were sewn onto it.

One hanging in particular depicted recent history (*historias ... novas*) and bore

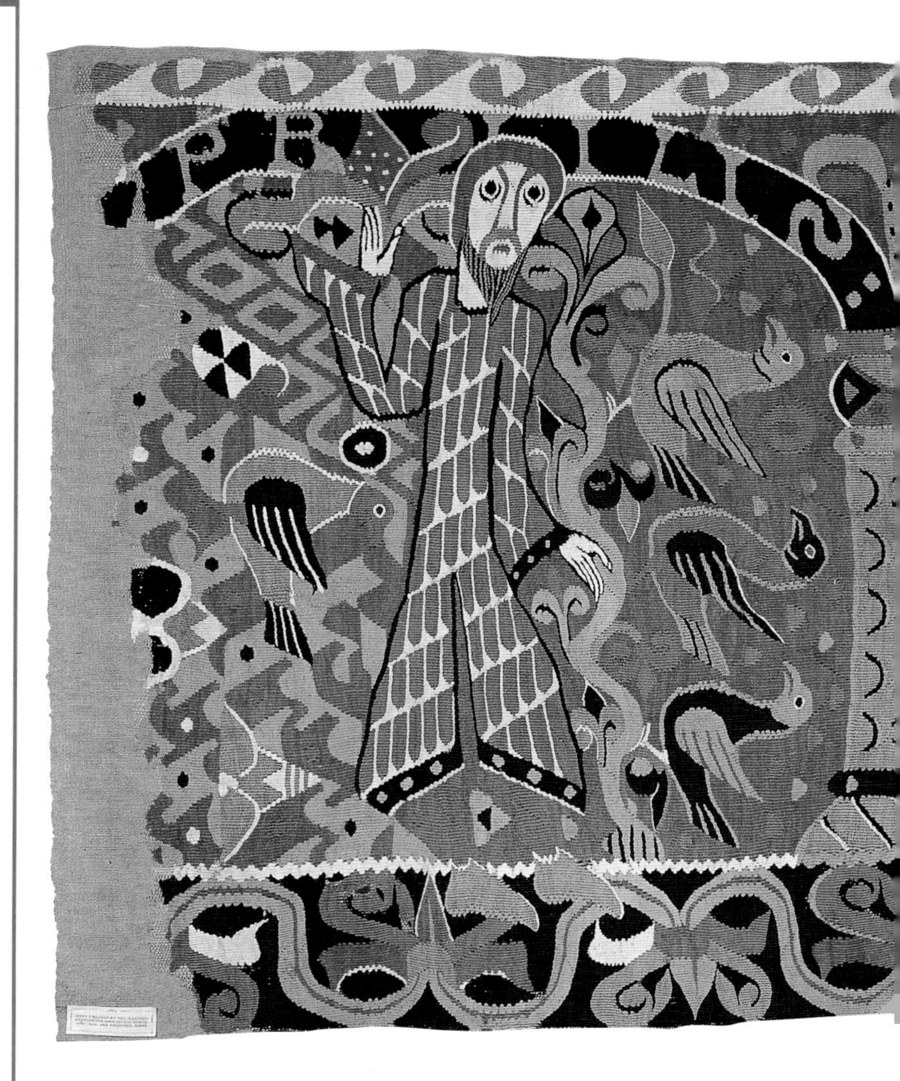

captions.[20] The story it told was that of William's conquest of England, beginning with the appearance of Halley's Comet (with no mention of Harold's voyage, nor of the Breton expedition, nor of the oath), and ending with the Norman conquest of Kent. It is an entirely secular narrative with no moral lesson, and it scarcely alludes to Harold and his perjury except in a passing reference to him as *parjurus*. But it furnishes some remarkable parallels to the Tapestry, notably the construction of

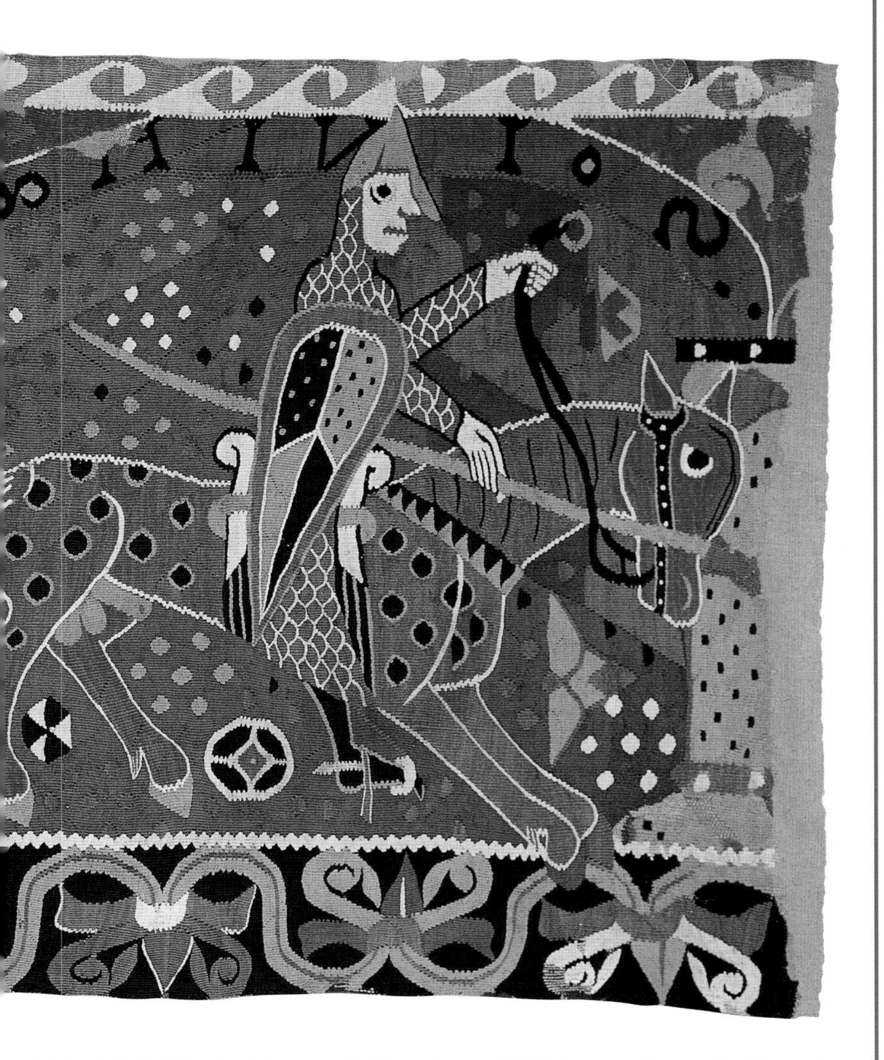

4. The Baldishol Hanging (Norway, early thirteenth century). This fragment, from a cycle of the months, shows April and May. Museum of Applied Arts, Oslo.

the fleet and the crossing of the Channel. Baudry also describes other hangings, of less interest in this context, illustrating sacred history from the Creation to the Flood, other episodes from the Bible, and scenes from Greek mythology.

This takes us a long way from Bayeux, for our thoughts are drawn to an early twelfth-century work, the famous Creation Tapestry preserved at Girona Cathedral in Catalonia (even if Baudry himself could not possibly have seen it).[21] It bears only the most distant relationship to the Bayeux Tapestry. A compact panel some 3.65m by 4.70m, with chain stitch embroidery forming a continuous surface entirely concealing the linen beneath, it has Christ enthroned in majesty in the centre, amidst concentric circles showing the six days of Creation and the months of the year. Thus neither its shape nor its needlework nor its pictorial composition have anything in common with the Bayeux Tapestry or its Scandinavian counterparts.

A recent critical verdict on the text observes that 'as a poet, Baudry constructs his own universe, but he constructs it out of real knowledge, not of the decorative scheme of the countess's chamber but of contemporary artefacts he knew' — which he drew on as much for the wall-hangings as for the floor-covering.[22] Prominent among them, no doubt, was the Bayeux Tapestry.

III

The style and spirit of the Tapestry

For a long time, people have seen the Tapestry in terms of modern media such as the comic strip, the animated cartoon, or even the cinema. But these comparative approaches need to be handled with care.

The Tapestry does have something in common with the modern comic strip, although its demarcation of scenes is less clear-cut. Both share a tendency towards over-simplification (every episode is focused on two or three heroes) and a taste for expressive, even excessive, gesture. While the Tapestry's captions are not exactly the same as 'word balloons' — for they do not purport to give the actual words or reactions of the characters — they do much the same job. And, like the comic strip, the Tapestry has little time for background, perspective, or subtle nuance. But, more relevantly, these are characteristics which, as well as its systematic use of bold colours without regard to the fine shades of real life, it shares with many manuscript illuminations of the eleventh century. Needless to say, their artistic purposes are worlds apart: mere escapism on the one hand, the beautifying of a cathedral for solemn festivals on the other.

Detailed studies have sought to establish resemblances with both animated cartoons and films on two levels, although the conclusions are not always entirely compelling.[23] Some parallels have been found on the level of narrative technique: continuous, or nearly continuous, narrative; and continuous movement indicated at key moments by the repeated use of almost identical patterns (when the fleet crosses the

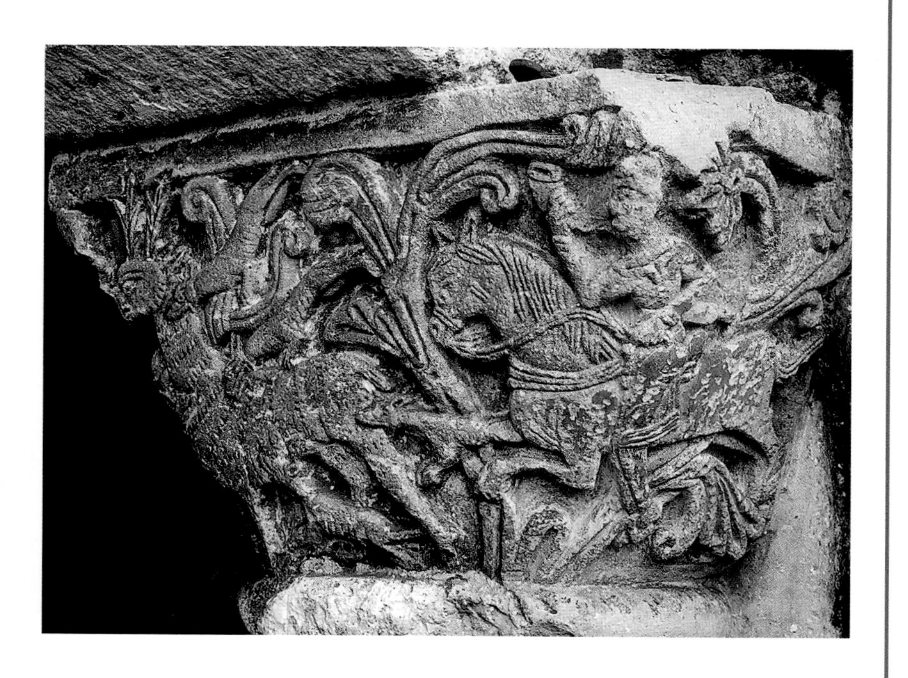

5. Capital from the doorway of the Priory of Goult (Orne), showing a deer-hunt.

Channel, and when the Normans advance and then charge at Hastings). It has even been suggested that the Tapestry employs flashback; and that at times it shows characters in successive moments of a single action, almost like a 'flick-book'. But the alleged examples are not that convincing. More plausible are the suggestions of 'slow motion' just before the action of the battle begins (scenes 50-51, pp. 228–234), and of the judicious interweaving of close-ups and wide-angles in particular episodes.

On another level, something analogous to the director's cut has been discerned: prologue, narrative crux, and denouement, along with a certain skill in the unfolding of action sequences. Here one can make some cautious comparisons both with classical artefacts such as Trajan's Column and the Antonine Column and with their medieval imitations such as the bronze column in the cathedral at Hildesheim, made in about 1030. These lengthy narrative reliefs of historical subjects (or scriptural subjects in the case of Hildesheim) use similar methods to demarcate particular sequences of action.

Yet for all that, it remains crucial to emphasise the uniqueness of the expressive techniques of the Tapestry. Comparions with other art-forms are, with two exceptions among the graphic arts, somewhat stretched. The exceptions are sculpture and pen-drawing.

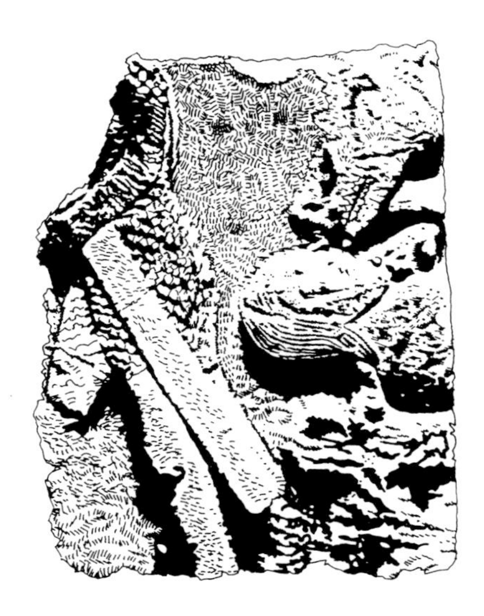

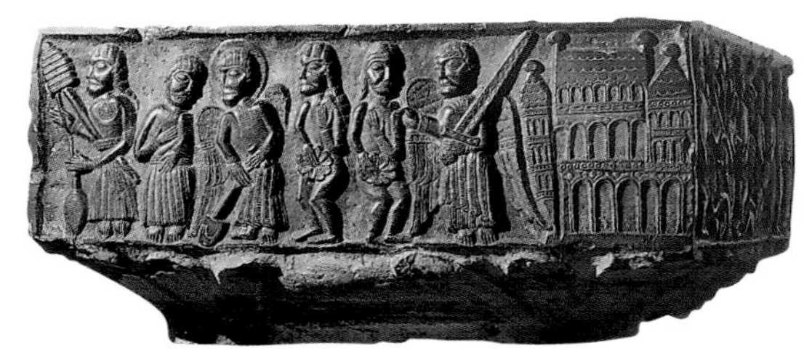

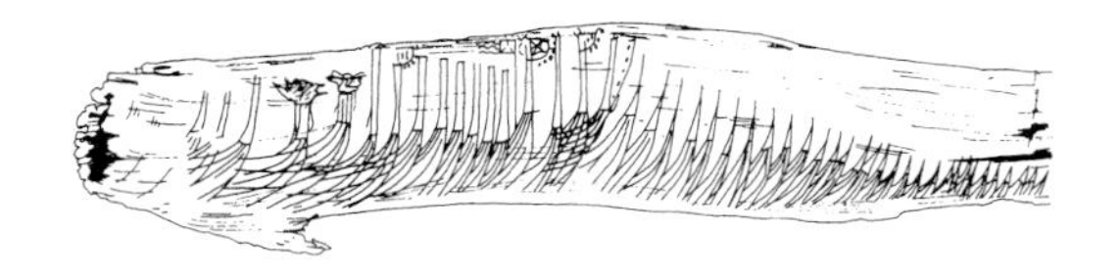

6. (top) Fragment of an early eleventh-century sculpted frieze found at Winchester. Height: 69.5cm. On the left is a man in a coat of mail similar to those on the Bayeux Tapestry. To the right, a wolf and the head of a recumbent man.

7. (middle) The story of Adam and Eve from the font at East Meon (Hampshire).

8. (bottom) Depiction of a fleet of Norwegian ships cut onto a piece of wood. Bergen, mid-thirteenth century.

A good deal of late-eleventh-century and twelfth-century sculpture is done in low relief, and is thus essentially graphic rather than plastic in character, with aesthetic values very close to those of the Tapestry. There are plenty of examples even in the Anglo-Norman world. A particularly striking resemblance is found in one of the scenes on the carved capitals in the doorway of the Priory of Goult (in Lande-de-Goult, Orne). The scene, which extends over two capitals, shows a deer-hunt. While the knight and the man on foot are depicted in civilian dress, the bearing and the harness of the horse, the general vigour of the scene, and above all the drawing of the trees call the Tapestry irresistibly to mind (fig. 5). That said, the carving is more mannered in its effect, and displays a fear of empty space which was not shared by the Tapestry's designer.[24]

Other examples include the fragments of a sculpted frieze discovered in 1965 by M. Biddle during excavations at Winchester Old Minster (demolished in 1093). One can make out a wolf and a warrior in chain-mail, perhaps part of a scene from the Nordic legend of Sigurd (fig. 6). Biddle himself made the connection with the Tapestry. But the original context for the frieze is entirely obscure.[25] Also of English provenance are various baptismal fonts carved from black Tournai marble, found in southern England, notably at Winchester Cathedral and at East Meon in Hampshire (fig. 7). These have images of buildings very like some of the Tapestry's drawings, although arguably the parallels are grounded in nothing more than the normal conventions for architectural drawing in the Romanesque period.[26] Particularly striking, on account of the military character of the scene, is the similarity to the carved doorhead of the church of St George's, Fordington (in the suburbs of Dorchester, Dorset), which has been interpreted as showing a story from the First Crusade, the miraculous intervention of St George (a knight armed with a lance bearing the

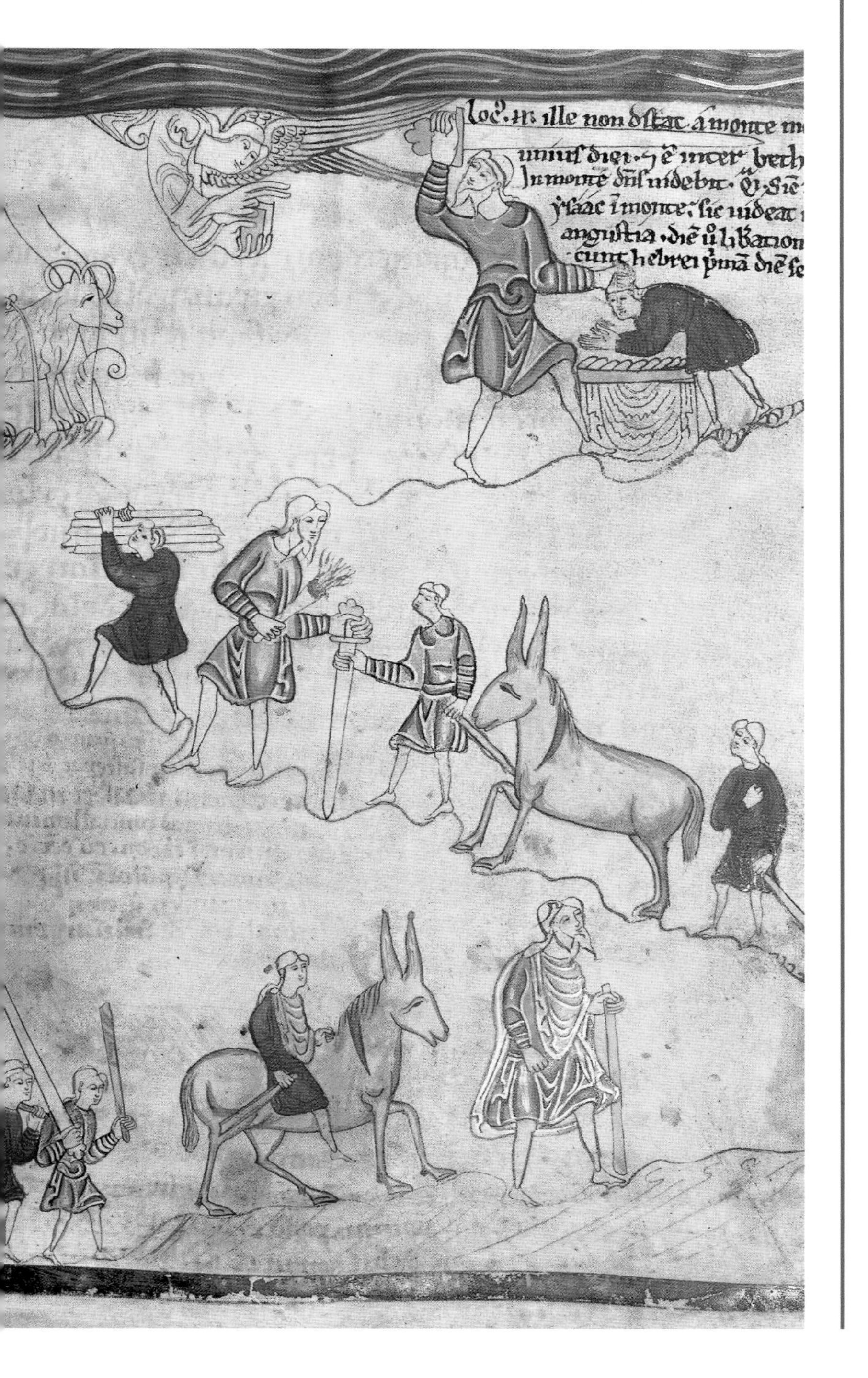

crusading banner) in favour of two crusaders kneeling before Antioch.[27] The equipment of the knights and crusaders is almost identical to that of the Tapestry's warriors. Dating from about 1100, the lintel is close to the Tapestry in both content and style.

Sculpted reliefs furnish still more parallels with the Tapestry's borders, notably for the lions in scenes 9 (pp. 109–110), 14 (pp. 125–126), 21 (p. 143), and 24 (pp. 156–157). These lions, arranged in facing pairs, are typical Norman Romanesque – and hardly naturalistic – with tails that pass between their hind legs and wind up around their backs to end in trefoils.[28] Some of the birds are reminiscent of those carved alongside the aforementioned hunting scene at Goult. And some of the signs of the zodiac, such as the fish in scene 17 (p. 133), are likewise part of the common currency of twelfth-century Anglo-Norman sculpture (as at Kilpeck in Herefordshire or Birkin in Yorkshire). Yet in the end all these similarities are relatively trivial, rooted in the aesthetic common ground of the

9. The story of Abraham and Isaac, from the Old English Hexateuch, produced at St Augustine's Abbey, Canterbury, c. 1030-50. London, British Library, Cotton MS Claudius B. IV, fol. 38.

Romanesque. None of them will sustain an argument for direct artistic influence.

A rather more intriguing parallel is found in the mid-thirteenth-century line-drawing carved on a 25cm piece of wood found about twenty-five years ago in excavations at the Bryggen (the old German or Hanseatic wharf) at Bergen in Norway (fig. 8).[29] Its bold, simple strokes show about thirty ships in line across, prows protruding in front of one another. Some of the prows have carved figureheads, like those on the Tapestry in the foreground of scenes 38-39 (pp. 197–203). The others are plain, except for three which are flying flags shaped like quarter-circles, just like the ones in scene 48 (p. 223). The little fleet heads towards the right in tight formation, and, despite the interval of two centuries, evinces the same essentially Nordic spirit as that shown on the Tapestry. No other medieval artefact presents us with a comparable naval scene.

It is the pen-drawings in eleventh-century manuscripts, however, especially English manuscripts, that most reward investigation in this context. Reference has been made above all to the illustrations in the Old English Hexateuch, probably produced at St Augustine's Abbey in Canterbury between 1030 and 1050. C. R.

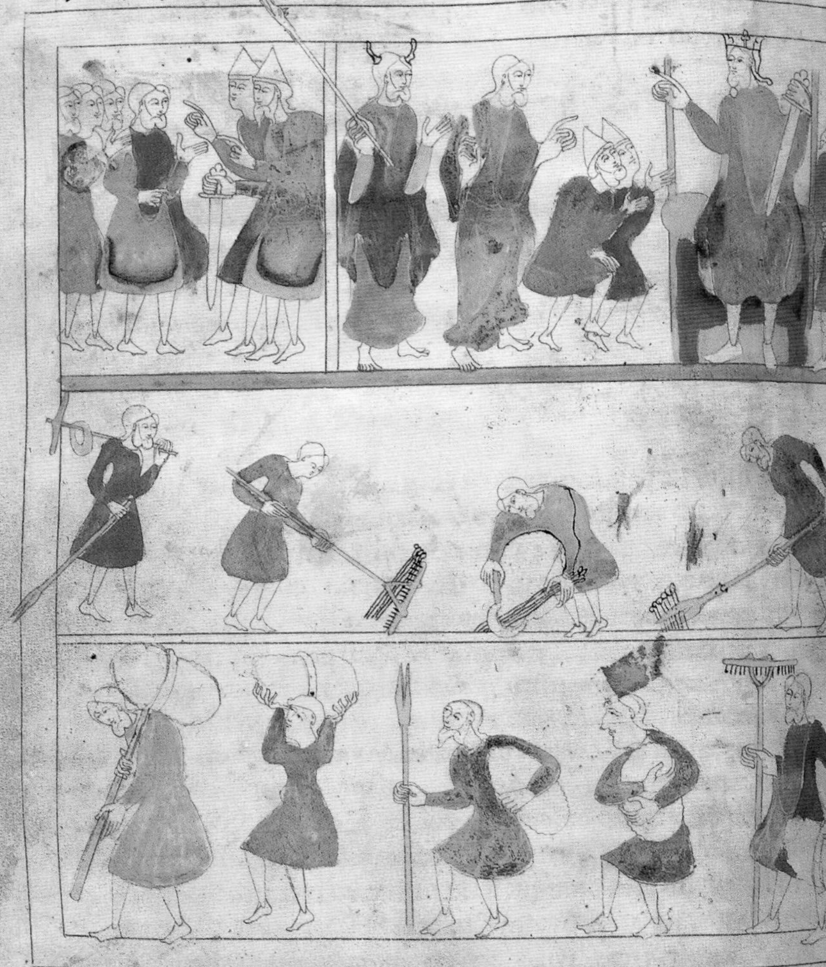

Dodwell pointed out the striking resemblances between some of its figures and various scenes in the Tapestry, such as the death of Edward the Confessor, the carts used for transporting weapons, and the battle scenes.[30] This is all quite convincing as regards particular detail and the then prevalent conventions for the portrayal of historical events, and certainly directs our attention towards the region responsible for the Tapestry's drawings. But there is none of the spirit of the Tapestry in these little scriptural miniatures, nor in any of the other biblical manuscripts that have been invoked in this context. Much the same goes for the comparisons that have been made with battle scenes: there is a clear common tradition in the iconography of war, but nothing more.[31] The mind behind the Bayeux Tapestry was no slave of convention. Nor is there anything more to be said for the comparisons that have been essayed with various eleventh-century continental manuscripts and with the drawings of Adémar of Chabannes. In the end, all we have are passing resemblances at the most.

There is not much more profit in the comparisons that have been drawn with certain Romanesque wall-paintings in a group of English churches known as the 'Lewes Group'. These share the Tapestry's practice of identifying the persons depicted by name.[32] But while there may be a relationship, it does not amount to direct influence.

This brings us to another relevant relationship, that between the Tapestry and the art of mosaic. Without going through all that is known about the pictorial floor mosaics of the eleventh century (and it is now a great deal), it is worth noting some resemblances. In each case, figures stand out from a monochrome background, drawn in coloured outlines and evenly coloured in, and often accompanied by explanatory Latin captions. The visual forms and means of expression are obviously closely related: no perspective and no subtle graduation in colour, just bold drawings in strong lines. Each genre draws heavily on the bestiary to stock the empty spaces. These similarities are most most marked in the best preserved cases, such as the celebrated floor mosaic in the cathedral of Otranto in Southern Italy, dating from around 1160 (figs. 11 and 12).[33] But they are also visible in the sparse fragments which have survived from the eleventh century. Floor mosaics, however, were not suited to the exposition of a continuous narrative.

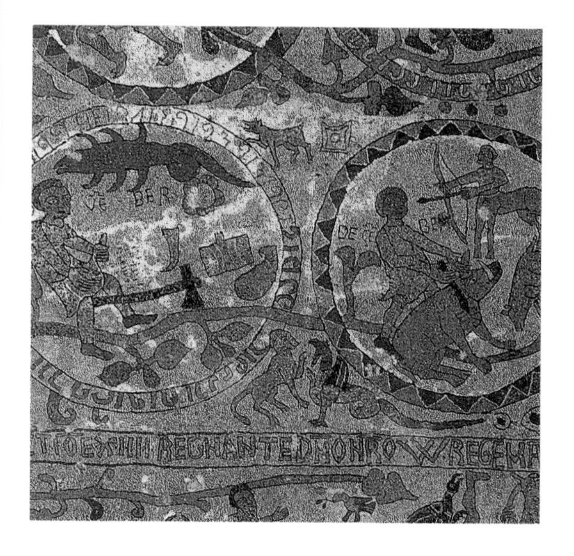

(above) 11. The floor mosaic at Otranto Cathedral (southern Italy, around 1160). This section, from the choir end of the nave, shows the signs of zodiac for November and December.

(opposite) 10. Harvest scenes from the Old English Hexateuch. London, British Library, Cotton MS Claudius B. IV, fol. 79v.

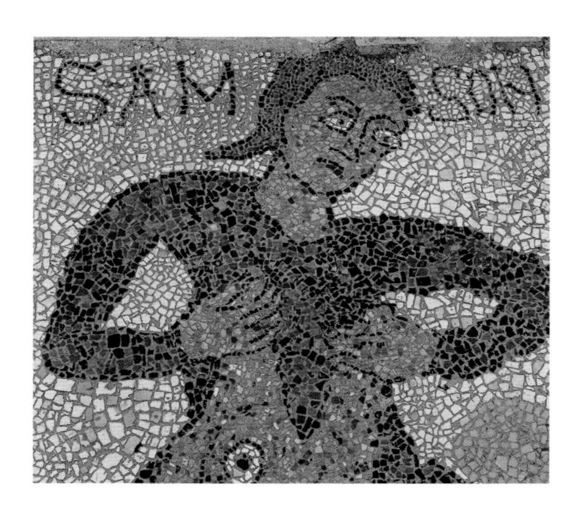

12. The floor mosaic at Otranto Cathedral (southern Italy, around 1160). Detail from the choir, showing Samson and the lion.

The Tapestry is of course innocent of perspective and the third dimension. Nevertheless, when removed from its protective glass and subjected to powerful lateral lighting (such as is for filming), a limited but suggestive effect of relief can be made out, which must have been more readily apparent before centuries of wear had flattened the embroidery. Moreover, though perspective in the strict sense is entirely absent, colour contrasts are used throughout the Tapestry to perform a similar function. Thus, for example, horses' legs in the background are almost always done in another, usually darker, coloured thread than those in the foreground. The same technique is used to distinguish the shields of William's guards (scene 15, p. 127), the shields hung on the sides of ships (scenes 5 and 39, pp. 101 and pp. 200–201), and above all the horses which tread on each other's heels. In crowd scenes, colour contrasts serve to distinguish individuals standing next to each other. Only in the case of buildings and ships is colour purely decorative, deployed merely for the sake of variety.

There is nothing, however, to suggest that the linen cloth (of which scarcely anything can be seen in its present state) had any markings to indicate which colours were to be used on it. These decisions seem to have been left to the discretion of the seamstresses.

One thing above all is lacking for a proper appreciation of the aesthetic of the Tapestry: knowledge of the precise setting in which it was displayed. Even granted that it was indeed Bayeux Cathedral, this does not get us very far, as the present-day structure is very different from the Romanesque original, of which only limited sections remain — notably the crypt and the bases of the west towers. We simply do not know whether the Tapestry was hung along the walls at eye level, or whether it was fixed to the pillars (although the former seems more likely). Its narrative continuity and progression would have been well suited to display around the ambulatory of the choir, but we do not know whether the choir at Bayeux had one: ambulatories were rare, though not unknown, in eleventh-century Normandy.

Notwithstanding the manifestly ecclesiastical milieu of those responsible for its creation and the evident moral purpose of its narrative, the Tapestry never sinks to the level of mere moralising. It might easily have done so. In the first third of the twelfth century, certain strands of the Anglo-Norman tradition of the Conquest tended strongly in that direction, as we can see from William of Malmesbury's anecdotes in the *Gesta regum*. This appears not so much in the story of Harold's perjury (which that author virtually glosses over) as in the circumstantial details: while awaiting a favourable wind at Saint-Valéry-sur-Somme, Duke William calmed his impatient troops by having St Valéry's relics brought out of the local church in a votive procession praying for a change in the wind; on the eve of the decisive battle, the Normans spent the night confessing their sins and took communion in the morning.[34] There is no sign of any of this on the Tapestry, which eschews such embellishments in order to maintain its narrative thrust.

Neither does the Tapestry succumb to the temptations of the heroic. It has often been pointed out that it finds no place for the sort of episodes that lent themselves to the medieval romance tradition. There is no sign of the *jongleur* (*joculator*, *mimus*) Taillefer who, according to Wace, Henry of Huntingdon, and the *Carmen de Hastingae Proelio*, marched at the head of the Norman force, juggling with his sword, before killing the first Englishman.[35] Nor is there any allusion to the Song of Roland (*Chanson de Roland*, *cantilena Rollandi*), which, according to William of Malmesbury and Wace, the Normans struck up as battle commenced.[36] Even if these fanciful traditions did not flower until the twelfth century, they might well have been present in germ fifty years before. In the same way, the Tapestry ignores the single combat, on horseback and then on foot, which later traditions conjured up in accordance with the conventions of classical epic, between Duke William and Gyrth, Harold's brother (in lieu of Harold himself), and of which we hear in the *Carmen* and Wace.[37]

It is also worth noting that the role of women, an integral component of the romances and *chansons de geste*, is kept to an absolute minimum, with the solitary and mysterious exception of Ælfgyva in scene 15 (pp. 128–129). Nothing is said of Matilda of Normandy, nor of Queen Edith (Edward the Confessor's wife, though she appears anonymously at his deathbed; scene 27, pp. 164–170), nor of Harold's mistress, Edith Swan-Neck, who is mentioned in *Domesday Book* and who, from the thirteenth century, figures in many stories about the discovery of Harold's body.[38] The world of the Tapestry is almost exclusively masculine — a monastic, arguably even a misogynistic, vision.

In short, the Tapestry rigidly avoids anything which might distract it from its purpose, eschewing anecdote and embellishment, the merely pious and the merely poetic alike.[39] In common with the great Romanesque masterpieces built soon after the Conquest, it achieves its effects by the most direct of methods.

IV

THE CAPTIONS

THE TAPESTRY'S SCENES ARE ACCOMPANIED almost throughout by a kind of running commentary in Latin, sewn in large capital letters along the top of the central band (although the ends of some longer phrases are fitted in lower, and a few proper names are placed elsewhere in order to identify particular individuals). In the first two thirds of the Tapestry, these texts are sewn in a dark blue thread which verges on black. In the final section, red and yellow are used, often in alternation and sometimes even within single words. Right at the end, around Harold's death, green thread is also used.

The only scenes without commentary are those where the action fills or even spills out of the middle band, and in any case speaks for itself, as in Harold's crossing from Bosham to Ponthieu, the construction of William's fleet, and the climax of the Battle of Hastings.

The captions are almost exclusively in clear Latin capitals, but there are some exceptions: E is sometimes rectangular and sometimes rounded; certain letters appear in uncial form as well as in capitals (h as well as H, m as well as M). Very occasionally, but crucially for establishing the geographical origin of the Tapestry, there are some distinctively Anglo-Saxon characters: the Æ found in Ælfgyva and Pevensæ, and the Đ in the name of one of Harold's brothers, Gyrth (GYRĐ).[40] The W is written with a repeated V, as in the name of Harold's other brother, Leofwine (LEVVINE). As usual in medieval scripts, Y has a point or dot. Abbreviations are not systematically avoided, but remain rare and entirely conventional: a tilde above a vowel in place of a final M in the accusative (though this is sometimes omitted[41]); E with a cedilla (Ȩ) for AE, and 7 for ET (once only, in scene 9, p. 109). And there are conventional contractions such as SCI for *sancti*, APLI for *apostoli*, and EPS for *episcopus*. Ligatures are extremely rare. Reading the text is relatively easy after a little basic instruction.

The words of the captions are almost always clearly demarcated, most often by a a pair of points (like a colon), with more important breaks in the prose indicated by three points. On two occasions a cross marks the start of a phrase (scenes 12 and 37, pp. 117 and 195). Needless to say, as in most texts from this period, the punctuation does not conform to modern conventions.[42]

The language, obviously, is Latin, equally intelligible on both sides of the Channel, and at that time the only language normally used for writing in Normandy. It was the only possible choice for a work destined to be displayed in a church. A few personal names, mostly in English, are not Latinised: that of King Edward right at the start and that of Harold in the first half, as well as those of the Breton Count Conan, the English Archbishop Stigand, Harold's two brothers, and the Normans Turold, Wadard, Vital, and Robert de Mortain. The same goes for the English place-names of Bosham, Pevensey (*Pevensæ*), and Hastings (*Hastinga*, *Hestinga*), as well as that of Beaurain (*Belrem*) in Picardy. The Duke of Normandy appears early on as *Wilgelm*, later as *Willelm* or *Willelmus*, the first form suggesting a pronunciation close to the modern English *William*. The author thus aims to keep key names in a clear and easily identifiable form, without the distortions of artificial Latinisation — perhaps connected with the tendency to avoid abbreviations. Utterly unpretentious, this is anything but the work of a pedant.

The Latin is for the most part very correct. However, three words in Old English creep into scene 45 (pp. 215–216): *at Hestenga ceastra* (in Latin this would be *ad Hastingae castra*). This is most significant. Here and there one finds non-classical but still perfectly clear words: *parabolant* (they parley), *caballi* for 'horses', and *milites* used in the sense of 'knights'. A slightly more serious lapse is the omission of the *–ur* termination of the deponent verb in the phrase *mirant(ur) stellam* (scene 32, pp. 176–178), although this may perhaps be explained as an abbreviation.[43] French place-names are given in archaic forms, such as *Rednes* for Rennes, or anglicised in their orthography, as with *Bagias* for Bayeux.[44] E. Maclagan was probably wrong, however, to take the usages *parabolant* (pp. 110–111) and *Stigant* (p. 175) as evidence for French linguistic influence. In fact, the Scandinavian personal name Stigant was latinised in both England and Normandy as *Stigandus*. In all, the Tapestry mentions a dozen place-names and fifteen personal names.

Although the author was concerned to keep things as accessible as possible, this did not prevent him from creating, if not a work of literature, then at least a coherent piece of prose. He never says more than he wants, and is studiedly ambiguous when it suits him. Thus when Odo is shown in the thick of the fight holding his staff, the word used for it is *baculum*, which might mean a commander's baton, a club, or a bishop's crook. The second possibility, which is quite plausible (see pp. 248–250), would be most compromising for a bishop, as it would be a breach of canon law.

The prose is extremely direct, consisting of short statements which are tied closely to the pictorial narrative by such words as *ubi* (where), *hic* (here) and *iste* (a strongly demonstrative personal pronoun, 'that one'). This is particularly well suited to the Tapestry's purpose, but it is worth noting that it is typical of historical writing in Old English. A. Crépin has noted how, in the *Anglo-Saxon Chronicle*, the word *her* (here, *hic*) refers 'to the line of the pascal table where the annalist notes the event'.[45] The same usage is found elsewhere, for example in inscriptions on Romanesque monuments on the Iberian peninsula, such as the doorway at Ripoll, the carved capitals at San Pedro de la Nave, not to mention various wall-paintings, but the connections seem neither as close nor as convincing.[46]

Although this close integration of text with image hardly lends itself to elaborate stylistic effects, there are still some striking touches — most notably the summary of William's address to his knights before the battle. He urges them *ut preparent se viriliter et sapienter ad prelium*, 'to prepare themselves manfully and wisely for the battle'. The phrase neatly captures the eleventh-century Norman spirit: courage and shrewdness were together the key to Norman success in England and Italy alike. Of course, the formula echoes the conventional attributes of the heroes of the *chansons de geste*: *sage et preux*, 'valiant and wise'. But it merits further exploration, which takes us once more into the Anglo-Saxon and Scandinavian world. Ealdorman Brihtnoth, the heroic warrior slain by the Vikings in 991, was a 'most courageous leader' (*dux fortissimus*), who, 'by virtue of his wonderful wisdom (*mirabilem sapientiam*) protected his folk manfully (*viriliter*)'. There is every chance that the phrase we find above scene 51 (pp. 232–234) was penned by an English hand — the more so in that it seems to have been unknown to William's Norman panegyrists, William of Poitiers and William of Jumièges.

There is a similar indication of an English mind behind the Latin words in the caption of scene 53 (pp. 242–244), *Hic ceciderunt simul Angli*

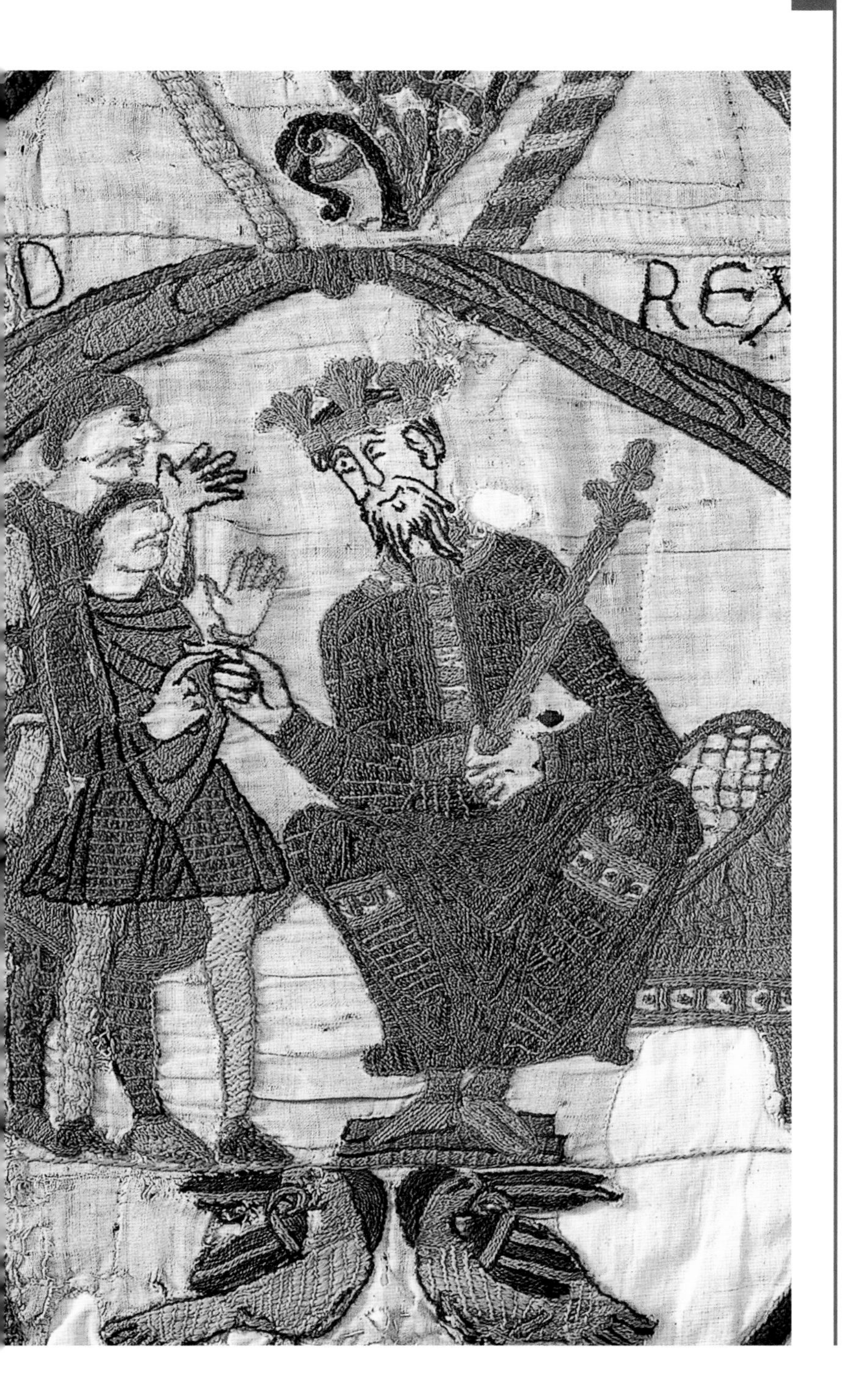

et Franci in prelio — 'Here English and French fell together in the fight'. In itself the sentiment could speak for victors or vanquished, as both were united in death through Harold's sin. But while tactfully respecting everybody's feelings, it is unmistakably English. The idea of describing the victors as 'French' would simply not have occurred to a Norman at this time, however appropriate it might seem given that the French tongue was one of the few things William's army had in common. It was not that long since the poet Garnier de Rouen, in a work dedicated to Duke William's uncle, the Archbishop of Rouen, had dreamed of 'wiping out the vainglorious French'.[47] And a century after Hastings, Wace was still referring to the conquerors as Normans more often than as Frenchmen. Yet from 1066 onwards, the royal administration in England used *Franci* for the conquerors, and official documents addressed the king's subjects as *Franci et Angli*.

It is also worth commenting on the title accorded to Harold. Before Edward's death he is consistently termed *Haroldus dux* or *dux Anglorum*, that is, he is put on the same level as William of Normandy. But from then until the battle, indeed until the very moment of his death, he is called king. Here, the author is clearly taking sides. In fact, until 1066 Harold was formally just an earl, although his real power was sufficient to justify the superior title used here. Indeed, one chronicler invented for him the unprecedented term *subregulus* (under-king). In 1066, he was unarguably the king, but the Anglo-Norman tradition, especially in the *Domesday Book*, tended to deny him that title, referring to him merely as *comes* (earl), when not disparaging him as *pseudorex* or even as *tyrannus* (tyrant, often used by Orderic Vitalis).

Despite the almost epic character of many episodes, the author hardly ever invokes poetic models. The nearest he comes to this is perhaps in scene 54 (p. 249), where Odo encourages the *pueros* (the 'lads' — in point of fact, the Norman knights) in what is possibly an allusion to Virgil. Apart from this, the prose is from start to finish as simple and direct as could be. Our author has no time for the expansive rhetoric and classical pastiche so dear to such contemporaries as William of Poitiers. At almost every point he uses the exact, even the technical word. His commitment to brevity and precision must have pleased his patrons: the Normans of the Conquest era prized efficiency above all things. He has no time for the tricks of trade of classical historiography, such as the speeches put into the mouths of protagonists. Edward the Confessor and Harold remain mute throughout. All we hear of Odo in scene 44 (p. 212) is that he said grace over the food. And when William addresses his troops just before the battle, his speech is summed up in a single phrase. Yet what an opportunity was lost! Recent work has emphasised how much of his success William owed to the stirring speeches he could deliver on the eve and in the heat of battle[48] — not to mention the negotiating skills he must have deployed over the preceding months to persuade the Norman barons to embark upon this risky venture. All the indications are, then, that this author was not writing for the sort of professionally literate readers who would have appreciated a more artful text, and that he had a becomingly modest sense of what was wanted from what we might call the Tapestry's librettist.

At a general level, the Tapestry steers purposefully clear of the kind of epic or heroic elaboration which could have obscured the basic story. Although is true that it contains most of the 'typical episodes that make up the *chansons de geste*: embassies, councils, pitched battles, sieges, stratagems, and the founding of abbeys to pray for the souls of the dead', it does so simply 'because they were the realities of war in the eleventh century'. They feature here without the 'stereotyped formulas' and 'epic clichés' of the *chansons de geste*.[49]

Finally, we should note that this kind of textual commentary must have been a standard feature of Romanesque narrative textiles. Baudry de Bourgueil remarks in his description of the imaginary tapestry in Countess Adela's chamber that 'writing explains the images and subjects so that anyone who can read can understand them … in fact one reads these cloths'.[50] This is what distinguishes these narrative textiles from similar medieval art-forms: on mosaics, the inscriptions were often only the signatures and marks of the craftsmen; even on the great mosaic of Otranto the captions are only labels of one or two words. But the Bayeux Tapestry manages to be at once a work of art and, to some extent, a work of literature.

V

THE CHARACTERS

THE BAYEUX TAPESTRY SHOWS 626 people in total. Fifteen of them are named, six of them more than once — which makes 53 names in all.[51] Of the named individuals, six are Norman, six English, and one Breton, the remaining pair being the Counts of Boulogne and Ponthieu. In the vast majority of cases, the names are written right over or beside the intended person. Only in the case of Turold is there some doubt about who is meant. Besides these personal names, twelve places are mentioned by name (one of them, Hastings, three times). The author was clearly more interested in people than in places. There are some significant omissions. One conspicuous absentee is Geoffrey de Montbray, Bishop of Coutances, who in and just after the events of 1066 was almost as important as Odo of Bayeux (who, in contrast, is mentioned twice and unmistakably appears anonymously twice more).[52] Among the places omitted are Winchester and London (or Westminster), where some crucial events unfolded.

Embroidery is not a medium which allows scope for the finer touches of physical or psychological portraiture. What matters is that the key figures appear in the right place and are readily identifiable, something which best achieved with the aid of distinctive attributes of clothing, weaponry, or setting.

Edward the Confessor, who appears in the opening scene and twice more (scenes 25 and 27, pp. 159 and 167), is a king and is therefore shown crowned (in scene 1 he also has a sceptre). When laid out in death, he no longer wears the crown. The figure of the king is entirely conventional, with no attempt at portraiture, though he is one of the few bearded figures on the Tapestry. Harold is even less distinctive. Before 1066 he lacks any distinguishing personal features, although in several scenes (2, p. 91; 4, p. 99; 9, p. 108; and 13, p. 121) he is shown with a falcon on his wrist (his taste for falconry is attested in some reliable sources). It is precisely this lack of distinguishing features which makes it impossible to be certain which figure is actually Harold in the scene showing his death (scene 57, pp. 256–257). Duke William himself fares no better. Sitting in state with drawn sword in scene 12 (p. 118), he is almost identical to the Count of Ponthieu in scene 9 (p. 110), and elsewhere he is indistinguishable from his own knights: he cannot even be made out on the ship carrying him to Pevensey.

Bishop Odo is recognisable by his large tonsure — at least when he is not wearing a helmet — but his costume has nothing remarkable about it, unlike that of Archbishop Stigand, who is shown at Harold's coronation in full pontifical vestments. But this is because, unlike Odo, Stigand is performing a public liturgical function. Bishops are not shown wearing mitres, but strictly contemporary texts such as the *De officiis* of Jean d'Avranches (Archbishop of Rouen) suggest that mitres were not yet considered essential episcopal attire.

Unnamed individuals can often be classified by social status, but only a small minority have distinctive dress or attributes. Clerics are always tonsured. In the entourage of the English kings, the rank of their closest associates — the *witan* (counsellors) and the housecarles (bodyguard) — is indicated by the great two-handed battle-axe (scene 29, p. 173), a legacy of the Danish influence dominant at the court earlier in the century.

The various emblems seen on the shields of the knights are often assumed to be heraldic escutcheons, but this is not in fact so, as formal heraldic bearings did not then exist. The emblems are simply identifying badges, extremely useful in combat, when helmets and chainmail obscured figures and faces.

Ethnic traits are portrayed only in the first part of the Tapestry. Until scene 23 (p. 155), Englishmen (or at least the important ones) are shown with moustaches, while the Normans are clean shaven. This distinction accords with the traditional pen-picture of the participants drawn two generations later by William of Malmesbury in a well-known anecdote: English scouts told Harold on the eve of the battle that 'almost everyone in that army looks like a priest, for their faces are shaved, upper and lower lips alike'.[53] The English, of course, were whiskered. In the early part of the Tapestry they are shown with their hair thick at the back of the head, while the Normans, Duke William foremost among them, have the nape of the neck shaved close and high. However, in the remainder of the Tapestry this distinction is no longer apparent — though of course most of the men are now shown in armour. (It is worth remarking in this context on the impossibility, in most cases, of distinguishing the Normans from the English by their military or naval equipment.)

There are no obvious ethnic prejudices evident in the drawings. Victors and vanquished alike appear as men of valour, and indeed look almost the same. The Tapestry does not stoop to caricature, and there is no sense of angels of light in conflict with agents of darkness. The contrast between the peoples comes down to a few matters of fashion which were soon forgotten. Far from imposing their shaving habits on the English, the Normans were soon sporting long hair and beards, to the horror of their moralists.[54]

In contrast with much medieval art, the Tapestry hardly ever depicts its major characters as figures of exceptional stature, looming over bystanders and drawing the attention of viewers. Almost the only example of this is King Edward in scenes 1 and 25 (pp. 89 and 159). However, some minor figures are drawn smaller, irrespective of their actual size, notably the almost dwarfish Turold in scene 10 (p. 113), the butchers in scene 40 (p. 207), and the Englishwoman and her son in scene 47 (p. 217). The diminutive figures of the bell-ringers in scene 26 (p. 161) and of the archers in the lower margin beneath the Norman cavalry in scenes 55-56 (pp. 250–255), however, may perhaps be intended to suggest some kind of perspective.

In the light of what has already been said, it is perhaps obvious that the Tapestry is not a particularly valuable source for the history of civilian clothing, which it reduces virtually to a single basic costume, irrespective of the differences there must have been between Norman and English dress. The only exceptions are King Edward, some of the clerics, and Turold. Not even William and Harold display any sartorial distinction. As usual, the different colours employed in the embroidery have more to do with a concern for aesthetic variety than with fidelity to actual colour.

The standard costume is of simple design: below, leggings, partly concealed by the tunic; and above, a short cloak held by a clasp at the shoulder. The head is mostly uncovered, although the look-out in scene 12 (p. 117) and some of the archers marching in the vanguard of the Norman army (scene 51, p. 235) have pointed hats, doubtless of cloth. The long cloak seems to be exclusive to princes, prelates and some of the clerics, while characters of middling rank have only the short cloak, which is also often worn by knights when in civilian dress. One or two figures have laced stockings, notably Duke William and one of his guards in scene 14 (pp. 125–126).[55]

Other than King Edward, few figures are shown with beards: two craftsmen in scene 36 (p. 189); the helmsman of the last ship in William's fleet (scene 38, p. 196); a cook (scene 42, p. 210); and one of William's table-companions in scene 43 (p. 212). There is nothing to suggest that a beard was the mark of any particular social rank. As for the women, there are only three, which precludes generalisation about their costume. They are the mysterious Aelfgyva (scene 15, p. 128), Queen Edith at King Edward's deathbed (scene 27, p. 166), and the Englishwoman driven out of her house by the Normans as they prepare for battle (scene 47, p. 217). All three wear long cloaks, and a veil covering the head and shoulders. The only possible hint of fashion is seen in the long sleeves of the anonymous Englishwoman.

VI

Soldiers, weapons and combat

As is evident from the inventory entry of 1476, viewers of the Tapestry have long seen it as a narrative of the Norman Conquest, that is, as primarily a work of military history. Today we take a different view, but the fact remains that the greater part of the story consists of feats of arms. This aspect inevitably, therefore, occupies an important part of this study.

The nature of the medium makes it easier to assess these military aspects at the individual than at the collective level. The arms, armour, and fighting techniques of the individual warriors are readily grasped, but not the tactical and strategic dimensions. It is clear enough, of course, that Norman tactics were based on heavy cavalry, while the English fought on foot. As Wace summed it up a century later, 'The Normans ... on horseback they are goodly knights / and well accustomed to the fight';[56] while 'The English knew not how to joust nor how to bear arms on horseback. They wielded axes and pikes, and fought with such weapons'.[57] But it is hard to go beyond this, because the designer, as we shall see, based almost all the combatants on a single model which is neither wholly English nor wholly Norman. He probably combined elements taken from both sides, doubtless with an English emphasis.

Archaeology, unfortunately, offers little help except with regard to the swords (coats of mail have rarely survived), and historical interpretations therefore vary considerably. For example, is the English force depicted on the Tapestry meant to be the *fyrd* (the mass levy), with the elite housecarles at its heart; or is it a more organised force, levied on the basis of one man for every five *hides* (the Old English *hide* meant a landholding adequate to support a family), as suggested by some valuable sources? In the end, this invaluable source for military history must remain uncertain, ambiguous, and contested. We shall not seek to extract from it more information than it can give.

Let us begin with a systematic examination of both the arms and the armour. Only three kinds of protective equipment are on show: helmets, hauberks (or coats of mail), and shields. The helmets are all of one kind: a cone-shaped headpiece, no doubt of iron, with a descending strip protecting the nose. Many seem to have been furnished with sideplates or thin vertical plates concealing the joins between the various parts. These helmets pose an interesting historical problem. Archaeological evidence suggests that there were not many of them around, and that they were mostly reserved for leaders. Thus, only one helmet survives from the whole of Norway, found in the tomb of Gjermundbu in Ringerike and dating from the early tenth century. They were more common in early eleventh-century England. The will of Archbishop Ælfric of Canterbury (c. 1003-04) includes a bequest of his best ship together with 60 coats of mail and 60 helmets (evidently enough for the entire crew). The profusion of helmets in the Tapestry is therefore somewhat surprising. Almost all the combatants wear them, except for the English infantry (perhaps the *fyrd*) drawn up on the hill between scenes 53 and 54 (pp. 245–248) and the substantial group of archers shown in the lower border supporting the final Norman assault in scenes 55 and 56 (pp. 250–255).

The shape of the helmets is clearly shown at the loading of the ships (scene 37, p. 192), where some are held by the nose-piece. They offer no protection for the cheeks or neck. They appear in various colours, but that probably reflects nothing more than the fancy of the seamstresses. The famous episode in scene 55 (p. 250) shows that they could be removed to facilitate recognition. There are no differences between the helmets of the leaders and those of the foot-soldiers. The design, known by specialists as the

Spangenhelm, is familiar from countless eleventh-century manuscript illustrations of Norman, English, and northern French provenance. It is also seen in the royal effigies on English coins from the reign of Cnut onwards.

The hauberk or coat of mail was also in general use. About 200 are depicted, worn by footmen as well as by knights, and by the English as well as the Normans. Their purpose is summed up by a Belgian text from the late tenth century: 'the hauberk is armour, an iron covering used by knights in combat; it repels the weapons of the foe'.[58] It was a traditional type of armour. Gaulish warriors were already using it at the beginning of the common era. Although the Romans made only limited use of it, the Germans were certainly familiar with it from the third century (witness the Danish finds at Vimose), and it is was also used by some horsemen at the time of the 'barbarian invasions'. But its heyday was from the tenth to the fourteenth centuries. After that it was nothing more than a supplement to plate-armour.

Like the helmet, the coat of mail appears in surprising numbers on the Tapestry for such an expensive item. Composed usually of interlocking iron rings, or less commonly of separate rings sewn onto a leather tunic, its manufacture required only limited raw material but immense quantities of manual labour, which put a very high price on it, as we know from various eleventh-century Norman sources. A Jumièges charter of circa 1045-49 records Roger I of Montgomery, an old liegeman of Duke Robert, receiving from the abbot, amongst other remuneration, 'one hauberk (elsewhere called armour) worth seven pounds'.[59] For comparison, a war-horse is valued in the same document at 30 pounds. These coats of mail were so valuable that they were often traded second-hand. Armour 'which once belonged to Robert de Troisgots' was sold to the church of Saint-Étienne in Caen for 11 pounds; in 1104 the Abbey of Mont-Saint-Michel accepted the gift of a horse and armour for which the owner, who had entered a monastery, had no further use.[60]

Further problems arise from the way that the Tapestry represents coats of mail. They all follow one pattern: a single piece comprising a mail tunic with mail leggings down to the knees, or in some cases, such as Duke William and Count Eustace (scenes 50 and 55, pp. 230 and 250), down to the feet. This all makes perfect sense for infantrymen, but is unthinkable for knights. So the Tapestry is most probably using a design based on English infantry armour, as seen in the coat of mail on the Winchester frieze fragment.[61] And another detail has tested the ingenuity of scholars. In five or six cases, the hauberk seems to have a kind of square breastplate over the upper part of the chest, clearly delineated in the embroidery by different coloured thread. It may have been removeable, as there seem to be four buttons fixing it at the corners. What was it? It could have been extra protection for a vulnerable area, but might simply have been a detachable flap to make the armour easier to get on and off. There is no way of deciding, but it does seem as though this feature, never seen on a foot soldier, was exclusive to a few high-ranking Norman knights: Duke William himself (scene 49, p. 225), some of his boon companions in scenes 21 and 22 (pp. 143–144), 40 (p. 207), 48 (p. 221), 49 (p. 224), and 55 (p. 251), and also Harold when he receives arms from William (scene 21, p. 143). The hauberks being loaded onto the ships (scene 37, pp. 192–193) all display this feature. And here the breastplates look rigid, in that they sometimes project above the level of the rods on which the hauberks are being carried. But given the limitations of the available archaeological evidence, this little mystery remains insoluble for now.

The coats of mail shown being loaded onto the ships reveal another detail not seen clearly elsewhere: the sleeves and leggings, both of them quite short, end in boldly delineated coloured borders, which might represent cloth or even leather.

It seems impossible to trust the testimony of the Tapestry as to the numbers of English infantry who wore a hauberk because, given its cost, it must have been the preserve of a small military elite. Despite the paucity of archaeological evidence, it is plausible that it was standard equipment for Harold's housecarles, but hardly for the bulk of his army. Most of the *fyrd* probably looked more like those in scene 54 (p. 245), with only a shield for protection.

The shields also pose problems, firstly as to shape. Early on they are mostly of an elongated kite shape, whether shown on the arms of knights (scene 7, pp. 105–106) or stowed at the sides of the ships (scene 5, p. 101). Round shields are the exception, seen on the arms of two English warriors (scene 52, pp. 240–241) and among the detritus of battle (scenes 53 and 57, pp. 242 and 259).[62] The long shields have no obvious boss, while the round ones display a stout pointed boss which may conceivably have had an offensive function. One or two of the long shields seem to have a central protrusion which may have been a vestigial boss (scenes 13 and 49, pp. 122 and 226). The kite-shaped shield appears in many continental manuscripts from the late tenth century onwards, and rapidly established itself as standard equipment for Norman knights.[63] Anna Comnena remarked on its prevalence among Bohemond's men at Dyrrhachium around 1100.[64] Viking shields found on ships in the Oslo fjord, in contrast, are round.[65] Upside down the long shield could serve in the field as, among other things, a makeshift table (scene 43, pp. 211–212). Only once do we get a clear view of the straps by which the shields were held (scene 17, pp. 134–135), as in general the bodies of the knights obscure them.

The decoration of the shields is another problem. Although archaeologists have found traces of colour on some surviving English and Scandinavian shields, there is no indication earlier than the Tapestry that this represented artistic decoration.[66] But the Tapestry's shields present a remarkable range of patterns and designs. Some look like heraldic designs, which has led some interpreters to see them as armorial bearings. But while this is simply anachronistic, there is a degree of resemblance in these emblems which means that they could have served as identifying badges. It is worth noting the considerable diversity of these designs.

While some shields are shown in a single colour (notably those on board ship), others are decorated with crosses of varying clarity, with spirals (one of the commonest motifs), with various patterns of studs, and with real or imaginary beasts — dragons perhaps, or else badly drawn lions or leopards. There is no apparent connection between these emblems and any particular social rank or military function.

As far as we know, the shields were made of wood (particularly from lime wood), with a leather covering and with metal studs (especially on the circular shields) around the rim and a metal boss at the centre. They would have been relatively cheap and thus in general use.

The offensive weapons on the Tapestry manifest greater variety: lance, sword, axe, bow, and perhaps club and crossbow (not to mention sticks and stones). The commonest weapon on show is the lance, mostly in the hands of knights but also at times of foot soldiers, whether in combat or not. Except for those set at sea, there is scarcely a scene without it. Its design is unproblematic: a two-metre shaft (to judge by the scale of the men), with a relatively slim, roughly triangular blade. The question of how it was used by mounted knights raises one of the most contested questions in the military history of the Middle Ages, that of 'mounted schock combat'. The traditional method

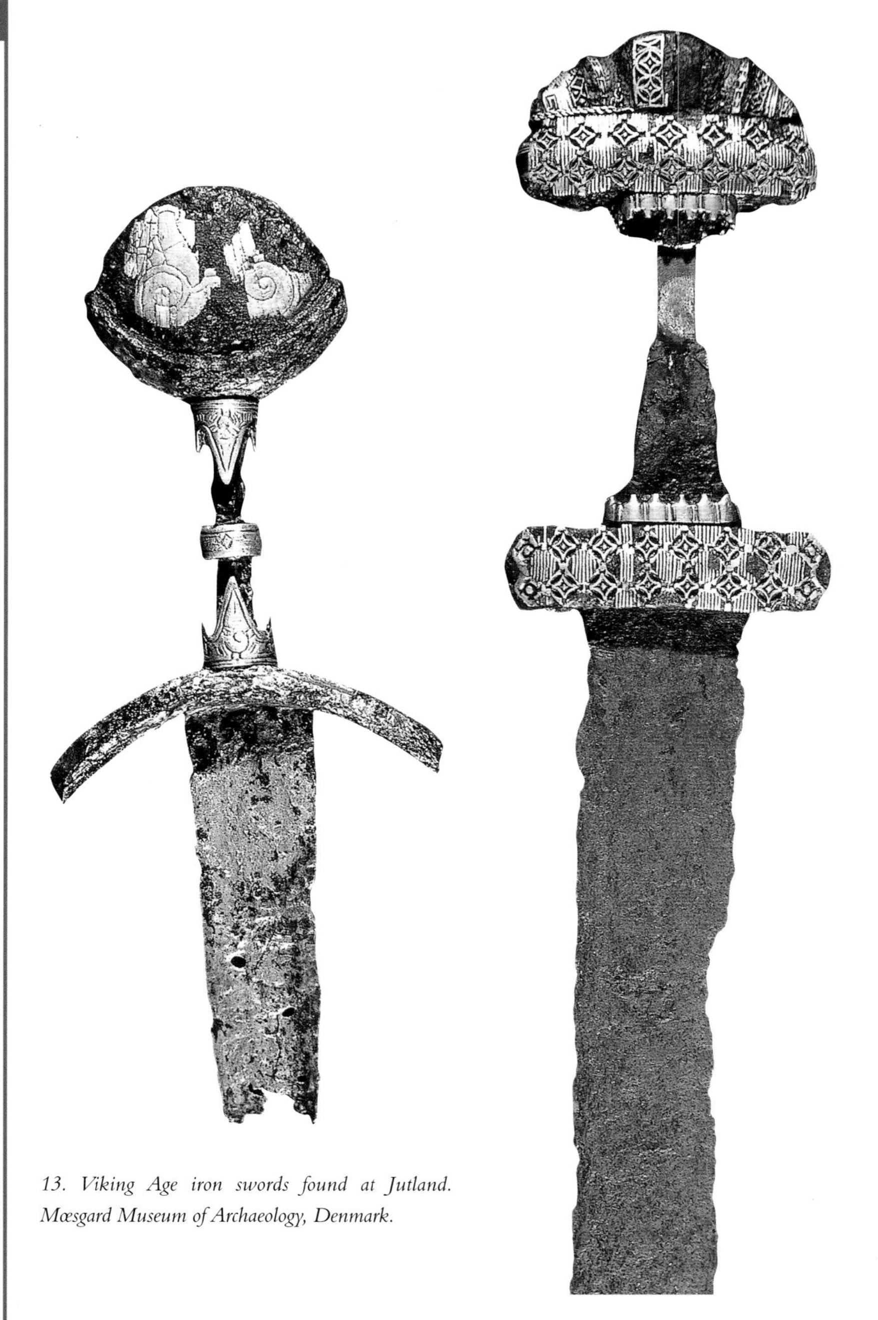

13. Viking Age iron swords found at Jutland. Mœsgard Museum of Archaeology, Denmark.

was for a horseman to grasp the lance halfway along the shaft, hold it aloft, and hurl it like a javelin. 'Mounted shock combat' involved couching it firmly under the right arm and charging to strike the enemy at chest height, which was not possible until the adoption of stirrups and high saddles had given the knight a firm seat. It is the first method which predominates on the Tapestry: the couched lance appears only two or three times (scene 52, p. 241).[67] The impact of this new tactic in 1066 should not be exaggerated. In any case it was most useful against other knights, but at Hastings the Normans faced only infantry.

The lances were fairly heavy, and are sometimes shown being rested on the stirrups by the knights as they marched. (scenes 40, 48, and 51, pp. 206, 221, and 234). It is only ever the knights who fly pennants or standards from their lances, never the foot-soldiers.

The swords, as far as can be told from their somewhat vague depiction, belong to what the leading expert, the Danish scholar Ada Bruhn Hoffmeyer, classifies as 'Group I transitional'. Dating from 1050-1100, this type is typified by a relatively broad, short blade, a handle ending in a hemispherical pommel, and with right-angled cross-pieces forming the guard.[68] It was neither specifically Norman nor English, but was common to most of western Europe and not vastly different from the swords in use at the end of the Viking era (fig. 13). Swords are seen most clearly where they are brandished by princes as an emblem of power, as by Guy of Ponthieu in scene 9 (p. 110) and by Harold in scene 30 (p. 175), as well as in the embarkation scene (37, p. 192). In the combat scenes, the shape of the pommel is almost indiscernible. Scabbards are rarely shown, although one can be seen on an English foot-soldier in scene 56 (p. 253), and four horses seem to have scabbards attached to their flanks: Count Guy's (scene 7, p. 105); one of those held by Turold (scene 10, p. 113); and those of Duke William where he greets Harold (scene 13, p. 122) and accepts the keys of Dinan (scene 20, p. 141). This feature may have been exclusive to princely mounts. In scene 9 (p. 109) there is a clear view of the belts and buckles on the two swords held point downwards in the presence of Count Guy. Curiously, the foot soldier about to behead an Englishman in scene 56 (p. 255) has two swords, one in his hand and the other at his side. Several knights, on the other hand, seem to have no sword to go with their lances and shields, though this may reflect nothing more than economy in the drawing.

The axes seen on the Tapestry have two very different functions: as tools in the hands of the woodmen and carpenters (scenes 35-36, pp. 183–185); and as weapons (not to mention their appearance in the hands of the butchers and foragers in scenes 40-41, pp. 207–209). The tools have simple, triangular blades, while the weapons often have a concave curve along the cutting edge. But it is not clear that in reality they were very different.[69] The military use of the axe, obviously a custom of Scandinavian origin, is restricted on the Tapestry to English infantry. The battle-axe was the weapon of choice for the housecarles, that originally Danish bodyguard which had, since the time of

Cnut, formed the entourage of the English kings. There is not a single axe on show at the loading of the Norman fleet.

The housecarles (from the Old Norse *hùskarlar*, literally 'house fellows') were free men devoted to the personal service of a prince or king. They are found in England for the first time in 1033, in Cnut's entourage. Later in the eleventh century, they were professional warriors, many of whom were rewarded with landed estates: *Domesday Book* refers to 25 of them. To judge from their names, they were mostly of Danish ancestry, even after the return of the Wessex dynasty in 1042.[70] In the rest of the Nordic world the term had less precise and often more peaceful connotations.[71]

In the Tapestry, the battle-axe is usually wielded with both hands, which precluded carrying a shield or a sword (except in one instance, in scene 54, p. 245). All the axe-men are equipped with helmets and hauberks, except for those on ceremonial duties at Harold's coronation (scene 29, p. 173). Such axes have been found at numerous archaeological sites, and in Scandinavia ornamental axes seem to have served as insignia of power, though there is no sign of this on the Tapestry.

Archers have a prominent place in the Tapestry's depiction of the Norman invasion force, but are seen only once in the English ranks (scene 51, p. 236), and not at all in the Breton campaign. Their first appearance is in scene 51 (p. 235), where four archers, only one of them in armour, support the advance of a unit of cavalry. They crowd the lower margin through scenes 55-56 (pp. 250–253), flanking the cavalry during the second assault.[72] They are armed with bows of average size and simple curvature, not comparable to the English longbows of the Hundred Years' War. They often wear a quiver at their back, with a supply of arrows, and some of them clutch bundles of arrows ready to use.

The importance of archery in 1066 is confirmed by the chronicles and is of considerable interest to the military historian, as was emphasised by the Norwegian archaeologist A. W. Brøgger in 1946. He argued that the deployment of archers at Hastings was a direct continuation of a Scandinavian tradition, as seen in particular at the Battle of Stiklestad (1033), in which St Olaf died.[73] William the Conqueror's tactical innovation was to co-ordinate his archers with traditionally French use of heavy cavalry: the task of the cavalry was to shatter the enemies' formation, that of the archers to harry them with continual fire. The chroniclers make particular mention of archery at the moment of Harold's death, when a 'hail of arrows' (*imber sagittarum*, says Henry of Huntingdon) fell upon the English ranks.[73b]

The employment of any other weapons is either poorly attested or purely conjectural. At the moment when William's knights hit the English line (scene 51, p. 236), a curious projectile is seen hurtling from the English ranks, a sort of shaft with three knobs on the end. It may perhaps represent a cluster of missiles launched in a volley, or else a crossbow bolt (of which more in a moment). But it is most probably simply a stone attached to a stick, as suggested by a passage of William of Poitiers in which he speaks of the English 'hurling weapons of all kinds … and stones fixed to sticks'.[74]

Objections have often been made to the notion that the crossbow formed part of the Norman arsenal in 1066, and certainly there is no sign of that weapon, then a recent invention, on the Tapestry. But the *Carmen de Hastingae Proelio* (whose authority is, as we shall see, somewhat suspect) refers to the presence of crossbowmen under the term *balistantes*, while the rather more reliable William of Poitiers talks of foot soldiers at the head of the army 'armed with arrows and crossbows [*balistis*]'.[75] Baudry de Bourgueil speaks in similar terms. The use of crossbows, then, seemed plausible both to contemporaries and to those writing in the early twelfth century. But the crossbow was unknown in England at that time. The suggestion that the only armoured archer (scene 51, p. 235) has a crossbow is mere wishful thinking: his bow is just like all the rest. If William did deploy crossbowmen, the Tapestry took no notice.[76]

Whatever the details, the weaponry depicted on the Tapestry was standard issue in late eleventh-century western Europe. More or less the same things can be seen on a Spanish ivory which once belonged to the shrine of the eponymous saint at San Millán de la Cogolla in the Rioja region and, at the other end of Christendom, on carved wooden panels from the church of Valthjofsstadhir in Iceland (now in the National Museum at Reykjavik): cone-shaped helmets with nose-pieces, coats of mail, even stirrups on long straps, and (on the ivory) kite-shaped shields. Heavy cavalry on the Norman model had caught on everywhere except among the English, who remained true to their custom of fighting on foot even though they rode to battle — as Harold does in the Tapestry (scene 49, pp. 226–227).

A knight's equipment was prodigiously expensive, and in most cases he had to meet the cost himself. Eleventh-century Norman charters furnish ample evidence for the price of warhorses. The custom was to repay donors or vendors to churches with mounts rather than in cash.[77] Over fifty such cases are known, with the value of the horses ranging from 14 *sous* to 30 *livres*, according to the quality and purpose of the animals. The average price was between 5 and 10 *livres*, this latter figure typical for a lady's palfrey. With warhorses the colour was also important — white horses were at a premium — and the usual price was between 8 and 12 *livres* a head. Over and above that were the bridle and saddle (priced in 1103 at 1 mark — about 8 *livres*); spurs (about 6 *deniers* in the twelfth century); and sword (a child's sword cost 14 *sous*).[78]

The Tapestry's horses have for a long time attracted the attention of specialists, who have considered from them several angles: breed, harness, horsemanship, and artistic convention.[79] One thing is clear: the depiction of the horses is as vivid as it is convincing. The designer of the cartoons knew his horses as well as, to judge from the naval scenes, he knew his ships. The horses on show are not of great height, and

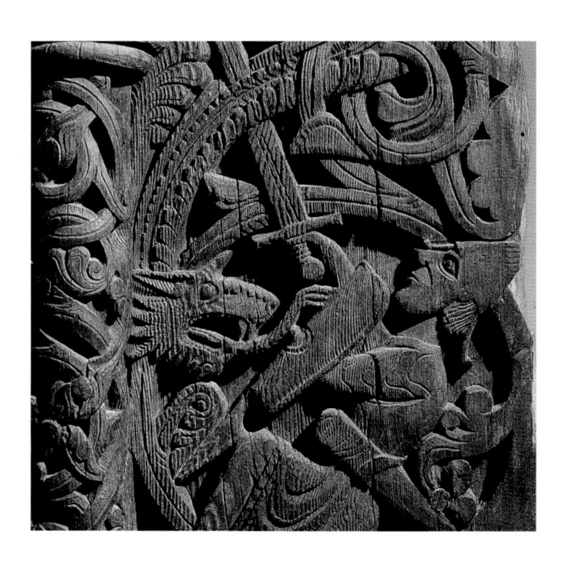

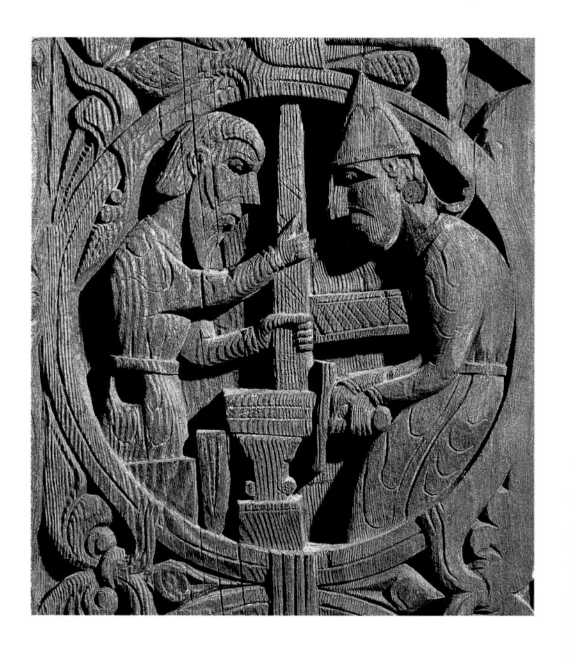

14 and 15. Details from a twelfth-century carved wooden doorway in the church of Hylestad (Norway) showing scenes from the Nordic saga of Sigurd. Above, Sigurd slays the dragon Fafnir. Below, Sigurd has the sacred sword reforged by Regin the smith. Oslo Historical Museum.

archaeological evidence confirms that the animals of this era were more the size of large ponies than of today's carthorses. Some writers have arbitrarily assumed that imposing chargers were reserved for great nobles such as Duke William or the Count of Ponthieu, but the Tapestry gives no warrant for this. Rather, it shows 'knights of some stature on relatively small mounts'.[80]

Documentary evidence takes us a little further. According to William of Poitiers, Duke William received horses from Gascony and the Auvergne, and also from the kings of Spain, who sent them to win his friendship.[81] Wace claims that the duke's mount at Hastings was a present from the king of Spain, brought to him by Walter Giffard, lord of Longueville-sur-Scie; and he frequently describes the Norman horses as 'Spanish', although modern scholars have doubts about the numbers of Spanish horses.[82] Our meagre knowledge of medieval equine breeds does not enable us to check this against the evidence of the Tapestry, although some specialists believe that an 'oriental' strain can be discerned there,[83] which would be consonant with Spanish origins.[84] But there is no reason to think that the majority of the Norman horses were of anything other than local origin: there were stud-farms in Normandy, mainly in the forested regions. The Tapestry's designer did not attempt to distinguish warhorses from packhorses and others in the way that contemporary usage did with its rich vocabulary of chargers, palfreys, workhorses, etc. Nor does he depict any striking equestrian feats, although William of Poitiers emphasised Duke William's reputation for horsemanship.[85]

The horses on the Tapestry are equipped with triangular stirrups, a recent innovation which revolutionised western cavalry tactics.[86] It derived, apparently, from the riders of the Steppes, or else from Iran, where heavy cavalry had been an essential military arm since the time of the Sassanids. In western art, the stirrup first appears in the tenth century, fixed at the end of a long strap which allowed the leg to be locked out: it was this which led to the aforementioned 'mounted shock combat'.

This new tactic for the lance, which in due course became standard practice, also required a sturdy high saddle which would seat the rider firmly enough to let him withstand the shock of frontal impact without falling off, as the Tapestry shows on several occasions. The Tapestry's saddles are symmetrical before and behind, the pommel much the same shape as the cantle or hind-bow. They must have been made partly of wood, as they do not seem to be merely fabric. The strap which attached the stirrups could be a weak point, for it might be grabbed in an attempt to unseat the rider (as in scene 53 pp. 246–247). While almost all the horses have a saddle-strap across the horse's breast, none has a crupper to the rear apart from the little packhorse in scene 41 (p. 209).

Bridle and bit are seen on most of the horses, as are the reins, which riders hold in their left hands. Even on board ship the horses are harnessed thus, with simple but doubtless effective tackle. The scale of the drawing does not enable us to see much of the horseshoes, but they were certainly in general use, and perhaps are sometimes indicated by nuances of colour in the embroidery (as in scenes 52 and 56, pp. 241 and 255). There is nothing to distinguish English harness from Norman.

One of the notorious difficulties about the battle-scenes on the Tapestry concerns the *vexillum sancti Petri*, the famous banner of St Peter, which was so crucial to the ideology of the whole enterprise. Bestowed by the pope as a sign of favour and approval, one had been accorded that very year by Pope Alexander II to the leader of the Patarini of Milan, a popular reforming group renowned for direct action.[87] So it was in current use. The subject was systematically explored by Carl Erdmann in 1935, and there is no doubt that William secured a papal banner.[88] But its exact appearance remains unknown. It is often reckoned, largely on the strength of the Tapestry, to have borne the sign of the cross. But the case is weakened by the fact that different interpreters think that they see it in different places. Several of them seem to have mistaken for it the lantern attached to the masthead of the duke's ship (scene 39, p. 201). Others identify it with the pennant brandished by the knight beside William when he shows his face to his troops in scene 55 (p. 251),[89] or else with that held by William himself in scene 46 (p. 217). It is fairly clear that it would have been attached to a lance. But plenty of Norman standards looked like these and bore the sign of the cross: there is one in scene 16 (p. 131), at the beginning of the Breton expedition, and that was certainly not blessed by the pope! So it is probably best to reserve judgement on this matter.

Harold's standard, whose place in his last stand is well attested by the chronicles, raises just as many questions. William of Poitiers reports that the victorious William sent it to the pope, and that it was

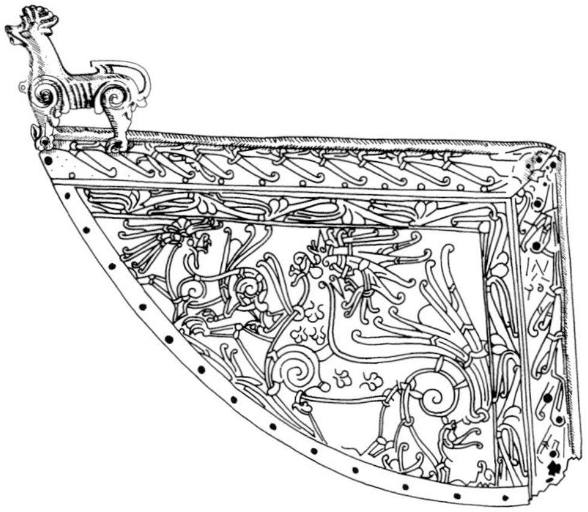

16. *Weathervane from the church of Heggen (Norway).*

embroidered in gold with the image of an armed man.[90] No doubt this was to some extent mere literary embellishment, as no such thing appears on the Tapestry. On the contrary, scene 57 shows clearly, in front of the mortally wounded king, a dragon fixed on a lance and flying horizontally in the wind. It might have been made of cloth, but not necessarily. For it is reminiscent of the metal standards, generally cut out of bronze plate, on Viking ships. They were often in the form of dragons, from the early eleventh to the late twelfth century. Several have survived to this day as weathervanes on churches, notably at Heggen (Buskerud) in Norway (fig. 16) and at Källunge and Söderala in Sweden, some of them cut out of bronze and others simply engraved on it.[91] The horizontal position of Harold's standard could well mean that it was of this type. On the other hand, neither the Norman nor the English ships on the Tapestry have such emblems, and nowhere else is Harold shown with a dragon-standard — neither on the Breton campaign (though his involvement in this was unexpected) nor at the start of the Battle of Hastings. Once more, the uncertainties remain considerable.

It is difficult to draw any useful conclusions about the other banners and standards fixed on lances in various places. They are mostly squares or rectangles of cloth with three short pennants on the outer side. Others are triangular, such as the one knocked to the ground by a charging knight in scene 53 (p. 242); and some are semi-circular (scene 48, p. 223). Almost all of them seem to belong to major figures, such as those addressed by Duke William in scene 50 (p. 231). Two of them are carried by members of a group of housecarls. To only one banner, that of Count Eustace of Boulogne (scene 55, p. 251), has any precise significance been plausibly attributed. The rest of them seem merely decorative.

The Tapestry, as we have said, is of only limited use to the historian of tactics and strategy. But it is relatively simple to locate it in the medieval development of the depiction of combat in art.[92] It is firmly conventional, especially in representing knightly combat and battle casualties. Some of the images represent eleventh-century innovations, borrowed from biblical illustrations, but most of them, as Jennie Kiff has shown, are based on models long familiar in English manuscripts. The innovations of the Bayeux designer are minor, such as showing multiple projectiles flying around the heads of the soldiers. The personal style of the artist is evident chiefly in the expressive grouping of the figures of knights and in the sheer scale of the battle sequence. Traditional images of combat were mostly confined to about half a dozen figures, with neither that sense of crescendo so evident in scenes 50-52 (pp. 230–240) nor that sense of the ebb and flow of a great battle which so powerfully struck the chroniclers of Hastings. The future of two great peoples was at stake, and the final outcome seemed more than once to hang in the balance. The designer of the Tapestry knew this and he had scope, the kind of scope denied to most artists of his time, cramped by the narrow confines of a page of manuscript. He had space and he knew how to use it. His achievement towers over the military art of the feudal era.

VII

The ships

The Bayeux Tapestry has long been recognised as a source of the utmost value for the naval history of north-western Europe in the eleventh century. In studying its images of ships one comes right up against some of the major problems it poses: the extent of its realism, the nature of its links with the English and Norman worlds, and the importance of the legacy of the Vikings shared by all the peoples of the North Sea shores. Images of ships, singly or in groups, always looking much the same, appear at four points on the Tapestry: Harold's voyage to France; his return home; after his accession; and above all when William's fleet set sail. They merit close examination, and so we shall discuss them here in more detail than is usual.

The varied nomenclature for seagoing vessels of the Viking Age (a nomenclature to which the Tapestry makes no allusion) is now beginning to be clearly understood. It shifted over time, and we shall focus on eleventh-century usage. Dismissing the spurious and barbarous term *drakkar* coined by the lexicographer A. Jal in 1836 (a term which had a bizarre afterlife in French historiography[93]), we find three key words. The first is *snekkja*, which remained current in Normandy until the twelfth century under the forms *isnecchia* or *esnèque*; in Scandinavia it denoted a vessel requisitioned for military service (the *leding*) — in Norway one of no more than about 40 oars.

Second is *langskip*, the longship (a word ultimately of classical Latin origin), a long, slender vessel built for primarily military purposes, and with more or less elaborate oceangoing variants such as the *hafskip*. Finally, there is *knörr*, or *canardus* in Norman Latin, used for a commercial vessel primarily designed to transport men, beasts, or goods. Besides these basic terms are a host of others, including *karfar*, chieftain's ships (of which those found in Norwegian royal ship burials are doubtless excellent examples); *skeidhir*, great ships of as many as 60 pairs of oars, of which the *drakar* (the correct spelling), decorated with dragon's head prows, were a variant; and *skutur*, low, light vessels used mainly for reconnaisance missions.[94]

Although the earliest and most spectacular archaeological finds, above all in Norway, furnished examples only of the first kind of ship, more recent discoveries in Denmark have retrieved equally good examples of the *langskip* and the *knörr*.

Various estimates, some of them highly debatable, have been offered as to the dimensions and capacities of the ships shown on the Tapestry. What is clear is that the drawings considerably simplify the reality, in particular by foreshortening — with some of the ships reduced to the scale of rowing boats (those in the background of the invasion fleet of 1066). Danish warships of the twelfth century carried on average 40 men, at once oarsmen, sailors, and warriors; and a similar figure emerges from thirteenth-century Norwegian sources. Only the chieftains' ships were larger. There is every reason to postulate similar figures for the ships of 1066.

The first archaeological find to cast light on the Tapestry was that made at Gokstad on the left bank of the Oslofjord, near Sandefjord. It was discovered in 1880 by Nicolay Nicolaysen and written up in 1882. Today it is on show in the Viking Ship Museum at Bygdøy near Oslo, as is the similar but even more spectacular vessel found in 1904 by Haakon Shetelig at Oseberg, a little to the south (fig. 17). This find was written up by him, Hj. Falk and A. W. Brøgger between 1917 and 1928.[95] A third find, made earlier (in 1867) on the eastern bank of the Oslofjord, at Tune (Rolsvøy) near Sarpsborg, was less interesting and far less complete. Besides these three, the Viking Ship Museum has some lesser exhibits, notably three rowing boats from Gokstad. All these vessels date from the ninth century.

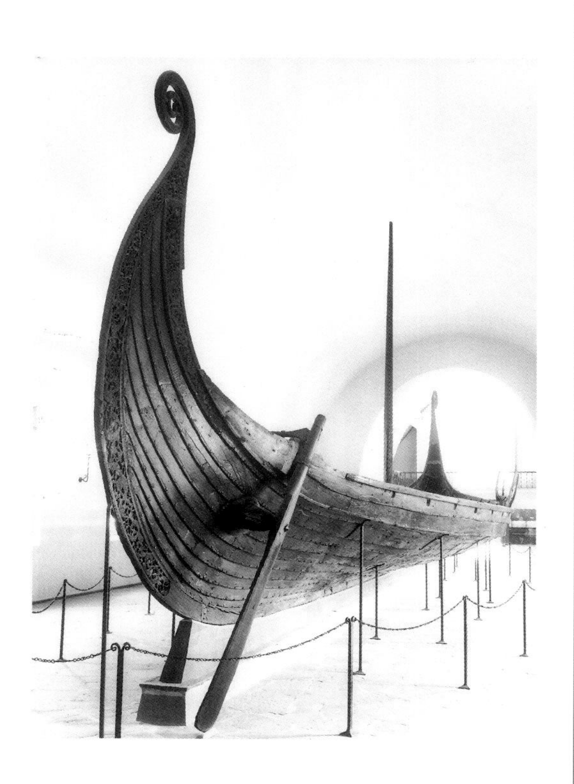

17. The Oseberg Ship (Norway). Viking Ship Museum, Bygdøy, Oslo.

Exceptional geological conditions — the presence of a blue clay in which organic materials such as wood and textiles are remarkably well preserved — give these three finds special value, but it must be remembered that the first two ships were found in royal burial mounds. The Oseberg ship in particular is of unique artistic significance, not only in terms of shipbuilding but also in terms of the grave goods interred with the body (sledges, a chariot, tent-posts, etc). It is the pinnacle of the Scandinavian art of the Viking Age. These finds have haunted the Norwegian imagination for a century. In 1892 a replica of the Gokstad vessel made an Atlantic crossing from Norway to the United States. However, finds of this kind can be deceptive. The Oseberg ship, a luxury vessel probably used for royal pleasure trips along the coast, is not the standard Viking vessel, and it differs significantly from the ships shown on the Tapestry. It is worth noting the dimensions: the Gokstad ship was 23.30 metres long and 5.25 metres broad, and the Oseberg ship was of the same order of magnitude at 21.45 metres long and 5.10 metres broad.

It is the Danish finds from Skuldelev, in the Roskilde fjord, that have really cast important new light on the Tapestry, as they are very ordinary vessels which were decommissioned after long service and scuttled for the strictly pragmatic purpose of blocking a channel. Five wrecks have been retrieved, dried out, and carefully preserved at the Viking Ship Museum in Roskilde.[96] Two are warships (nos. 2 and 5), two are trading vessels (nos. 1 and 3; nothing like them had been found before), and one is a ferry or fishing-boat (no. 6). One of the warships (no. 5) is a perfect match for the rotted vessel whose outlines were revealed in 1935 by the excavation of a ship-burial at Ladby (near Kerteminde, on the Danish island of Fionie). It is also the nearest thing to the ships shown on the Tapestry. Its prow survives (as does that of no. 3), and is unadorned. Carbon-dating suggests that these ships were built between 910 and 1080. They were all built mainly of oak, with some fir and lime. The warship (no. 5) was about 18 metres long and 2.60 metres broad, with a draught of about 1.10 metres. It was clinker-built with seven boards each side (the Tapestry never shows more than five boards). It had 12 oars per side, requiring a crew of 24 oarsmen. Though less well preserved than that of Gokstad and a far cry from the splendour of the Oseberg vessel, these ships from Skuldelev are certainly more informative for our purposes, typical of the run-of-the-mill shipping of the time.

It should be borne in mind that only one of the Viking ships actually used in coastal raids on western Europe is currently known to us — and in pretty poor shape, as it was burned prior to being buried. Dating from the second half of the tenth century, it was discovered in 1906 by P. du Châtellier and L. Le Pontois at Locmaria on the isle of Groix.[97] It presents several interesting features for our purposes, notably the large number of round shields (from 14 to 20) attached to the sides, as well as the remains of an ornate prow reminiscent of that found at Ladby. The tomb in which it was found was doubtless that of a Viking chief.

Besides these celebrated examples, which any study of the Tapestry must take into account, there are other, less spectacular finds to be considered: the Klåstad ship (from the western coast of the Oslofjord, c. 800) and the Askekärr ship from the lower Göttaälv, both of them capacious cargo vessels, slightly pointed fore and aft; and the ship found in 1967 on the Baltic island of Rügen at the Slav-Scandinavian trading station of Ralswiek. These are all variants of the sort of trading ship represented by no. 1 of the Skuldelev finds.[98]

The principal artistic sources for Viking ships are the extraordinary engraved steles from the Swedish island of Gotland which have been investigated by S. Lindqvist and E. Nylén.[99] About 380 survive, from between the fifth and the twelfth centuries. A good number of them, from about the beginning of the eighth century, have, alongside runic inscriptions and scenes from Norse mythology, the image of a ship with a square sail, headed no doubt for the nether world with its armed crew (fig. 18). These images provide our earliest evidence as to the nautical instruments available to the Vikings. The ships are strikingly similar to those on the Tapestry, with the same kind of sails, similar figureheads fore and aft (often in the form of animal heads), steering-oars, and, often enough, round shields hung along the side. The crewmen are often wielding swords, and sometimes seem to be wearing cone-shaped helmets. Sometimes lances are stacked fore or aft. There is only one notable difference: the rigging. A kind of lozenge-patterned netting keeps the sail in shape, and the cords

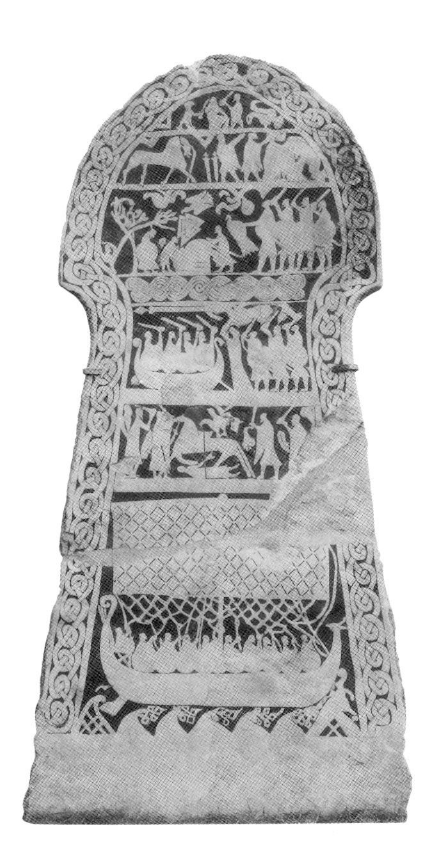

18. Eighth-century engraved stone from Lärbro. Now in the Bunge Museum (Gotland).

at the ends are held by the men on board. This was probably, as we shall see, because those sails were made from wool. But otherwise the similarities are striking. Only some of the oldest steles (perhaps from the sixth century) show boats with oars but without sails. Mostly there is only one ship on each stele. These images from Gotland are of especial importance because they are the only sources prior to the Tapestry which give us any sense of what Viking sails were like.[100]

Looking more closely at the Tapestry's nautical scenes, it seems that, without distinguishing clearly between different types of vessel in its rather schematised depictions of ships, the Tapestry nevertheless implies a distinction by assigning two separate functions to them. Most of the ships carry men (it is not possible to distinguish soldiers from sailors), but some carry not only men but also horses (up to ten). Documentary sources likewise distinguish ships by their cargo: Baudry de Bourgueil writes of the ships that 'one carries men, another horses', and Wace says much the same.[100b]

This transportation of horses by sea is important, and has often been seen as a technique recently acquired by the Normans, who would have seen the Byzantines doing this in Calabria, and would have used it themselves for the first time during their first landings in Sicily, around 1060. This interpretation rests primarily on the evidence of the *Carmen de Hastingae Proelio*, which has Apulians, Calabrians, and Sicilians in Duke William's army (line 259). The mention of Sicily, though, is an anachronism: the Norman conquest of that island had barely begun in 1066. And the general suspicion which now surrounds the reliability of the *Carmen* also casts doubt on this passage.[101] Another interpretation sees in it simply a continuation of a Viking practice, a possibility confirmed by experiments with copies of the Ladby ship.[102] But this must be somewhat doubtful, as the alleged precedents date back to the years 866-892! In fact, the Normans could have learned Byzantine techniques in other ways. Normans had been serving as Byzantine mercenaries since 1035 at the latest, and some had even taken part in 'amphibious operations' such as Georgios Makarios's unsuccessful assault on Syracuse. Mediterranean influence, then, remains a plausible though not a compelling hypothesis.

Almost all the ships on the Tapestry have figureheads fore or aft (sometimes both), usually in the shapes of animal heads. These ornaments are a real problem for naval archaeologists, as none have turned up in excavations (the spiral prow on the Oseberg ship is a reconstruction). So they are known only from pictorial sources, chief among them the Gotland steles and the Tapestry itself. It was once thought that the figureheads dredged up at various times from the Scheldt, at Moerzeke and Zele were from Viking ships, but unfortunately they have been shown to be far older, dating from the sixth to eighth centuries. Their intentions are manifestly the same: to arouse fear in the enemy, and perhaps to work some magic, by adorning the ship with the head of a dragon ready to strike.[103] It is clear that, in the ninth and tenth centuries, these dragon figureheads (from which one type of ship, the *dreki*, took its name) could be removed when the voyage was over and the ships had been drawn up onto the shore (as in scene 39, pp. 204–205, where in one case there is a clear view of the fixing pegs). It is not likely that every ship in a fleet would have such ornaments. Several of the ships on the Tapestry lack them, not only those being readied for launch but also some of those at sea, such as the first and last cavalry transports in scenes 38-39 (pp. 196–203), as well as the smaller vessels in the background.

Some of the figureheads are in the form of large flowers (scenes 24 and 38, pp. 156 and 198), while that in scene 4 (p. 99) is a simple post. But the dragon's head is the norm and, whether placed fore or aft, it is always facing forwards. Some are more elaborate than others, with tongues stuck out or with curls on their necks like a man's hair (reminiscent, this, of the metal spirals found near the prow of the Ladby ship). They were probably painted in bright colours.

Still more challenging is the appearance on the Tapestry of ships with shields fixed at the back, singly or in pairs. Though seen on both English (scene 5, p. 101) and Norman (scene 38, pp. 196–198) ships, there is no archaeological evidence for this. It has been suggested that they may be signals for communicating instructions to the fleet.[104] There is no reason to think that they are there to protect the helmsman.

Nothing on the Tapestry suggests any difference between English and Norman vessels. Clearly the artist had only a single model in mind, and, given what can be deduced about his identity, it was probably English rather than Norman. Not that there is likely to have been much to choose between the ships from either side of the Channel. Even the words in use were related: the Norman *esnèque* corresponds to the Old English *snacc*, both of them deriving from the Old Norse *snekkja*. The north-western shores of Europe were bound up in a single maritime culture that had been profoundly affected by the Vikings, and this was as true of ducal Normandy as of the English kingdom.

This is not the place to spell out the sea-going strengths of these ships, strengths which have been tested during the past century in replicas of the Gokstad, Ladby, and Skuldelev vessels. These sizeable but streamlined boats were quick, supple enough to weather heavy seas, and, stabilised by their keels, easy to steer — but wretchedly uncomfortable. There was no shelter from the spray. Space was strictly limited, even in the trading ships. The absence of a hold had serious drawbacks, but left them with a very shallow draught which permitted river navigation. There has been endless discussion of their ability to hold a course across or even against the wind, and the question remains open.[105] The Tapestry sheds no light on any of this.

What the Tapestry does show, however, is the steering. At the rear of the ships, even when under sail, an oar is always put out on the right-hand side, 'to starboard' (from the Nordic *stjornbordhi*, the 'steering board', that is, the side with the steering oar). This massive oar is of a manifestly different design from the rest. It is in effect a side-mounted rudder, the only type of rudder known on the northern seas prior to the twelfth century, when rudders began to be mounted on the stern-post. At the top is a short perpendicular tiller, as in scene 4 (p. 99), and about a third of the way down it is fastened to the side of the boat in some way which is only shown very roughly (scene 5, p. 101). Several shapes of rudder are shown, of which the rarest is the straight oar (scene 4, p. 99). The most common kind is broad and curved, with a kind of curl back at the bottom.

Marine archaeologists have identified a number of these steering-oars from the Viking Age and the eleventh century. One which closely resembles those on the Tapestry was netted in 1958 by Danish fishermen off the Jutland coast at Vorsaa, and is now housed in the Frederikshaven Museum. Made of oak, it is 2.80 metres long (1.82 metres for the blade), with an almost circular handle and three holes in it for the fastenings, which suggests that it could be attached in two different positions.[106] Everything was designed so as to minimise drag while allowing the ship to be kept on course (fig. 19). Similar steering-oars have been been recovered from Denmark, Sweden, and most recently from England — some from the Suffolk coast (though these are straight rather than curved),[107] and some, dating from the late tenth or early eleventh centuries, from the Thames at London. A drawing carved on a rune-stone from Tulstrup in Scandinavia shows a vessel with a steering-oar curved at the end like many of those on the Tapestry. In general, the later rudders are bigger and heavier, less like ordinary oars than those in use at the beginning of the Viking Age. In this regard, then, the archaeological data agree perfectly with the evidence of the Tapestry, and nothing could testify more forcefully both to the sharp eye of its designer and to the rootedness of its images in Nordic tradition.

When the voyage was over and the ship had been dragged up onto the shore, the rudder was detached even before the mast was struck, if scene 39 (pp. 202–203) is to be believed. But it was held in place by nothing more than a few straps.

Along with the Gotland steles, the Tapestry is our principal source for the sails and rigging of these ships, as archaeological evidence, it need hardly be said, is virtually non-existent. But the lack of perspective in what are inevitably schematic drawings makes its testimony hard to interpret. Most commentators agree that the sails are rectangular, although they could just as easily be trapezoid, as almost all of them are shown billowing in the wind, which distorts their shape. Each sail hangs from a yard-arm slung perpendicular to the single central mast. As shown, the sails are multicoloured, but this may be nothing more than a whim of the seamstresses. Written sources show that the sails were made from woollen cloth, which would not have been very tough: hence, on the Gotland steles, that lozenge-patterned network of leather ribbing. But there is no sign of such reinforcement on the Tapestry's sails: presumably linen and canvas had by then replaced wool.

In several cases (notably scene 38, pp. 196–201), the sail is held at the bottom in a remarkable way, apparently by a man beside the pilot at the back of the boat, if not by the pilot himself. This evidently had something to do with the steering, but it is hard to believe that one man could have withstood strong winds unaided. There must have been some system of cords, and even perhaps pulleys, to facilitate this task, but there is no sign of it. Rigging is reduced in the Tapestry to a handful of cables running to the sides of the ship from the masthead, or from the junction of the mast and the yard-arm. This simple system, which has been tested in modern reconstructions, allowed the mast to be easily lowered and dismounted once land was reached, as in scene 39 (p. 203): beached ships are always shown without masts. But the Tapestry cannot show us the keelson (the wooden block, in Danish the *mastefisk*, into which the mast was stepped), nor the keel which supported it.

The ships shown on the Tapestry could make way under sail or by rowing, and had no need of harbours: such were their main advantages. For a major voyage such as crossing the Channel they relied chiefly on sail. The oars were simply for manoeuvring close to shore, as seen twice on the Tapestry: three crewmen are pulling on oars at Harold's ill-fated departure (scene 4, p. 99), and two are shown with oars on his arrival at Ponthieu, when the anchor is being let down (scene 5, pp. 102–103). None of the Norman boats in scenes 38-39 is shown at such a moment, but several of them, notably those drawn up on the shore at Pevensey, clearly have holes for oars along the uppermost planks of their sides. Similar features are seen on various Scandinavian images of ships (e.g. on a stone from Iona), but with the exception of the Ralswiek vessel, they are not to be seen on any of the archaeological finds.

The fact that ships were hauled ashore after voyages is well known, and this was still customary in Normandy at the end of the twelfth century. A ship famously foundered off Dieppe in 1183 because it had been too long on dry land and was only refurbished when it was actually back in the water.[108] So there was no call for elaborate harbours, and the Tapestry shows no such thing. But makeshift shelters (*naust* in Old Norse)

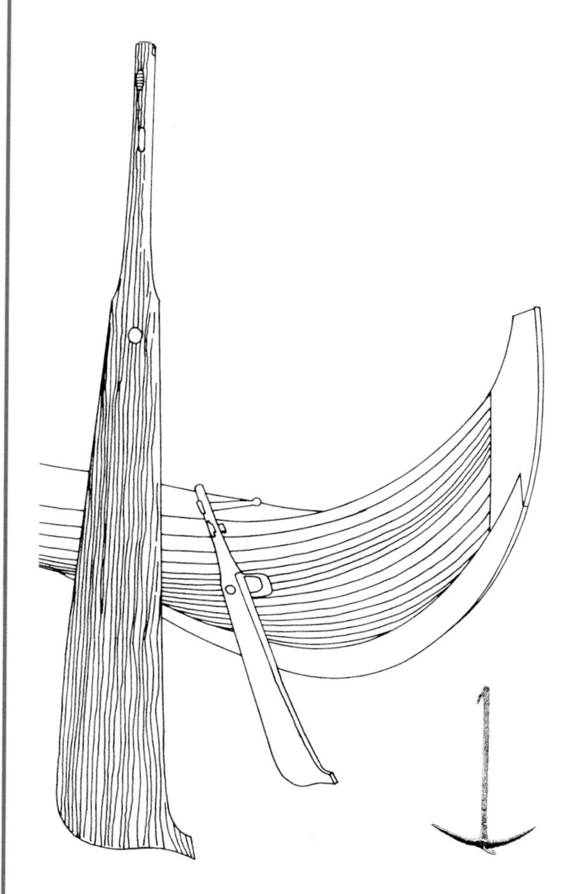

19. (left) Eleventh-century steering-oar or side-rudder from Vorsaa (Jutland); the drawing in the background is a hypothetical reconstruction. (right) Ninth-century anchor found at Ribe (Jutland), 1.50m long.

were rigged up when ships had to spend a long time ashore. Anchors were employed when the boats had to spend time moored offshore, as in scenes 7 and 34 (pp. 104 and 182). These look identical to those recovered at Oseberg, Ladby, and Ribe (in south-western Denmark).

The Tapestry's way of showing the planks of the ships' sides in varying colours is probably meant to represent the 'clinker-built' (or 'shiplap', i.e. overlapping timber) construction typical of Viking vessels. As evident from scene 36 (p. 185), the carpenters prepared the planks separately, presumably near the timber-yard, but they were assembled to form the ship near to where it would be launched, so as to minimise the problems of transporting timber from forest to seashore.[109]

Unlike some of the ships seen on the steles, but like those recovered by archaeologists, the ships on the Tapestry are not equipped with rams. The prows of its ships are barely distinguishable from the sterns, and both ends are decorated in much the same ways.

The importance of depth-sounding for coastal navigation is well-known, but the Tapestry shows it in action only once, where the English ship brings news of Harold's accession to the throne (scene 34, p. 182). At the prow stands a crewman who seems to be not only looking out for land but also sounding the depth as they approach the coast.

The helmsman was easily the most important man on board, and in both Old English and Old Norman, *stirman*, a word of Scandinavian origin, denoted someone who combined the positions of master, captain, and navigator. We know that although King Edward only rarely went to sea, he employed one Thorkell (a Danish name) in this capacity. According to *Domesday Book*, he was rewarded with land in Worcestershire. He also had a *rector navis regis* ('steersman of the royal ship') at Brabiston in Norfolk.[110] All the great princes had servants of this kind. Duke Robert (the Conqueror's father) employed one Restaud, rewarding him with the little island of Jethou, between Guernsey and Sark. William himself evidently had a steersman in 1066 — according to Orderic Vitalis, his name was Stephen son of Airard, and his son in turn was accorded hereditary rights to the office by Henry I in 1120. Stephen himself, according to *Domesday Book*, was rewarded with lands in Berkshire (far enough from the sea!). The *ministerium esneccae regis* ('service of the king's ship') remained an important position throughout the Anglo-Norman period, down to the reign of Henry II.[111]

For all the delicate questions it raises, the Tapestry is universally recognised as one of the principal sources for the marine archaeology of the Middle Ages. In artistic terms, it is also the most successful depiction of a fleet on the high seas between the ceramics of the Greeks and the early modern era: other attempts at such scenes in Romanesque art and medieval illumination are crude and schematic, in settings too restricted to do justice to the subject.[112] But in the embroidery of the Tapestry, there is a real sense of the sea, of open waters really traversed by the fleets, and not merely of coast-hugging vessels or particular incidents. As with the cavalry action in the battle scene, one feels here that rare gift, the blending of first-hand experience with authentic artistic inspiration in a rendering of a great event in its full breadth. And yet this neither detracts from the historical value of the images nor from their narrative impact: each tableau deserves consideration in its own right.

VIII

The buildings and the environment

The Tapestry shows a number of buildings of various kinds, civil, military, and religious. These have aroused considerable interest among commentators, and are not always easy to interpret. Some of the pictures, plainly, are merely symbolic; others, though less numerous, are fairly realistic; and they all open important windows onto the thought and technique of the Tapestry's designer.

It has been shown recently that the depiction of palaces on the Tapestry stands in an iconographic tradition with roots stretching back to the late Roman Empire, albeit in some cases with significant variations.[113] Three palaces are portrayed, and though none is named, they are probably to be identified as Winchester (scene 1, pp. 88–89), Rouen (scene 14, pp. 125–127), and Westminster (scenes 25, 27, and 33, pp. 159, 165, and 177–180). They are all shown in cross-section, reduced to a kind of canopy supported on columns and flanked on one side or both by turrets. Lanterns and other roofing features may appear above the canopy, which sometimes has curtains hanging from it: in scene 27 (p. 165), at the death of King Edward, these curtains, as in classical convention, are knotted around the columns.

The images of Winchester and Westminster conform closely to classical iconography, but not so the other structures, such as the house where Harold makes merry with his companions (scene 4, p. 97), the keep at Rouen (scene 12, p. 119), and the great hall of that palace (scene 14, pp.125–127). These are distinctive buildings displaying some original features. The first was a leisure building of a kind known in the Middle Ages as a *laubia* or 'lodge', of which only the first floor was occupied.[114] The second is one of the first stone keeps known in western Europe, the 'Old Tower' of Rouen, whose imposing bulk passed into proverb (no doubt resembling the Tower of London, it was demolished after the French conquest of Normandy in 1204): the Tapestry's designer must have heard tell of it. The third was hardly less celebrated: a great hall belonging to the same palace complex. Several like it still survive in both England and Normandy. What passes for Guy of Ponthieu's residence, in contrast (scene 9, pp. 109–110), is little more than a conventional outline, with no distinguishing features.

One particular detail was long puzzled over. Some of the views of palaces, such as Winchester (scene 1, pp. 88–89) and Rouen (scene 12, p. 119), show a curious pattern of multicoloured lozenges on the outside walls which frame the doors. Is this merely a decorative motif of the seamstresses, or does it, as has been suggested, show animal skins hung on wooden walls to reduce the risk of fire? The most plausible explanation has in fact been advanced by R. Gem, after a close examination of late eleventh-century Norman remains at Westminster. There, traces of glazed tiles arranged in a vertical *opus reticulatum* have been found, notably on the western wall of the ancient monastic refectory.[115] The multicoloured roof-tiles (scenes 3, 9, and 10; pp. 97, 109–110, and 113–116), however, cannot be explained in this way. There is no archaeological evidence for the use of colour-glazed tiles in roofing, and no reason to think that the shingles (wooden tiles) which covered some buildings were painted. In short, this feature is most likely a figment of the artists' imagination. The picture of Bosham church (scene 3, p. 95) shows clearly how the shingles were attached.

There are other noteworthy details. The great hall of the palace at Rouen (scene 14, pp. 125–127) faithfully reproduces a typical feature of the Norman architecture of that time in the blind arcade of semicircular arches running along the top of the long wall. It is reminiscent of the long-since demolished great hall at the Abbaye-aux-Dames of Caen, as seen in an eighteenth-century engraving.[116]

Yet that said, the views of palaces on the Tapestry are not very realistic. Most of their features are thousand-year-old stereotypes: the hangings wrapped around the columns in scene 27 (p. 165) look like those of the purely symbolic image of Theodoric the Great's palace in the Basilica of S. Apollinare Nuovo, Ravenna. Some of the smaller buildings — like the trees, as we shall see — are little more than visual punctuation marks, such as that which divides scenes 24 and 25 (p. 158), which symbolises the distance between Harold's landfall and Edward's palace; or that in scene 15 (p. 129) which separates the unspecified location of the Ælfgyva episode from the departure of the Breton expedition. Often, though not always, these little structures separate people looking to their right from others who are facing left.

The views of churches look rather more realistic and susceptible of precise architectural interpretation — though both are English. While much of the drawing of Bosham church (which Harold visits before leaving for France: scene 3, p. 93) is purely fanciful, its most distinctive feature is perfectly recognisable in the tall, narrow chancel arch of the still extant Anglo-Saxon structure (fig. 20). And while the view of

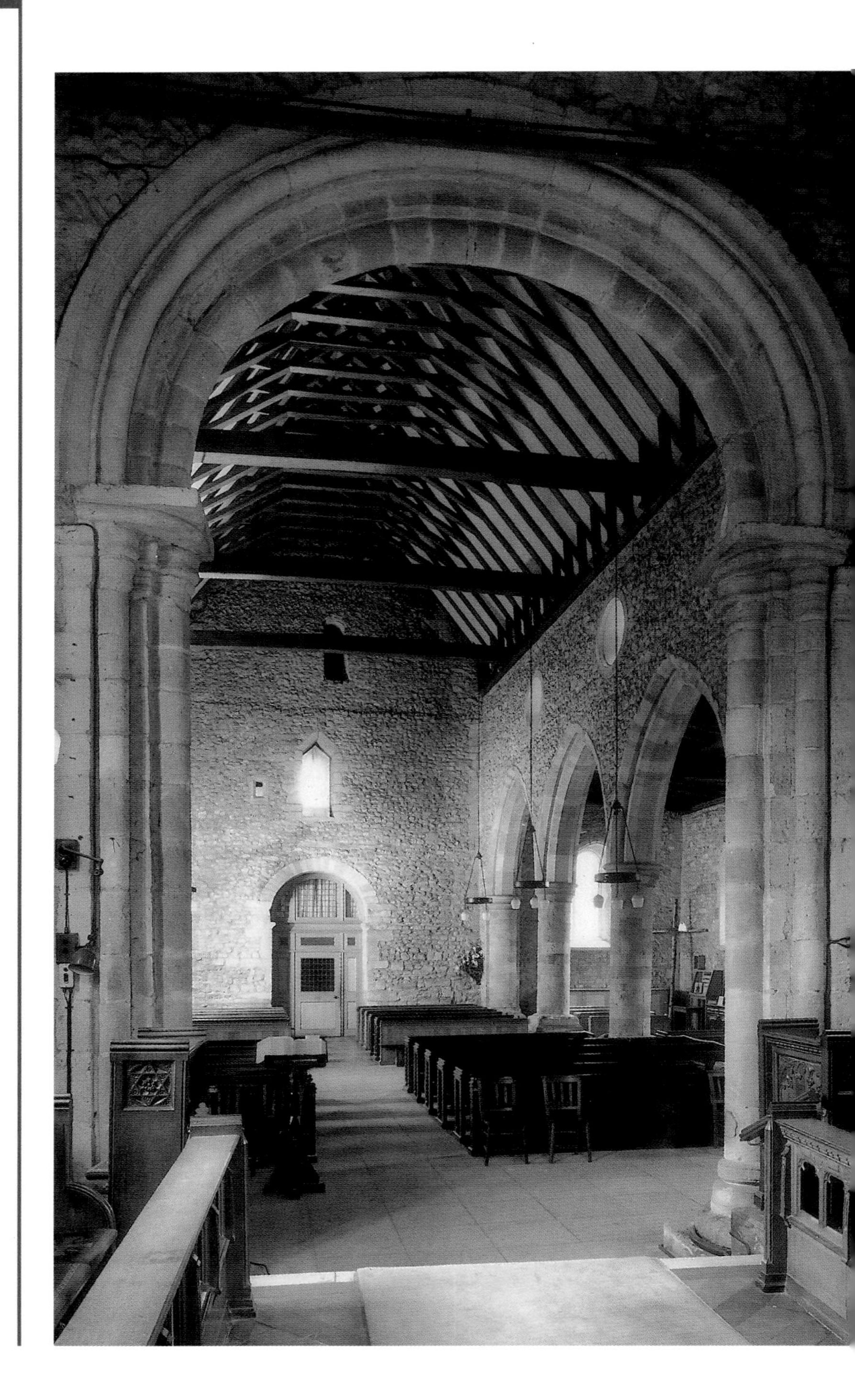

the abbey church of Westminster (scene 26, pp. 162–163) combines interior with exterior features, it does this so skilfully that the building's relationship with the nave at Jumièges, long appreciated by archaeologists, is quite evident.[117]

The Tapestry's most valuable architectural testimony concerns the 'motte and bailey' castle, which was introduced to England in the years following 1066.[118] It shows five examples, three of them in Brittany (Dol, Rennes, and Dinan), one at Bayeux and one at Hastings. The first four were permanent constructions, while the last was a field fortification put up immediately after the Norman landing. Archaeologists have recognised the particular value of the Tapestry's testimony, which has been corroborated by digs at sites such as Abinger (Surrey)[119] and the Motte d'Olivet in the Grimbosq forest (in the Calvados region of Normandy). The late eleventh-century motte was a mound of earth (often based on a natural rise) with a ditch dug around the base and a steep wooden gangway leading to a wooden fort at the top. Details, of course, could vary. Thus at Dol (scene 18, p. 136) the fort seems to be raised above ground level by timber props, a feature which is not seen at Rennes or Dinan (though possibly indicated at Hastings). The picture of Hastings shows us how quickly these fortifications could be thrown together with such basic tools as picks and shovels. And it seems likely that the drawings of the Breton mottes are based on the sort of castles that the first Norman lords made familiar in England. For by 1064 Dol, Dinan, and Rennes were almost certainly built at least in part from stone (of which there was no shortage in Rennes, a town of Roman origin).[120] But whatever their limitations, the Tapestry's images of castles retain enormous importance for archaeologists, far more detailed than other surviving images.[121]

One notable architectural feature of the Tapestry is the 'hogback'

(opposite) 20. Chancel arch of the parish church of Holy Trinity, Bosham (Sussex), looking from the choir.

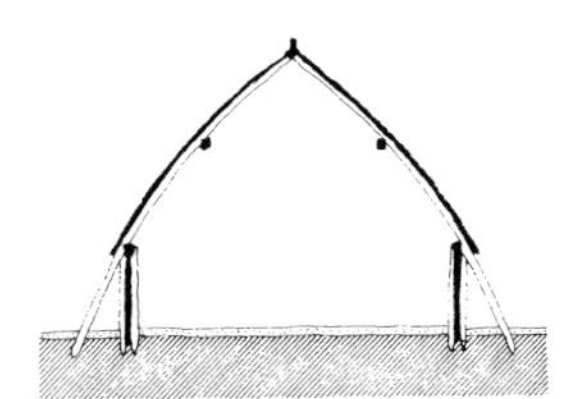

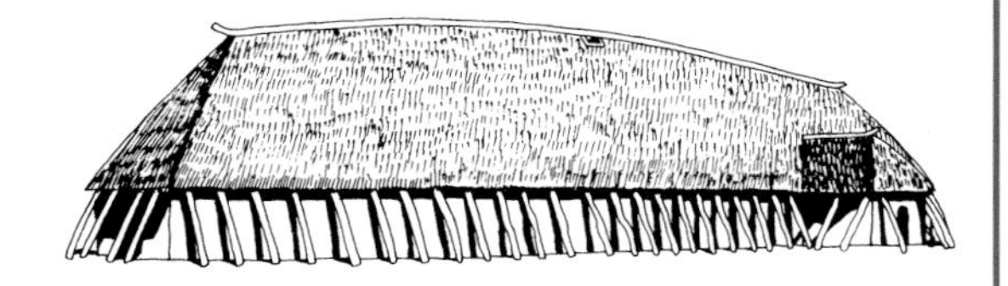

21. Reconstruction of a house at Fyrkat (Denmark). Note the hogback roof.

roof seen, for example, on the highest part of the castle at Dinan (scene 19, pp. 140–141), on the watch-tower (scene 24, p. 157), and, though a little less clearly, on the English house torched by the Normans (scene 47, pp. 217–218). This is no mere artistic fancy. It was a common feature of eleventh-century vernacular buildings not only in England (as seen in funeral monuments made in the form of houses) but also in Normandy (excavations at Mirville in the Pays-de-Caux) and Denmark (at Trelleborg, Fyrkat, and Aggersborg; fig. 21). The groundplan for buildings with this kind of roof usually shows gently curved long walls, but this cannot be seen on the Tapestry.[122]

But like most pictures of buildings from this period, those on the Tapestry represent generic types rather than specific structures. Only in the cases of Bosham church and Westminster Abbey do the drawings suggest direct knowledge of the actual buildings.

There is not much to say about the Tapestry's depiction of terrain. From scene 7 (p. 104), outdoor scenes are indicated purely symbolically by a wavy or bumpy line at the bottom. On two occasions in the narrative of the Battle of Hastings, steep or rising ground is shown: when the two armies are advancing unseen towards each other (scenes 49-50, p. 227); and just before the final assault (scenes 53-54, pp. 245–248). In this second case, the embroidery seems to suggest the presence of traps dug at the foot of the hill (see also scene 53, p. 242).

The sea is indicated equally rudimentarily, by two or more roughly parallel and gently wavy lines. Fish appear in the lower margin of one of the sea scenes (scene 17, pp. 133–134). But after scene 50 the lower margin is integrated into the narrative.

In the central narrative band of the Tapestry, the natural world is reduced to a few trees, drawn with no particular concern for realism.

They look more like strapwork than vegetation, and hardly ressemble even the trees often depicted in medieval sculpture. Many of them serve merely to punctuate the narrative or to indicate that action is taking place outdoors. There are 39 trees besides those shown in the ship-building scenes. The last tree appears in scene 50 (p. 230), as the one in scene 58 (p. 267) is the work of a restorer. The only tree to play any special part in the story is that in scene 11 (p. 117), in which a look-out is perched to observe the comings and goings of messengers between Ponthieu and Normandy. The trees themselves usually stand on little coloured hillocks. Few bear any distinct foliage, and the little that is shown is ornamentation rather than representation.

IX

THE BORDERS

ALTHOUGH THEY ARE FAR FROM EYE-CATCHING, the borders of the Tapestry have been as closely studied by experts as the rest of it, and raise as many tricky questions – which we shall not be trying to solve here. Three kinds of subjects occupy the borders. First are the merely decorative individual motifs, usually birds and beasts, real or imaginary, separated from each other by pairs of slanting lines which are themselves often filled in with little floral or foliated patterns or crosses. Then, mainly in the first half, there are scenes of people engaged in various activities, apparently based on episodes drawn from classical fables. Finally, in a few places, the main action of the Tapestry encroaches onto the borders either directly, as in the battle scenes and the Channel crossings; or indirectly, as in scene 17 (pp. 133–134), where the fish appropriate to the estuary shown in the main scene appear in the lower border. But this is rare except in the closing stages of the Battle of Hastings.

The animal motifs call for little comment. They are rarely realistic.[123] Thus, as in Romanesque sculpture, the lions almost always have tails which, as already noted, pass between their hind legs and wind around their backs to end in clubs or in clusters of leaves. The dogs and the occasional deer are unremarkable, though the appearance of a pair of camels (scene 13, pp. 121–122) is more surprising. The birds are sometimes at rest and sometimes in flight. Among the mythical birds are a number of chimaeras (the winged beasts in scenes 35, 36, and 40; pp. 183, 185–187, and 207), some dragons (scenes 15-16, pp. 129–132), two female centaurs (scenes 10 and 11, pp. 113–116, upper border), and two winged centaurs (scene 2, p. 91). There is no special significance in the orientation of the animals, which sometimes face the same way, sometimes face each other, and sometimes stand back to back. One can comment on their variety, but there is nothing remarkable in their depiction or their arrangement.

It is the action scenes that have attracted the most attention, with all commentators agreeing that some of them illustrate episodes from well-known fables. Others, however, simply represent scenes from everyday life which, though unconnected with fables, are not without a certain interest: the hounds in pursuit of a hart (scene 12, pp. 117–118), the man bringing down birds with a sling (scene 10, p. 113), the bear-baiting (scene 11, pp. 116–117), and the sowing and ploughing (scene 10, pp. 114–115). It has long been realised that this last scene furnishes the earliest surviving picture of the harrow (the earliest written reference to which dates from 1096) as well as providing valuable evidence for the history of the plough (although, rather implausibly, the plough here is drawn by but a single animal, and an ass at that).

Considerable scholarly effort has gone into identifying the fables illustrated in the borders, with important contributions being made by both H. Chefneux and M. L. Herrmann.[124] Such familiar tales as the Crow and the Fox, the Wolf and the Lamb (scene 4, p. 98), the Wolf and the Crane (scene 5, pp. 100–101), and perhaps the Two Pigeons have long been recognised. But it is not so clear how the Tapestry's designer knew these tales, whether through Latin reworkings such as the *Romulus* or the Avianus, or through a now lost Old English version (wrongly attributed to Alfred the Great as early as the twelfth century), or simply by oral tradition. It has been claimed that there are close connections between these elements of the Tapestry and the illuminations in a Limousin manuscript of Prudentius preserved at Leiden, but there is in fact no reason to think even that they have a single common source, for both simply draw on stock eleventh-century imagery.[125]

It does not seem sensible to try to trace other images in the borders to more obscure fables. There is no reason to suppose that the designer of the Tapestry had access to rich literary resources. Nor is there much to be said for the idea that some of these early

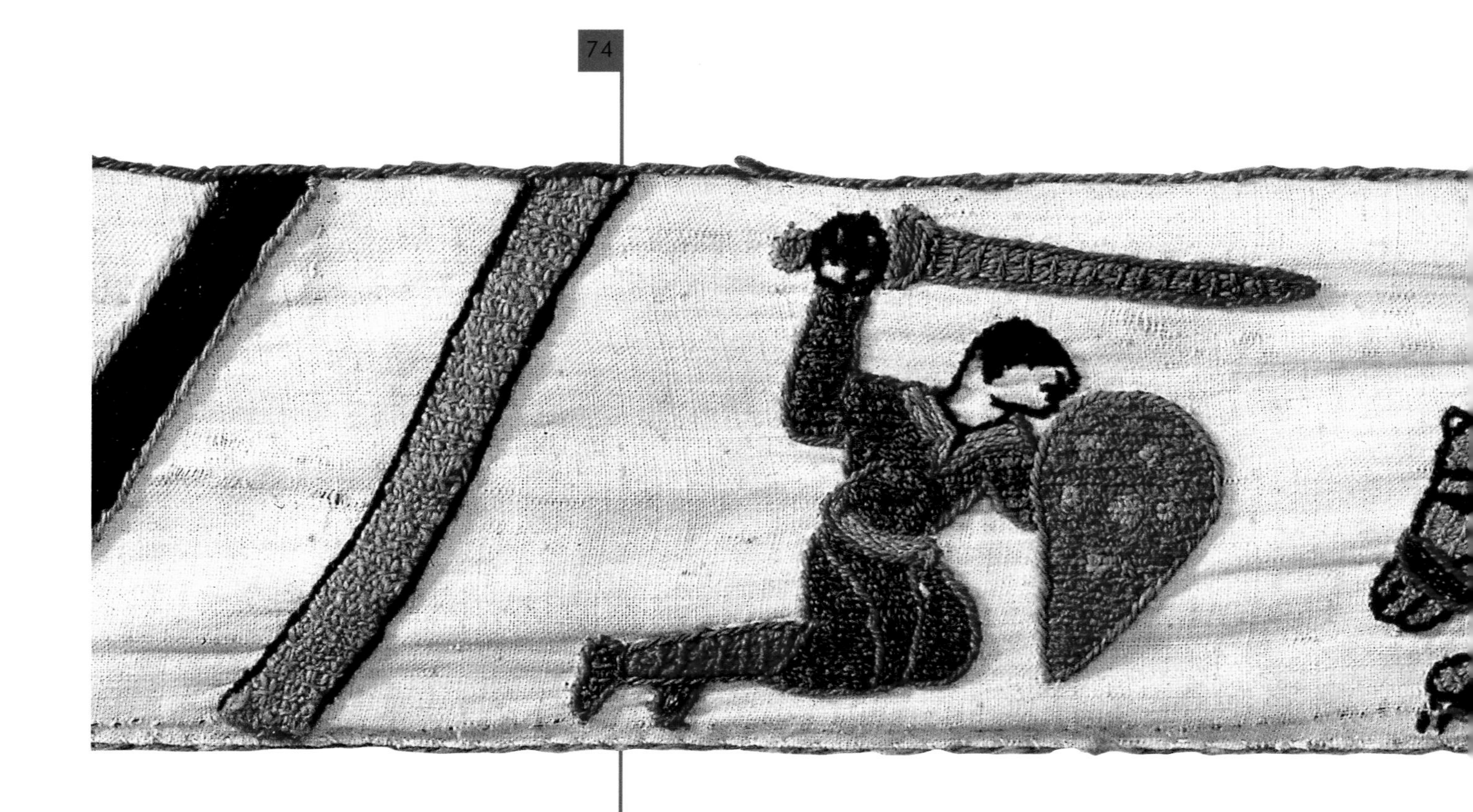

scenes from fables are repeated towards the end of the Tapestry: the images in question seem to be mere decorative motifs. However, the Fox and the Crow appear twice (scenes 4 and 16, pp. 98 and 131), as do the Wolf and the Crane (scene 5, bottom, pp. 100–101; and scene 24, top, p. 157), though for no apparent reason.

There is no doubt, however, about the fertile, lively, and at times bawdy imagination of the designer. Here it is worth commenting on the possibility of significant connections between the main storyline of the Tapestry and the border scenes, although this has only been seriously canvassed with respect to a few particular cases, most notably that of the obscene male nude shown beneath the mysterious episode of Ælfgyva and the clerk (scene 15, p. 127). But the apparently erotic significance of this juxtaposition is much diminished by the appearance of another male nude beneath the preceding scene, where William greets Harold at Rouen: no hint of illicit sex there. Nor, just before that, is there any obvious connection between Harold's departure for Rouen (scene 13, p. 120) and the encounter between an aroused Adam and an embarrassed Eve in the lower margin. But there

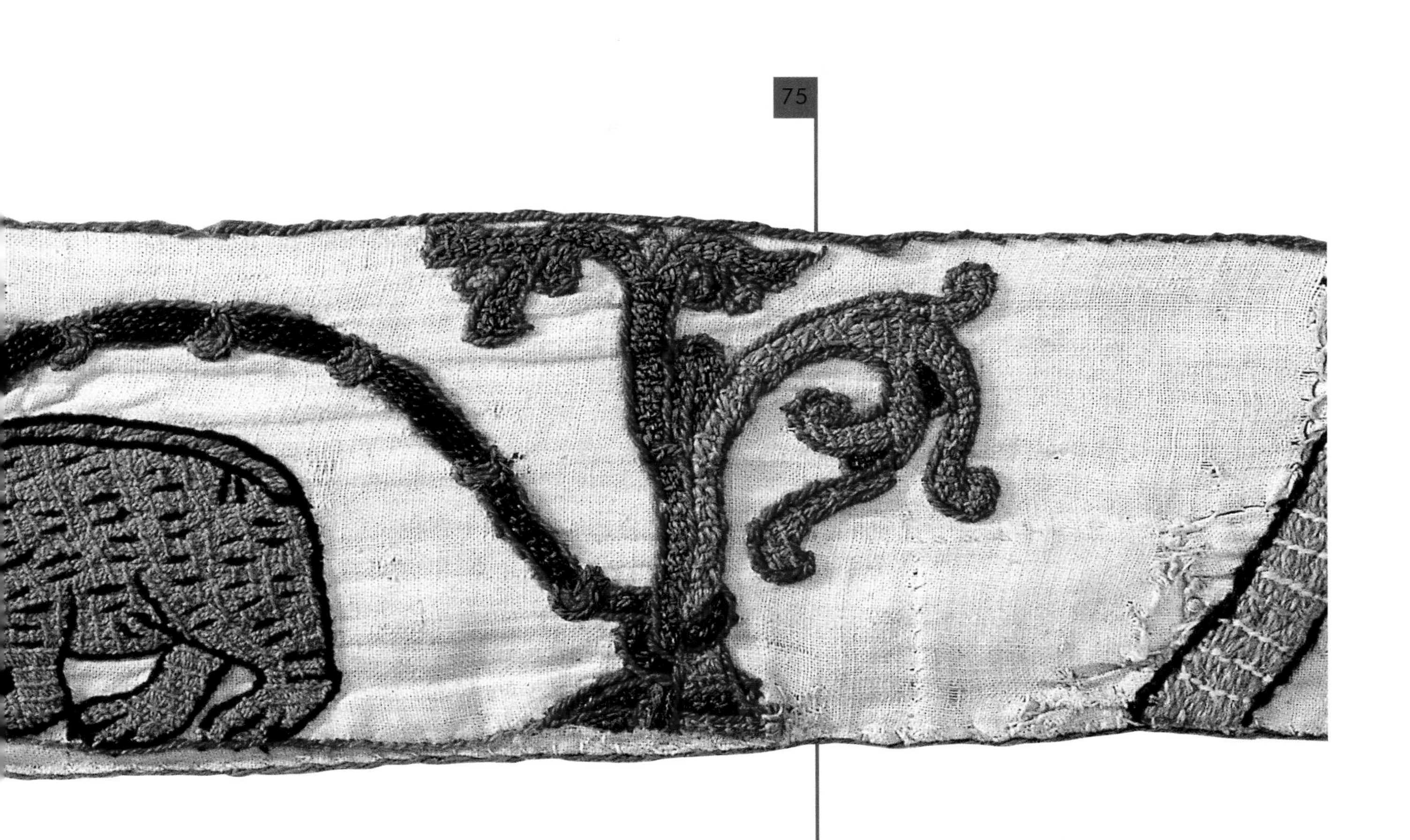

may be something in the idea that the pair of fish beneath scene 17 (p. 133) alludes to Pisces and thus to the date when William entered Brittany.

Modern sensibilities sometimes find it faintly shocking that obscene images can appear in avowedly religious contexts, whether in the modillions of a Romanesque church or in the *sheila-na-gig* (a mythical name) of pious medieval Ireland. But the Tapestry's occasionally bawdy images are thus not out of keeping with medieval sensibilities. They are mostly found in the earlier part of the Tapestry, though they last appear in scene 48. It is sometimes possible to find a connection with some familiar fable (as in scene 48, p. 222), but not usually. But all this is, quite literally, marginal. At the key moments, such as Harold's coronation, William's Channel crossing, and the climax of the Battle of Hastings, the borders offer no such distractions. (The naked and dismembered corpses in the closing scene (pp. 262–263), in any case partly the work of restorers, are of an entirely different character.)

X

THE HISTORICAL BACKGROUND

THE BAYEUX TAPESTRY IS NOT THE WORK OF A HISTORIAN. It tells the story in its own distinctive way, focusing on the moral lesson: the terrible consequences which followed the violation of a solemn oath sworn upon sacred relics. Anything that does not serve this purpose is deliberately excluded. Nevertheless, a proper understanding of the Tapestry requires a more exact knowledge of the facts, at least insofar as we can ascertain them — which is not always as far as we would like: while the chroniclers tell us a great deal about William after the Conquest, they are much less generous with information about what led up to it.

This brief account attempts to summarise the current scholarly consensus on the background and course of the Battle of Hastings, emphasising those aspects which cast light on the Tapestry and striving to maintain a balance between the contrasting Anglophile and Norman prejudices which mar so much of the historiography of the years 1064-66.[126] But it does not aspire to the status of absolute truth: some element of subjectivity is unavoidable.

The first task is to introduce the *dramatis personae*, taking careful note of the connections between them.

King Edward, whose notorious piety earned him the posthumous epithet 'the Confessor', was of the royal House of Wessex, the son of the English King Ethelred II by his second wife Emma, the sister of Duke Richard II of Normandy (Duke William's grandfather). Born in

England around 1005, Edward twice took refuge in Normandy, to evade the Danish conquerors Svein Forkbeard and Cnut. His second exile, lasting about 25 years, was doubtless varied by occasional visits to Flanders. Emma's decision to accept Cnut as her second husband in order to retain her position as queen led to a breach between mother and son, and Edward came to feel much closer to his Norman than to his English relatives. Following the death of Cnut's last son, Edward was unanimously recognised as king by the English, but on his return to the land of his birth he brought with him a substantial Norman and Flemish entourage which played an important part at his court for the next ten years. Several of these men were rewarded with prominent ecclesiastical or military positions.

Edward's merits as king have been the subject of much debate. Though unquestionably intelligent, his Norman upbringing and his lack of training in the arts of war left him ill-equipped for his role. He was never able to break free of the rival factions and pursue a genuinely independent policy, except perhaps briefly in 1051-52. Yet neither was he ever fully reconciled to the Anglo-Danish hegemony of Godwin's clan after 1052.

This Anglo-Danish faction, which had previously supported Cnut and his sons, and which eventually secured the downfall and exile of most of Edward's Norman entourage, was led first by Earl Godwin (something of a parvenu in the Anglo-Saxon aristocracy), and then, after his death in 1053, by Harold – Godwin's son by a Danish mother. Godwin had in effect forced Edward to marry Harold's sister, Edith, in 1045, and the marriage was never happy. Godwin's extensive and faction-ridden kin-group included a number of fiercely unruly personalities, notably his eldest son, Svein, who died in exile after murdering his brother Beorn, and Tostig, Earl of Northumbria from 1055 until 1065, who was to play a crucial role in the events of 1066, in the course of which he met his death. Harold had several other brothers: Leofwine and Gyrth, who fell by his side at Hastings, and the young Wulfnoth, who was sent to Normandy as a hostage in 1051, along with Harold's nephew Hakon.

Harold seized the crown in January 1066, but as the mere brother-in-law of the late king he was rejected by certain nobles — not least his brother Tostig. But Harold's trump card was his relationship with the

Danish king, Svein Estrithson, who inherited Cnut's claim to England.

William of Normandy, born in 1028, was the bastard son of Duke Robert the Magnificent by a woman from Falaise named Herlève (Arlette). After his father died in 1035 on his way back from a pilgrimage to Jerusalem, William was acknowledged as duke — though not without some opposition: it took him until about 1050 to impose his authority on Normandy itself. In 1063 he extended his power to the neighbouring county of Maine, and he had a kind of protectorate over north-east Brittany. In 1051 he married Matilda of Flanders, whose father, Count Baldwin V (1035-67), was at that time Regent of France following the death of the Capetian King Henri I.

William inherited his father's and grandfather's predilection for the House of Wessex and antipathy for the Danes. It is just possible that Duke Robert the Magnificent may have considered an expedition to England to vindicate the claim of his cousin Edward to the throne; and it is likely that in 1051 William himself made a brief visit to England to see King Edward and discuss the succession with him. William's mother had married a Norman viscount, Herluin de Conteville, and William was very close to his two half-brothers, her sons, the talented Odo (d. 1097), whom he made Bishop of Bayeux in 1049 and Earl of Kent in 1066-67, and Robert, to whom he granted extensive domains in Cornwall and south-west England.

Duke William's political and military talents are beyond dispute. He was a worthy leader for a people who, in the course of the eleventh century, made war a national industry and conquest almost a vocation. As pious as his cousin Edward, but immeasurably his superior in practical matters, William had managed in the 1050s to forge a valuable alliance with the reforming wing of the clergy while safeguarding his ducal power over the bishops of Normandy. This delicate balancing act earned him credit with the papacy which he was to exploit to the full in 1066. For he was able to present himself as the champion of the Church against the upstart Anglo-Danish Archbishop of Canterbury, Stigand, who had already made himself *persona non grata* at Rome. William's marriage to Matilda not only ended a long-standing rivalry with Flanders but also brought him a valuable ally in the Pas-de-Calais.

Conspicuous by their absence from the Tapestry, the other major players of 1066 were based in Scandinavia. The Age of the Vikings had not yet come to a close, and as late as 1086 the kinsmen of Cnut still dreamed of vindicating their family's claim to the English throne. The king of Denmark in 1066 was Svein Estrithson, Harold Godwinson's cousin. The king of Norway, Harald Hardrada, may not have had any hereditary claim, but could remember the approaches which Emma had made towards his predecessor, Magnus the Good. More to the point, he was the Viking spirit incarnate. A veteran who had seen service under the Byzantine Emperors and the Princes of Russia, he yearned only for further military glory once he had seized power in Norway. As King Svein of Denmark was preoccupied with domestic problems Harald was the only Scandinavian prince to take a direct part in the events of 1066.

Finally, although the Tapestry completely ignores him and he fares little better in the chronicles, we should nevertheless take heed of the last surviving scion of the House of Wessex, Edgar Atheling, grandson of a half-brother of Edward. Returning to England in 1056 from a long exile in Hungary, this somewhat anodyne and almost tragicomic figure would survive another fifty years, gathering around himself a motley band of die-hard Anglo-Saxon loyalists whose epitaph might be 'too little, too late'.

In September 1051, Edward the Confessor seemed to have broken free. He had banished Godwin and his sons, appointed a Norman to the key position of Archbishop of Canterbury, and without doubt envisaged Duke William as his eventual successor. But William, as yet barely secure upon his own throne and far more concerned with his immediate prospects in Maine, was in no position to respond. So, faced with a two-pronged attack by Godwin from Flanders and by Harold from Ireland, Edward had to come to terms. On 14 September 1052 Godwin and his cronies returned to power stronger than ever. Edward was but a pawn in their hands, and most of the Normans he had brought to England were banished, starting with the new archbishop of Canterbury. He had to hand over key positions to former henchmen of Cnut. One of the Danish king's brothers was given control of several Midlands counties, and Tostig, one of Godwin's sons, was made Earl of Northumbria The deaths of various relatives of Edward's who had been summoned back from Hungary put the succession in doubt.

It seems possible that, in 1064, Edward revisited the possibility of making William his successor, and that, in his turn, William, now firmly in control of both Normandy and Maine, was at last free to take the idea seriously. Certainly it is hard to believe that Harold's mission to Normandy, the subject of the first movement of the Tapestry's narrative, had nothing to do with the succession. However, there was no immediate solution to the problem. Since Godwin's death in 1053, his two most powerful sons, Harold and Tostig, had been at loggerheads, notably over a dispute between Tostig and lesser magnates in Northumbria which had erupted into open conflict in 1063. The feuding brothers had sought to interest the Scandinavian kings Svein and Harald in their quarrel, and Tostig also enjoyed the support of Baldwin V of Flanders, William's father-in-law. Thus, despite the traditional enmity between Flanders and Normandy, the duke and the count found a common enemy in Harold in 1066 — a crucial development, as Flanders was able not only to furnish a sizeable contingent of William's army but also to assist him in crossing the Channel.

Edward's sudden death on 5 January 1066 brought all this intrigue to a head — and also marks the start of the second movement of the Tapestry's narrative. But while the Tapestry follows events around the Channel in some detail, it completely ignores the part played by Tostig and Harald Hardrada. There is not so much as a hint of the importance of northern England and the Scandinavian connection. Neither the Tapestry nor, indeed, any of the contemporary chronicles tells us when the Normans first realised that they were going to benefit from the opening of a second front against Harold. It is not inconceivable that, perhaps through the mediation of Flanders, there may have been some co-operation between William and Tostig; and it is hard to believe that William knew nothing of Norwegian intervention until the defeat of Tostig and Harald Hardrada at Stamford Bridge on 25 September. But none of this had any bearing on the moral tale which the Tapestry set out to tell. William of Poitiers may have attached great importance to the intelligence despatched to Duke William by Robert fitz Wimarch, a Norman in Edward's service, but the Tapestry gives no inkling of it.[127] It follows the duke's preparations without further reference to events in England until the opposing forces begin to scout each other out at Hastings (scene 49-50, pp. 224–225). This focus on the duke gives the story both coherence and dramatic effect.

The other conspicuous omission on the Tapestry is any allusion, other perhaps than the use of the term 'Franci' for William's troops, to the multinational character of the invasion force. We know of the important part played not only by Bretons (who appear on the Tapestry only as William's enemies in the events of 1064) but also by Flemings, Poitevins, and many other adventurers who flocked to the Norman standard. But this had no relevance to the Tapestry's moral theme, and was of no special interest to the English, for whom it was enough that their enemies all spoke one language.

There is no need to draw out at length all the connections between the Tapestry's narrative and the abundant written sources for the Norman Conquest.[128] Suffice it to say that the Tapestry's testimony is among the most valuable in that, though less precise than the Latin and French chronicles, it is far more vivid, and its probable early date lends it especial interest. The chronicles do shed light on the Tapestry (and *vice versa*), but the thesis that the Tapestry was dependent on some particular written source no longer seems tenable.

Two minor texts, however, seem to have a particular relationship with the Tapestry: Baudry de Bourgueil's poem (written between 1085 and 1102), because it purports to describe a wall-hanging that told the story of Hastings; and the prose account found in the *Historia Novorum* of Eadmer, a monk of Canterbury.[129] Written before 1107, Eadmer's account seems to embody an English tradition very close to that of Bayeux, as it too makes the whole story hinge on Harold's oath, giving considerable attention to his voyage to Normandy in 1064, and jumping straight from his arrival back in England to the death of Edward the Confessor.[130] Nevertheless, there are differences. Eadmer is far less favourable to the Normans, ignores the Breton expedition, and has nothing to say about Bishop Odo.

The Norman point of view inevitably predominates in the three main chronicle sources: the *Gesta Normannorum Ducum* of William of Jumièges, a brief enough account, but early, written towards 1070; the more fulsomely rhetorical *Gesta Guillelmi* of William of Poitiers, written around 1073-75 (or, according to R. H. C. Davis, as late as 1077); and finally the perceptive and lively, at times gossipy, story found in the *Historia Ecclesiastica* of Orderic Vitalis, a monk of Sainte-Evroult of mixed English and French parentage who laboured long over his work, which was not finished until about 1140.

One source often put forward as particularly close to the events is the *Carmen de Hastingae Proelio*, a Latin poem attributed to Bishop Guy of Amiens (1058-75). Sadly, the attribution is spurious, and if Guy wrote anything about Hastings it no longer survives.[131] For, as R. H. C. Davis and George Garnett have shown, the poem cannot be contemporary and its testimony cannot be relied upon.[132] It was an essentially literary exercise and its picturesque details are not to be taken at face value.

There is more to be said for the other twelfth-century Anglo-Norman chronicles, despite their late date. William of Malmesbury's *Gesta regum Anglorum*, from about 1125, has useful information on William's fleet and on his prolonged wait at Saint-Valèry-sur-Somme. Henry of Huntingdon's *Historia Anglorum* (around 1130) has left its mark on later historiography thanks to its picturesque anecdotes, such as the story of Taillefer, the Normans' feigned flight, and the knights who were killed plunging into the ditch. Finally, the late French poem, the *Roman de Rou*, commissioned by Henry II around 1170, gains special value from the fact that its author, the Jerseyman Wace, was a canon of Bayeux. He must have known the Tapestry, and was doubtless influenced by it: he certainly seems to allude to some of its scenes and significant details, although he does not cover everything or everyone mentioned on it. He also had access to other sources, whether written or oral.[133] After Wace, however, the Norman tradition becomes increasingly standardised and unremarkable.

The parallel tradition of the *Anglo-Saxon Chronicle*, a family of essentially annalistic texts written in Old English, originating in the ninth century and ending around 1155, remains of considerable value in clarifying the facts of the story. The Norman Conquest is covered in versions of the chronicle compiled at the abbeys of Winchester, Abingdon, Worcester, and Peterborough. A lost recension, diverging from these, was the basis for a Latin version produced around 1130. Traditionally ascribed to 'Florence of Worcester' (though it was probably the work of a monk named John), this furnishes much material of real interest. However, the Norman Conquest is far from centre-stage in this tradition, whose main focus is on earlier events and monarchs. Finally, various monastic chronicles produced in twelfth-century England add valuable testimony on specific details: notably the chronicles of Battle Abbey, which William founded to commemorate his victory, and of the abbey of Hyde, near Winchester, which pays particular attention to the fates of Edward the Confessor and Harold.

NOTES TO PART ONE

CHAPTER I

1 The following paragraphs are dependent on S. Bertrand, 'Étude sur la Tapisserie de Bayeux', *Annales de Normandie* 10 (1960), pp. 197-206; and on his chapter in the French translation of F. M. Stenton's *The Bayeux Tapestry*, pp. 77-80.

2 V. Beziers, *Histoire sommaire de la ville de Bayeux* (Caen, 1773), p. 53.

2a *Les Monuments de la Monarchie française* (5 vols. Paris, 1729-33), vols. 1, pp. 371-79 (a partial description, based on Lancelot's work) and 2, pp. 1-29, for a full account.

3 For this, see the paper read by Sylvette Lemagnen at the cultural centre of Cerisy-la-Salle in October 1999 (forthcoming). Neither the war-time German research nor that conducted during the relocation of the Tapestry in 1984 has yet been published.

4 Notably R. Drögereit, 'Bemerkungen zum Bayeux-Teppich', *Mitteilungen des Instituts für österreichische Geschichtsforschung* 70 (1962), pp. 257-93, arguing that the Tapestry was dependent on William of Poitiers.

5 See M. D. Legge, 'Bishop Odo in the Bayeux Tapestry', *Medium Ævum* 56 (1987), pp. 84-85.

6 J. M. Bouvris, 'La dédicace de l'église cathédrale de Bayeux', *Société des Sciences, Arts et Belles-Lettres de Bayeux* 28 (1982), pp. 3-16.

7 These were set out by R. N. Sauvage in his definitive article 'La Tapisserie de la reine Mathilde à Bayeux', *Bibliothèque de l'École des Chartes* 82 (1921), pp. 157-65, in the wake of the book by A. Levé, *La Tapisserie de la reine Mathilde* (Paris, 1919). See also W. R. Lethaby, 'The Perjury at Bayeux', *Archaeological Journal* 74 (1917), pp. 136-38, repr. in the invaluable collection of R. Gameson (ed), *The Study of the Bayeux Tapestry* (Woodbridge, 1997), pp. 19-20. But we cannot accept Sauvage's opinion that the Tapestry was a work of secular origin, only later brought from England to Bayeux, an opinion that was partly revived in C. R. Dodwell, 'A brief note on the secular aspects of the Bayeux Tapestry', *Gazette des Beaux-Arts* 68 (1966), pp. 227-32.

CHAPTER II

8 For the fullest technical detail see S. Bertrand, *La Tapisserie de Bayeux et la manière de vivre au onzième siècle* (La Pierre-qui-Vire: Zodiaque, 1966), pp. 23-.

9 A. Andersson, *L'Art scandinave* II (La Pierre-qui-Vire: Zodiaque, 1968), fig. 244 & colour plate 399.

10 *L'Art scandinave* II, plate 248 and colour plate 382.

11 Scandinavian parallels to the Tapestry are conveniently summarised by A. Geijer in his articles on 'bildvävnad' and 'broderi' in *Kulturhistorik Leksikon for nordisk Middelalder* (Copenhagen, 1956), vol. I, cols. 535-40; and vol. II, col. 263; with references to further literature.

12 *Liber Eliensis*, ed. E. O. Blake, Camden Society 3rd series, 92 (London, 1962), p. 136 (book II, ch. 36).

13 D. Whitelock, *Anglo-Saxon Wills* (Cambridge, 1930), pp. 14 and 64. *Liturgica Historica*, ed. E. Bishop (Oxford, 1918), p. 401.

14 *Memorials of St Dunstan*, ed. W. Stubbs (London, 1874), p. 12; *Guillaume de Poitiers, Histoire de Guillaume le Conquérant*, ed. R. Foreville (Paris, 1952), pp. 256-58; for an English version, see *The Gesta Guillelmi of William of Poitiers*, ed. & tr. R. H. C. Davis and M. Chibnall (Oxford, 1998), pp. 176-77; O. Lehmann-Brockhaus (ed.), *Lateinischen Schriftquellen zur Kunst in England, Wales und Schottland vom Jahre 901 bis zum Jahre 1307* (5 vols. Munich, 1955-60), vol. 3, p. 24.

15 Liutprand of Cremona, *Antapodosis*, II, 31.

16 *Historia S. Florentii*, ed. Marchegay and Mabille, *Chroniques des églises d'Anjou* (Paris, 1869), pp. 306-07: 'quosdam mirae pulchritudinis pannos, sagittariis et leonibus caeteris quibusdam animantibus figuratus'.

17 Editions by L. Delisle, *Mémoires de la Société des Antiquaires de Normandie* 28 (1873), pp. 187-224; P. Lauer, *Mélanges d'Histoire offerts à M. Ch. Bémont* (Paris, 1913), pp. 43-56; K. Hilbert, *Baldricus Burguliensis Carmina* (Heidelberg, 1979); Baudry de Bourgueil, *Poèmes*, ed. J. Y. Tillette (Paris, 1998). For an English translation of the description of the tapestry (lines 205-578), see S. A. Brown, *The Bayeux Tapestry: History and Bibliography* (Woodbridge, 1988), pp. 167-77

18 J. Y. Tillette, 'La chambre de la comtesse Adèle', *Romania* 151 (1981), pp. 145-71, at p. 147.

19 X. Barral I Altet, *Els mosaics de paviment medievals a Catalunya* (Barcelona, 1980), p. 5; and especially 'Un pavement du XIIe siècle décrit par Baudry de Bourgueil', *Dumbarton Oaks Papers* 41 (1987), pp. 41-54.

20 Baudry, lines 234-35 and 562-68.

21 See P. de Palol, *El tapis de la Creació de la catedral de Girona* (Barcelona, 1986; Supplement to *Quaderns d'estudis medievals*, 2). See also Jean Ainaud de Lasarte, *Catalogue Romane* II (La Pierre-qui-Vire: Zodiaque, 1961), plates 78-80 and colour plate 12.

22 The verdict is that of X. Barral I Altet, 'Un pavement', p. 41.

CHAPTER III

23 Above all Marie-Thérèse Poncet, *Étude comparative des illustrations du Moyen Âge et des dessins animés* (Paris, 1952) and M. Parisse, *La Tapisserie de Bayeux: un documentaire du XIe siècle* (Paris, 1983).

24 L. Musset, *Normandie romane* I (3rd edn. La Pierre-qui-Vire: Zodiaque, 1987), pp. 295-96, plates 117-21.

25 M. Biddle in the exhibition catalogue *Vikingerne I England* (Aarhus, 1981), p. 167.

26 L. Musset, *Angleterre romane* I (La Pierre-qui-Vire: Zodiaque, 1983), pp. 325 and 373, plates 122 and 150. The same conventions underlie the cave drawing at Sika in Uppland (Sweden), which schematically depicts a church beside a pseudo-runic text. It probably dates from the early twelfth century. See *Upplands runniskrifter* U 529, p. 403.

27 S. Alford, 'Romanesque architectural sculpture in Dorset: a selective catalogue and commentary', *Dorset Natural History and Archaeological Society Proceedings* 106 (1984), pp. 1-22, at pp. 1-5.

28 On the Romanesque lions of Normandy see M. Baylé, 'Les siècles romans en Basse-Normandie', *Art de Basse-Normandie* 92 (1985), pp. 130-31.

29 Bergen, Bryggens Museum. It is no doubt a schematic representation of the *leidang* (naval levy) of the Norwegian kings, whose capital was then at Bergen.

30 C. R. Dodwell, 'L'originalité iconographique de plusieurs illustrations anglo-saxonnes de l'Ancien Testament', *Cahiers de civilisation médiévale* 14 (1971), pp. 319-28. See also R.

Gameson, 'The Origin, Art, and Message of the Bayeux Tapestry', in his *Study of the Bayeux Tapestry*, pp. 157-211, at pp. 168-69, for some fascinating observations on the possible links with drawings in tenth- and eleventh-century English manuscripts.
31 J. Kiff, 'Images of war: illustrations of warfare in early eleventh-century England', *Anglo-Norman Studies* 7 (1984), pp. 177-94.
32 D. Park, 'The "Lewes Group" of wall paintings in Sussex', *Anglo-Norman Studies* 6 (1893), pp. 200-25.
33 See also P. Belli D'Elia, *Pouilles romanes* (La Pierre-qui-Vire: Éditions Zodiaque, 1987), plates 29-40.
34 William of Malmesbury, *De Gestis Regum Anglorum*, ed. W. Stubbs (2 vols. London, 1887-89), vol. 2, pp. 300 and 302.
35 C. Warren Hollister, 'The *Carmen de Hastingae Proelio*', *English Historical Review* 93 (1978), pp. 241-61, at p. 248. Wace, ed. Holden, vol. 2, pp. 183-84, lines 8013-38. Burgess and Van Houts, p. 181. *Carmen de Hastingae Proelio*, lines 389-407. Henry of Huntingdon, *Historia Anglorum*, ed. and tr. D. Greenway (Oxford, 1996), pp. 392-93.
36 See, among others, D. D. R. Owen, 'The epic and history: *Chanson de Roland* and *Carmen de Hastingae Proelio*', *Medium Ævum* 51 (1982), pp. 18-34, at pp. 31-32.
37 *The Carmen de Hastingae Proelio of Guy, Bishop of Amiens*, ed. C. Morton and H. Muntz (Oxford, 1972), p. 30, from verse 470; and Wace, ed. Holden, vol. 2, p. 214, lines 8819-28 (Burgess and Van Houts, p. 190).
38 She only appears anonymously at Edward the Confessor's death-bed (scene 27, p. 164 et seq.).
39 But is this consistent with the at times positively indecent gusto of some of the borders in the first part? This is one of the enigmas of the medieval mind.

CHAPTER IV

40 This is an Anglo-Saxon letter, long obsolete in written English, though still used in Icelandic, representing the voiced 'th'.
41 Thus for *Edwardu* (scene 25, p. 159) and *rege* (scene 49, p. 224).
42 For these aspects of the captions I have relied on the comments made by R. I. Page in his review of D. M. Wilson in *Antiquity* 60 (1986), pp. 156-57.
43 Or else perhaps the deponent form had lapsed into disuse.
44 This is the view of R. Lepelley, 'Contribution à l'étude des inscriptions de la Tapisserie de Bayeux: Bagias et Wilgelm', *Annales de Normandie* 14 (1964), pp. 313-21; tr. as 'A Contribution to the Study of the Inscriptions in the Bayeux Tapestry', in *Study of the Bayeux Tapestry*, ed. Gameson, pp. 39-45.
45 A. Crepin, 'Étude typologique de la Chronique Anglo-Saxonne', in J. Poirion, *La chronique et l'histoire au Moyen Âge* (Paris, 1984), pp. 137-51, at p. 140.
46 J. Vives, 'Inscripciones hispanicas y los *capitula biblica*', *Estudios dedicados a Menendez Pidal* VII, I (Madrid, 1957), pp. 477-84.
47 *Francos debellare superbos*.
48 J. Bliese, 'William the Conqueror, William the Orator', *The Anglo-Norman Anonymous* III, 2 print 1985, pp. 3-4.
49 These citations are drawn from R. Louis, 'Y a-t-il une "Geste de Guillaume le Conquérant"?', *Annales de Normandie* 3 (1953), pp. 15-21, at p. 20.
50 Baudry, lines 564 onwards.

CHAPTER V

51 Including the name of Eustace of Boulogne, now illegible thanks to damage in the upper border of scene 55 (p. 251).
52 L. Musset, 'Un grand prélat normand du XIe siècle: Geoffroy de Montbray, évêque de Coutances (1048-1083)', *Revue de département de la Manche* 25 (1983), pp. 3-17.
53 William of Malmesbury, *De Gestis Regum Anglorum*, ed. Stubbs, vol. 2, p. 301.
54 See in particular the sermon delivered in 1105 by the Bishop of Sées Serlon in the church of Carentan. Orderic Vitalis, *Historia ecclesiastica*, ed. M. Chibnall (6 vols. Oxford, 1968-80), vol. 6, pp. 64-66.
55 In several scenes, the tunics seem to be split very high, almost to the waist. The only specific study of costume in the Tapestry is the rather cursory contribution of J. L. Nevinson 'The Costumes', in F. M. Stenton (ed), *The Bayeux Tapestry: a comprehensive survey* (2nd edn. London, 1965), pp. 70-75.

CHAPTER VI

56 Wace, ed. Holden, t. II, p. 173, lines 7763-66 (Burgess and Van Houts, p. 178).
57 Wace, ed. Holden, t. II, p. 206, lines 8603-8 (Burgess and Van Houts, p. 188).
58 'Les Miracles de Saint Eugène à Brogne', ed. D. Misonne, *Revue Bénédictine* 76 (1966), pp. 231-91, at p. 267.
59 *Chartes de Jumièges*, ed. J. J. Vernier (Rouen, 1916), vol. 1, p. 69, no. 22. The work required is estimated at 140 hours or more by R. Allen Brown, 'The Status of the Norman Knight', in *War and Government in the Middle Ages*, ed. Gillingham and Holt (Cambridge, 1984), pp. 18-32, at p. 28.
60 Cartulaire de Saint-Étienne de Caen, no. 202; Cartulaire du Mont-Saint-Michel, no. 79.
61 N. P. Brooks and H. E. Walker, 'The Authority and Interpretation of the Bayeux Tapestry', *Anglo-Norman Studies* 1 (1979), pp. 1-34, at pp. 19-20.
62 Though the heavy restoration to scene 58 renders its testimony unreliable.
63 Kiff, 'Images of War', pp. 183-86. See also M. Pastoureau, 'La naissance des armoiries', *Le XIIe siècle. Mutations et renouveau*, ed. F. Gasparri (Paris, 1994), pp. 163-92.
64 P. Schreiner, 'Zur Ausrüstung, des Krieges in Byzanz', *Les Pays du Nord et Byzance* (Uppsala, 1981), pp. 215-36, at p. 233.
65 In most cases only the metal boss survives, but they can number thirty or forty.
66 D. M. Wilson, *The Archaeology of Anglo-Saxon England* (Cambridge, 1976), p. 19; G. Bersu, *Three Viking Graves in the Isle of Man* (London, 1966), pp. 60-65.
67 See the indispensable observations of Sawyer in his contribution to P. H. Sawyer and R. H. Hilton, 'Technical Determinism: the Stirrup and the Plough', *Past and Present* 24 (April 1963), pp. 90-100, esp. pp. 93-94. See also the recent contribution of J. Flori, 'Encore l'usage de la lance ... la technique du combat chevaleresque vers l'an 1100', *Cahiers de civilisation médiévale* 31 (1988), pp. 43-240.
68 A. B. Hoffmeyer, *Middelalderens Tvæggede sværd* (Copenhagen, 1954), p. 34 and vol. 2, plate IV.

69 The Old Norse *bolöx* was used for both purposes. See H. Falk, *Altnordische Waffenkunde* (Heidelberg, 1914), p. 113.
70 For this last point see N. Hooper, 'The Housecarls in England in the Eleventh Century', *Anglo-Norman Studies* 7 (1984), pp. 161-76.
71 M. Wilde-Stockmeyer, *Slaverei auf Island* (Heidelberg, 1978), pp. 48-49.
72 There must be some reservations about the mounted archer in the final scene (scene 58), which has been heavily restored.
73 A. W. Brøgger, *Stiklestadslaget* (Oslo, 1946). See also L. Musset, 'Récentes contributions scandinaves à l'exégèse de la Tapisserie de Bayeux', *Bulletin de la Société des Antiquaires de Normandie*, 51 (1948-51), pp. 275-79.
73b Henry of Huntingdon, *Historia Anglorum*, ed. Greenway, pp. 394-95.
74 William of Poitiers, ed. Foreville, p. 188 (Davis and Chibnall, pp. 128-29).
75 *Carmen de Hastingae Proelio*, ed. Morton and Muntz, p. 22, line 338. William of Poitiers, ed. Foreville, p. 184 (Davis and Chibnall, p. 126-27).
76 It has been suggested that the crossbow was excluded from the Tapestry because it was reckoned an immoral and inhumane weapon: it was soon to be prohibited by the Church on these grounds at the Lateran Council of 1139. This is the view of the editors of the *Carmen de Hastingae Proelio* (appendix C, p. 112). But it does not seem very plausible. See also the rather debateable C. Gaier, 'Quand l'arbalète était une nouveauté', *Le Moyen Âge* 99 (1993), pp. 210-29.
77 L. Musset, 'Réflexions sur les moyens de paiement en Normandie aux XIe et XIIe siècles', *Cahiers des Annales de Normandie* 22 (Caen, 1989), pp. 69-70.
78 Pancarte de Saint-Gabriel.
79 Above all by L. G. M. Champion, *Les chevaux et les cavaliers de la Tapisserie de Bayeux* (Caen, 1907). R. H. C. Davis, 'The Warhorses of the Normans', *Anglo-Norman Studies* 10 (1987), pp. 67-81 emphasises the relatively small stature of the horses of that time.
80 Champion, *Les chevaux et les cavaliers*, p. 47.
81 William of Poitiers, ed. Foreville, p. 26 (Davis and Chibnall, pp. 16-17)
82 Wace, ed. Holden, vol. 2, p. 164, lines 7535-42 (Burgess and Van Houts, p. 175). A. M. Bautier, 'Contribution à l'histoire du cheval au Moyen Âge', *Bulletin philologique et historique du Comité des Travaux Historiques et Scientifiques* (1976), pp. 209-49. We do know, however, that William had occasional contacts with the king of Castile, regarding possible marriage alliances.
83 Champion, *Les chevaux et les cavaliers*, p. 44.
84 R.H. and A.M. Bautier, 'Contribution à l'histoire de l'élevage du cheval au Moyen Âge', *Bull. philol. et hist. du Comité...* , 1976, pp. 209-249. It is known, however, that William had intermittent contacts with the king of Castile, including the arrangement of matrimonial plans.
85 William of Poitiers, ed. Foreville, p. 26 (Davis and Chibnall, pp. 16-17).
86 For this last point see B. S. Bachrach, 'Animals and Warfare in Early Medieval Europe', *Settimane di studio del Centro Italiano di Studi dull'Alto Medioevo, Spoleto* 31 (1983), pp. 707-51, esp. p. 744.
87 *Vita S. Arialdi*, ed. F. Baethgen, *Monumenta Germanicae Historica ... Scriptores* 30, pars II (Leipzig, 1934), pp. 1059-60, c.
88 C. Erdmann, *Die Entstehung des Kreuzzugsgedankens* (Stuttgart, 1935), pp. 181-83.
89 But some commentators attribute this banner to Eustace of Boulogne. See C. Morton, 'Pope Alexander II and the Norman Conquest', *Latomus* 34 (1975), pp. 362-82, at p. 367.
90 William of Poitiers, ed. Foreville, p. 224 (Davis and Chibnall, pp. 152-53).
91 P. C. Schramm, *Herrschaftszeichen und Staatssymbolik* (Stuttgart, 1955), pp. 655-62; T. J. Arne, Söderalaflöjeln, *Hälsingerunor*, 1949.
92 J. Kiff, 'Images of War', pp. 177-94.

Chapter VII

93 For the rise of this spurious term, which combines a barbarism and a solecism with a misunderstanding, see the excellent note by G. Nondier, 'Sur le lancement de drakkar', *Études Normandes* 41 (1992), no. 4, pp. 90-92.
94 For the terminology, see above all H. Falk, *Altnordisches Seewesen* (Heidelberg, 1912); N. Bjørgo, 'Skibstypar i nørron samtidssoger', *Sjøfartshistorisk Årbok* (Bergen, 1965); O. Crumlin Pedersen, *Traeskibet* (Copenhagen, 1968); R. Malmros, 'Leding og skjaldekvad', *Aarbøger for nordisk Oldkyndighed og Historie* (1985), pp. 89-139.
95 N. Nicolaysen, *Langskibet fra Gokstad ved Sandefjord* (Kristania, 1882); A. W. Brøgger, H. Falk, H. Shetelig, *Osebergfunnet* (4 vols. Oslo, 1917-28).
96 See above all O. Olsen, O. Crumlin Pedersen, 'The Skuldelev Ships', *Acta Archaeologica* 29 (1958), pp. 161-75 and 38 (1967), pp. 73-174; and also the same authors' more accessible work, *Fem vikingskibe fra Roskilde fjord* (Roskilde, 1969). As a result of an early error, the wrecks are numbered 1, 2, 3, 5, and 6.
97 M. Müller-Wille, 'Das Schiffsgrab von der Île de Groix (Bretagne)', in B. Arrhenius et al., *Das archäologische Fundmaterial III der Ausgrabung Haithabu* (Neumünster, 1978. Berichte über die Ausgrabungen in Haithabu 12), pp. 48-84.
98 For further detail see the general account by A. W. Brøgger and H. Shetelig, *Vikingskipene, deres forgjængere og etterfølgere* (Oslo, 1950), as well as the excellent survey by S. McGrail, 'Ships, Shipwrights and Seamen', in *The Viking World*, ed. J. Graham-Campbell (London, 1980), pp. 36-63.
99 S. Lindqvist, *Gotlands Bildsteine* (2 vols. Stockholm, 1941-42); E. Nylén, *Bildstenar* (Visby, 1978).
100 Scholars have generally recognised the value of the Tapestry for nautical archaeology, but have often failed to realise that invaluable information is to be derived from the documentary sources of the time, especially saints' lives, which often cast important light on everyday matters.
100b Baudry, line 354; Wace, ed. Holden, vol. 2, pp. 125-26, lines 6481-6504 (Burgess and Van Houts, p. 163).
101 As has been vigorously argued by D. P. Waley, 'Combined Operations in Sicily, AD 1069-1078', *Papers of the British School at Rome* 22 (1954), pp. 118-26.
102 Above all by C. M. Gillmore, 'Naval Logistics of the Cross-Channel Operation, 1066', *Anglo-Norman Studies* 7 (1984), pp. 105-31; see also J. H. Pryor, 'Transportation of Horses by Sea during the Era of the Crusades', *Mariner's Mirror* 68 (1982), pp. 9-27 and 103-26.
103 On this last point see R. L. S. Bruce-Mitford, 'A New Wooden Ship's Figure Found in the Scheldt', *Acta Archaeologica* 38 (1976), pp. 199-209.
104 Crumlin Pedersen, *Træskibet*, p. 36.

105 See S. Haasum, *Vikingatidens segling och navigation* (Stockholm, 1974), though his conclusions are highly debatable.
106 O. Crumlin Pedersen, 'Side-røret fra Vorsaa', *Kuml* (Aarhus, 1960), pp. 106-16.
107 G. Hutchinson, 'The Southwold Side-Rudders', *Antiquity* 60 (1986), pp. 219-21. See also G. J. Marcus, *The Conquest of the North Atlantic* (London, 1980), p. 50.
108 L. Musset, 'Les périls de mer dans l'État anglo-normand', *Revue du Nord* special no. 1 (1986), pp. 413-21, at p. 419.
109 Crumlin Pedersen, 'The Skuldelev Ships' (1967), p. 160.
110 For this see A. Williams, 'Land and Power in the Eleventh Century: the Estates of Harold Godwineson', *Anglo-Norman Studies* 3 (1980), pp. 171-87, esp. p. 179.
111 For the last point see R. H. Lindemann, 'Channel Crossings by English Royalty, 1066-1216', University of Virginia PhD dissertation, 1981, p. 225 (and pp. 261-83 for comment on the use of 'esnèque' in England.
112 An exception must be made for the striking image of a fleet engraved on the thirteenth-century wooden baton (fig. 8) found at Bergen during excavations in the Bryggen, as mentioned above.

Chapter VIII

113 This is largely drawn from the invaluable thesis of Alain Labbé, *L'architecture des palais et des jardins dans les chansons de geste* (Paris, 1987).
114 M. Cagiano de Azevedo, 'Laubia', *Studi Medievali* 10 (1969), pp. 431-69, esp. pp. 446 and 459-60.
115 U. T. Holmes, 'The Houses of the Bayeux Tapestry', *Speculum* 34 (1959), pp. 179-83; and R. D. H. Gem, 'The Romanesque Rebuilding of Westminster Abbey' *Anglo-Norman Studies* 3 (1980), pp. 33-60, at pp. 59-60.
116 See below, footnote 124.
117 Gem, 'Romanesque Rebuilding'.
118 See the careful and helpful comments of M. M. Gauthier in *Bull. Soc. Nat. Antiq. France* (1989), p. 54, arguing that most of the images of mottes on the Tapestry are schematic and symbolic rather than realistic.
119 B. Hope-Taylor, 'The Norman Motte at Abinger (Surrey) and its Modern Castle', in *Recent Archaeological Excavations in Britain*, ed. R. L. S. Bruce-Mitford (London, 1956), pp. 223-49.
120 This might be the reason why the depiction of the ground in the image of the motte at Rennes is different from that elsewhere, but I doubt it.
121 The possibility that the colouring of the tower at Dol (scene 18, p. 136) has some technical significance rather than being merely ornamental has been raised. But as with the colouring of the vertical timbers in the châteaux at Rennes and Dinan, it is impossible to be sure.
122 On the use of this type of roof on wooden buildings in the eleventh century, see P. Halbout and J. Le Maho, *Aspects de la construction de bois en Normandie du Ier au XIVe siècle* (Caen, 1985), p. 61, with further references to English publications on the subject. See also J. Le Maho, *La motte seigneuriale de Mirville* (XIe-XIIe siècles) (Rouen, 1984).

Chapter IX

123 W. B. Yapp, 'Animals in Medieval Art: the Bayeux Tapestry as an Example', *Journal of Medieval History* 13 (1987), pp. 15-73.
124 H. Chefneux, 'Les fables dans la Tapisserie de Bayeux', *Romania* 60 (1934), pp. 1-35 and 153-94; L. Herrmann, 'Apologues et anecdotes de la Tapisserie de Bayeux', *Romania* 65 (1939), pp. 376-82, and *Les fables antiques de la broderie de Bayeux* (Brussels, 1964). Herrmann's book tends to exaggerate the number of classical subjects depicted on the Tapestry. Refer also to the helpful comments of H. Prentout, *Études sur quelques points d'histoire de Normandie* III (Caen, 1926), pp. 60-61.
125 Leiden, Codex Vossius Latin 8, 15. See also D. Gaborit-Chopin, 'Les dessins d'Adémar de Chabannes', *Bulletin Archéologique du Comité des Travaux Historique et Scientifiques*, n. s. 3 (1976), pp. 163-225, which revisits in part a German study by Georg Thiele, *Der illustrierte lateinische Aesop in der Handschrift des Ademar Codex Vossianus Lat. Oct. 15* (Leiden, 1905).

Chapter X

126 These are expounded throughout F. M. Stenton, *Anglo-Saxon England* (3rd edn. Oxford, 1971). See also D. C. Douglas, *William the Conqueror* (London, 1964); M. de Boüard, *Guillaume le Conquérant* (Paris, 1984); and the handy little study by D. Whitelock, D. C. Douglas, C. H. Lemmon, and F. Barlow, *The Norman Conquest: Its Setting and Impact* (London, 1966).
127 William of Poitiers, ed. Foreville, p. 170 (Davis and Chibnall, pp. 116-17).
128 The best survey of the relationship between the Tapestry and the chronicles is the article by Brooks and Walker, 'Authority and Interpretation of the Bayeux Tapestry' *Battle*, I, 1976, pp. 1-34.
129 See R. D. Wissolik, 'The Monk Eadmer as Historian of the Norman Succession: Körner and Freeman Examined', *The American Benedictine Review* 30, I (1979), pp. 32-43.
130 Eadmer, *Historia Novorum*, ed. M. Rule (Rolls Series. London, 1884), pp. 6-8.
131 *The Carmen de Hastingae Proelio of Guy, Bishop of Amiens*, ed. C. Morton and H. Muntz (Oxford, 1978). Morton and Muntz favour the traditional attribution.
132 R. H. C. Davis, 'The *Carmen de Hastingae Proelio*', *English Historical Review* 93 (1978), pp. 241-61; G. Garnett, 'Coronation and Propaganda: some implications of the Norman claim to the throne of England in 1066', *Transactions of the Royal Historical Society*, 5th series, 36 (1986), pp. 91-116. D. D. R. Owen, 'The Epic and History: *Chanson de Roland* and *Carmen de Hastingae Proelio*', *Medium Aevum* 51 (1982), pp. 18-34, draws attention to the epic concerns of the *Carmen*
133 *Roman de Rou*, Ed. A.J. Holden (Paris 1970-1973), 3 vols.

Part Two | Commentary

THE ENSUING DETAILED EXAMINATION OF THE TAPESTRY seeks to elucidate the issues which arise from each scene without lapsing into a blow-by-blow narrative of the events of 1064-66. It presupposes a knowledge of what has been said in the introduction, and hence tries to avoid repeating the general observations made there. While it cannot be exhaustive, it strives to cast light on as many details as possible, even if definitive solutions cannot be offered for all the problems raised. It focuses on the central narrative band of the Tapestry: the borders are considered only occasionally, when they contain something of special interest.

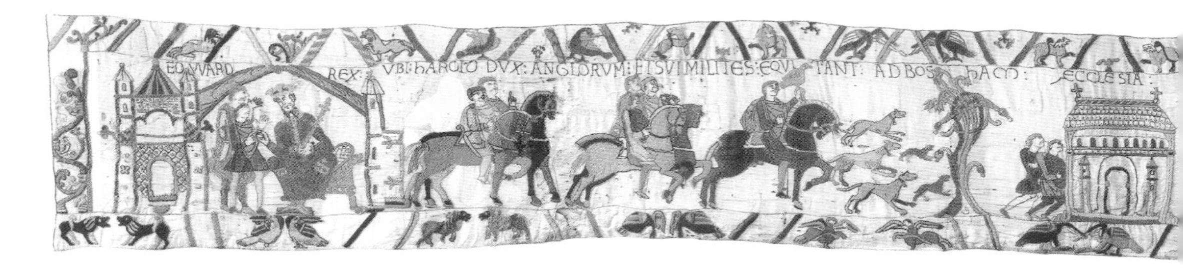

The Tapestry has suffered at both ends from centuries of being folded and unfolded for its annual display, and some serious damage can be seen here at the start, along with some significant attempts at restoration, particularly in the vertical border at the left and the lower border. In the captions, the obvious anachronism 'Edward' is the work of restorers, as elsewhere the spelling is invariably 'Eadwardus'. In the early eighteenth century the legible text began at 'REX', and the initial 'V' of 'VBI' was missing. There is no reason to believe, however, that anything important has been lost: this plunge straight into the action makes an entirely plausible start.

Edward the Confessor is seen enthroned in one of his palaces — probably Winchester, then in effect the English capital. He is apparently giving instructions to two Englishmen who stand on his right in civilian dress. One of them must be Harold. The king, seated on a plump cushion, is shown in accordance with the iconographic conventions for royalty at that time 'in majesty' on a low throne (its arms carved in the form of beasts' heads, its feet in the form of lions' paws). And he has his *regalia*, the insignia of royal rank: on his head the crown, with its crudely executed *fleur-de-lys* decorations; and in his right hand the sceptre. Note that these are not identical with the insignia bestowed upon Harold after Edward's death (scenes 29-30, pp. 173–175). The crown shown in scene 29 (p. 173) is rather different from this, although that on Harold's head in scene 30 (p. 175) is much the same. And Edward is not shown here with the orb that Harold holds aloft at his coronation. The opening scene, then, is not the solemn 'crown-wearing' ceremony practised by the English kings. The *regalia* serve merely to identify the seated figure as a king.

The palace follows the usual Romanesque conventions, but two features are worthy of note. On the left, the lozenge pattern shown around the doorway has an actual counterpart on another eleventh-century palace, Westminster. And the open door on the right, at the bottom of the turret just behind the horsemen, has trefoil ironwork at the level of the hinges, of a pattern that can still be seen on some surviving eleventh-century church doors such as those in North Yorkshire at Stillingfleet (whose strap-hinges show Viking-style ships) and at Staplehurst in Kent. There is a clearer view of strap-hinges in scene 47 (pp. 218–219).

(Eadwardus) rex.

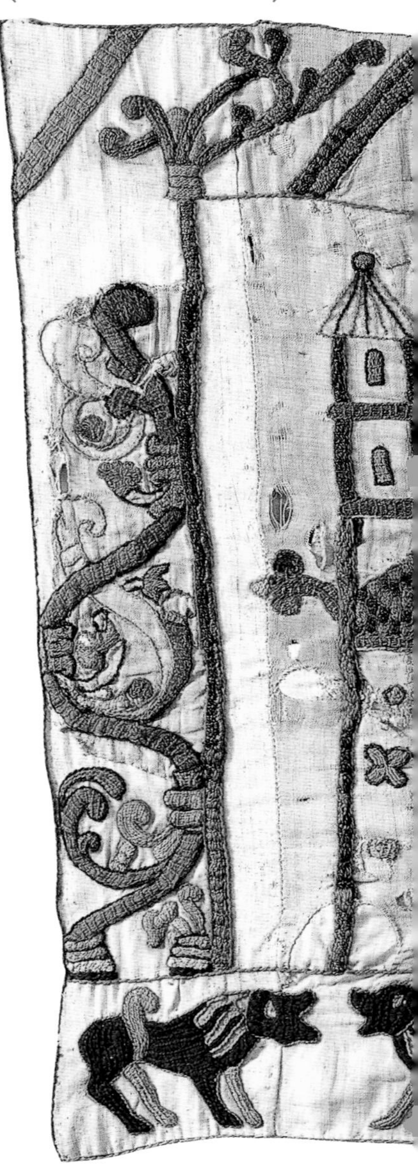

Scene 1

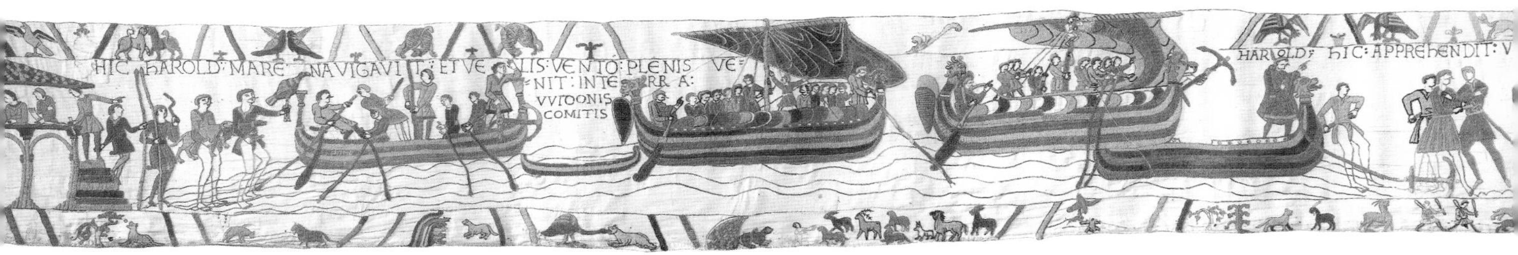

(U)BI HAROLD...

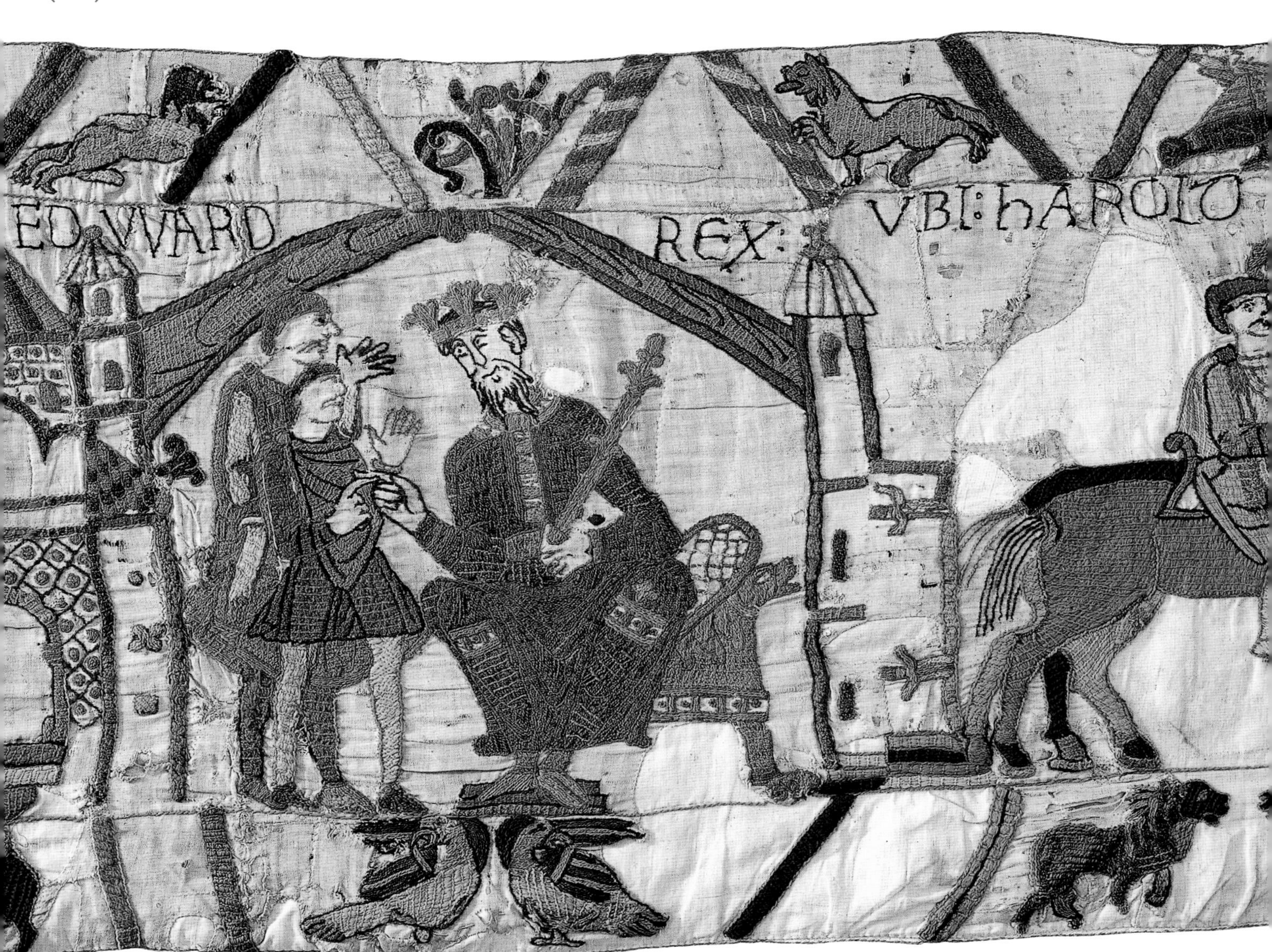

King Edward. Where Harold …

90

... Harold dux Anglorum et sui milites

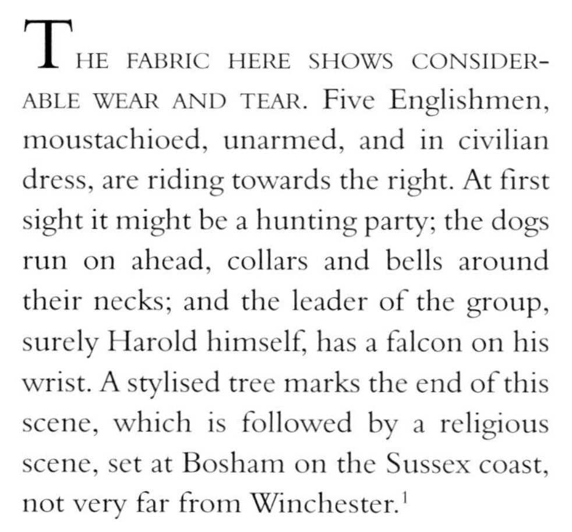

THE FABRIC HERE SHOWS CONSIDERABLE WEAR AND TEAR. Five Englishmen, moustachioed, unarmed, and in civilian dress, are riding towards the right. At first sight it might be a hunting party; the dogs run on ahead, collars and bells around their necks; and the leader of the group, surely Harold himself, has a falcon on his wrist. A stylised tree marks the end of this scene, which is followed by a religious scene, set at Bosham on the Sussex coast, not very far from Winchester.[1]

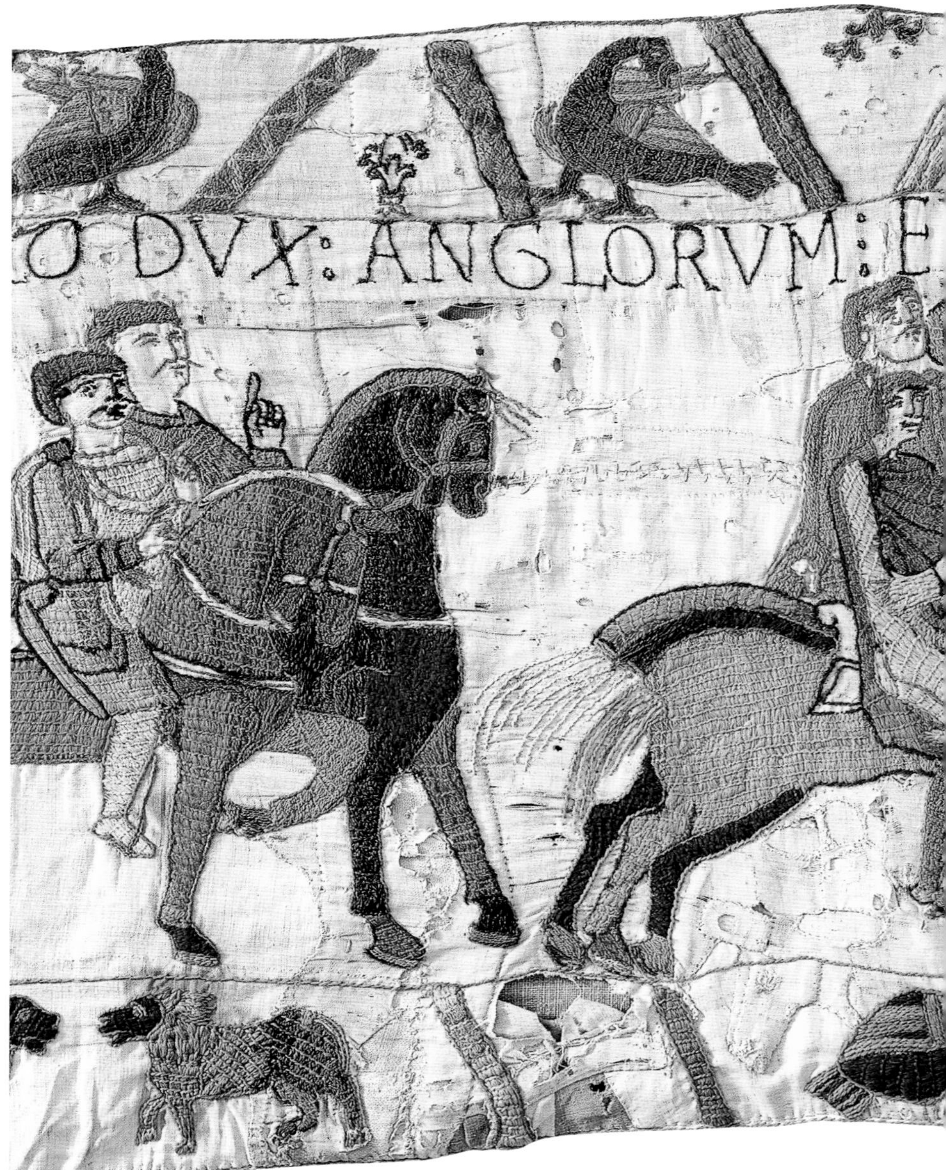

[1] See A. Taylor, 'Bosham', *Anglo-Norman Studies* 14 (1991), pp. 1-23.

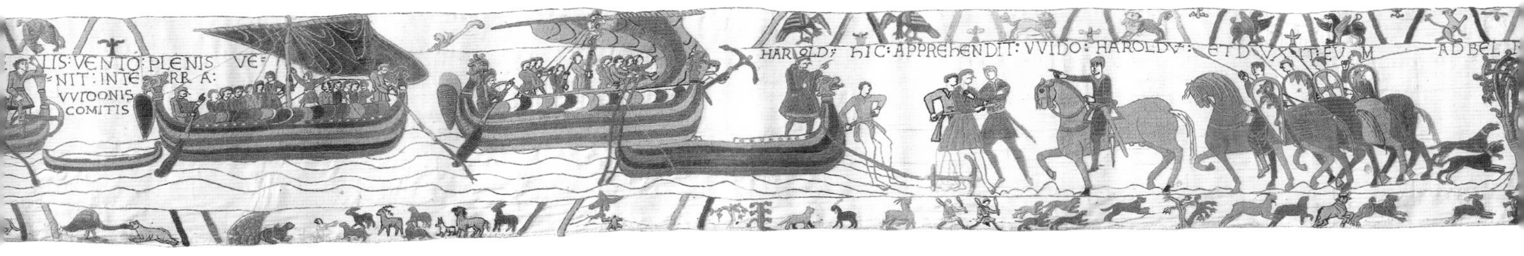

EQUITANT AD BOSHAM.

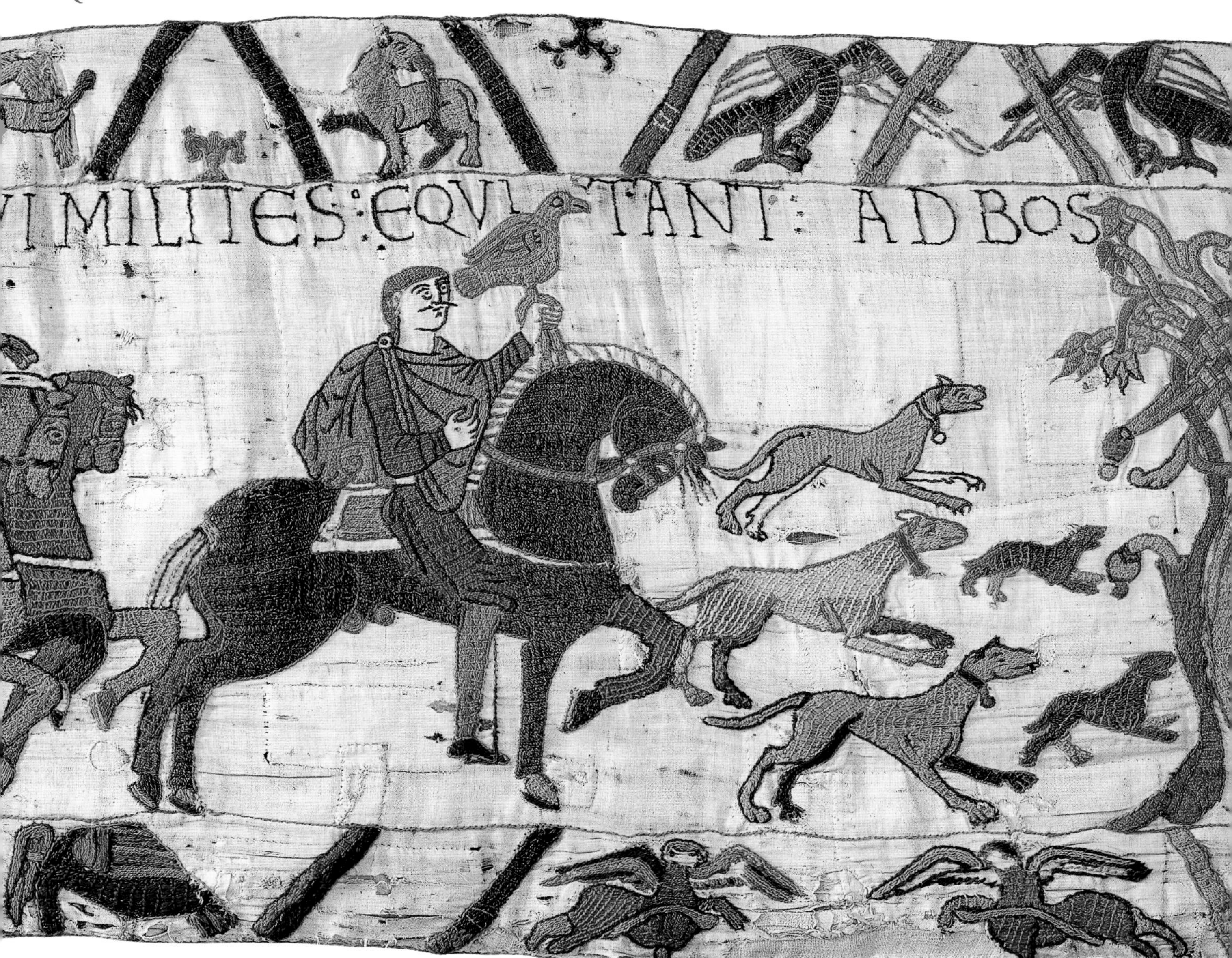

Harold, Duke of the English, and his knights ride to Bosham.

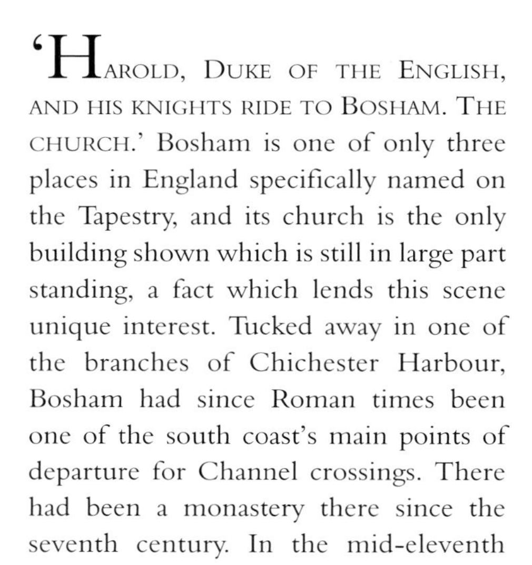

'HAROLD, DUKE OF THE ENGLISH, AND HIS KNIGHTS RIDE TO BOSHAM. THE CHURCH.' Bosham is one of only three places in England specifically named on the Tapestry, and its church is the only building shown which is still in large part standing, a fact which lends this scene unique interest. Tucked away in one of the branches of Chichester Harbour, Bosham had since Roman times been one of the south coast's main points of departure for Channel crossings. There had been a monastery there since the seventh century. In the mid-eleventh century the area belonged to Harold, who had inherited it from his father, Earl Godwin. For a family based at the royal court in Winchester, Bosham provided an invaluable escape-route in times of trouble, as in 1051-52.[2] The church itself had been bestowed by Edward upon one of his chaplains, a distant Norman relative named Osbern who was to become Bishop of Exeter in 1072. Osbern annexed it to his episcopal see, and in the twelfth century it became a collegiate church, surviving until its dissolution in 1548.

Bosham is clearly one of the most important places on the Tapestry, yet among the documentary sources for Harold's ill-fated journey of 1064, only two texts mention it, both of them from the twelfth century: William of Malmesbury's *Gesta Regum*, and Wace.[3] This furnishes a powerful argument for the independence of the Tapestry from the Norman chroniclers of the eleventh century, William of Jumièges and William of Poitiers.

The church itself, dedicated to the Holy Trinity, and built in part from material salvaged from Roman ruins, is relatively small, but well preserved. The eleventh-century elements still intact are the west tower (not shown on the Tapestry), a small section of the nave and choir, and, most significantly, the entire chancel arch dividing the two (fig. 20, p. 68). It is this which the Tapestry's

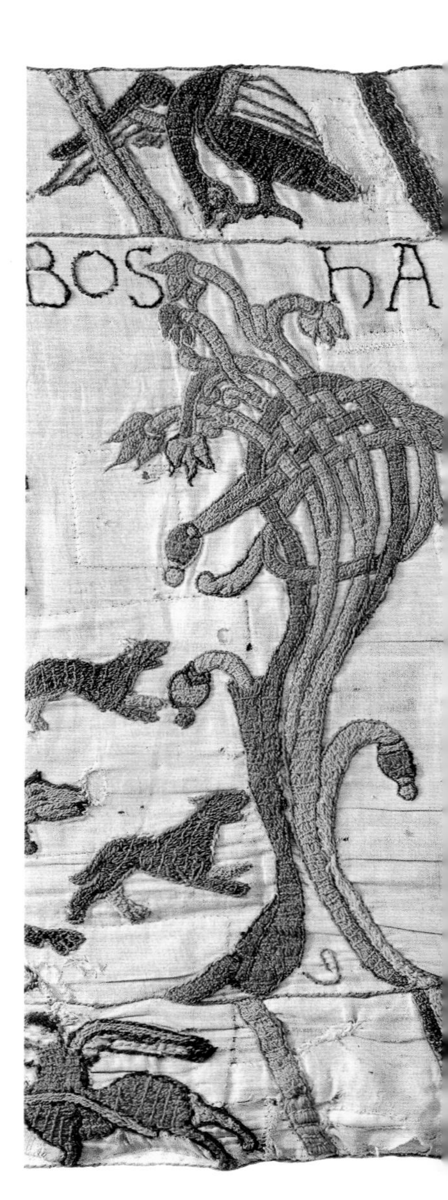

SCENE 3

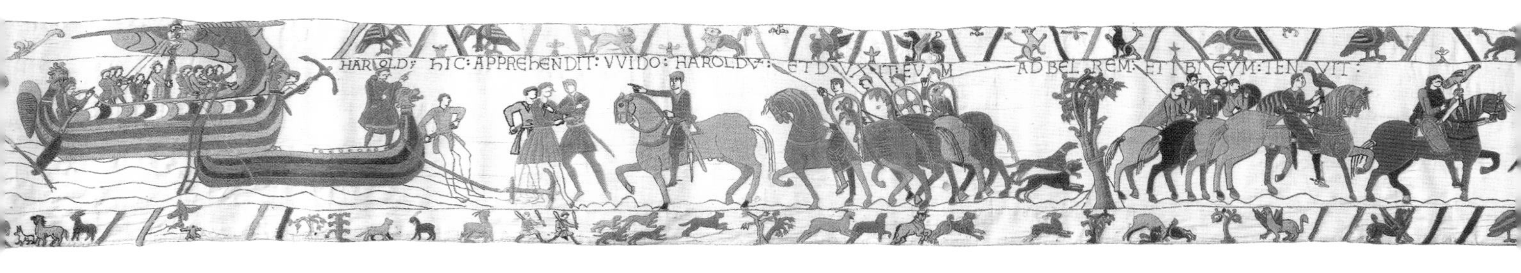

Ecclesia

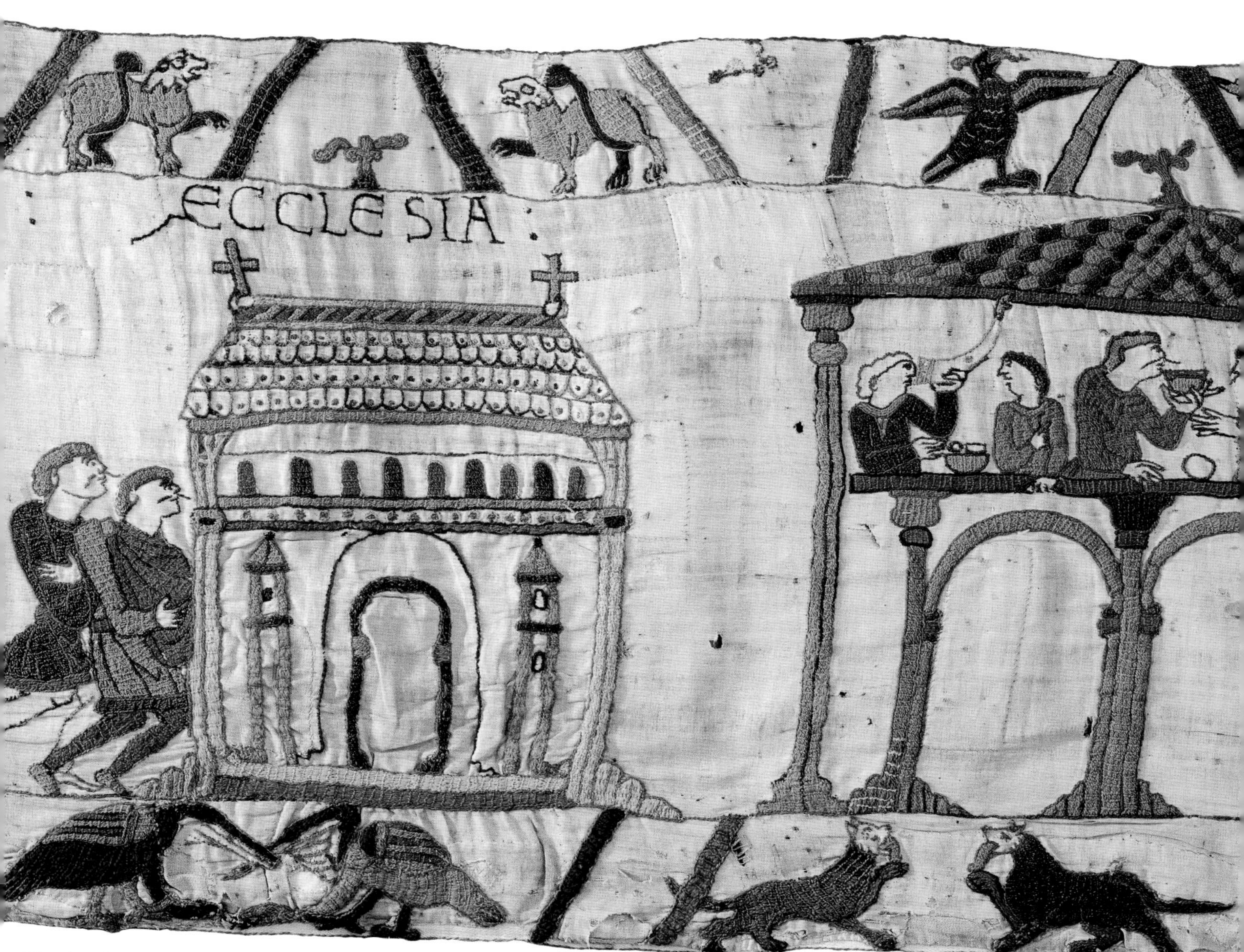

The church.

designer makes the visual key to identifying the church: a high and rather narrow round arch resting on piers with moulded bases and projecting capitals. At 6 metres high and 2.90 metres wide, the actual arch matches the proportions of the embroidered image — proportions typical of the Anglo-Saxon architecture of the time — and its capitals accord with those suggested by the Tapestry.[4] The artist is startlingly true to the actual building, which he must have known.

The rest of the drawing makes no attempt at realism or perspective, though the nine little windows under the roof perhaps allude to those which lit the church. It is not clear whether the slender, pointed turrets either side of the arch represent façade decoration or actual structures, though the crosses above the gables were probably authentic. But these interpretative difficulties simply reflect the limitations of the medium: emphasis on a key feature has to take precedence over any attempt at an accurate overall view.

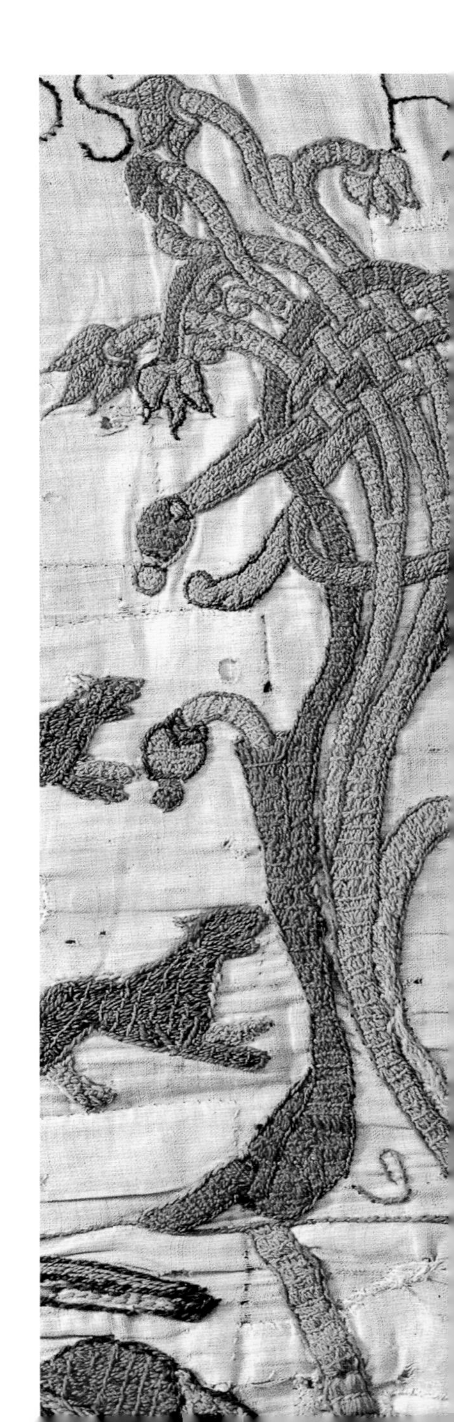

[2] A. Williams, 'Land and power in the 11th century: the estates of Harold Godwineson', *Anglo-Norman Studies* 3 (1980), pp. 171-87, esp. p. 185.
[3] Wace, ed. Holden, vol. 2, p. 95, line 5614 (Burgess and Van Houts, p. 154).
[4] L. Musset, *Angleterre romane*, vol. 1 (La Pierre-qui-Vire: Zodiaque, 1983), pp. 81-83, with photographs (plate 16).

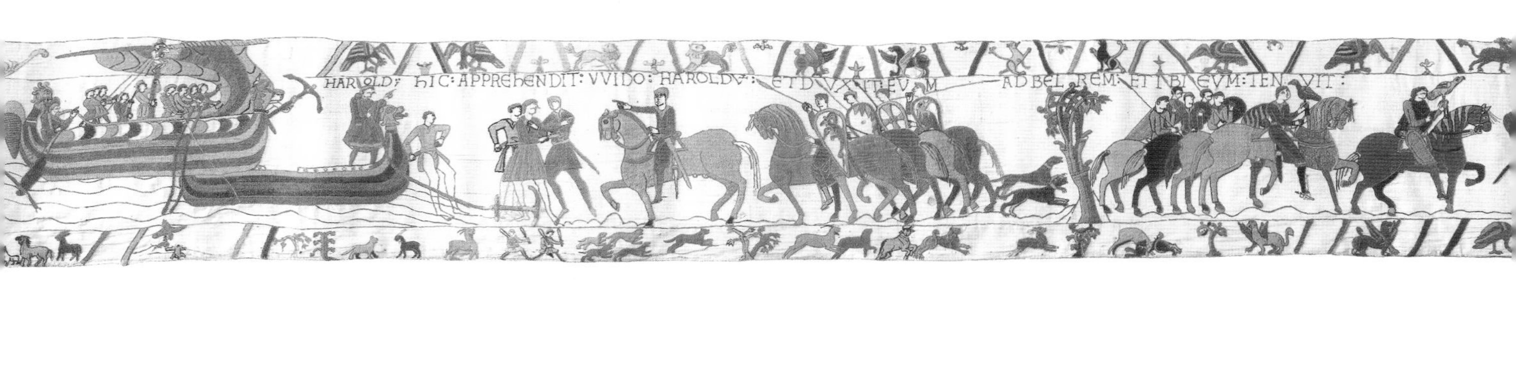
HAROLD: HIC: APPREHENDIT: VVIDO: HAROLDV: ET DVXIT EVM AD BELREM: ET IBI EVM TENVIT:

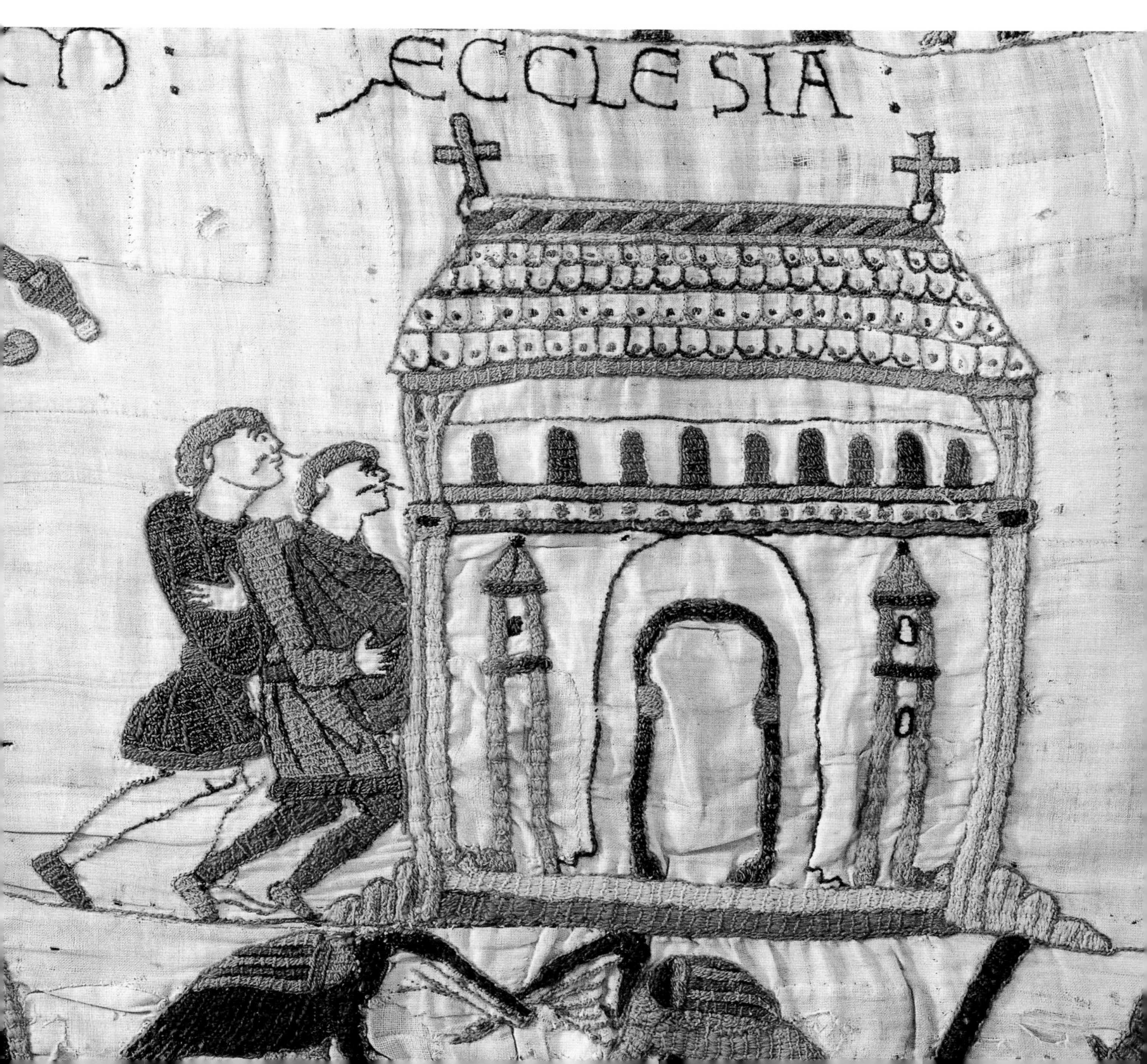
ECCLESIA :

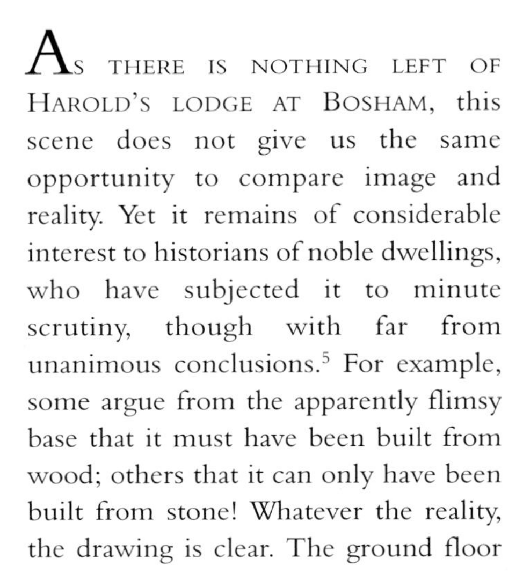

As there is nothing left of Harold's lodge at Bosham, this scene does not give us the same opportunity to compare image and reality. Yet it remains of considerable interest to historians of noble dwellings, who have subjected it to minute scrutiny, though with far from unanimous conclusions.[5] For example, some argue from the apparently flimsy base that it must have been built from wood; others that it can only have been built from stone! Whatever the reality, the drawing is clear. The ground floor consists of three large arches carried by columns with moulded capitals; on the first floor a banqueting hall runs the length of the building, and a staircase outside leads down to the beach for embarkation. The sloping roof, perhaps made from variously coloured tiles, culminates in an indistinct ornament which blends into one of the flowers that decorate the Tapestry's borders. The building has been convincingly identified as of a kind frequently mentioned in medieval texts as a *laubia* or lodge, typically open to the elements on the ground floor, with a solarium above.

The five figures on this upper floor are seen only at half length, evidently seated at a table, of which we see only the top, with some pots on it. They are drinking mead or ale, two of them from capacious horns, but the central figure — quite possibly Harold himself — from some kind of cup. It is presumably the end of the meal: the figure at the right is pointing seawards and seems to be calling on the others to go and get on board the awaiting ship. Some have taken this man for a Norman messenger, as he seems to have his neck shaved. But this is very speculative. The drinking-horns are of course typically Anglo-Saxon, and are not seen at the Tapestry's other meal (scene 43, p. 212), that of the Normans at Hastings. Plenty of drinking-horns survive from both pre-Conquest England and Scandinavia: there were seven, made from the ox-horn, in the Sutton Hoo tomb, and they could also be made from glass. The mouth of the horn was usually decorated with bands of precious metal.

The cups might possibly be metal, but were more probably made from 'turned' wood, perhaps maple, like several found at Sutton Hoo. Their rims might also be fitted with decorative bands. Harold's use of a cup (if it is Harold) might hint at the impact of new customs emanating from the Continent while his companions are clearly happy with traditional ways. The key features of this scene are too typical of the time and the place to support the idea that it derives from some conventional stereotype of a royal banquet. It looks more like a little ceremony of departure or leave-taking — almost 'one for the road'.

[5] See in particular A. Hamilton Thompson, 'The English house', in G. Barraclough (ed), *Social Life in Early England* (London, 1966), p. 142; and M. Cagiano de Azevedo, 'Laubia', *Studi medievali* 10 (1969), pp. 431-69, at pp. 446 and 459-60.

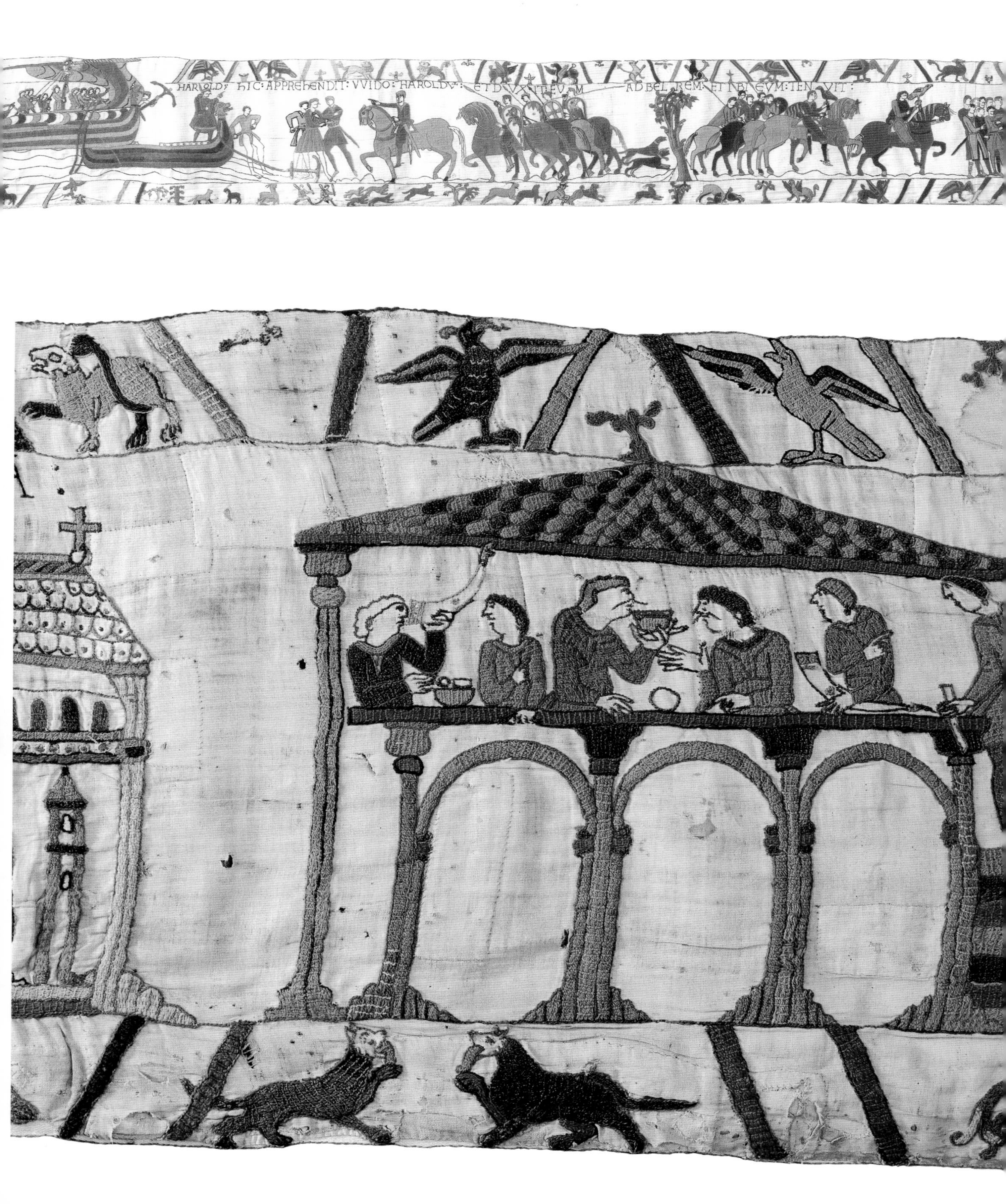
HAROLD: HIC: APPREHENDIT: VVIDO: HAROLDV:

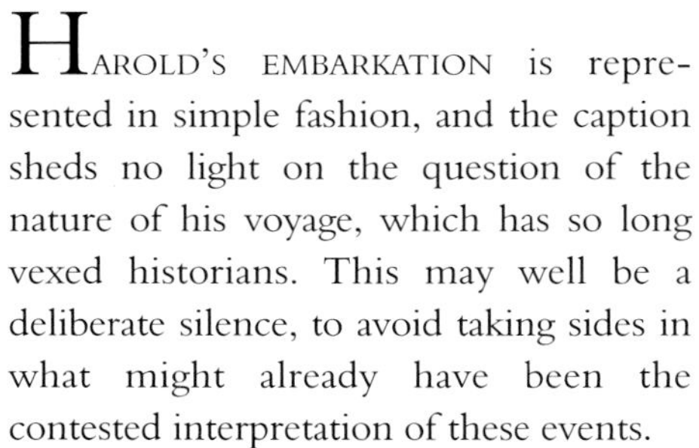

HAROLD'S EMBARKATION is represented in simple fashion, and the caption sheds no light on the question of the nature of his voyage, which has so long vexed historians. This may well be a deliberate silence, to avoid taking sides in what might already have been the contested interpretation of these events.

Two Englishmen stand in shallow water, barefoot and hitching up their tunics. The one in front — undoubtedly Harold — has a falcon on his wrist, and both are carrying dogs (each fitted with a collar). It looks like a hunting party. Following behind on the beach are two underlings carrying oars or poles and some kind of handle. This scene, unlike that of William's embarkation later on (scene 37, pp. 192–195), shows no loading of weapons or supplies.

That Harold is once again shown with a falcon is no mere picturesque fancy on the part of the designer. We have it on good authority that he was passionate about falconry. In a discussion of hunting birds, the twelfth-century author Adelard of Bath notes in passing that Harold owned books on the subject — no doubt they fell into William's hands later.[6] Clearly Harold's English contemporaries knew all about this passion of his, even if no Norman source mentions it. (Hawks and hounds appear only once more on the Tapestry, in scene 14, pp. 124–125.)

The studied neutrality of the caption is set in perspective by the controversies which have raged ever since the eleventh century over the motive for Harold's voyage. Every conceivable explanation has been canvassed: Edward the Confessor sent him on a mission concerning the succession; he was to negotiate the release of his brother and his nephew, Wulfnoth and Hakon, who had been Norman hostages for twelve years (a suggestion, this, of the near-contemporary Eadmer, later endorsed by Wace); he was considering marriage to one of William's daughters; it was just a fishing trip that went wrong in a storm (this was William of Malmesbury's idea — but why take hawks and hounds on a fishing trip?).[7]

The one thing we know for certain is that, when he set off, his destination was not the place he ended up, Ponthieu, the region of the Seine estuary. But it is far from clear whether his destination was Normandy or, as has been suggested, Flanders.[8] If we but knew, we would have a key not only to the Tapestry but also to Norman policy towards England in the years before 1066. But the only possibility clearly excluded by the Tapestry is the notion that the events of 1064 represented a mere concatenation of chance circumstances. For the opening scene shows that Harold received some kind of commission from Edward, or at least that he discussed a proposed voyage with him and received his approval for it. And this scene shows a man setting off on a serious voyage, not some pleasure trip: *pace* William of Malmesbury, he is not boarding a fishing-

HIC HAROLD MARE

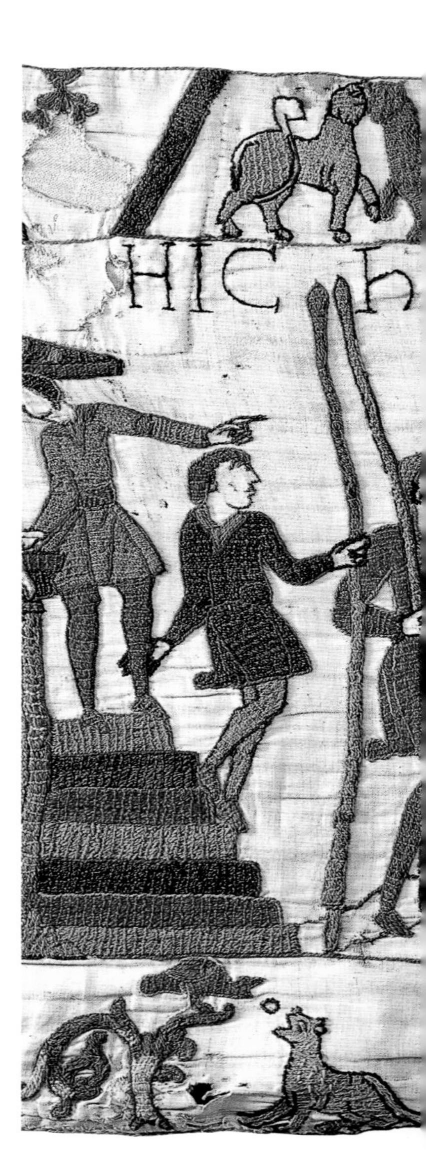

SCENE 4

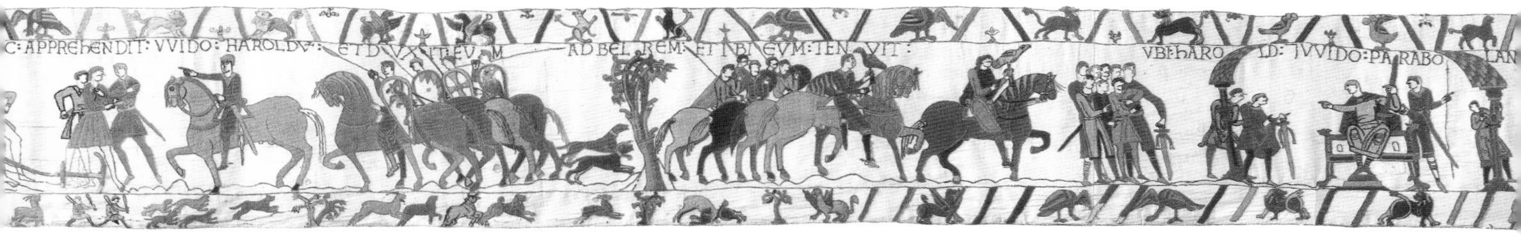

NAVIGAVIT…

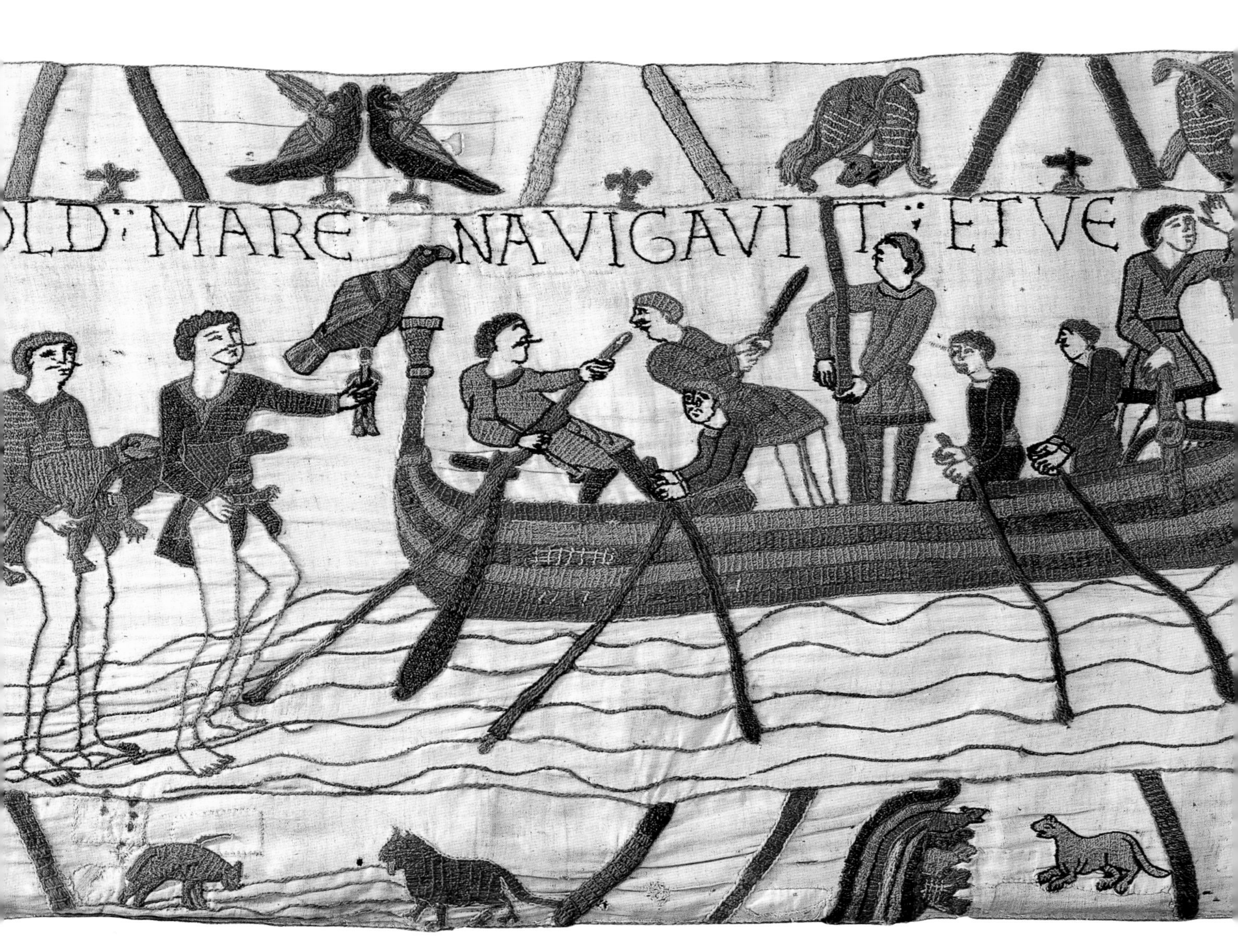

Here Harold sailed by sea …

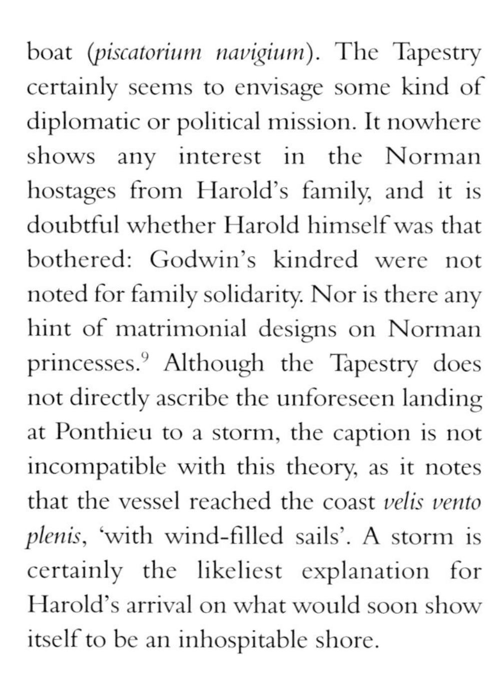

boat (*piscatorium navigium*). The Tapestry certainly seems to envisage some kind of diplomatic or political mission. It nowhere shows any interest in the Norman hostages from Harold's family, and it is doubtful whether Harold himself was that bothered: Godwin's kindred were not noted for family solidarity. Nor is there any hint of matrimonial designs on Norman princesses.[9] Although the Tapestry does not directly ascribe the unforeseen landing at Ponthieu to a storm, the caption is not incompatible with this theory, as it notes that the vessel reached the coast *velis vento plenis*, 'with wind-filled sails'. A storm is certainly the likeliest explanation for Harold's arrival on what would soon show itself to be an inhospitable shore.

[6] C. H. Haskins, 'King Harold's Books', *English Historical Review* 37 (1927), pp. 398-400. See also H. R. Loyn, *Harold Son of Godwin* (Hastings, 1966), p. 16 and note 30.

[7] Wace, ed. Holden, vol. 2, pp. 88-89 (lines 5435-41) and 94 (lines 5581-96) (Burgess and Van Houts, pp. 151 and 153). Eadmer, *Historia Novorum*, ed. M. Rule, p. 6.

[8] Some quite ludicrous destinations have also been proposed. In the early thirteenth century the great Icelandic author Snorri Sturluson suggested that he was heading for Wales when a storm blew him off course to Normandy (*The Saga of Harald Hardrada*, ch. 76).

[9] P. Grierson helpfully emphasised that Harold had doubtless been despatched by Edward on at least one diplomatic mission regarding the succession before this. His voyage to Flanders in 1056 could have been undertaken with the aim of persuading Edward Atheling, a possible heir to the throne, to return from Hungary. See *English Historical Review* 51 (1936), pp. 90-97. A mission to Normandy in 1064 might also have had a bearing upon the succession.

THE TAPESTRY'S FIRST NAUTICAL SCENES ARE OF A PEACEFUL CHARACTER. There are no weapons on show, no horses on board and no armour worn, although the customary shields are hung along the ships' sides. The designer is therefore free to illustrate some interesting details not visible on the warships of 1066, such as the manoeuvring of the last ship in the line as it leaves Bosham. Two sailors lean back on their poles to lever it away from shore while others bend their slender oars with the strain of getting under way (though there is no sign of rowlocks or even of holes for the oars). As the French coast looms, a sailor on the third ship sounds the depths with a pole, while two oarsmen assist the manoeuvres of the ship ahead. The ships out at sea are under sail, and the third vessel is towing a long-boat of the kind known from Viking finds in Norway. A half-naked boy clings to the mast of the

... ET VELIS VENTO P

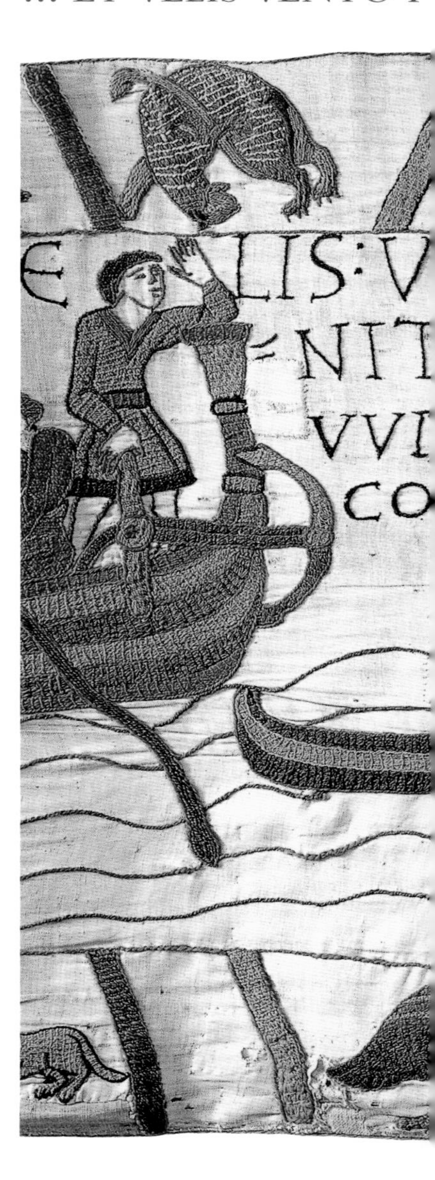

SCENE 5

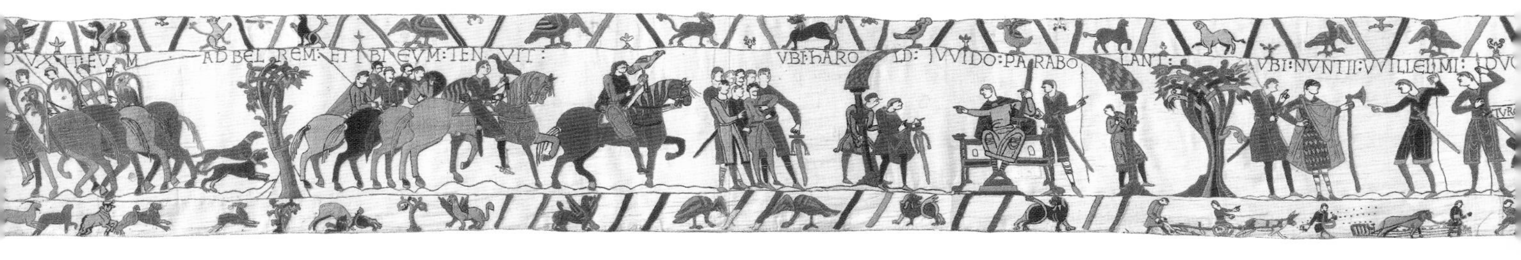

S VENIT IN TERRA WIDONIS COMITIS.

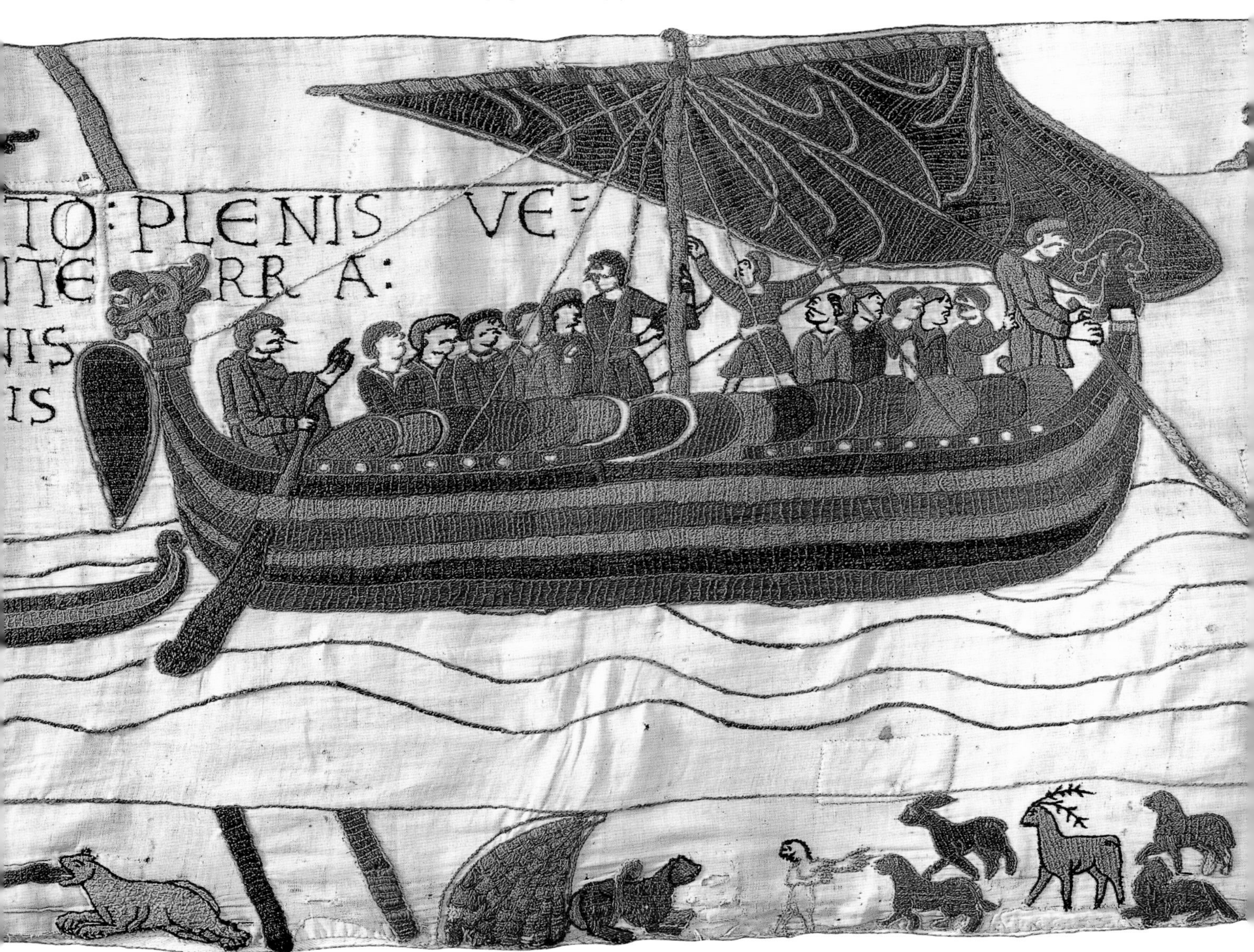

…and with wind-filled sails arrived in the land of Count Wido.

ship that is nearing land, ready to drop the sail, while four seamen haul on cables and a fifth takes a firm grip on the mast; there is a particularly clear view of the anchor at the bows.

Unlike the Norman ships of 1066, these four English ships all have a gap halfway along their uppermost boards, boards which, on two of these vessels, also have holes for the oars. There is no archaeological evidence for this feature. But apart from these minor differences, the English ships are much the same as the Norman ones, with the same steering and rigging.

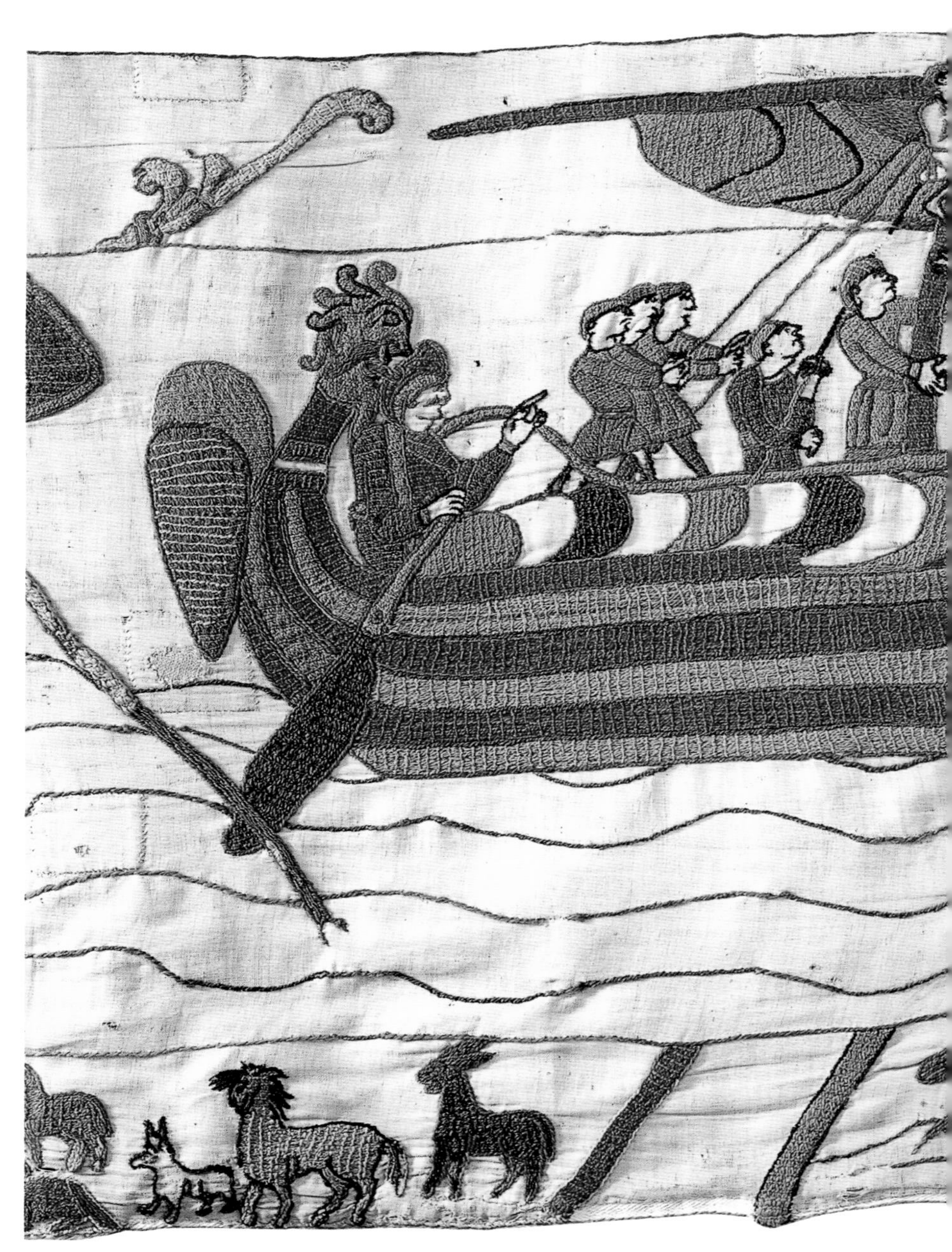

Scenes 5–6

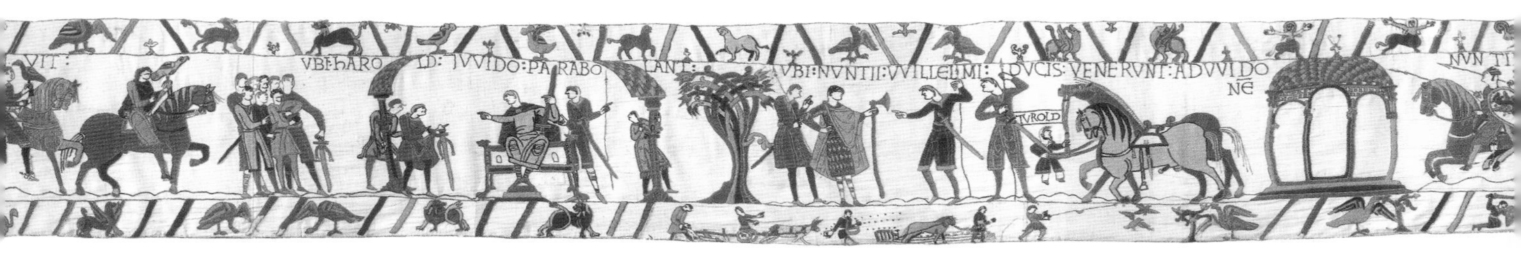

Harold.

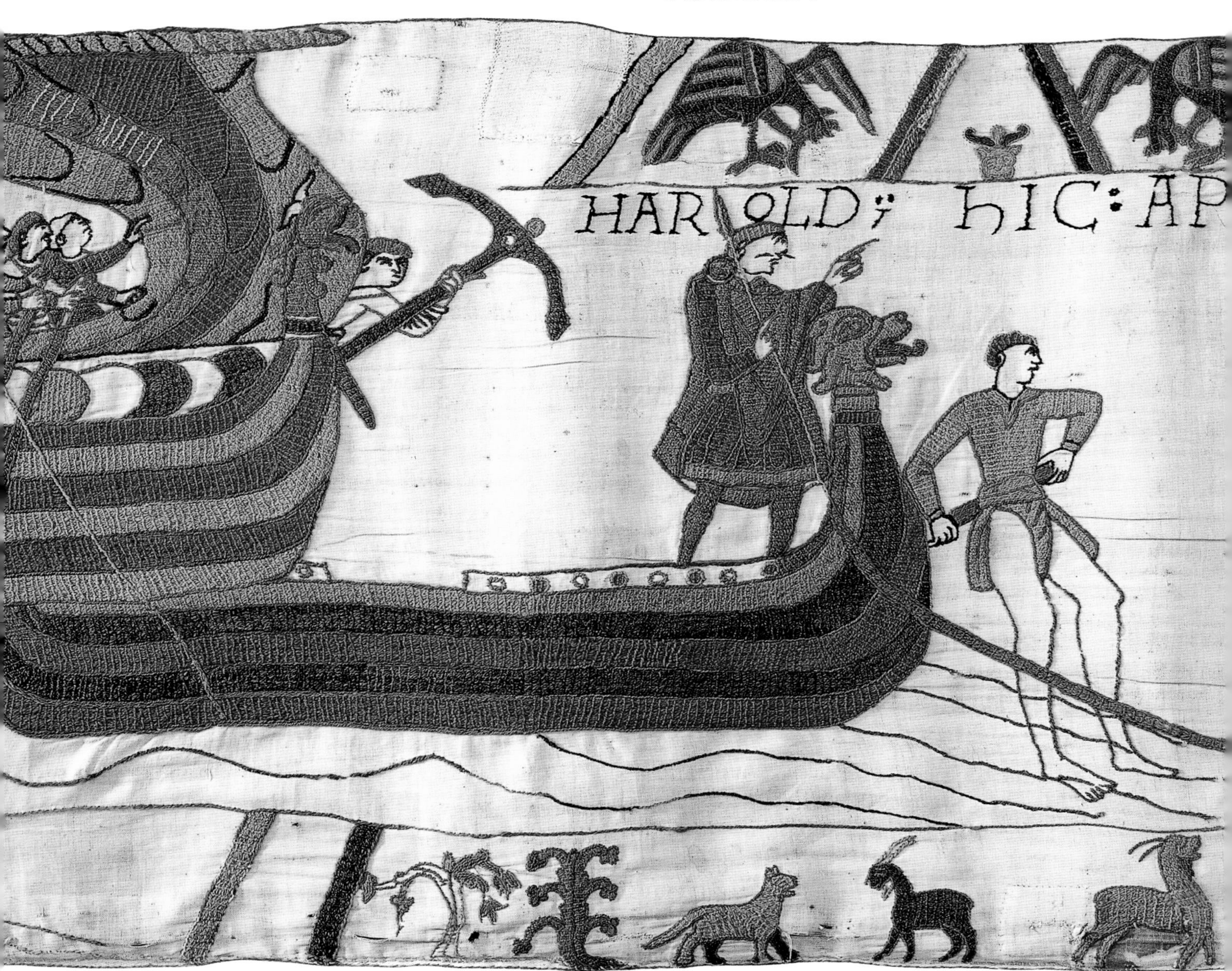

Harold.

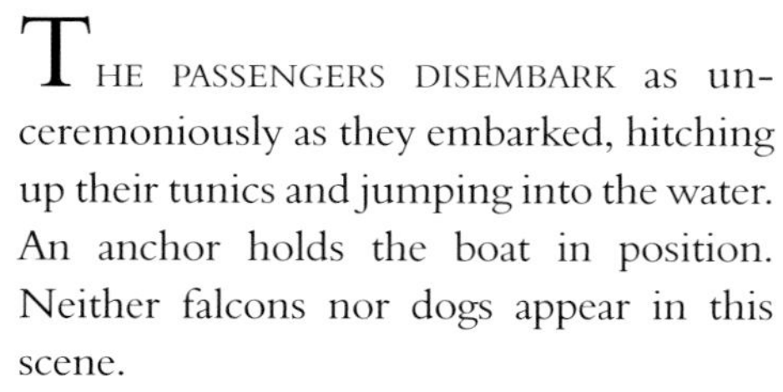

THE PASSENGERS DISEMBARK as unceremoniously as they embarked, hitching up their tunics and jumping into the water. An anchor holds the boat in position. Neither falcons nor dogs appear in this scene.

As soon as he comes ashore, Harold is seized by two armed men, apparently on the orders of a mounted knight who, sword at his side, directs operations with a gesture of command. The caption simply gives his name, Wido — that is, Guy. It does not give his title, but he was the Count of Ponthieu. Several eleventh- and twelfth-century texts spell out the awful truth about what is going on. At this time it was common along the coasts of north-west Europe to treat shipwreck victims as fair game, sometimes even selling them into slavery. Contemporary commentators found it shocking, at least in this instance. William of Poitiers describes it as a 'horrible and barbaric custom, contrary to all Christian justice', while William of Malmesbury records that 'by the barbaric and lawless custom of this region, those who survived a shipwreck faced new perils on land'.[10] It was not until the 1150s, in the early years of Henry II's reign, that this custom was finally suppressed in the Angevin Empire.[11] But for a recently established coastal lordship such as the County of Ponthieu, this peculiar variant on the salvage business was an important source of revenue.

Guy I of Ponthieu is a well-known figure who inherited the county after the death in battle of his brother, Enguerrand II, in 1053. Enguerrand had been struggling in vain against Norman power, and Guy had to acknowledge himself Duke William's vassal in 1059. He may well have been present, with his brother and son, in William's host at the battle of Hastings.[12] He died in 1100. The Anglo-Norman chroniclers pay him little attention. William of Malmesbury dismissed him as a *semivir*, 'but half a man', perhaps because of his behaviour towards Harold in this episode, which was not only brutal and mercenary, but almost inexplicable: at this time Ponthieu enjoyed close ties with England, and the Abbot of Saint-Riquier, the foremost monastery in the region, was a friend of Harold's brother-in-law, King Edward.[13]

[10] William of Poitiers, ed. Foreville, p. 102; William of Malmesbury, *De Gestis Regum Anglorum*, ed. Stubbs, vol. 1, p. 279.

[11] William of Newburgh, ed. Howlett, vol. 1, p. 282; for comment, see W. L. Warren, *Henry II* (London, 1979), p. 209.

[12] If we can believe the *Carmen de Hastingae Proelio*, verse 537 (see the edition by Morton and Muntz, p. 34; and commentary, pp. 116-20). See also D. Douglas, 'Companions of the Conqueror', *History* 27 (1943), pp. 129-47, at p. 139.

[13] Hariulf, *Chronique de l'abbaye de Saint-Riquier*, ed. F. Lot (Paris, 1894), p. 237.

HIC APPREHENDIT V

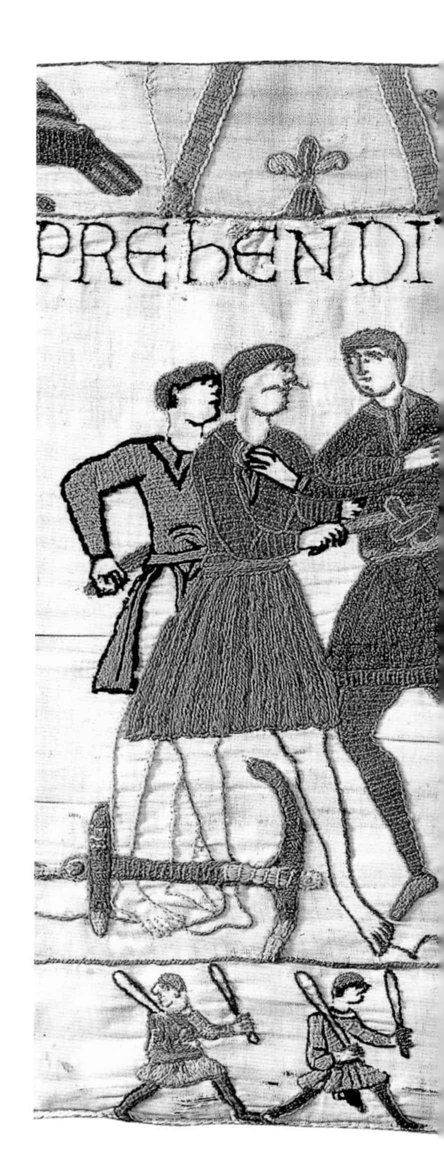

SCENE 7

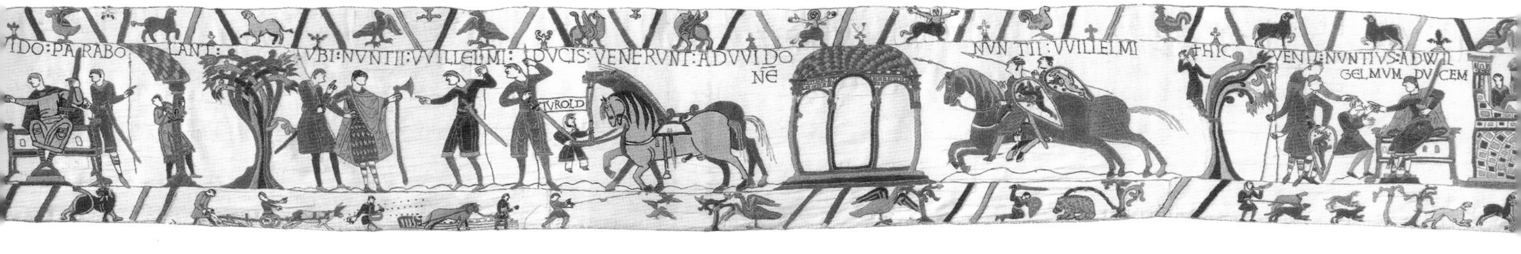

O HAROLDUM ET DUXIT EUM...

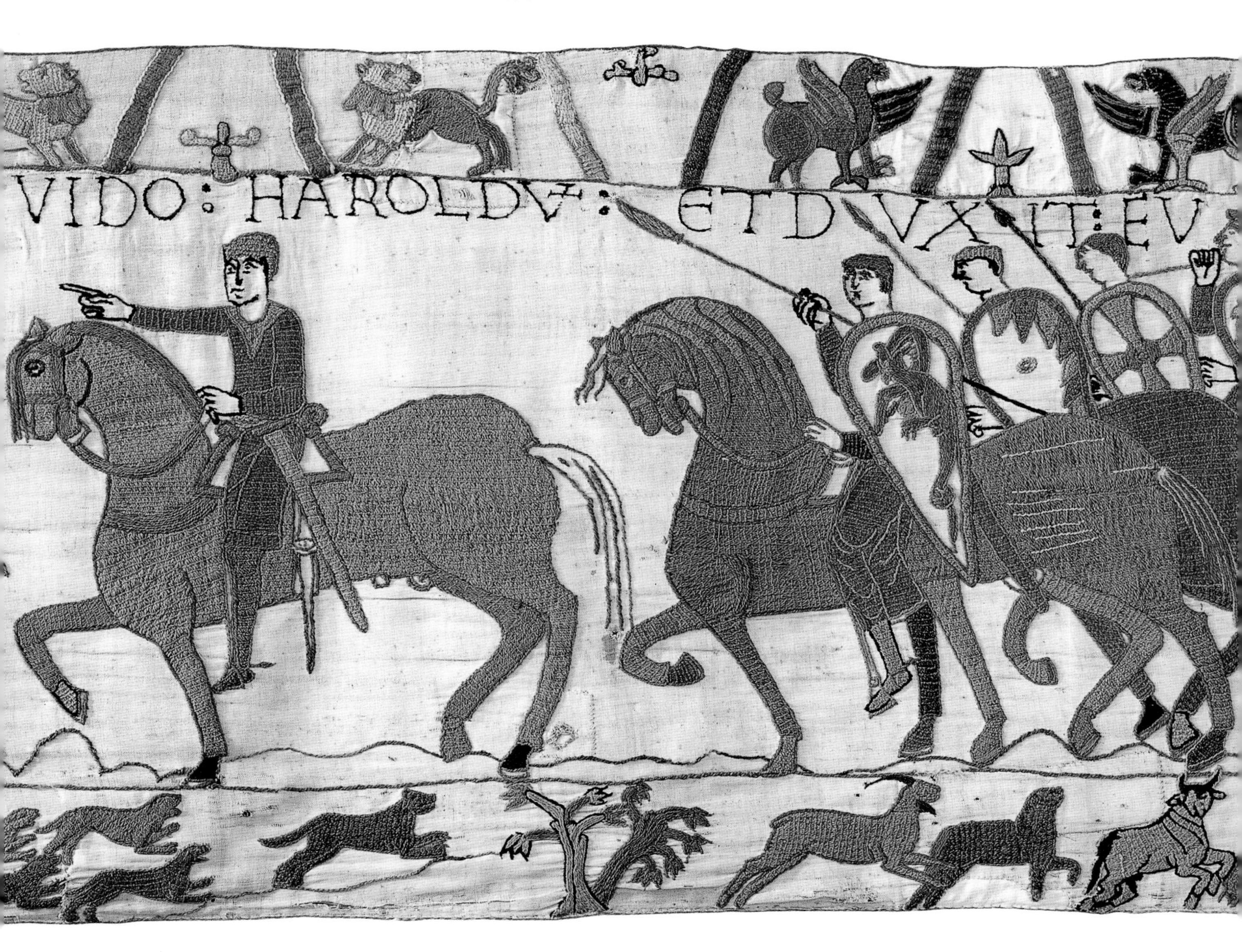

Here Wido apprehended Harold and took him …

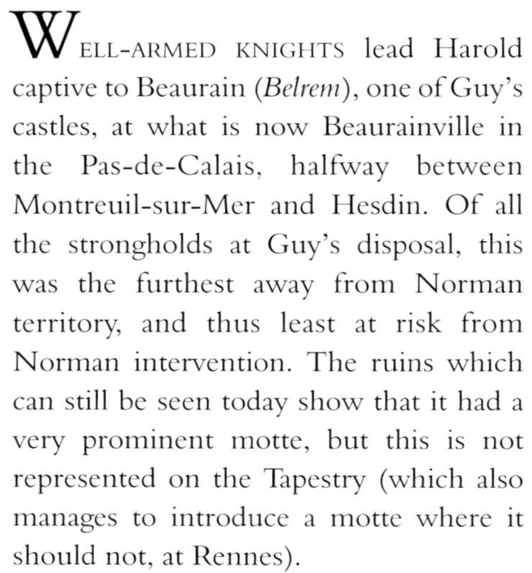

Well-armed knights lead Harold captive to Beaurain (*Belrem*), one of Guy's castles, at what is now Beaurainville in the Pas-de-Calais, halfway between Montreuil-sur-Mer and Hesdin. Of all the strongholds at Guy's disposal, this was the furthest away from Norman territory, and thus least at risk from Norman intervention. The ruins which can still be seen today show that it had a very prominent motte, but this is not represented on the Tapestry (which also manages to introduce a motte where it should not, at Rennes).

Harold's treatment here is better than at his capture. Although he is still surrounded by a detachment of knights, he is accorded the honours of rank: like Guy himself, he is shown with a falcon on his wrist, and his hounds are running along behind. His escorts are not in armour, but his captive status is unambiguous: the caption emphasises that Guy 'held' (*tenuit*) him.

... ET DUXIT EUM AD BELREM ET IBI EUM TENU

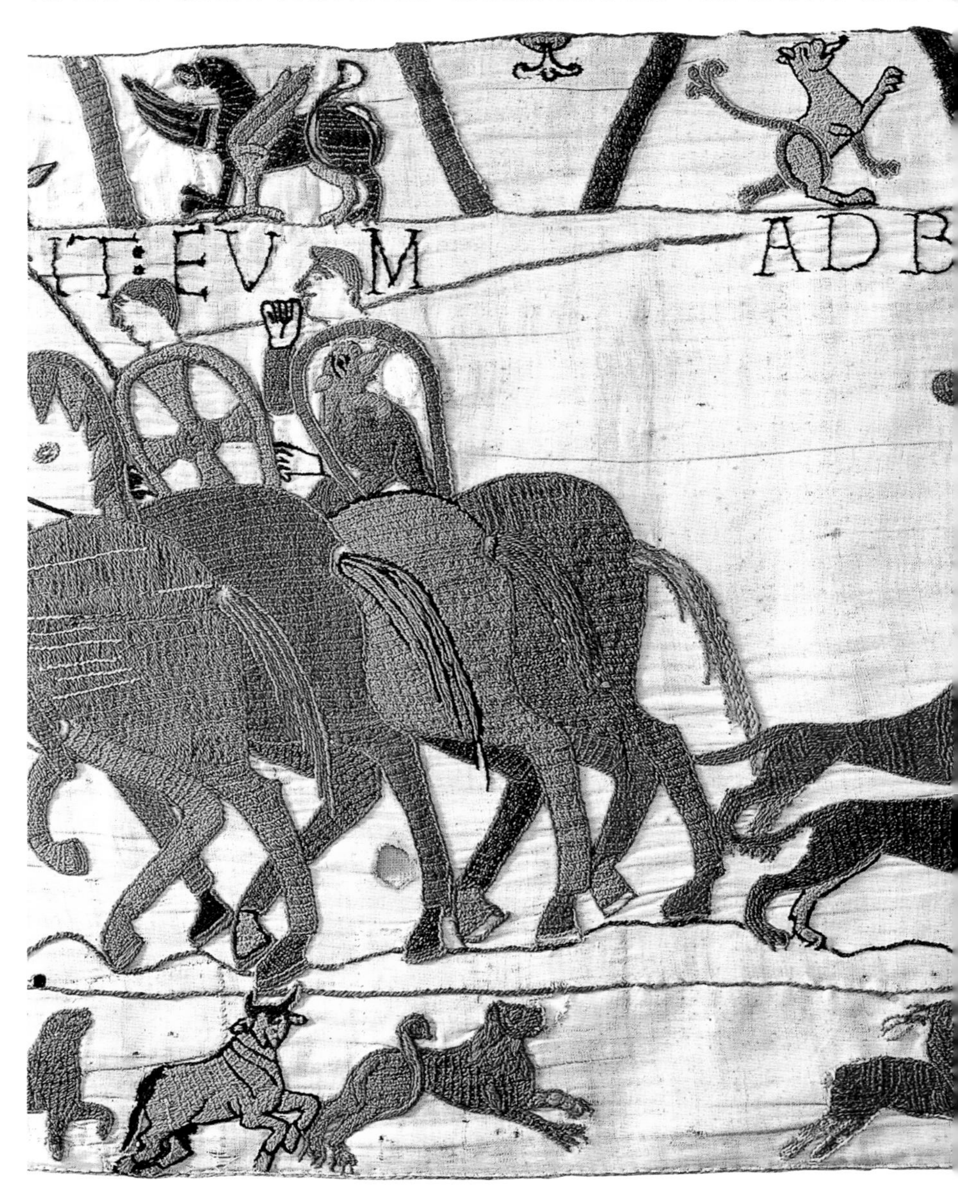

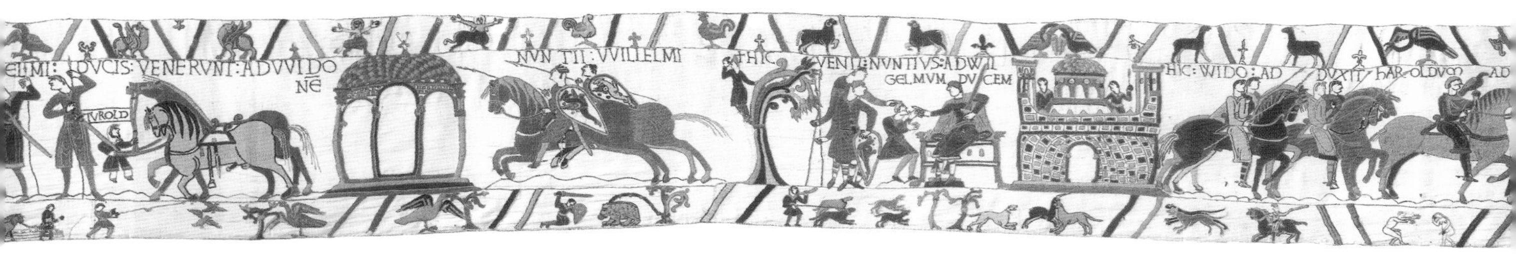

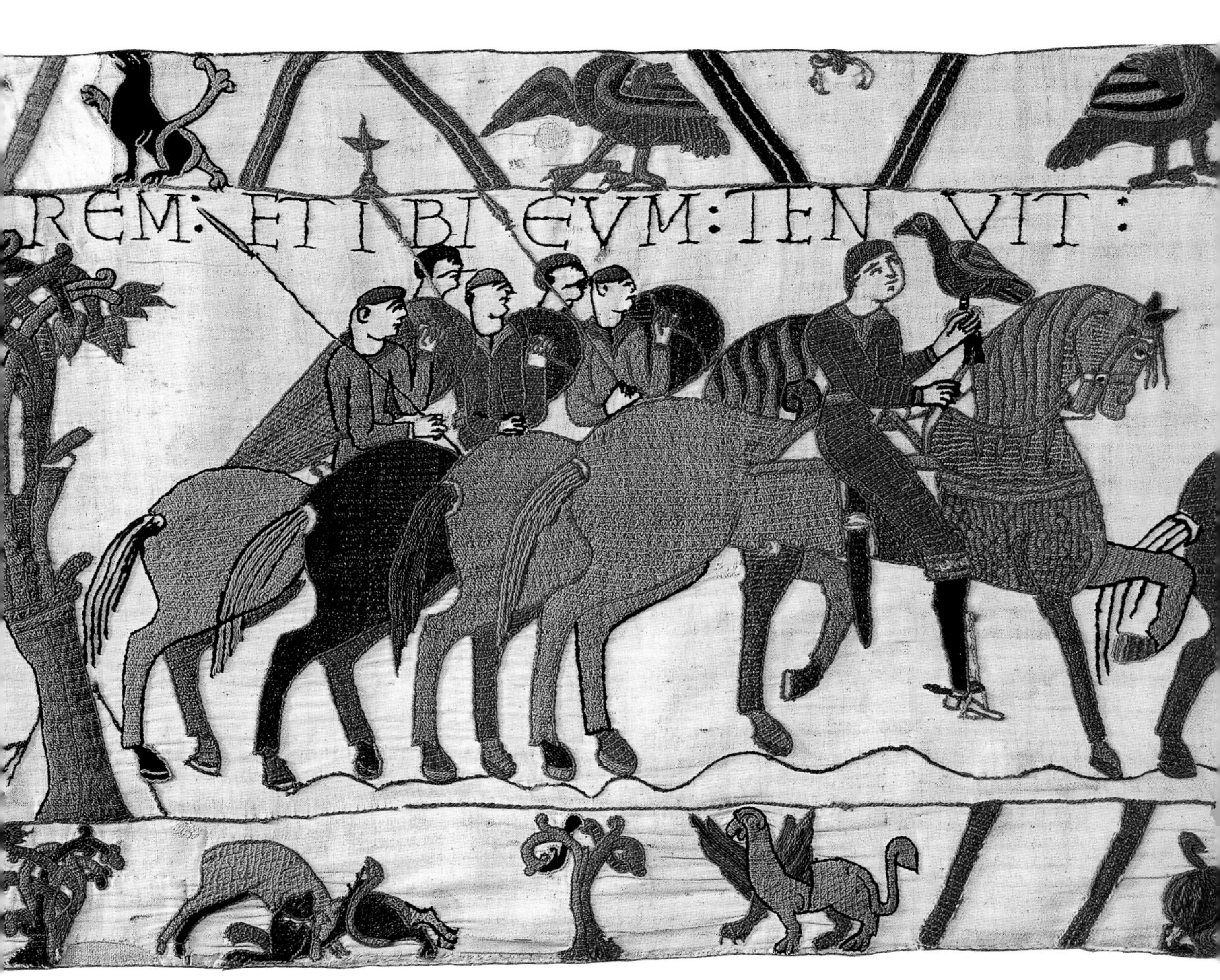

…and took him to Beaurain and held him there.

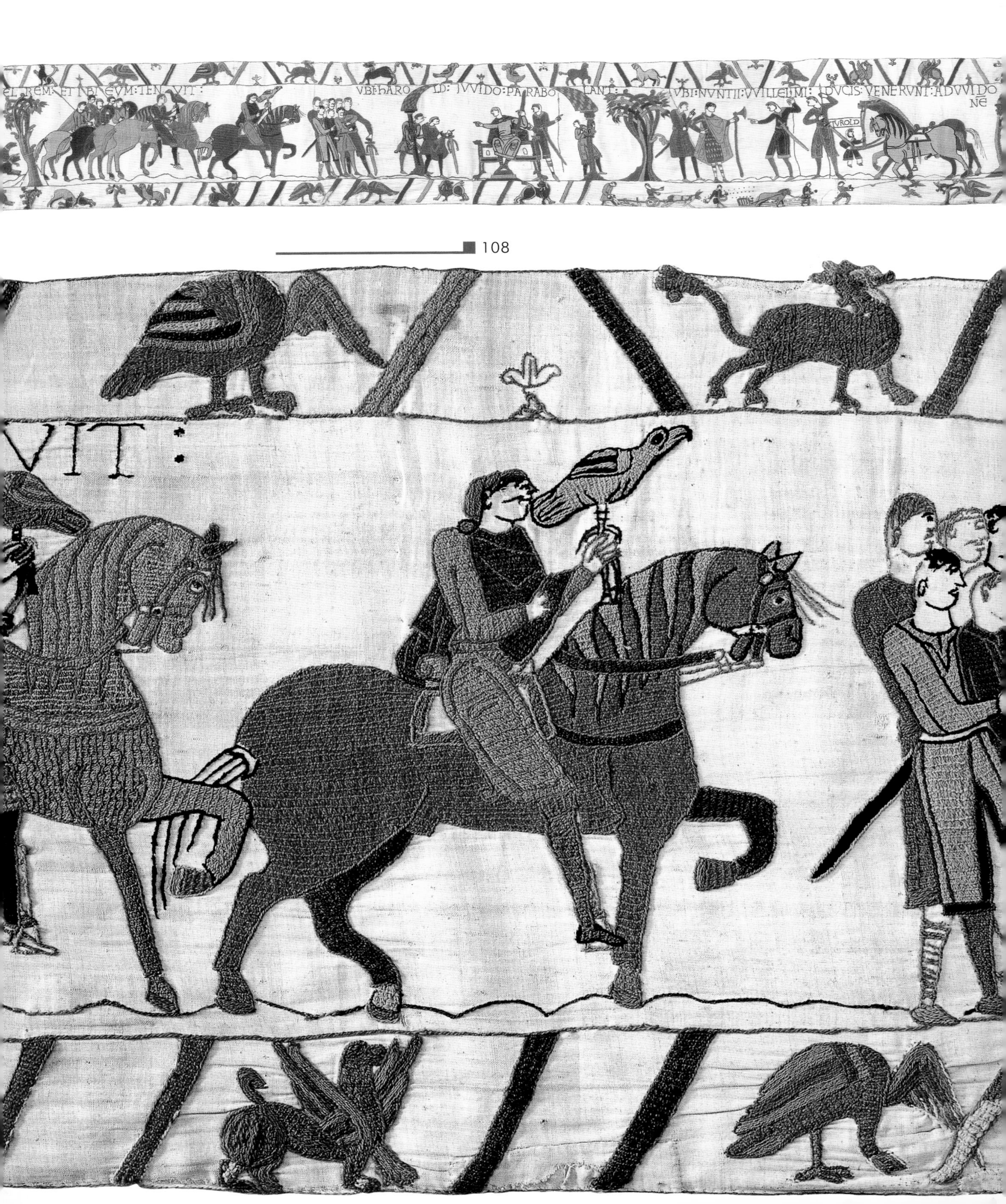

108

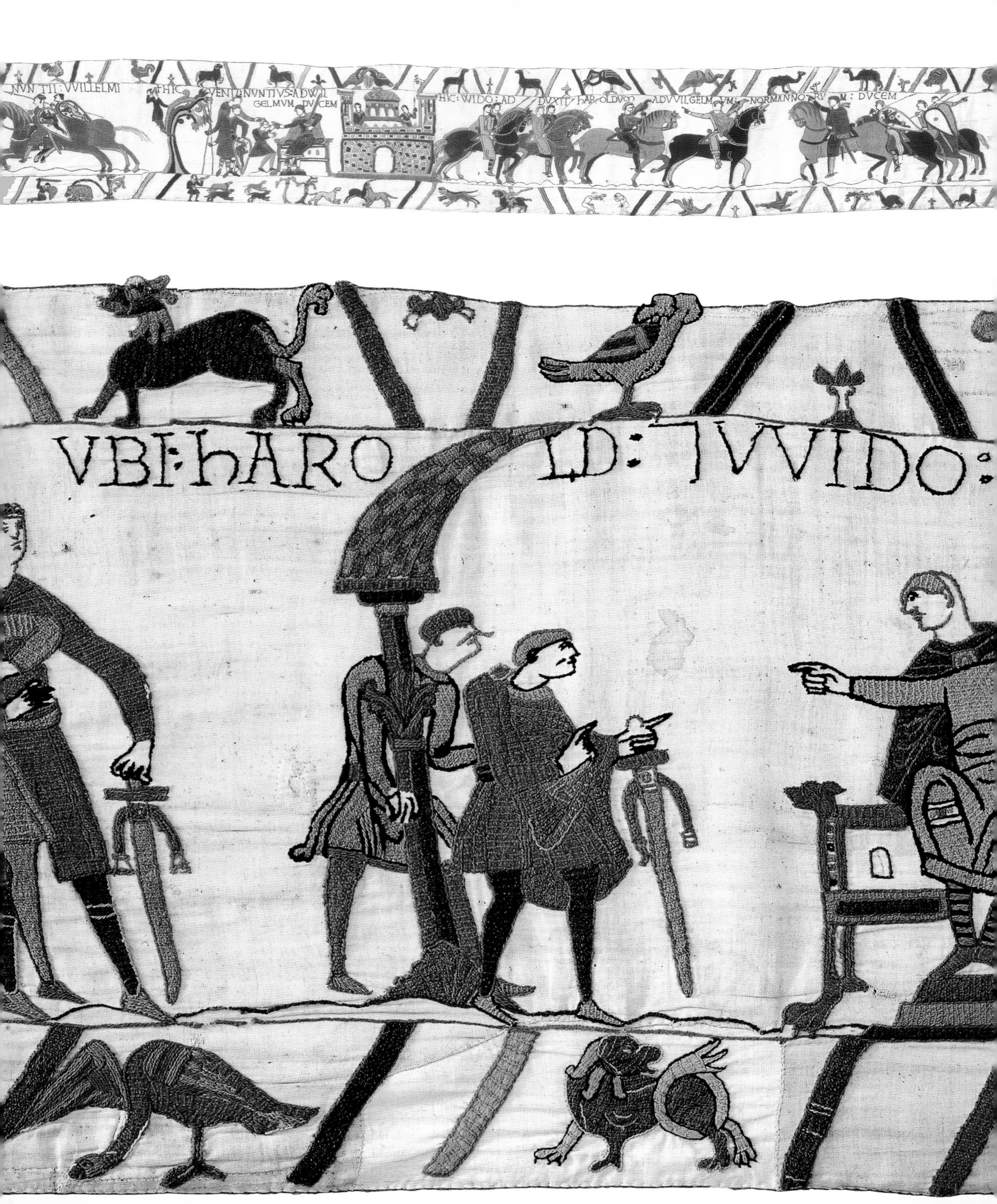
NVN TII: VVILLELMI
HIC VENIT: NVNTIVS: AD WIL GELMVM DVCEM
HIC: WIDO: AD DVXIT HAROLDVM AD VVILGELM VM: NORMANNO RV M: DVCEM
VBI: HARO LD: 7 VVIDO:

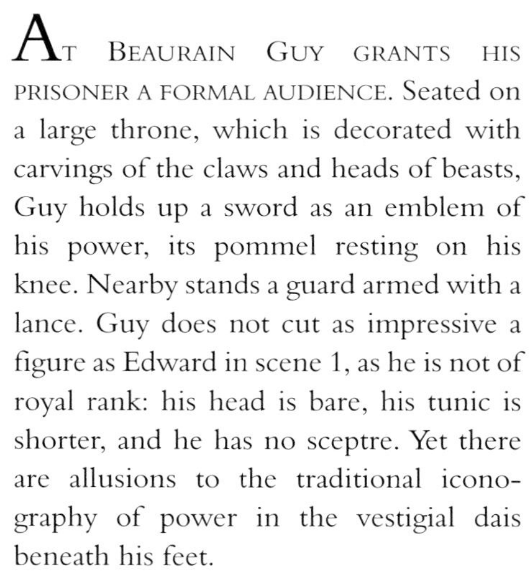

AT BEAURAIN GUY GRANTS HIS PRISONER A FORMAL AUDIENCE. Seated on a large throne, which is decorated with carvings of the claws and heads of beasts, Guy holds up a sword as an emblem of his power, its pommel resting on his knee. Nearby stands a guard armed with a lance. Guy does not cut as impressive a figure as Edward in scene 1, as he is not of royal rank: his head is bare, his tunic is shorter, and he has no sceptre. Yet there are allusions to the traditional iconography of power in the vestigial dais beneath his feet.

In the background to the left, a group of eight men witnesses the scene, some of them English, some French. Harold approaches on foot, proffering his sword in its unbuckled belt (p. 109). We are not told the subject of their conversation, but it is no doubt Harold's ransom. Negotiations over the prisoner would soon be under way with the Norman court. Harold is hardly in a position of strength, and appears suitably deferential to his captor. Even a noble prisoner usually had a hard time in the eleventh century.

The focus then shifts to an episode which will continue through the next two scenes (11-12, pp. 116–119), namely the comings and goings of messengers between Ponthieu and Duke William at Rouen. Some scholars claim that the Tapestry gets the story back to front here, seeing in scene 10 (pp. 111–112) a discussion between Count Guy and William's envoys, followed in scene 11 (pp. 116–117) by what should have preceded it, the sight of those same envoys, they argue, riding from Rouen towards Ponthieu. But this is hardly compelling. There were most probably several exchanges between Ponthieu and Normandy before terms were agreed for handing Harold over to the duke. Such, at least, is the account of the near-contemporary Eadmer.[14]

A stylised tree marks the change of scene, and there are several noteworthy features in what follows. First of all, Guy himself, guarded as usual by his spearmen, is now shown armed with a great battle-axe as a status symbol. As elsewhere on the Tapestry this weapon is associated exclusively with an English milieu (and archaeological evidence confirms its essentially Anglo-Scandinavian character), it seems that the designer has unconsciously transported Anglo-Saxon customs across the Channel.

[14] See in particular the claims of R. D. Wissolik, 'Duke William's messengers: an "insoluble reverse-order" scene of the Bayeux Tapestry', *Medium Aevum* 51 (1982), pp. 102-7. Eadmer has two missions: one from Harold to Normandy; and the other from Normandy to Ponthieu, ordering Guy to set Harold free, and threatening to use force if necessary. See Eadmer, *Historia Novorum*, ed. Rule, pp. 6-7.

(U)BI HAROLD ET V

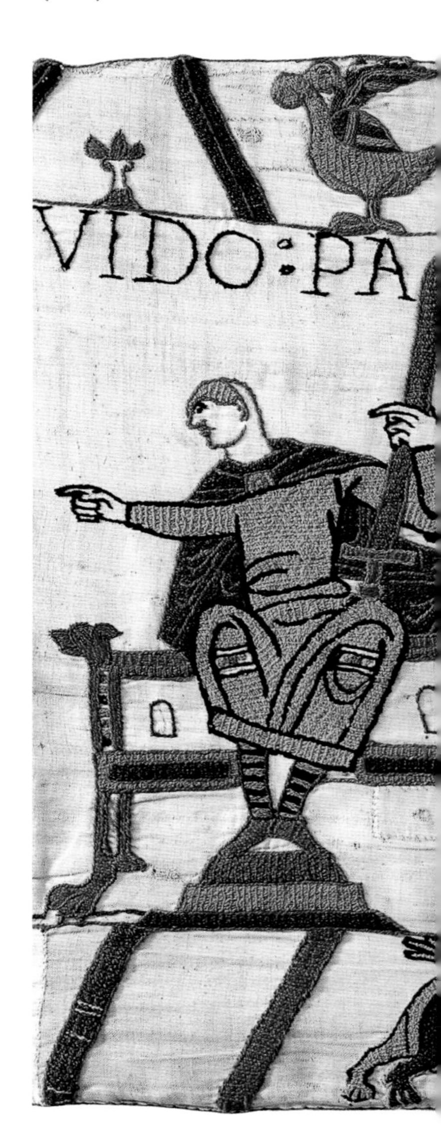

SCENES 9–10

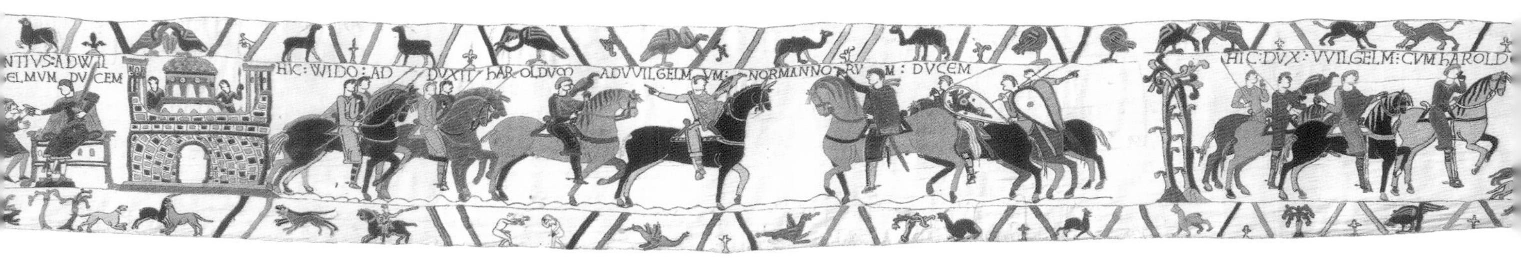

O PARABOLANT. UBI NUNTII...

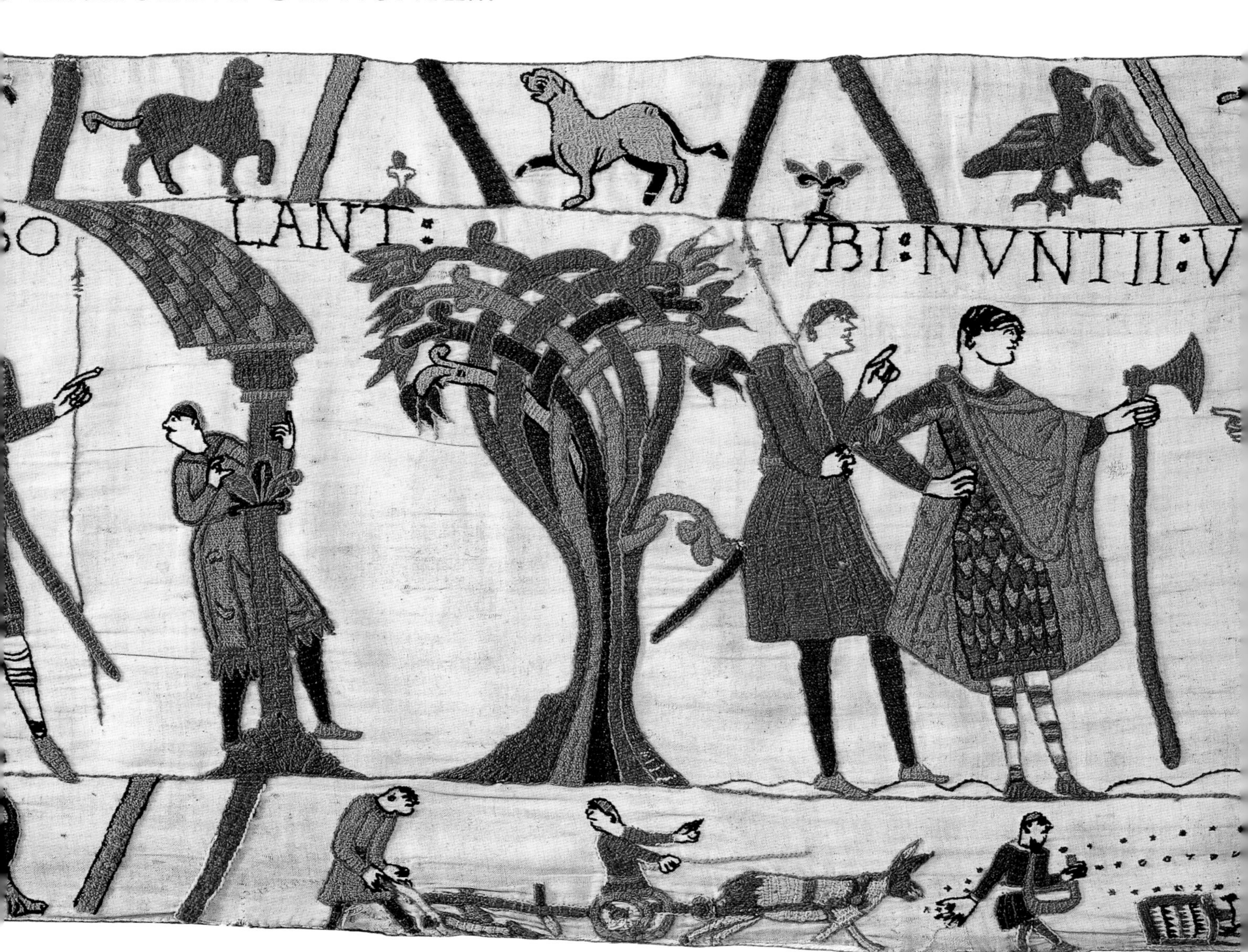

Where Harold and Wido parlay. Where messengers …

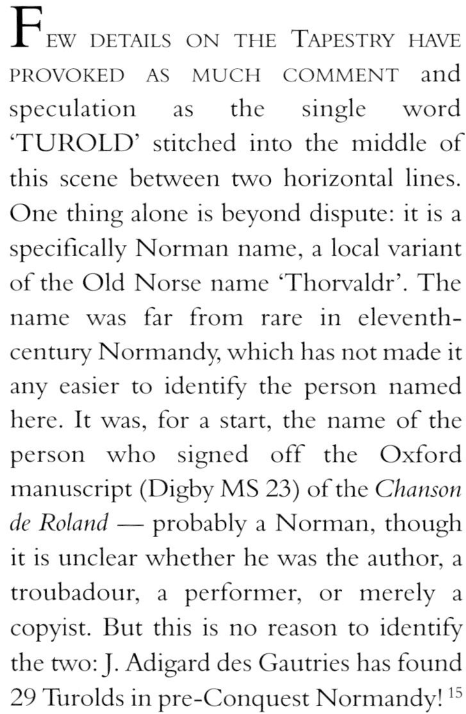

Few details on the Tapestry have provoked as much comment and speculation as the single word 'TUROLD' stitched into the middle of this scene between two horizontal lines. One thing alone is beyond dispute: it is a specifically Norman name, a local variant of the Old Norse name 'Thorvaldr'. The name was far from rare in eleventh-century Normandy, which has not made it any easier to identify the person named here. It was, for a start, the name of the person who signed off the Oxford manuscript (Digby MS 23) of the *Chanson de Roland* — probably a Norman, though it is unclear whether he was the author, a troubadour, a performer, or merely a copyist. But this is no reason to identify the two: J. Adigard des Gautries has found 29 Turolds in pre-Conquest Normandy! [15]

The first problem is whether the name is meant to indicate the tall fellow standing just to the left, or the bearded little figure below, holding the horses' bridles. Each has had his advocates. The tall fellow is one of William's messengers, and if this is Turold, then, as R. Lejeune has argued forcefully, he might well have been a member of the duke's entourage (or else of Bishop Odo's).[16] There would still be several Turolds to choose from, notably the post-Conquest Abbot of Peterborough, a son of the Viscount of Montfort-sur-Risle; but also a future vassal of Odo, mentioned under Norfolk in the *Domesday Book* (which in addition has several entries under Kent and Essex for one Raoul, son of Turold).[17] But none of these possibilities carries any real conviction.

As for the strange little figure with his pointed beard, slashed tunic, and white leggings, is he really a dwarf, or is his diminutive scale simply an index of humble social standing? This was a familiar enough convention in medieval art, although it is not used anywhere else on the Tapestry.[18] Lejeune contends that his unusual clothing is the typical costume of a minstrel or jester, but while this is possible, there is no evidence for it from the Anglo-Norman world: the only reliable parallel adduced is from far-away Catalonia.

[15] *La Chanson de Roland: texte établi d'après le manuscrit d'Oxford*, ed. G. Moignet (Paris, 1969), p. 276, 'Ci falt la geste que Turoldus declinet'. See pp. 15-16 for a discussion of the name and of the meaning of 'declinet'. J. Adigard des Gautries, *Les noms de personnes scandinaves en Normandie de 911 à 1066* (Lund, 1954. Nomina Germanica 11), pp. 342-47.

[16] R. Lejeune, 'Turold dans la Tapisserie de Bayeux', *Mélanges René Crozet* (Poitiers, 1966), vol. 1, pp. 419-25.

[17] See H. Prentout, 'Essai d'identification des personnages inconnus de la Tapisserie de Bayeux', *Revue Historique* 176 (1935), pp. 15-19 (Gameson, *Study of the Bayeux Tapestry*, pp. 25-26); and also H. E. J. Cowdrey, 'Towards an interpretation of the Bayeux Tapestry', *Anglo-Norman Studies* 10 (1988), pp. 49-65, at p. 50 (Gameson, *Study of the Bayeux Tapestry*, p. 94).

[18] P. E. Bennett, 'Encore Turold dans la Tapisserie de Bayeux', *Annales de Normandie* 30 (1980), pp. 3-13.

Ubi nuntii Willel

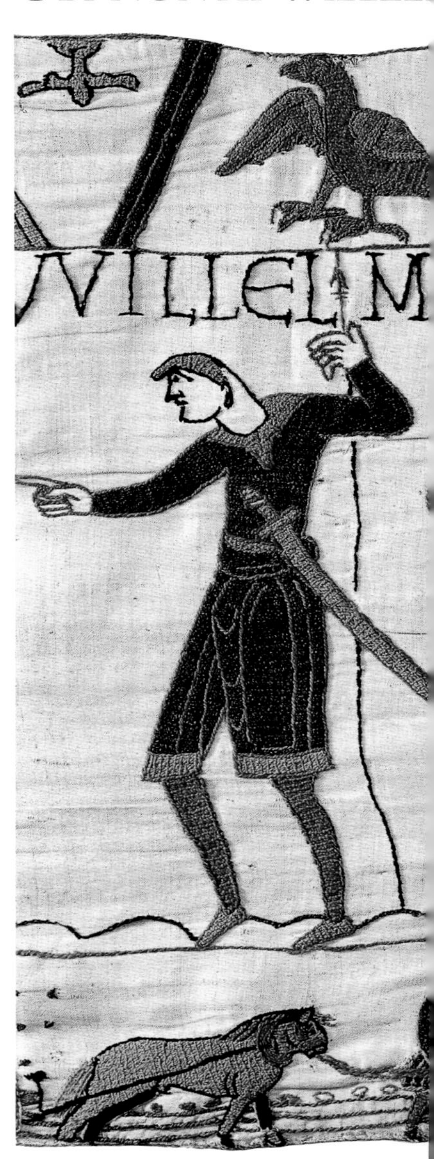

Scene 10

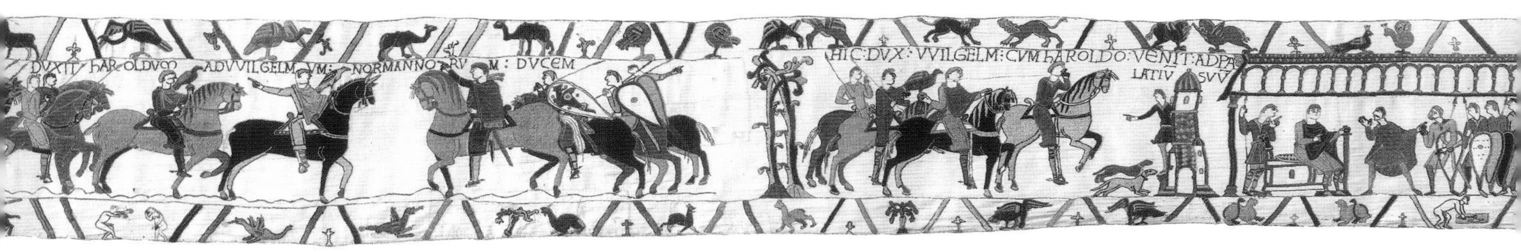

UCIS VENERUNT AD WIDONEM. TUROLD.

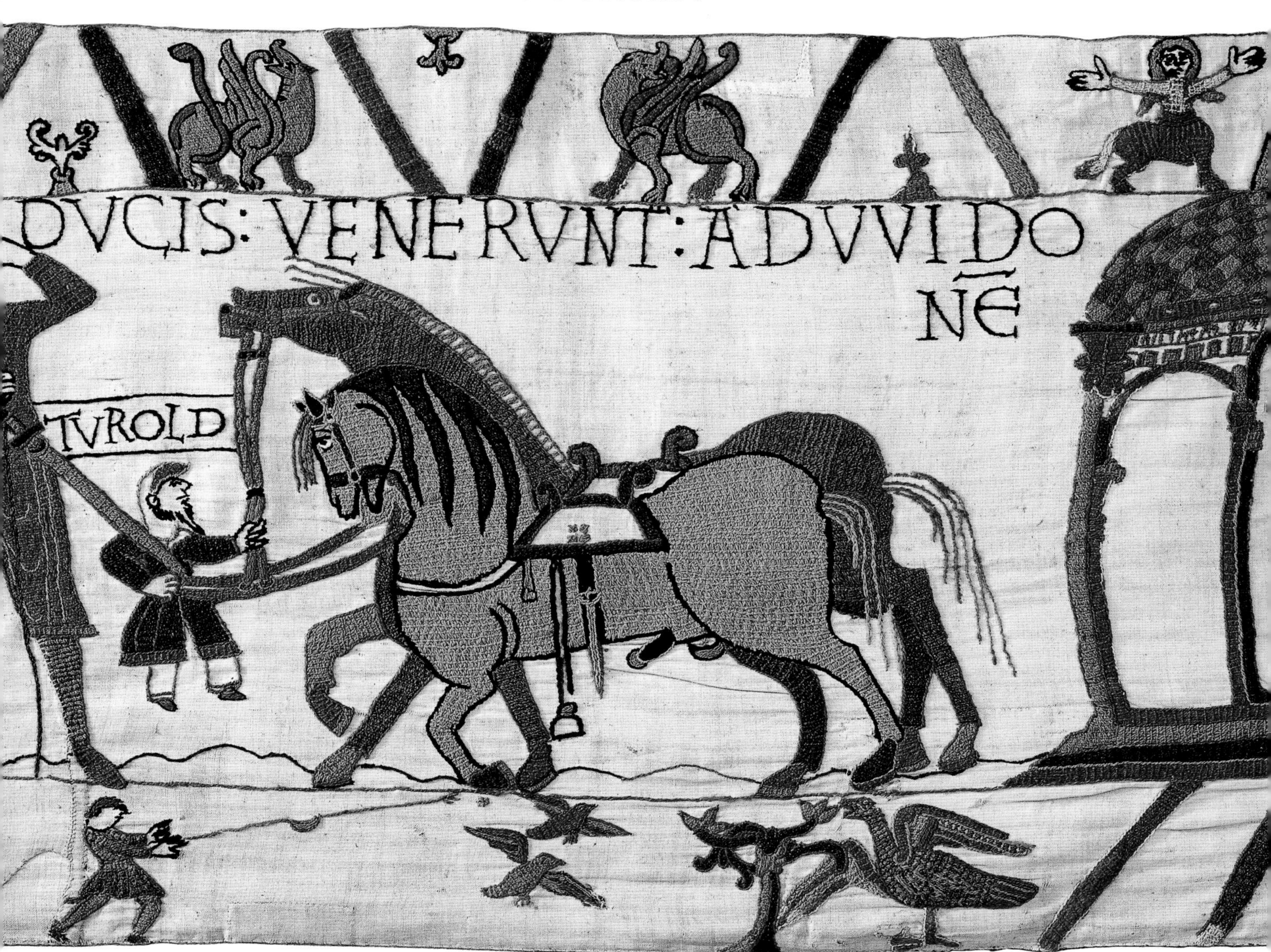

Where messengers of Duke William came to Wido. Turold.

THE LOWER BORDER OF THIS SCENE IS RIGHTLY FAMOUS for its depictions of agricultural activities — ploughing, sowing, and harrowing. The realism of the first image is questionable: the plough is drawn by a single beast, and an ass at that, rather than the usual horses or oxen. The picture of the plough itself is very clear, with wheels towards the front, coulter and ploughshare behind, and a second peasant at the back controlling the 'stilt' or handle. But it is rather stereotyped, owing more to the pictorial conventions of manuscript illumination than to the reality known from archaeological evidence. The third image in the series is more plausible. It is the earliest surviving picture of a harrow, then a recent invention. (The earliest documentary attestation of the harrow comes from much the same time, in some ecclesiastical legislation of 1096.[19]) It is not clear whether it is made from iron, or from wood (which seems more likely). It might even be a wooden frame with metal teeth.

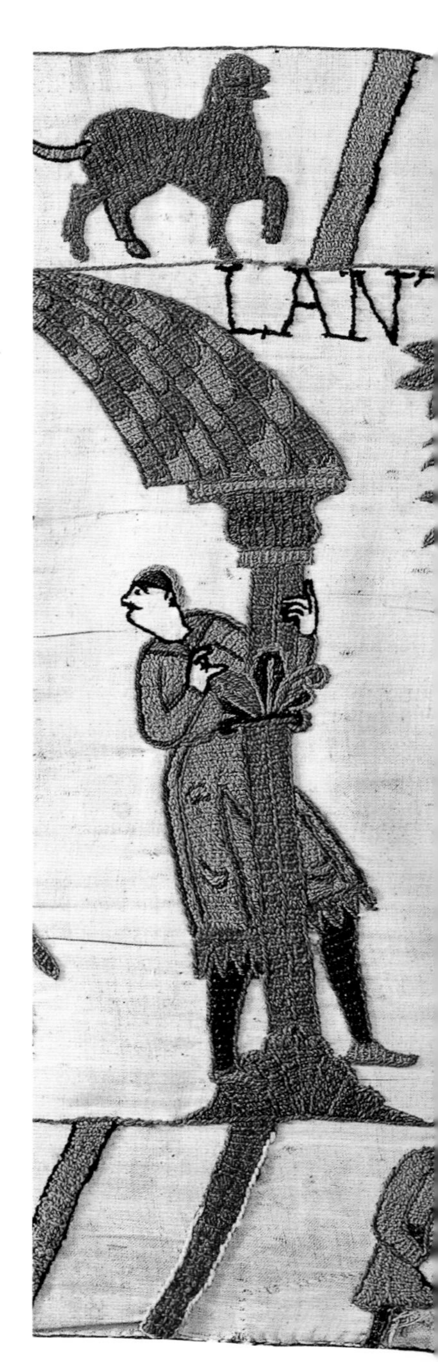

[19] Orderic Vitalis, *Historia Ecclesiastica*, ed. Chibnall, vol. 5, p. 20. See also A. M. Bautier, 'Contribution à l'histoire du cheval au Moyen Âge', *Bulletin philologique et historique du Comité des Travaux Historiques et Scientifiques* (1976), pp. 209-49, at p. 226.

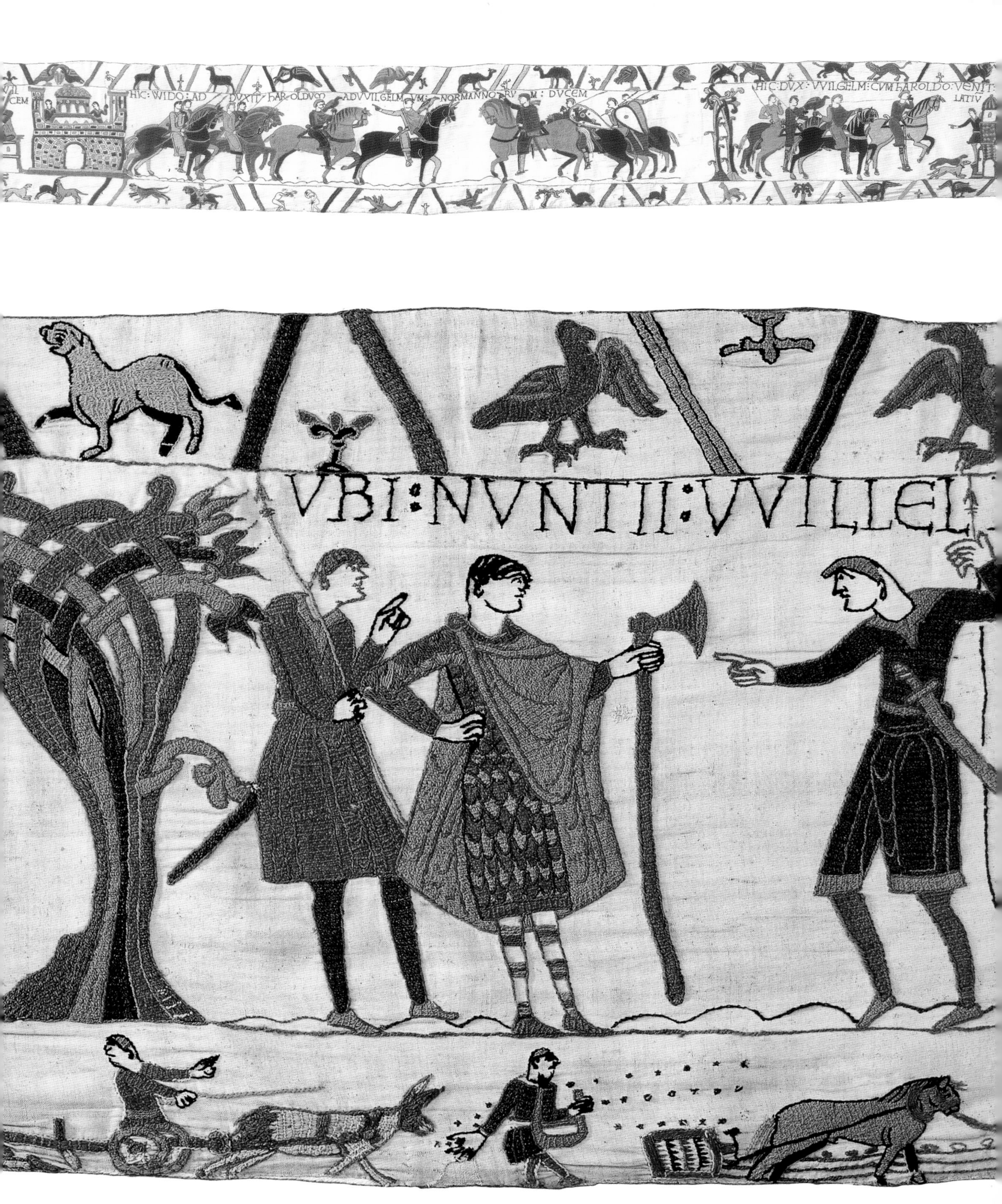
HIC: WIDO: AD DUXIT HAROLDUM AD UUILGELMUM: NORMANNORUM: DUCEM
HIC: DUX: UUILGELM: CUM HAROLDO: VENIT:
LATIU
UBI: NUNTII: UUILLEL

Nuntii Willelmi.

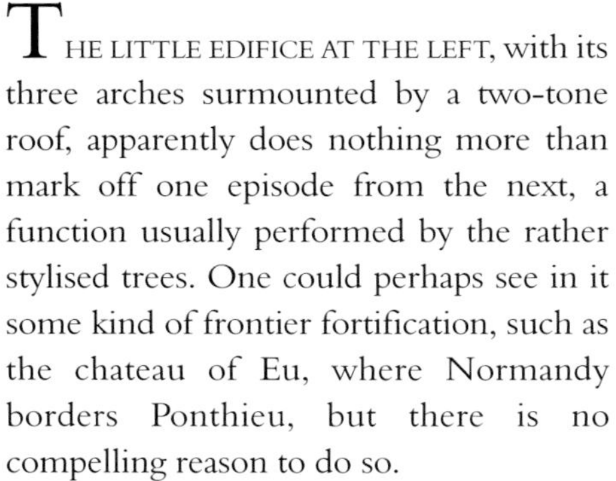

The little edifice at the left, with its three arches surmounted by a two-tone roof, apparently does nothing more than mark off one episode from the next, a function usually performed by the rather stylised trees. One could perhaps see in it some kind of frontier fortification, such as the chateau of Eu, where Normandy borders Ponthieu, but there is no compelling reason to do so.

Beside it ride two of William's messengers, armed but not armoured (they have swords, shields, and lances, but neither helmets nor hauberks), and clearly in haste. This is no mere elegant variation on the more sedate riding scenes elsewhere on the Tapestry. It fits with the evidence of the more reliable chroniclers, such as William of Poitiers and, above all, Eadmer.[20] Eadmer comments on the haste (*festinato*) with which the *nuntii Willelmi* (the same words as on the Tapestry) headed for Ponthieu, with the message that if Guy did not immediately accede to the Norman demands, 'he should be in no doubt that Duke William of Normandy would come to Ponthieu in force to settle the matter'. The weapons of the envoys no doubt served to underline the message. Guy, as we know, acquiesced. After all, his county was in effect a Norman dependency.

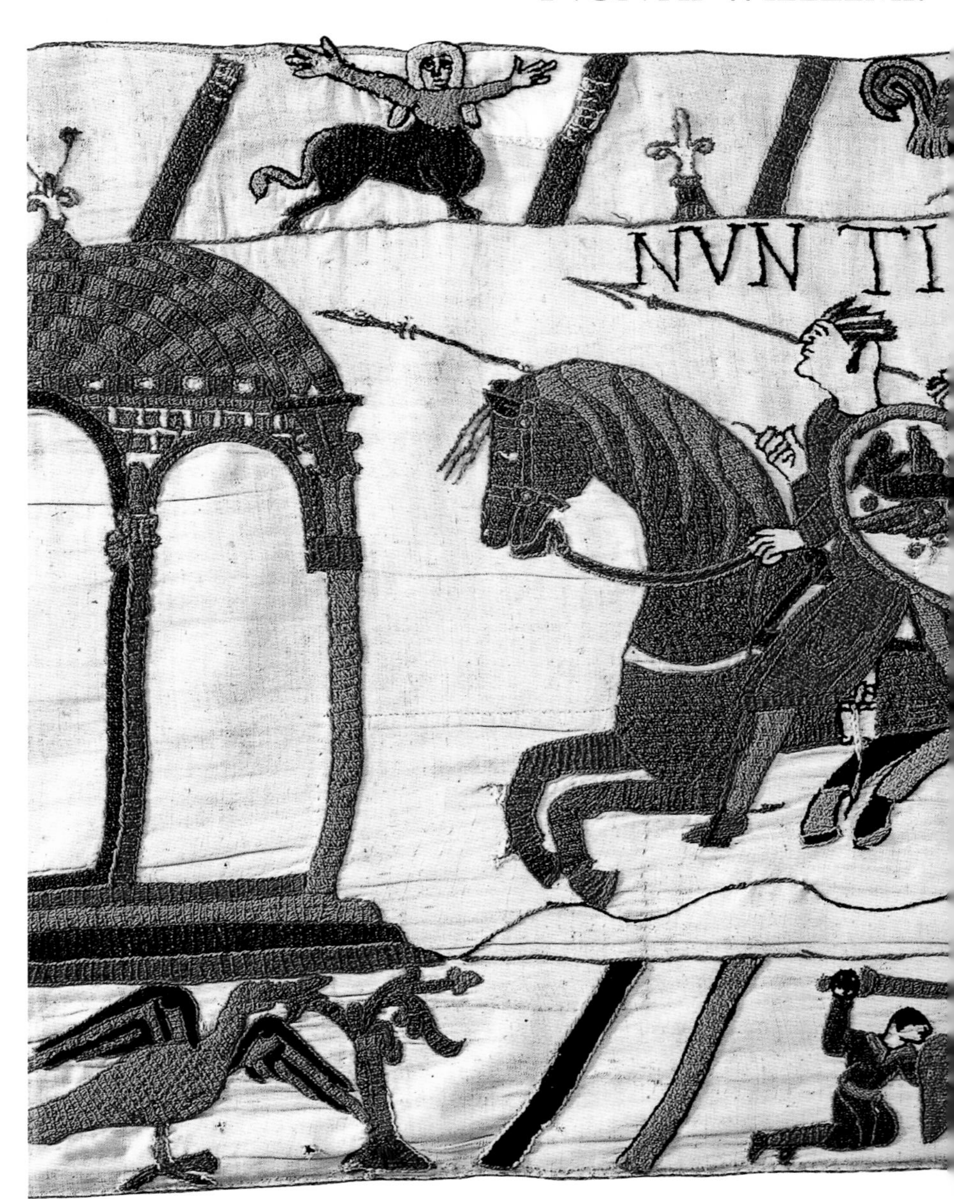

[20] Guillaume de Poitiers, ed. Foreville, p. 102 (Davis and Chibnall, pp. 68-69); Eadmer, *Historia novorum*, ed. Rule, p. 7.

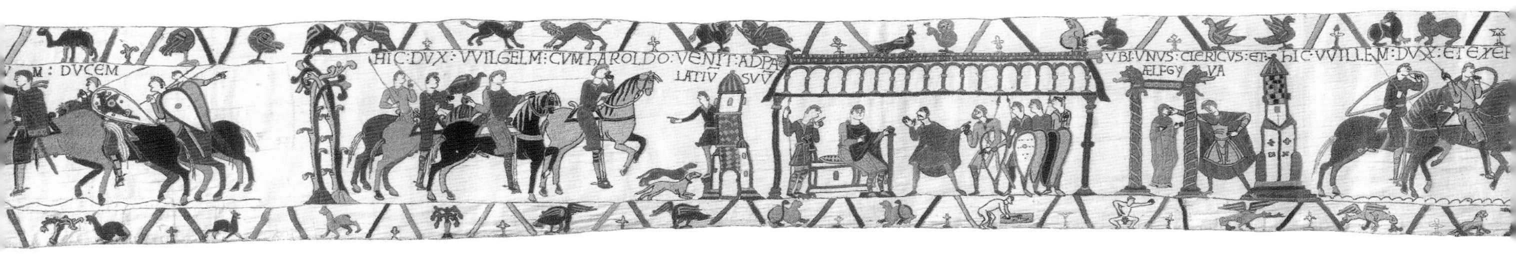

+ Hic venit nuntius...

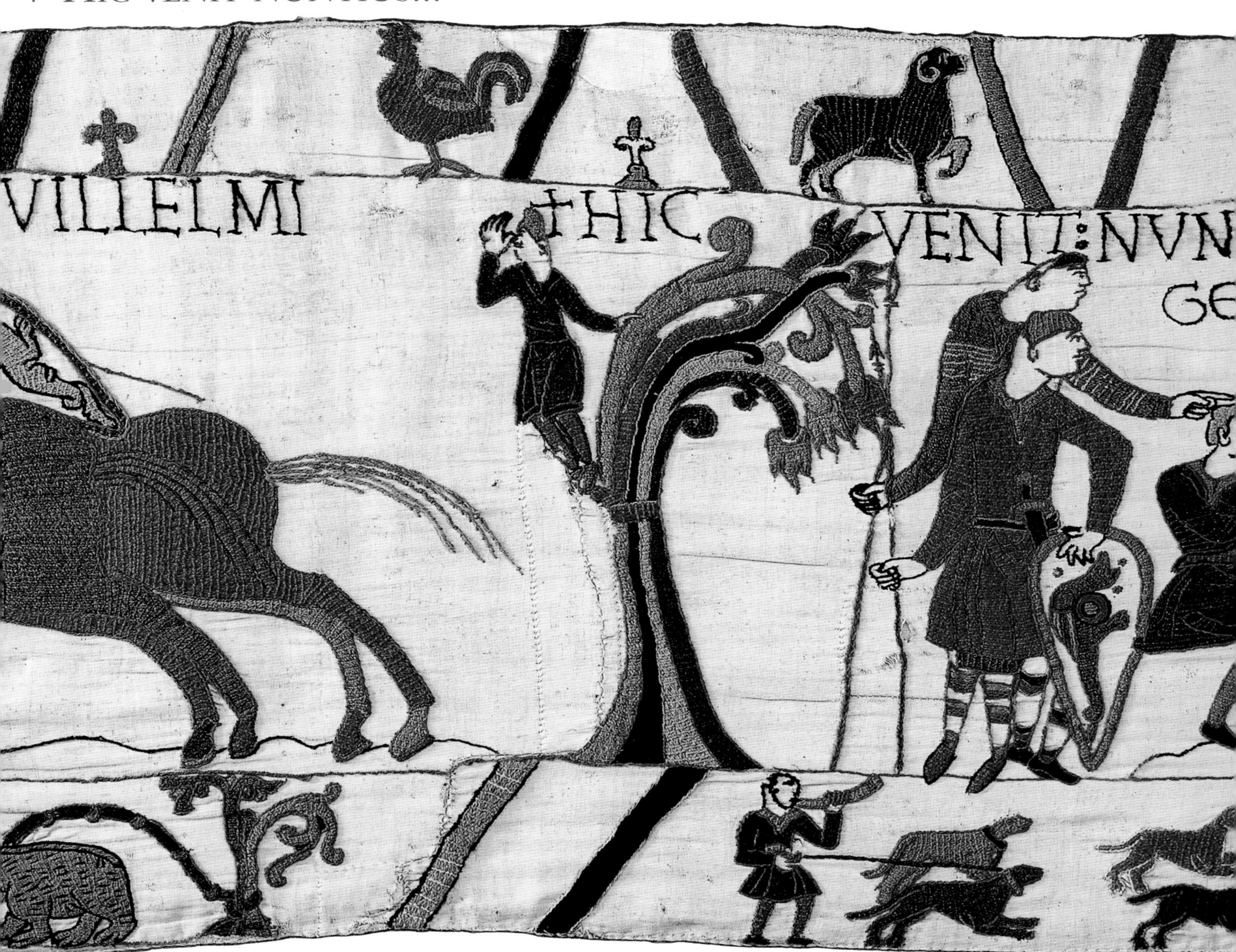

William's messengers. + Here a messenger comes …

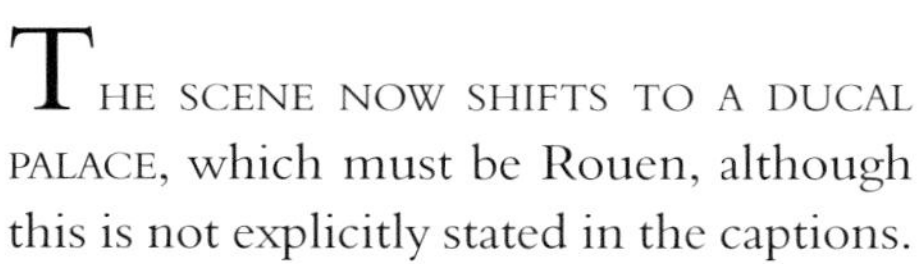

THE SCENE NOW SHIFTS TO A DUCAL PALACE, which must be Rouen, although this is not explicitly stated in the captions.

Escorted by two armed guards, a messenger presents himself to Duke William, who is seated upon a throne almost identical to that of Count Guy in scene 9 (p. 110), and, like Guy, holding a large sword in his left hand. These would seem to be the Tapestry's conventional attributes for a ruler of less than royal rank.

The action unfolds in the shadow of a large fortified structure of elaborate design but without a motte. There is every reason to identify this as the famous 'Tower of Rouen', one of the earliest known stone castles, erected by William's grandfather, Duke Richard II, in the early eleventh century. Its sheer size became proverbial among the Normans. The castle was at one and the same time a royal residence, a military and administrative centre, and a state prison. Razed to the ground in 1203-04, it has left no trace today. Situated on the bank of the Seine, it was next door to the rather less daunting building shown in scene 14 (pp. 124–125). A blunt assertion of Norman power, it stands in marked contrast to the less massive edifices depicted on the Tapestry thus far. The central structure, flanked by the two guards, may represent one of the palace's chapels. The colours are probably nothing more than artistic licence.

The figure who stands before William beneath the caption *nuntius* is not a messenger from Count Guy. With his moustache and his unshaven head he would appear to be an Englishman, almost certainly a messenger from Harold.

HIC VENIT NUNTIU

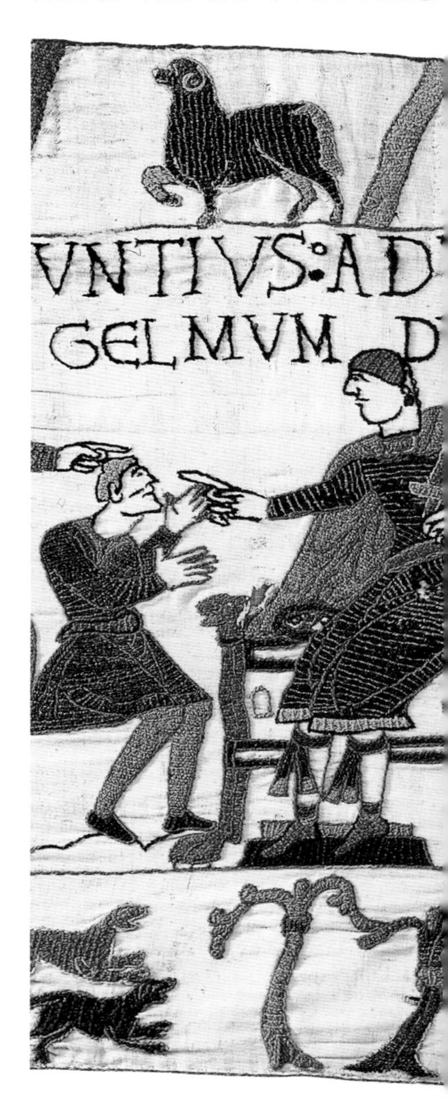

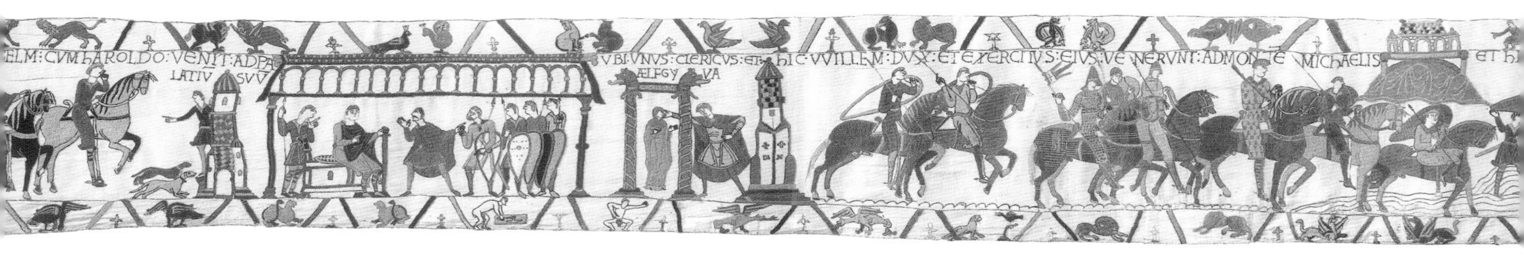

AD WILGELMUM DUCEM.

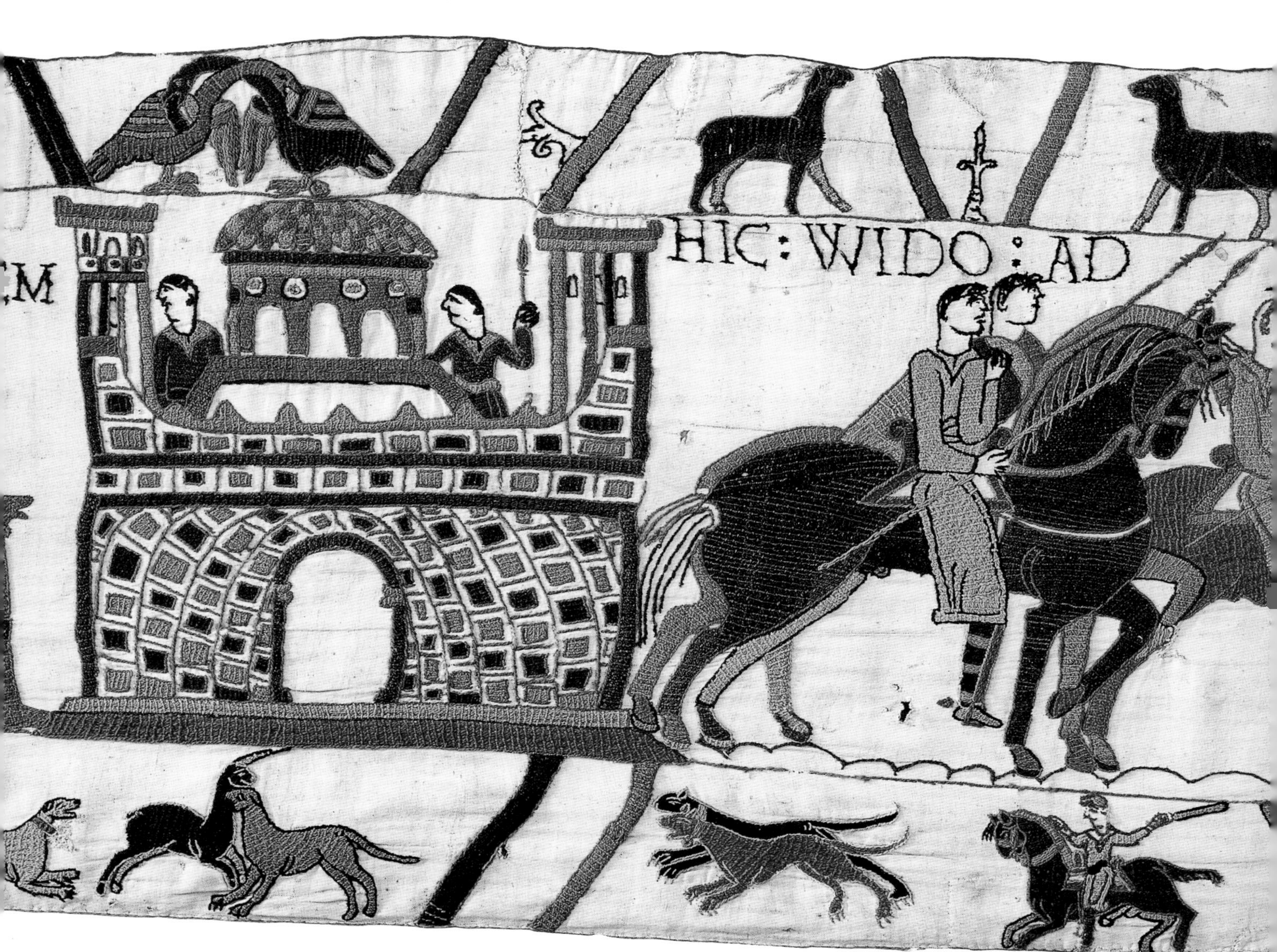

Here a messenger comes to Duke William.

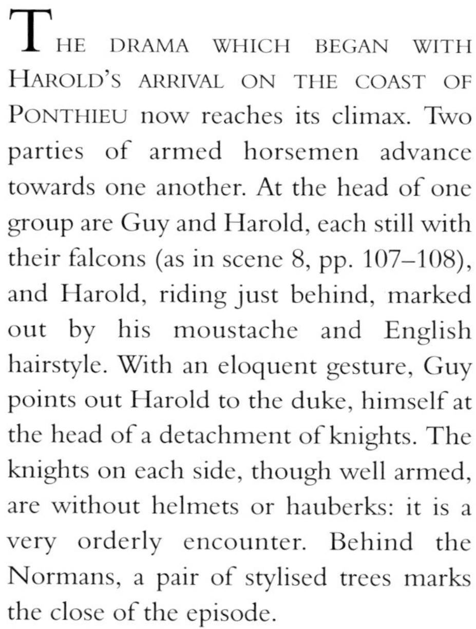

THE DRAMA WHICH BEGAN WITH HAROLD'S ARRIVAL ON THE COAST OF PONTHIEU now reaches its climax. Two parties of armed horsemen advance towards one another. At the head of one group are Guy and Harold, each still with their falcons (as in scene 8, pp. 107–108), and Harold, riding just behind, marked out by his moustache and English hairstyle. With an eloquent gesture, Guy points out Harold to the duke, himself at the head of a detachment of knights. The knights on each side, though well armed, are without helmets or hauberks: it is a very orderly encounter. Behind the Normans, a pair of stylised trees marks the close of the episode.

William of Poitiers reports that Harold was handed over to William at Eu, on the frontier between Normandy and Ponthieu.[21] But there is nothing of that here. The Tapestry glosses over such historical and geographical details, concentrating on the broad outlines of the story.

HIC WIDO ADDUXIT

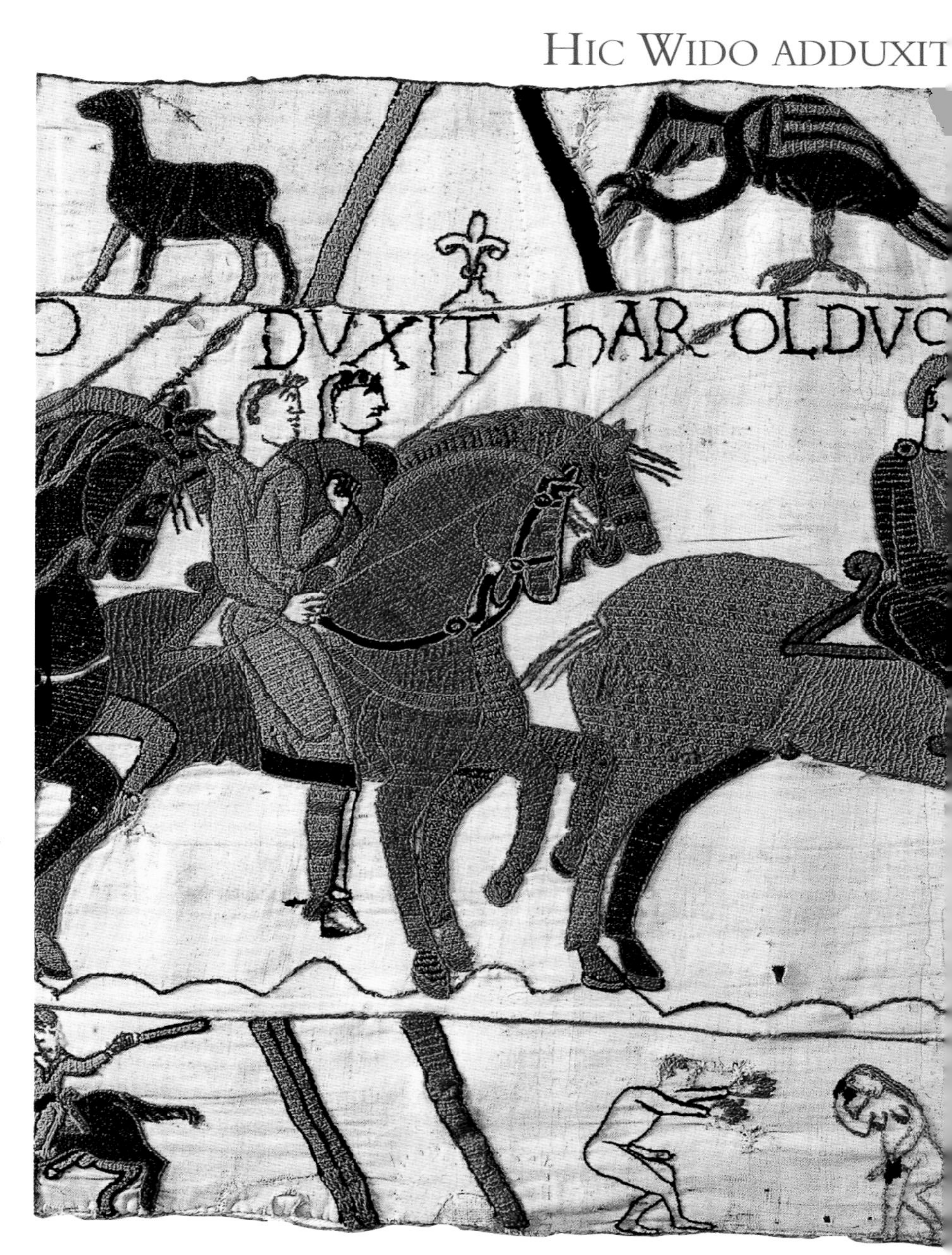

[21] William of Poitiers, ed. Foreville, p. 102 (Davis and Chibnall, pp. 68-71). He goes on to claim that William rewarded Guy with grants of 'substantial and rich lands, and large sums of money'. But the Tapestry says nothing of this.

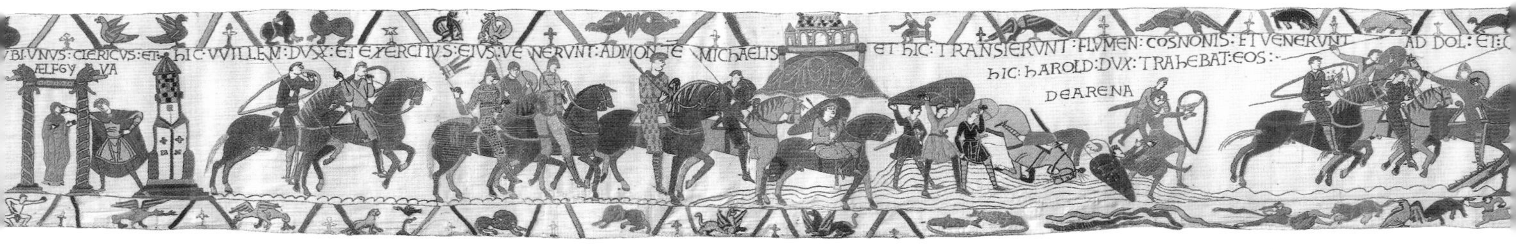

HAROLDUM AD WILGELMUM NORMANNORUM DUCEM.

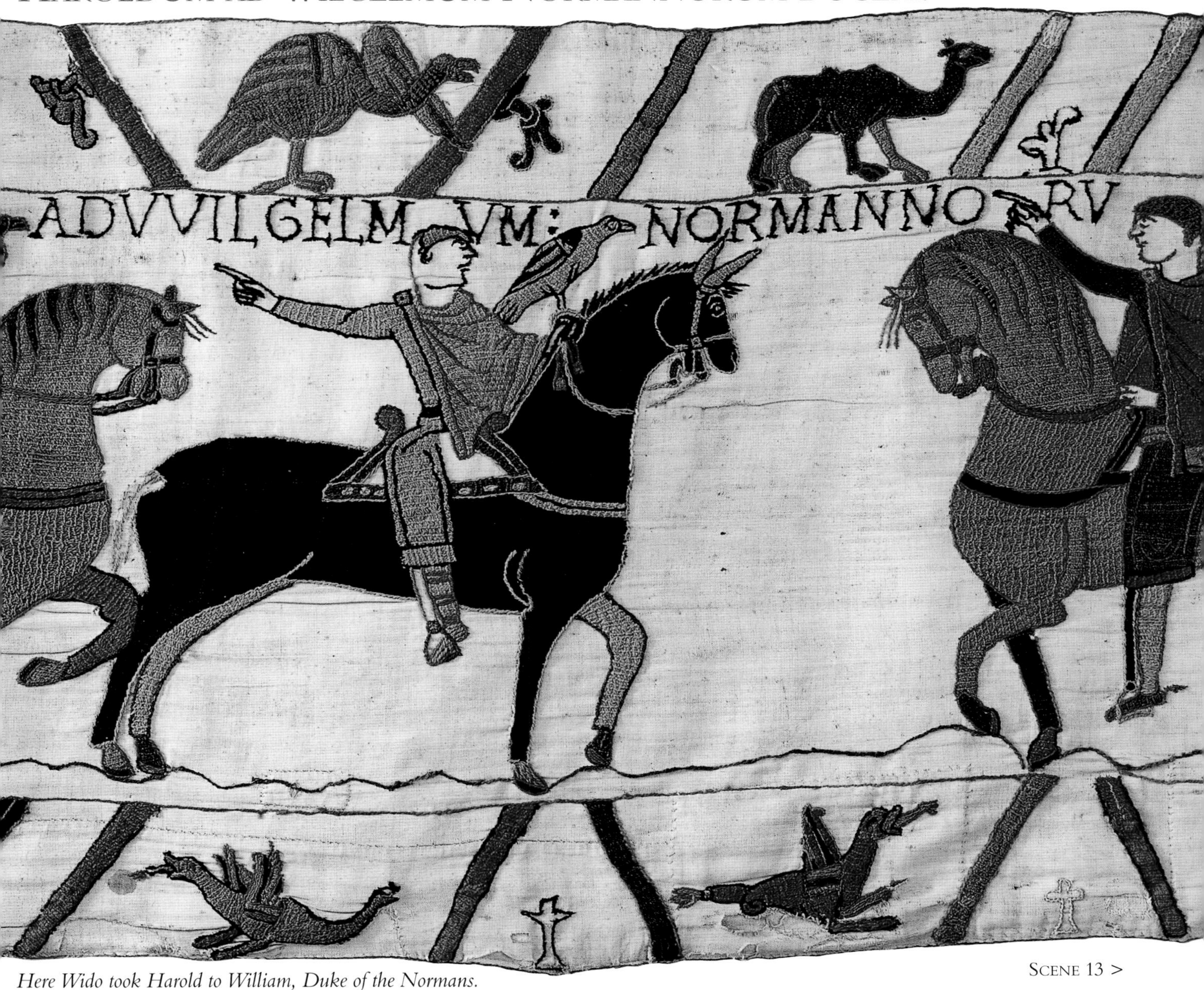

Here Wido took Harold to William, Duke of the Normans.

SCENE 13 >

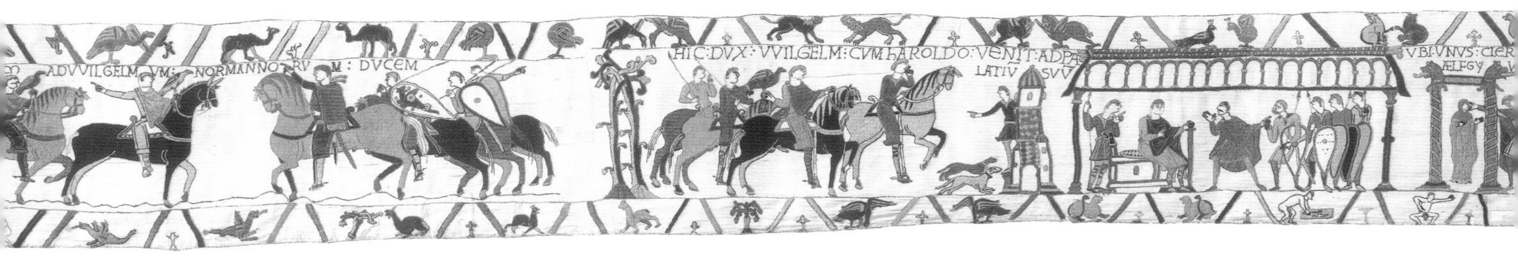
ADVVILGELM VM: NORMANNO RV M : DVCEM
HIC: DVX: VVILGELM: CVM HAROLDO: VENIT: AD PA
LATIV SVV
VBI: VNVS: CLER
ÆLFGY

122

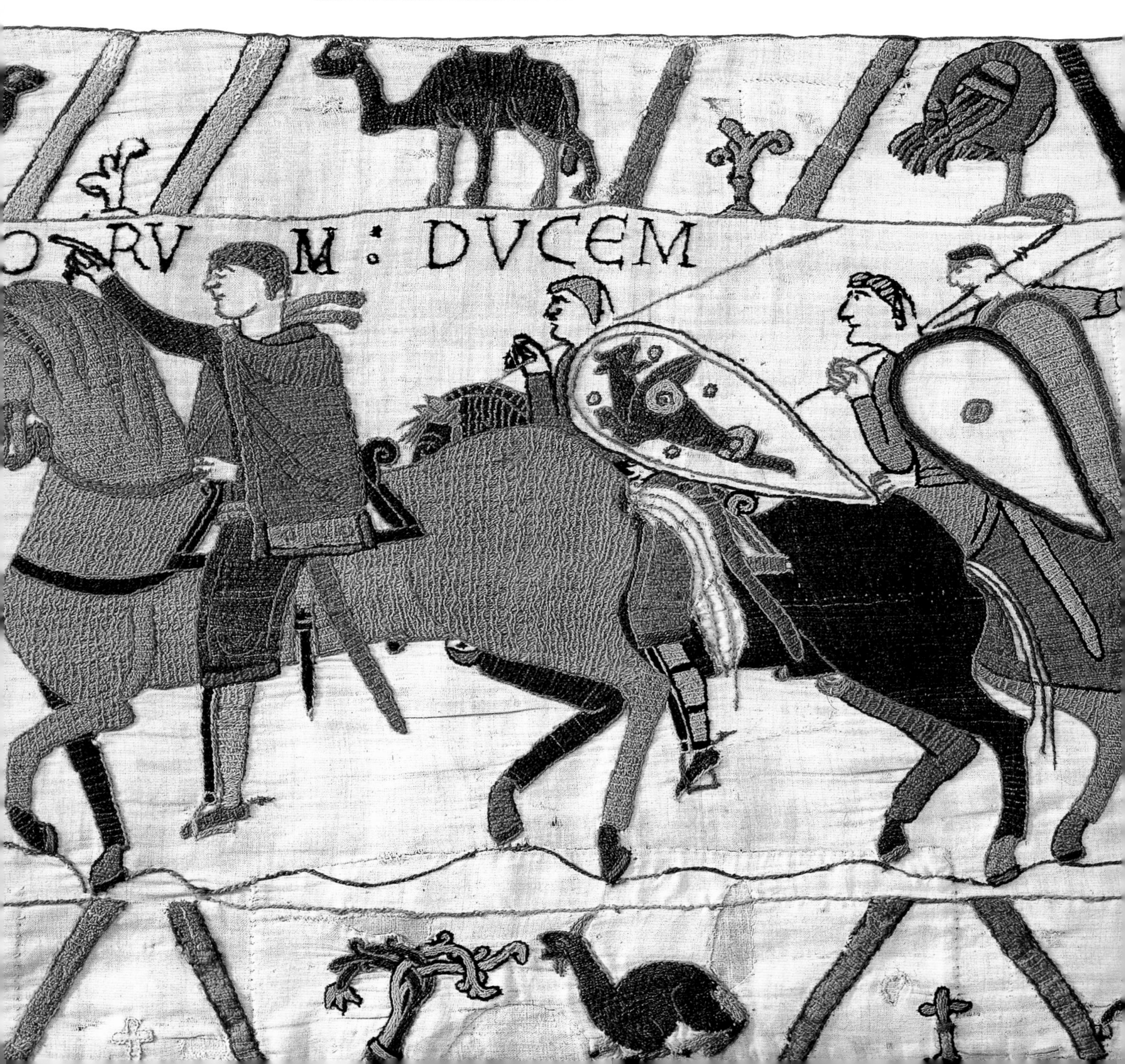
RV M : DVCEM

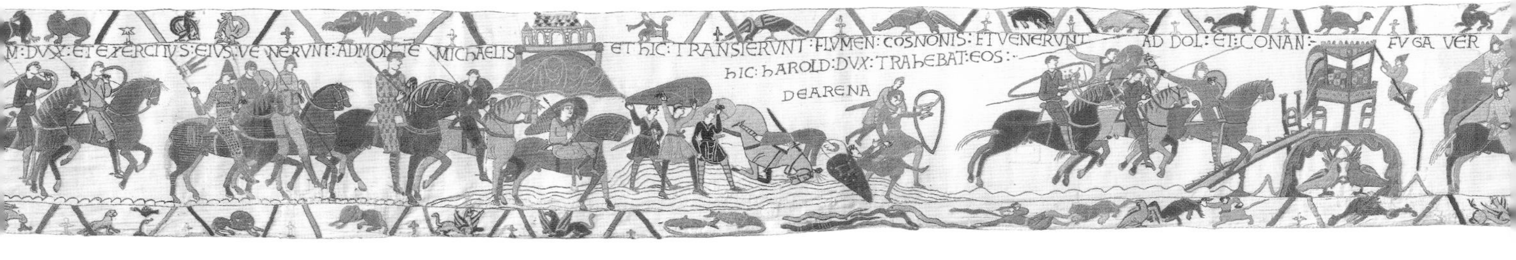

M:DVX:ET EXERCITVS:EIVS:VENERVNT:ADMONTE MICHAELIS ET HIC:TRANSIERVNT:FLVMEN:COSNONIS:ET VENERVNT AD DOL:ET:CONAN: FVGA VER

HIC:HAROLD:DVX:TRAHEBAT:EOS:

DEARENA

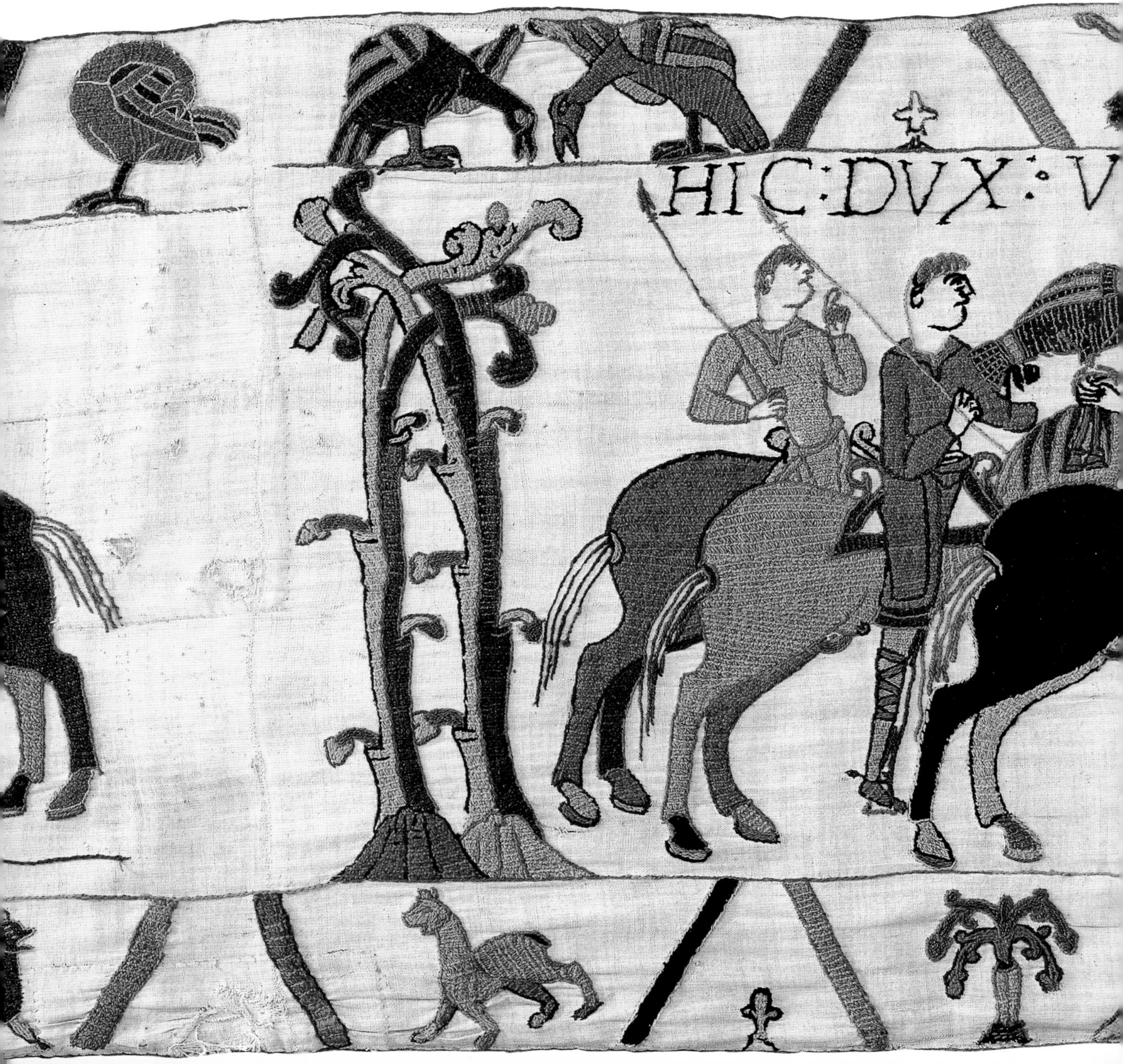

HIC:DVX:V

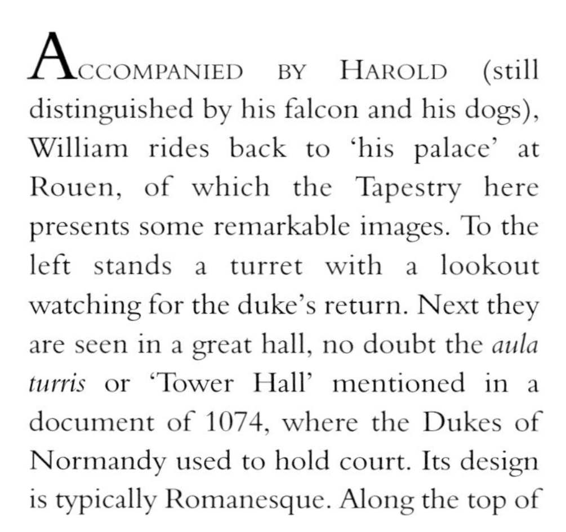

Hic dux Wilgelm

Accompanied by Harold (still distinguished by his falcon and his dogs), William rides back to 'his palace' at Rouen, of which the Tapestry here presents some remarkable images. To the left stands a turret with a lookout watching for the duke's return. Next they are seen in a great hall, no doubt the *aula turris* or 'Tower Hall' mentioned in a document of 1074, where the Dukes of Normandy used to hold court. Its design is typically Romanesque. Along the top of the walls runs a blind arcade of semicircular arches, a common feature of Norman buildings of the period, whether ecclesiastical or vernacular (the latter of course rather rare). The great reception hall at the Abbaye-aux-Dames de Caen, founded by the Conqueror, had this kind of decoration, at least at the gable-ends, as we know from an Engelmann lithograph of the demolition of the hall in the early nineteenth century. The hall was presumably of considerable size, perhaps comparable to the 'Hall of the Exchequer' built a generation later for Henry I's palace at Caen and still standing today.

In the great hall the duke is seated on a throne similar to that in scene 12 (p. 118), holding his sword with the point resting on the ground. A solitary guard, armed with a lance, stands behind him. William is welcoming Harold, who gestures towards the four armed men behind him (oddly, they have four lances but five shields!). This is probably something to do with preparations for the imminent expedition against Brittany.

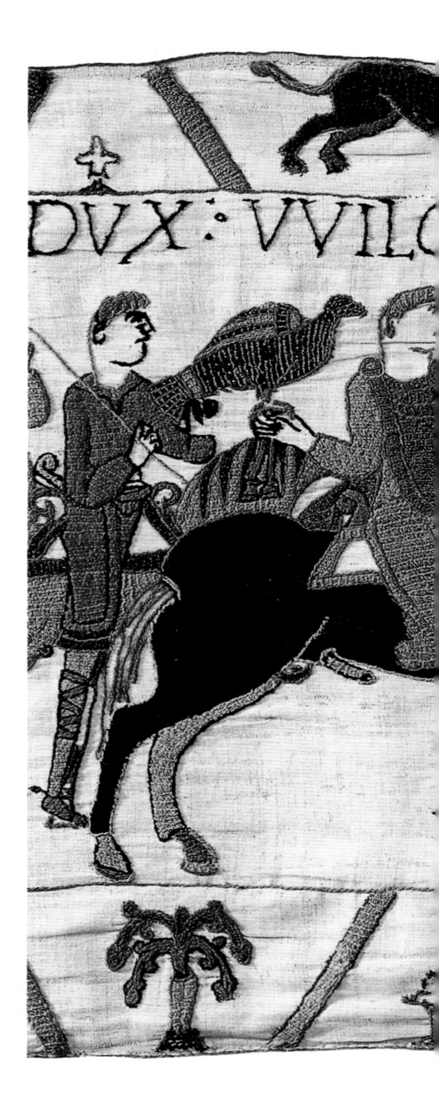

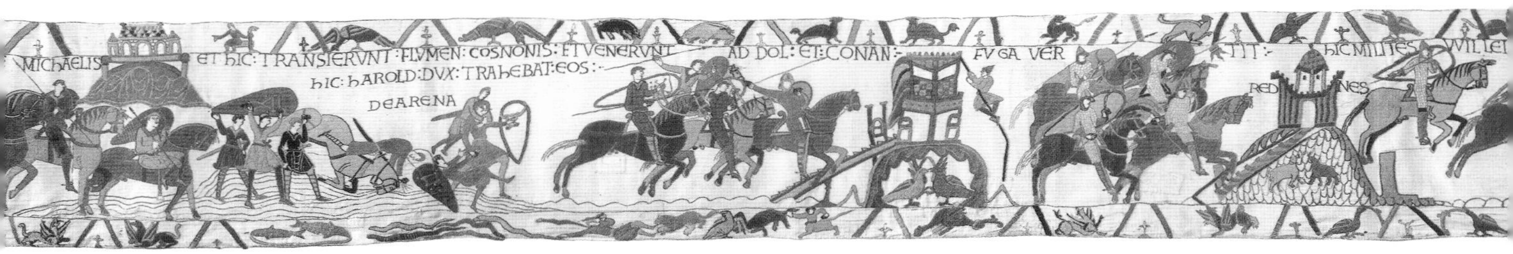

CUM HAROLDO VENIT AD PALATIUM SUUM.

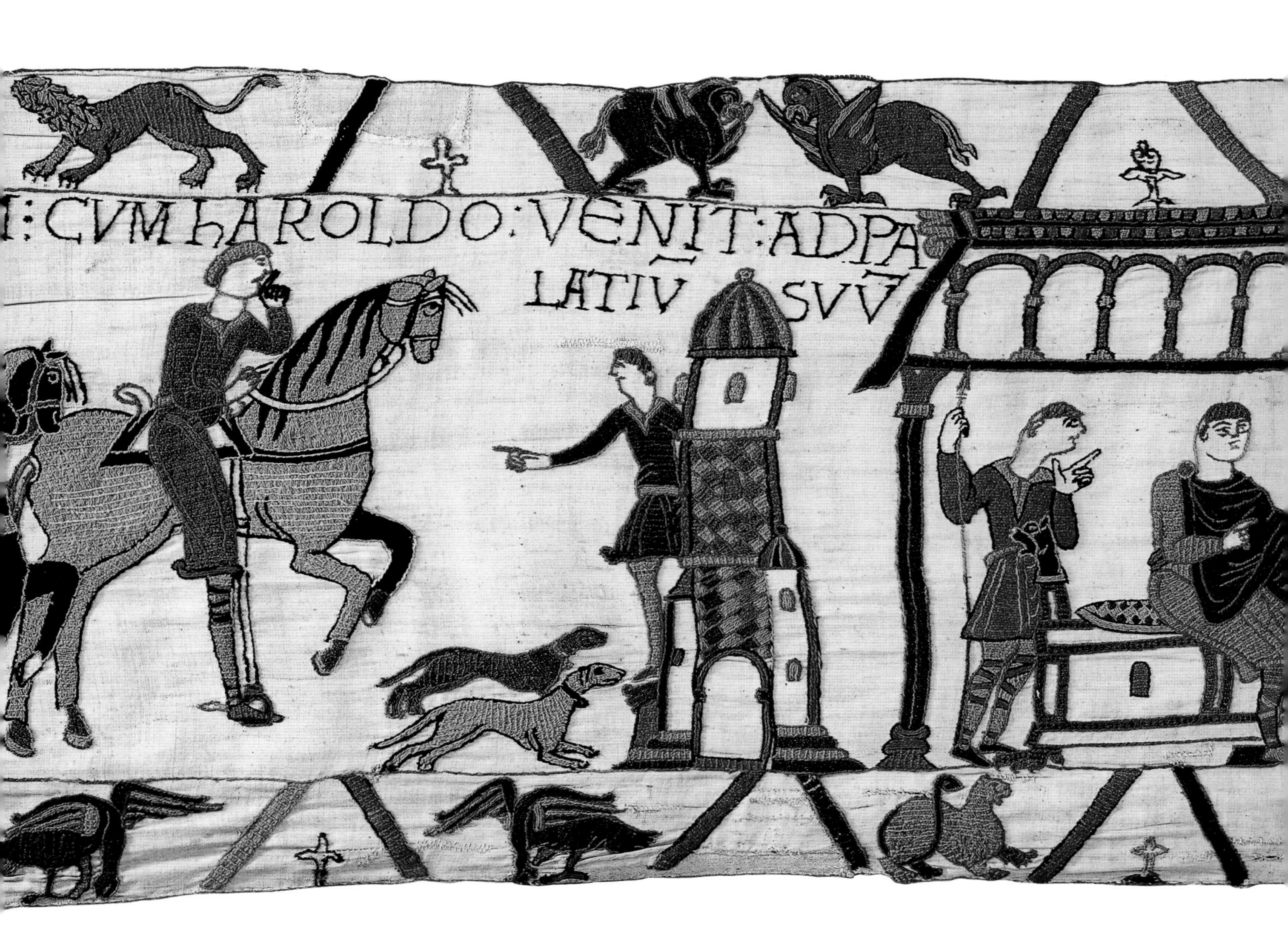

Here Duke William came with Harold to his palace.

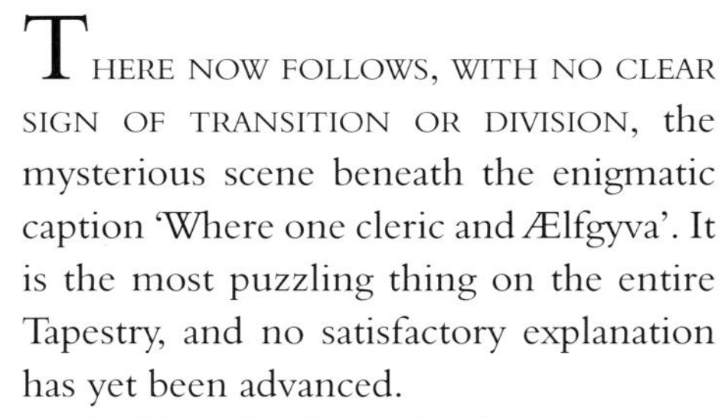

THERE NOW FOLLOWS, WITH NO CLEAR SIGN OF TRANSITION OR DIVISION, the mysterious scene beneath the enigmatic caption 'Where one cleric and Ælfgyva'. It is the most puzzling thing on the entire Tapestry, and no satisfactory explanation has yet been advanced.

Sticking firmly to the facts, we see a little building supported by two spiral columns surmounted by capitals in the form of dragons' heads. Within it stands a woman, her head covered, wearing a full-length robe. She is apparently being slapped in the face by a slim, tonsured man who stands outside, in front of a turret that rests on four steps.

Two questions immediately suggest themselves, although neither of them has an easy answer. First, just what is this little building? Only one distinctive answer has been proposed, though it is distinctly implausible: that it is a *seidhhjallr*, a ritual edifice from which Nordic prophetesses, or *völur*, gave out their oracles. The cleric, on this theory, is intervening to prevent some act of sorcery.[22] But this is all rather tendentious. There is no obvious indication of magic or paganism. Secondly, is there any connection between this and the obscene figure in the border just beneath? Several commentators have inferred that Ælfgyva was mixed up in some sexual scandal. But this, too, is far from compelling. In the absence of any obvious explanation it has even been suggested that somehow an entirely unrelated drawing has strayed into the Tapestry. But this, though not inconceivable, seems very far-fetched indeed.

The name Ælfgyva is the only real clue, but research into it, while throwing up various candidates, remains inconclusive. Ælfgyva was one of the commonest English women's names of the eleventh century. It was what the English chose to call Emma (d. 1051), the sister of Duke Richard II (and thus Duke William's great-aunt) and mother of Edward the Confessor, when she crossed

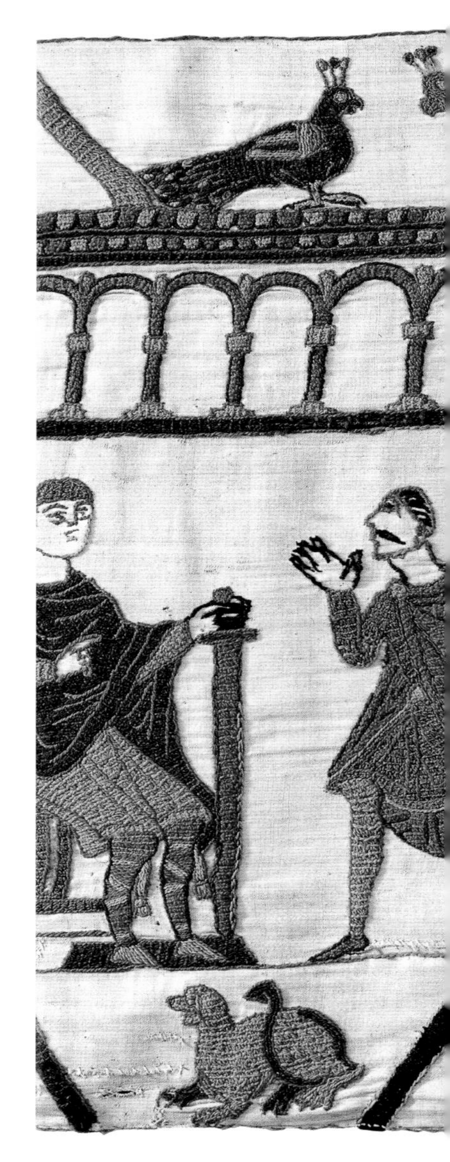

SCENES 14–15

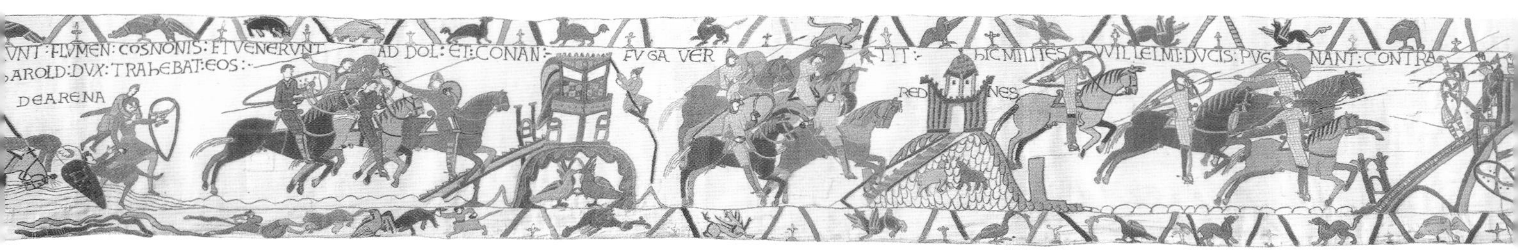

Ubi unus clericus et Ælfgyva.

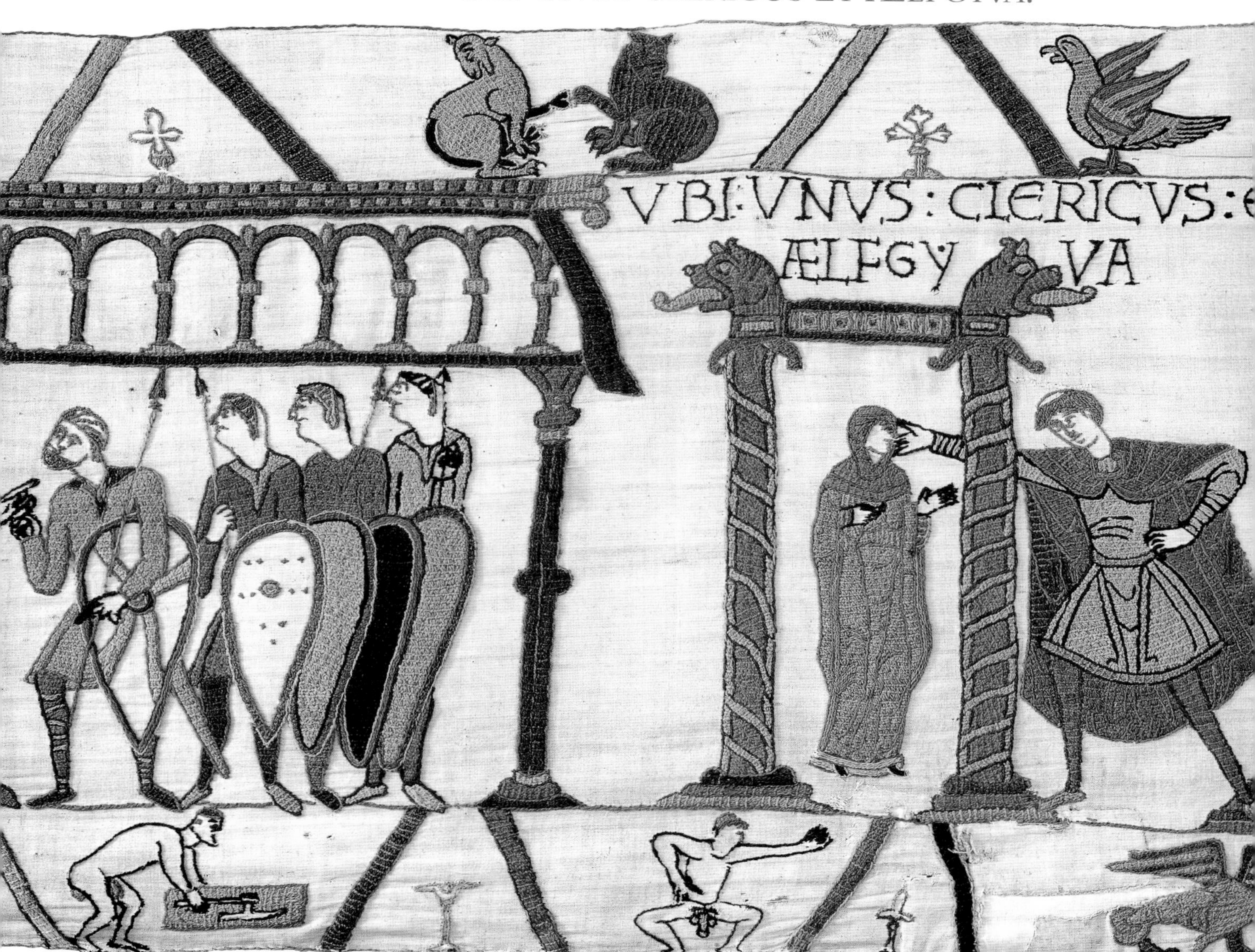

Where one cleric and Ælfgyva.

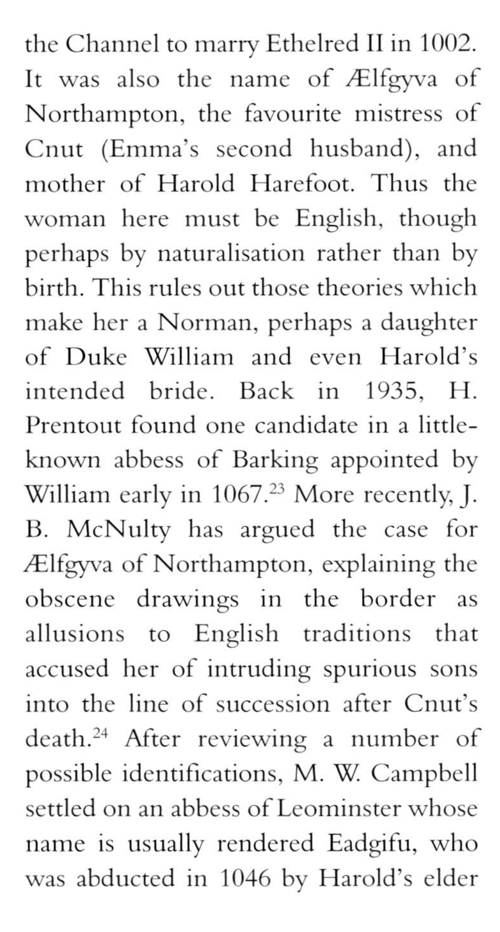

the Channel to marry Ethelred II in 1002. It was also the name of Ælfgyva of Northampton, the favourite mistress of Cnut (Emma's second husband), and mother of Harold Harefoot. Thus the woman here must be English, though perhaps by naturalisation rather than by birth. This rules out those theories which make her a Norman, perhaps a daughter of Duke William and even Harold's intended bride. Back in 1935, H. Prentout found one candidate in a little-known abbess of Barking appointed by William early in 1067.[23] More recently, J. B. McNulty has argued the case for Ælfgyva of Northampton, explaining the obscene drawings in the border as allusions to English traditions that accused her of intruding spurious sons into the line of succession after Cnut's death.[24] After reviewing a number of possible identifications, M. W. Campbell settled on an abbess of Leominster whose name is usually rendered Eadgifu, who was abducted in 1046 by Harold's elder brother, Swein. He links this well-known scandal with Harold's attempt in 1064 to secure the release of some of his relatives then in Normandy as hostages,[25] but neither the Tapestry nor the chronicles hint at any such connection. The identity of Ælfgyva therefore remains a mystery.

There is rather more consensus, however, over the nature of the blow to the woman's face. It has long been recognised that this was a mnemonic technique widely used at that time and attested by both Norman and English sources. The blow would have been meant to make sure that Ælfgyva never forgot what she was witnessing — perhaps Harold's agreement with William prior to its solemnisation by the oath sworn on the relics.

All that can be said about the two structures in this scene is that the use of spiral columns to frame human figures is found in English sculpture of that period, for example in the effigy of Bishop Herbert Losinga in Norwich Cathedral.[26]

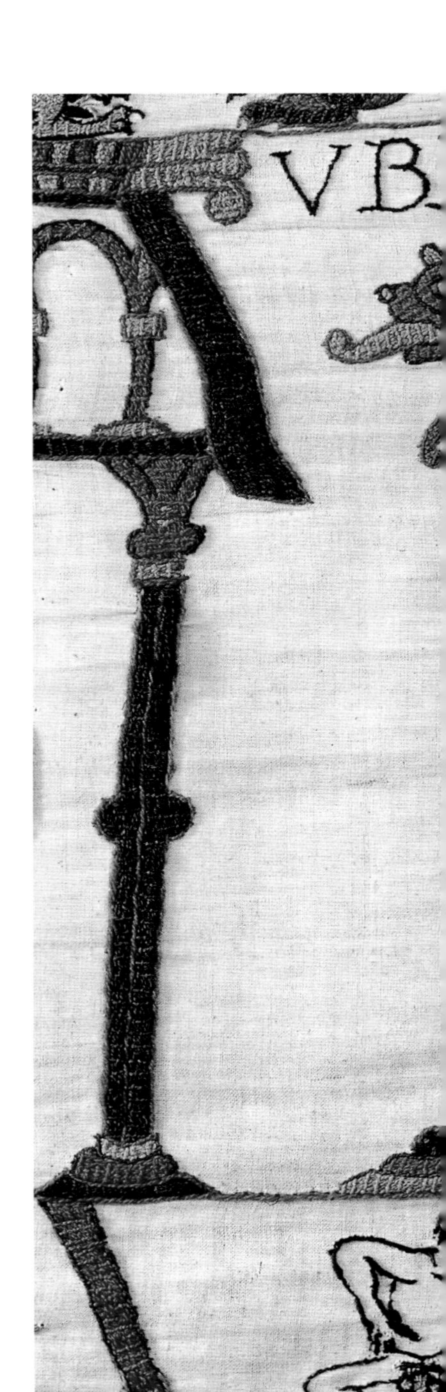

[22] V. Kül, 'Hlidhskjalf og Seidhhjallr', *Arkiv för nordisk Filologi* 75 (1960), pp. 84-112, at pp. 87-88.

[23] H. Prentout, 'Essai sur l'identification des personnages inconnus de la Tapisserie de Bayeux', *Revue Historique* 176 (1935), pp. 14-38, at pp. 25- (Gameson, *Study of the Bayeux Tapestry*, pp. 22-25).

[24] J. B. McNulty, 'The Lady Ælfgyva in the Bayeux Tapestry', *Speculum* 55 (1980), pp. 659-68.

[25] M. W. Campbell, 'Ælfgyva, the mysterious lady of the Bayeux Tapestry', *Annales de Normandie* 34 (1984), pp. 127-45. E. F. Freeman, 'The identity of Ælfgyva in the Bayeux Tapestry', *Annales de Normandie* 41 (1991), pp. 117-34, identifies her as Queen Emma!

[26] See E. Fernie, 'The Spiral Piers of Durham Cathedral', *Medieval Art and Architecture at Durham Cathedral* (British Archaeological Association, III; 1986), p. 51; and also the illustration in L. Musset, *Angleterre romane*, I (La Pierre-qui-Vire: Zodiaque, 1983), p. 266 and plate 88.

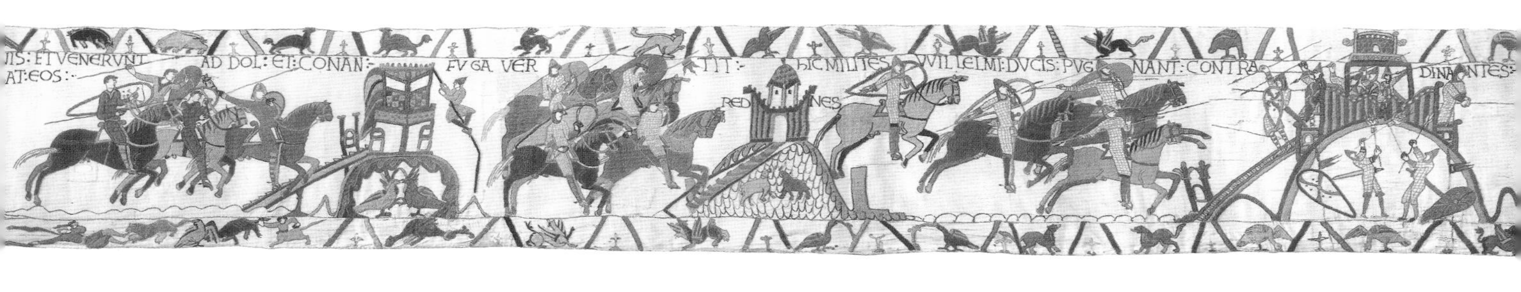

IS: ET VENERVNT
AT: EOS:
AD DOL: ET: CONAN:
FVGA VER
TIT:
RED
NES
HIC MILITES
VVILLELMI: DVCIS: PVG
NANT: CONTRA
DINANTES:

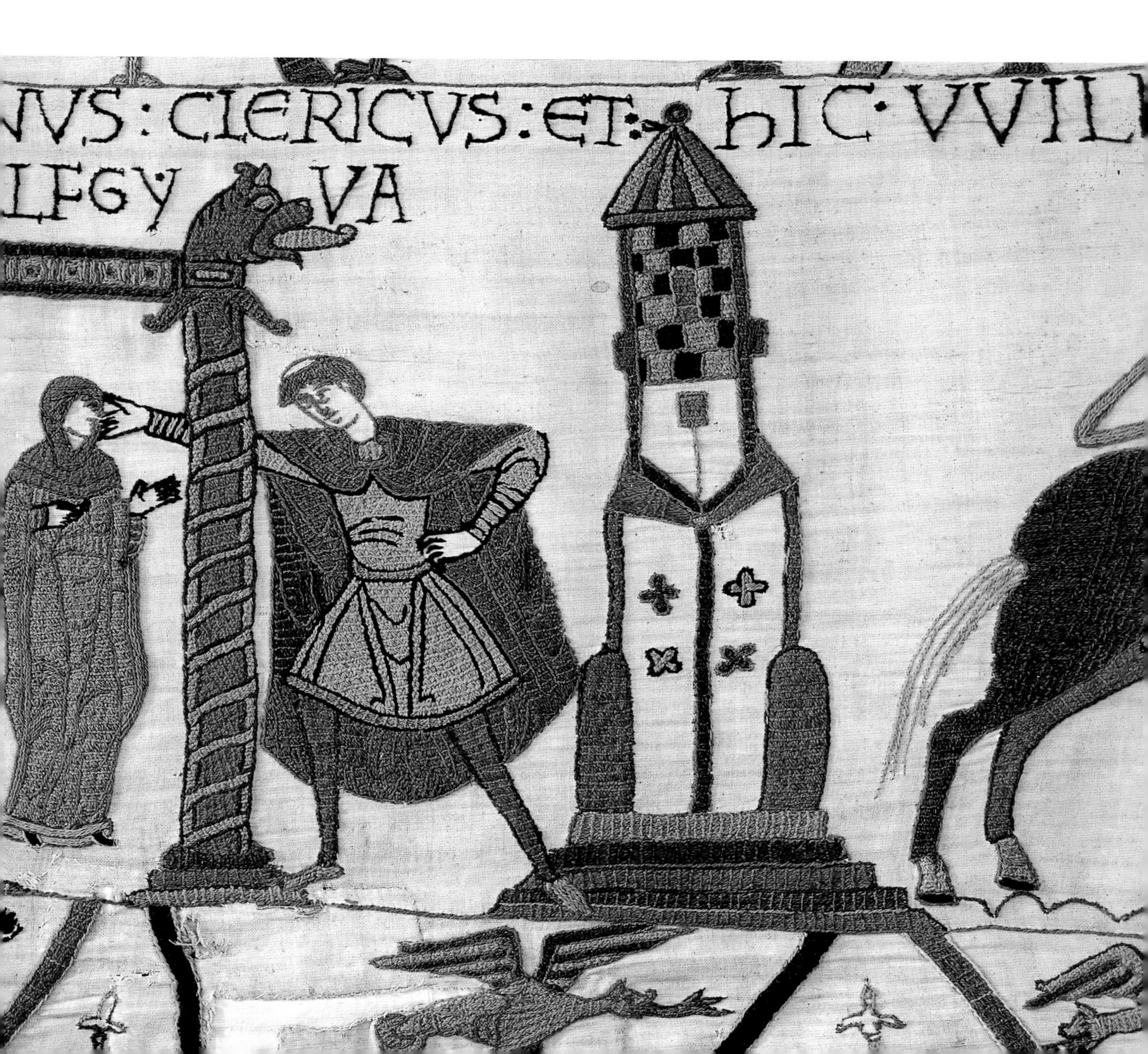

NVS: CLERICVS: ET:
HIC·VVIL
LFGY
VA

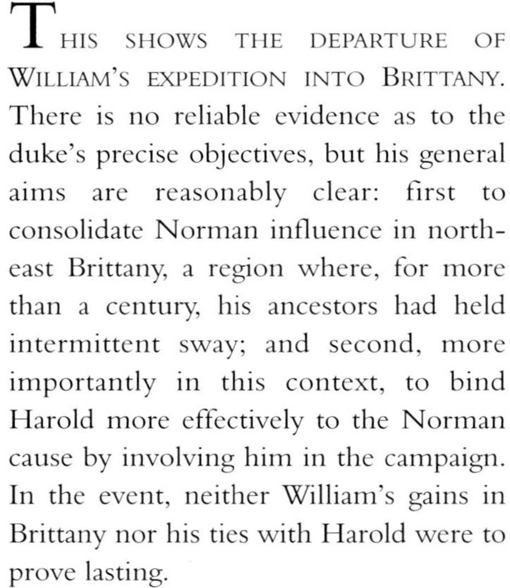

THIS SHOWS THE DEPARTURE OF WILLIAM'S EXPEDITION INTO BRITTANY. There is no reliable evidence as to the duke's precise objectives, but his general aims are reasonably clear: first to consolidate Norman influence in north-east Brittany, a region where, for more than a century, his ancestors had held intermittent sway; and second, more importantly in this context, to bind Harold more effectively to the Norman cause by involving him in the campaign. In the event, neither William's gains in Brittany nor his ties with Harold were to prove lasting.

The Norman force is crossing the Couesnon (marking the border with Brittany) at a ford in an area of shifting sands in sight of Mont-Saint-Michel.

For no apparent reason, the relative scale of the drawings of human figures varies here: Duke William, carrying a commander's baton, is much larger than his companions, such as the horseman two places ahead of him, who has hitched up his legs to keep them out of the water.

At first sight, the image of Mont-Saint-Michel in the background — a little church perched on top of a little round hill — looks distinctly unrealistic. Yet in fact it betrays a degree of genuine knowledge (the site was, after all, a major pilgrimage destination). Even today the abbey church rests directly on the rock at only one point, about halfway along, at the crossing. So while the Tapestry offers us a stylised view rather than the Romanesque church as it actually was (still less as it is now: a portion of the nave is all that survives from that time), it is striving to convey some sense of its distinctive siting on the rock.

The Normans probably crossed the Couesnon not at Pontorson, as one does today, but further downstream, where the little river flows into the sea and there is indeed a view of Mont-Saint-Michel. The Couesnon, it is worth noting, is the only body of water explicitly named on the Tapestry.[27]

[27] On Mont-Saint-Michel at this time see the articles by J. Vallery-Radot and Y. M. Froidevaux in *Millénaire du Mont-Saint-Michel*, t. 5 (1993), pp. 35-61 and 68-82.

HIC WILLELM DUX

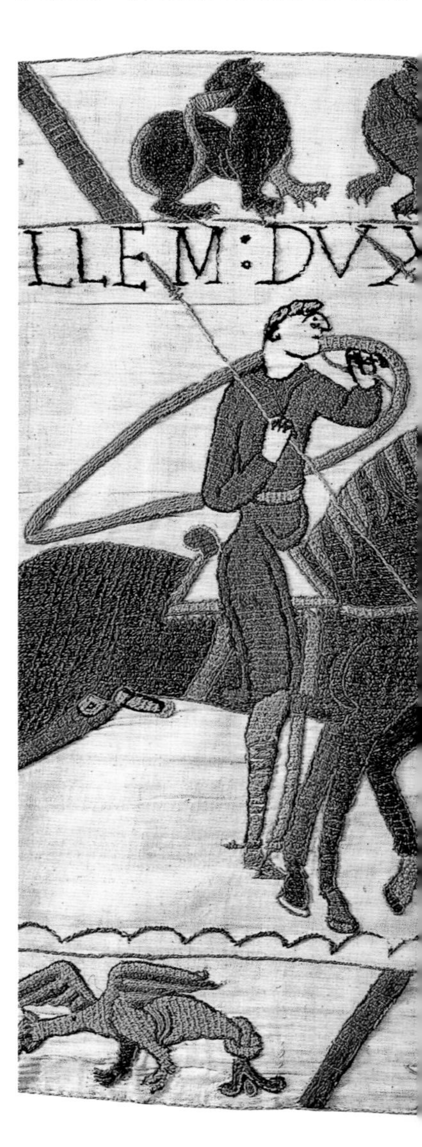

SCENE 16

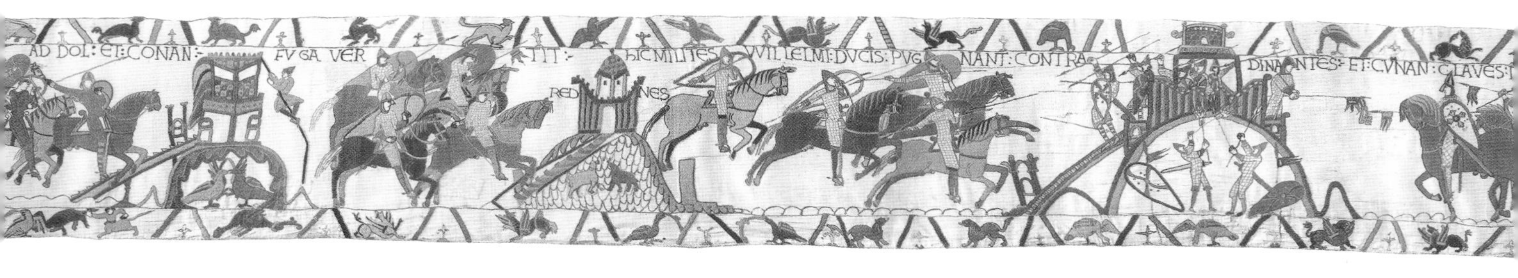

XERCITUS EJUS VENERUNT AD MONTEM MICHAELIS

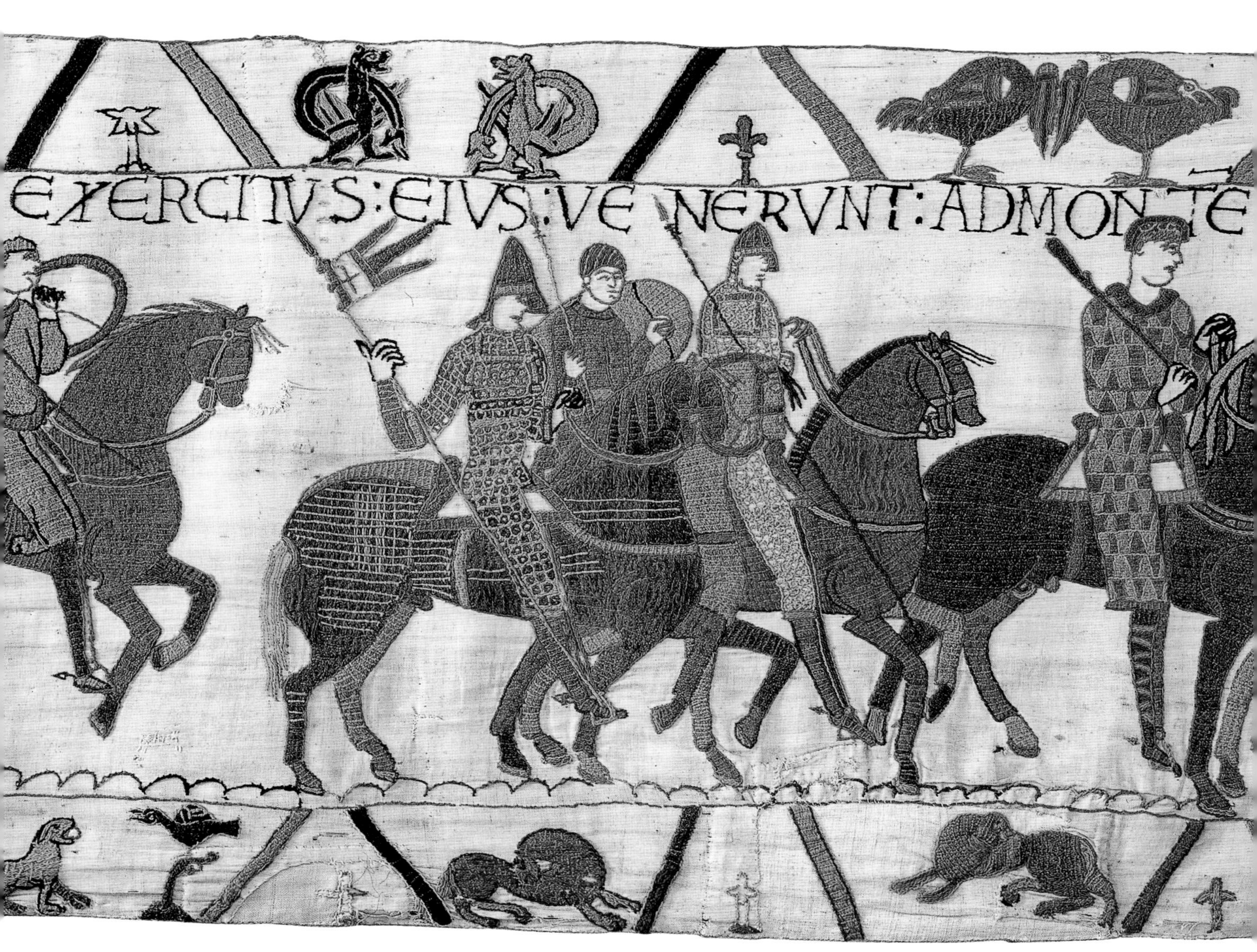

Here Duke William and his army came to Mont (Saint) Michel …

SCENES 16–17 >

132

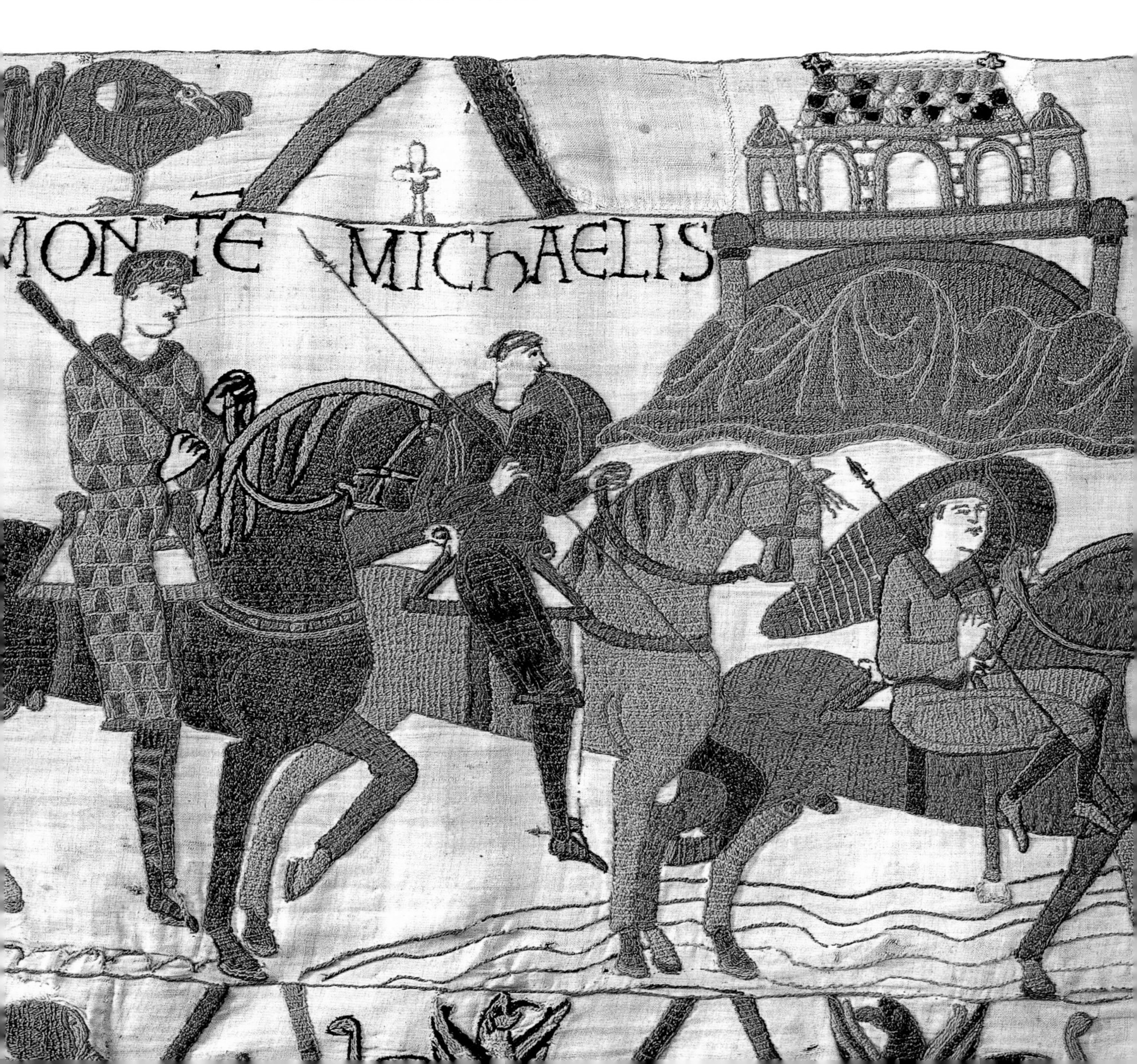

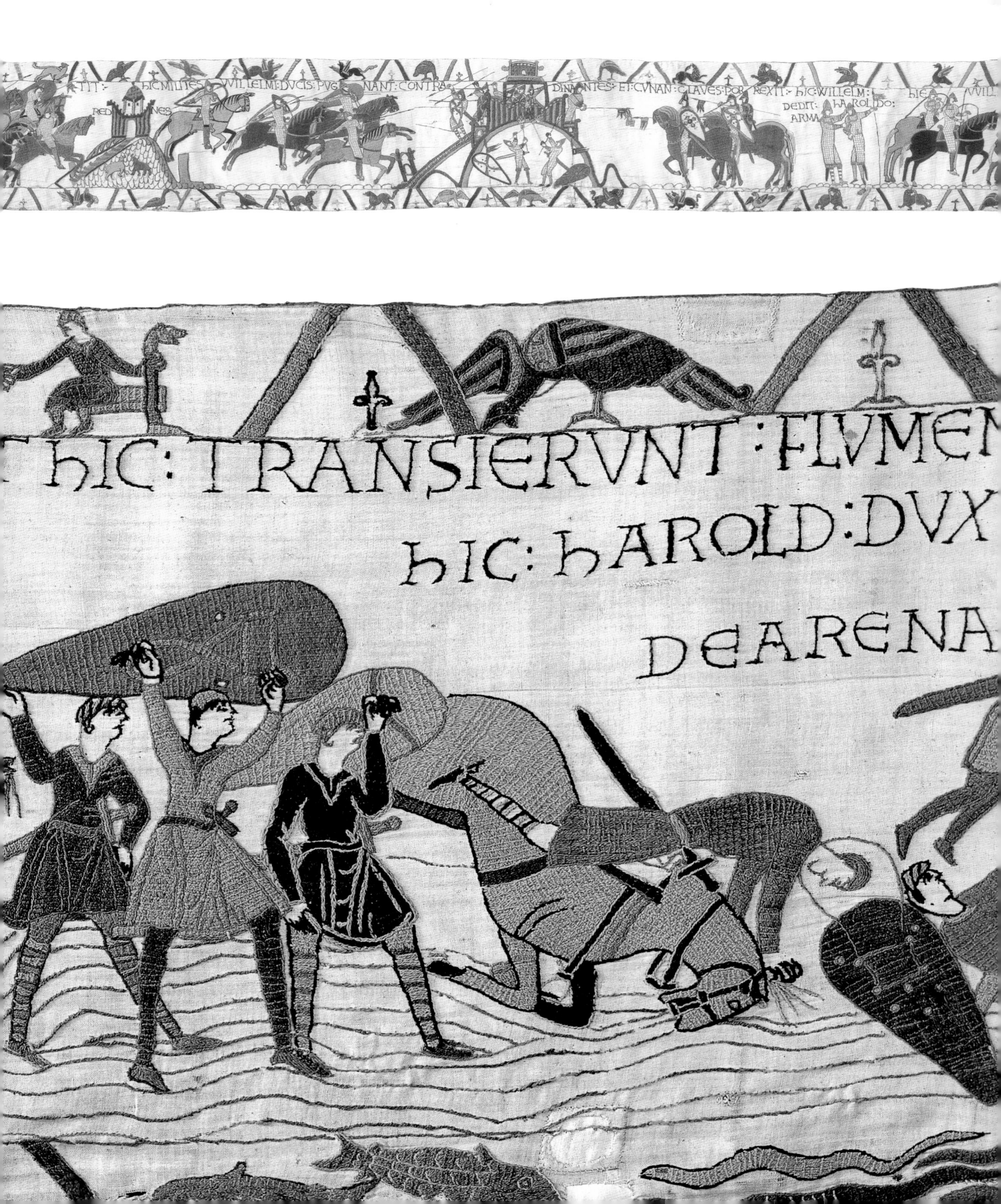
HIC: TRANSIERUNT: FLUMEN
HIC: HAROLD: DUX
DE ARENA

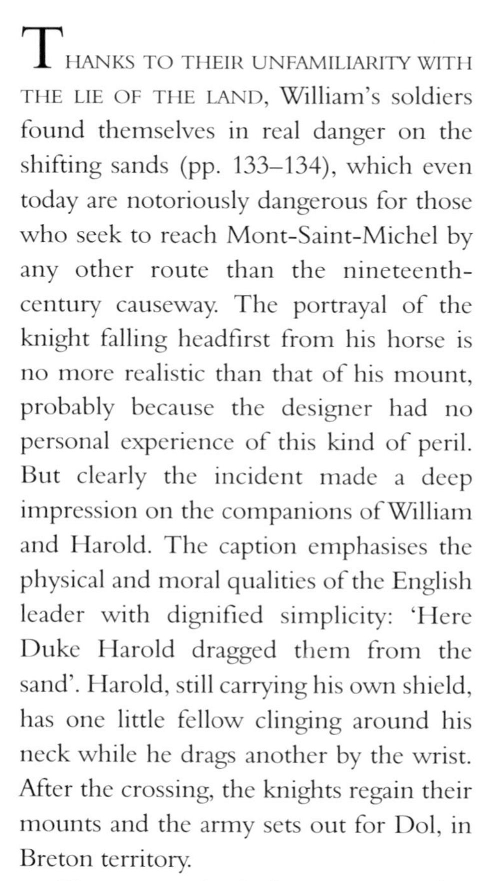

Thanks to their unfamiliarity with the lie of the land, William's soldiers found themselves in real danger on the shifting sands (pp. 133–134), which even today are notoriously dangerous for those who seek to reach Mont-Saint-Michel by any other route than the nineteenth-century causeway. The portrayal of the knight falling headfirst from his horse is no more realistic than that of his mount, probably because the designer had no personal experience of this kind of peril. But clearly the incident made a deep impression on the companions of William and Harold. The caption emphasises the physical and moral qualities of the English leader with dignified simplicity: 'Here Duke Harold dragged them from the sand'. Harold, still carrying his own shield, has one little fellow clinging around his neck while he drags another by the wrist. After the crossing, the knights regain their mounts and the army sets out for Dol, in Breton territory.

The presence in the lower margin of an image of two fishes, back to back but connected by some kind of ribbon, has been taken as an allusion to the zodiacal sign of Pisces and thus as a veiled chronological reference placing the expedition in late February or early March. But in the absence of any comparable references on the Tapestry, this remains highly speculative; and while we cannot date the Breton expedition more precisely than 1064, it almost certainly began later in the year.

ET HIC TRANSIERUNT FLUMEN COSNONIS ET

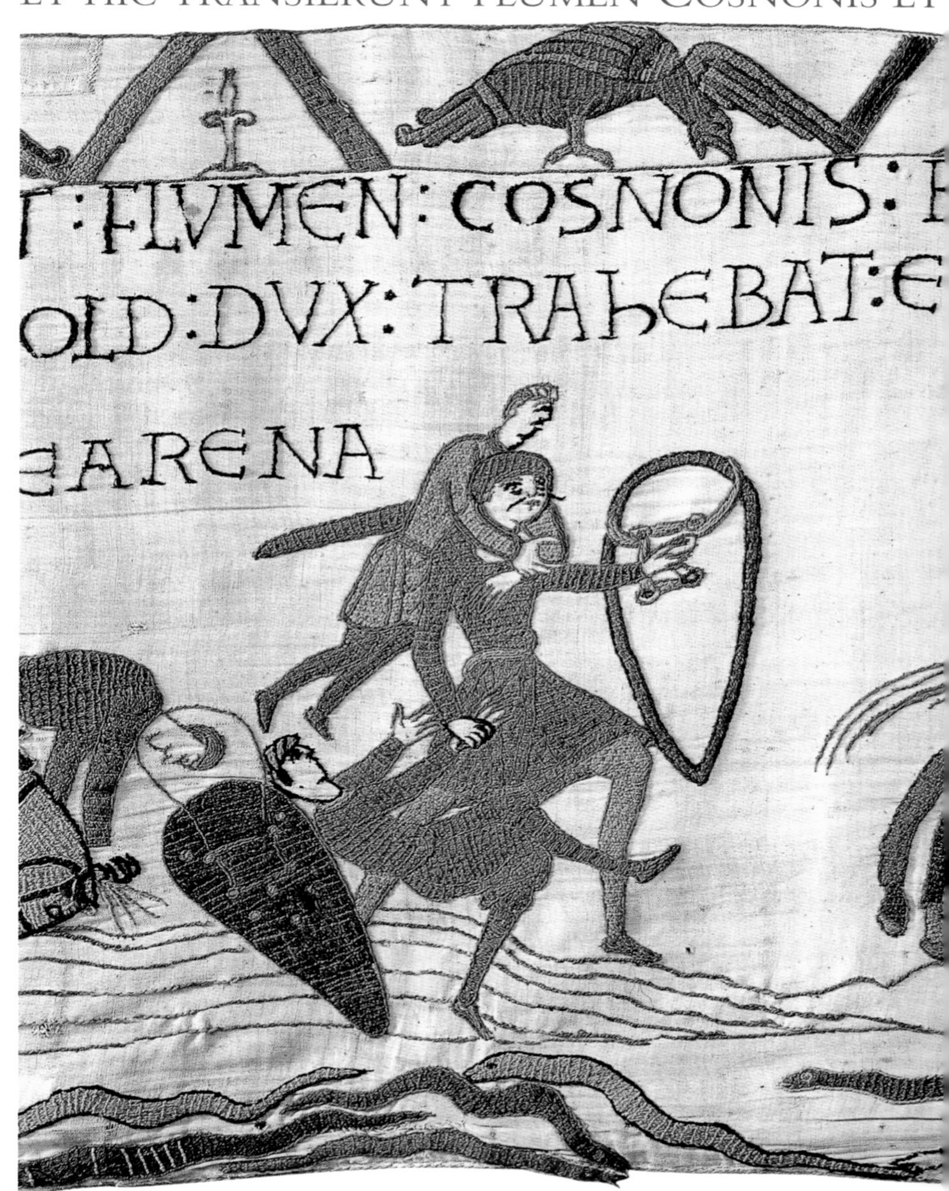

Scene 17

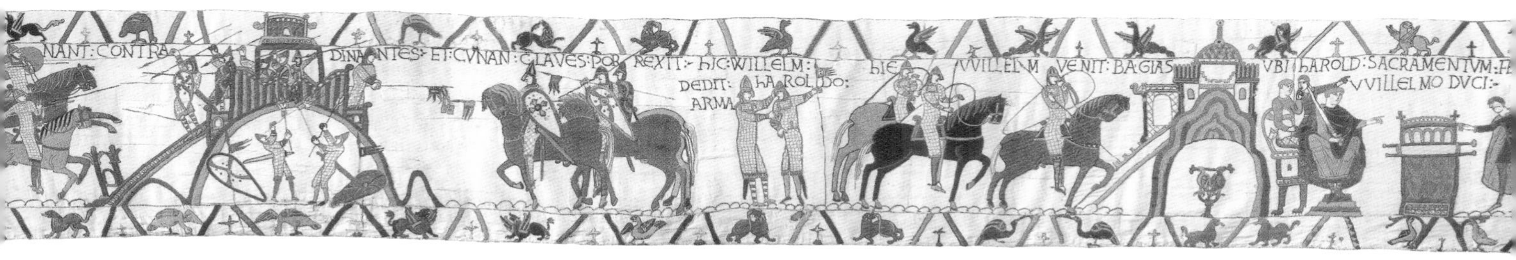

ENERUNT AD DOL. HIC HAROLD DUX TRAHEBAT EOS DE ARENA.

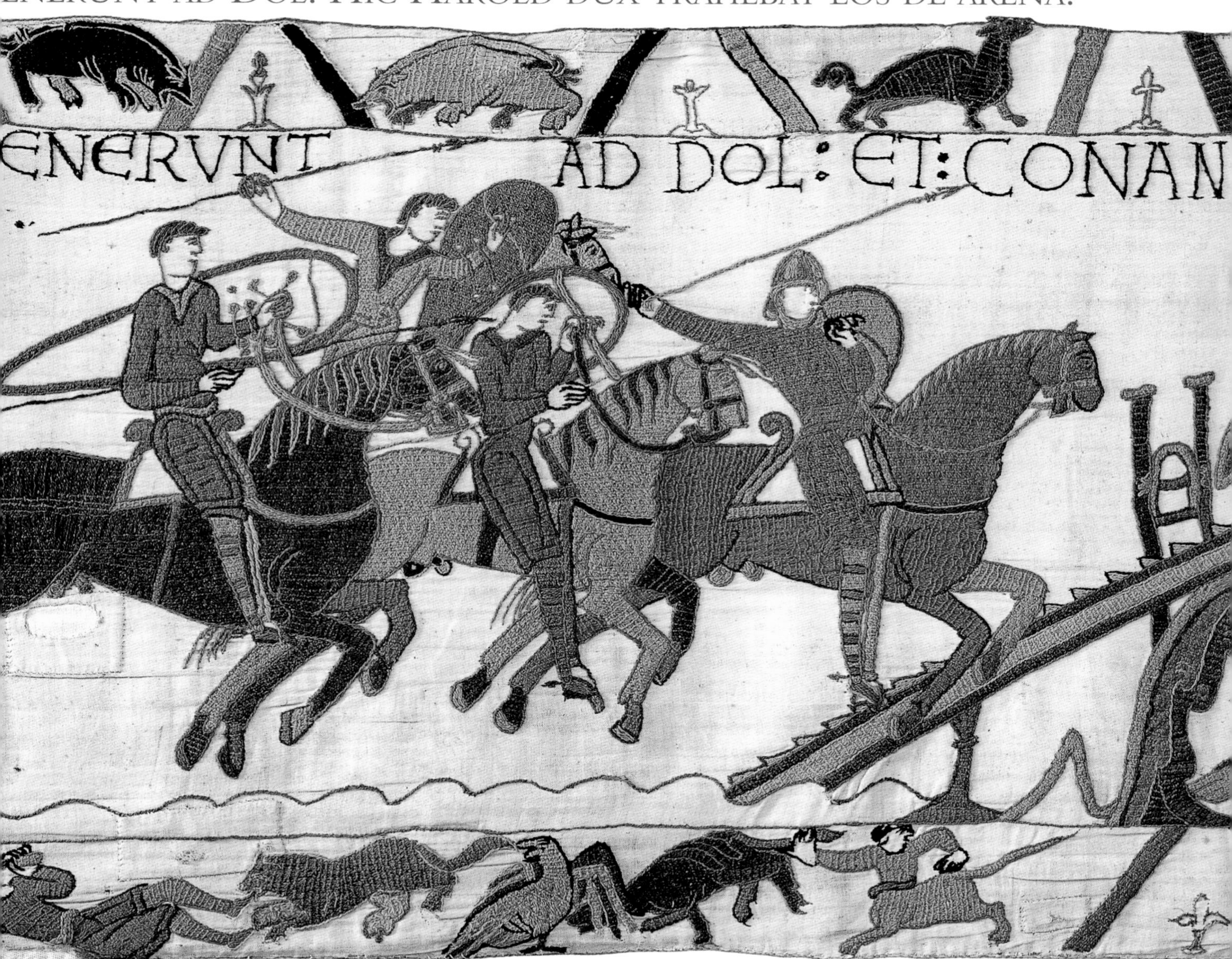

...and here they crossed the River Couesnon and came to Dol. Here Duke Harold dragged them from the sand.

Et Conan fuga vertit.

There is not much documentary evidence for the Breton expedition which occupies the next few scenes (pp. 136–141). Freeman pointed out as long ago as 1870 that it is not mentioned in any reliable Breton source. Only the Norman chroniclers mention it, chief among them William of Poitiers. According to him, Ruallon of Dol rose up against Count Conan II of Brittany, appealing to William of Normandy for aid. William of Jumièges says nothing about it, though, and the *Carmen de Hastingae proelio* confines itself to vague talk about Duke William's activities *finibus occiduis* ('on the western frontier'). William of Malmesbury and Orderic Vitalis refer to it only in passing.[28]

Conan, named twice in the captions (scenes 18 and 20, pp. 136 and 141), is Conan II (1040-66), descended from the Counts of Rennes. He aspired to control over the whole of Brittany, but had a firm grip only on its eastern half. Even there he had rivals, notably the Counts of Penthièvre. The captions do not accord him a title (the title of Duke of Brittany became current only in the twelfth century). Ruallon de Dol (who is neither named nor depicted on the Tapestry) was the steward

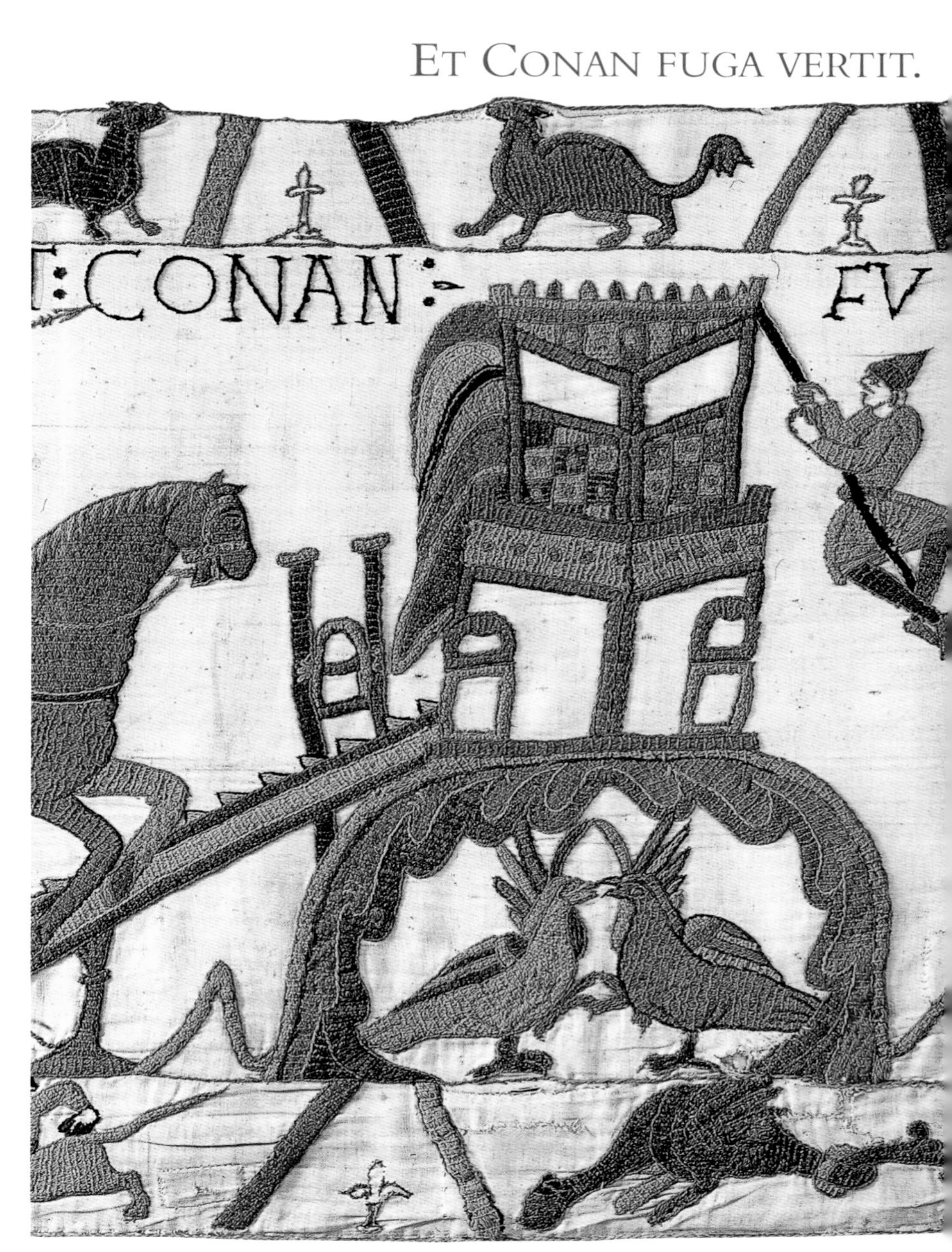

Scene 18

[28] Guillaume de Poitiers, ed. Foreville, p. 110 (Davis and Chibnall, pp. 74-75; *Carmen de Hastingae Proelio*, ed. Morton and Muntz, p. 2, verse 21; William of Malmesbury, *De Gestis Regum Anglorum*, ed. Stubbs, vol. 1, p. 279; Orderic Vitalis, ed. Chibnall, vol. 2, p. 136. E. A. Freeman, *The History of the Norman Conquest of England* (2nd edn. 4 vols. Oxford, 1870-76), vol. 3, pp. 711-12.

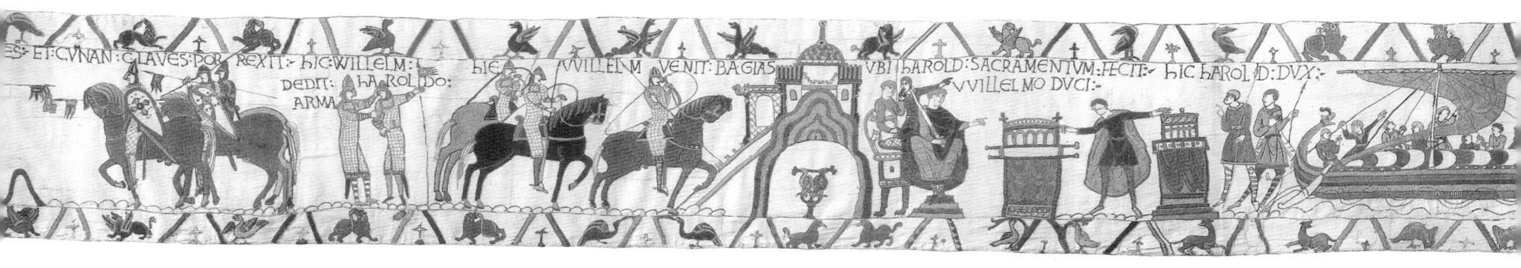

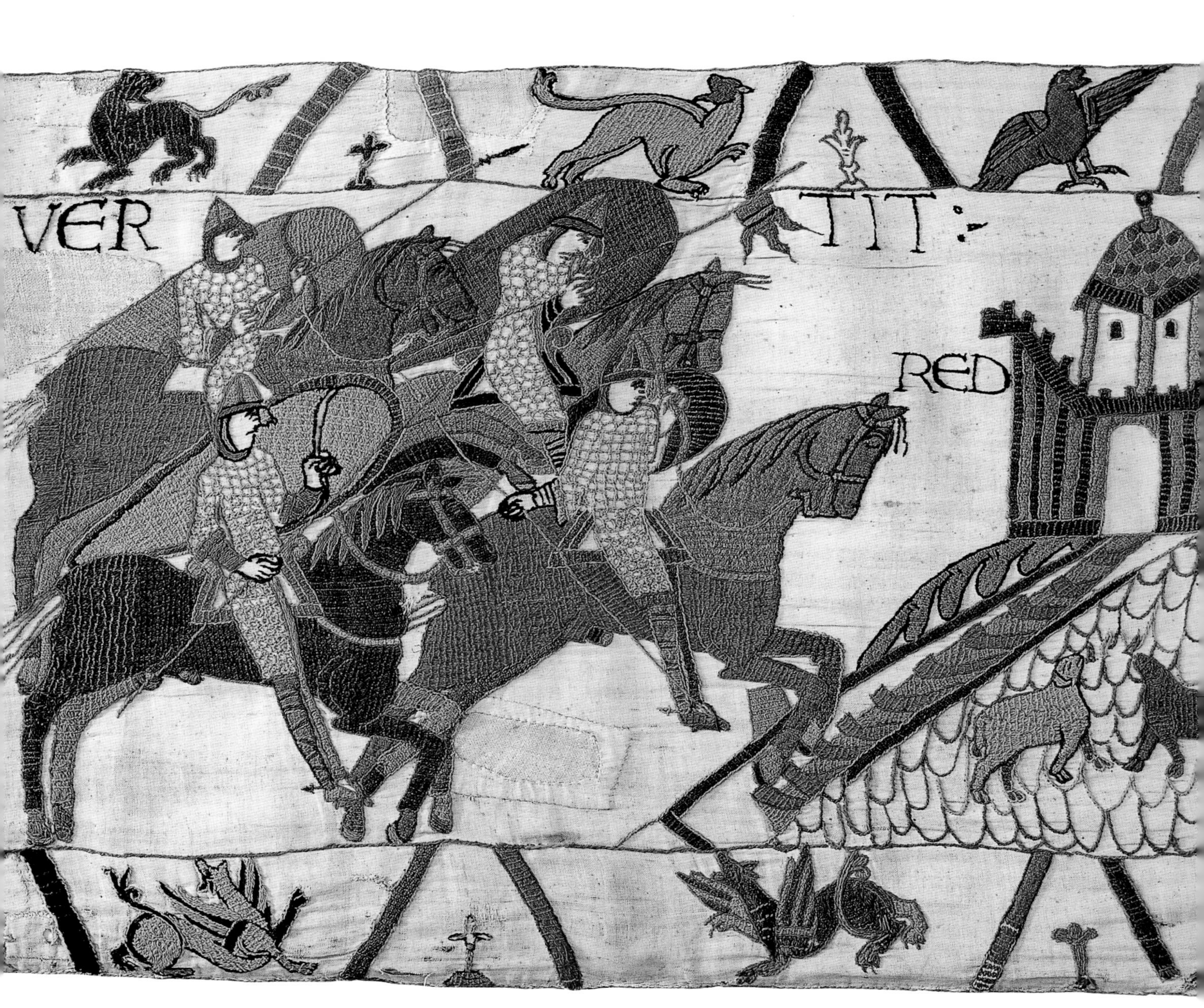

And Conan turned and fled.

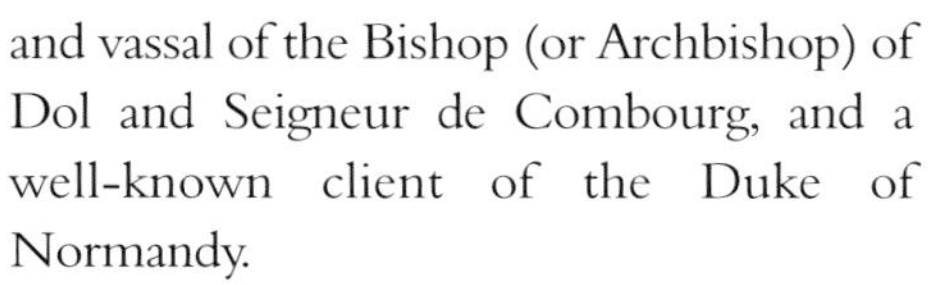

and vassal of the Bishop (or Archbishop) of Dol and Seigneur de Combourg, and a well-known client of the Duke of Normandy.

The Tapestry, however, ignores the political background to concentrate on the military aspects of the campaign and their connection with the oath which Harold subsequently swore to William. It makes no allusion to Ruallon's eventual fate: he had to take refuge with his Norman patron, who bestowed Pontor-son upon him. William's adventure was rather less glorious than the Tapestry suggests.

The story told here is sketchy in the extreme. After the crossing of the Couesnon comes the attack on Dol with Conan's flight to Rennes, and then the attack on Dinan and its surrender to the Norman besiegers. The depiction of the three castles at Dol, Rennes, and Dinan is somewhat problematic in that, as was said before, they were probably built at least in part of stone by this time (see above, p. 69). The detail of a slight figure, presumably Conan, escaping from Dol down a rope (p. 136), calls to mind a commonplace of medieval chronicles, several of which, for example, tell such a story of the siege of Antioch in 1098.[29]

[29] On these *funambuli*, see R. H. C. Davis, 'William of Poitiers and his history of William the Conqueror', *The Writing of History in the Middle Ages: essays presented to Richard William Southern* (Oxford, 1981), pp. 71-100, at p. 82; see also Orderic Vitalis, ed. Chibnall, vol. 5, p. 98.

REDNES. HIC MILITES WILLELMI DUCIS PUG

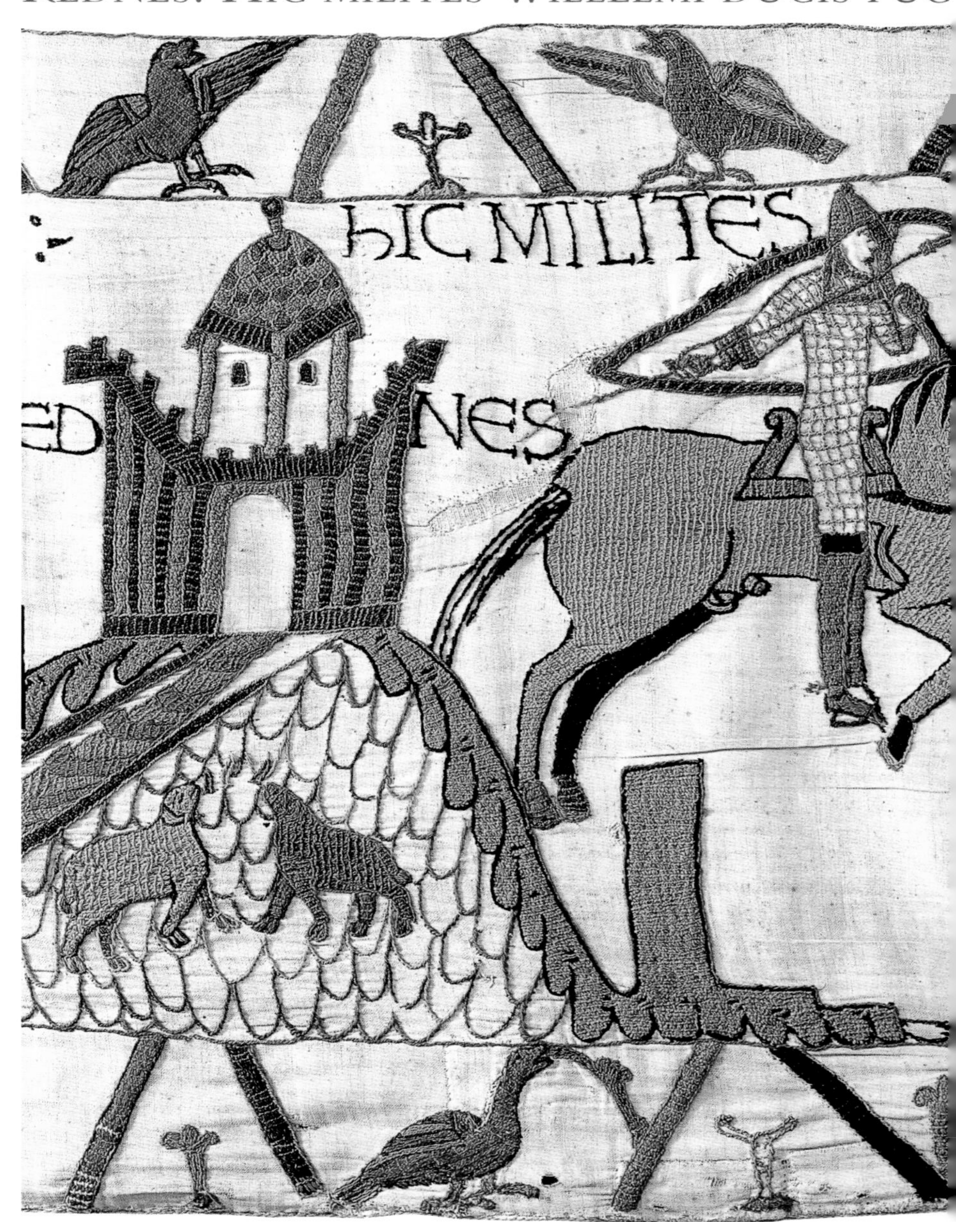

SCENES 18–19

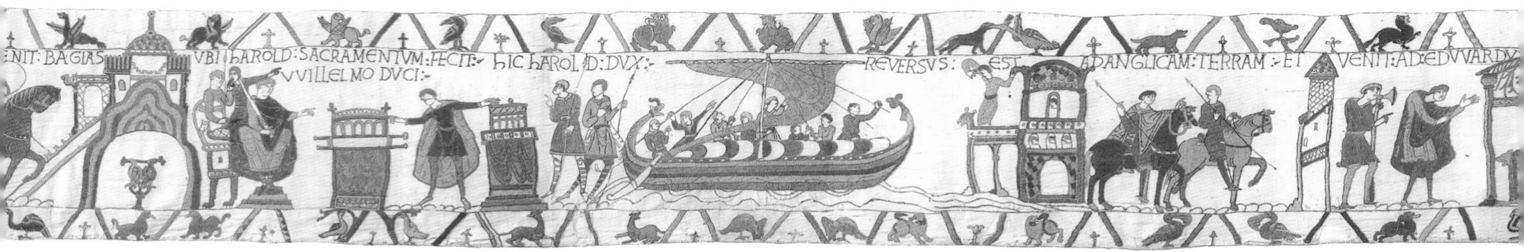

NT…

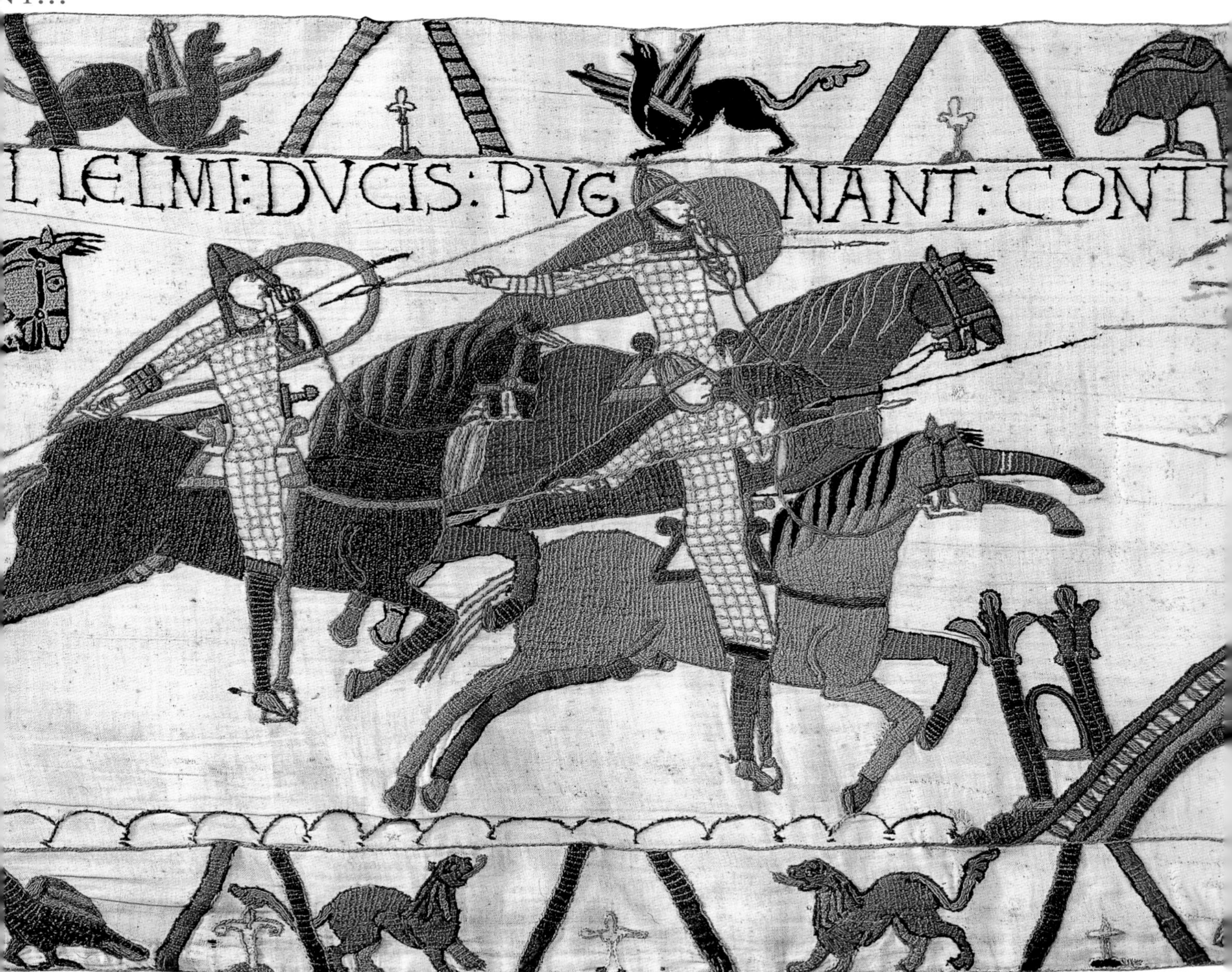

Rennes. Here Duke William's knights fight …

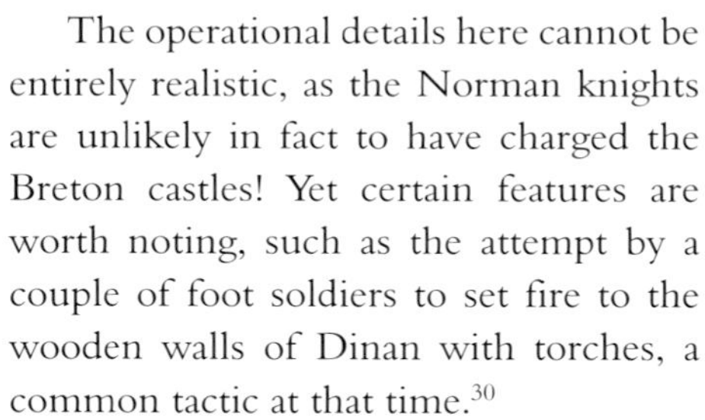

The operational details here cannot be entirely realistic, as the Norman knights are unlikely in fact to have charged the Breton castles! Yet certain features are worth noting, such as the attempt by a couple of foot soldiers to set fire to the wooden walls of Dinan with torches, a common tactic at that time.[30]

Conan is specifically named as the figure shown surrendering the keys of Dinan, hanging at the end of his lance, to one of the besiegers. The pair of keys might seem unduly bulky, but excavations at Trelleborg in Denmark turned up keys of a comparable size (used, no doubt, for opening a similarly massive gate).[31]

Both the pair of birds depicted on the motte at Dol and the pair of beasts on that at Rennes would seem to be merely decorative, drawn from the same bestiary as those that fill the borders.

... CONTRA DINANTES ET CUNAN CLAVES PO

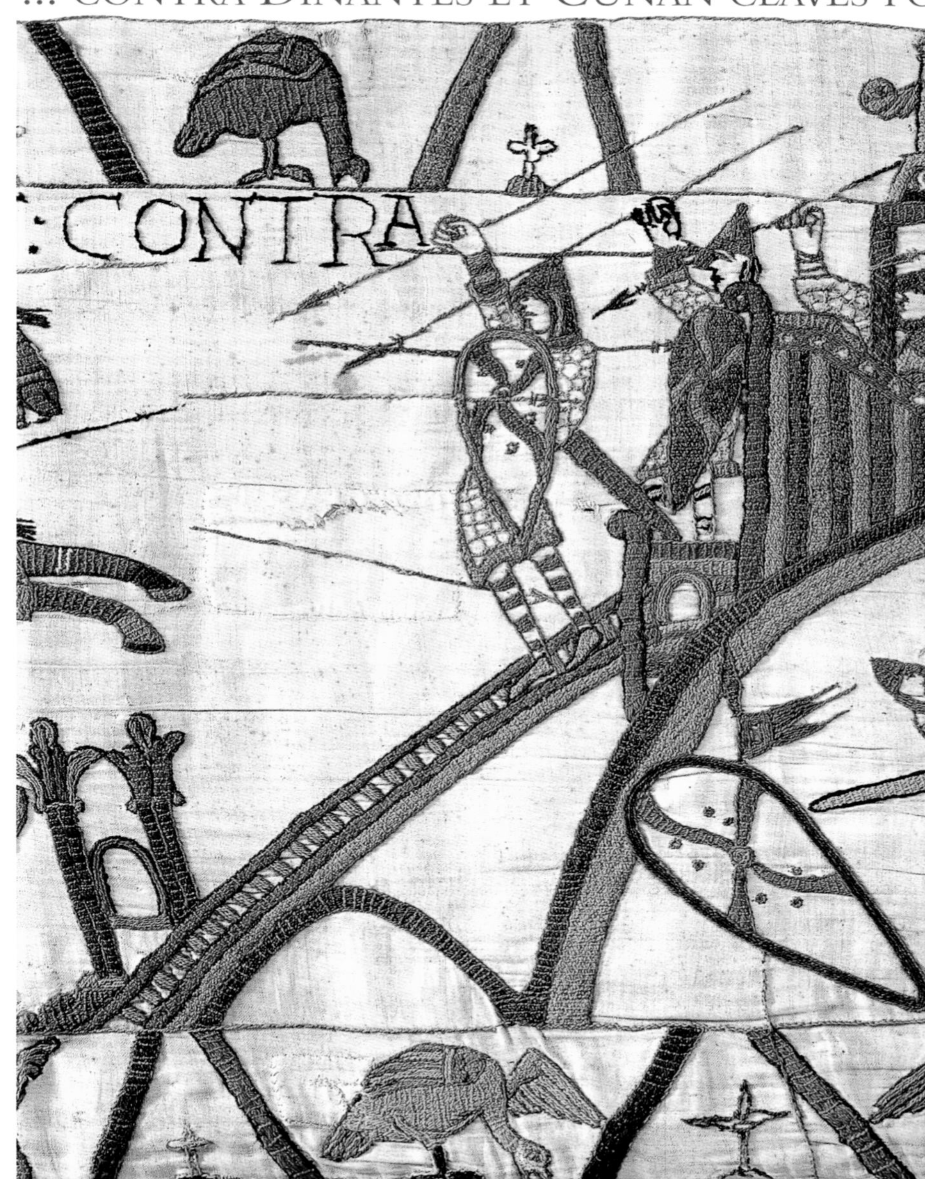

[30] On the 'old castle' (*viel chastel*) of Rennes, see J. P. Leguay, 'Le paysage urbain de Rennes au milieu du XVe siècle', *Mém. Soc. d'hist. et d'archéol. de Bretagne* 54 (1977), pp. 69-116, at p. 77; and N. Y. Tonnerre & A. Chèdeville, *La Brétagne féodale* (Rennes, 1987), p. 415, for an explanation of the scales here shown covering the motte.

[31] P. Nørlund, *Trelleborg* (Copenhagen, 1948), p. 125 and plate 21.

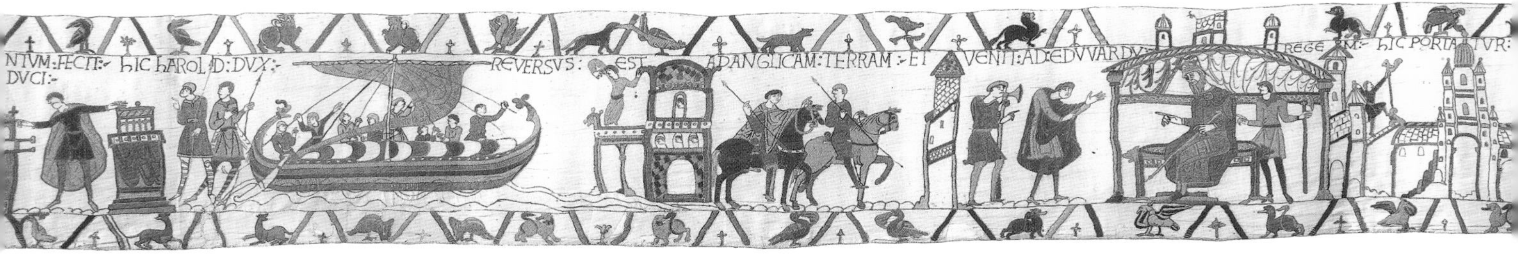

IT.

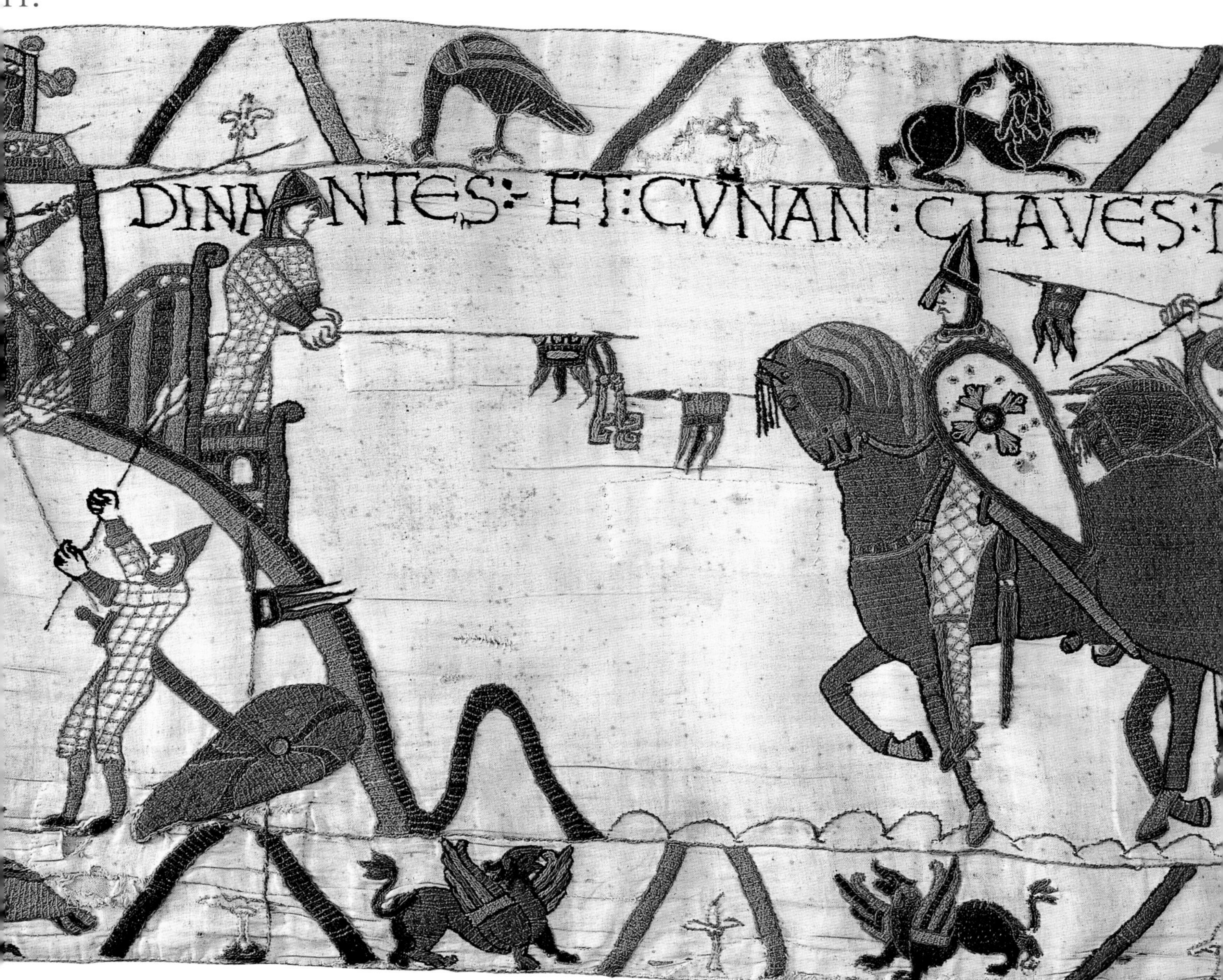

...against Dinan and Conan hands over the keys.

Hic Willelm dedit

The caption is clear: 'Here William gave arms to Harold'. On their return from Brittany, Duke William, in his full armour, hands the similarly accoutred Harold a helmet and perhaps a sword. This has frequently been read as one of the earliest surviving depictions of the ceremonial 'dubbing' of a knight, albeit according to the simple forms of the eleventh century rather than the more elaborate and even religious rituals developed later in the Middle Ages. As Frank Barlow observed, the Tapestry might be an exact illustration of the transaction Orderic Vitalis reports as having taken place between Lanfranc and Henry (later King Henry I) in 1086: the bestowal of the *lorica* or coat of mail (which Harold is already wearing here), the placing of the helmet on the head, and the presentation of the *militiae cingulum*, the 'belt of knighthood'.[32] This was manifestly a Norman ritual, and its adoption by Harold is an indication of the interest he took in French customs, something which was remarked upon in the contemporary account of the life of Edward the Confessor.[33] According to Orderic Vitalis, Edward, an even more notorious admirer of things continental, had already adopted this custom in bestowing the *cingulum militiae* upon his squire Robert of Rhuddlan.[34]

Others have read this scene, however, as a symbolic recognition by Harold of William's future overlordship of England.[35] But there is nothing to suggest this: the context points rather to a recognition by William of the military prowess displayed by Harold during the Breton expedition. The gift of a helmet is manifestly a mark of honour. There is no reason to go further than this. Even talk of 'dubbing' may be tendentious: William's gesture is not the traditional knightly dubbing which was an indispensable part of chivalric initiation.

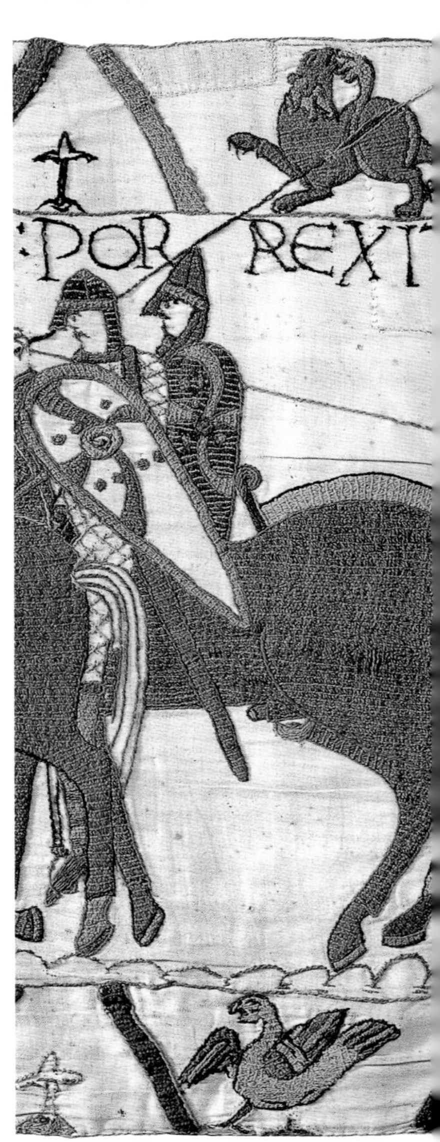

Scene 21

[32] F. Barlow, *William Rufus* (London, 1983), p. 24; see also Orderic Vitalis, ed. Chibnall, vol. 4, p. 120.
[33] *Vita Eduardi regis*, ed. Barlow, p. 32.
[34] Orderic Vitalis, ed. Chibnall, vol. 4, p. 136: 'ab illo [i.e. Edward] cingulum militiae accepit'.
[35] J. Flori, 'Les origines de l'adoubement chevalreseque', *Traditio* 35 (1979), pp. 209-72, at p. 285. Flori offers various other highly questionable interpretations of the Tapestry.

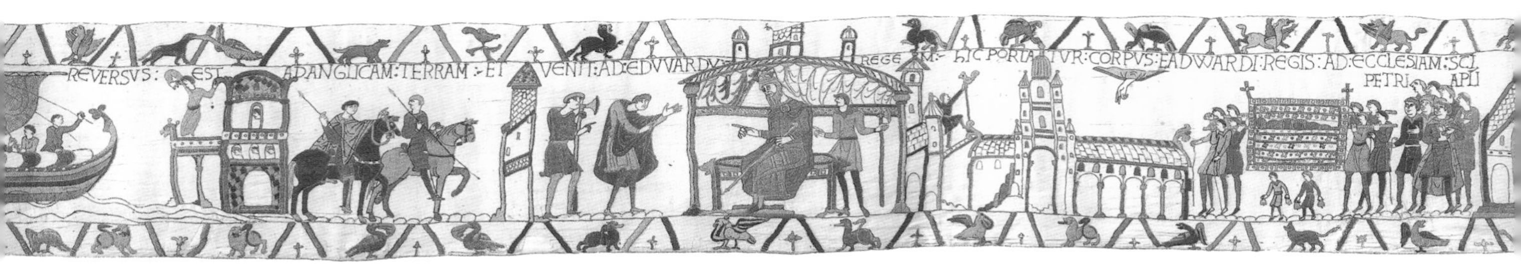

HAROLDO ARMA. HIE [SIC] WILLELM...

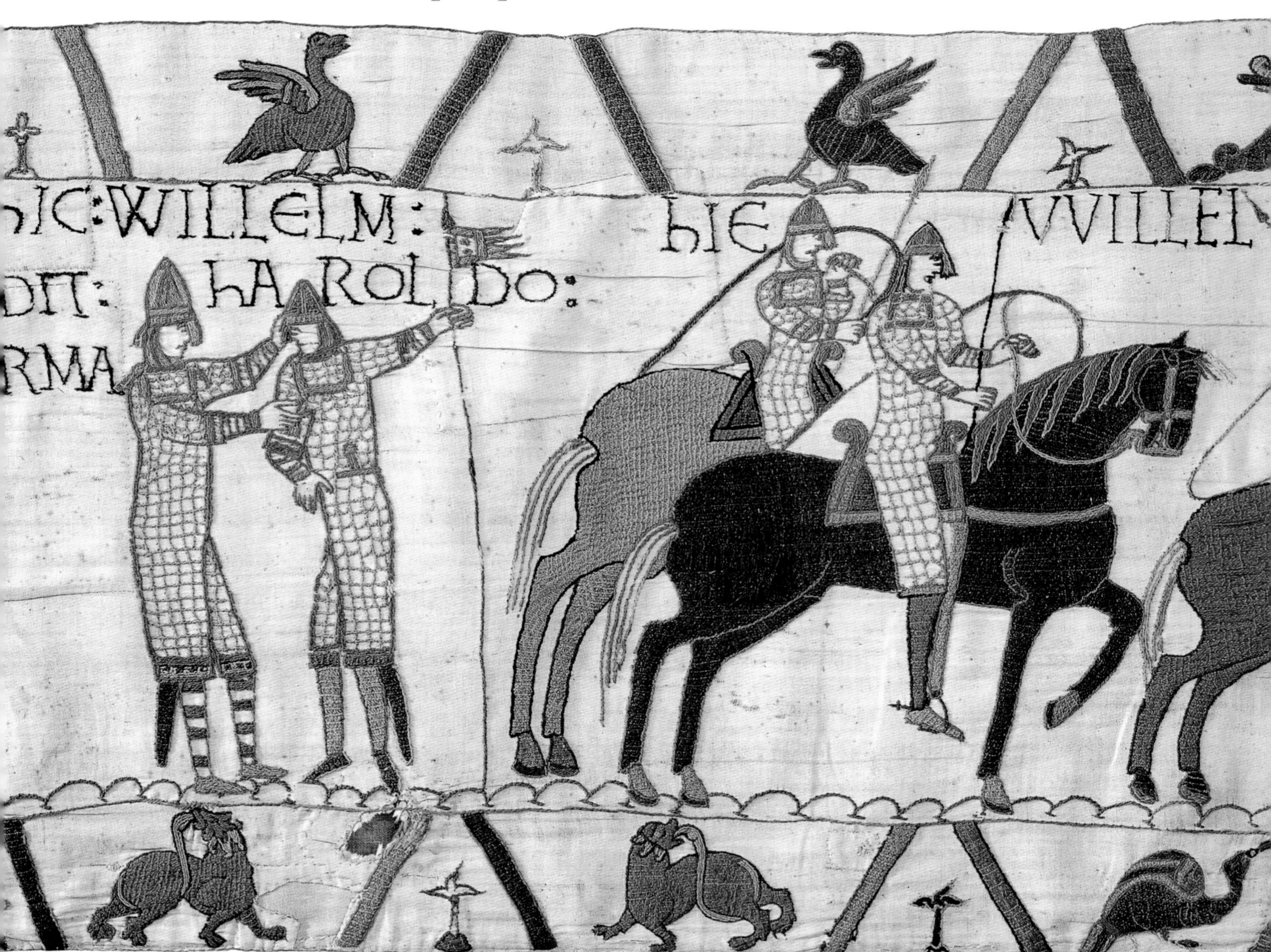

Here William gave arms to Harold. Here William …

Hie (sic) Willelm

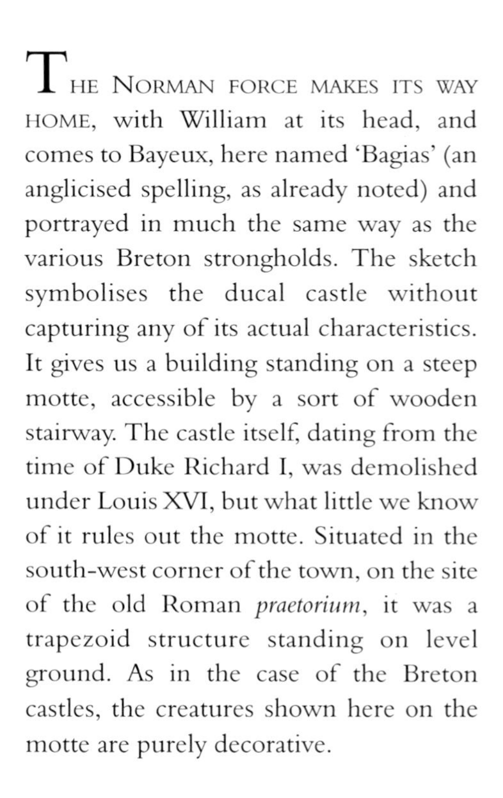

The Norman force makes its way home, with William at its head, and comes to Bayeux, here named 'Bagias' (an anglicised spelling, as already noted) and portrayed in much the same way as the various Breton strongholds. The sketch symbolises the ducal castle without capturing any of its actual characteristics. It gives us a building standing on a steep motte, accessible by a sort of wooden stairway. The castle itself, dating from the time of Duke Richard I, was demolished under Louis XVI, but what little we know of it rules out the motte. Situated in the south-west corner of the town, on the site of the old Roman *praetorium*, it was a trapezoid structure standing on level ground. As in the case of the Breton castles, the creatures shown here on the motte are purely decorative.

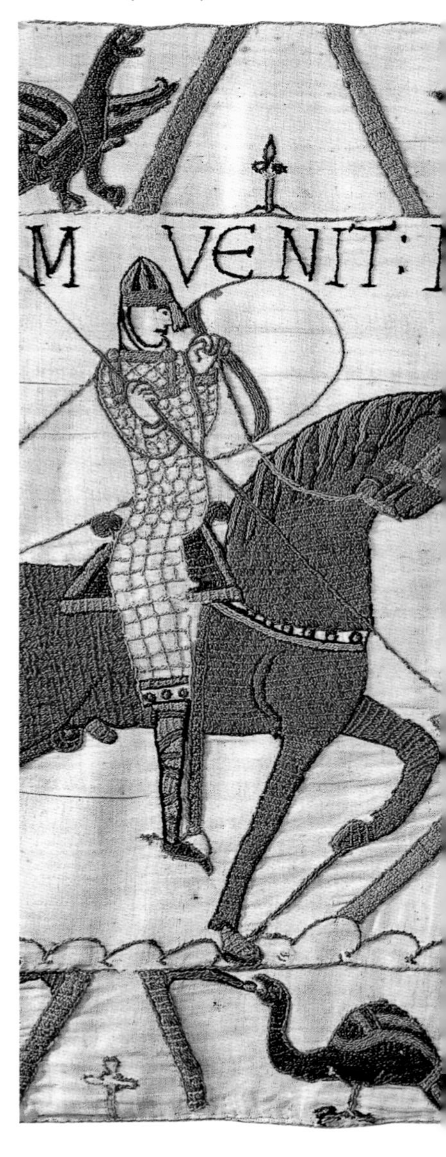

Scenes 22–23

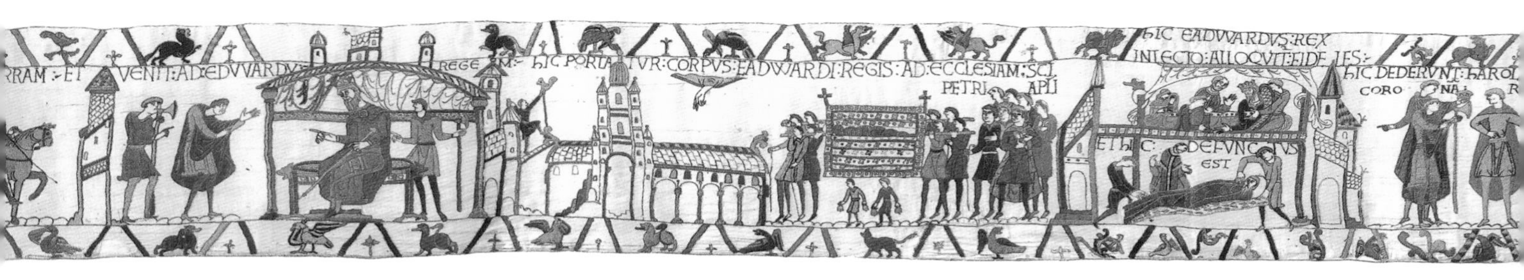

ENIT BAGIAS. UBI HAROLD SACRAMENTUM FECIT WILLELMO DUCI.

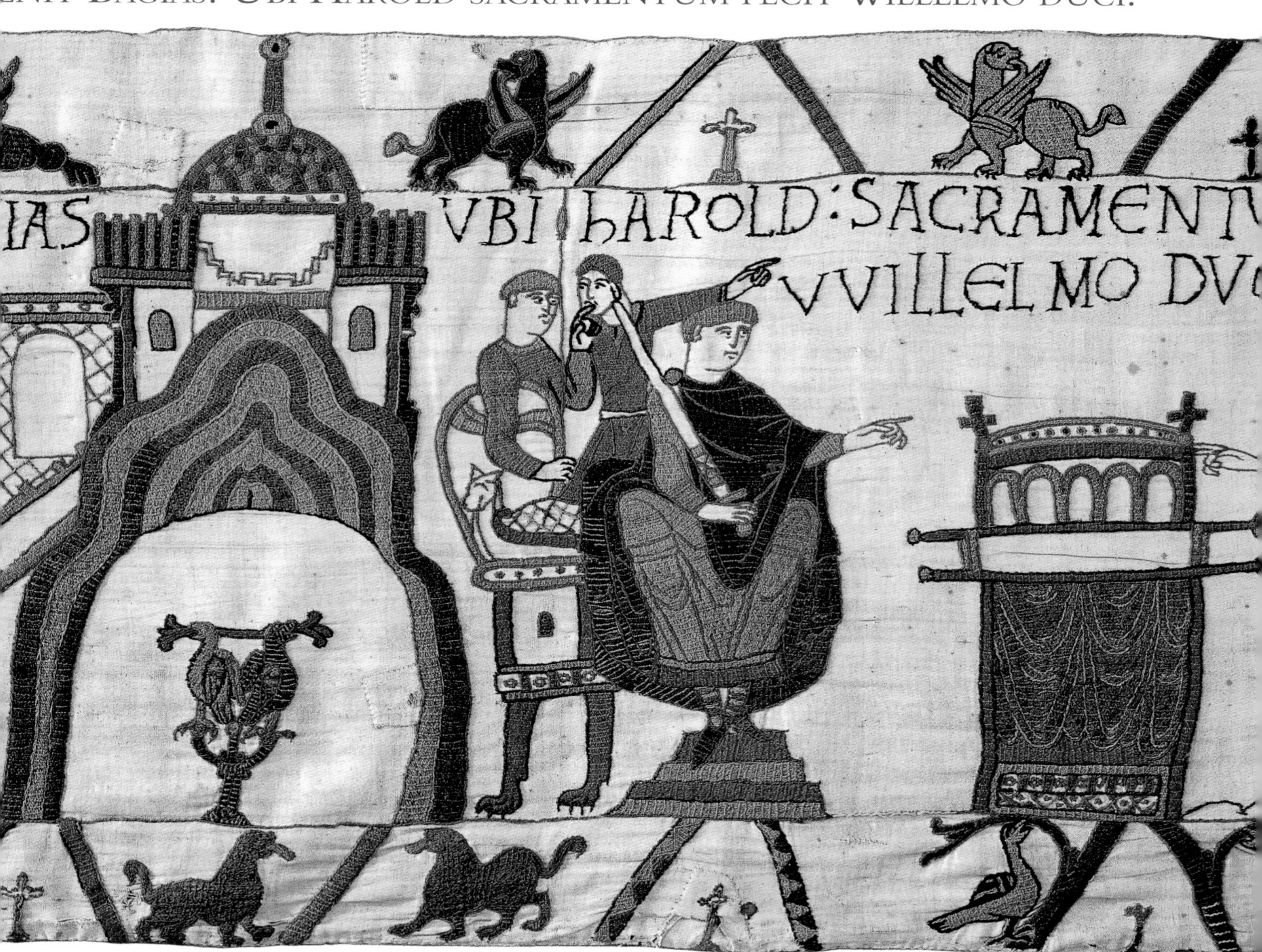

Here William came to Bayeux. Where Harold took an oath to Duke William.

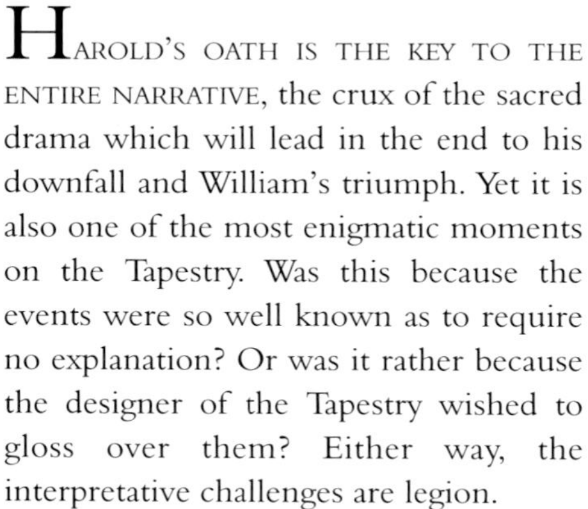

Harold's oath is the key to the entire narrative, the crux of the sacred drama which will lead in the end to his downfall and William's triumph. Yet it is also one of the most enigmatic moments on the Tapestry. Was this because the events were so well known as to require no explanation? Or was it rather because the designer of the Tapestry wished to gloss over them? Either way, the interpretative challenges are legion.

The action unfolds in the presence of Duke William, seated on his throne and bearing his sword, with a spearman on guard behind him. As with the earlier scenes of this kind, the setting is a ducal residence. But the chroniclers disagree as to which it was. According to William of Poitiers, the oath was taken at Bonneville-sur-Touques, a ducal castle of the first order, situated in the hinterland of Trouville and thus close to the route William would have followed in returning from Brittany and Bayeux to Rouen.[36] Bonneville, part of the diocese in which William of Poitiers served as an archdeacon, was not famous for any shrines or relics (though the ducal chapel may perhaps have housed some). Wace, in contrast, places the oath-taking at Bayeux itself, amidst a solemn assembly (a 'parliament') and in the presence of relics which the duke had had gathered there.[37] A rather inferior source, the *Vita Haroldi* compiled towards 1206, sets it in the shade of an oak-tree, the 'perjured

Ubi Harold sacramentum fecit Willel

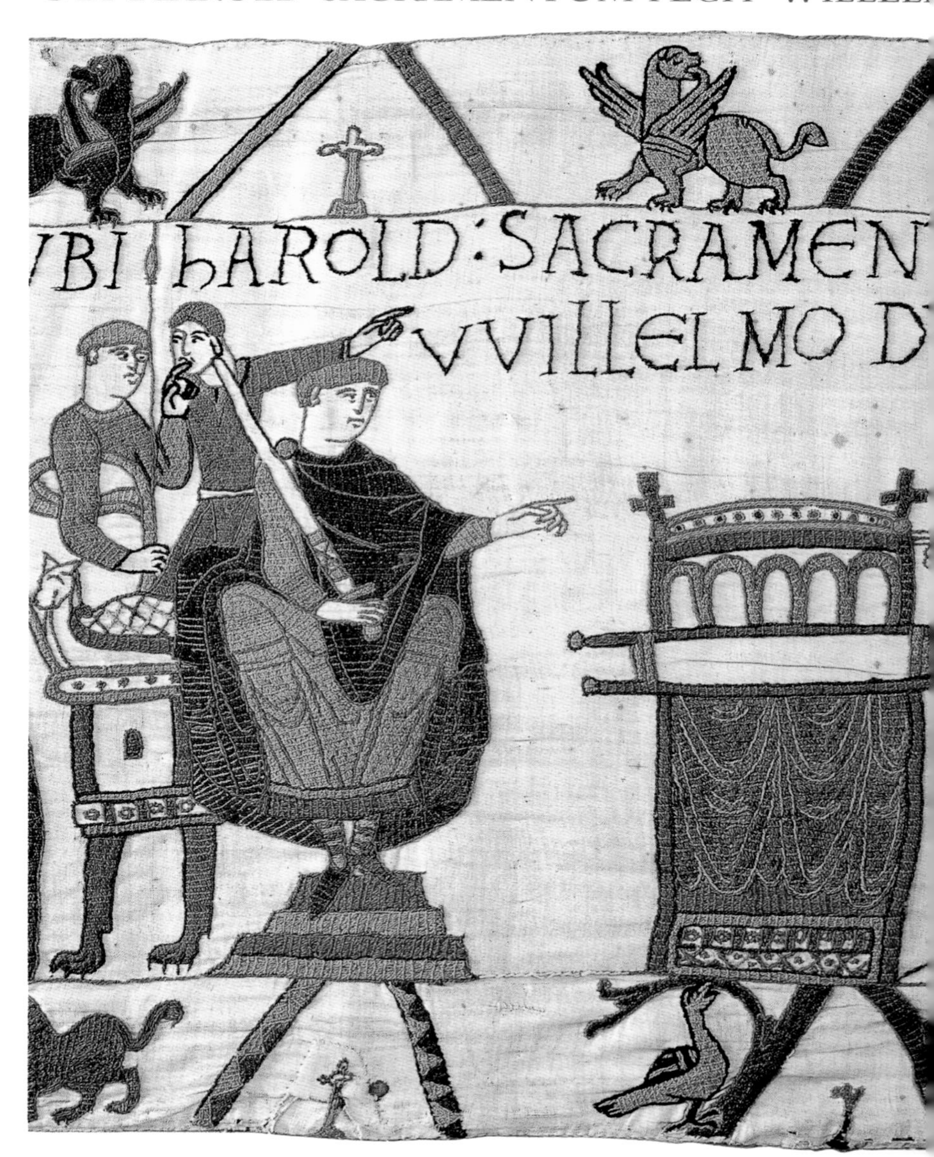

Scenes 23–24

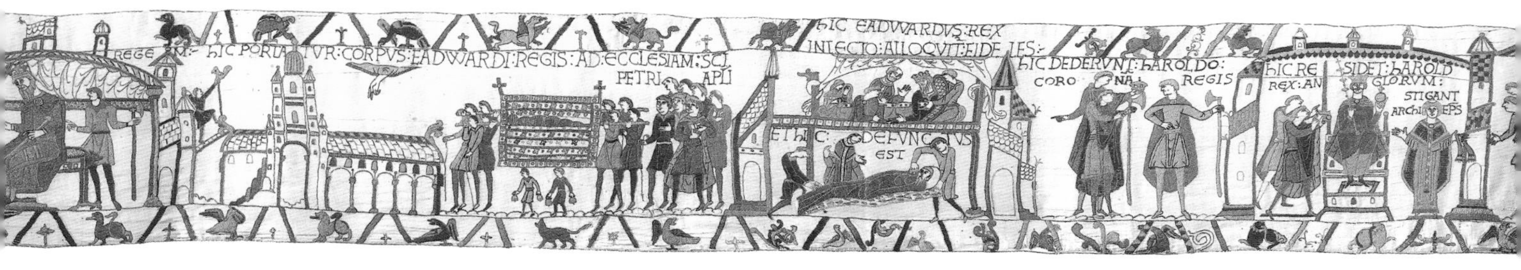

UCI.

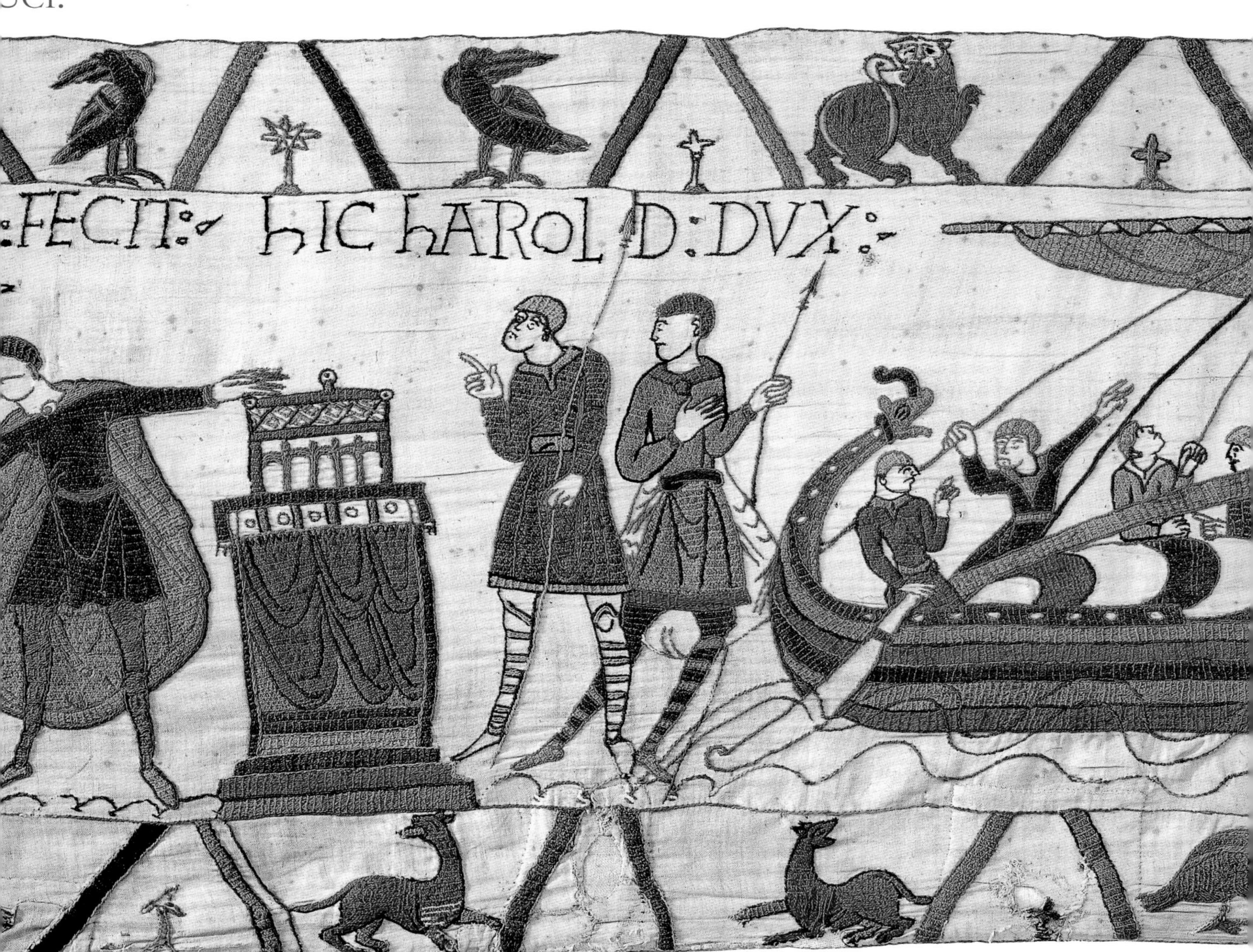

Where Harold took an oath to Duke William.

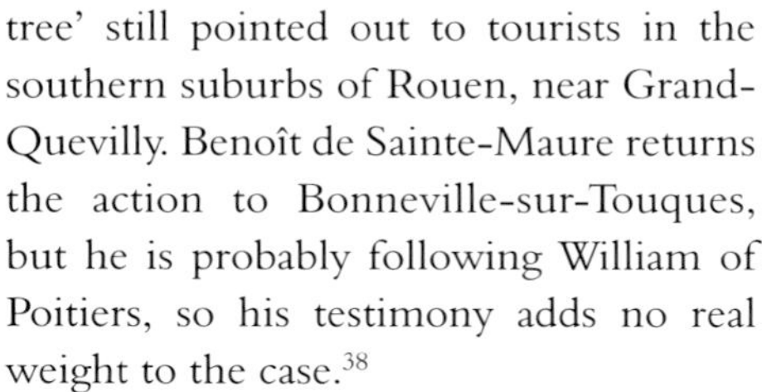

tree' still pointed out to tourists in the southern suburbs of Rouen, near Grand-Quevilly. Benoît de Sainte-Maure returns the action to Bonneville-sur-Touques, but he is probably following William of Poitiers, so his testimony adds no real weight to the case.[38]

At first sight, the Tapestry seems to support the case for the oath having been taken at Bayeux. But it has recently been pointed out that the captions make no definite statement to this effect.[39] There is no necessary logical or grammatical connection between the phrases 'Here William came to Bayeux' and 'Where Harold took an oath to Duke William'. In the latter phrase, 'VBI' ('where') simply refers to the place on the Tapestry, not to any specific geographical location. On this reading, the oath could have been taken anywhere between Bayeux and wherever it was that Harold embarked for England. Thus it could indeed have been Bonneville.

On the other hand, Michel de Boüard argues that William of Poitiers and the Tapestry could actually have been describing two distinct oaths. For William refers to an oath taken prior to the Breton expedition while that mentioned on the Tapestry is taken afterwards. The former, taken at Bonneville, would have related to the English succession, while the latter, taken at Bayeux, would have been the customary oath of fealty sworn after the ceremonial bestowal of knightly arms.

As the Tapestry gives no architectural background for this scene, we cannot tell if it is set in a cathedral or a castle. Nor do the other sources help us decide between a secular or an ecclesiastical context for the oath. Local patriotism could have made William of Poitiers insist on Bonneville because it was in his diocese, while Wace, a canon of Bayeux, could have been led into error either by a hasty reading of the Tapestry or by a local tradition based on it. The choice is a delicate one, but on the whole I incline to Bayeux, as this fits better with the fact that the Tapestry was clearly destined for Bayeux and has always been kept there.

[36] William of Poitiers, ed. Foreville, p. 105 (Davis and Chibnall, pp. 70-71).
[37] Wace, ed. Holden, vol. 2, pp. 97-98 (Burgess and Van Houts, pp. 154-55).
[38] *Vita Haroldi*, ed. F. Michel, *Chroniques anglo-normandes*, vol. 2 (Rouen, 1836), pp. 185-86. Benoît de Saint-Maure, *Chronique des Ducs de Normandie*, ed. C. Fahlin (3 vols. Uppsala, 1951-67), vol. 2, pp. 481-82.
[39] M. Parisse, *La Tapisserie de Bayeux* (Paris, 1983), p. 138.

Ubi Harold sacr

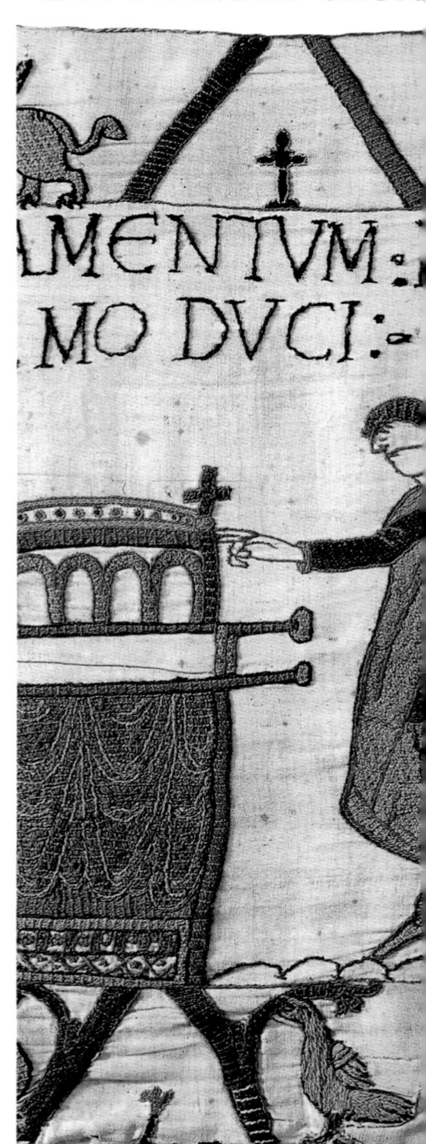

Scene 23

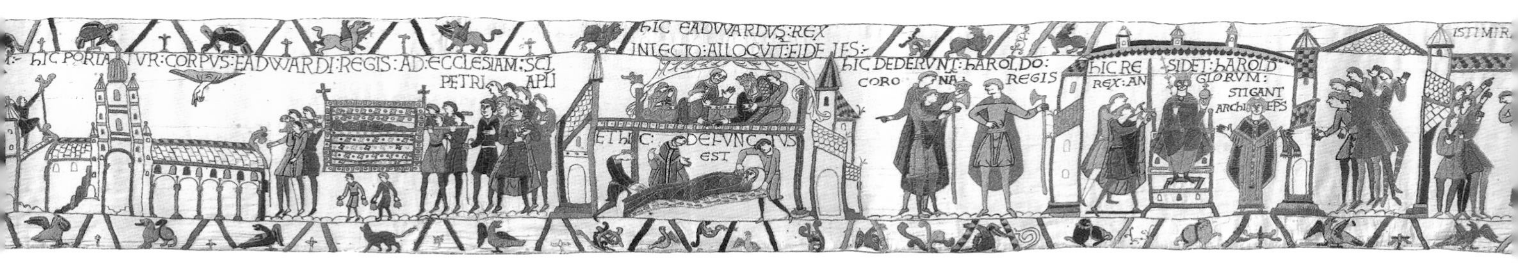

NTUM FECIT WILLELMO DUCI.

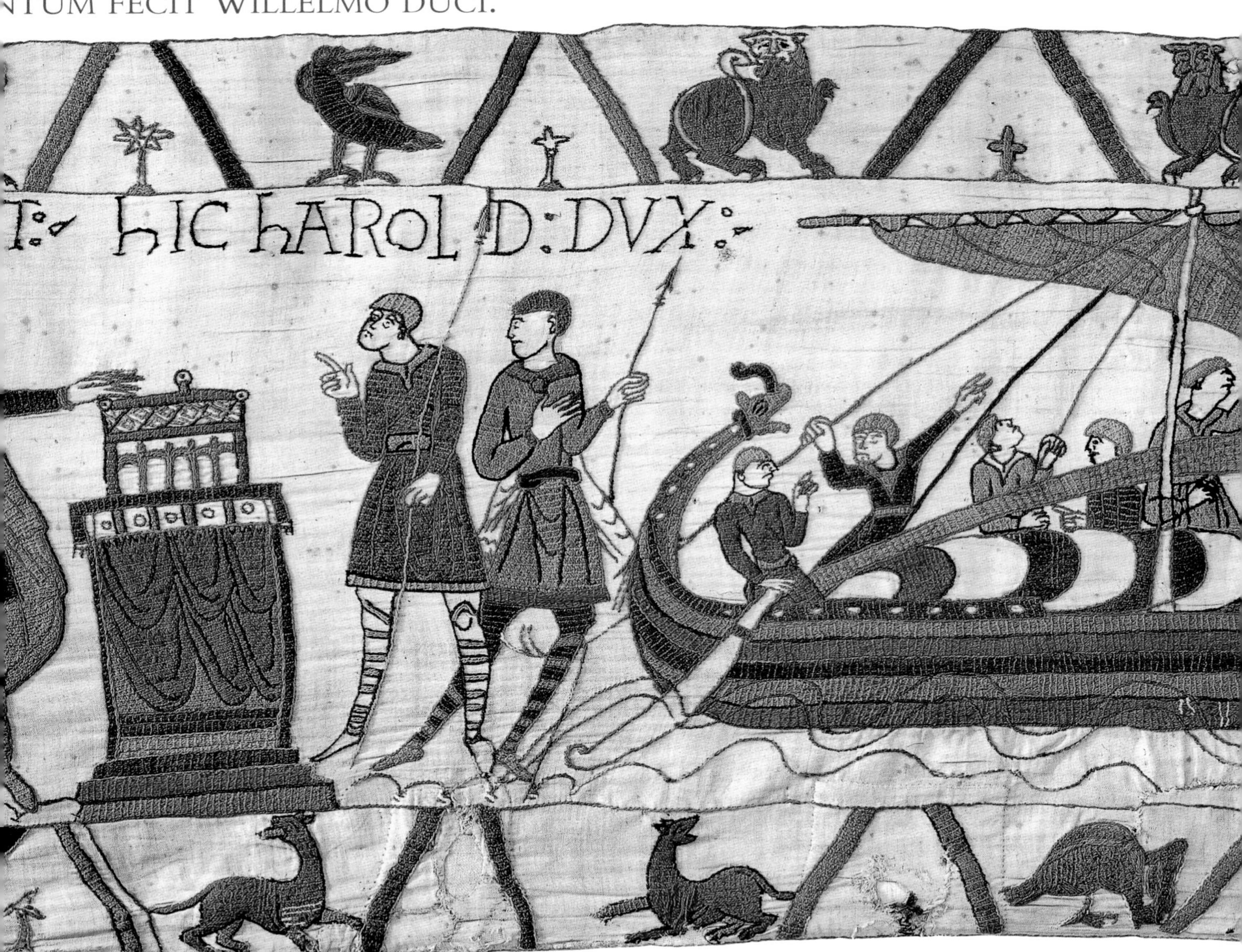

Where Harold took an oath to Duke William.

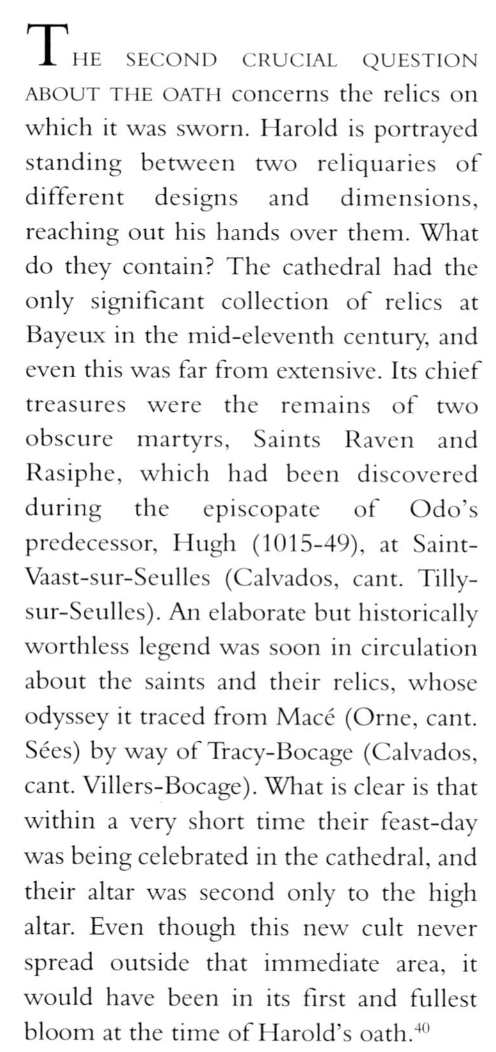

THE SECOND CRUCIAL QUESTION ABOUT THE OATH concerns the relics on which it was sworn. Harold is portrayed standing between two reliquaries of different designs and dimensions, reaching out his hands over them. What do they contain? The cathedral had the only significant collection of relics at Bayeux in the mid-eleventh century, and even this was far from extensive. Its chief treasures were the remains of two obscure martyrs, Saints Raven and Rasiphe, which had been discovered during the episcopate of Odo's predecessor, Hugh (1015-49), at Saint-Vaast-sur-Seulles (Calvados, cant. Tilly-sur-Seulles). An elaborate but historically worthless legend was soon in circulation about the saints and their relics, whose odyssey it traced from Macé (Orne, cant. Sées) by way of Tracy-Bocage (Calvados, cant. Villers-Bocage). What is clear is that within a very short time their feast-day was being celebrated in the cathedral, and their altar was second only to the high altar. Even though this new cult never spread outside that immediate area, it would have been in its first and fullest bloom at the time of Harold's oath.[40]

We know nothing of any relics that there might have been at Bonneville. But Wace provides a clue as to what might have been going on at Bayeux. The duke, he reports, 'ordered all the holy relics to be assembled in one place'.[41] William would thus have brought together some of the duchy's most sacred relics, as he had done before in 1047 to add solemn authority to a peace council that met in a suburb of Caen (now known as Sainte-Paix). The most celebrated relics of Rouen, those of St Ouen and St Catherine, had been brought over for it.[42] It has recently been emphasised that in the eleventh century it was common to solemnise peace councils with relics,[43] and resolving the English succession would have been the best way of ensuring the peace of north-western Europe. The cathedral treasury might well have been augmented with relics from elsewhere for such an occasion.

The two reliquaries are highly ornate, hung with fine cloths, and decorated along their sides with the blind arches which were typical decorative motifs for such artefacts. The one on the right is of a conventional rectilinear design, and seems to be standing on an altar. But the one on the left, placed on a kind of bier decked with precious hangings (which Wace calls a 'paile', and Burgess translates as a silk cloth), has a curved lid in the shape of the hogback roofs seen on several of the buildings on the Tapestry. Intriguingly, we know of a Danish reliquary dating from the early eleventh-century which had precisely this feature. Until 1945 it was to be found in the cathedral treasury at Cammin (or Kamien) in what was then Germany but is now Poland. The reliquary itself

UBI HAROLD SACR

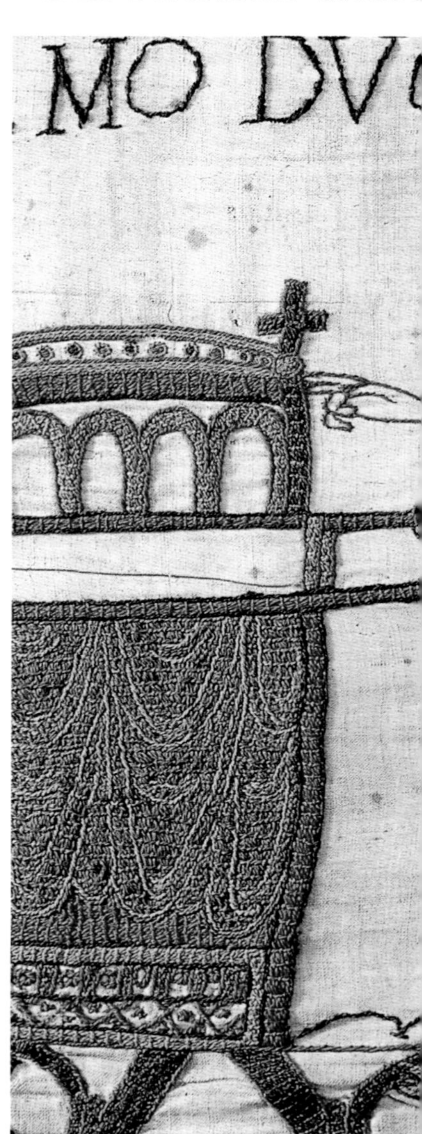

SCENE 23 (detail)

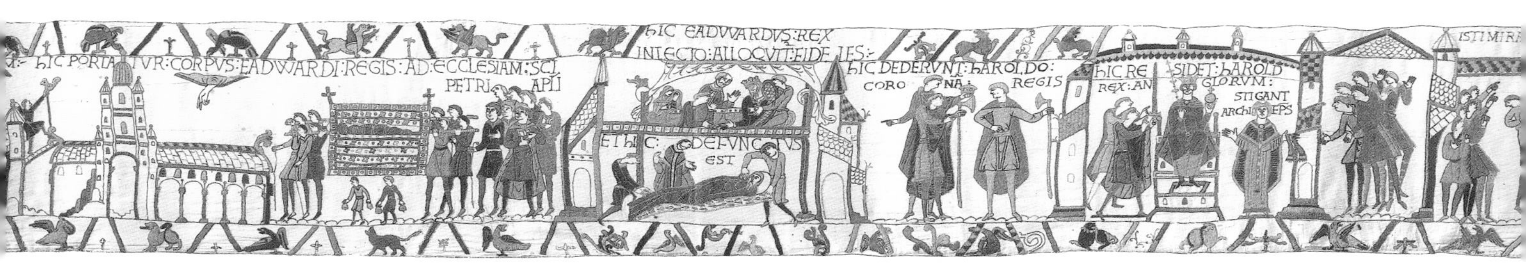

NTUM FECIT WILLELMO DUCI.

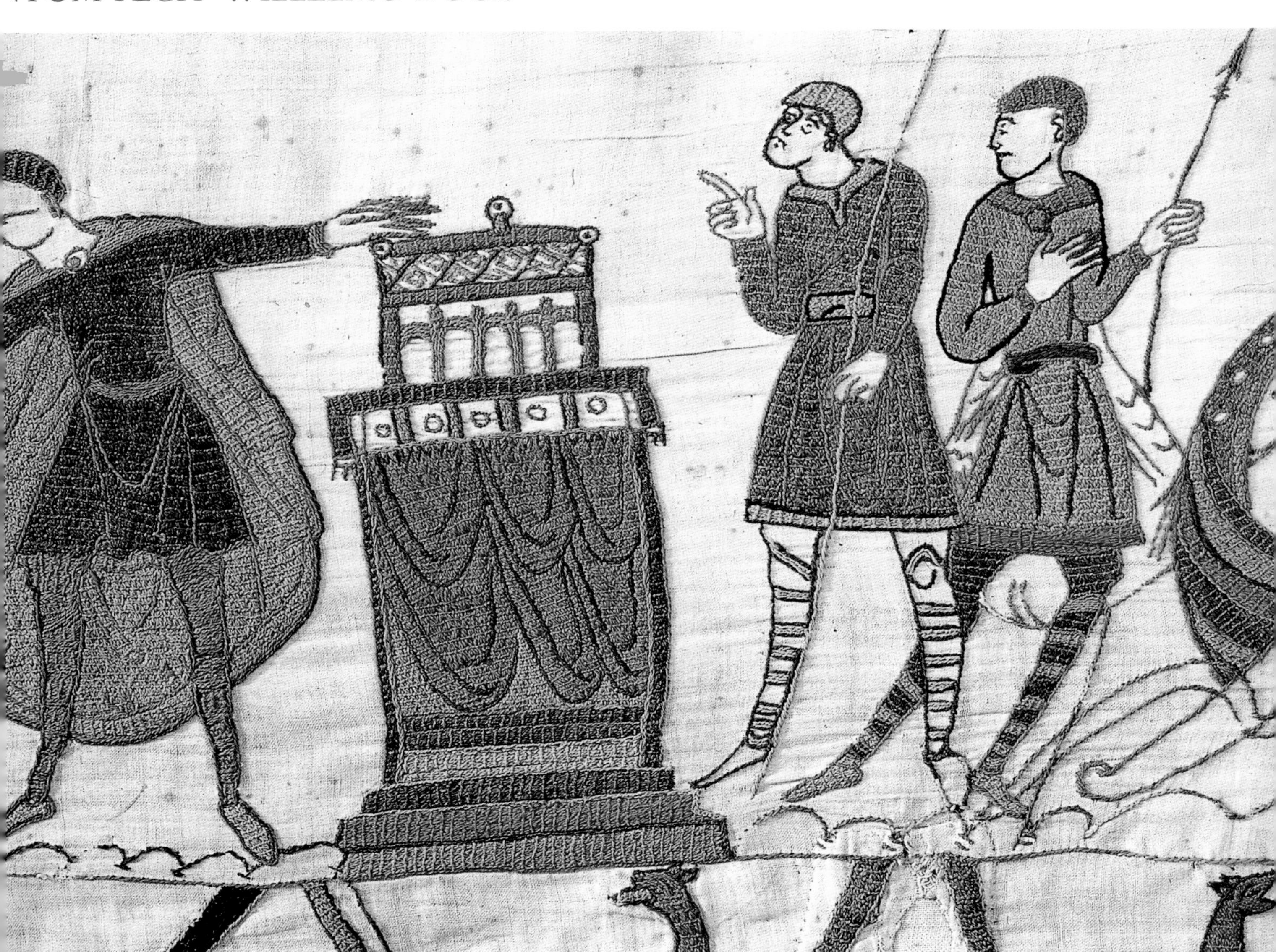

Where Harold took an oath to Duke William.

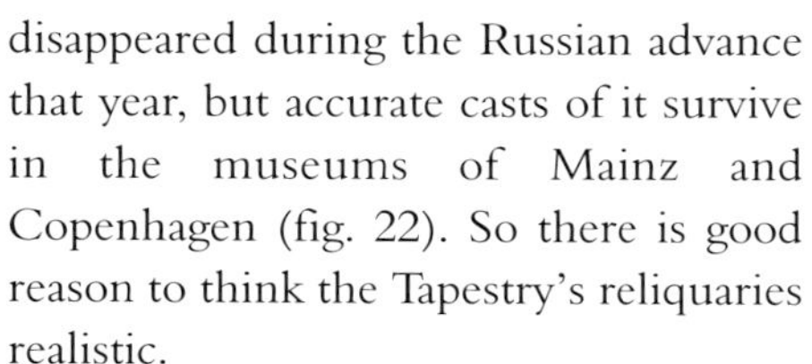

disappeared during the Russian advance that year, but accurate casts of it survive in the museums of Mainz and Copenhagen (fig. 22). So there is good reason to think the Tapestry's reliquaries realistic.

The reliquary upon which Harold swore is described in two twelfth-century texts (Wace and the Hyde chronicle, which know of but one reliquary[44]) as the 'bull's-eye' (*oculum bovis*) from the impressive round gemstone that adorned it. There is no sign of this on the Tapestry, which may indicate that Wace's account represents a narrative tradition independent of that of the Tapestry. The Hyde chronicle adds that among the 'infinite multitude of relics of saints' contained in the reliquary the least remarkable were those of St Pancras. But this is scarcely credible, for while St Pancras was widely venerated in England and also in Flanders, there are few signs of his cult anywhere in Normandy, and none at Bayeux.[45]

Wace's account of the oath claims, uniquely, that Harold had no idea what was really in the chest and therefore did not fully realise the significance of what he was doing. But the Hyde chronicle says just the opposite: 'he knew perfectly well that he could not provoke such a great martyr with impunity'. So the two texts tend to cancel each other out. But Wace's claim is pretty far-fetched. Harold could scarcely have been oblivious of the significance of an oath sworn upon relics. Max Förster found conclusive testimony to the familiarity of this custom in Anglo-Saxon times in a whole series of texts, including a law of Ethelred II from about 997.[46]

[40] B. de Gaiffier, 'Les saints Raven et Rasiphe vénérés en Normandie', *Analecta Bollandiana* 89 (1961), pp. 303-19. For the account of their lives, translation, and miracles, see *Acta Sanctorum*, July, V, pp. 390-94.

[41] Wace, ed. Holden, vol. 2, p. 97, verses 5685-86 (Burgess and Van Houts, p. 154): 'toz les corsainz fist demander / e en un leu toz assenbler'.

[42] *Miracula S. Audoeni, A. A. SS. Aug.*, IV, p. 834, C. 51; *Miracula S. Catharinae*, ed. Poncelet, *Analecta Bollandiana* 22 (1903), p. 435, C. 25.

[43] See J. F. Lemarignier's comment in discussion in *Cristianizzazione ed organizzazione ecclesiastica delle campagne nell'Alto Medioevo = Settimane di studio del Centro Italiano di Studi sull'Alto Medioevo, Spoleto* 28 (1980), pp. 269-70.

[44] Wace, ed. Holden, vol. 2, p. 98, verses 5691-94 (Burgess and Van Houts, p. 154); *Liber Monasterii de Hyde*, ed. Edwards, p. 290. This latter text is rather fanciful, and asserts that William betrothed one of his daughters to Harold.

[45] D. Bernstein, 'The blinding of Harold and the meaning of the Bayeux Tapestry', *Anglo-Norman Studies* 5 (1982), pp. 40-64. There is no particular reason to identify the 'bull's-eye' with the round knob on top of the reliquary on the right. For the cult in Flanders, see W. Wattenbach, 'Reliquien in Gent', *Neues Archiv* 8 (1883), pp. 366-77.

[46] M. Förster, *Zur Geschichte des Reliquien Kultus in Altengland* (Sitzungsberichte der Bayerischen Akademie der Wissenschaften. Philosophisch-historisch Abteilung 8. Munich, 1943), pp. 17-19.

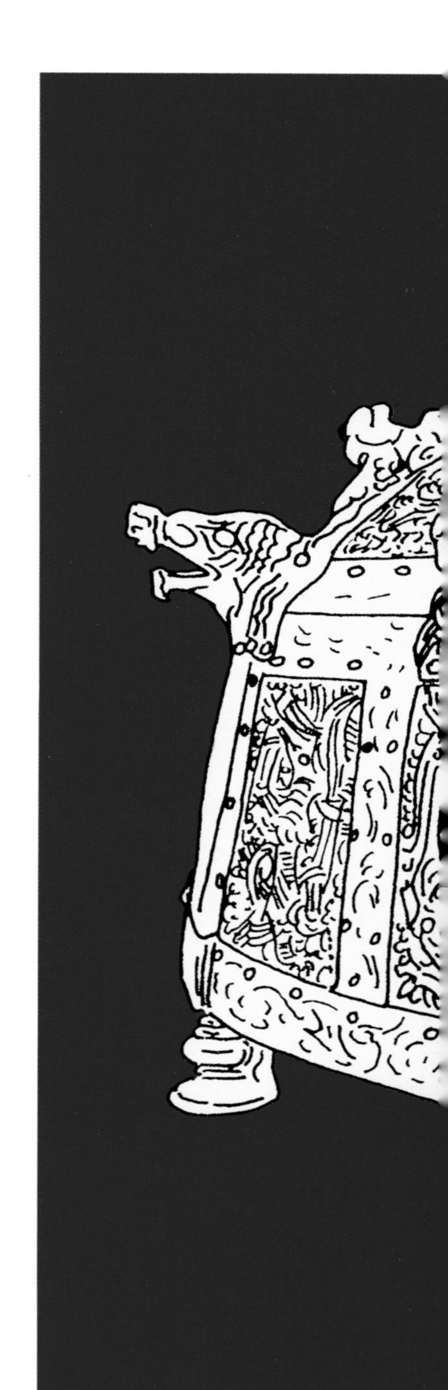

22. The Cammin (Pomerania) Reliquary, from a cast belonging to Copenhagen museum.

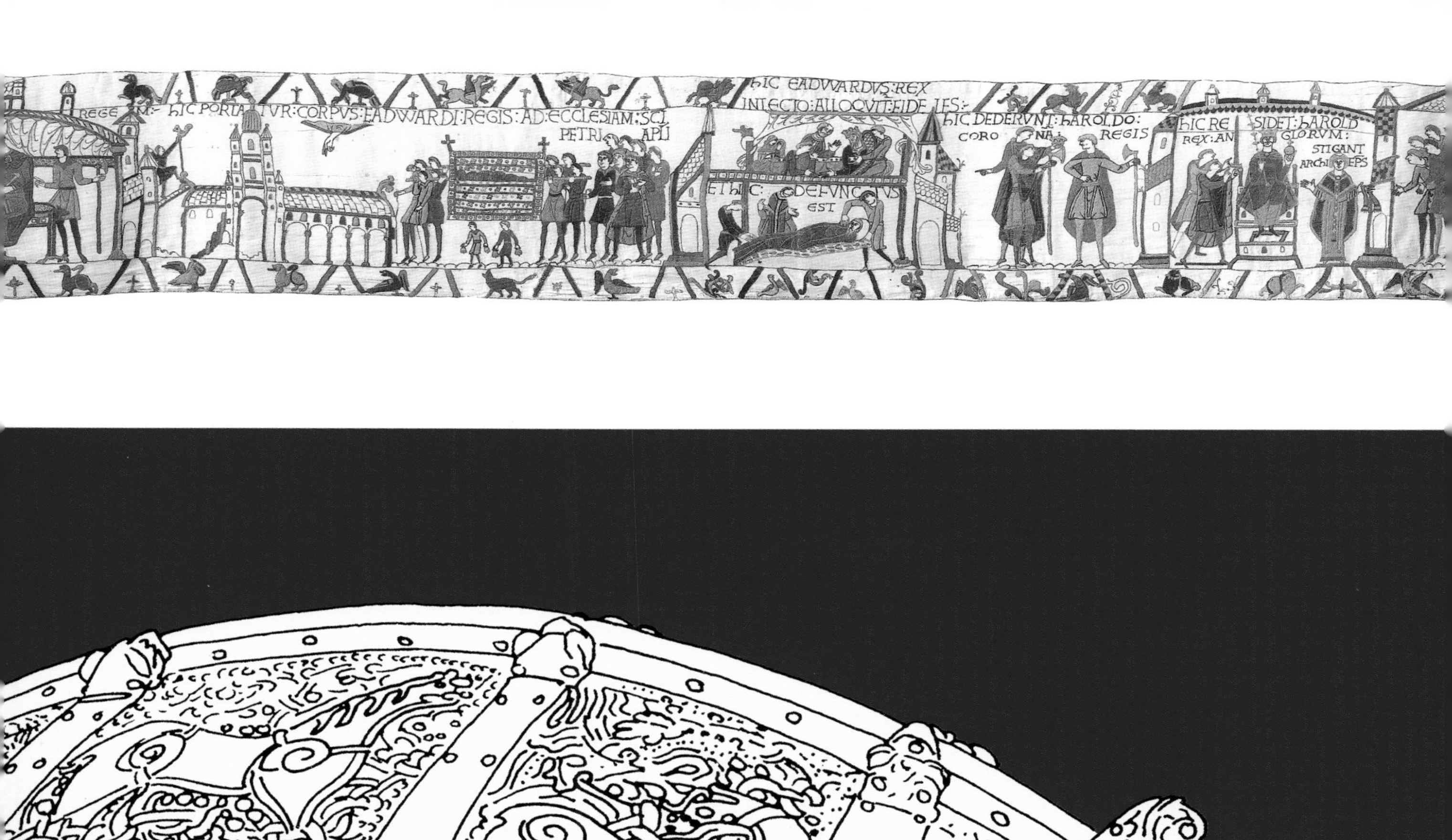
REGE
HIC PORTATUR: CORPUS: EADWARDI: REGIS: AD: ECCLESIAM: SCI
PETRI APLI
HIC EADWARDUS: REX
IN LECTO: ALLOQUIT: FIDELES:
ET HIC DEFUNCTUS EST
HIC DEDERUNT: HAROLDO:
CORO NA: REGIS
HIC RESIDET: HAROLD
REX: ANGLORUM:
STIGANT
ARCHIEPS

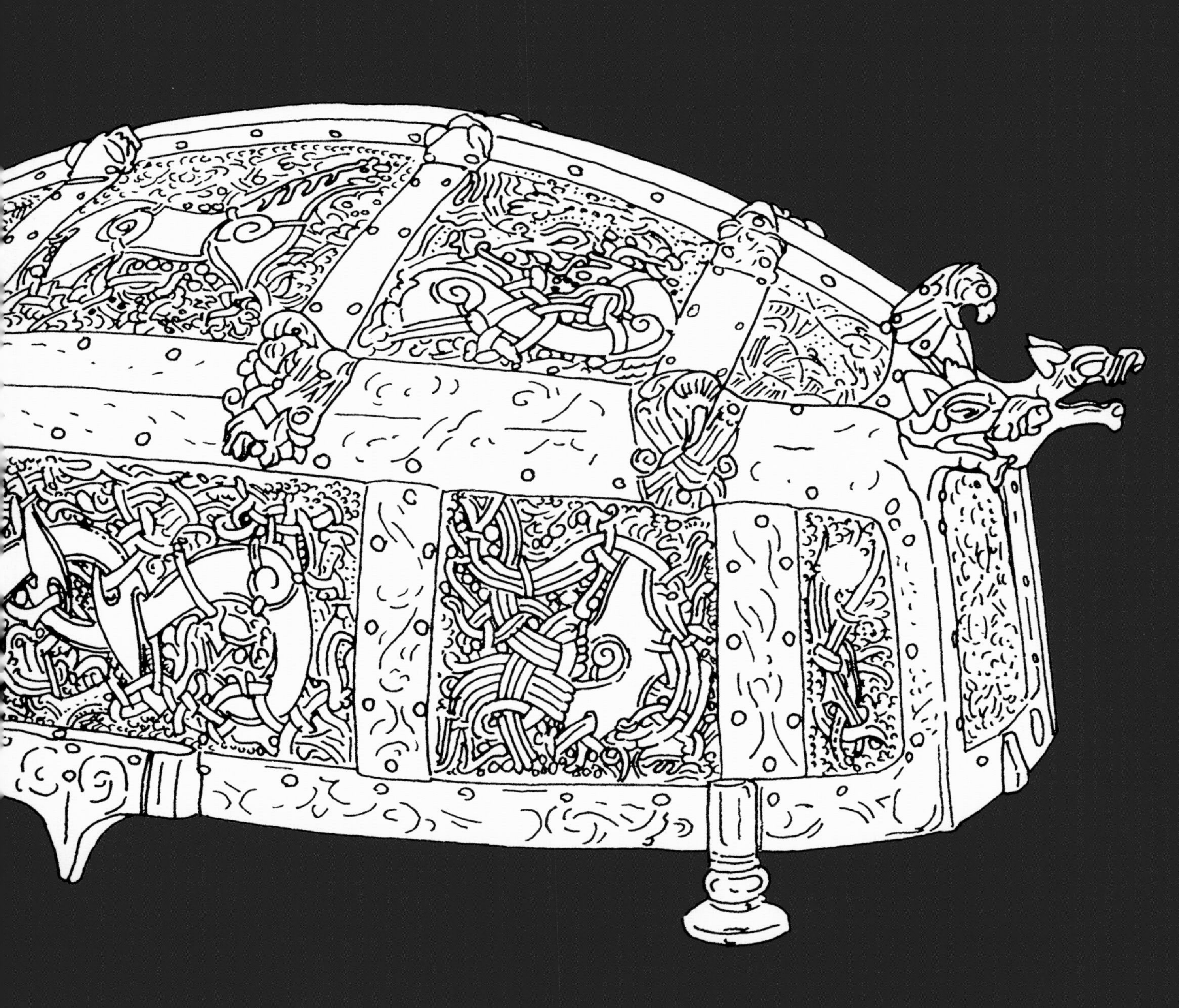

THE CRUCIAL QUESTION FOR THE HISTORIAN remains that of what Harold actually swore, and the Tapestry's vagueness on this could well be deliberate. Perhaps even then there were conflicting accounts of the oath. Modern scholars for the most part agree that the oath concerned the succession to the English throne and that Harold bound himself to respect William's claim to it. Anything more than this is mere speculation, though it does look as though, whatever its precise terms, the oath left a bitter aftertaste in English mouths. The 'Life of Edward the Confessor' describes Harold as 'too prone to oaths, more's the pity'.[47] The chronicler of the abbey of Saint-Riquier in Picardy gratuitously credits him with another broken oath, by which he allegedly promised King Edward that he would promote the succession of Edgar Atheling.[48] An unfortunate reputation for perjury therefore hung about Harold's name even outside Normandy.

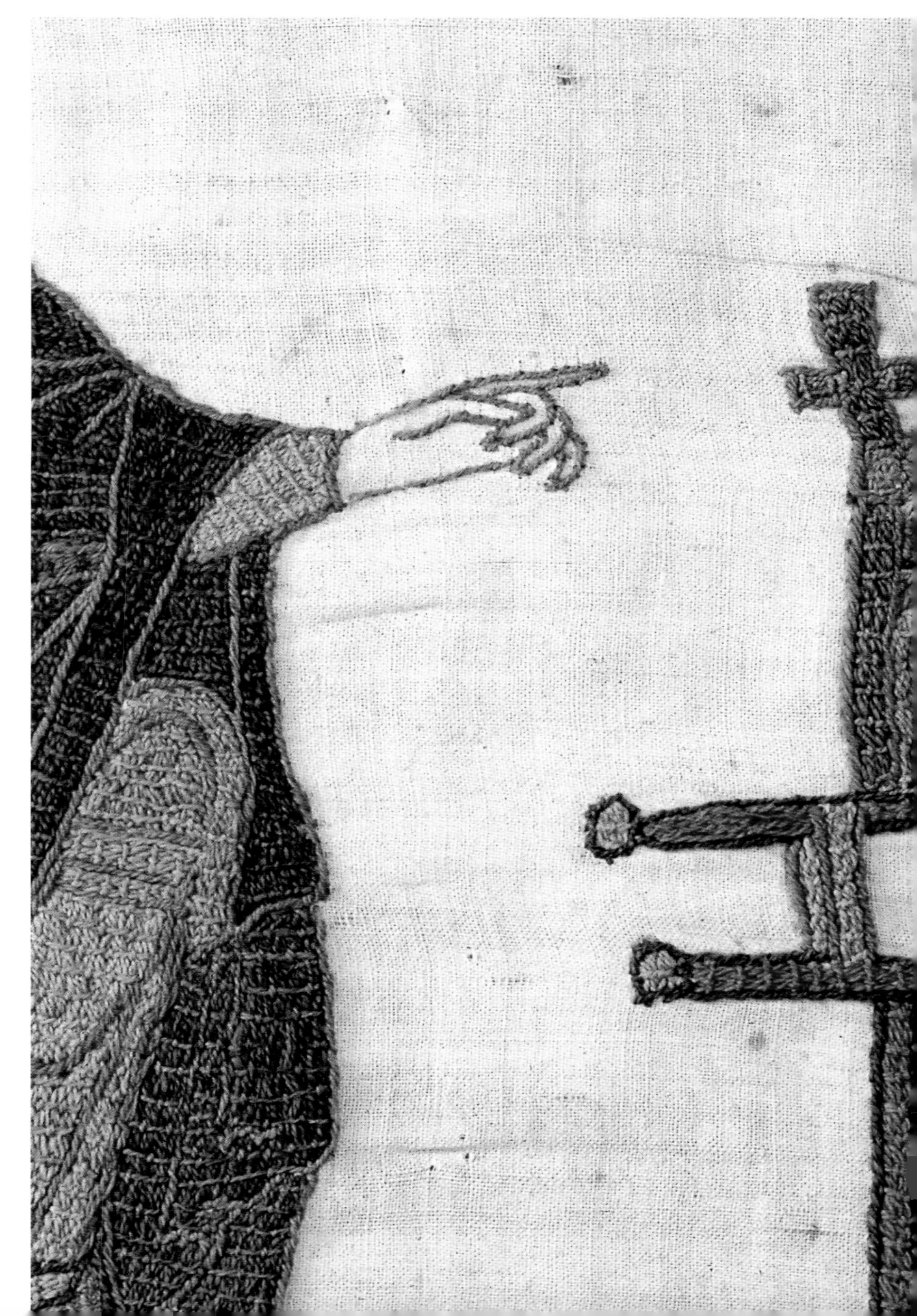

[47] *Vita Edwardi*, ed. Barlow, p. 62: 'ad sacramenta nimis, proh dolor, prodigus'.
[48] Hariulf, *Chronique de l'abbaye de Saint-Riquier*, ed. Lot, p. 241.

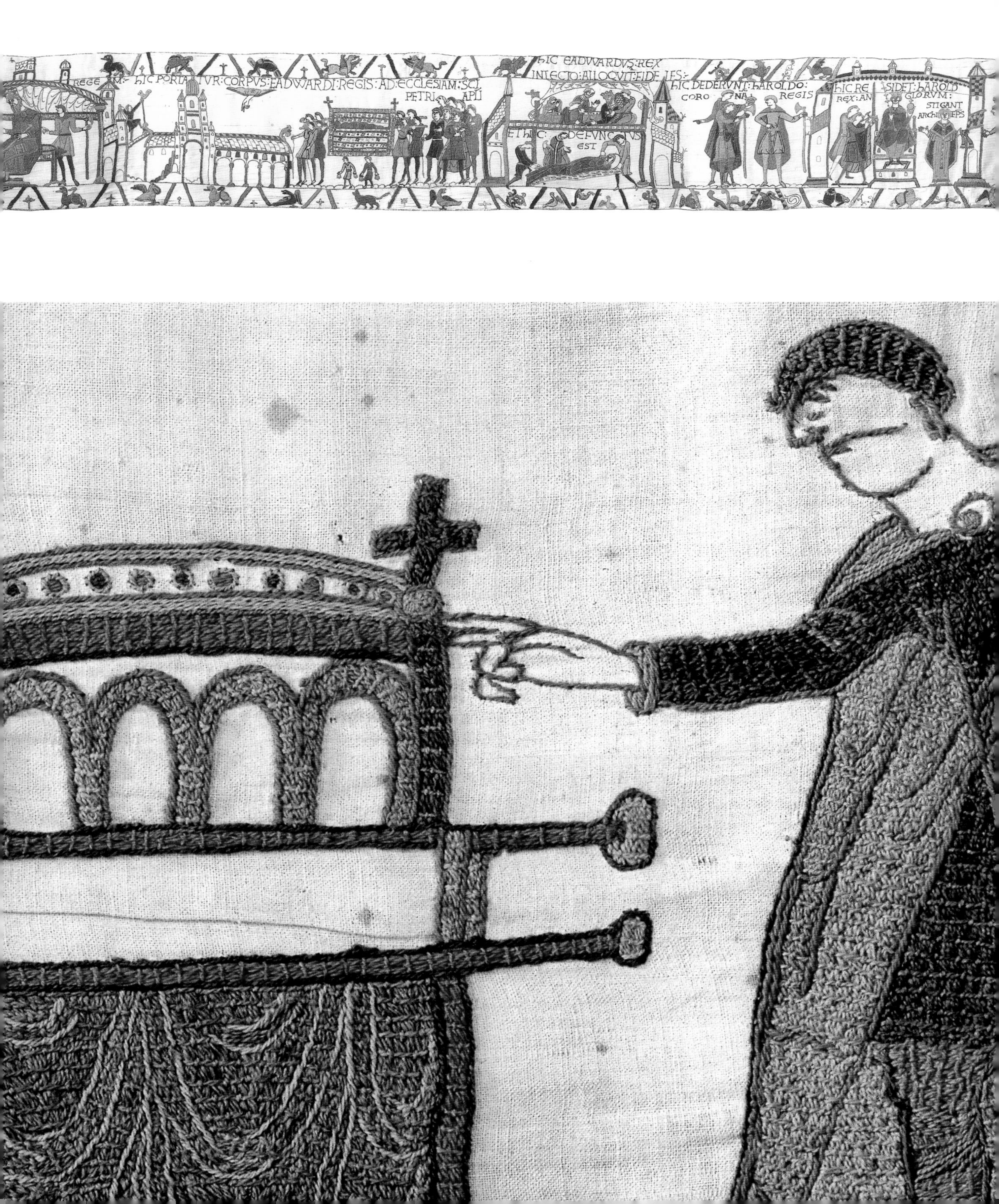

REGE
HIC PORTATUR CORPUS EADWARDI REGIS AD ECCLESIAM SCI PETRI APLI
HIC EADWARDUS REX IN LECTO ALLOQUIT FIDELES
ET HIC DEFUNCTUS EST
HIC DEDERUNT HAROLDO CORONA REGIS
HIC RESIDET HAROLD REX ANGLORUM
STIGANT ARCHIEPS

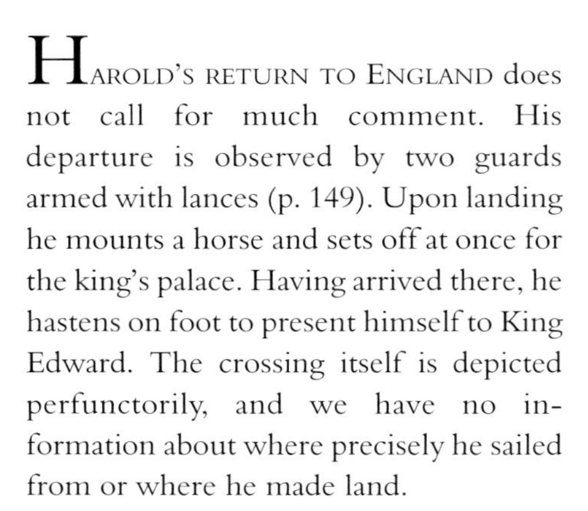

HAROLD'S RETURN TO ENGLAND does not call for much comment. His departure is observed by two guards armed with lances (p. 149). Upon landing he mounts a horse and sets off at once for the king's palace. Having arrived there, he hastens on foot to present himself to King Edward. The crossing itself is depicted perfunctorily, and we have no information about where precisely he sailed from or where he made land.

One can perhaps hazard some conjectures as to his landfall from the apparently urban character of the structure from which a look-out watches for his arrival. The building seems to be a house which opens onto the street by means of an archway. Three faces peer out from the three windows of the rather cramped first storey; the second floor, with but one window, sits under a hogback roof. It looks rather like the kind of building described in the following terms in the cartulary of Oseney Abbey: 'a shop [*schopa*] with a sun-room [*solarium*] above and a cellar [*celarium*] beneath', although there is nothing on the Tapestry to suggest that the ground-floor is a cellar (i.e. a store for merchandise).[49] The animal's head adorning the parapet of the balcony protruding towards the sea suggests that this extension at least, if not the whole building, was of timber construction. As to the location of the house, Southampton or Dover would be the most obvious possibilities, depending on whether the royal palace in the next scene is meant to be Winchester or Westminster.

HIC HAROLD DUX R

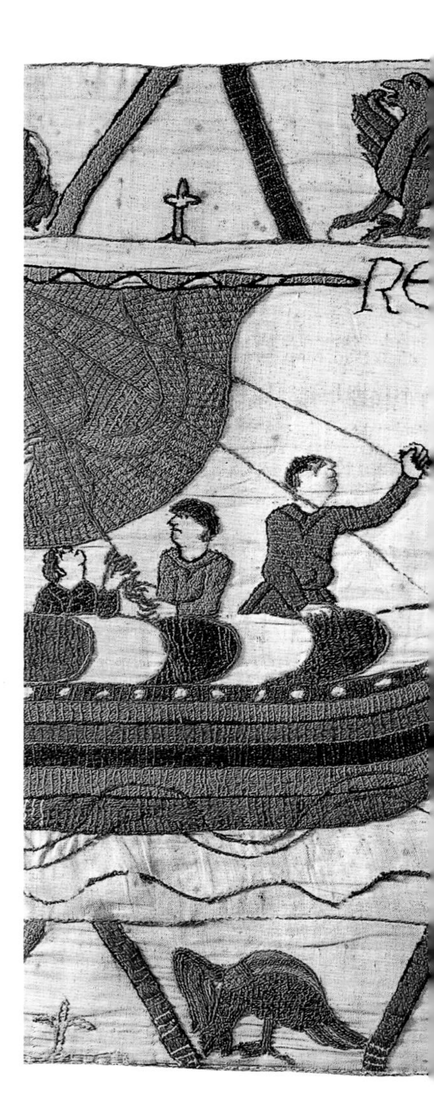

SCENE 24

[49] U. T. Holmes, 'The houses of the Bayeux Tapestry', *Speculum* 34 (1969), pp. 179-83, at p. 192.

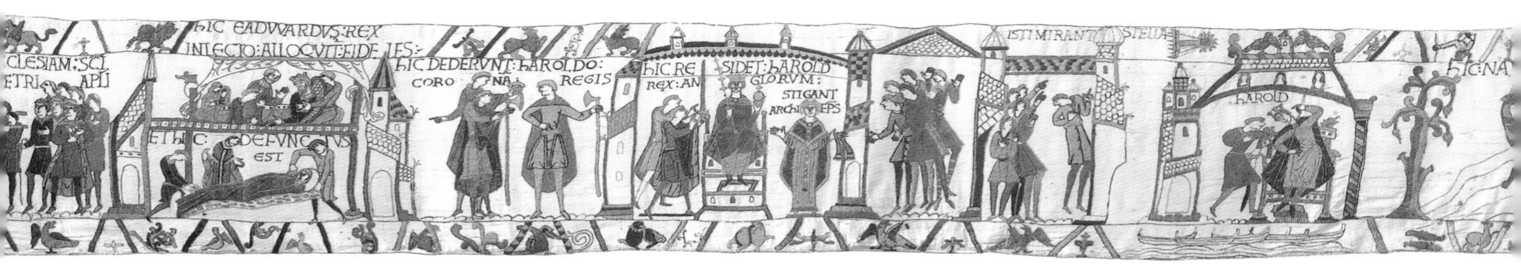

SUS EST AD ANGLICAM TERRAM...

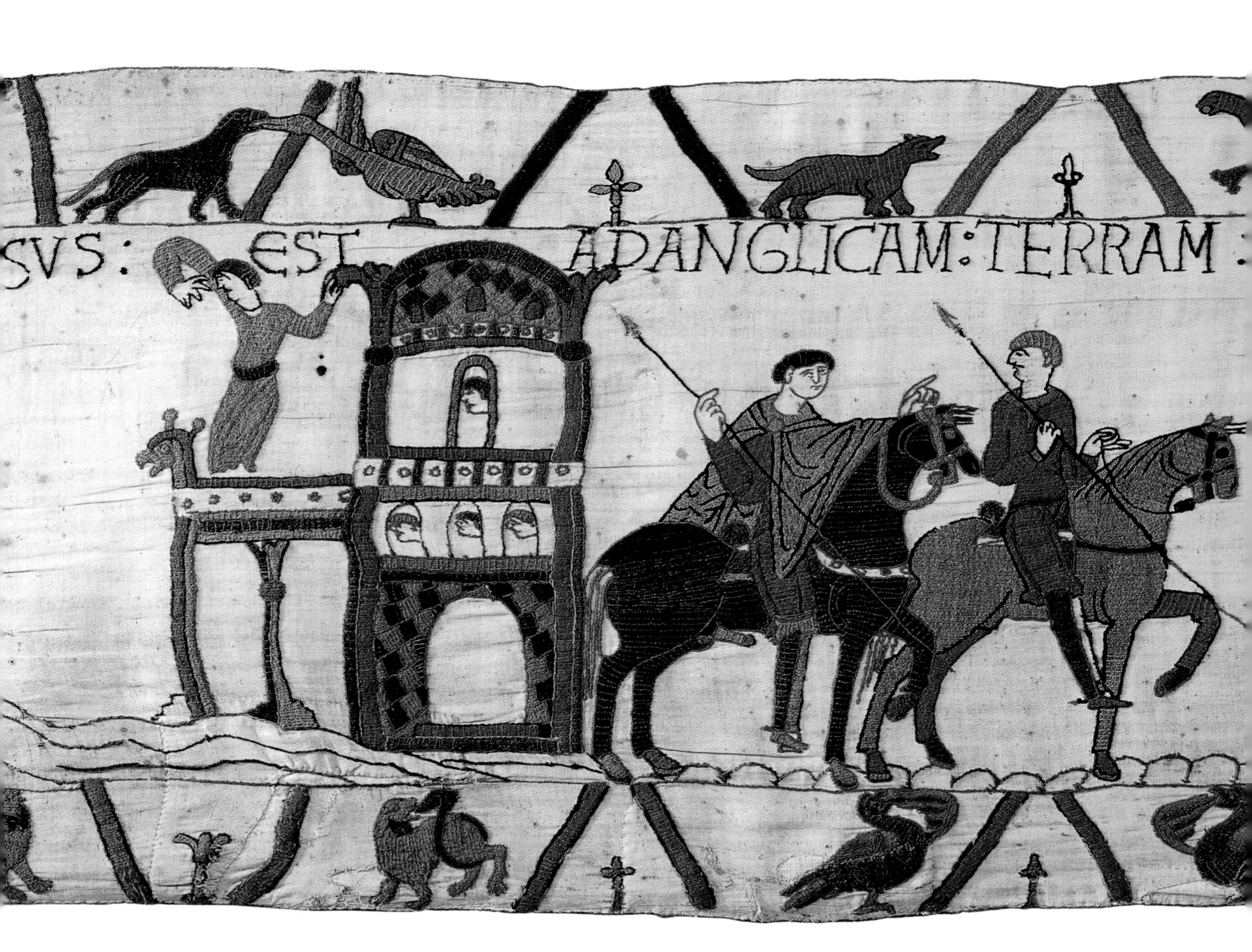

Here Duke Harold returned to the English land …

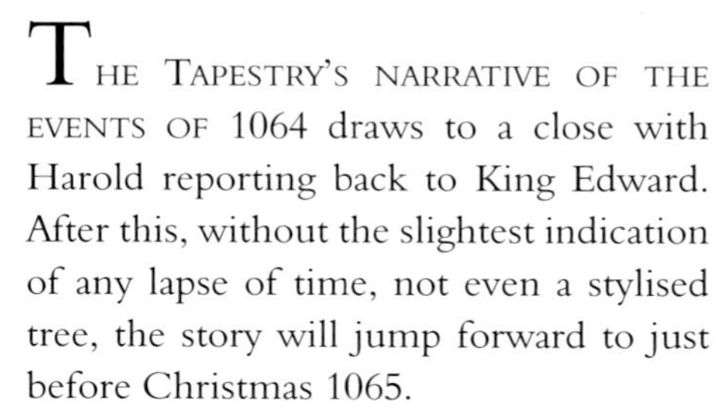

The Tapestry's narrative of the events of 1064 draws to a close with Harold reporting back to King Edward. After this, without the slightest indication of any lapse of time, not even a stylised tree, the story will jump forward to just before Christmas 1065.

King Edward receives Harold in a palace, but it cannot certainly be identified with that of Westminster, where he is next seen (scene 27, p. 165), as this palace is schematic rather than realistic. Edward himself is seated not on a throne, but on a bench covered with a cushion. He has the same robes and insignia as in the opening scene of the Tapestry. This is the last time he appears in good health, but he seems older and more tired, his head and neck lolling to one side. His physical decline is more marked than his age would lead us to expect. He was over 60, which was a great age by the standards of the time. Hardly any English king since the ninth century had reached such an age, and neither Harold nor William would do so (both dying violent deaths, the former at about 45, the latter at 59).

Edward and Harold are each attended by a guard armed with the housecarl's characteristic battle-axe. As usual, the caption tells us nothing of what is going on, preferring to gloss over controversial topics. Harold approaches his sovereign in an attitude of self-abasement, but whether out of shame over what happened in Normandy or out of merely conventional deference is far from clear.

... ET VENIT AD EDW

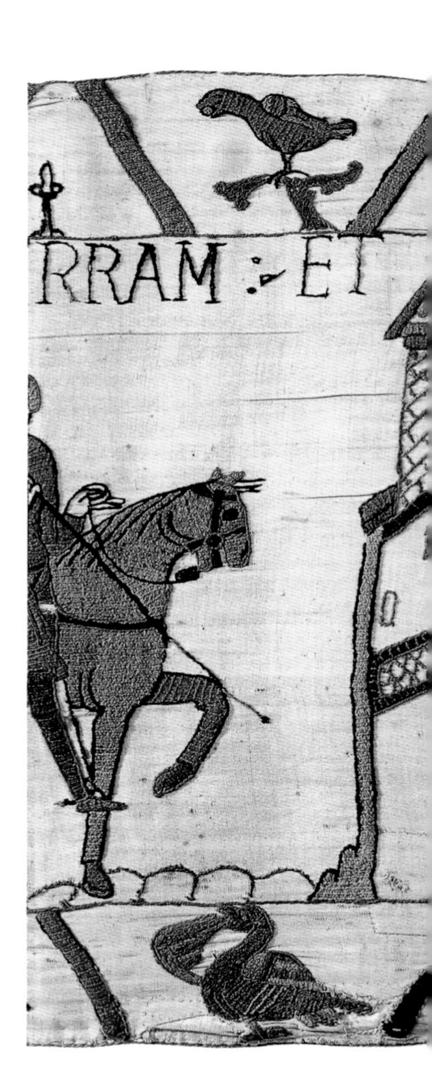

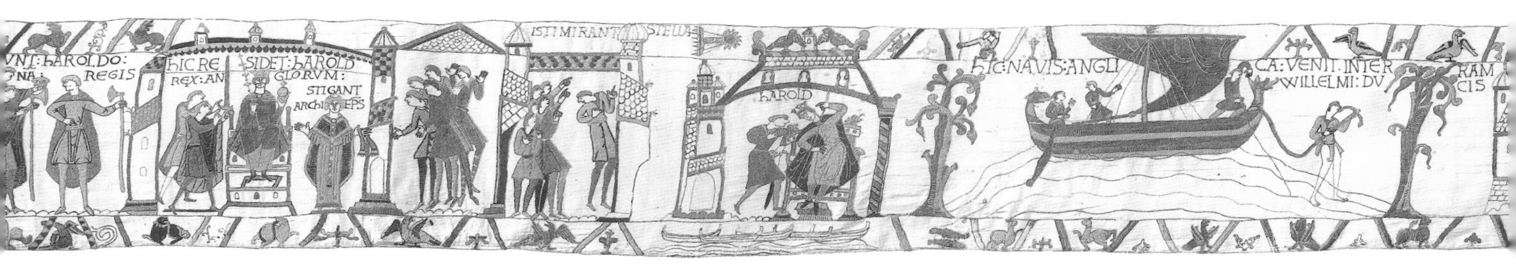

M REGEM.

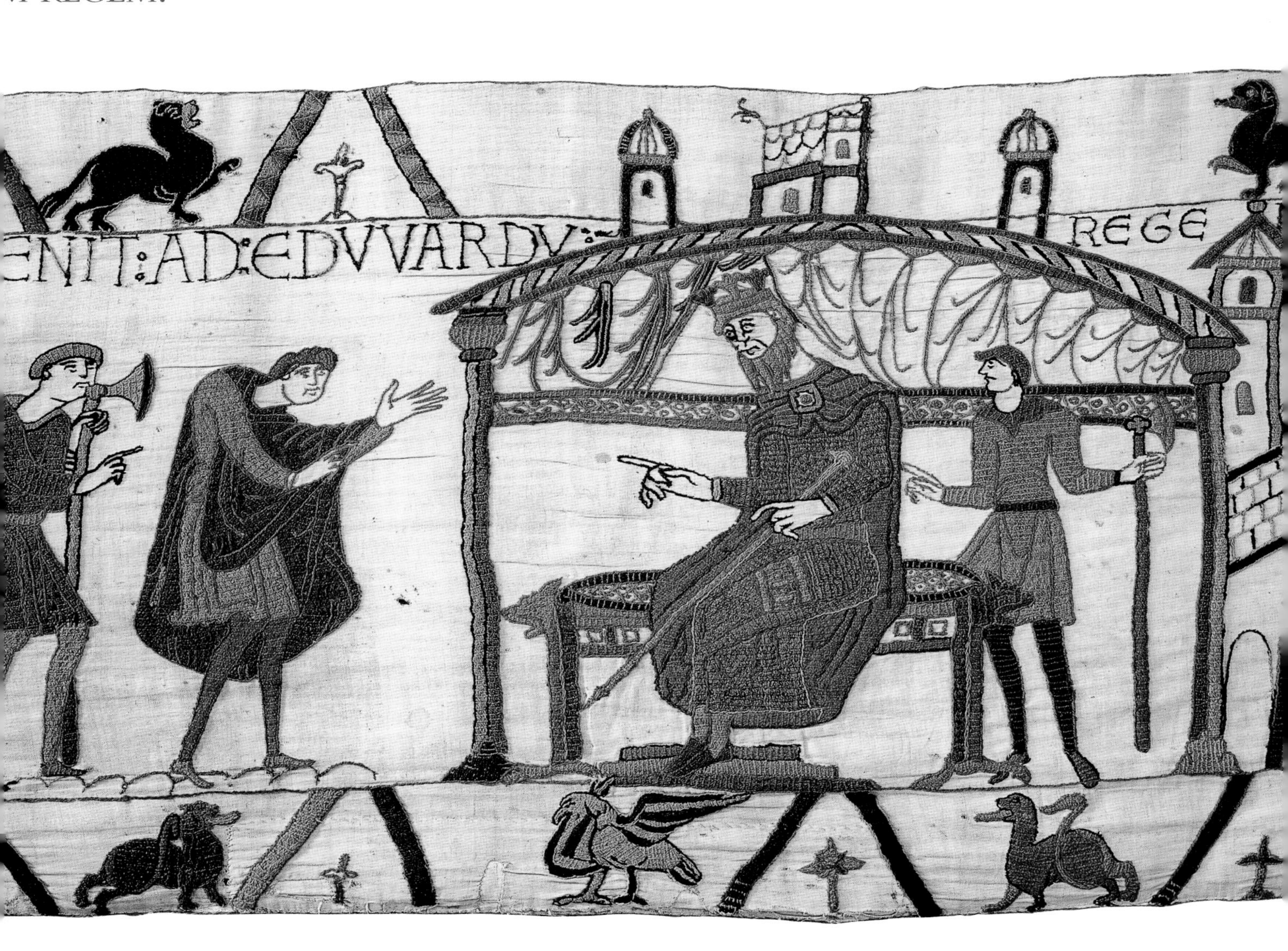

...and came to King Edward.

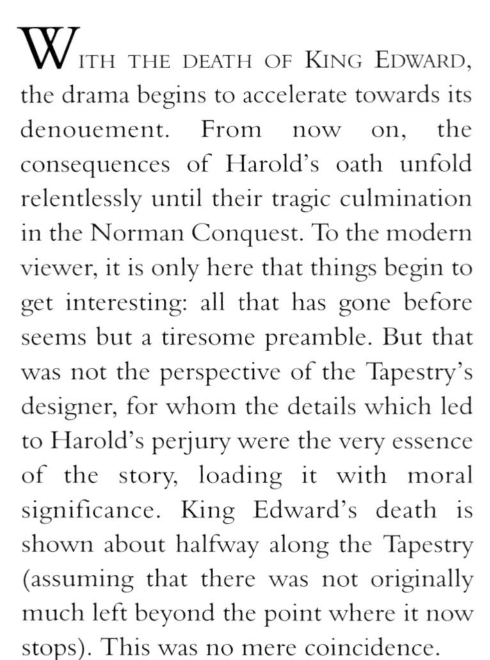

With the death of King Edward, the drama begins to accelerate towards its denouement. From now on, the consequences of Harold's oath unfold relentlessly until their tragic culmination in the Norman Conquest. To the modern viewer, it is only here that things begin to get interesting: all that has gone before seems but a tiresome preamble. But that was not the perspective of the Tapestry's designer, for whom the details which led to Harold's perjury were the very essence of the story, loading it with moral significance. King Edward's death is shown about halfway along the Tapestry (assuming that there was not originally much left beyond the point where it now stops). This was no mere coincidence.

It is possible to put a reasonably precise date on this crucial episode. Christmas 1065 saw Edward at Westminster not only to celebrate the festival but also to witness the consecration of the newly-built abbey church and to convene an assembly of magnates and councillors. His poor health ruled out longer journeys (for example to Gloucester, where he had spent Christmas in 1052 and 1062). The palace of Westminster, just outside London, was quite comfortable enough.

Anglo-Saxon custom differed from that of Normandy in not providing for the succession ahead of the ruler's death. William had been acknowledged as heir by the nobility of Normandy before the departure of his father, Duke Robert, for the Holy Land on a pilgrimage from which he would never return. Nothing of this kind had ever been attempted in England. Hence the particular importance of the events surrounding Edward's deathbed. Various options for the succession faced him at Westminster that winter: to designate an heir himself, or to leave the matter to the discretion of the *witan*, the traditional royal councillors. Among possible heirs the leading contenders were Edgar Atheling (grandson of his half-brother Edmund), whom the Tapestry ignores but whose claim was taken seriously by many contemporaries; and Harold, Edward's brother-in-law — though this would have gone against the traditions of English kingship, in that Harold could not boast descent from Cerdic, the perhaps mythical founder of the Wessex dynasty. Although nothing is spelled out, the Tapestry seems to imply that Edward chose Harold and thus, whether or not he knew of the oath, unleashed heavenly vengeance on his kingdom.

Hic portatur corp

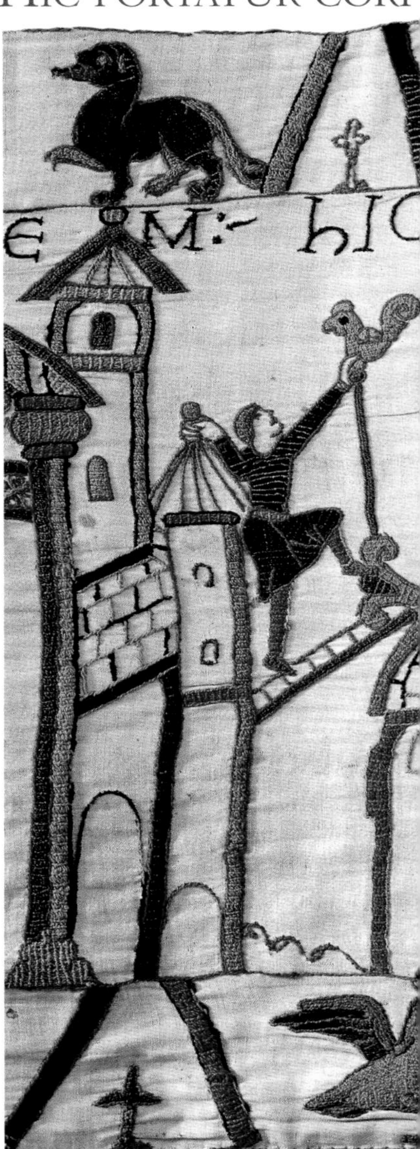

Scene 26

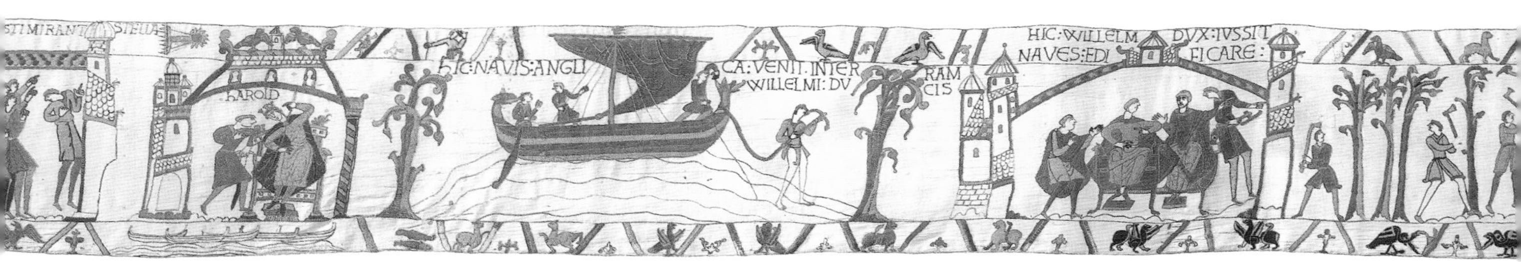

ADWARDI REGIS AD ECCLESIAM SANCTI PETRI APOSTOLI.

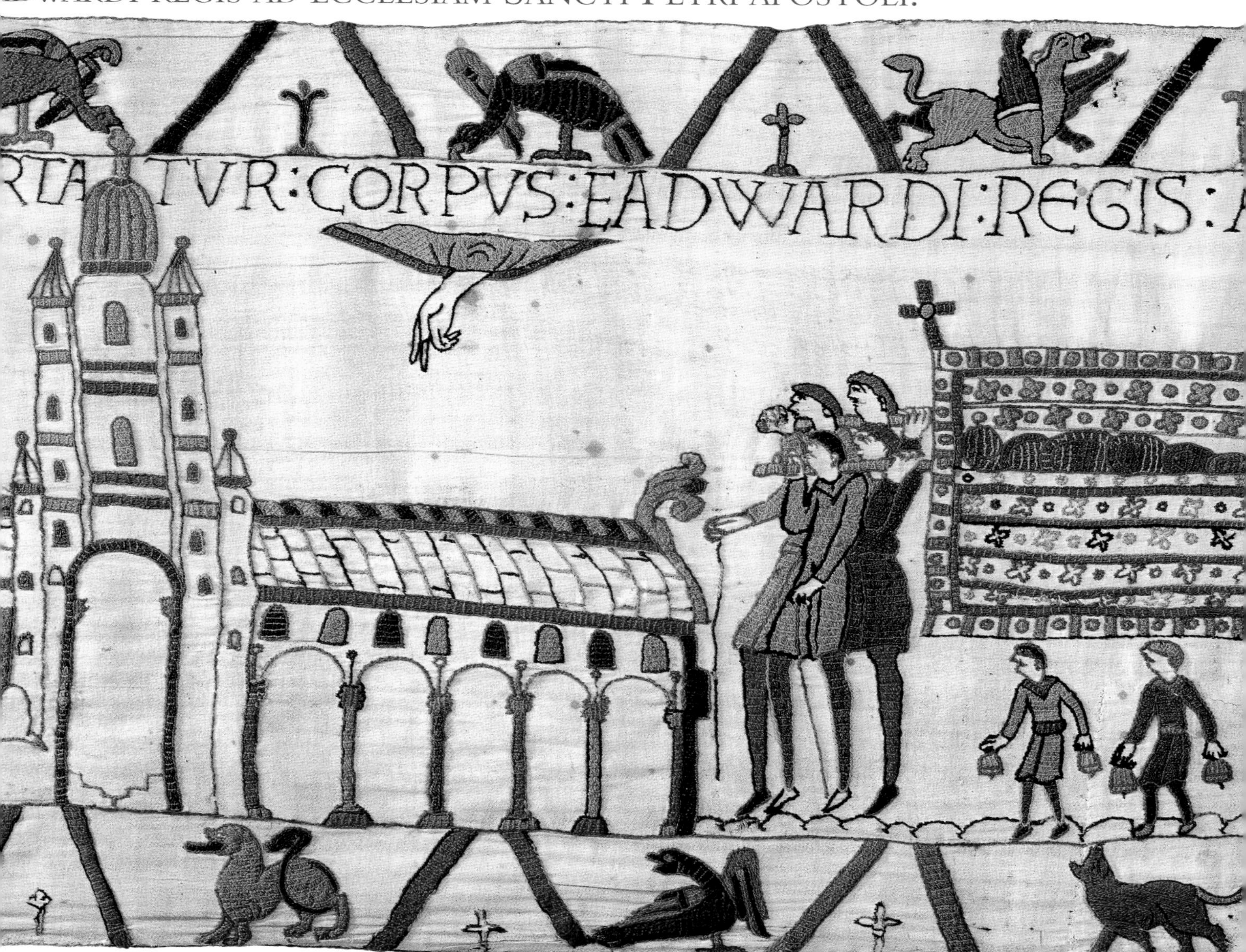

Here the corpse of King Edward is borne to the church of the Apostle Saint Peter.

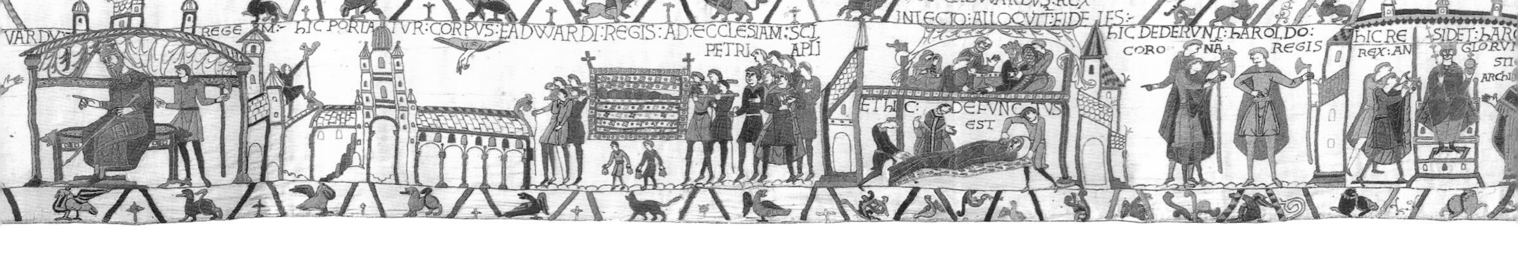

SCENES 26-28 MAKE SENSE ONLY AS AN ENSEMBLE, and merit close attention not only to their narrative contribution but also to their visual details. The chronological problem posed by the Tapestry's ordering of events has already been noted: Edward's funeral is shown before his death! But it is also worth noting that this episode is described in greater detail than anything except the Battle of Hastings — marking it out as of crucial importance. The events shown here all took place in the ten days from 28 December 1065 (the dedication of the abbatial church of St Peter at Westminster) to 6 January 1066 (the coronation of King Harold). The action is packed: at one stage (scene 27, p. 171), successive scenes are, uniquely, shown one above the other.

It all begins with the consecration of Westminster Abbey, symbolised by the workman placing the weathercock on the roof of the choir — then, as today, the traditional 'topping-out' ceremony for churches. This is the first illustration of that custom, which is also attested in Anglo-Norman documentary sources from this epoch. A letter from Bishop Wulfstan of London, written in about 993, refers to a golden cock on top of Winchester Cathedral: *stat ei vertice gallus aureus*; and in the mid-eleventh century, Geoffrey of Montbray, Bishop of Coutances, had a cock placed on top of his newly finished cathedral.[50]

The depiction of the abbey church itself offers much of interest. As usual on the Tapestry, it combines interior and exterior features in a single view. Of all the Tapestry's buildings, this is the easiest to interpret, with its structure clearly drawn from the north side. To the right is the nave, of five bays, with arches on two levels, but no towers. In the centre stands the crossing, supporting a massive tower which is flanked by bell-towers. To the left is the apse, perhaps two bays long. This is entirely consistent with what is known of the actual building, which was the first sizeable church erected in England in the Romanesque style already fashionable on the Continent, and especially in Normandy. In effect, it was the English manifesto for the new style that was to sweep all before it. Archaeologists have established that the abbey was very like that of Jumièges, then also approaching completion (its dedication took place in 1067).[51] The structural and decorative prominence accorded to the central tower (a lantern-tower, to judge by the windows) was at this time an unmistakeably Norman characteristic. The only non-Norman features are the carved finials, perhaps of floral design, at either end of the crest of the roof.

Practically nothing of Edward's church survives today, but archaeological investigations suggest a ground-plan in

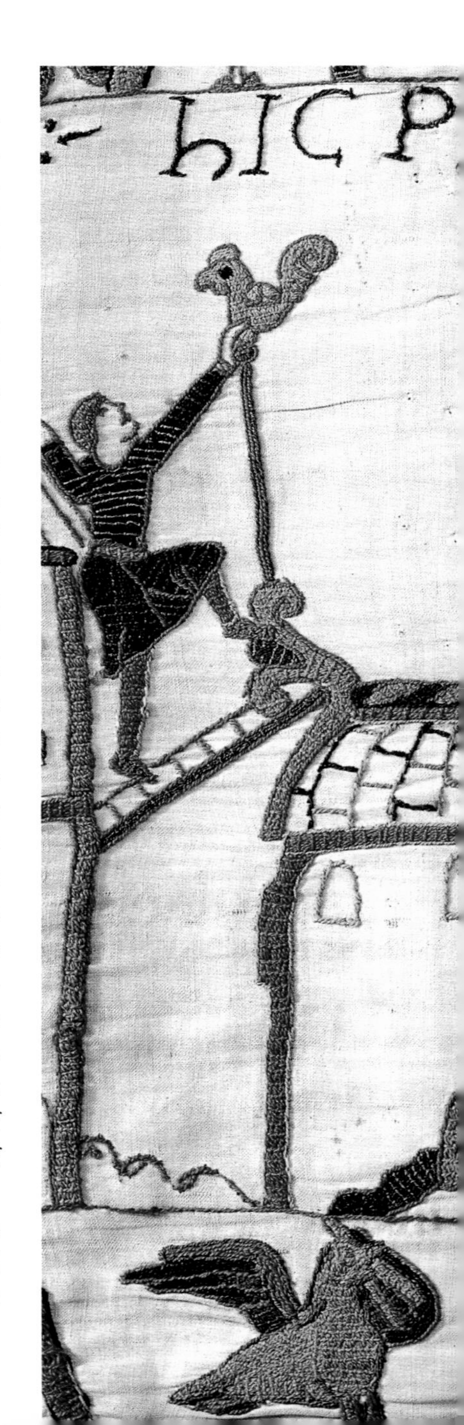

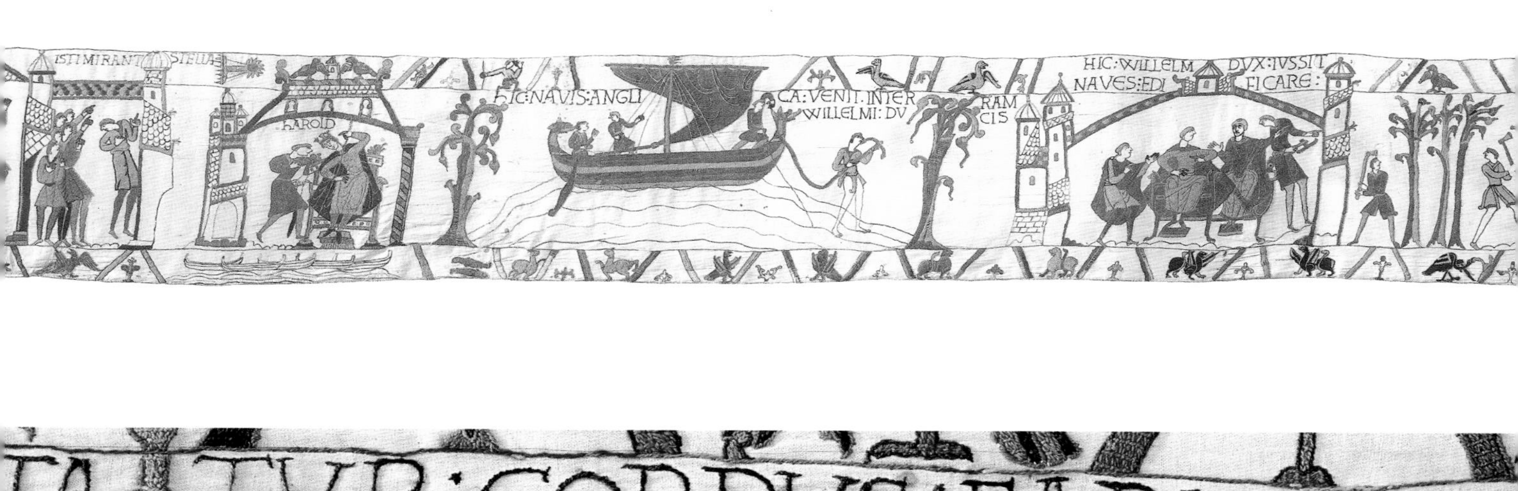
ISTI MIRANT STELLA
HAROLD
HIC:NAVIS:ANGLI
CA:VENIT.INTER
WILLELMI:DU
RAM
CIS
HIC:WILLELM DUX:IUSSIT
NAVES:EDI FICARE:

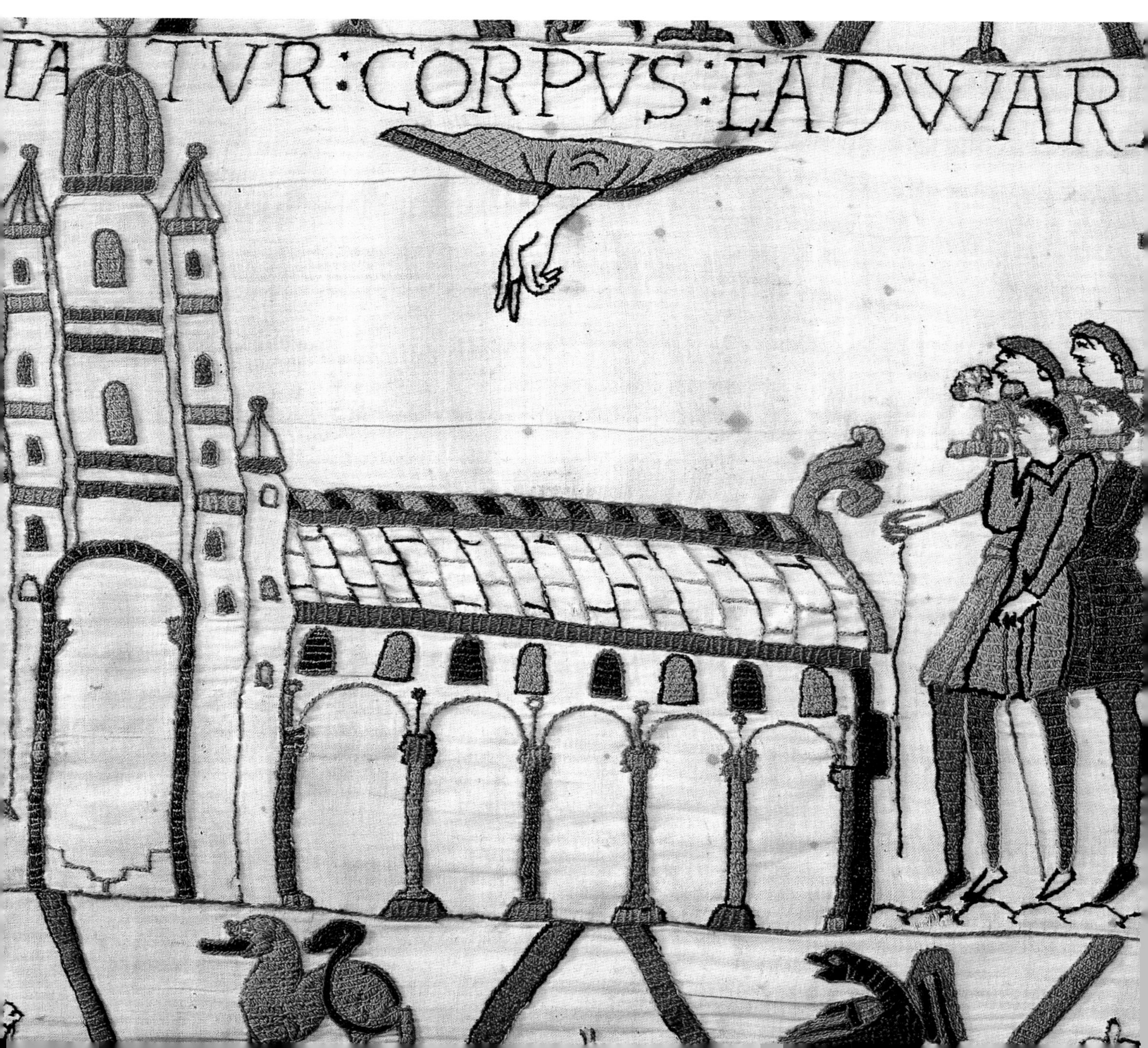
TA TUR:CORPUS:EADWAR

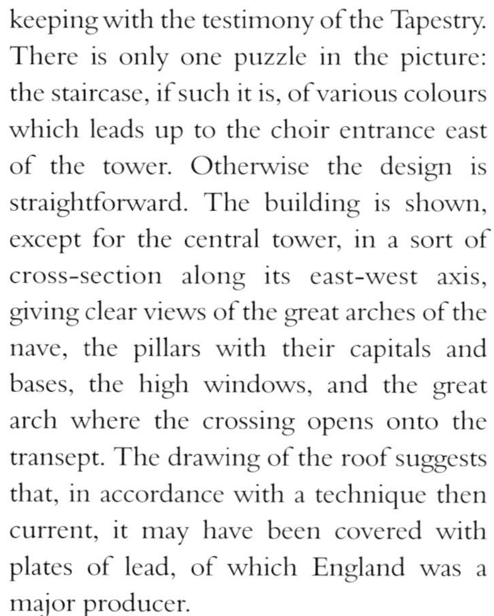

keeping with the testimony of the Tapestry. There is only one puzzle in the picture: the staircase, if such it is, of various colours which leads up to the choir entrance east of the tower. Otherwise the design is straightforward. The building is shown, except for the central tower, in a sort of cross-section along its east-west axis, giving clear views of the great arches of the nave, the pillars with their capitals and bases, the high windows, and the great arch where the crossing opens onto the transept. The drawing of the roof suggests that, in accordance with a technique then current, it may have been covered with plates of lead, of which England was a major producer.

Above the nave appears the hand of God making a gesture of benediction. It is unclear whether this is an allusion to the consecration of the sanctuary or simply an anticipation of the next scene, in which case it might be a sign of the welcoming into heaven of Edward's soul at the moment that his body was being taken to the church for the funeral ceremonies.

[50] S. Lindgrén and J. Neumann, 'Viking weathervane practices', *Fornvännen* 88 (1983), pp. 197-203, at p. 201; *Gesta Gaufridi*, ed. *Gallia Christiana*, t. 11, *instr.* col. 223.

[51] R. H. M. Gem, 'The Romanesque rebuilding of Westminster Abbey', *Anglo-Norman Studies* 3 (1980), pp. 33-60, esp. pp. 36-37; E. Fernie, 'Reconstructing Edward's Abbey at Westminster', *Romanesque and Gothic: Essays for George Zarnecki* (Woodbridge, 1987).

THE ACTUAL ORDER OF EVENTS NOW TAKES US TO THE UPPER SECTION of the following scene, undoubtedly set next door to the abbey in the palace of Westminster, where Edward was staying when he fell ill on Christmas Eve 1065. He probably suffered a stroke. The view of the palace is reminiscent of that in the first scene (p. 88). On the right is a kind of extension, doubtless a turret-stairway leading to the first floor where the king is confined to his bed. As usual with the Tapestry's palace interiors, ample draperies frame the king. In this case they presumably represent the curtains around his bed, and the classical convention by which they are shown wound loosely around the posts or columns permits a clear view of the principal figures.

Edward himself, distinguished by the crown with its fleurs-de-lys, is obviously very ill. A servant props him up on a pillow. At his bedside are a layman and a cleric. The latter, recognisable by his tonsure, seems to be gesturing for some assistance. These two men can be plausibly identified as Harold and Archbishop Stigand. At the foot of the bed are two veiled women, one of them probably Harold's sister Edith. The best accounts of Edward's life, such as that written by Osbert of Clare in 1138, confirm the presence of these three at his deathbed, along with another of the king's relatives, one Robert, who does not appear on the Tapestry.[52]

The caption above describes the scene:

(HIC) EADWARDUS R

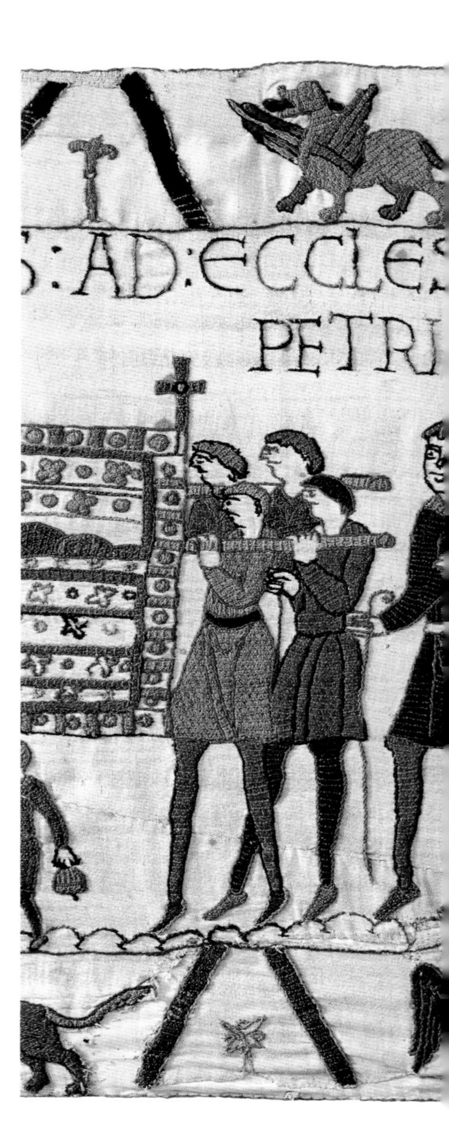

SCENES 26–27–28

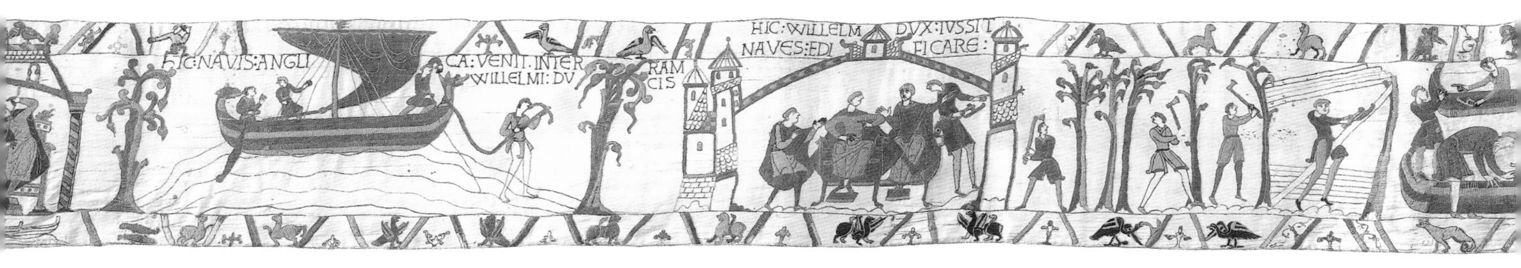

N LECTO ALLOQUITUR FIDELES, ET HIC DEFUNCTUS EST.

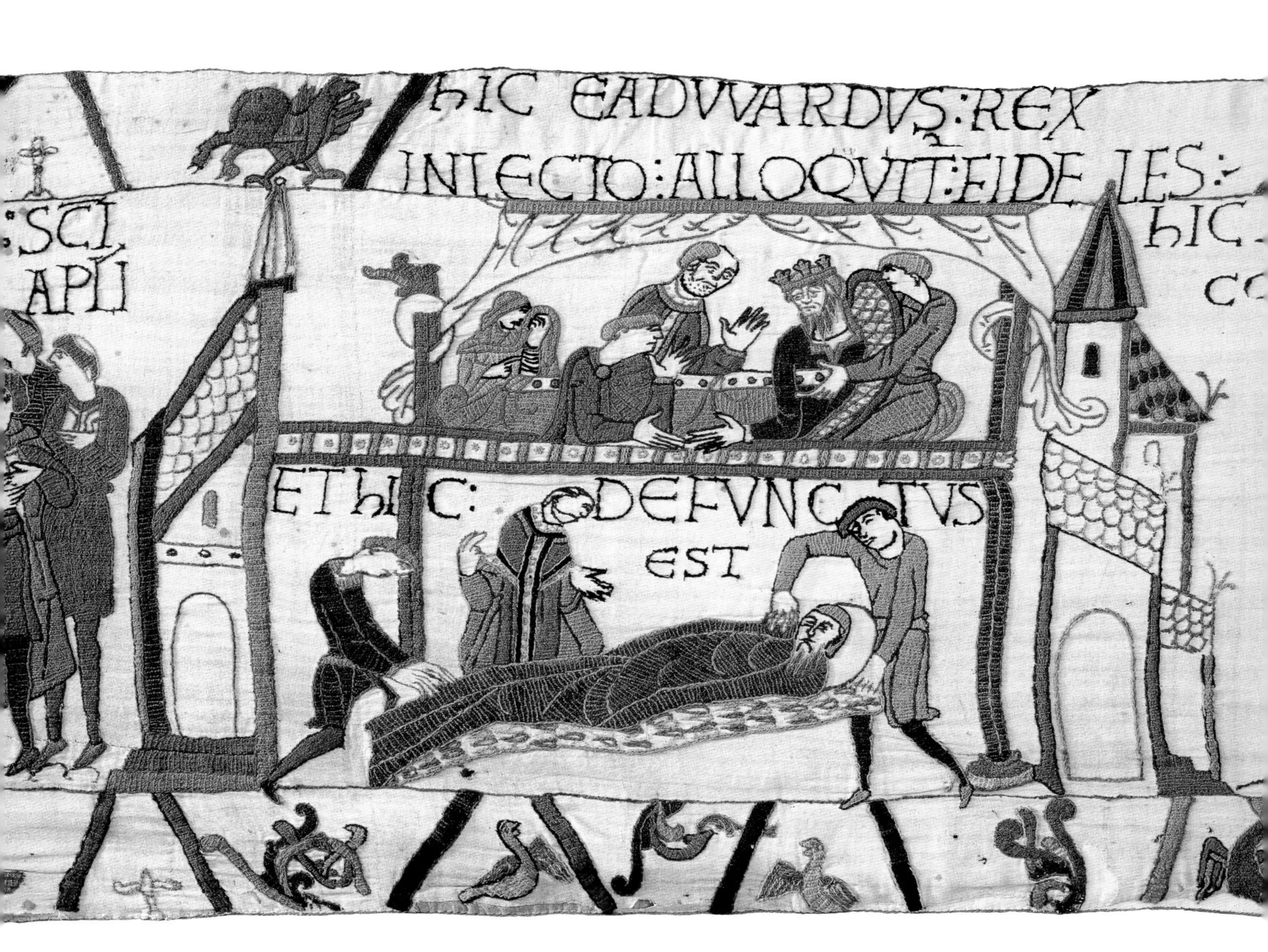

Here King Edward speaks with his followers on his bed, and here he died.

'Here King Edward speaks with his followers on his bed'. But, as usual, it studiously passes over exactly what was said (crucial though this was for the future of the English monarchy), doubtless because the English and Norman traditions differed radically on the subject. The Norman tradition maintained that Edward confirmed Duke William's claim to the throne, previously agreed in 1051. The English tradition was by no means unanimous. According to some recensions of the *Anglo-Saxon Chronicle*, Edward bequeathed the crown to Harold. According to the 'Life of King Edward', he entrusted both his widow and his kingdom to Harold's protection, though without naming him as his successor (something which was not strictly in his power anyway, as it required the assent of the *witan*, the 'wise men'). Such protection might have been meant to last only until William came to make good his claim. But in the absence of any official record of the pious king's last will, there is no way to decide between the rival accounts. Given the general sense that he died of some kind of stroke, he may not even have been in any position to voice his wishes.[53] The earliest documentary source, Eadmer's *Historia Novorum*, shares the Tapestry's reticence on the subject. It seems that even in the first generation after the Conquest this was a contested question with little hope of a definitive answer. What is beyond all doubt is that the Tapestry studiously refrains from taking sides.

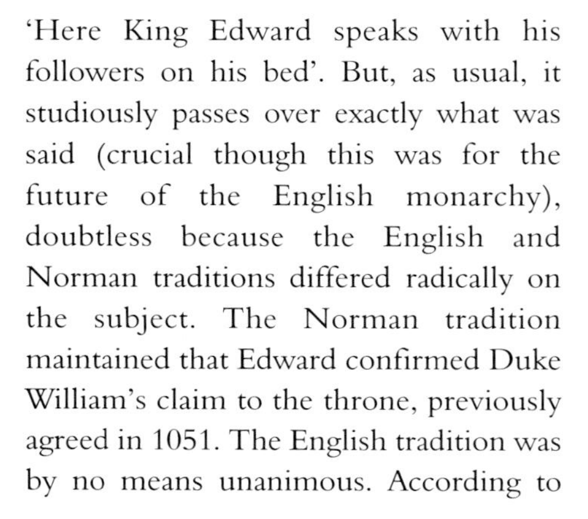

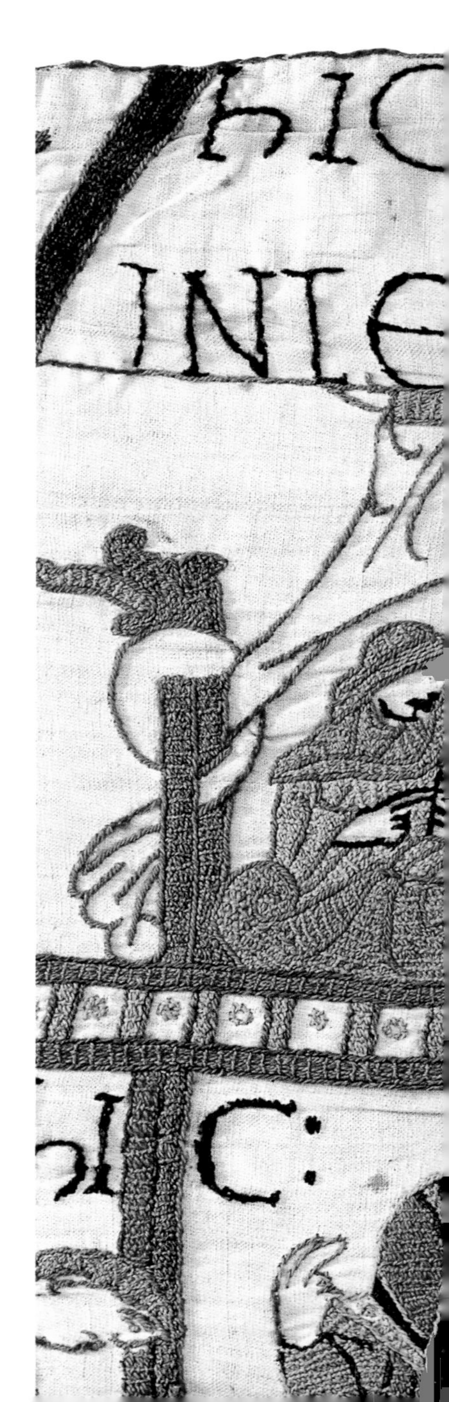

[52] *Vie de saint Édouard*, ed. M. Bloch, *Analecta Bollandiana* 41 (1926), pp. 108-9. See also F. Barlow, *Edward the Confessor* (London, 1970), p. 247.
[53] Barlow, *Edward the Confessor*, pp. 247-50, discusses Edward's death.

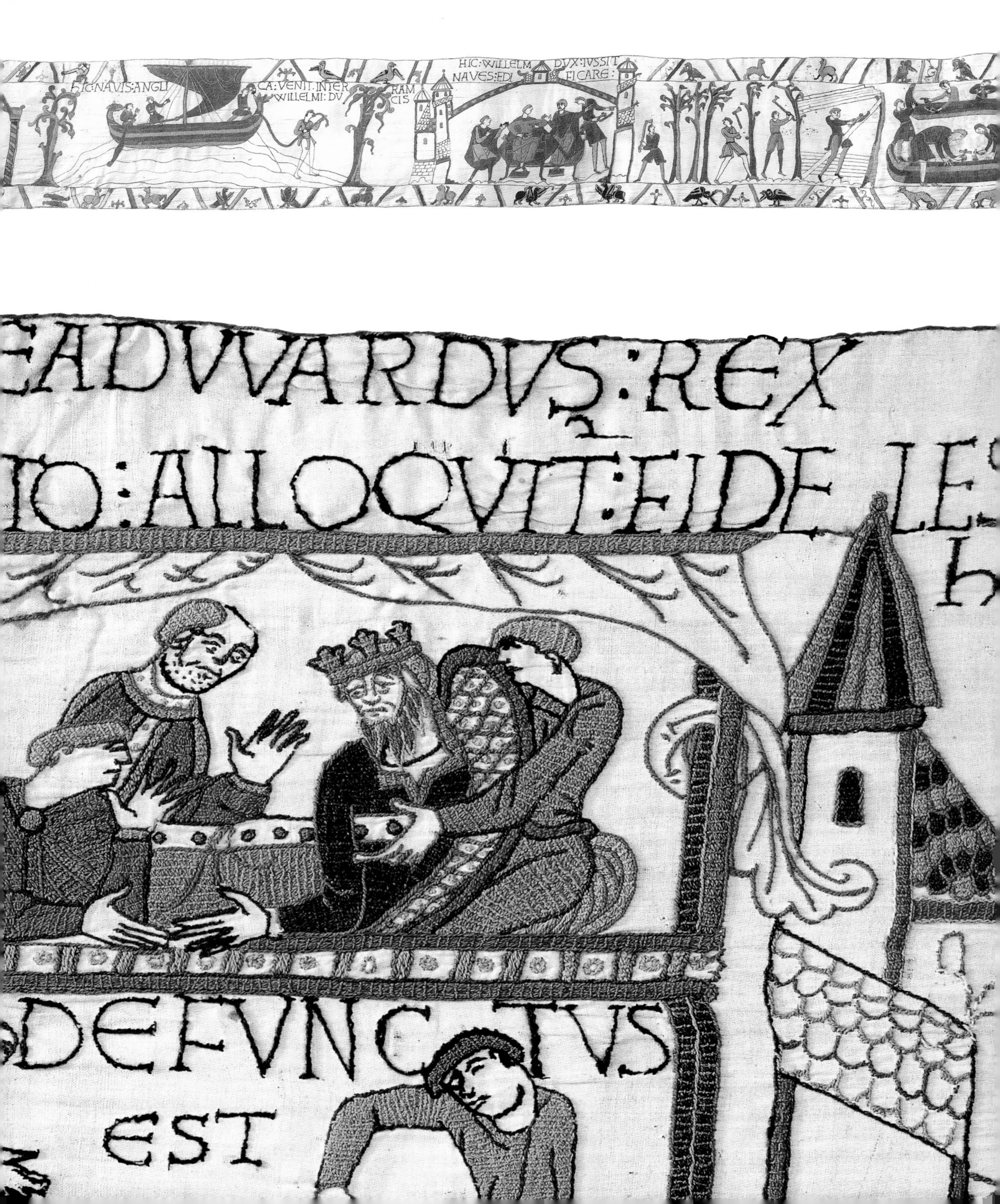
HIC: NAVIS: ANGLI
CA: VENIT: INTER
WILLELMI: DV
RAM
CIS
HIC: WILLELM
DVX: IVSSIT
NAVES: EDI
FICARE:
EADWARDVS: REX
IO: ALLOQVIT: FIDE LE
DEFVNCTVS
EST

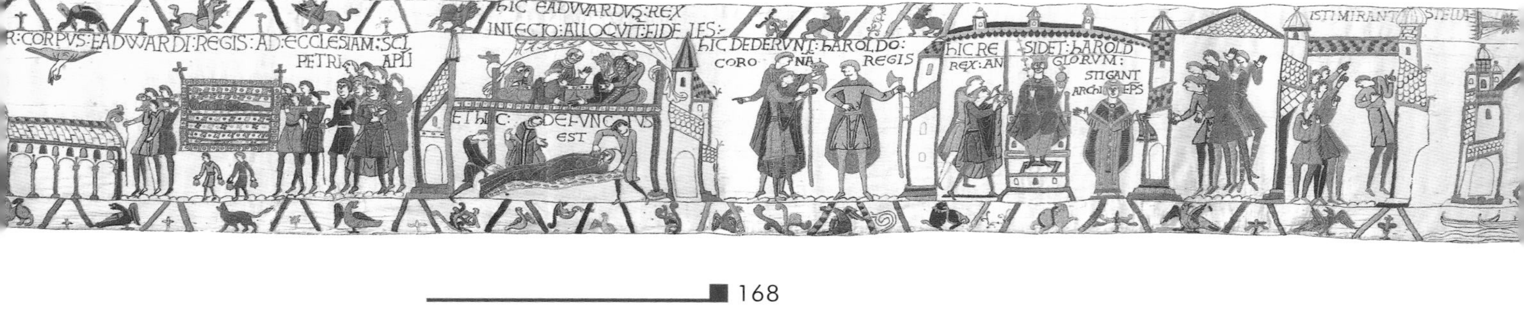

THE LOWER SECTION OF THIS SCENE shows the dead king's faithful servants attending to his corpse in the presence of a priest. Now stripped of his crown, he is being wrapped in a dark winding-sheet — the same as that in which, in the previous scene, he is shown on his way to burial. To judge by medieval practice, the winding-sheet was probably of leather, as in the case of King Valdemar the Great of Denmark (d. 1182), whose tomb in the church of Sankt-Bendt in Ringsted was opened by Danish archaeologists in 1855 to reveal that his corpse had been wrapped in an animal's hide (fig. 23).[54]

William the Conqueror himself was wrapped in ox hide when his corpse was taken from Rouen to Caen for burial in 1087. And according to the nineteenth-century archaeologist Father Cochet, the same was done in 1108 for Hugh of Grandmesnil, a Norman lord who died in England but was buried back in Normandy, and for both Henry I in 1135 and Henry II in 1183 (the former's corpse was transported from Lyons-la-Forêt for burial at Reading; and the latter from Martel in the Midi for burial at Rouen). In short, this was a common enough practice for persons of high rank.[55]

[54] R. A. Olsen, N.-J. Hansen, E. Kjærsgaard, *Skt. Bendts Kirke i Ringsted* (Copenhagen, 1978), p. 41.
[55] Abbé Cochet, 'Notice sur des sépultures chrétiennes trouvées en mars 1871 à Saint-Ouen de Rouen', *Mém. de la Soc. des Antiq. de Normandie* 28, p. 505.

23. The tomb of Valdemar the Great at Ringsted (Denmark) when opened in 1855. Compare this with the burial of Edward the Confessor.

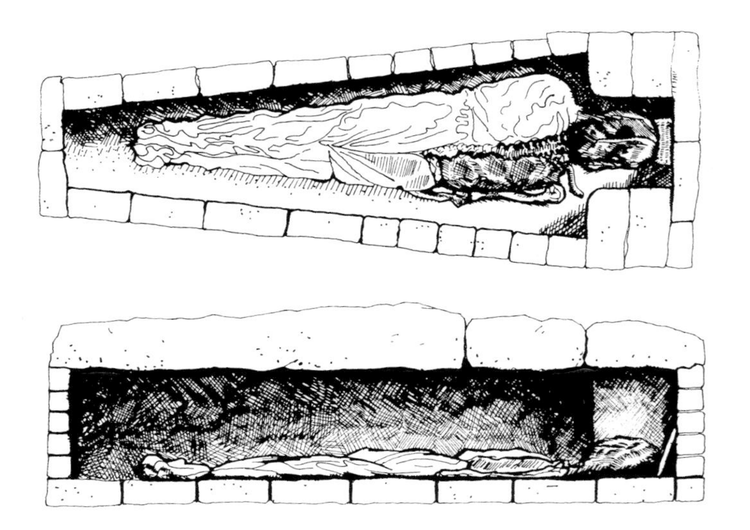

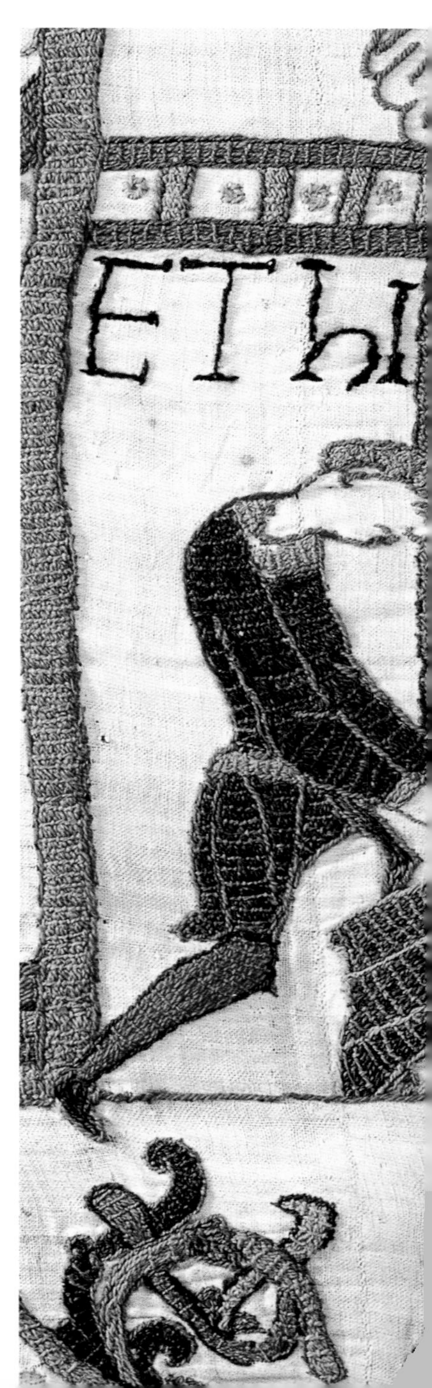

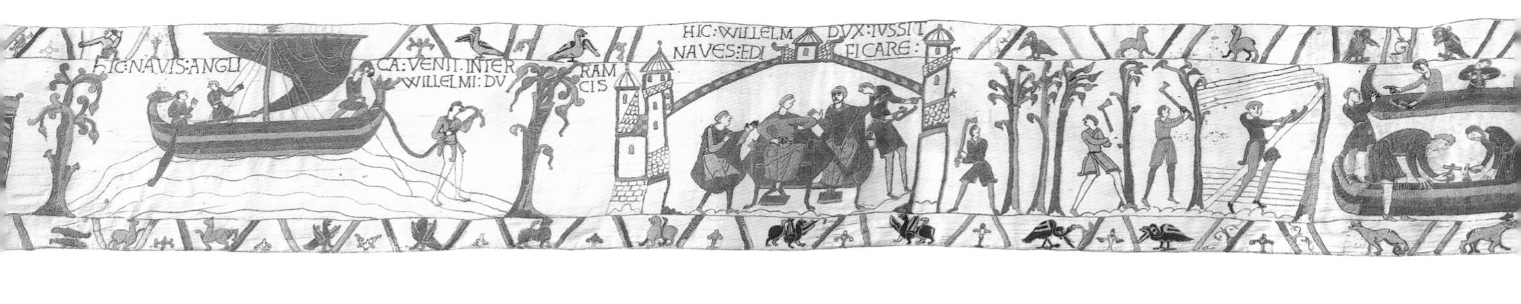
HIC:NAVIS:ANGLI
CA:VENIT.INTER
WILLELMI:DU
RAM
CIS
HIC:WILLELM
DUX:IUSSIT
NAVES:EDI
FICARE:

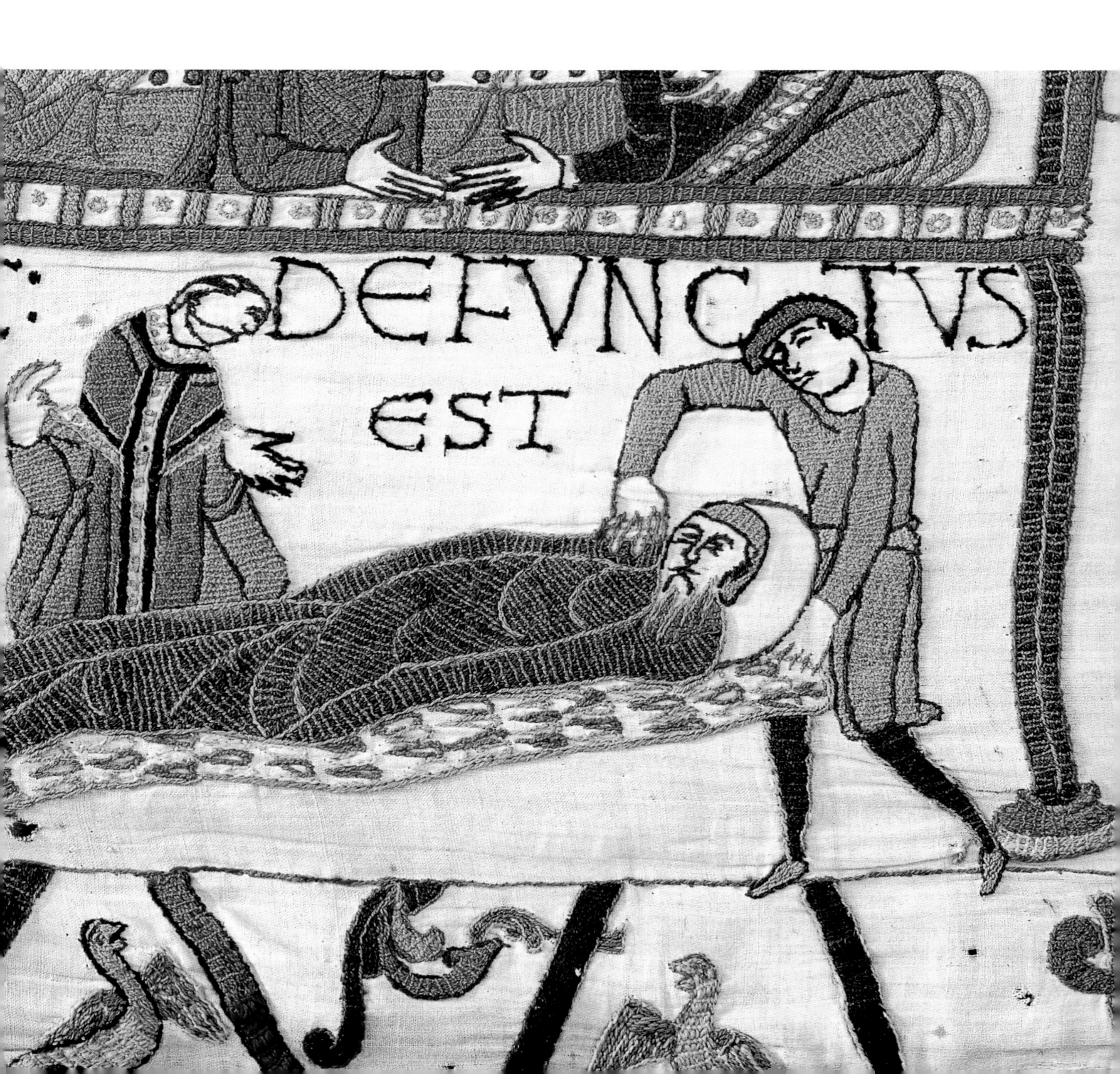
DEFVNC TVS
EST

Hic portatur corp

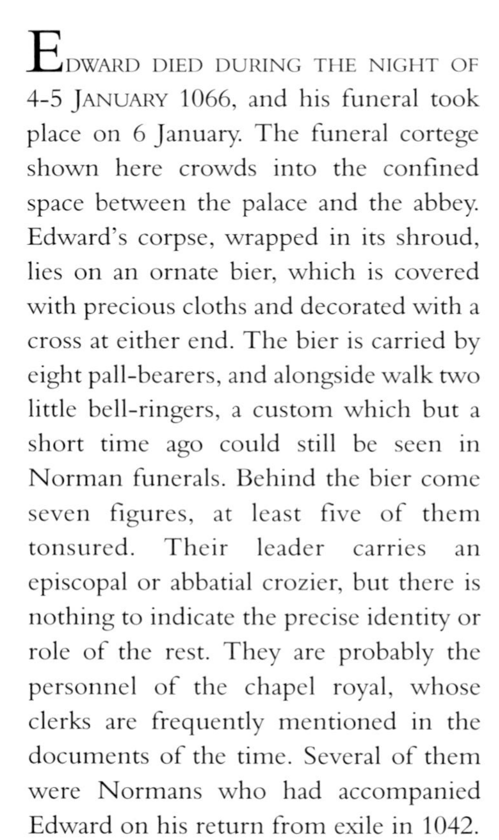

Edward died during the night of 4-5 January 1066, and his funeral took place on 6 January. The funeral cortege shown here crowds into the confined space between the palace and the abbey. Edward's corpse, wrapped in its shroud, lies on an ornate bier, which is covered with precious cloths and decorated with a cross at either end. The bier is carried by eight pall-bearers, and alongside walk two little bell-ringers, a custom which but a short time ago could still be seen in Norman funerals. Behind the bier come seven figures, at least five of them tonsured. Their leader carries an episcopal or abbatial crozier, but there is nothing to indicate the precise identity or role of the rest. They are probably the personnel of the chapel royal, whose clerks are frequently mentioned in the documents of the time. Several of them were Normans who had accompanied Edward on his return from exile in 1042.

Here the Tapestry bids farewell to Edward, without explicitly stating that he was buried in Westminster Abbey (unlike his predecessors, who were almost always buried at Winchester). His tomb, later redesigned in the Gothic style and altered even subsequently to that, still stands in the choir of the abbey church.

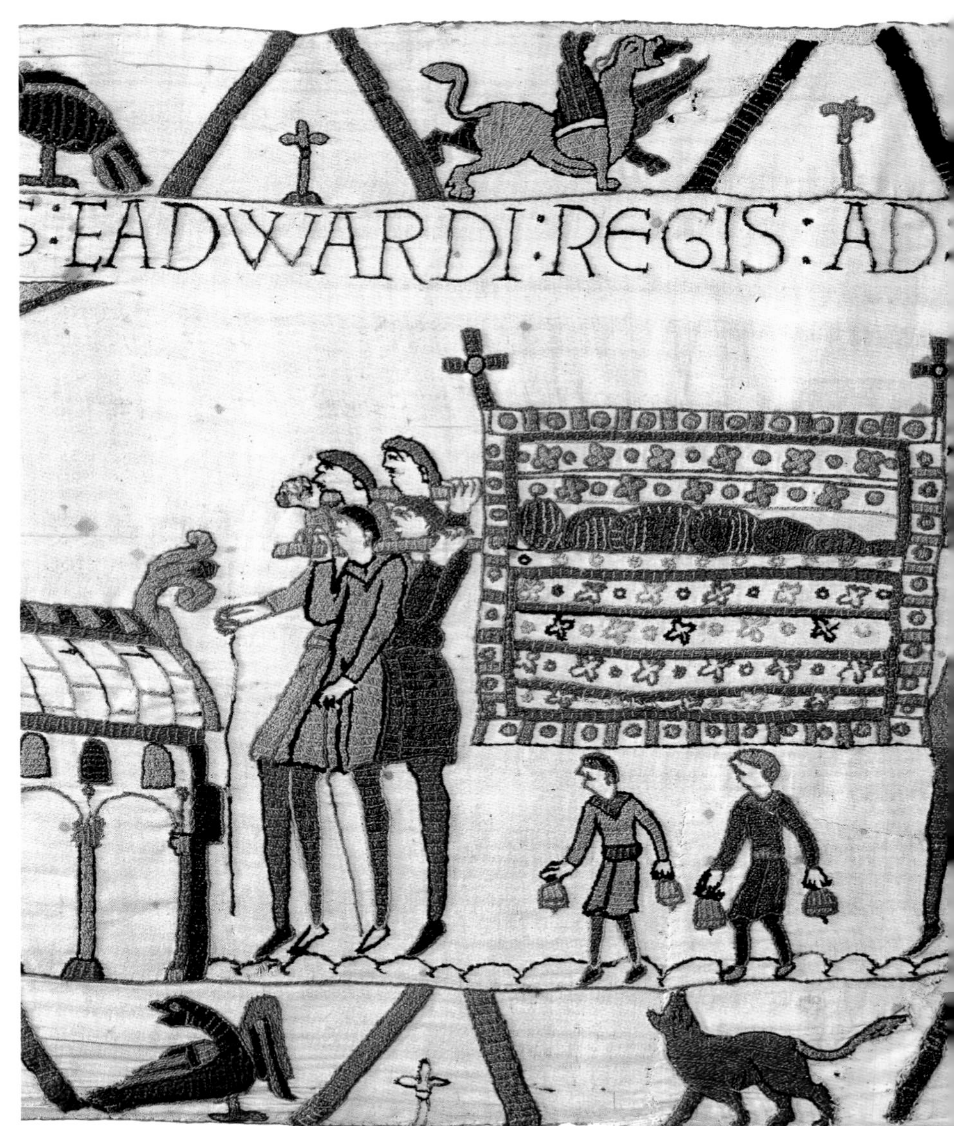

Scenes 26–27–28

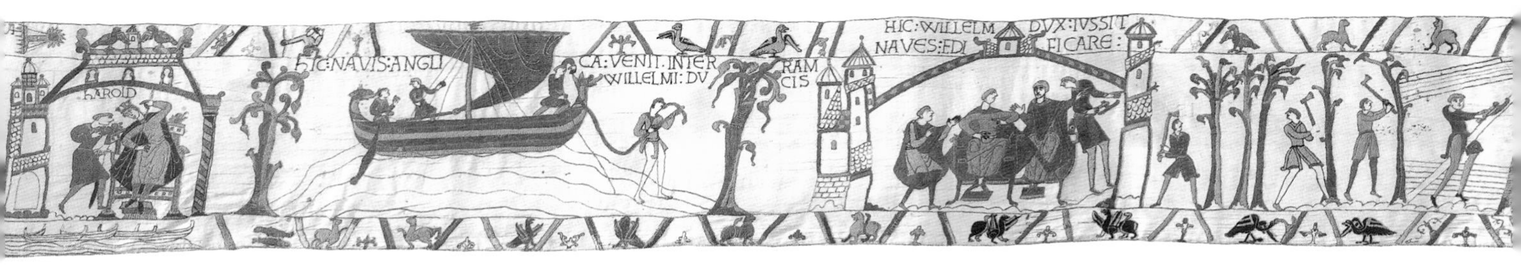

ADWARDI REGIS AD ECCLESIAM SANCTI PETRI APOSTOLI.

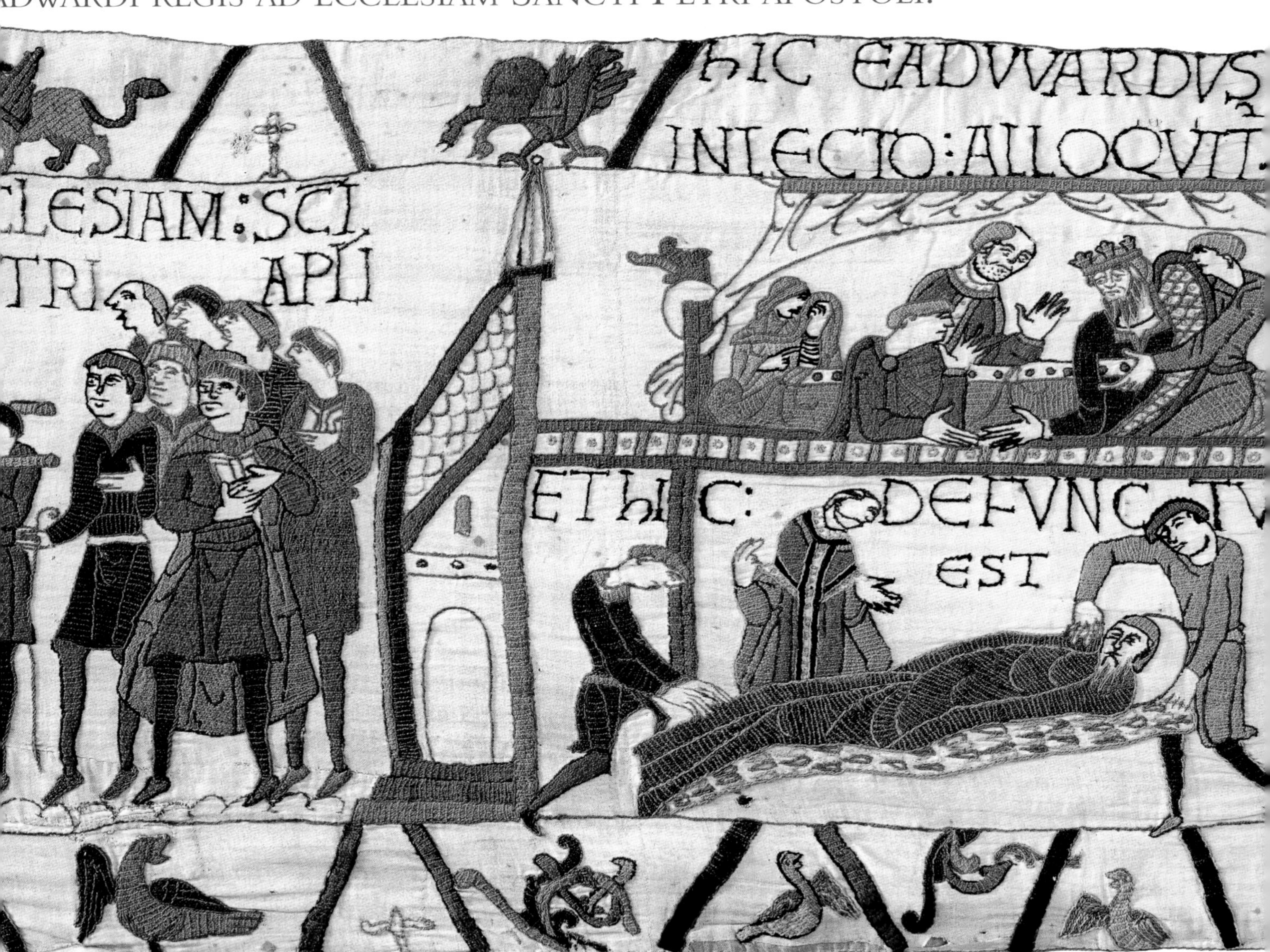

Here the corpse of King Edward is borne to the church of the Apostle Saint Peter.

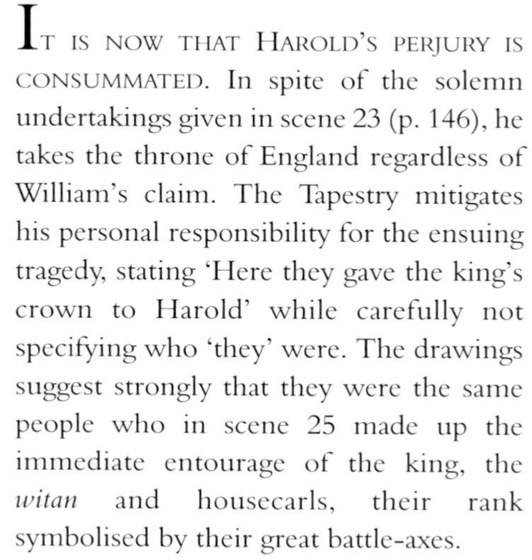

It is now that Harold's perjury is consummated. In spite of the solemn undertakings given in scene 23 (p. 146), he takes the throne of England regardless of William's claim. The Tapestry mitigates his personal responsibility for the ensuing tragedy, stating 'Here they gave the king's crown to Harold' while carefully not specifying who 'they' were. The drawings suggest strongly that they were the same people who in scene 25 made up the immediate entourage of the king, the *witan* and housecarls, their rank symbolised by their great battle-axes.

The *witan* or 'wise men' who had gathered for the dedication of the abbey church certainly did not have an unfettered right to dispose of the succession as they saw fit. The convention was that they selected the best qualified male in the House of Wessex. In most cases this was of course the eldest son of the deceased king, though there had been exceptions, such as the decision fifty years earlier to turn to the Danish dynasty. But in 1066 they faced a serious problem. Edward had no children, his brothers were all dead, and his closest male kindred were the descendants of his half-brother Edmund Ironside. These relatives had only just returned from an exile in Hungary which had lasted so long that they were virtually foreigners. The only one old enough to assume power had died in 1057, and his son, Edgar Atheling, a boy of but ten or twelve years, was in no position to take on the burdens of kingship in such delicate circumstances. The *witan* would barely have given him a thought. Moreover, Harold hurried things in such a way that they could not deliberate for long. On 6 January 1066, the day after Edward's death and the very evening of his burial, their choice fell upon Harold who, though not of the blood royal, had in effect exercised the powers of the king for some time and was at least the late king's brother-in-law. The Tapestry's direct narrative here makes perfect sense: there simply were no other realistic candidates.

The crown seems to have been conferred upon Harold in the open air outside the palace of Westminster. The person proffering it has no distinguishing features, and the crown itself is neither that which Edward wore nor that which Harold himself wears elsewhere (scenes 30 and 33, pp. 175 and 180). Lacking fleurs-de-lys ornaments, it is closed with a sort of cap on top. The reason for the difference is obscure. The ceremony would appear to be entirely secular, with no clergymen appearing here at all.

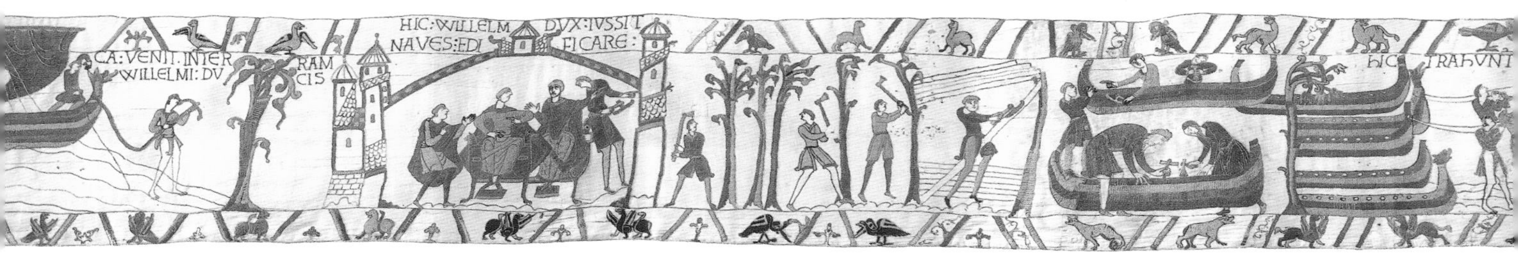

Hic dederunt Haroldo coronam regis.

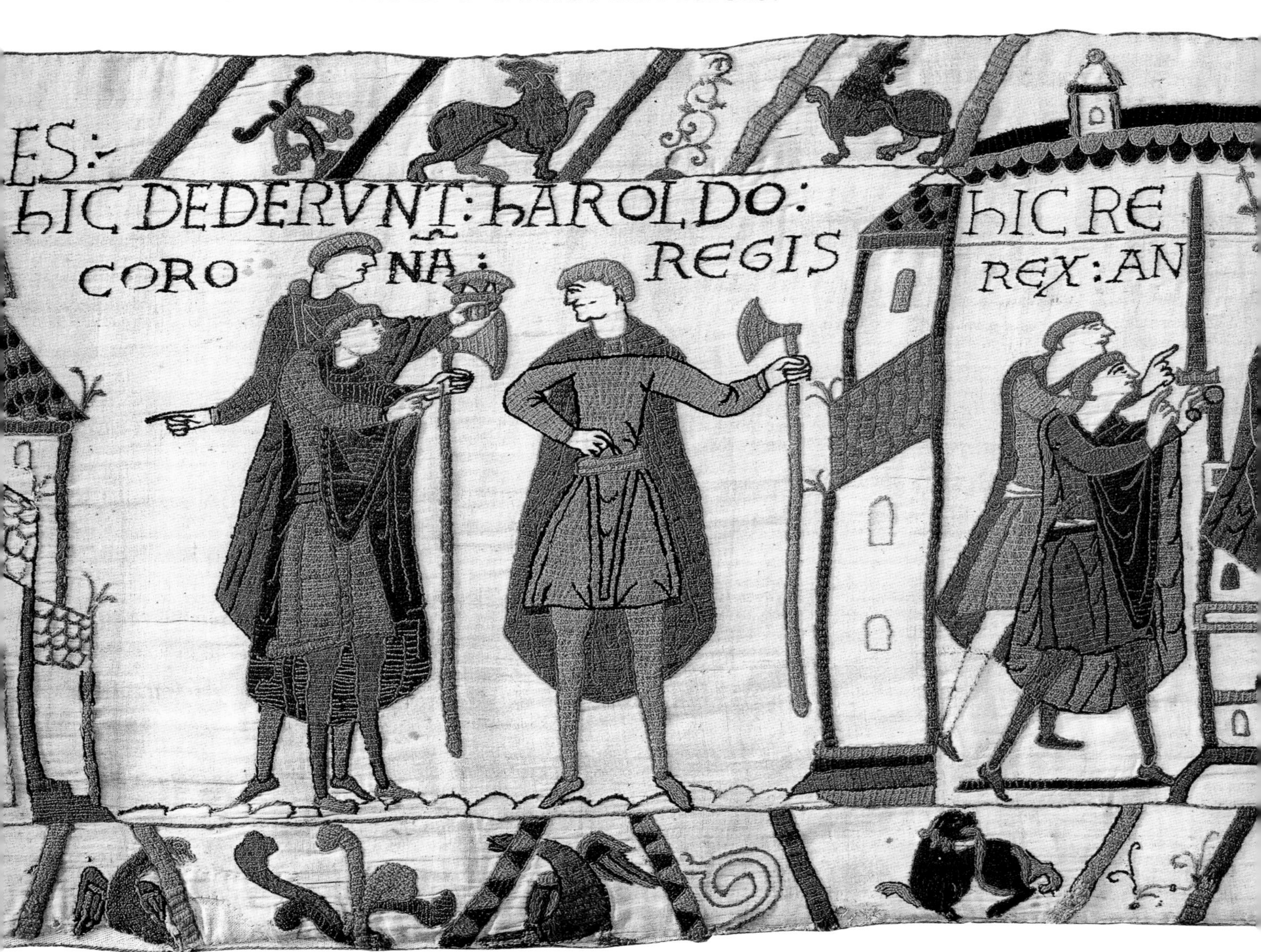

Here they gave the king's crown to Harold.

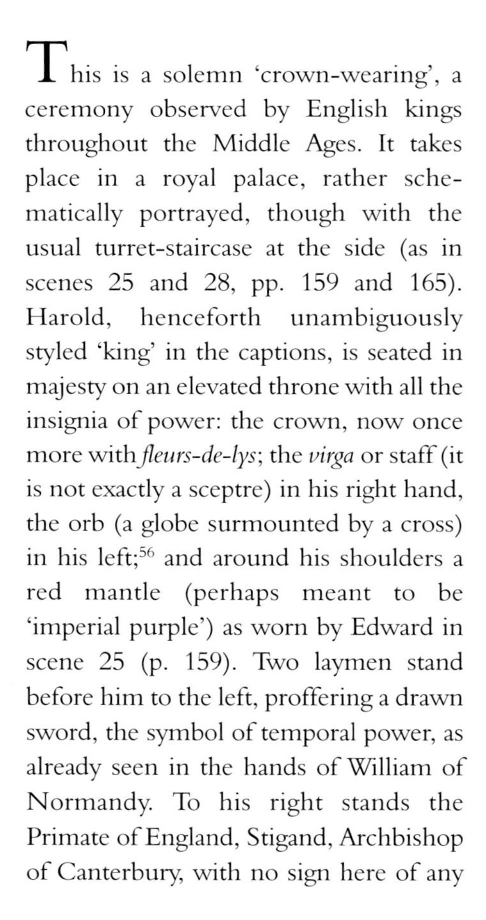

This is a solemn 'crown-wearing', a ceremony observed by English kings throughout the Middle Ages. It takes place in a royal palace, rather schematically portrayed, though with the usual turret-staircase at the side (as in scenes 25 and 28, pp. 159 and 165). Harold, henceforth unambiguously styled 'king' in the captions, is seated in majesty on an elevated throne with all the insignia of power: the crown, now once more with *fleurs-de-lys*; the *virga* or staff (it is not exactly a sceptre) in his right hand, the orb (a globe surmounted by a cross) in his left;[56] and around his shoulders a red mantle (perhaps meant to be 'imperial purple') as worn by Edward in scene 25 (p. 159). Two laymen stand before him to the left, proffering a drawn sword, the symbol of temporal power, as already seen in the hands of William of Normandy. To his right stands the Primate of England, Stigand, Archbishop of Canterbury, with no sign here of any such irregularity in his canonical status as was urged against him in Norman propaganda. He is wearing his episcopal vestments and holding his stole (or maniple, worn in the usual eleventh-century way). His presence in this scene suggests that he is performing some kind of liturgical function: although it does not seem to be an actual coronation, it is certainly not far removed from one. He is extending his arms in a gesture of welcome, unquestionably associating himself with what is being done.

The emphasis on Stigand's presence may reflect Norman propaganda. When William replaced Stigand with Lanfranc in 1070, it was argued that the support he had shown for Harold had compromised his status under canon law. This in turn might even suggest 1070 as a *terminus a quo* for the design of the Tapestry, which could be emphasising the parallel between Harold's usurpation and that of the archbishop, the 'invader of the metropolitan see (i.e. Canterbury) who wrested the *pallium* from Archbishop Robert, whom he had displaced by force and trickery'. This was old news in 1066, though, as Robert had been displaced in 1051 and Stigand had not taken any direct part in the affair. The official Norman view was that the see of Canterbury, like the throne itself, was formally speaking vacant: but it is curious that it took William four years to reach this conclusion.[57]

In an adjoining room, five laymen look on through an open door, probably representing the element of popular acclamation which was a customary feature of medieval succession and coronation rituals.[58]

[56] For the orb Harold is holding see P. E. Schramm, *Sphaira Globus, Reichsapfel* (Stuttgart, 1958), p. 117.
[57] The citation is from *Canterbury Professions*, ed. M. Richter (Torquay, 1973), p. 32. See also F. Barlow, *The English Church, 1000-1065* (2nd. edn. London, 1979), p. 304 and G. Garnett, 'Coronation and Propaganda', pp. 91-116, at p. 108. Norman sources, among them William of Poitiers, emphasise Stigand's role in Harold's succession, but English sources attach more importance to the irreproachable Ealdred, Archbishop of York, to whom William the Conqueror himself turned at the end of that year.
[58] J. L. Nelson, 'The Rites of the Conqueror', *Anglo-Norman Studies* 4 (1981), pp. 117-32, at p. 127.

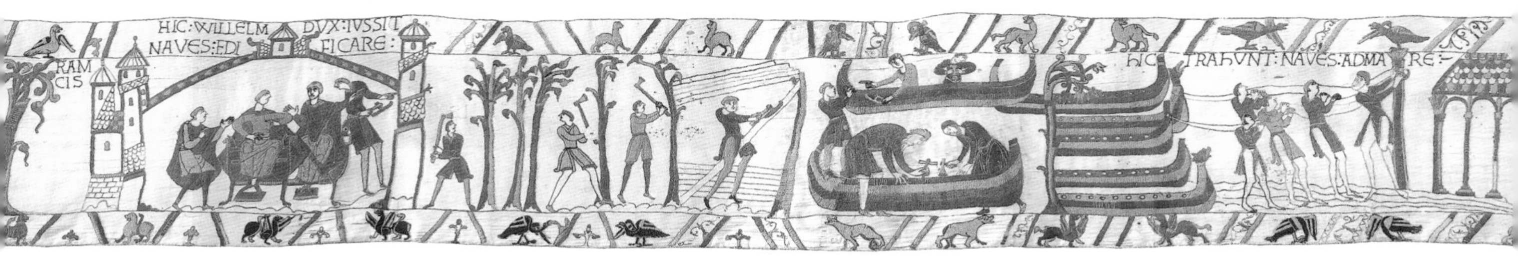

HIC RESIDET HAROLD REX ANGLORUM. STIGANT ARCHIEPISCOPUS.

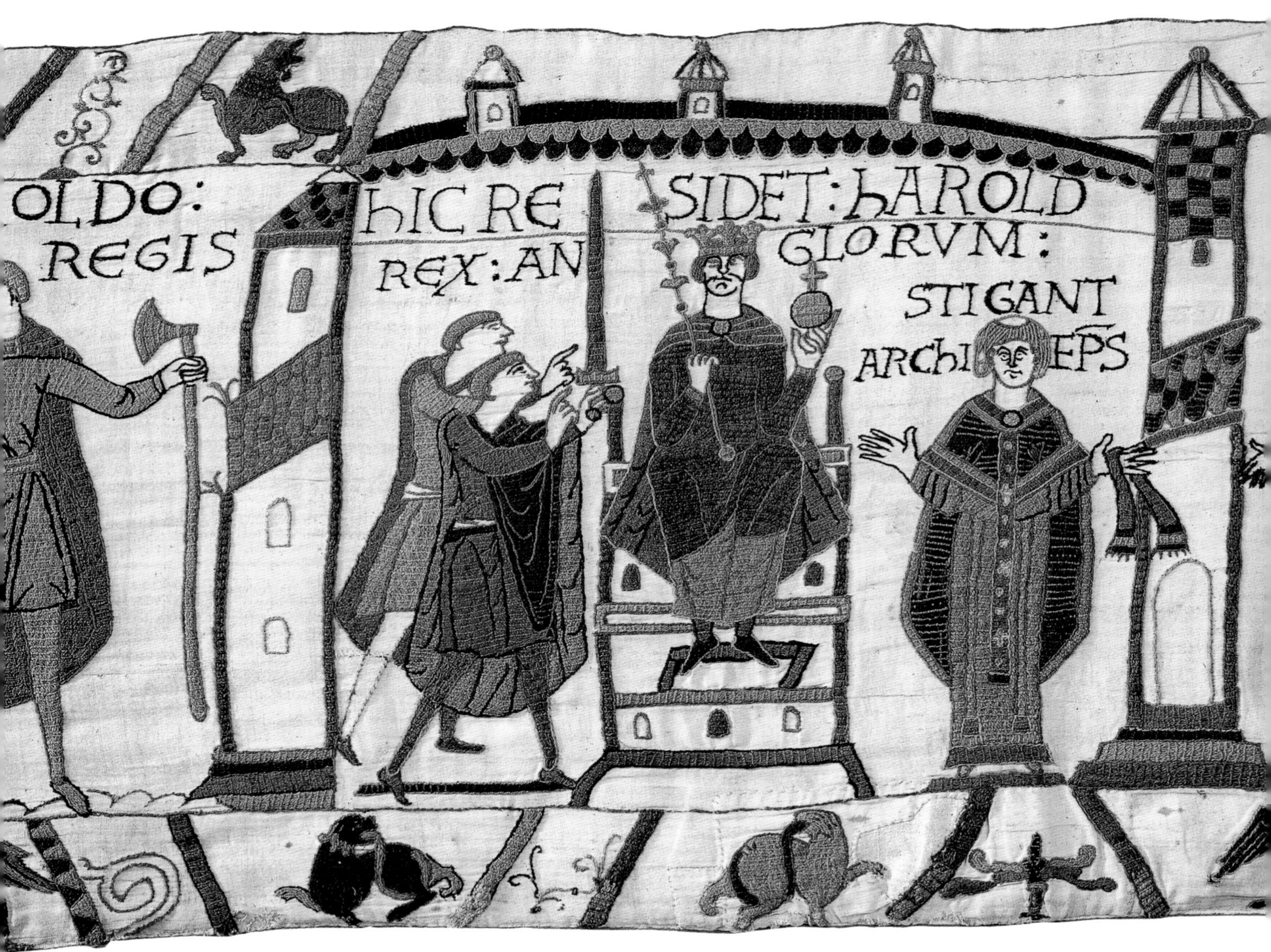

SCENE 30

Here sits Harold, King of the English. Archbishop Stigand.

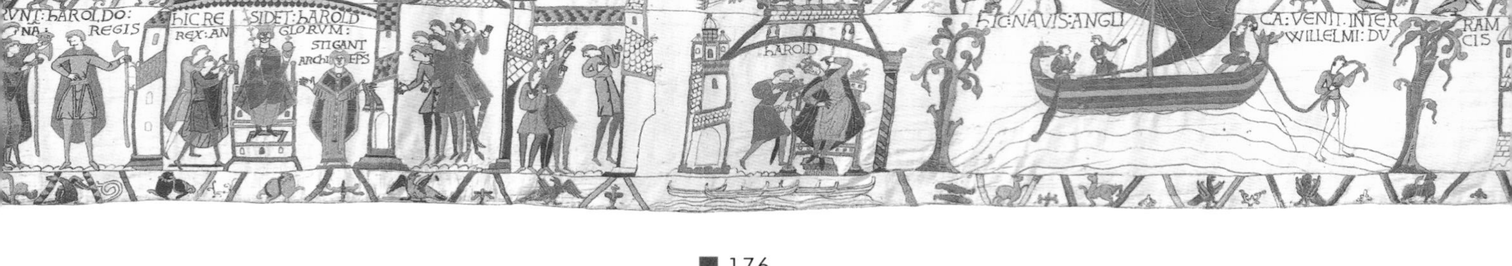

Isti mirant stella(m

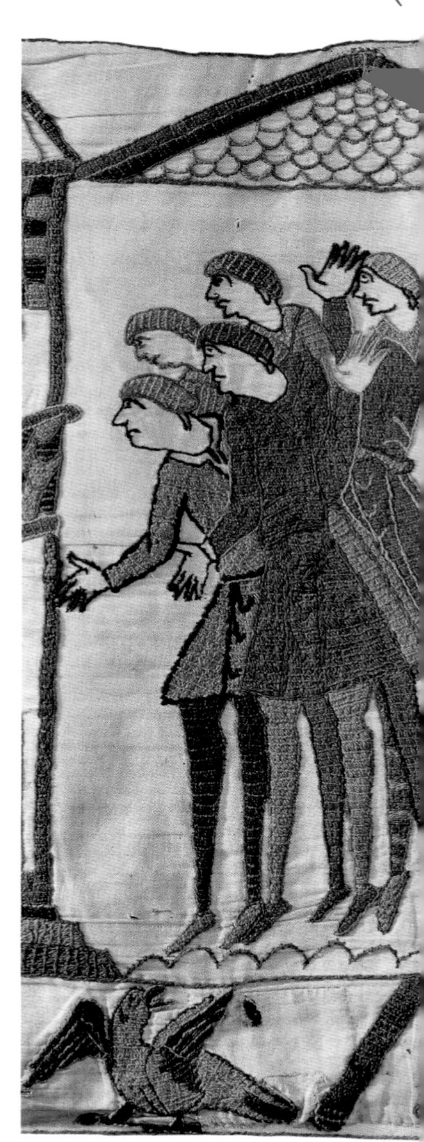

Scenes 31–32–33

'They wonder at the star.' Thus the caption describes this famous episode. Six Englishmen stand outside the royal palace pointing with evident astonishment at the appearance of an unexpected star in the sky. The star is portrayed as a kind of cogwheel trailing a tail that ends in a crossbar shooting out flames. We know that this was the regular visit of Halley's Comet, named after E. Halley, the English astronomer who identified its 76-year cycle in 1682 (its last visit was in 1986), and this, although it has undergone slight restoration, is the earliest picture of it.[59] In 1066 it was visible within five months of Harold's accession, from 24 April to 1 May.

By 1066 there was already a well-established traditional understanding of comets. Isidore of Seville summed up ancient lore on the subject in his *Etymologies*, describing them as 'stars that trail flames like hair' — which is probably what the Tapestry is trying to show here — and adding that 'when this kind of star appears, it portends famine, plague, or war'. Almost every medieval chronicle that mentions a comet connects its appearance with some such catastrophe. The comet of 1066 was linked with Harold's defeat and death not just in England and Normandy but almost throughout Europe. It is rare indeed for a chronicle to relate the comet to anything else, and even when they do so, it is not to the exclusion of the Battle of Hastings. Thus some Icelandic accounts connect it in addition with the defeat and death of Harald Hardrada at Stamford Bridge, while Adam of Bremen finds additional significance for it in the fall of his own Archbishop Adalbert and in a disaster which befell his compatriots in their perennial conflict with the Slavs.

The comet made a deep impression throughout the West, even where it did not come to be seen as of local historical significance. The Anglo-Saxon Chronicle, like the Tapestry, gives it special attention, mistakenly declaring that the like had never been seen in the heavens before, and linking it with the attempted landing of Harold's brother and foe, Tostig, on the Isle of Wight. Baudry de Bourgueil gives it a prominent place on his fictional tapestry, saying in effect: 'we all saw it ten times or more; it shone brighter than all the stars and but for its length might have been a second moon; it dragged a long tail behind; old men were amazed, and declared that it presaged great things, while women beat their breasts; but no one knew what it foretold and each interpreted it in their own way'. Stripped of the literary flourishes, that is pretty much what the Bayeux Tapestry shows. Wace speaks of a 'great star' which 'shone for fourteen days', adding that such stars appear when a new king is to take the throne.[60] A memorable Latin

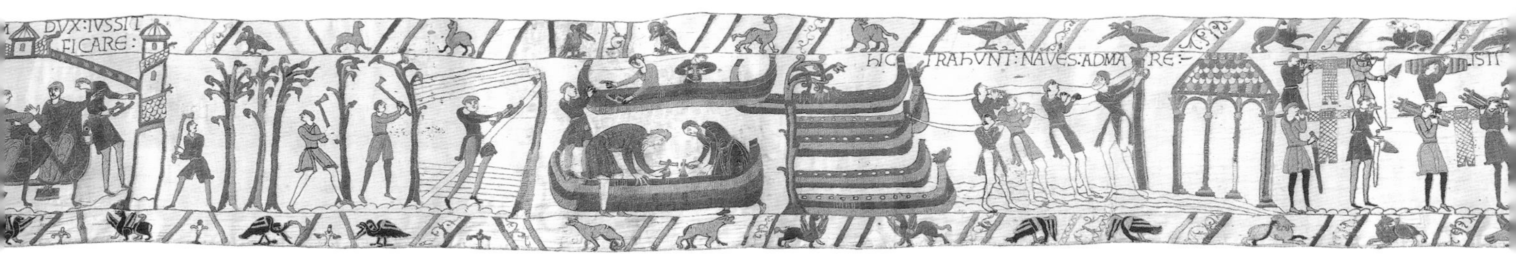

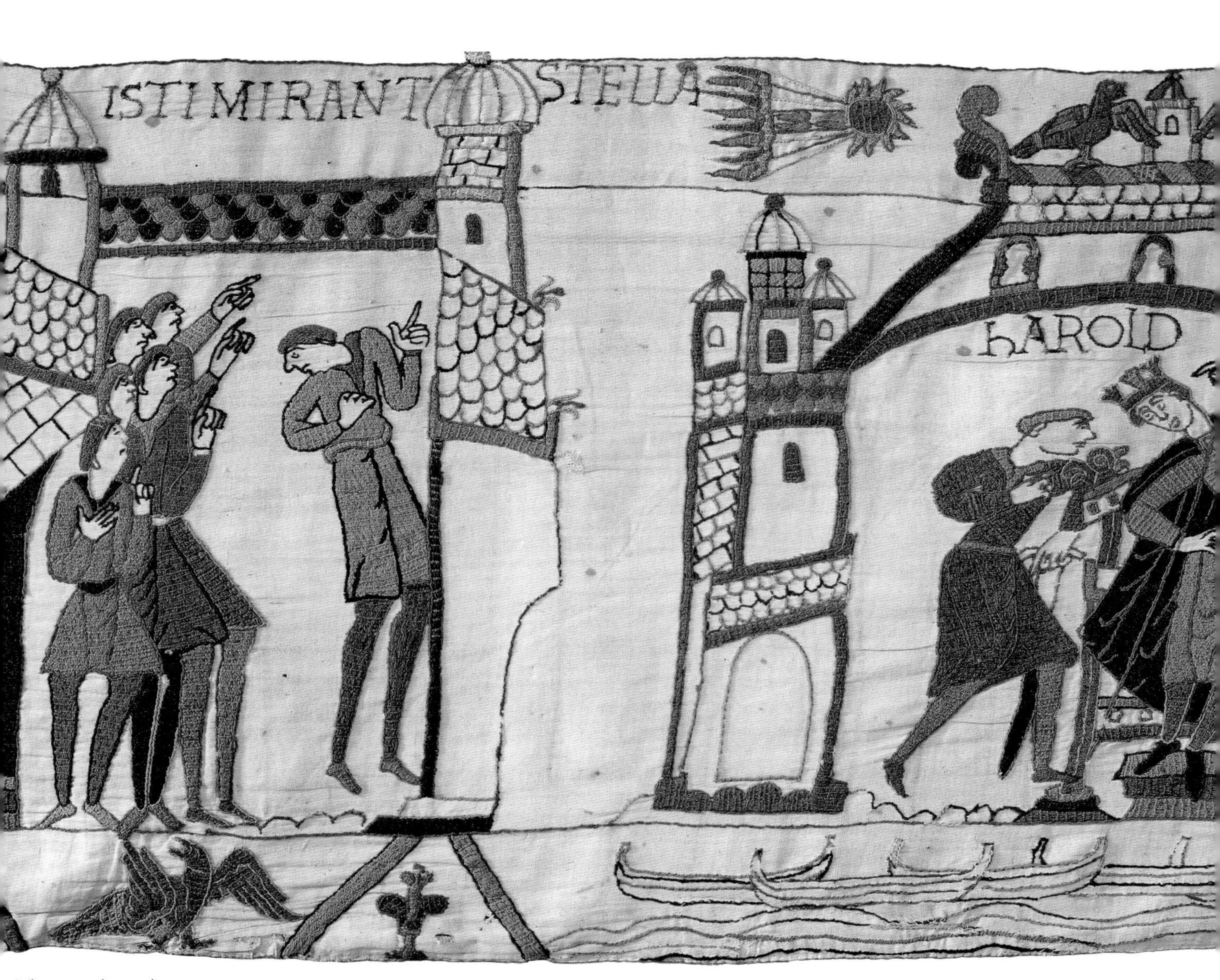

They wonder at the star.

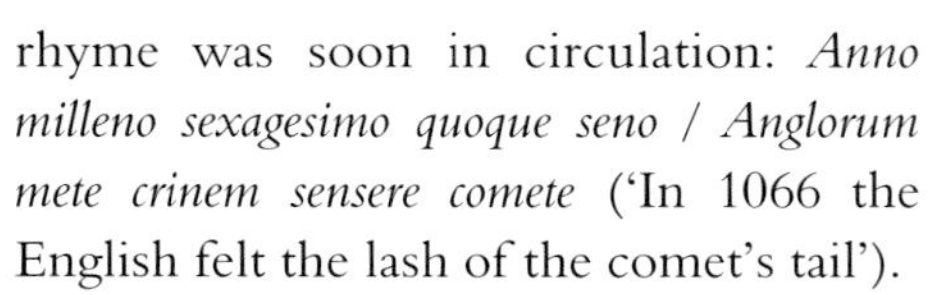

rhyme was soon in circulation: *Anno milleno sexagesimo quoque seno / Anglorum mete crinem sensere comete* ('In 1066 the English felt the lash of the comet's tail').

Except for the fact that this is one of the few points at which the narrative encroaches on the upper border, there is thus nothing distinctive about the Tapestry's portrayal of the comet. It simply follows the learned opinion of the time, basing its drawing on literary models.

It is worth noting, however, that the Tapestry here sacrifices chronological precision to narrative effect. The comet did not in fact appear, as is here implied, straight after Harold's accession, but four and a half months later — by which time William must long since have heard about the proceedings at Westminster, even though the Tapestry shows the news reaching him afterwards (scene 35, p. 183). But the Tapestry's reversal of strict chronological order is clearly meant to highlight the immediate judgement of divine providence upon Harold's perjury.

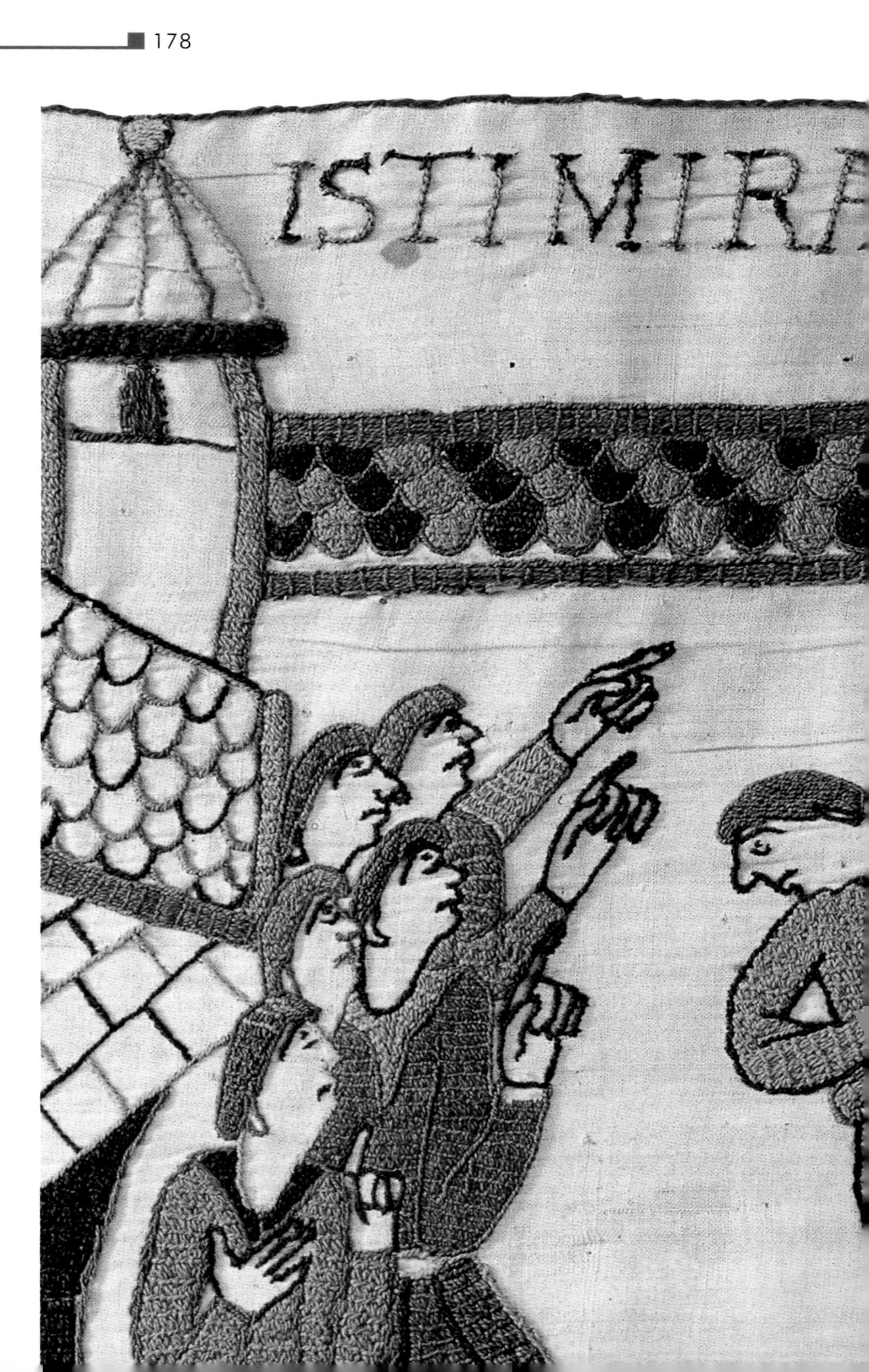

[59] The comet of 1066 and its interpretation were the subject of a conference held at Bayeux in 1986, whose proceedings were published in 1991. See in particular L. Musset, 'Le comète de Halley et l'influence sociale et politique des astres', pp. 7-12. The commentary here also avails itself of numerous unpublished communications.

[60] Baudry, ed. Lauer, p. 45, lines 243-58; Wace, ed. Holden, vol. 2, pp. 119-20, lines 6319-28 (Burgess and Van Houts, p. 161).

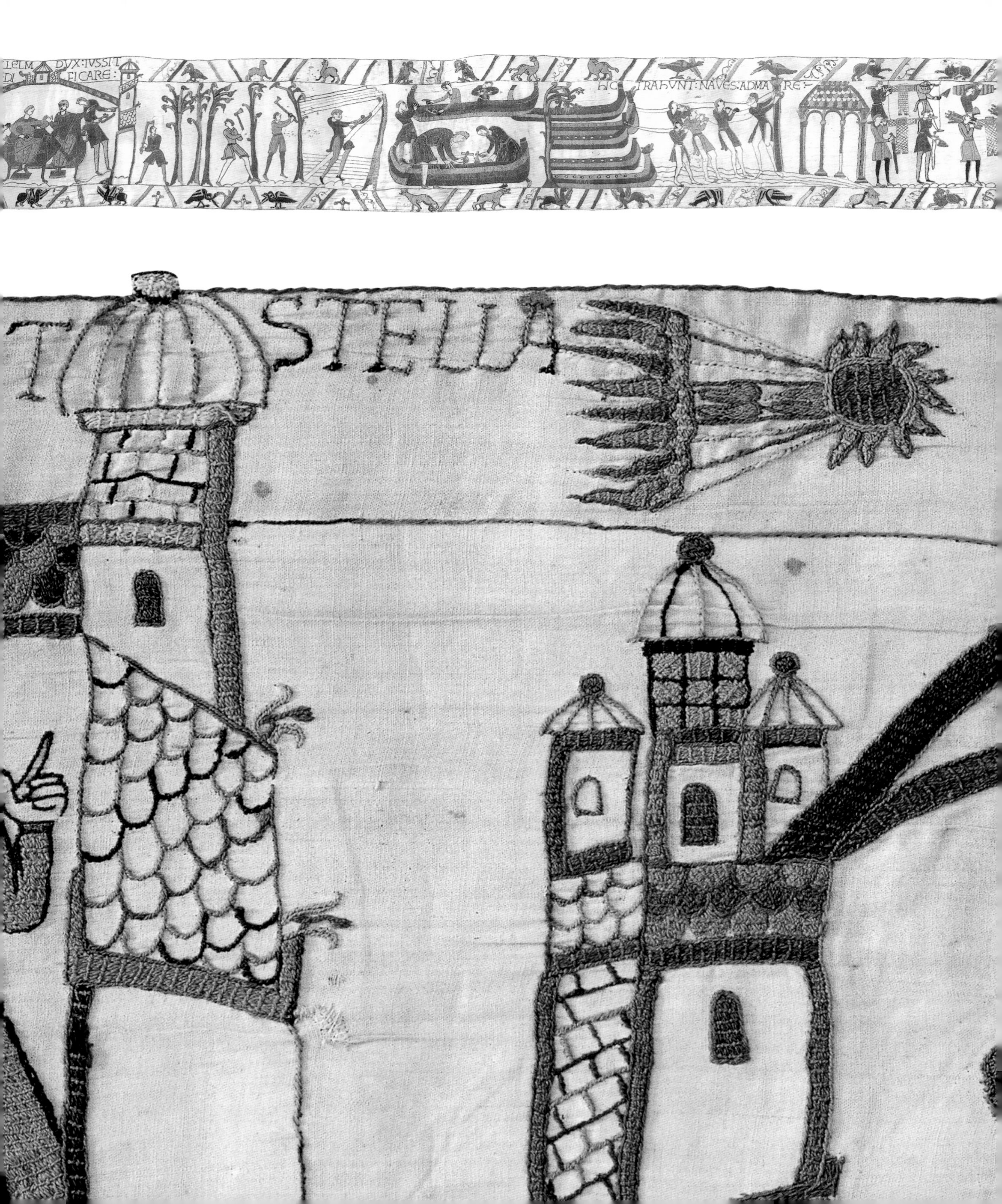
IELM DVX:IVSSIT
DI FICARE:
HIC TRAHVNT:NAVES:ADMA RE:
STELLA

HAROLD. HIC NAV

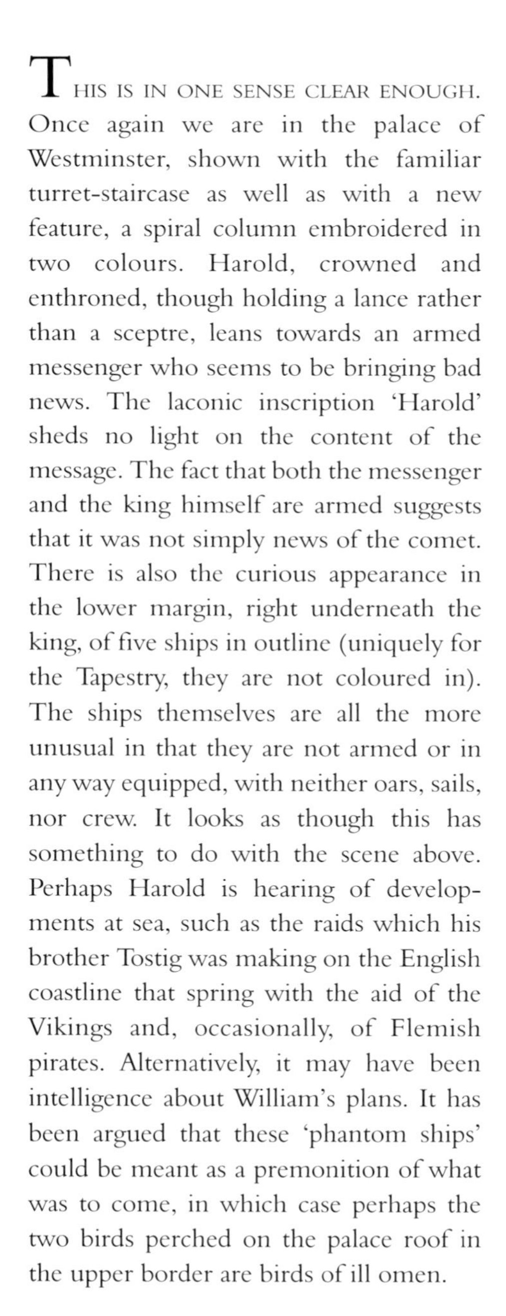

THIS IS IN ONE SENSE CLEAR ENOUGH. Once again we are in the palace of Westminster, shown with the familiar turret-staircase as well as with a new feature, a spiral column embroidered in two colours. Harold, crowned and enthroned, though holding a lance rather than a sceptre, leans towards an armed messenger who seems to be bringing bad news. The laconic inscription 'Harold' sheds no light on the content of the message. The fact that both the messenger and the king himself are armed suggests that it was not simply news of the comet. There is also the curious appearance in the lower margin, right underneath the king, of five ships in outline (uniquely for the Tapestry, they are not coloured in). The ships themselves are all the more unusual in that they are not armed or in any way equipped, with neither oars, sails, nor crew. It looks as though this has something to do with the scene above. Perhaps Harold is hearing of developments at sea, such as the raids which his brother Tostig was making on the English coastline that spring with the aid of the Vikings and, occasionally, of Flemish pirates. Alternatively, it may have been intelligence about William's plans. It has been argued that these 'phantom ships' could be meant as a premonition of what was to come, in which case perhaps the two birds perched on the palace roof in the upper border are birds of ill omen.

'HERE AN ENGLISH SHIP COMES TO THE LAND OF DUKE WILLIAM', reads the caption. Obviously it is carrying news of Harold's accession. The vessel has a skeleton crew: a couple of sailors and a couple of passengers. It is shown nearing the shore and being anchored in the same way as the foremost ship in scene 6 (pp. 103–104). There is nothing to indicate where precisely the Channel was crossed, nor who the messengers were, though it is known that there were close commercial ties between London and Rouen.

From this scene onwards the Tapestry abandons the practice of distinguishing Englishmen from Normans by hairstyle, possibly because a different designer is now in charge. In this context it is also worth noting that since scene 17 (p. 135) the English have not been shown with moustaches.

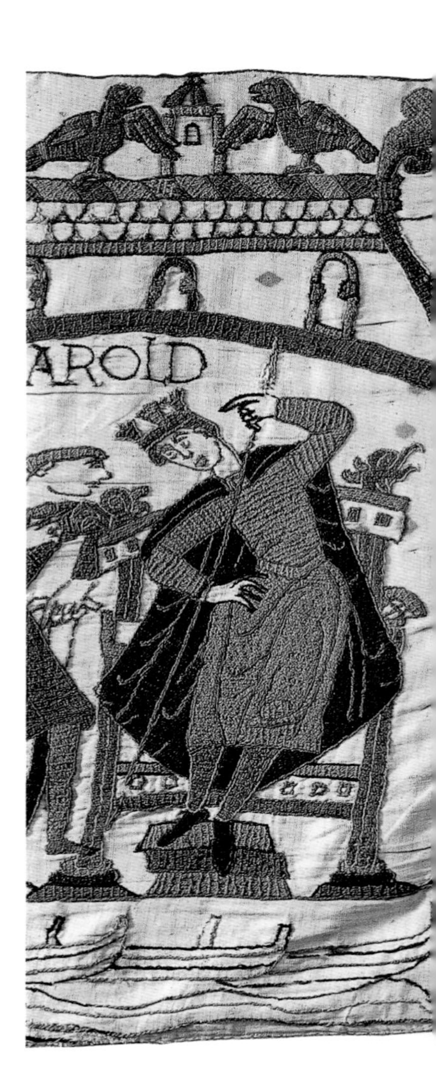

SCENES 33–34

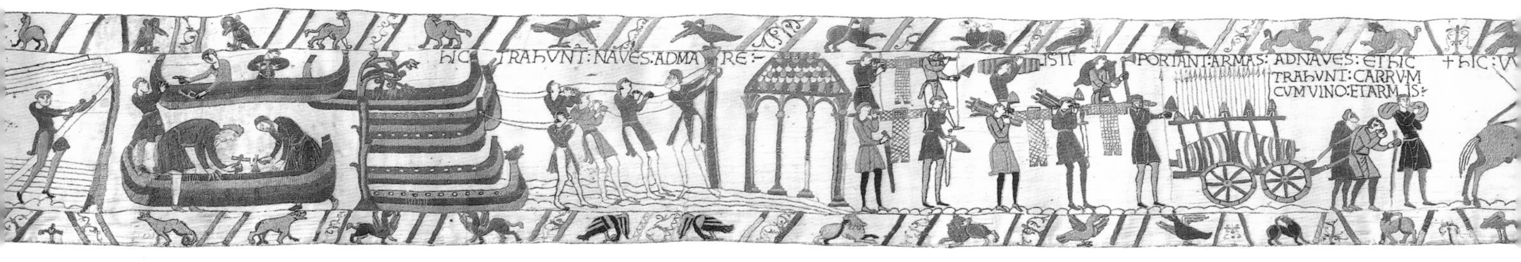

ANGLICA...

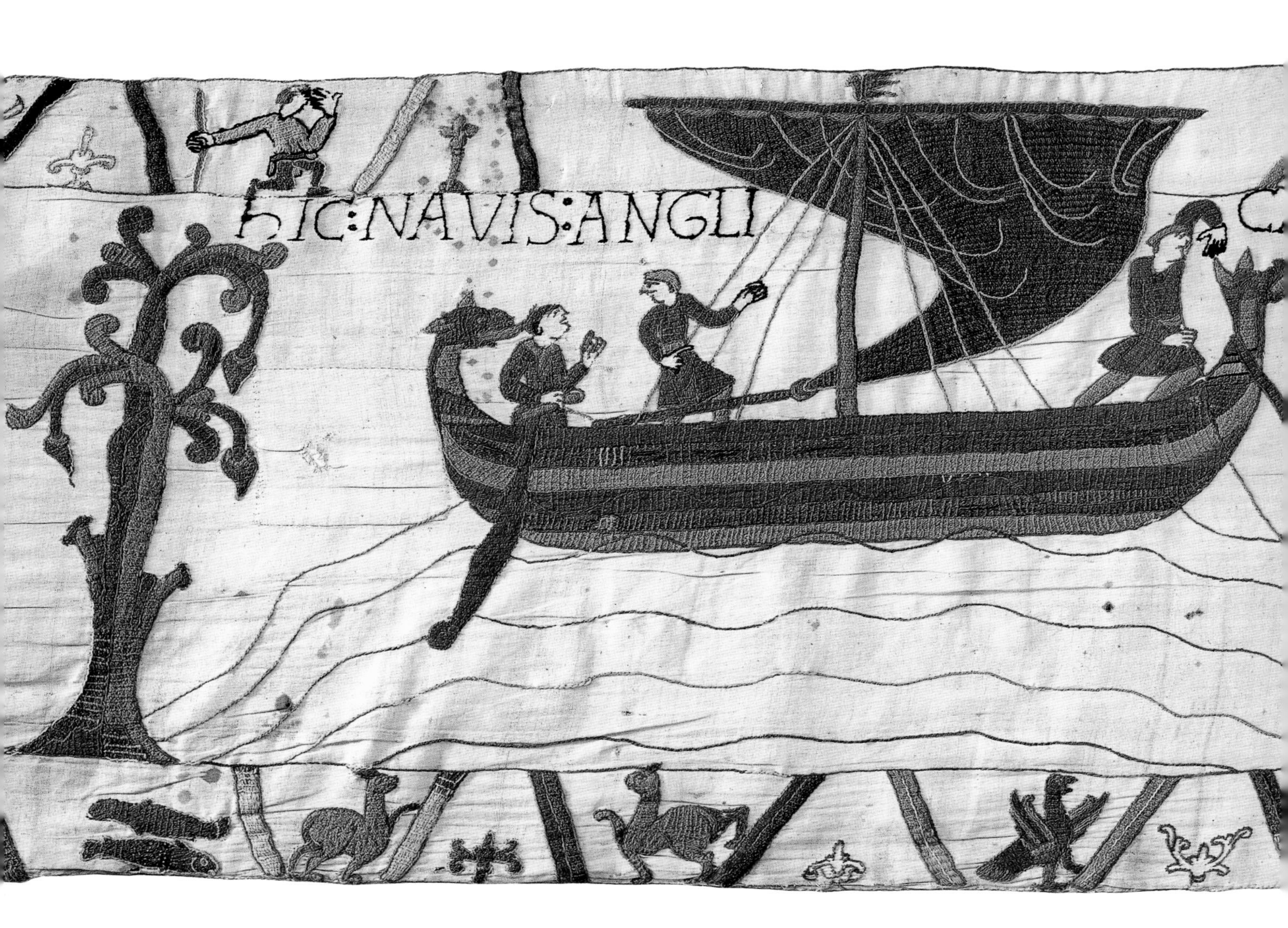

Harold. Here an English ship …

■ 182

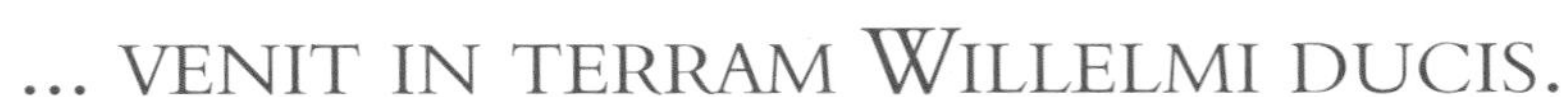

... VENIT IN TERRAM WILLELMI DUCIS. HIC WILLELM DU

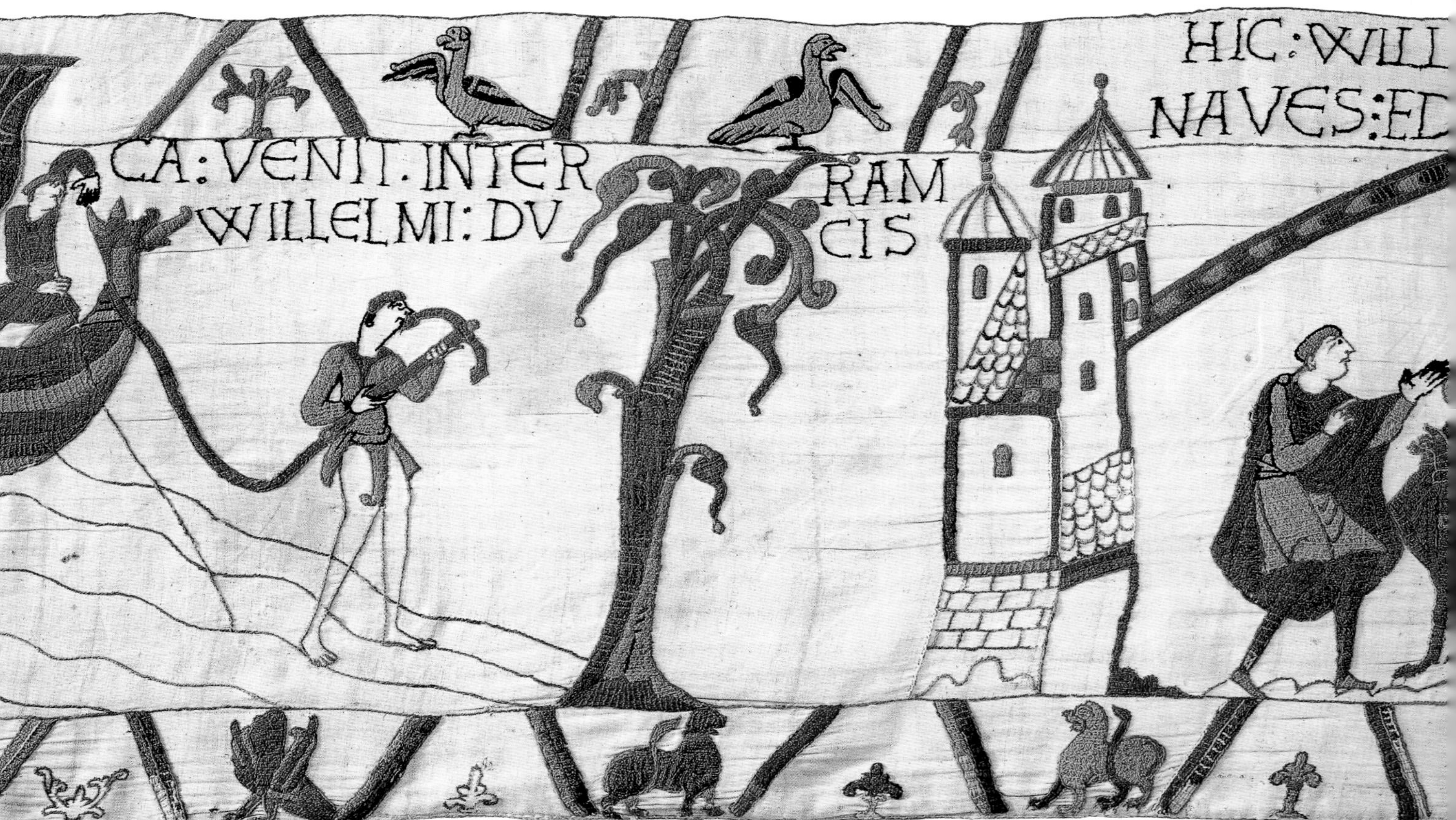

THE SCENE IS ONCE MORE A DUCAL PALACE, most probably Rouen (but just possibly Lillebonne). The portrayal is in any case stylised in the extreme. William, shown here without any insignia of rank, sits upon a throne whose arm-rests end in carved animal heads. It looks more like a business meeting than a ceremonial occasion. On the duke's right is a messenger bringing the latest news. To his left a clergyman stands on a little square of carpet, or perhaps a footstool (the duke's feet are resting on something similar), making an eloquent gesture. This is almost certainly Bishop Odo. Beside him stands a shipbuilder with a broadaxe, being given the orders for the construction of the fleet. The caption tells us everything: 'Here Duke William ordered ships to be built'. The Tapestry glosses over the lengthy deliberations at the Norman court and the discussions which, as we know from the chroniclers, William had with his barons at Lillebonne and Bonneville-sur-Touques early that year.

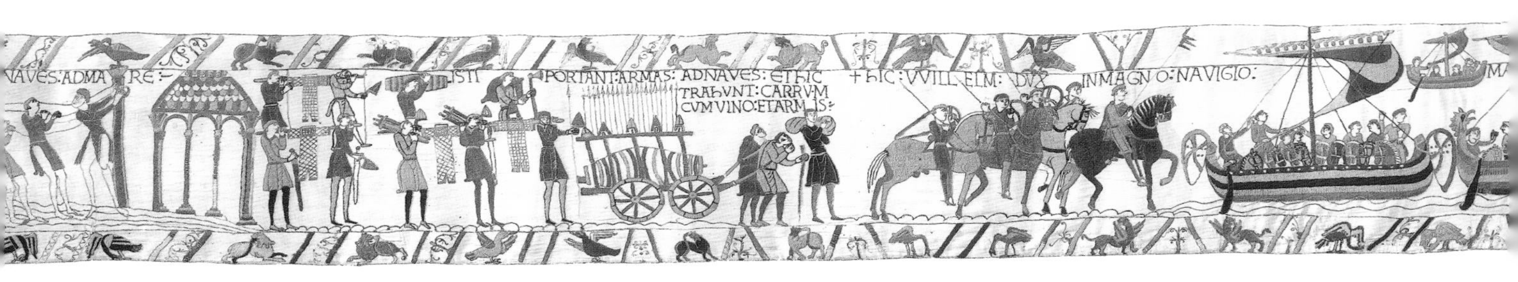

USSIT NAVES EDIFICARE.

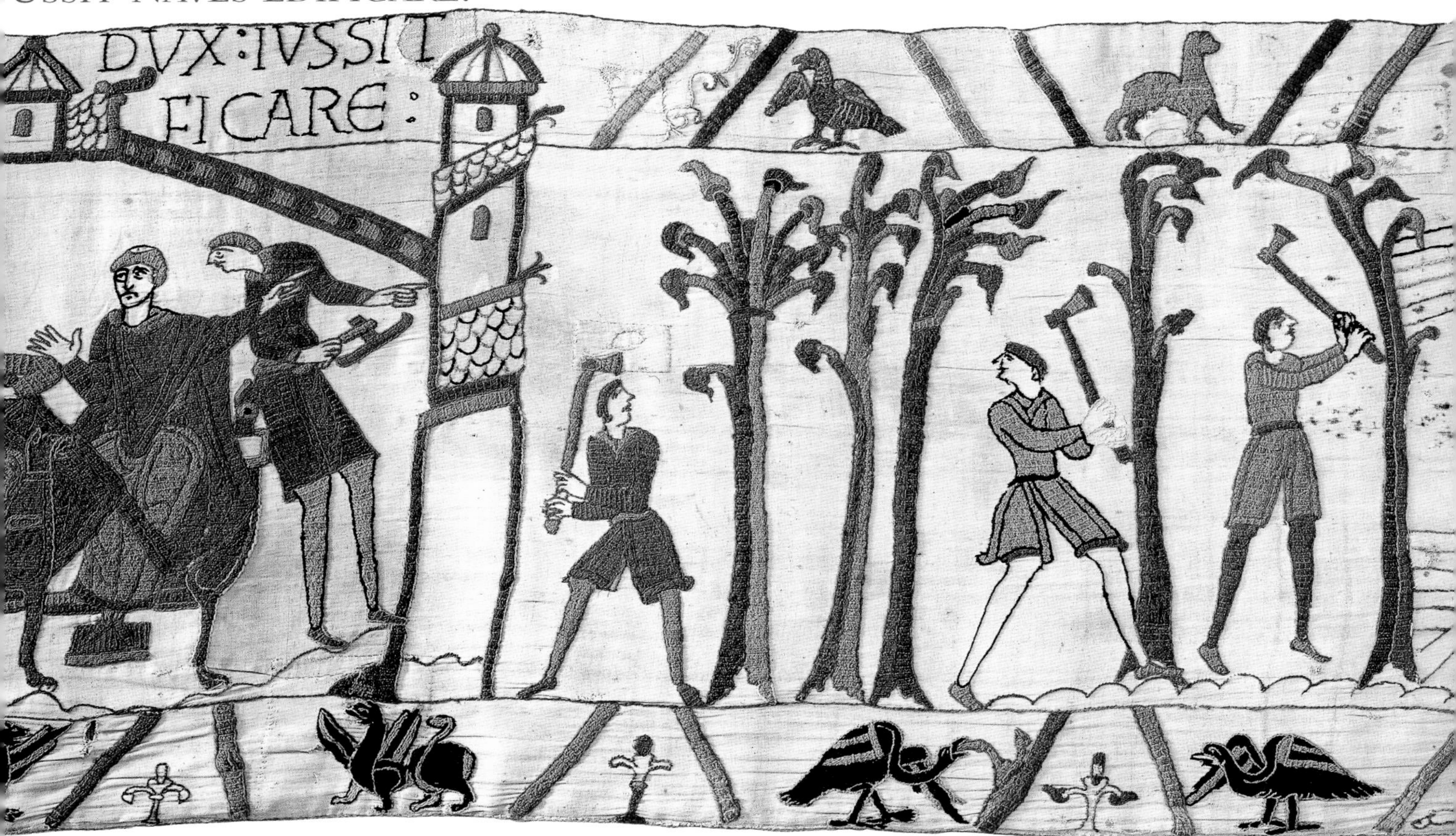

... comes to the land of Duke William. Here Duke William ordered ships to be built.

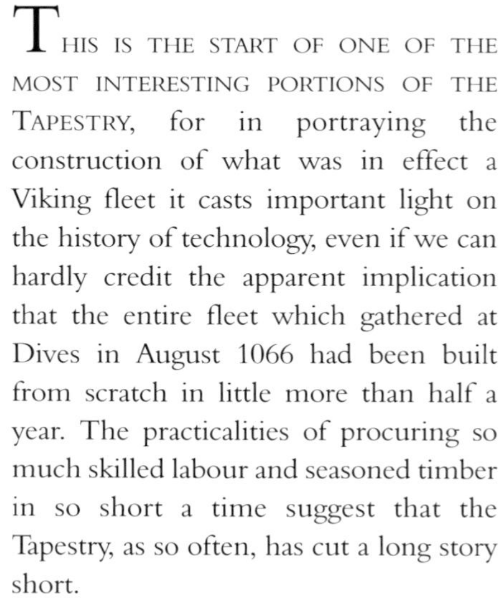

THIS IS THE START OF ONE OF THE MOST INTERESTING PORTIONS OF THE TAPESTRY, for in portraying the construction of what was in effect a Viking fleet it casts important light on the history of technology, even if we can hardly credit the apparent implication that the entire fleet which gathered at Dives in August 1066 had been built from scratch in little more than half a year. The practicalities of procuring so much skilled labour and seasoned timber in so short a time suggest that the Tapestry, as so often, has cut a long story short.

Eleventh- and twelfth-century traditions generally agree that most of the ships in the Norman fleet were already in service before William decided upon his invasion. Some of them doubtless belonged to the duke himself. Others would have been requisitioned from his subordinate lords and knights on the basis of some kind of levy whose rules are now unknown, though they might well have resembled those current in Scandinavia (the so-called *leidhangr*) and England, which in both cases were becoming more systematic and monetarised in the course of the eleventh century.[61] The only documentary references to the procedures followed in 1066 are rather late and highly unreliable, though for want of anything better historians have sought to draw some conclusions from them. Yet these conclusions are trivial enough, such as the supposed name of William's own ship, the *Mora* (the 'noiraude' or 'dark-haired maid') allegedly presented to him by his wife Matilda.

SCENE 36

The spurious document published in 1845 as the 'Catalogue of those who furnished vessels for Count William's expedition to England' purports to give the names of fourteen of Normandy's leading barons who between them supplied a thousand ships (though the figure for the fleet derived from other sources does not exceed 756) by virtue of feudal obligations akin to those of knight service.[62] But the text is most probably a twelfth-century flight of fancy and is full of glaring errors, the most egregious of which is that Matilda was rewarded for the *Mora* with the earldom of Kent. In fact, until his arrest in 1082, Bishop Odo was the sole tenant of that fief, and he had no immediate successor; while Matilda was never granted any earldom. The catalogue also credits certain Norman lordships with absurdly large naval contingents: Fulke d'Aunou, who held only one coastal territory (Foulbec, at the mouth of the Risle) is said to have provided forty vessels, while Roger de Beaumont, whose estates were entirely landlocked, is supposed to have provided sixty. If anything can be salvaged from this text (which is extremely doubtful),

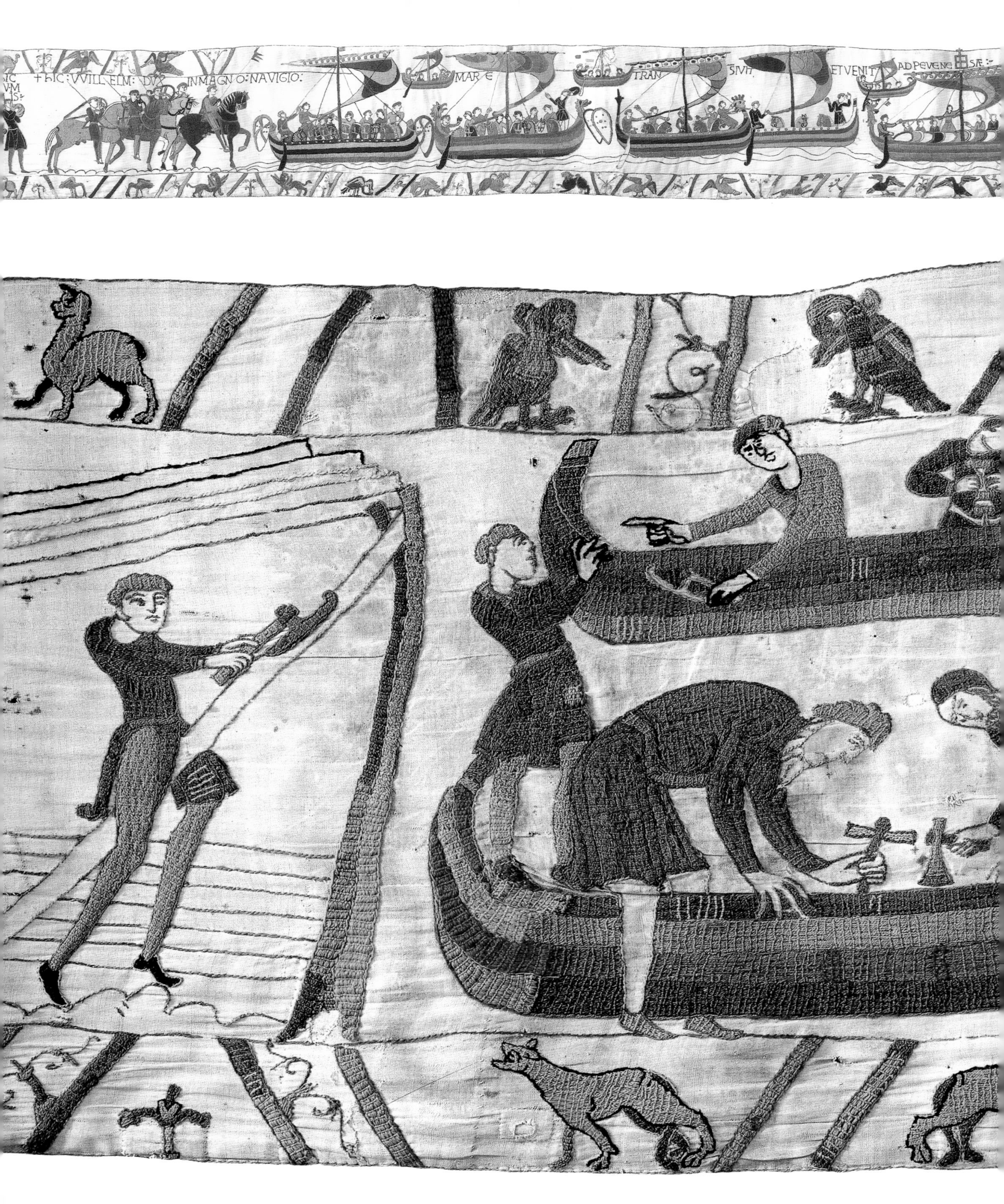
+HIC: VVILL ELM: DUX
IN MAGNO: NAVIGIO:
MARE
TRAN
SIVIT
ET VENIT
AD PEVENESÆ:

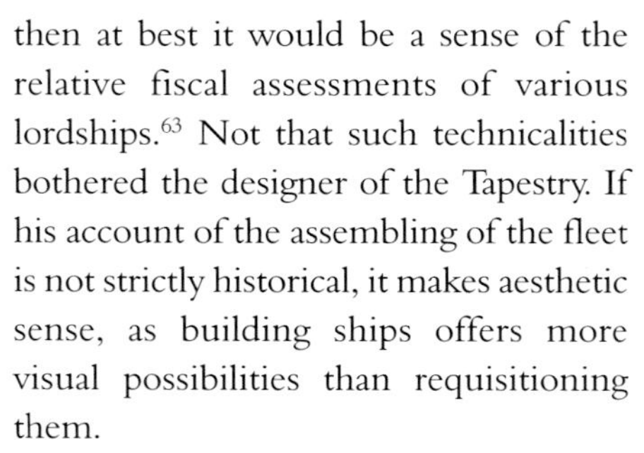

then at best it would be a sense of the relative fiscal assessments of various lordships.[63] Not that such technicalities bothered the designer of the Tapestry. If his account of the assembling of the fleet is not strictly historical, it makes aesthetic sense, as building ships offers more visual possibilities than requisitioning them.

The interpretation of this section of the Tapestry is made easier by some helpful external evidence. First of all, there is invaluable archaeological evidence if not from actual Viking construction yards then at least from two repair yards: one at Fribrødre Bæk in Denmark, and the other at Paviken on the Swedish island of Gotland. In addition, there is the literary evidence of Baudry de Bourgueil, whose imaginary wall-hangings echo the Tapestry's description of ship building. He expatiates at some length on the activities of the woodmen who fell timber at the prince's command and of the shipwrights who fashion oars, masts and other components from all sorts of woods: oak, holly, ash, and fir. In short, 'you see the forest march towards the shore'. Baudry's fleet is of 3000 vessels, some for foot soldiers, some for knights, and some for the horses. In an interesting but otherwise unconfirmed aside, he notes that workmen were recruited 'from all over the world' (*ex toto … orbe*) for this enterprise, which might indicate that the shipbuilding techniques depicted need not be merely Anglo-Norman.[64]

[61] L. Musset, 'Problèmes militaires du monde scandinave (VIIe-XIIe siècles)', *Settimane di studio del Centro Italiano di Studi sull'Alto Medioevo, Spoleto* 15 (1968), pp. 229-291.

[62] 'Catalogus suppeditantium naves ad expeditionem Willelmi comitis in Angliam', ed. J. A. Giles, *Scriptores rerum gestarum Willelmi Conquestoris* (London, 1845), pp. 21-22.

[63] See in particular G. M. Gillmore, 'Naval Logistics of the Channel Operation 1066', *Anglo-Norman Studies* 7 (1984), pp. 105-31, at pp. 119-21. There is also an important article by E. Van Houts, 'The Ship List of William the Conqueror', *Anglo-Norman Studies* 10 (1987), pp. 159-83, which includes an excellent reproduction of the only manuscript (from the second half of the twelfth century) but tends to a conclusion I doubt, namely that the document is useful and derived originally from Fécamp. My opinion remains the same: this is a record of fiscal capacity, not of real ships supplied. C. Warren Hollister also attempts to rehabilitate the list in 'The Greater Domesday Tenants-in-Chief', in *Domesday Studies*, ed. J. C. Holt (Woodbridge, 1987), pp. 219-48, proposing various emendations to the published text, but scarcely rendering it any more plausible.

[64] Baudry, ed. Lauer, p. 47, verses 331-57, esp. 335 and 347.

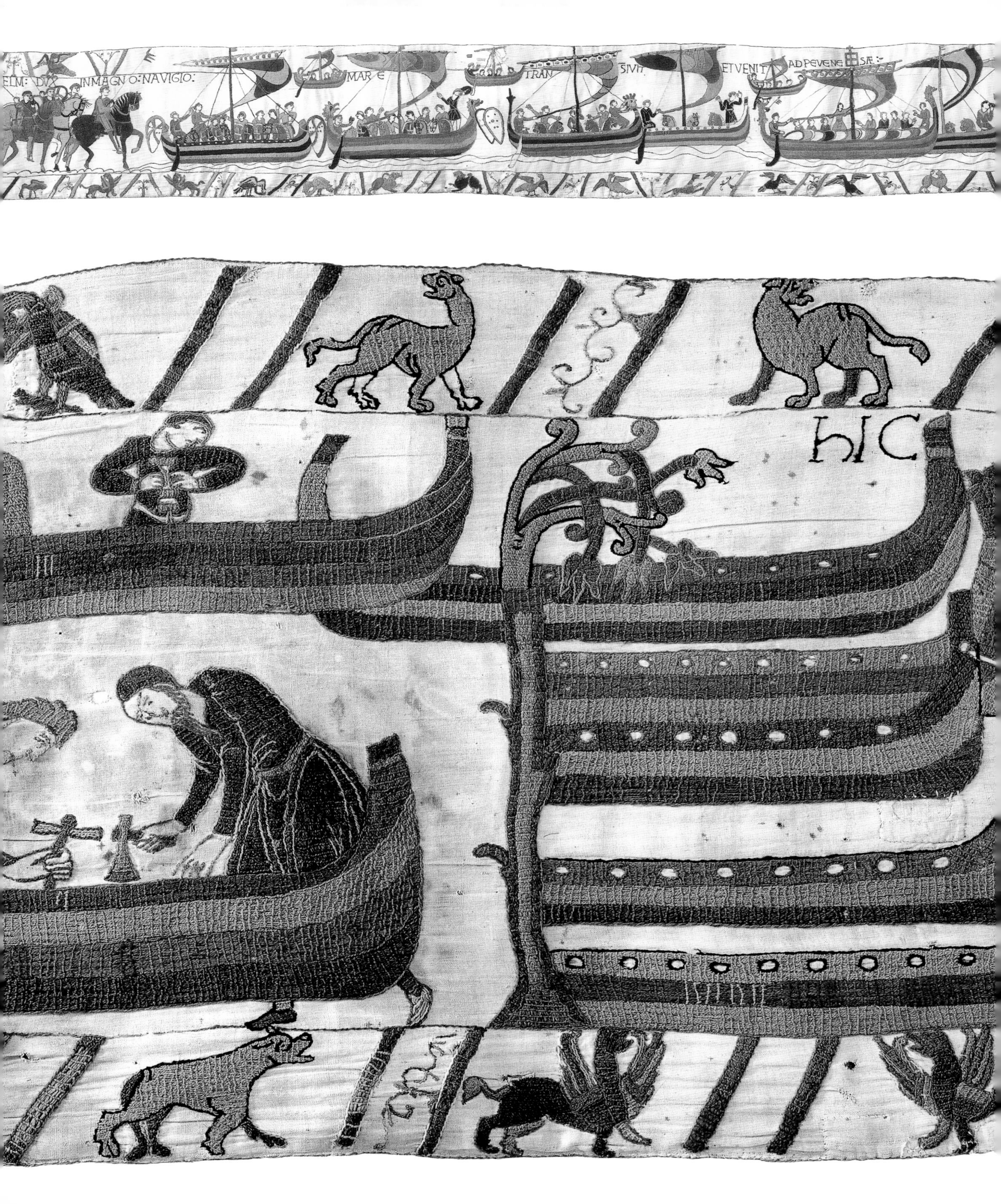
ELM: DUX
INMAGN O: NAVIGIO:
MAR E
TRAN
SIVIT
ET VENIT
AD PEVENE
SÆ:
HIC

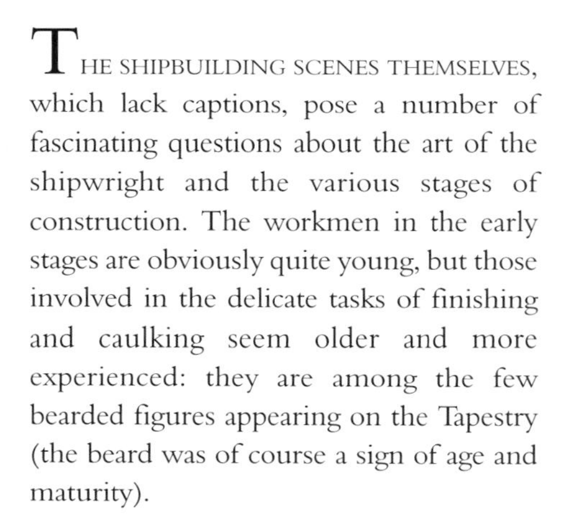

THE SHIPBUILDING SCENES THEMSELVES, which lack captions, pose a number of fascinating questions about the art of the shipwright and the various stages of construction. The workmen in the early stages are obviously quite young, but those involved in the delicate tasks of finishing and caulking seem older and more experienced: they are among the few bearded figures appearing on the Tapestry (the beard was of course a sign of age and maturity).

The shipwrights' toolkit seems to consist of three tools: the wood-axe, the broadaxe, and the hammer. The wood-axes are rather different from the battle-axes which served the English as weapons or as symbols of rank. The workman's axe was smaller and virtually triangular, with a straight rather than a curved blade, and can probably be identified with what was known in Old Norse as a *boløx*, which was used for felling trees and could also serve as a hatchet. Many examples have turned up in excavations.[65]

The construction process is shown in four stages. First the trees (as unrealistically drawn as ever) are felled, and then they are cut up into planks and planed with a broadaxe,[66] a task which would have been carried out not in the forest but at the shipyard, where the finished timbers are assembled to form the hulls.[67] The final touches are applied by the older, bearded craftsmen, one of whom wields a mallet, with which he is caulking the vessel to render it watertight. The oarports were probably made last, when the detachable figureheads were fitted fore and aft.

[65] S. Horn-Fuglesang, *Some Aspects of the Ringerike Style* (Odense, 1980), pp. 146-47.

[66] The broadaxe is identical to one found at the port of Hedeby in 1979. See O. Crumlin Pedersen, 'Aspects of Viking-Age Shipbuilding', *Journal of Danish Archaeology* 5 (1986), p. 285.

[67] See O. Olsen and O. Crumlin Pedersen, 'The Skuldelev Ships', II, *Acta Archaeologica* 38 (1967), p. 160.

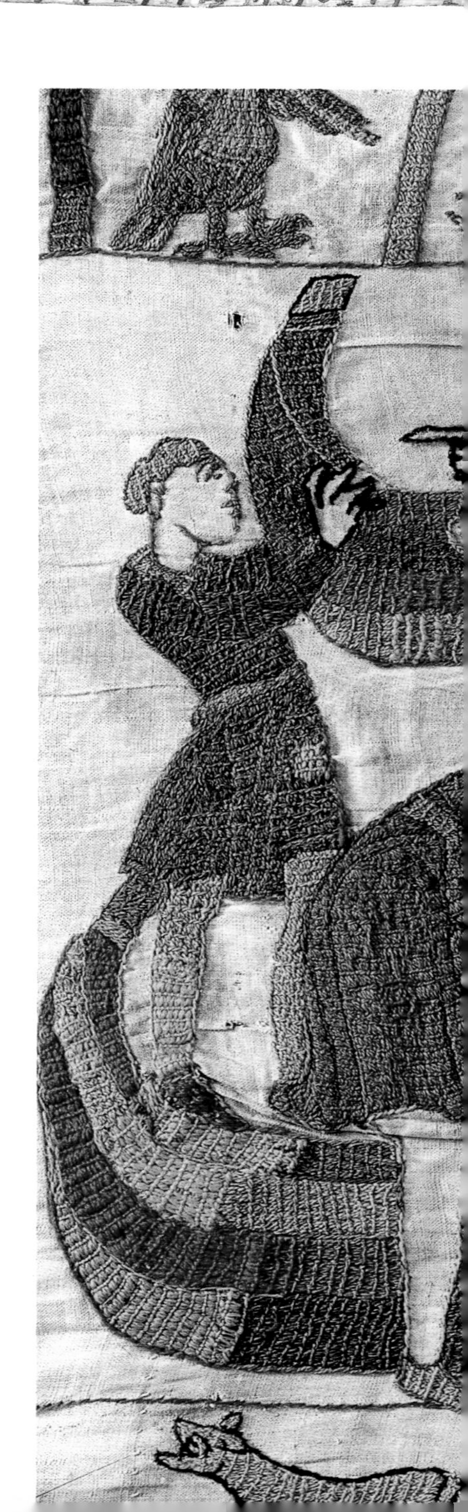

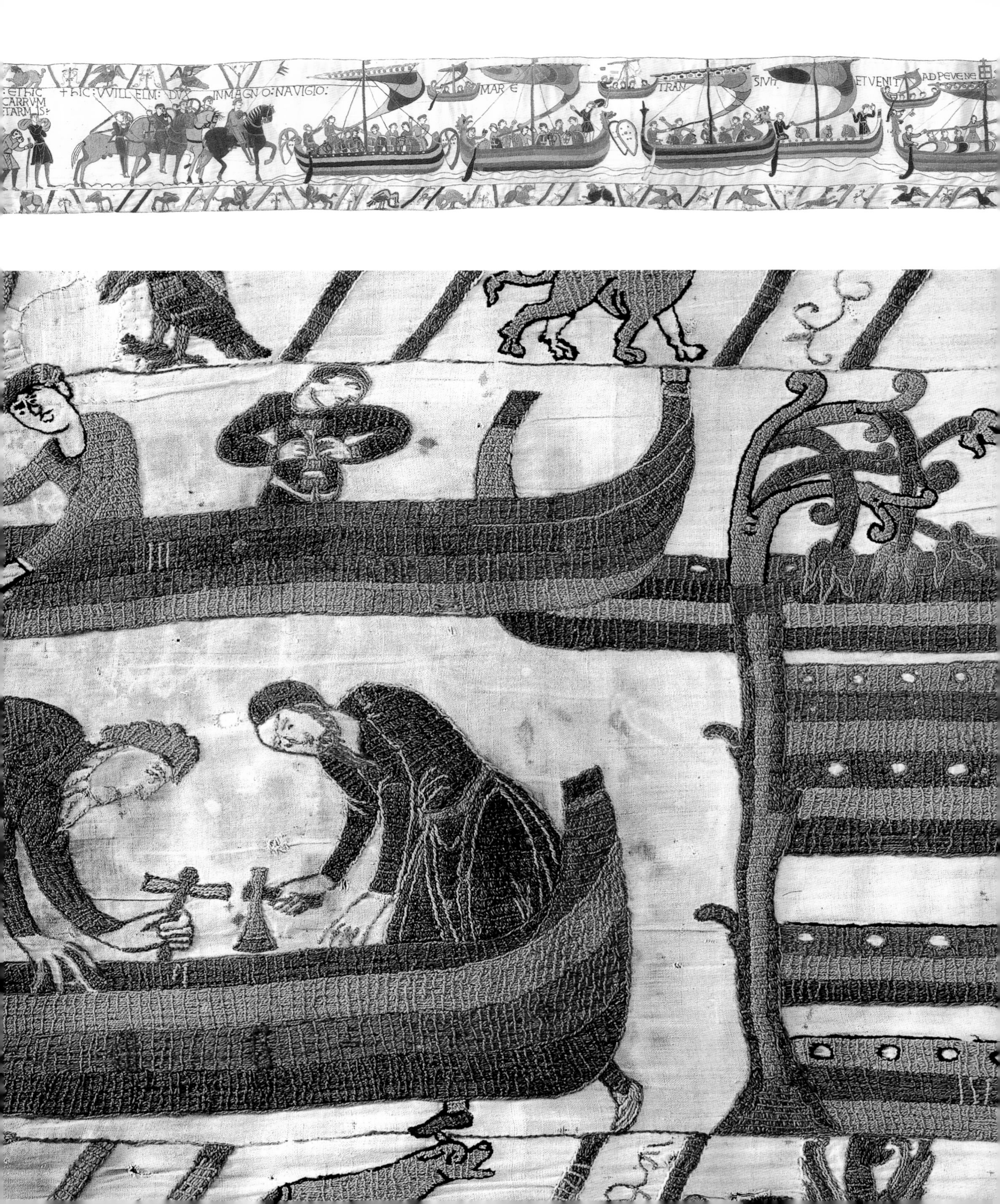
ET HIC CARRVM ET ARMIS
HIC VVILLELM DUX IN MAGNO NAVIGIO MARE TRANSIVIT ET VENIT AD PEVENE

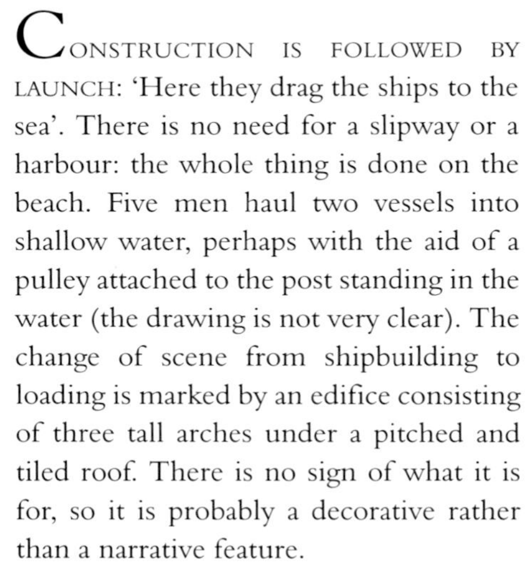

HIC TRAHUNT NAVE

CONSTRUCTION IS FOLLOWED BY LAUNCH: 'Here they drag the ships to the sea'. There is no need for a slipway or a harbour: the whole thing is done on the beach. Five men haul two vessels into shallow water, perhaps with the aid of a pulley attached to the post standing in the water (the drawing is not very clear). The change of scene from shipbuilding to loading is marked by an edifice consisting of three tall arches under a pitched and tiled roof. There is no sign of what it is for, so it is probably a decorative rather than a narrative feature.

Although the location is not specified, much of this was probably taking place at the mouth of the Touques, near the major ducal residence at Bonneville, and helpfully close to a large forest (the present-day forest of Saint-Gatien, inland from Trouville). But the main rendezvous for the ducal fleet was a little further west at Dives (and Cabourg), then a port of some importance. The Dives estuary, then much wider than it is today, was the base for much maritime activity, in particular for the Norman whaling fleets that operated under the aegis of the abbey of Fécamp (and soon afterwards also of the abbey of Saint-Étienne de Caen) and formerly under ducal authority.[68] The area, moreover, was well served by a network of roads, the 'chemins sauniers', or 'salt roads', connecting the salt-pans of Escanneville (at Gonneville-sur-Merville), Sallenelles, and Dives with Falaise and the Norman interior. About halfway between Haute-Normandie and the Cotentin, the area was thus almost perfect for the concentration of Norman forces ahead of the invasion.[69] The traces of eleventh-century occupation found in 1982 at Bavent, a few kilometres south-west of Dives, probably mark the holding camps where William's troops waited until embarkation.[70]

[68] L. Musset, 'Les baleiniers normands du Xe au XIIIe siècle', *Revue d'Histoire Economique et Sociale* 42 (1964), pp. 147-61; and 'Les ports en Normandie du Xie au XIIIe siècle', *Autour du pouvoir ducal normand* (Caen, 1985; Cahiers des Annales de Normandie, 17), p. 118.

[69] L. Musset, 'Les chemins sauniers de la Normandie médiévale', *Annales de Normandie* 33 (1983), pp. 175-79.

[70] See various notes by C. Pilet, esp. in *Annales de Normandie* 33 (1983), p. 311.

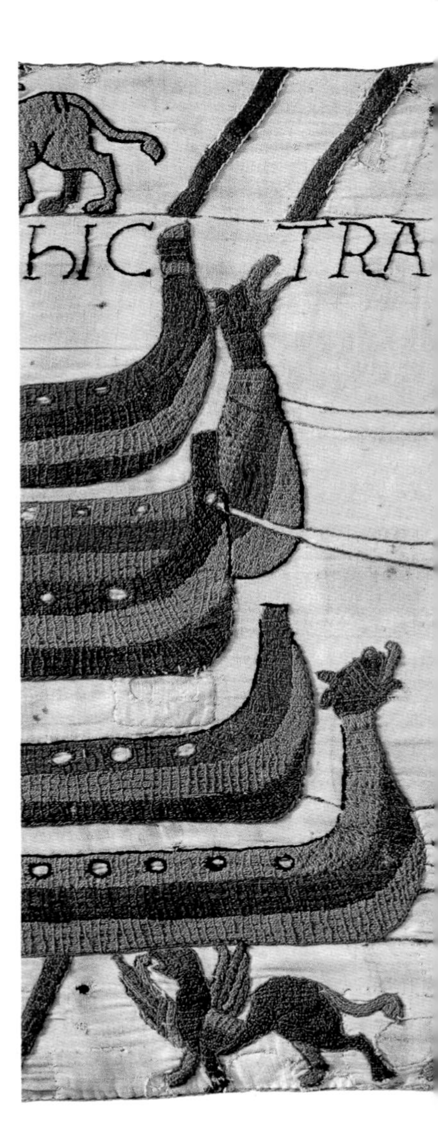

SCENE 36 (continued)

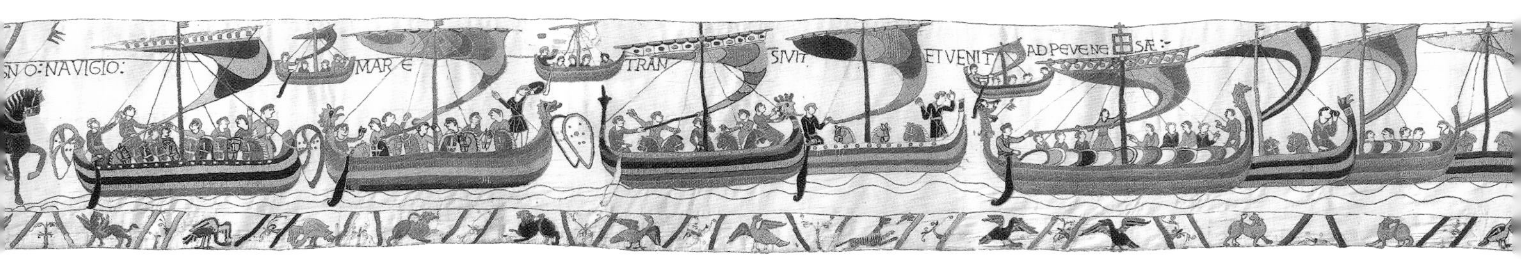

D MARE.

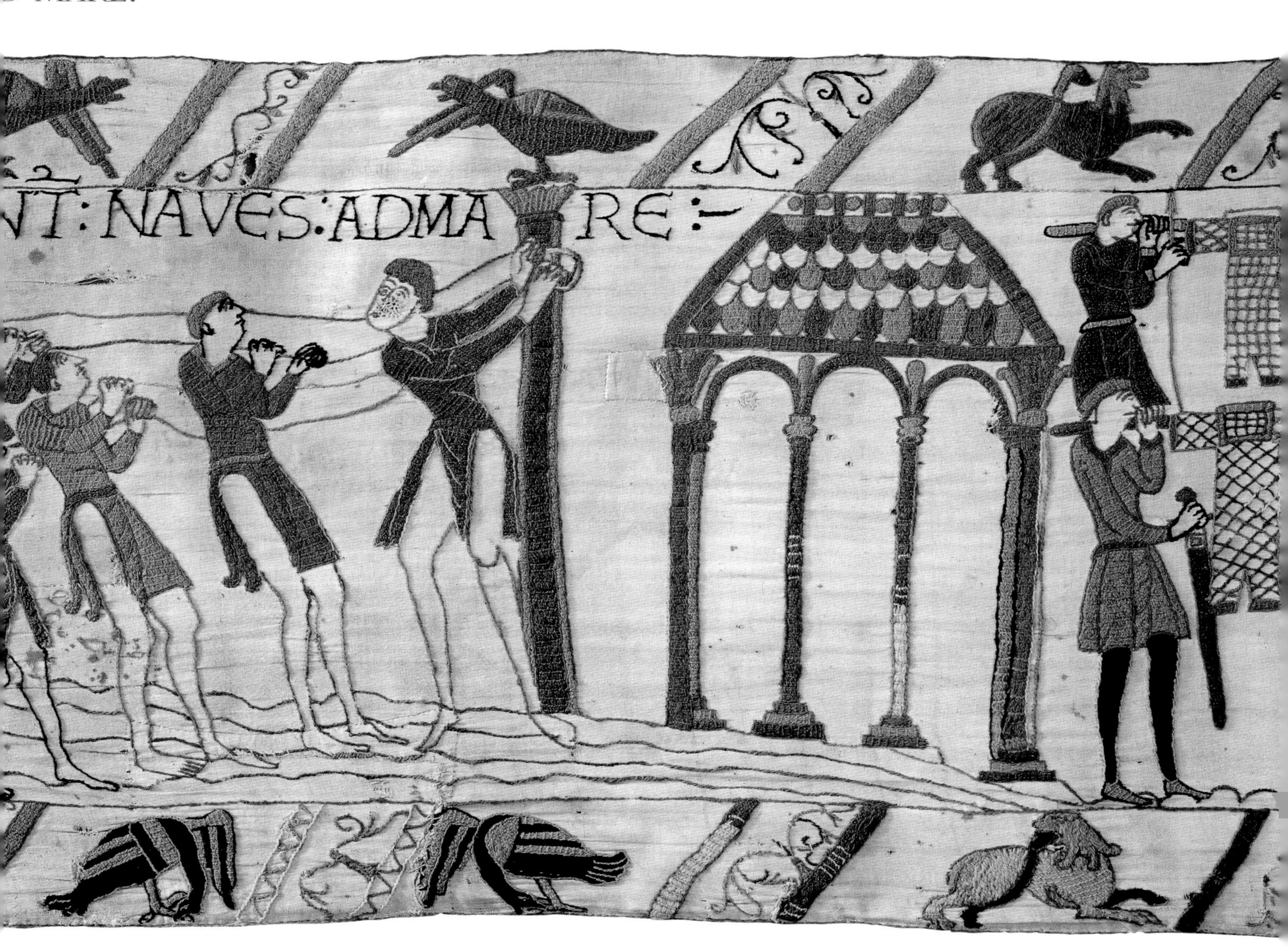

Here they drag the ships to the sea.

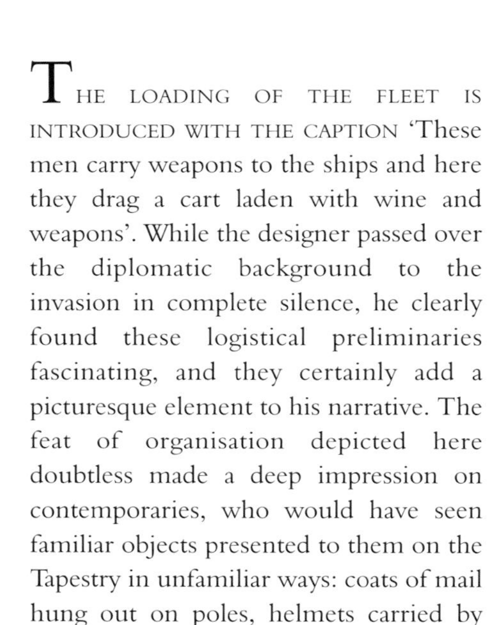

Isti portant armas

THE LOADING OF THE FLEET IS INTRODUCED WITH THE CAPTION 'These men carry weapons to the ships and here they drag a cart laden with wine and weapons'. While the designer passed over the diplomatic background to the invasion in complete silence, he clearly found these logistical preliminaries fascinating, and they certainly add a picturesque element to his narrative. The feat of organisation depicted here doubtless made a deep impression on contemporaries, who would have seen familiar objects presented to them on the Tapestry in unfamiliar ways: coats of mail hung out on poles, helmets carried by their nose-pieces, and swords in bundles.

The cargo is carried to the ships by men, not by beasts of burden. It has been pointed out that the four-wheeled cart which two men are dragging by a harness is not of Norman but of English design, akin to those seen in Anglo-Saxon Old Testament illuminations: 'a platform with sides made from poles placed at intervals and joined by a single horizontal bar'.[71] This must be the sort of cart that the designer saw around Canterbury every day.

The loading scene concentrates on armaments: there is no sign of the oars, rigging, or other marine equipment visible on the ships in the next scene. Nor do we see much of the more mundane side of an army's commissariat. Except for the sack on the shoulders of the man in front of the cart, this army's provisions seem to come down to wine, conveyed in casks (as on the cart), kegs or wineskins (on the shoulders).

The prominent place of wine may seem surprising to those who know modern Normandy, but in 1066 cider had not yet become fashionable. Its first documented appearance was some years after the Conquest, and until the thirteenth century it was largely confined to the regions of Bessin and the Pays d'Auge. Wine, on the other hand, was produced in several parts of ducal Normandy, notably in the Seine valley (towards Vernon), around Argences (to the east of Caen), and south of Avranches. Whatever the quality, there was plenty of it, and it may be that the consumption of wine struck the English as one of the distinctive characteristics of Norman culture.[72]

[71] C. E. Dodwell, 'L'originalité iconographique de plusieurs illustrations anglo-saxonnes de l'Ancien Testament', *Cahiers de civilisation médiévale* 14 (1971), pp. 319-28, at p. 326.

[72] Although Domesday Book shows that, in 1086, England itself still possessed some vineyards, albeit doubtless less productive.

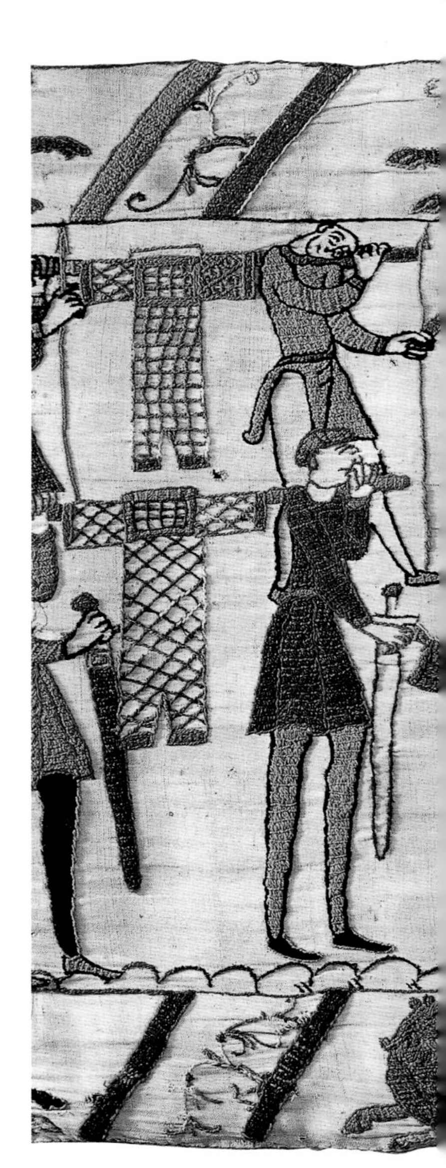

Scene 37

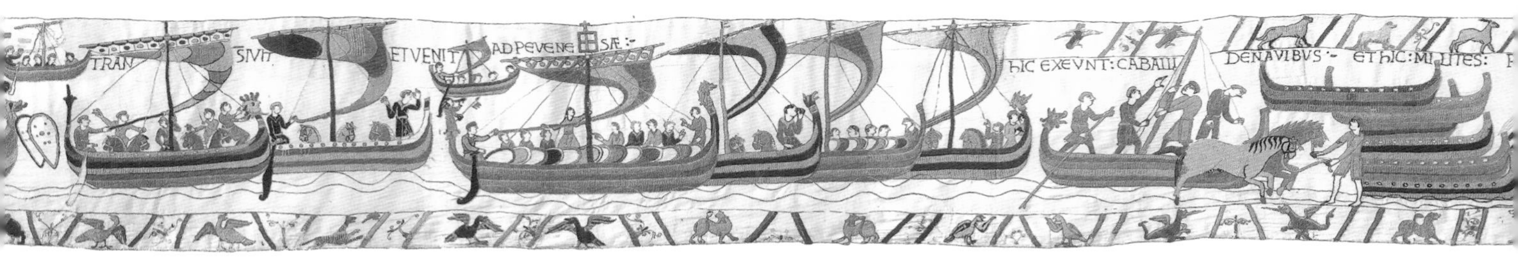

D NAVES ET HIC TRAHUNT CARRUM CUM VINO ET ARMIS

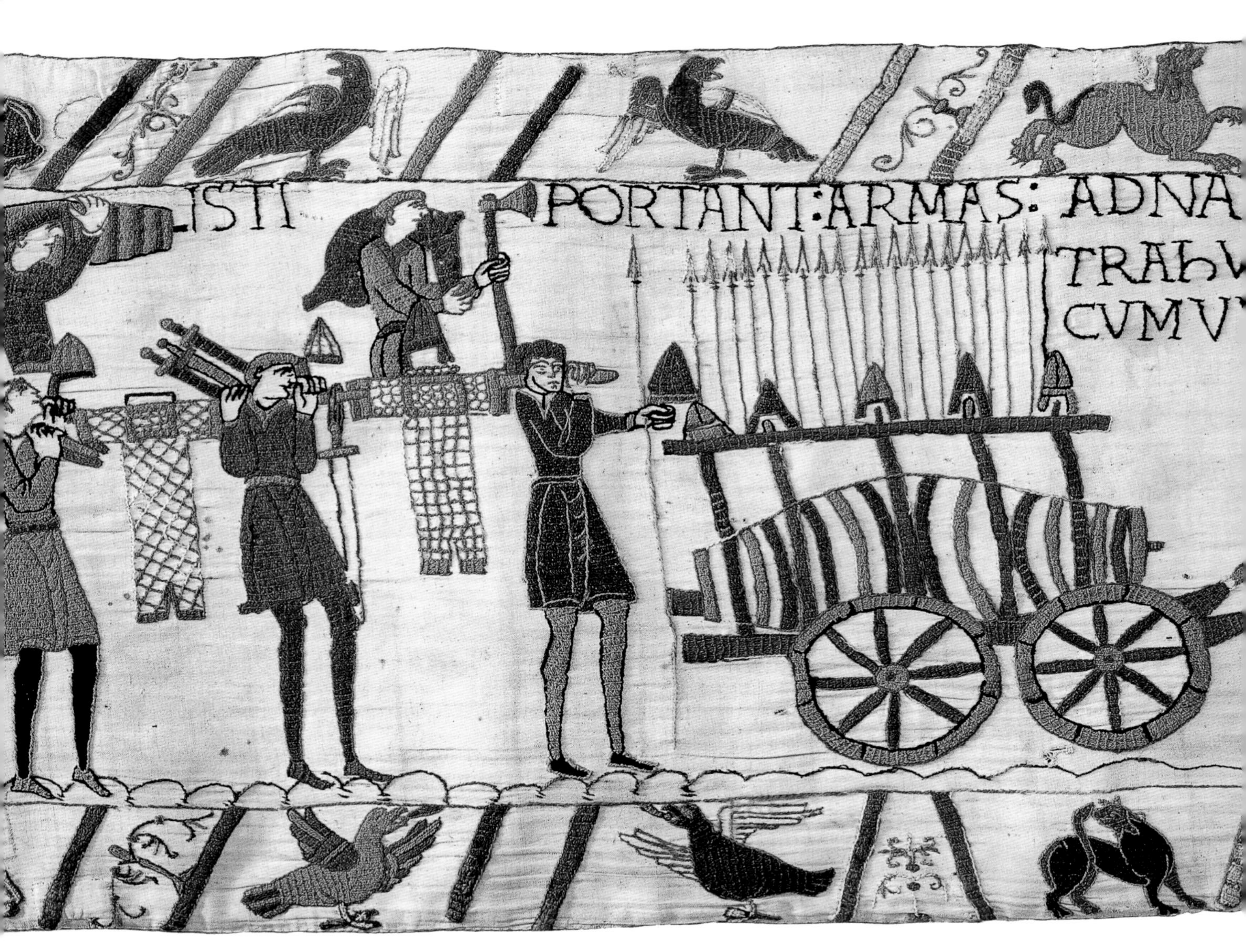

These men carry weapons to the ships and here they drag a cart laden with wine and weapons.

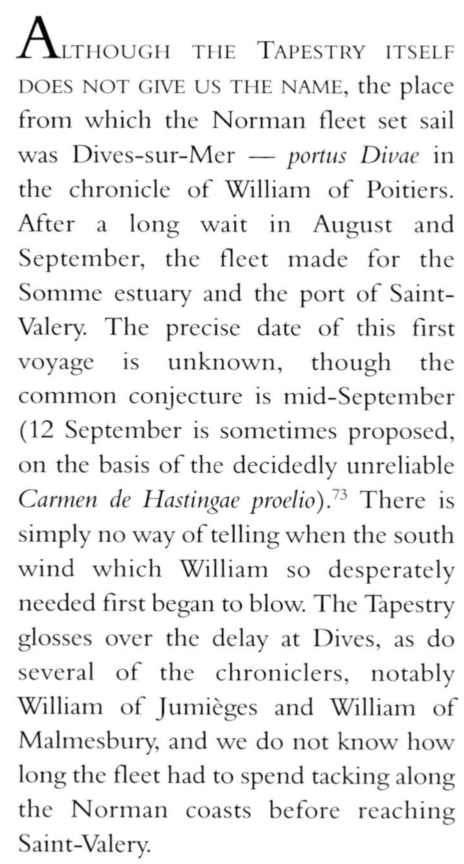

ALTHOUGH THE TAPESTRY ITSELF DOES NOT GIVE US THE NAME, the place from which the Norman fleet set sail was Dives-sur-Mer — *portus Divae* in the chronicle of William of Poitiers. After a long wait in August and September, the fleet made for the Somme estuary and the port of Saint-Valery. The precise date of this first voyage is unknown, though the common conjecture is mid-September (12 September is sometimes proposed, on the basis of the decidedly unreliable *Carmen de Hastingae proelio*).[73] There is simply no way of telling when the south wind which William so desperately needed first began to blow. The Tapestry glosses over the delay at Dives, as do several of the chroniclers, notably William of Jumièges and William of Malmesbury, and we do not know how long the fleet had to spend tacking along the Norman coasts before reaching Saint-Valery.

The view of William himself embarking in company with four of his knights brings us to the vexed question of the number of troops he took across the Channel. William of Poitiers suggests an impressive 50,000 men; the chronicle of Saint-Maixent, of little value in this regard, a more modest 14,000. Modern historians tend to go still lower, reckoning on 7,000 men, or 8,000 at the very outside.[74] But there is no secure basis for estimating the size of William's army, nor indeed that of Harold's — though the English force was probably slightly larger. Irrespective of the numbers involved, it was no inconsiderable feat, under the conditions of the eleventh century, to assemble and embark such a force, and to keep it in good order for the nearly two months which elapsed between its assembly and its eventual landing in England.

THIS PHASE OF THE TAPESTRY, then, has considerably simplified historical reality in the interests of providing a smooth and continuous narrative. It omits the councils of Norman barons which took place in the first half of the year, conflates into a single event the embarkation at Dives and the sailing from Saint-Valery, and ignores the long delays at both places. Nor does it go into any detail about the composition of the army, which included contingents not only from Normandy but also from Brittany, Maine, Picardy, Flanders, and even Poitou. Nor finally does it bother enumerating those who 'came over with the Conqueror', the real list of whom has long dismayed genealogists with its brevity.[75] All that matters is the implacable manifestation of divine providence in the form of the Norman invasion. The headlong narrative is interrupted at the most for the occasional picturesque moment as in scenes 42 and 43 (pp. 210–211 and 212).

[73] William of Poitiers, ed. Foreville, pp. 150-51 (Davis and Chibnall, pp. 102-3). *Carmen de Hastingae Proelio*, line 76]

[74] William of Poitiers, ed. Foreville, pp. 150-51 (Davis and Chibnall, pp. 102-3. M. de Boüard, *Guillaume le Conquérant* (Paris, 1984), p. 295; C. H. Lemmon, *The Field of Hastings* (3rd. edn. St Leonards, 1951), p. 18, offers a more detailed breakdown — 3,000 horse, 4,000 foot, and 1,000 bowmen — which, unlike the medieval figures, is not unreasonable.

[75] The only reliable list is that prepared by D. C. Douglas, 'Companions of the Conqueror', *History* 28 (1943), pp. 130-47. The lists deposited at the Saint-Prix chapel in the castle of Falaise and at the church of Dives-sur-Mer are of no scholarly value, simply gathering up names of lineages which are not attested outside the pages of Domesday Book. Scarcely two or three names need to be added to the 32 that Douglas listed (five of which are uncertain).

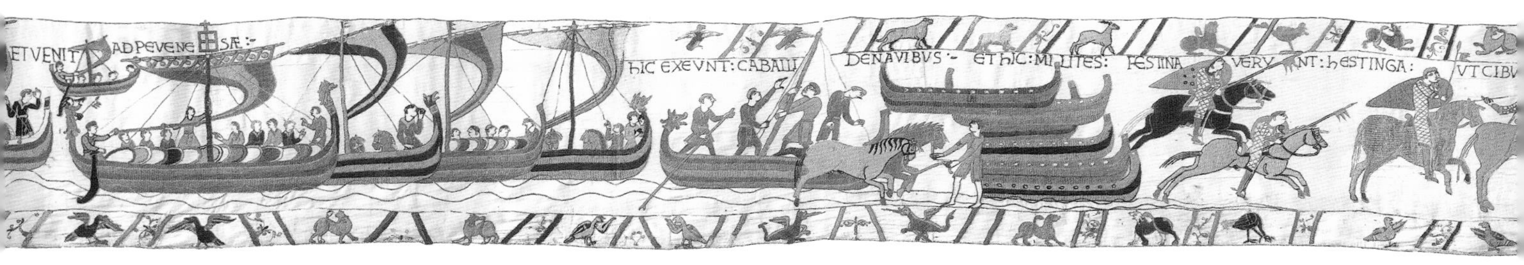

... CUM VINO ET ARMIS. + HIC WILLELM DUX...

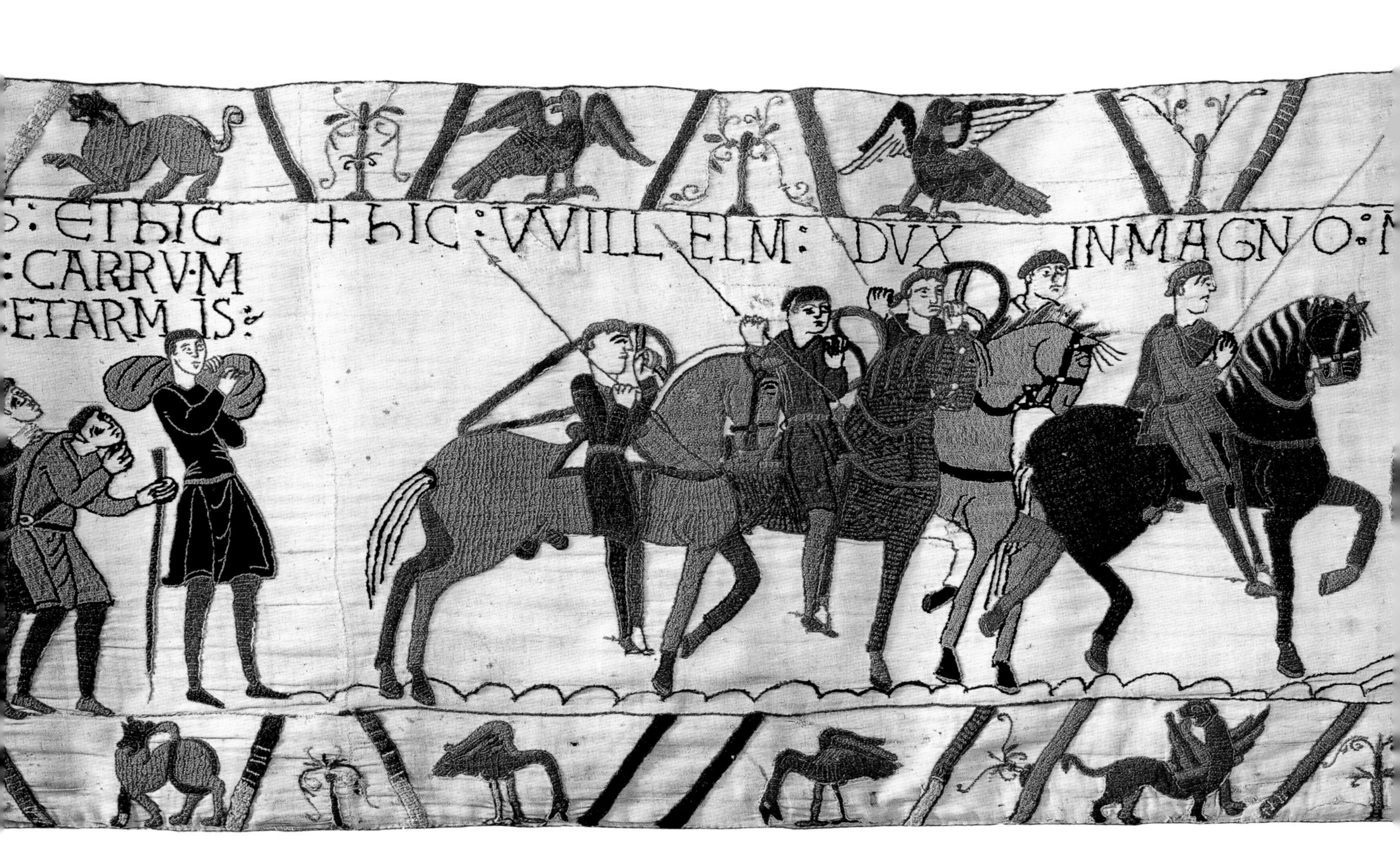

...laden with wine and weapons. + Here Duke William ...

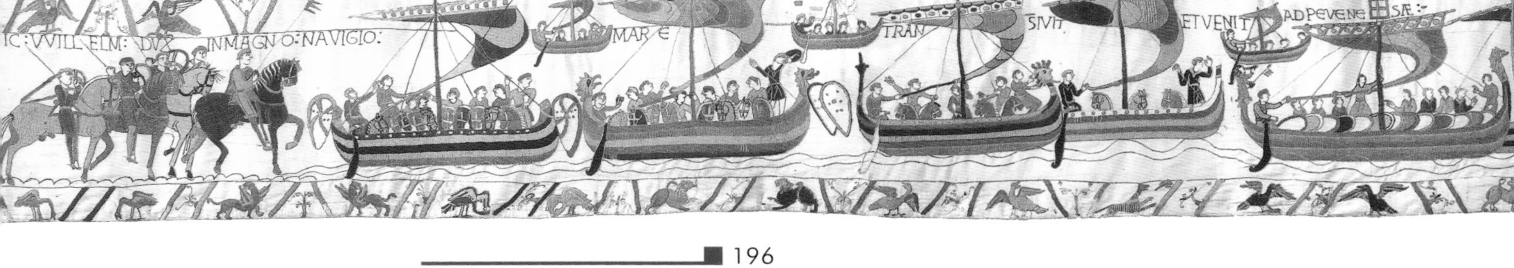

196

THE CHANNEL CROSSING OF THE NORMAN FLEET (pp. 196–203) is without doubt one of the most famous scenes on the Tapestry. Having dealt already with the general nautical issues which arise from it, we shall concentrate here on specific details. Nine ships are shown in the foreground and three in the background. Six of them are carrying horses, which, of course, the English would subsequently have seen as a decisive element in the campaign. All the vessels have their masts raised and their sails set, and although oarports are visible on three of them, there is no sign of oars being used at any stage. Only one ship is being manoeuvred with a pole, and that is the one seen approaching the English shore, with its mast being lowered and its horses disembarked, just before it is dragged up onto the beach. Only two of the ships have shields fixed along the gunwales.

Not all of the ships have figureheads. There are none visible on the ships drawn up on the beach, nor on the ships in the background, perhaps in the latter case because they are portrayed in much smaller scale. Nor is there anything on the rearmost vessel. Among the figureheads one in particular stands out, and has attracted considerable scholarly attention. The fifth ship from the left in the line occupying the foreground, almost certainly the duke's own, is decorated at the stern with a small human figure carrying a short lance and pennant in its left hand and blowing a horn held in its right. This detail was familiar to the twelfth-century chroniclers. According to the *Brevis relatio*, the duke's ship (which it reckoned to have been commissioned by Matilda) had at its prow 'a little golden boy pointing to England with his right hand, and holding an ivory horn to his mouth with his left hand'.[76] Wace refers to 'what sailors call the *brant*' (a Norman term, derived from an Old Norse word for a prow) as decorated with an image in copper of a boy armed with a drawn bow and arrow pointed towards England.[77] So the figure on the ship's stern is no mere flight of fancy, but the artist's impression of a feature which caught the imagination of contemporaries.

The duke's vessel is also distinguished by the curious emblem at the masthead, a crossed square with a further cross on top. There are two possible interpretations of this. One suggestion is that it is the famous *vexillum sancti Petri*, the papal banner sent to William by Alexander II. The other, more mundane view sees in it a lantern meant to help the fleet stay together by night, as described by Wace: 'The duke had a lantern placed on the top of his ship's mast, so that the other ships could see it and hold their course behind him'.[78] Both William of Poitiers and the *Carmen de Hastingae Proelio* mention a lantern, and the use of lanterns for such purposes is attested in an entirely independent source, the *Miracles of St Thomas Becket*, in an

... IN MAGNO NAVIGIC

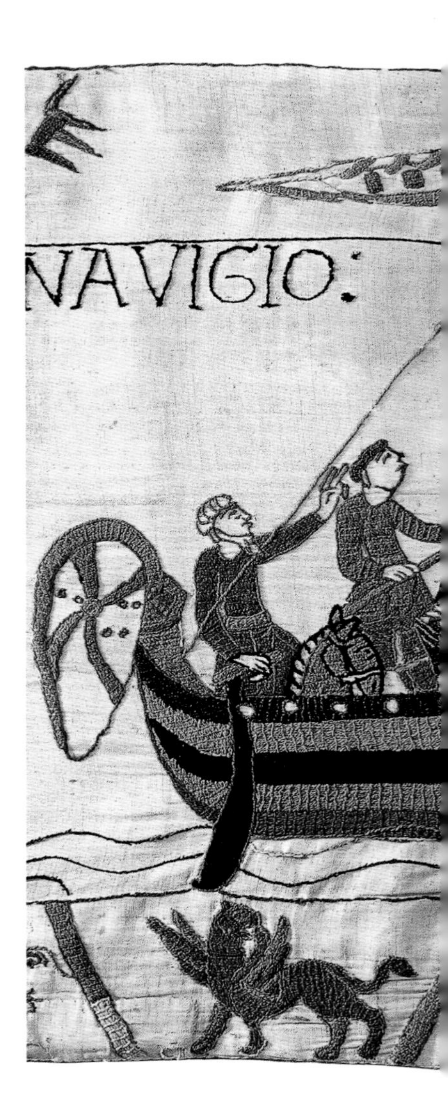

SCENE 38

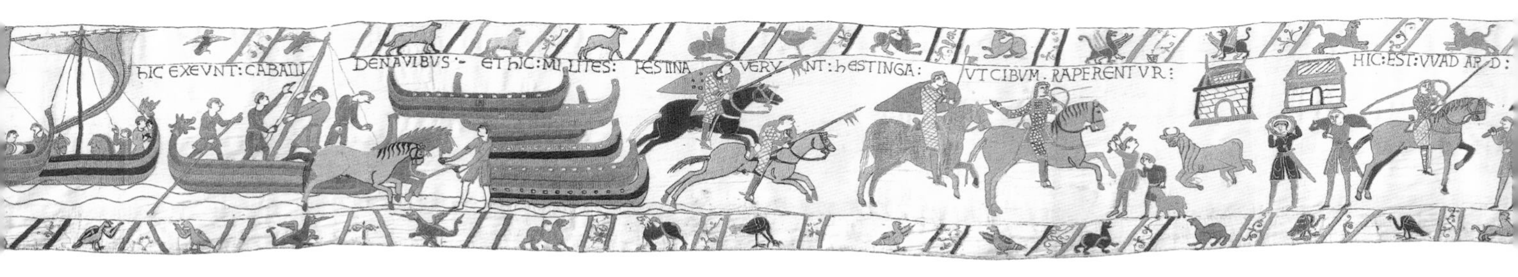

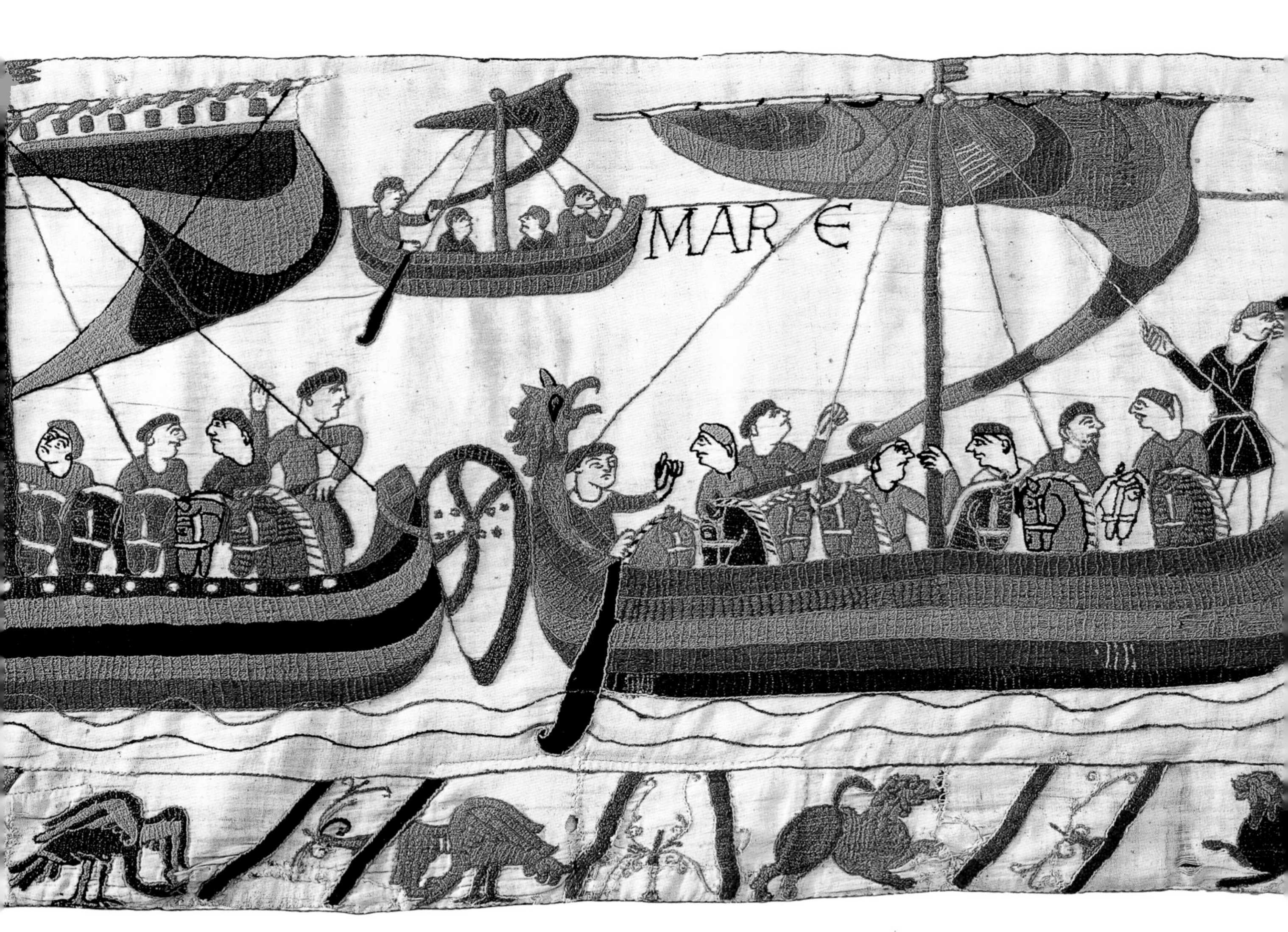

…in a great ship …

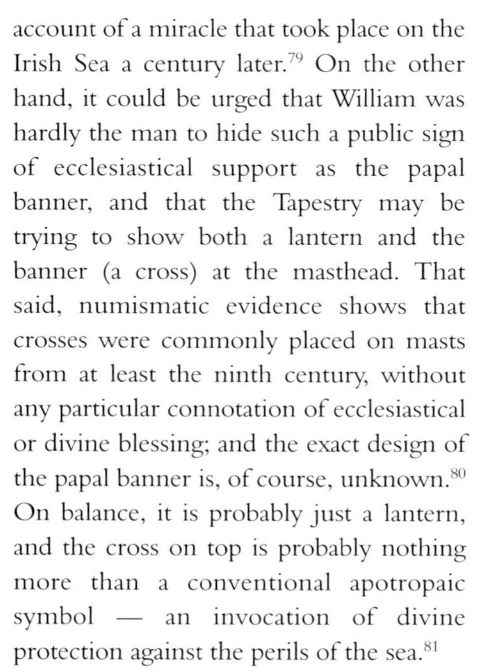

account of a miracle that took place on the Irish Sea a century later.[79] On the other hand, it could be urged that William was hardly the man to hide such a public sign of ecclesiastical support as the papal banner, and that the Tapestry may be trying to show both a lantern and the banner (a cross) at the masthead. That said, numismatic evidence shows that crosses were commonly placed on masts from at least the ninth century, without any particular connotation of ecclesiastical or divine blessing; and the exact design of the papal banner is, of course, unknown.[80] On balance, it is probably just a lantern, and the cross on top is probably nothing more than a conventional apotropaic symbol — an invocation of divine protection against the perils of the sea.[81]

The artistic merits of the depiction of the Norman fleet deserve special comment, as it goes far beyond the rather static images typical of Romanesque and medieval nautical scenes. The Tapestry's ships are shown in motion, their sails spread before the wind and straining at their ropes. And although the duke's vessel is in full view, the others are mostly shown one behind another, almost jostling each other, to give the impression of a crowded sea.

... MARE TRANSIVIT...

As is well known, William crossed the Channel during the night of 27-28 September 1066. It was a quick crossing, assisted by the strong southerly wind for which he had been waiting since August.

As soon as the fleet reached Pevensey (whose name is written with the typically Old English 'Æ'), the landing commenced, providing the Tapestry with further picturesque scenes. The Tapestry gives the site no distinguishing features, although even today the remains of a Roman fort are clearly visible. All that it

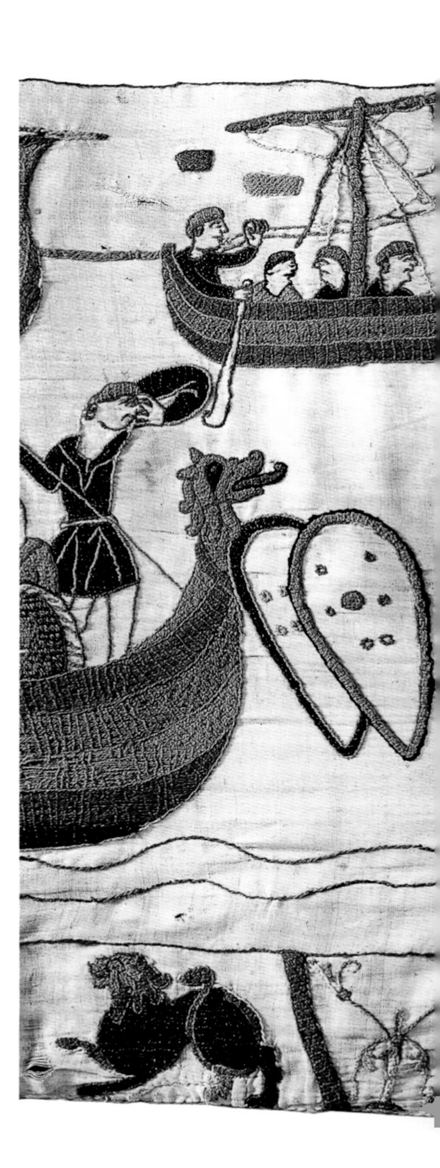

Scene 38

[76] *Brevis relatio*, ed. J. A. Giles, *Scriptores rerum gestarum Willelmi Conquestoris* (London, 1855), p. 22 (appendix).

[77] Wace, ed. Holden, vol. 2, p. 124, verses 6453-57 (Burgess and Van Houts, p. 163).

[78] Wace, ed. Holden, vol. 2, p. 124, verses 6447-50 (Burgess and Van Houts, p. 163).

[79] William of Poitiers, ed. Foreville, p. 162; *Carmen de Hastingae Proelio*, verse 8; *Miracula S. Thomae*, ed. Robertson, vol. I, p. 527.

[80] V. Fenwick, 'A New Anglo-Saxon Ship', *International Journal of Nautical Archaeology* 12 (1983), pp. 174 et seq.

[81] Scholars remain on the whole sceptical about identifying the object at the masthead with the papal banner. See C. Erdmann, *Die Entstehung des Kreuzzugsgedankens* (Stuttgart, 1935), pp. 181-83; C. Morton, 'Pope Alexander II and the Norman Conquest', *Latomus* 34 (1975), pp. 362-82, at p. 367. We know for certain only that it could be affixed to a lance. There was certainly nothing special about crosses on flags and banners in the Middle Ages, and they by no means implied papal sanction. The national flag of Denmark, for example, the *Dannebrog*, a white cross on a red background, which became the model for all the other Scandinavian flags, was traced to the early thirteenth century, but in fact dates from the fifteenth century and has no connection with the papacy.

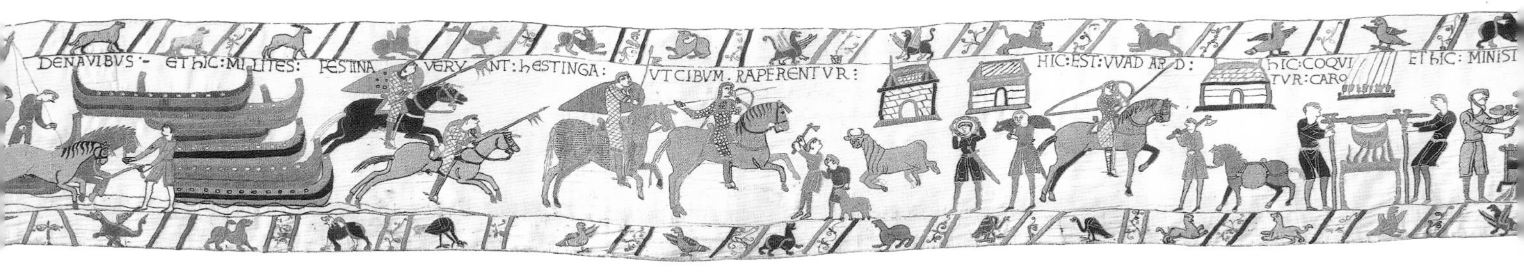

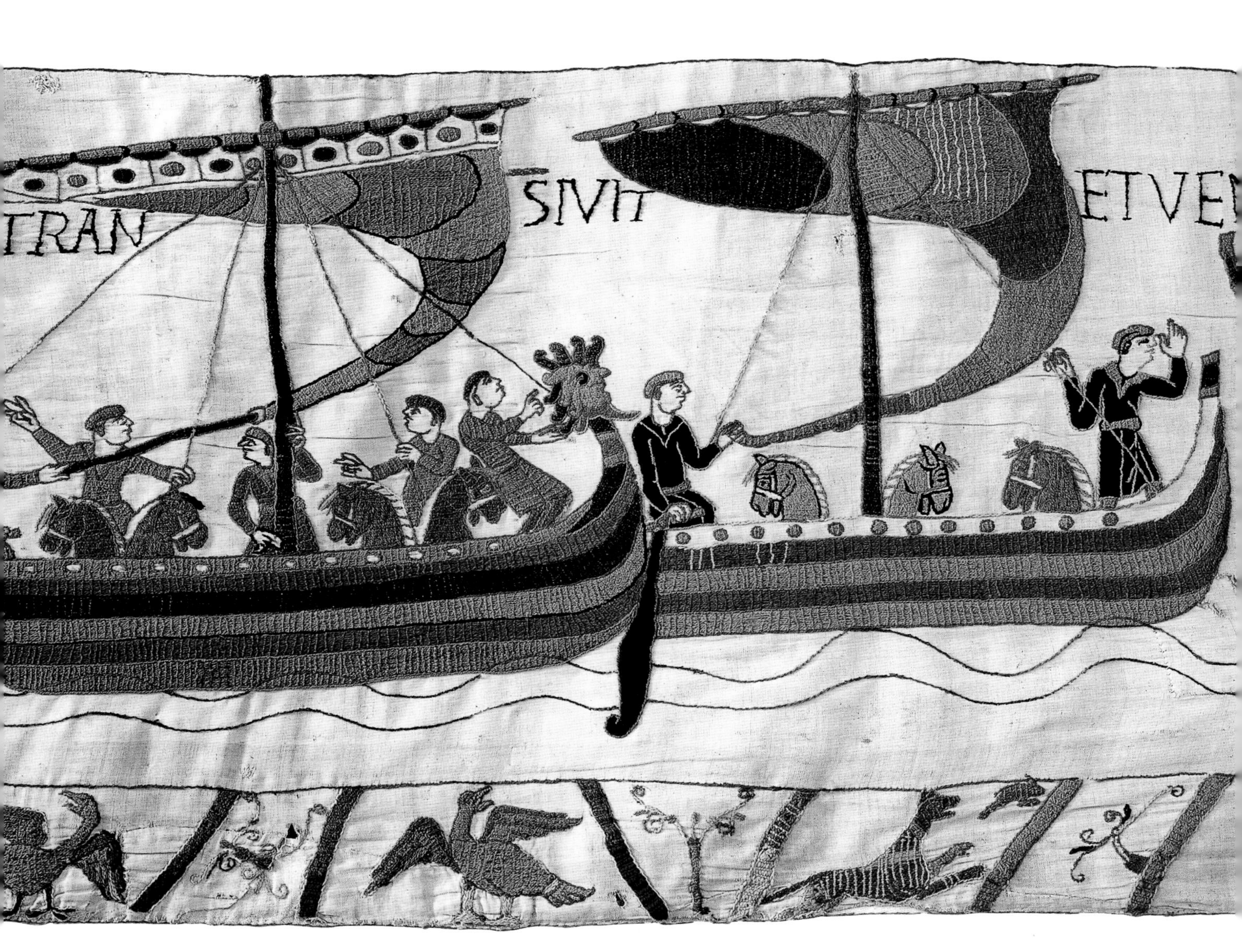

…crossed the sea …

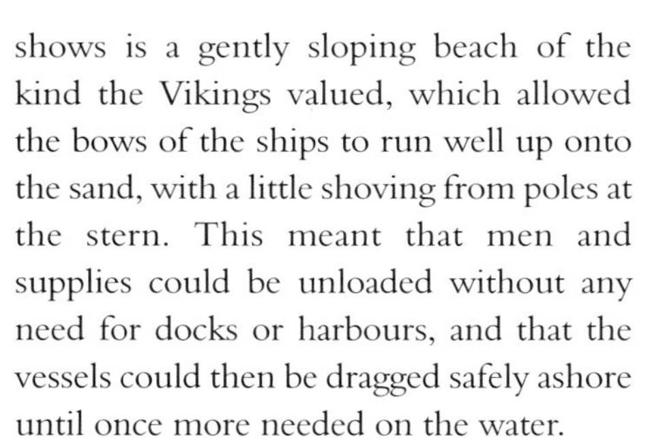

shows is a gently sloping beach of the kind the Vikings valued, which allowed the bows of the ships to run well up onto the sand, with a little shoving from poles at the stern. This meant that men and supplies could be unloaded without any need for docks or harbours, and that the vessels could then be dragged safely ashore until once more needed on the water.

Pevensey was clearly not chosen by accident.[82] There were sound strategic as well as tactical reasons for the choice. A direct assault on the south coast of England from the nearest points in Normandy would have brought William to the region of the Solent, the Isle of Wight, and western Sussex. But this would have meant establishing a bridgehead in the Godwin heartlands of Southampton, Hayling Island, and Bosham, where fierce resistance was to be expected from Harold's followers.[83] Further east, the shortest possible Channel crossing would have brought the invaders to Dover, whose topography and Roman fortifications made it a very hard target. But between the two lay Pevensey. Today it is hardly the most maritime of locations, lying a mile or so inland amidst salt-flats. But the coastline has pushed well south since the eleventh century, when today's drained marshland was a lagoon open to the tides, with two good channels to the sea. It was navigable to small boats as late as the seventeenth century.[84] Pevensey had attracted the attention of the Romans, who called it Anderita and made it part of their chain of coastal forts against the Saxons. And it retained its importance in Anglo-Saxon times: Domesday Book credited it with 52 burgage tenures.

There was no garrison to repel the Normans, however, and William made it the headquarters of his bridgehead, taking advantage of the ancient fortifications. Subsequently he bestowed the town on his half-brother Robert of Mortain, who repaired the Roman walls and erected a castle within them. Pevensey retained its strategic importance in the next generation. In the Anglo-Norman civil war of 1101 it was there that Henry I chose to await the invasion of his brother Robert Curthose (who in fact landed at Portsmouth).[85]

[82] The Viking predilection for this kind of shoreline is illustrated with numerous examples by B. Almgren, *Vikingatåg och vikinga skepp* (Uppsala, 1963; excerpts from the journal *Tor* for 1962 and 1963).

[83] This was brought to light by R. Fleming, 'Domesday Estates of the King and the Godwines', *Speculum* 58 (1983), pp. 987-1007, at p. 1001.

[84] A. J. F. Dulley, 'Excavations at Pevensey, Sussex', *Medieval Archaeology* 11 (1967), pp. 209-32. See also F. Aldworth and D. Frere, *Historical Towns in Sussex: an Archaeological Survey* (London, 1976), pp. 46-47.

[85] W. Hollister, 'The Anglo-Norman Civil War, 1101', *English Historical Review* 88 (1973), pp. 315-44, at p. 325.

... ET VENIT AD PEVEN

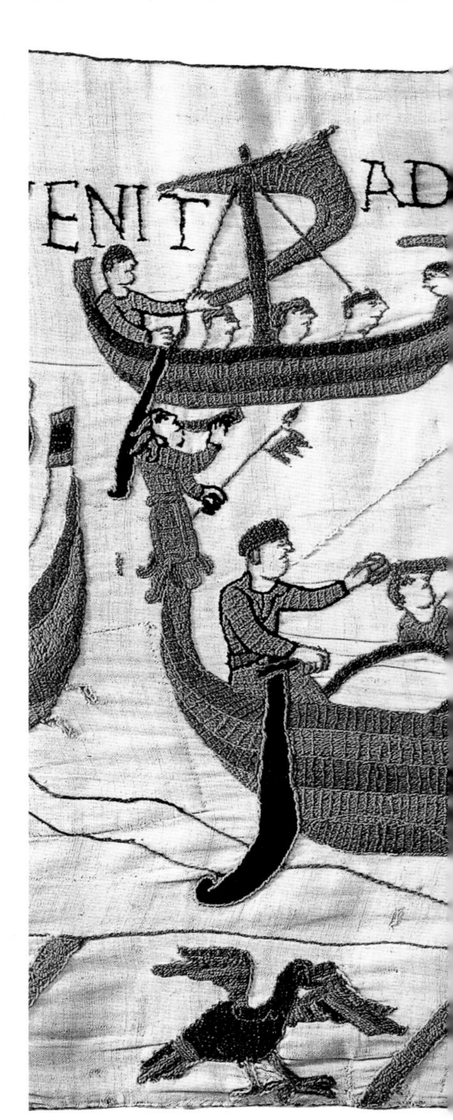

SCENES 38–39

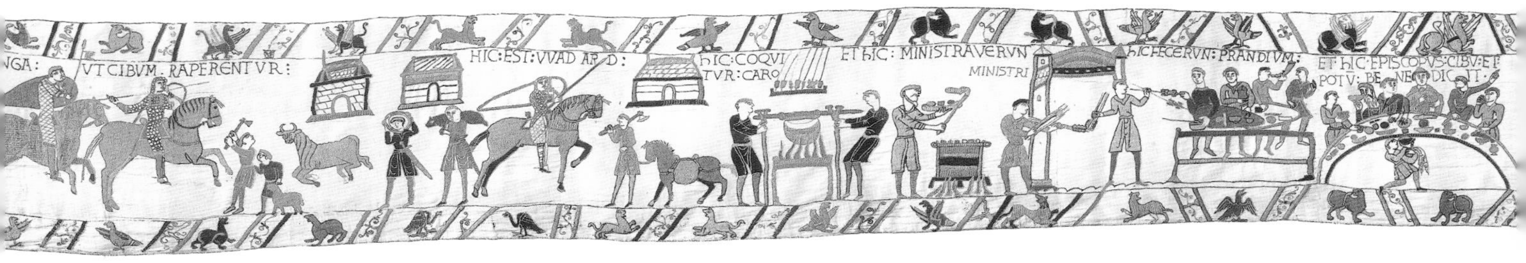

E.

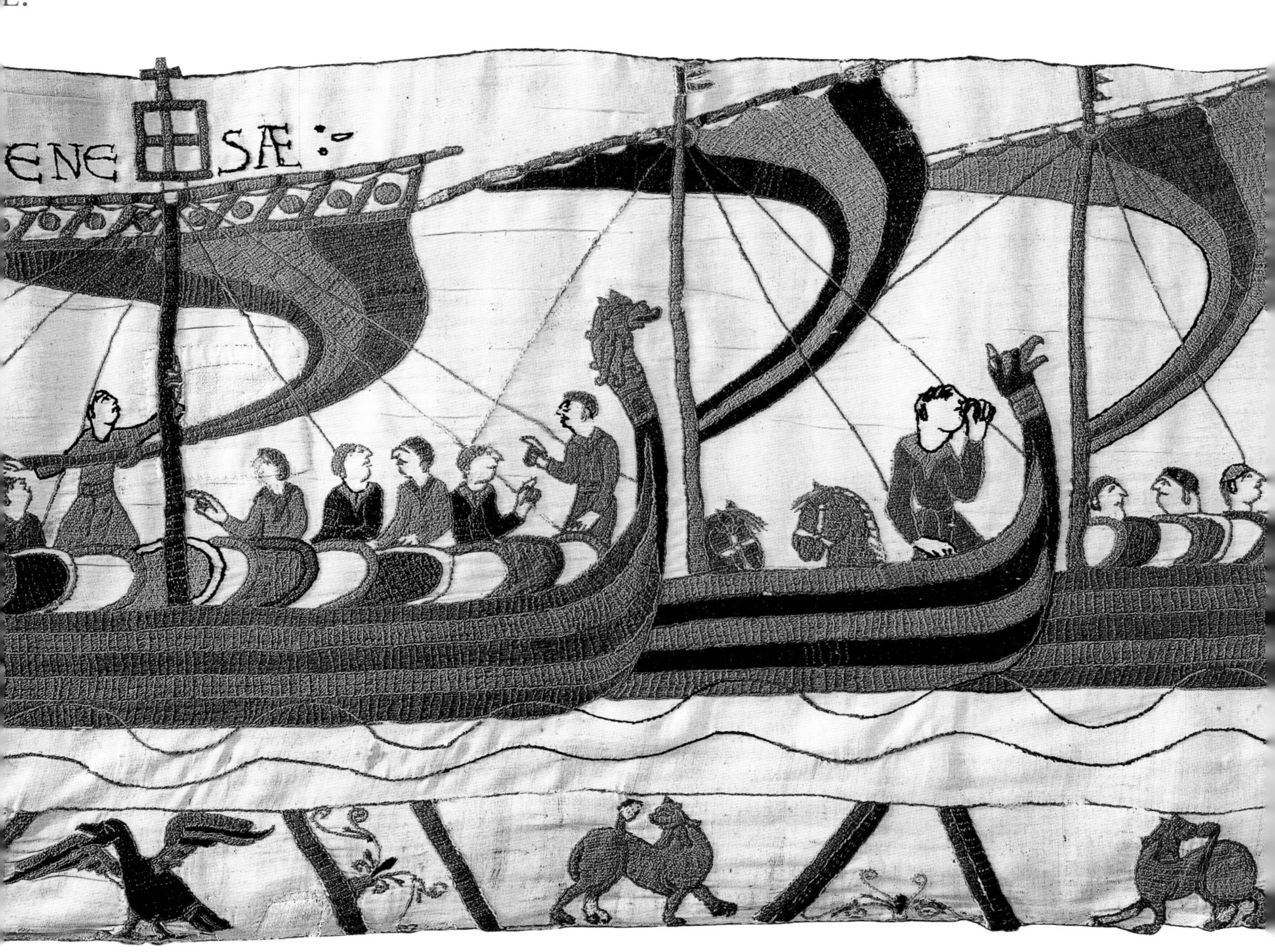

… and came to Pevensey.

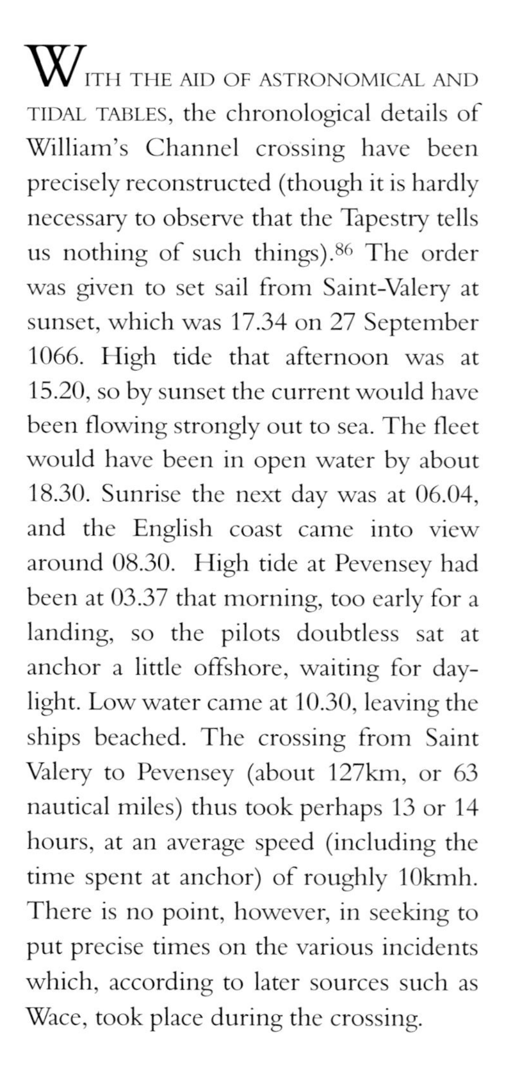

WITH THE AID OF ASTRONOMICAL AND TIDAL TABLES, the chronological details of William's Channel crossing have been precisely reconstructed (though it is hardly necessary to observe that the Tapestry tells us nothing of such things).[86] The order was given to set sail from Saint-Valery at sunset, which was 17.34 on 27 September 1066. High tide that afternoon was at 15.20, so by sunset the current would have been flowing strongly out to sea. The fleet would have been in open water by about 18.30. Sunrise the next day was at 06.04, and the English coast came into view around 08.30. High tide at Pevensey had been at 03.37 that morning, too early for a landing, so the pilots doubtless sat at anchor a little offshore, waiting for daylight. Low water came at 10.30, leaving the ships beached. The crossing from Saint Valery to Pevensey (about 127km, or 63 nautical miles) thus took perhaps 13 or 14 hours, at an average speed (including the time spent at anchor) of roughly 10kmh. There is no point, however, in seeking to put precise times on the various incidents which, according to later sources such as Wace, took place during the crossing.

[86] This paragraph is based on C. H. Lemmon, 'The Campaign of 1066', in D. Whitelock, D. C. Douglas, C. H. Lemmon, and F. Barlow, *The Norman Conquest* (London, 1966), p. 88; and J. Laporte, 'Les opérations navales en Manche et mer du Nord pendant l'année 1066', *Annales de Normandie* 16 (1976), pp. 3-42. The precise times given by the authors differ by a few minutes.

HIC EXEUNT CABALLI

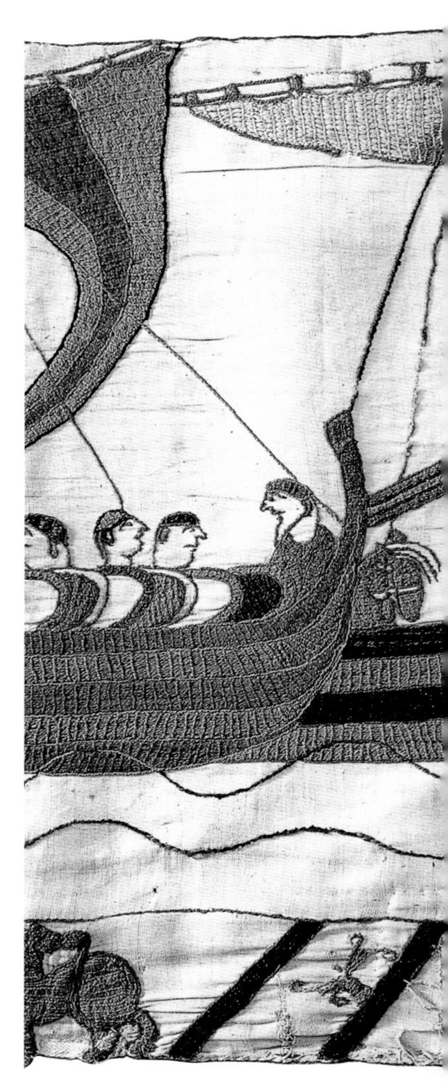

SCENE 39

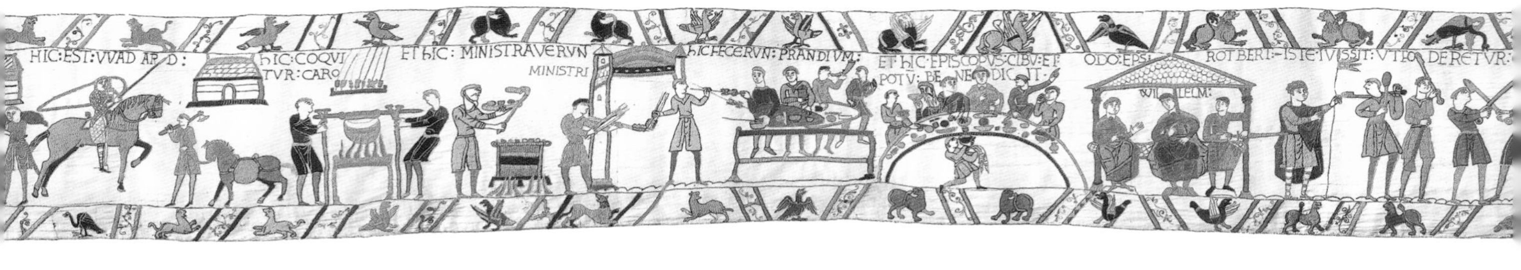

DE NAVIBUS.

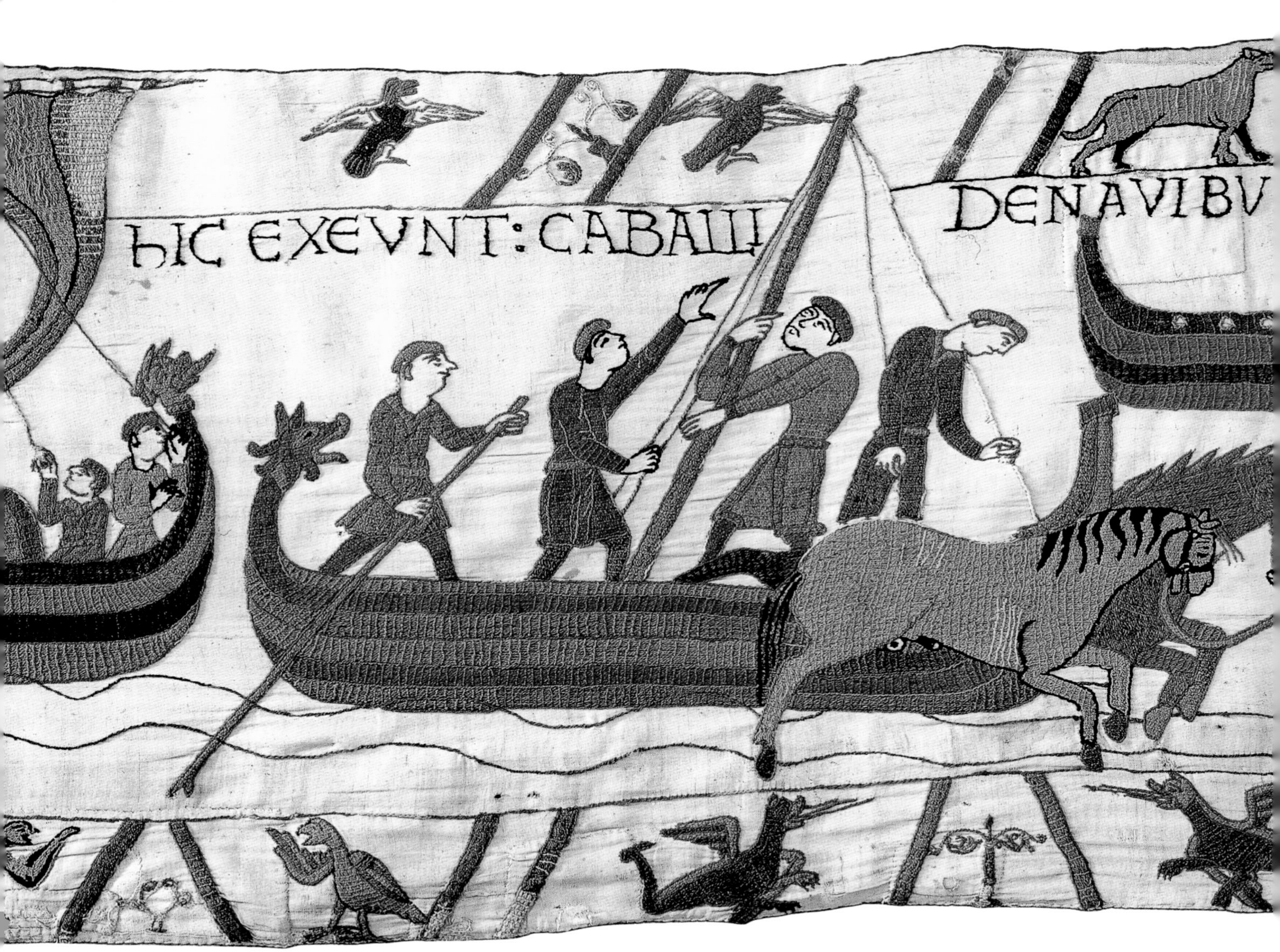

Here the horses leave the ships.

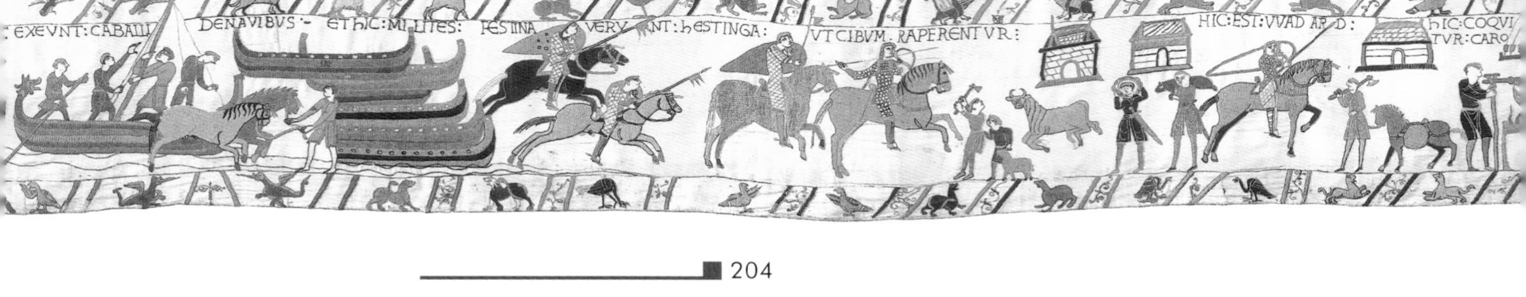

THE FIRST TASKS ON REACHING LAND were to strike the masts and get the horses ashore. Modern reconstructions carried out with replica Viking ships have shown just how closely the Tapestry's images of the horses correspond with the realities of this operation.[87] Unloading the horses was crucial: hence its specific mention in the caption 'Here the horses leave the ships'.

Then the ships (six of them in the picture) were drawn up onto the sands. Masts, sails, oars, and shields were removed, as were the figureheads that decorated the troop ships. Reconnaissance parties dash off to reconnoitre the interior, detachments of mail-clad but bareheaded knights, lances and shields at the ready. It soon becomes clear that there is no organised English resistance. The chronicles inform us that Harold had not long before stood down both the fleet which guarded the Channel and the troops which he had stationed along the coast: the men were needed back home to help with the harvest, and by then the real danger seemed to be from the north, where the Norwegians had landed on the Humber. That same northerly wind which had so long detained William south of the Channel had worked in favour of Harald Hardrada. Having landed on the Ouse at Riccall around 15 September, Harald and Tostig had rapidly established good relations with the Scandinavian settlers of Lindsey (north Lincolnshire) and Yorkshire, and had already taken York.

On news of this Harold had headed north on a forced march. The northern earls, Edwin and Morcar, were crushed at Fulford on 20 September. Harold himself met the Norwegians at Stamford Bridge, just east of York, on 25 September, where both Harald and Tostig fell in battle. Harold allowed the surviving Norwegians and their allies to return home in their ships.

These decisive events, amply documented in English sources, are completely ignored not only by the Tapestry but also by the majority of the Norman writers, even those, such as Baudry de Bourgueil, who were not simply concerned with tracing the disastrous consequences of Harold's perjury. Yet their importance to the Norman cause can hardly be exaggerated. Not only did the defeat of the Norwegians eliminate another rival for the English crown, but the campaign drew Harold away from the south at the crucial moment and weakened his forces before the final encounter.

[87] Masts often had to be lowered even while rowing. See R. Malmros, 'Leding Og. Skjaldekvad', *Aarbøger for nordisk Oldkyndighed og Historie* (1985), pp. 89-139, at p. 100.

ET HIC MILITES FEST

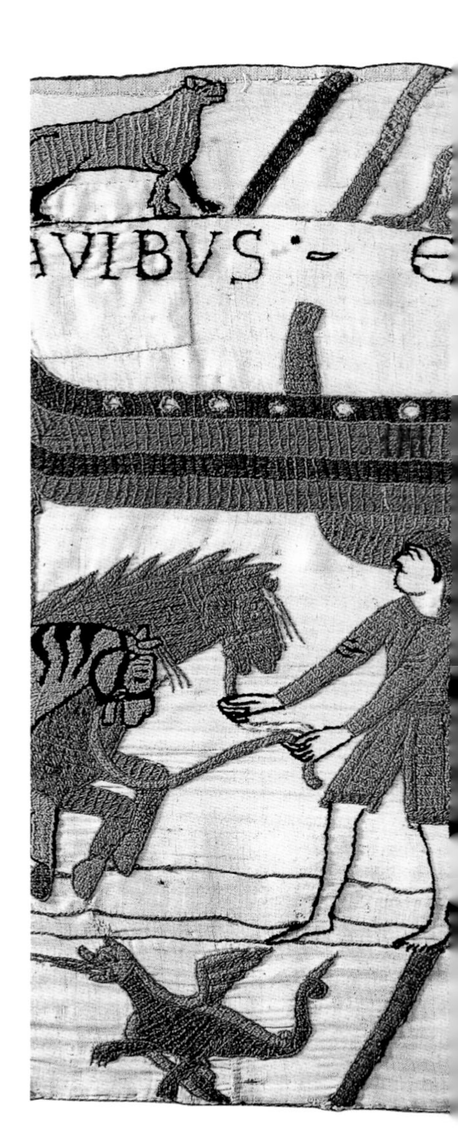

SCENES 39–40

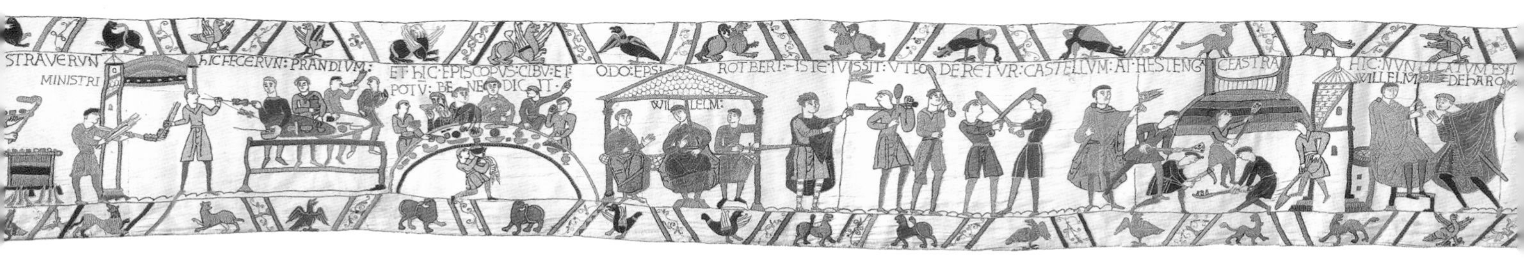

ERUNT HESTINGA...

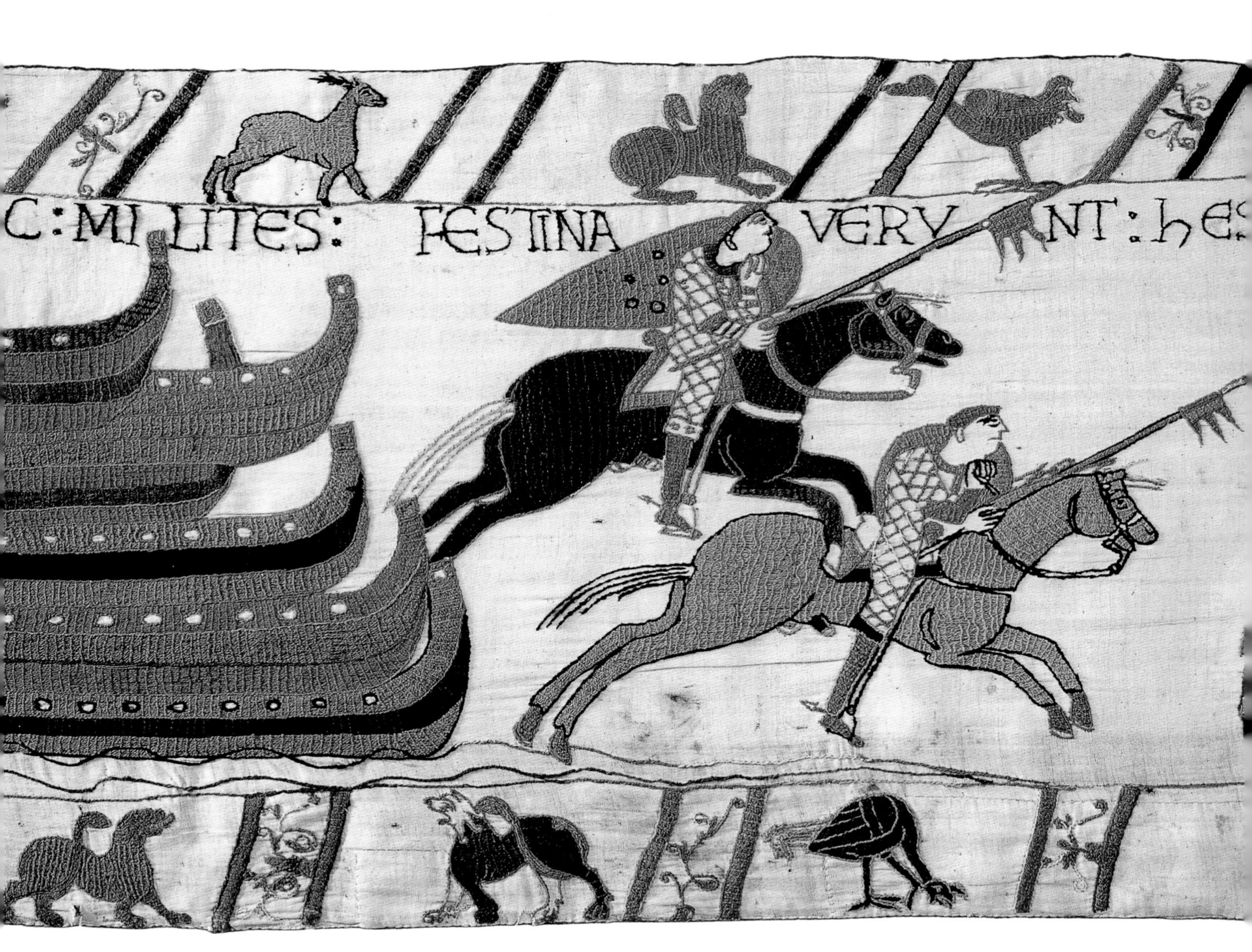

And here the knights hurried to Hastings …

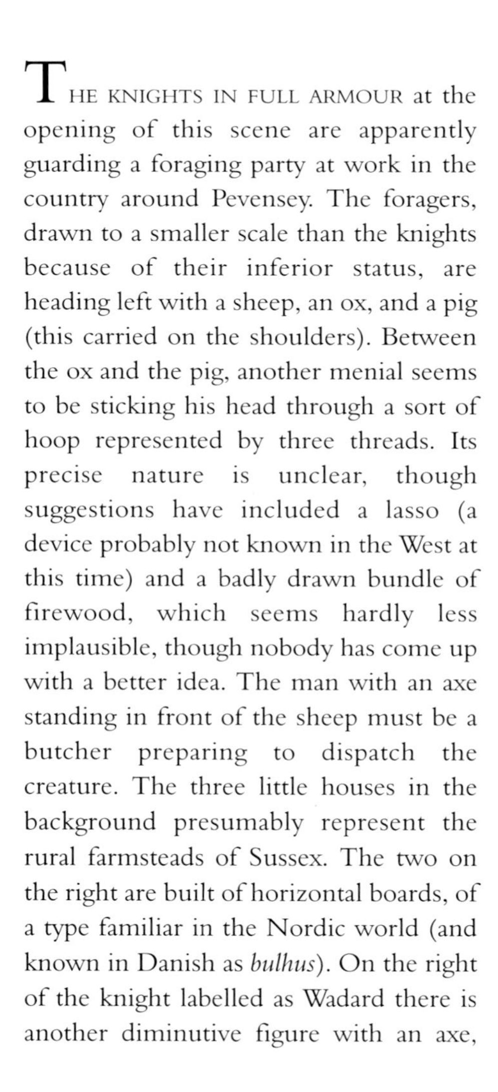

... UT CIBUM RAPERENTUR

THE KNIGHTS IN FULL ARMOUR at the opening of this scene are apparently guarding a foraging party at work in the country around Pevensey. The foragers, drawn to a smaller scale than the knights because of their inferior status, are heading left with a sheep, an ox, and a pig (this carried on the shoulders). Between the ox and the pig, another menial seems to be sticking his head through a sort of hoop represented by three threads. Its precise nature is unclear, though suggestions have included a lasso (a device probably not known in the West at this time) and a badly drawn bundle of firewood, which seems hardly less implausible, though nobody has come up with a better idea. The man with an axe standing in front of the sheep must be a butcher preparing to dispatch the creature. The three little houses in the background presumably represent the rural farmsteads of Sussex. The two on the right are built of horizontal boards, of a type familiar in the Nordic world (and known in Danish as *bulhus*). On the right of the knight labelled as Wadard there is another diminutive figure with an axe,

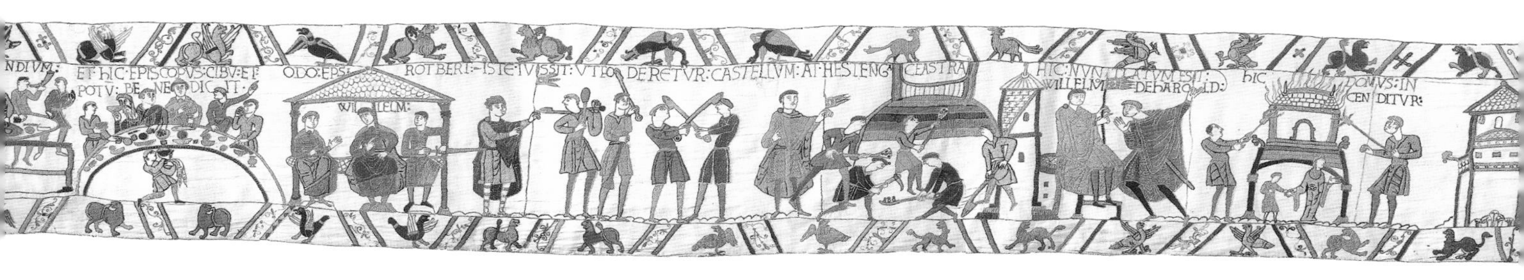

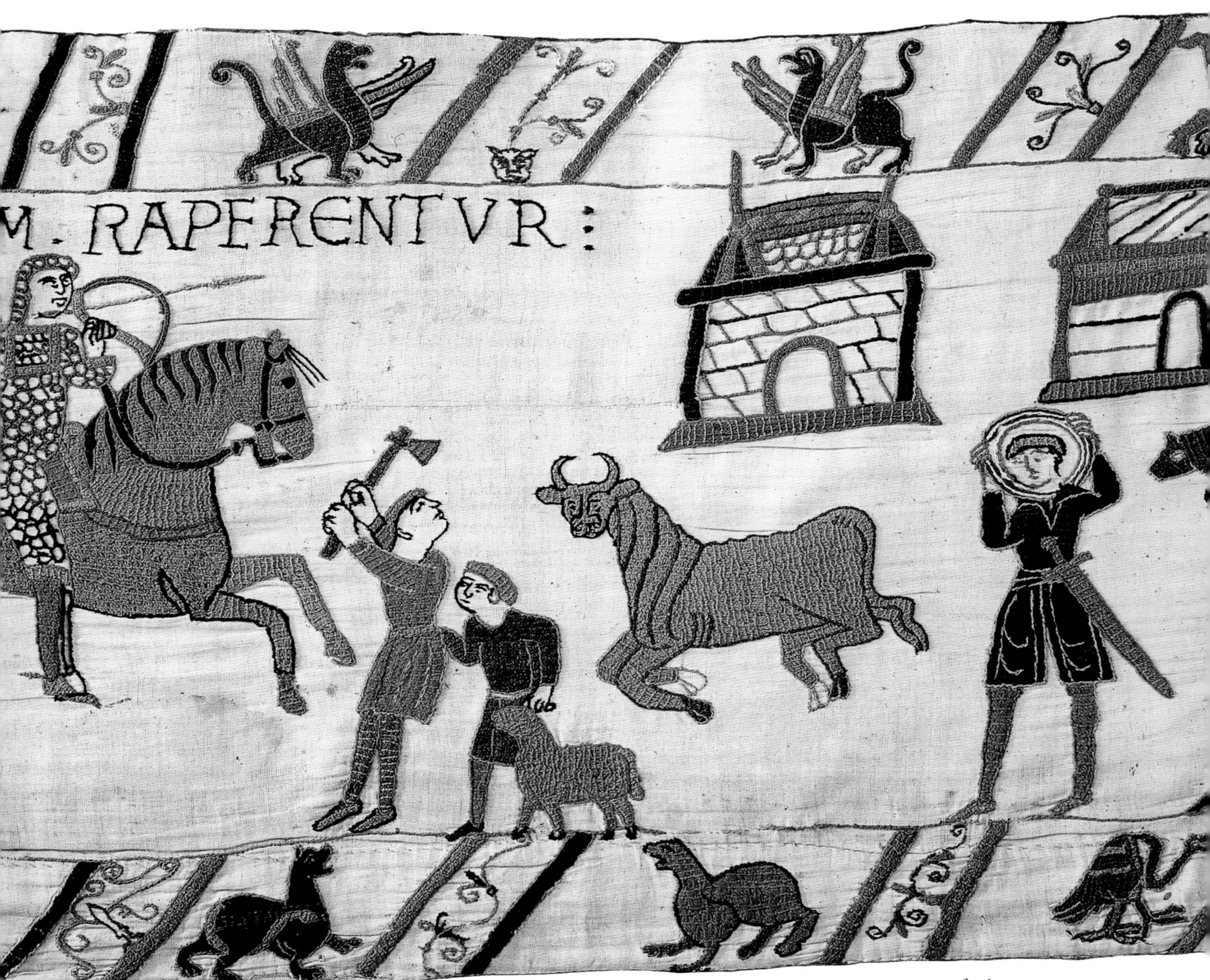

…to get food.

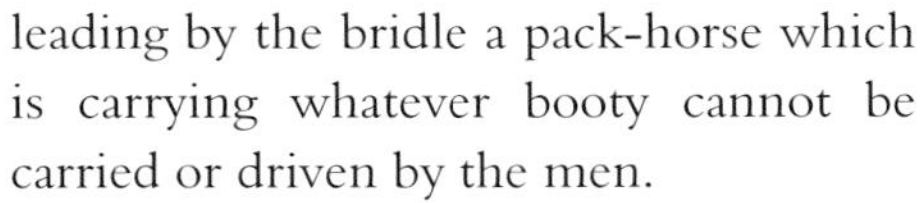

Hic est Wadard.

leading by the bridle a pack-horse which is carrying whatever booty cannot be carried or driven by the men.

In the midst of this scene appears Wadard, the only figure drawn on the larger scale. Mail-clad but bareheaded, he is riding towards the right. Although no particular reason can be given for his prominence here, his identity at least has been established beyond doubt. Wadard was a vassal of Bishop Odo, and is named in numerous sources, notably the cartulary of the Abbey of Saint-Pierre de Préaux (near Pont-Audemer).[88] *Domesday Book* shows that Wadard later had substantial landholdings in Kent. From Odo he held six houses in Dover as well as farms at Farningham, Maplescomb, Nurstead, Buckwell, and Combe Grove. And besides these he held Milton Regis from the king and two other portions of land from St Augustine's Abbey at Canterbury.[89]

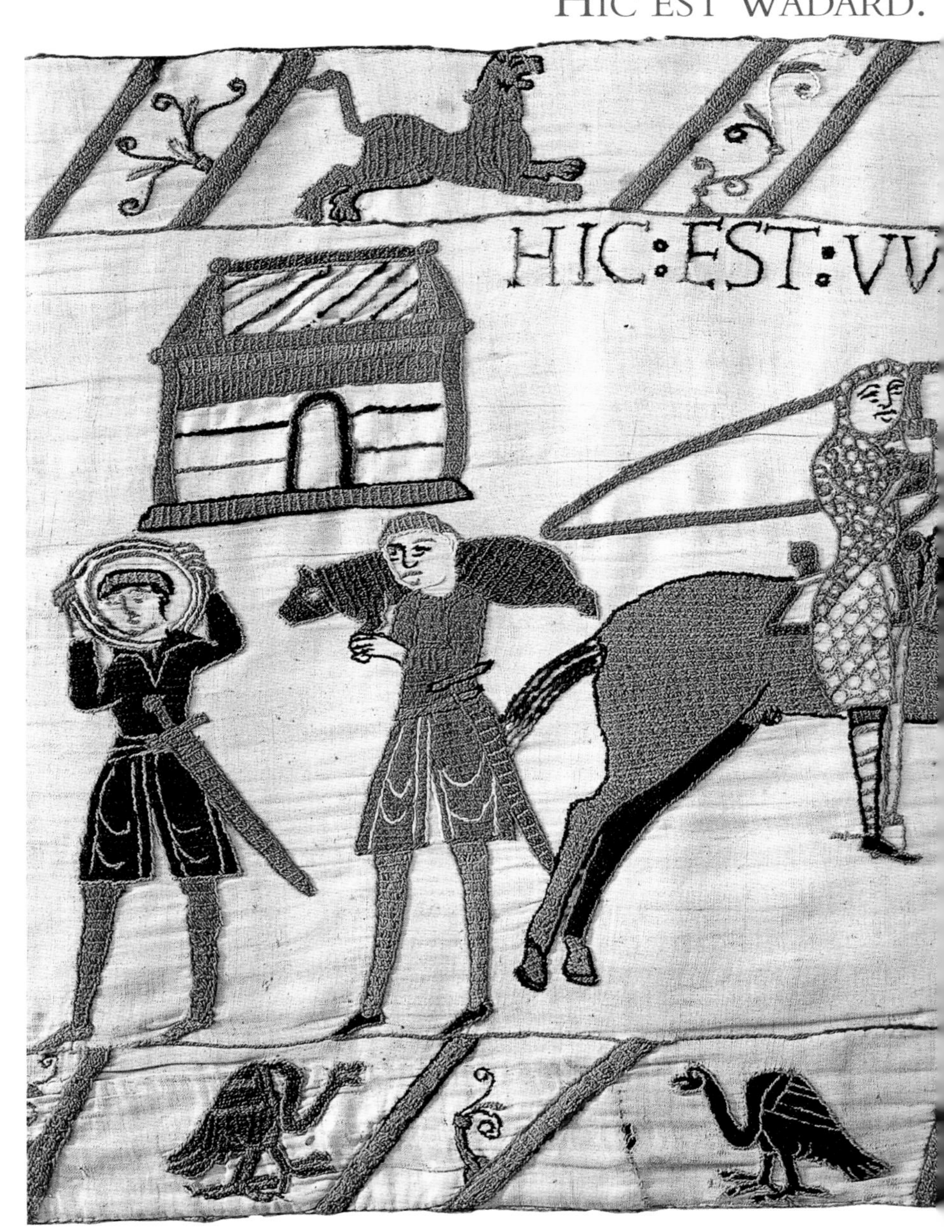

[88] See above all H. Prentout, 'Essai d'identification des personnages inconnus de la Tapisserie de Bayeux', *Revue historique* 176 (1935), pp. 14-21 (Gameson, *Study of the Bayeux Tapestry*, pp. 26-28). See also Cartulaire de Préaux, Archives de l'Eure, H 711, nos. 294, fol. 102r; and 416, fol. 136r. As Prentout observed, the link between Wadard and Odo could well have been forged not far from Préaux, in the Basse-Risle area, the patrimony of Viscount Herluin de Conteville, Odo's father and Duke William's father-in-law.

[89] *Domesday Book*, vol. I, p. 6, col. 2; p. 7, col. 1, etc.

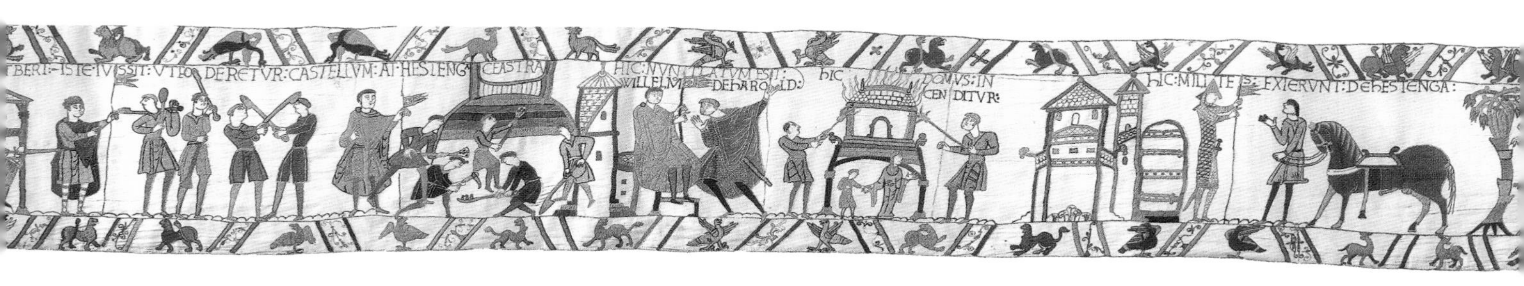

Hic coquitur caro...

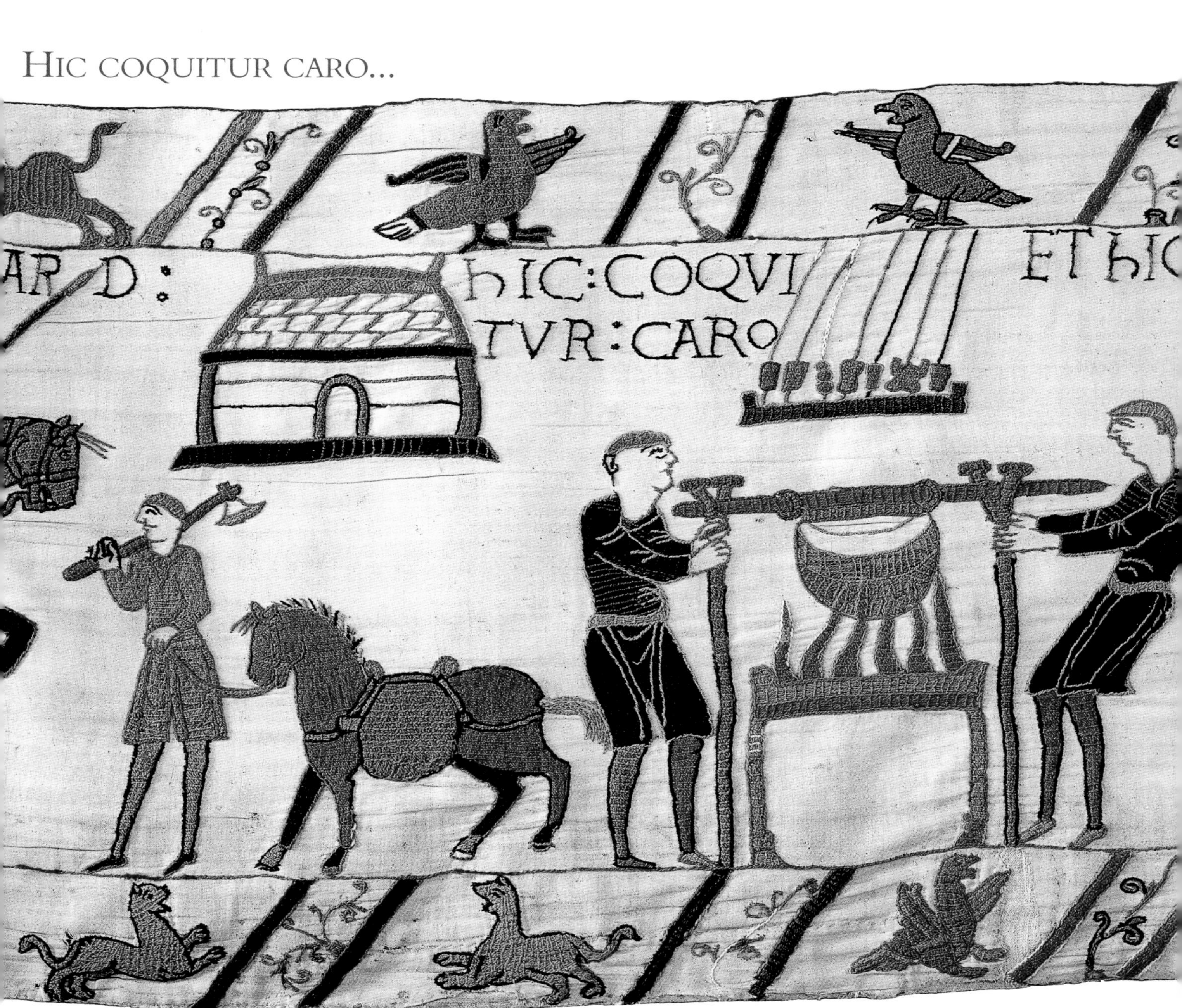

Here is Wadard. Here meat is cooked …

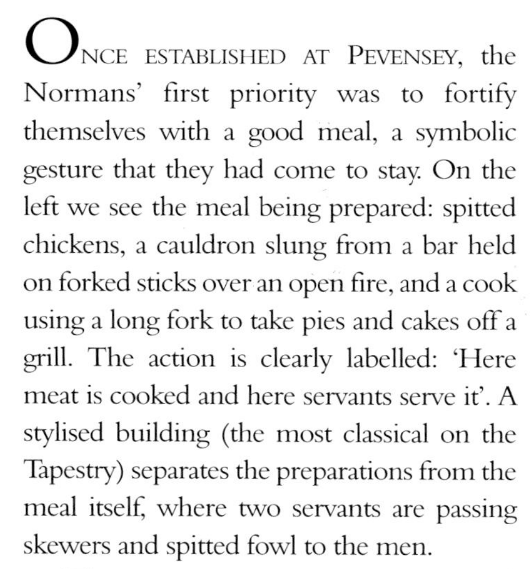

Once established at Pevensey, the Normans' first priority was to fortify themselves with a good meal, a symbolic gesture that they had come to stay. On the left we see the meal being prepared: spitted chickens, a cauldron slung from a bar held on forked sticks over an open fire, and a cook using a long fork to take pies and cakes off a grill. The action is clearly labelled: 'Here meat is cooked and here servants serve it'. A stylised building (the most classical on the Tapestry) separates the preparations from the meal itself, where two servants are passing skewers and spitted fowl to the men.

The common troops eat at makeshift tables (shields resting face down on trestles), while their leaders are seated at a rather poorly drawn horseshoe table (p. 212). The scene is clearly modelled on the iconographical tradition of the Last Supper familiar from manuscript illuminations.[90] Bishop Odo sits in the place of honour, recognisable by his tonsure and labelled simply as 'the bishop' (although he was not the only bishop present, there is no doubt whom the Tapestry means by this title). His right hand makes a blessing over the food and drink. Five men are seated with him at the table, one of them, to judge by the beard, of advanced years. A servant curtseys before them, bearing a cup and a napkin.

On the table are plates and cups (the latter shown side on), two fish, and a knife, just as in depictions of the Last Supper. Indeed, an eleventh-century manuscript of the Gospels still found at Canterbury has an illumination that may have directly inspired this scene.[91] No chairs are visible at any of the tables, makeshift or not. One of the diners at the common table is putting a horn to his lips, either as a trumpet or as a drinking vessel. Given the way he is holding it, the former seems more likely, in which case he may be giving the signal for the start of the meal.

[90] L. H. Loomis, 'The Table of the Last Supper in Religious and Secular Iconography', *Art Studies* 5 (1927), pp. 71-90.
[91] Brooks and Walker, 'Authority and Interpretation', pp. 15-16 (Gameson, Study of the Bayeux Tapestry, pp. 75-76).

... ET HIC MINISTRA

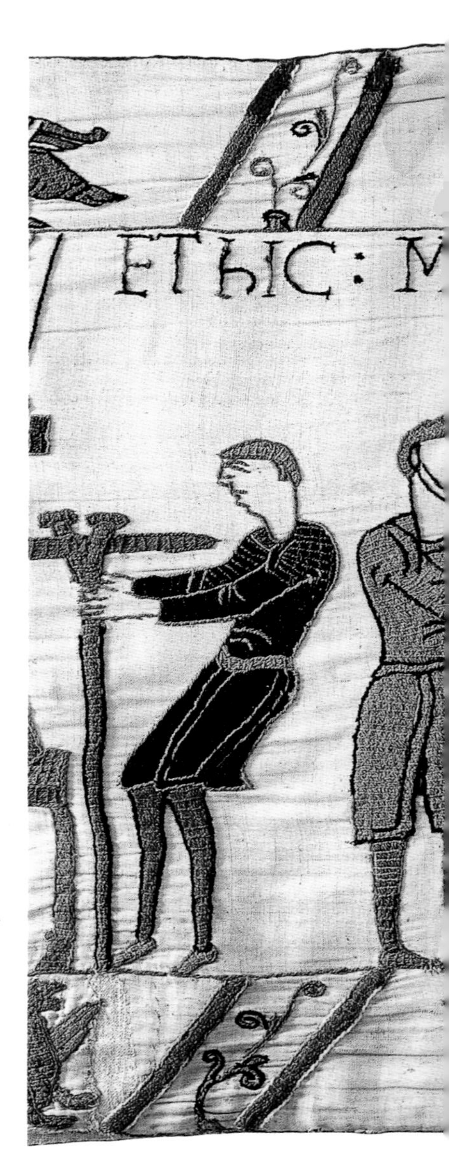

Scenes 42–43

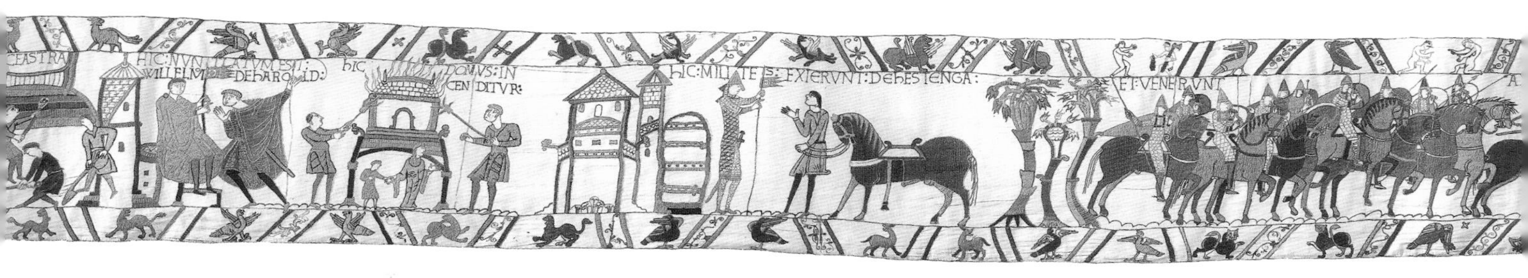

RUNT MINISTRI. HIC FECERUNT PRANDIUM...

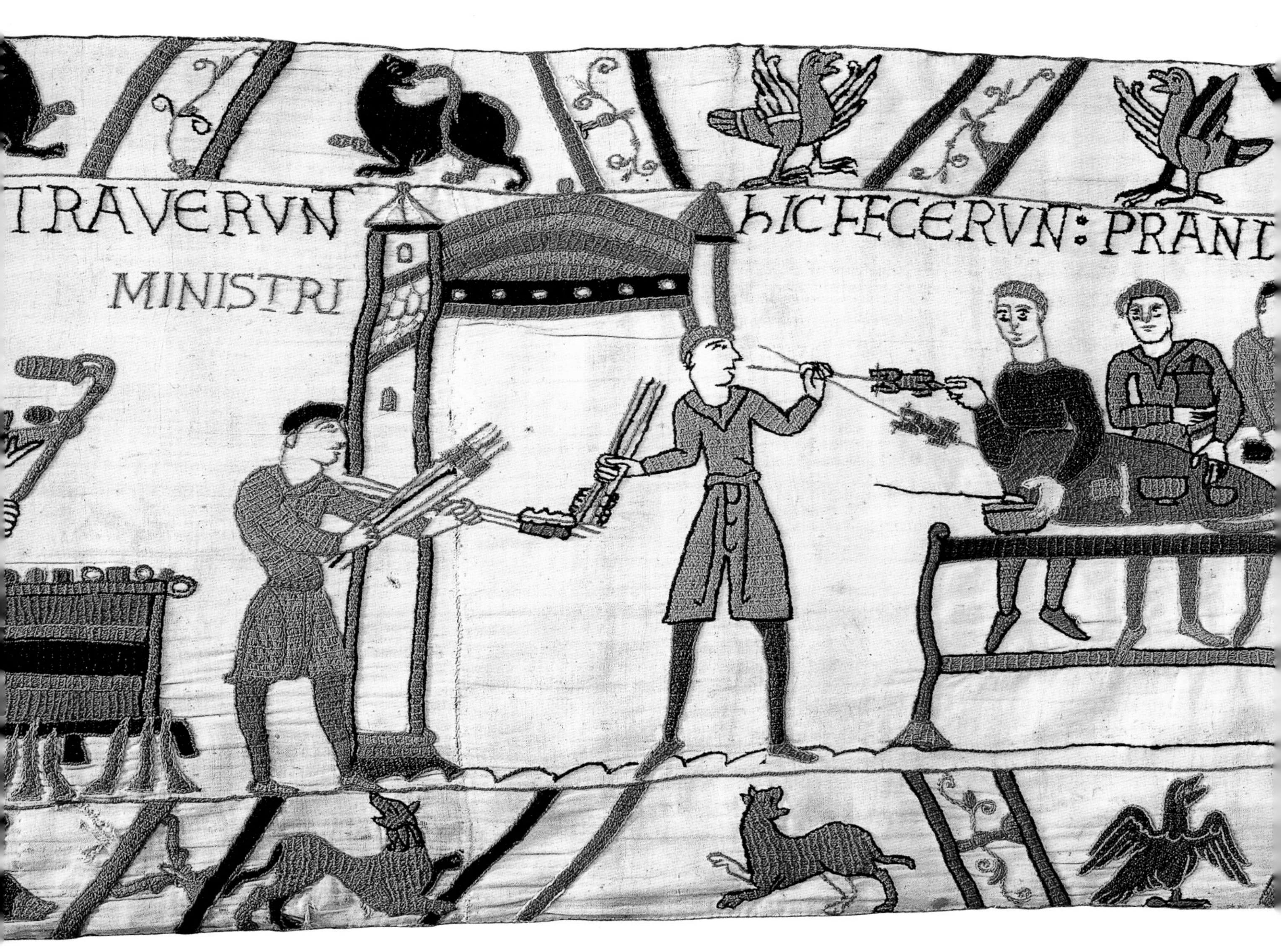

…and here servants serve it. Here they have a meal …

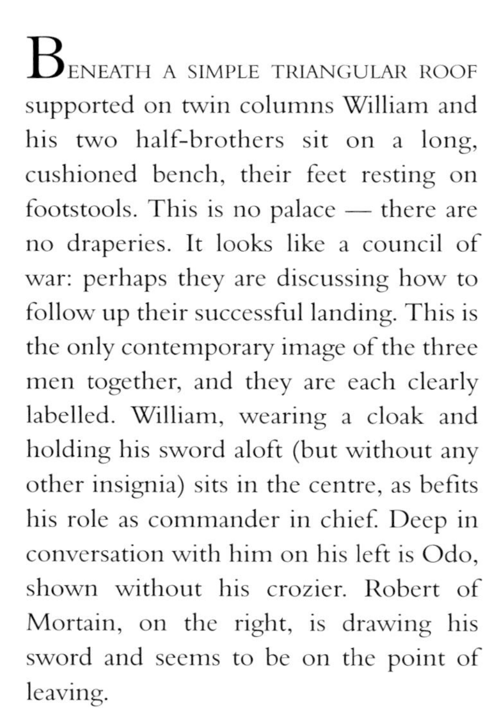

Beneath a simple triangular roof supported on twin columns William and his two half-brothers sit on a long, cushioned bench, their feet resting on footstools. This is no palace — there are no draperies. It looks like a council of war: perhaps they are discussing how to follow up their successful landing. This is the only contemporary image of the three men together, and they are each clearly labelled. William, wearing a cloak and holding his sword aloft (but without any other insignia) sits in the centre, as befits his role as commander in chief. Deep in conversation with him on his left is Odo, shown without his crozier. Robert of Mortain, on the right, is drawing his sword and seems to be on the point of leaving.

... ET HIC EPISCOPUS CIBU(M) ET POTUM BEN

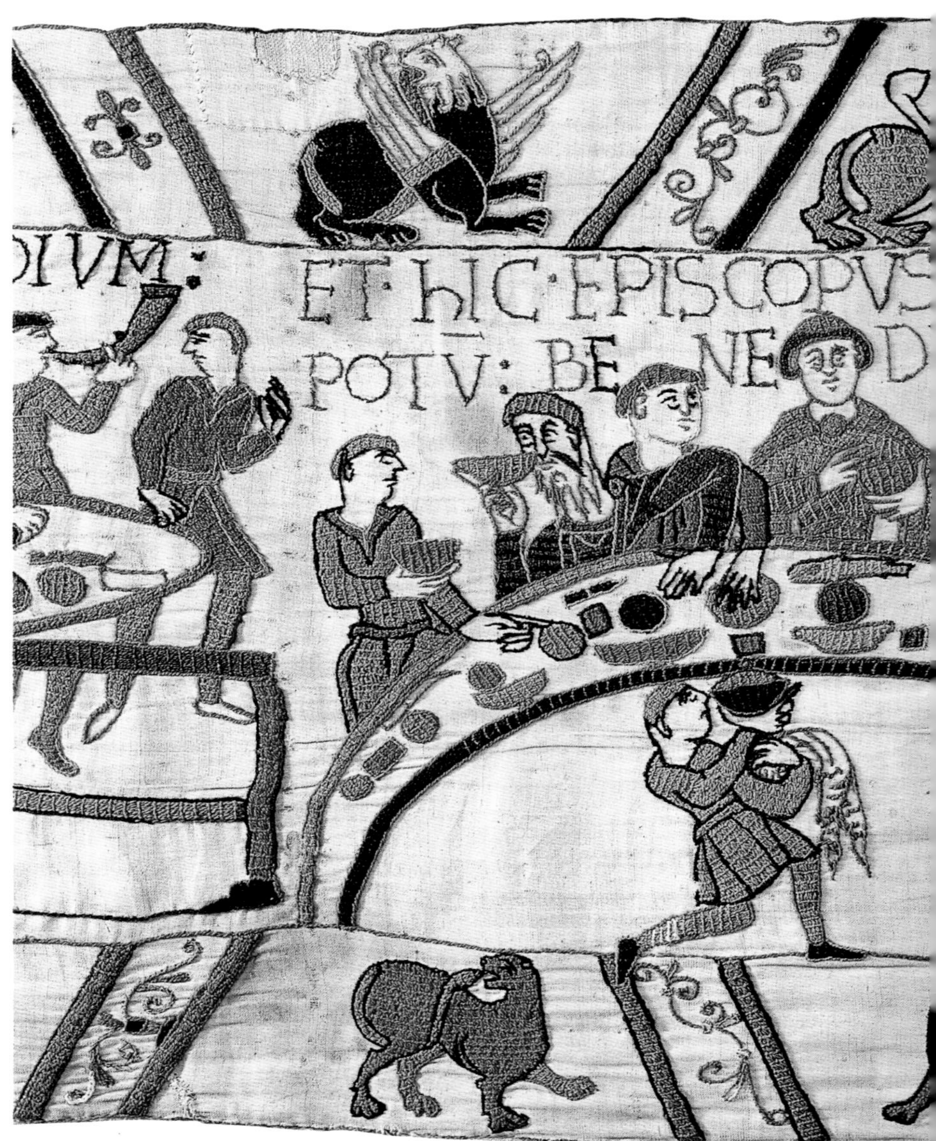

Scenes 43–44

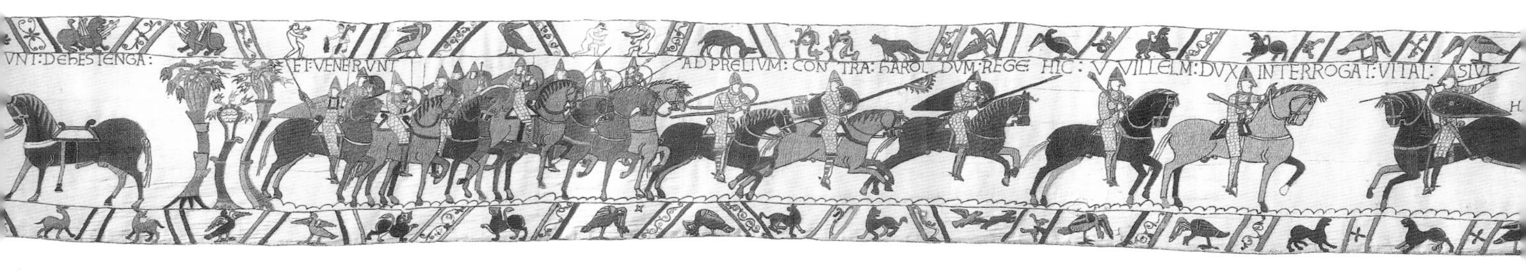

ICIT. ODO EPISCOPUS. WILLELM. ROTBERT.

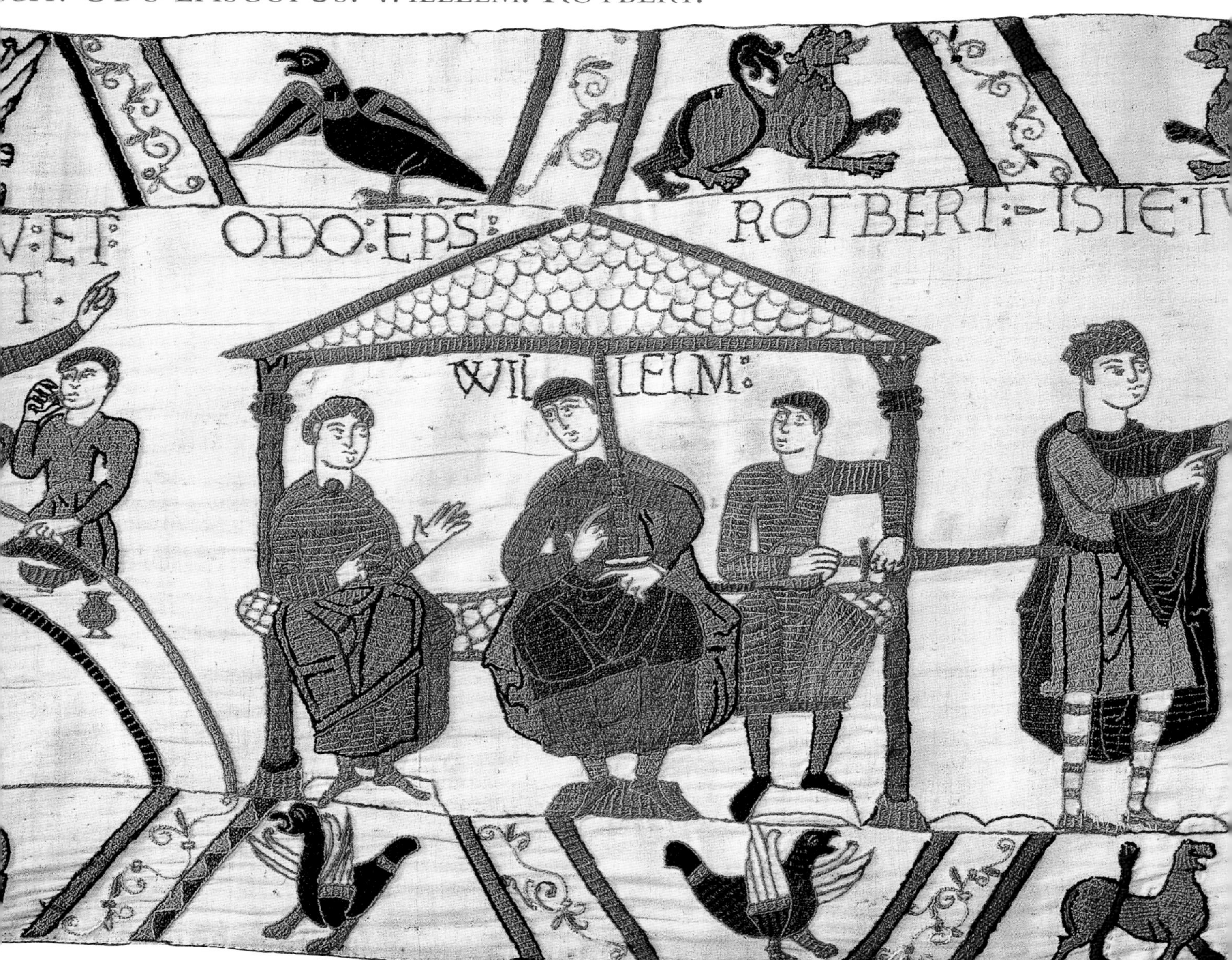

…and here the bishop blesses the food and drink. Bishop Odo. William. Robert.

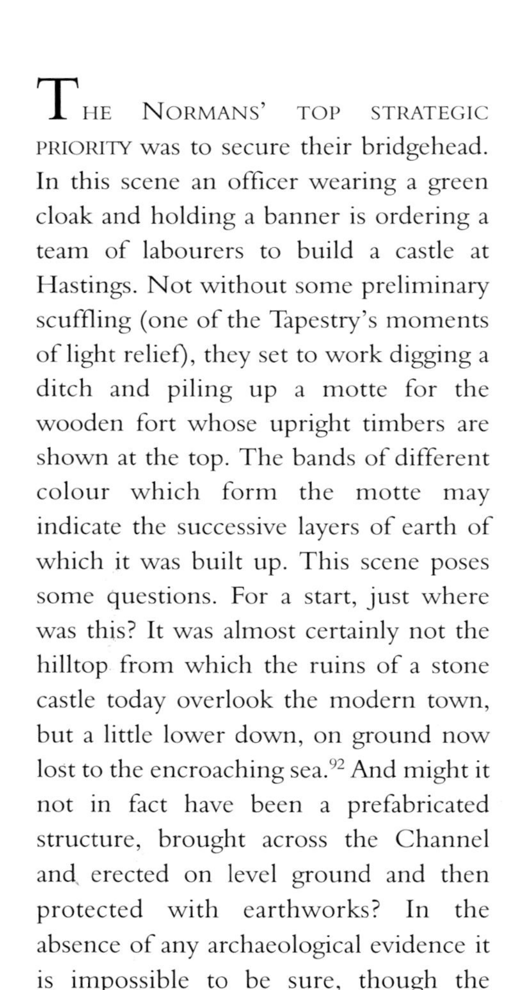

The Normans' top strategic priority was to secure their bridgehead. In this scene an officer wearing a green cloak and holding a banner is ordering a team of labourers to build a castle at Hastings. Not without some preliminary scuffling (one of the Tapestry's moments of light relief), they set to work digging a ditch and piling up a motte for the wooden fort whose upright timbers are shown at the top. The bands of different colour which form the motte may indicate the successive layers of earth of which it was built up. This scene poses some questions. For a start, just where was this? It was almost certainly not the hilltop from which the ruins of a stone castle today overlook the modern town, but a little lower down, on ground now lost to the encroaching sea.[92] And might it not in fact have been a prefabricated structure, brought across the Channel and erected on level ground and then protected with earthworks? In the absence of any archaeological evidence it is impossible to be sure, though the temporary structure was probably the ancestor of the more substantial edifice whose ruins are visible today.

The chronicles do confirm, however, that a castle was indeed constructed within days of the landing. It is mentioned not only by William of Jumièges and William of Poitiers (who has two castles, one at Hastings and the other at Pevensey) but also by the *Anglo-Saxon Chronicle*.[93] According to Orderic Vitalis, William entrusted it to Humphrey of Tilleul.[94]

The workmen's shovels are rustic implements, relatively small and obviously easy to use, but perhaps not that suitable to large-scale works. They are of a distinctively medieval and English design, made from wood except for a strip of metal (here indicated by darker thread) to strengthen the digging edge: excavations in England have turned up plenty of these metal strips (metal was, of course, expensive and in limited supply, and hence would not be used for the entire blade). At the top of the shaft these English shovels had an open handle for the hand to pass through, a feature also seen on German tools but not on those used in France. They are also quite different from Scandinavian shovels, which were entirely wooden and lacked these distinctive handles.

[92] F. H. Baring, 'Hastings Castle, 1050-1150', *Sussex Archaeological Collections* 57 (1915), pp. 120-25; J. F. A. Mason, 'The Companions of the Conqueror: an Additional Name', *English Historical Review* 71 (1956), pp. 61-69; B. A. Barker and K. J. Barton, 'Excavations at Hastings Castle', *Archaeological Journal* 75 (1968), pp. 303-05.

[93] William of Jumièges, ed. Marx, p. 134; William of Poitiers, ed. Foreville, p. 168 (Davis and Chibnall, pp. 114-15); *Anglo-Saxon Chronicle*, 1066, manuscript D.

[94] Orderic Vitalis, ed. Chibnall, vol. 2, p. 220.

Iste jussit ut fode

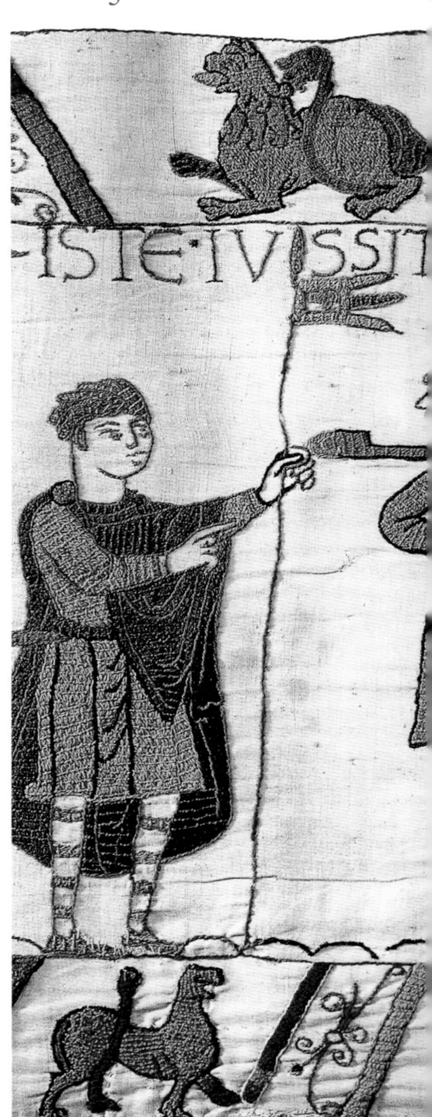

Scene 45

ETUR CASTELLUM “AT HESTENGA CEASTRA”.

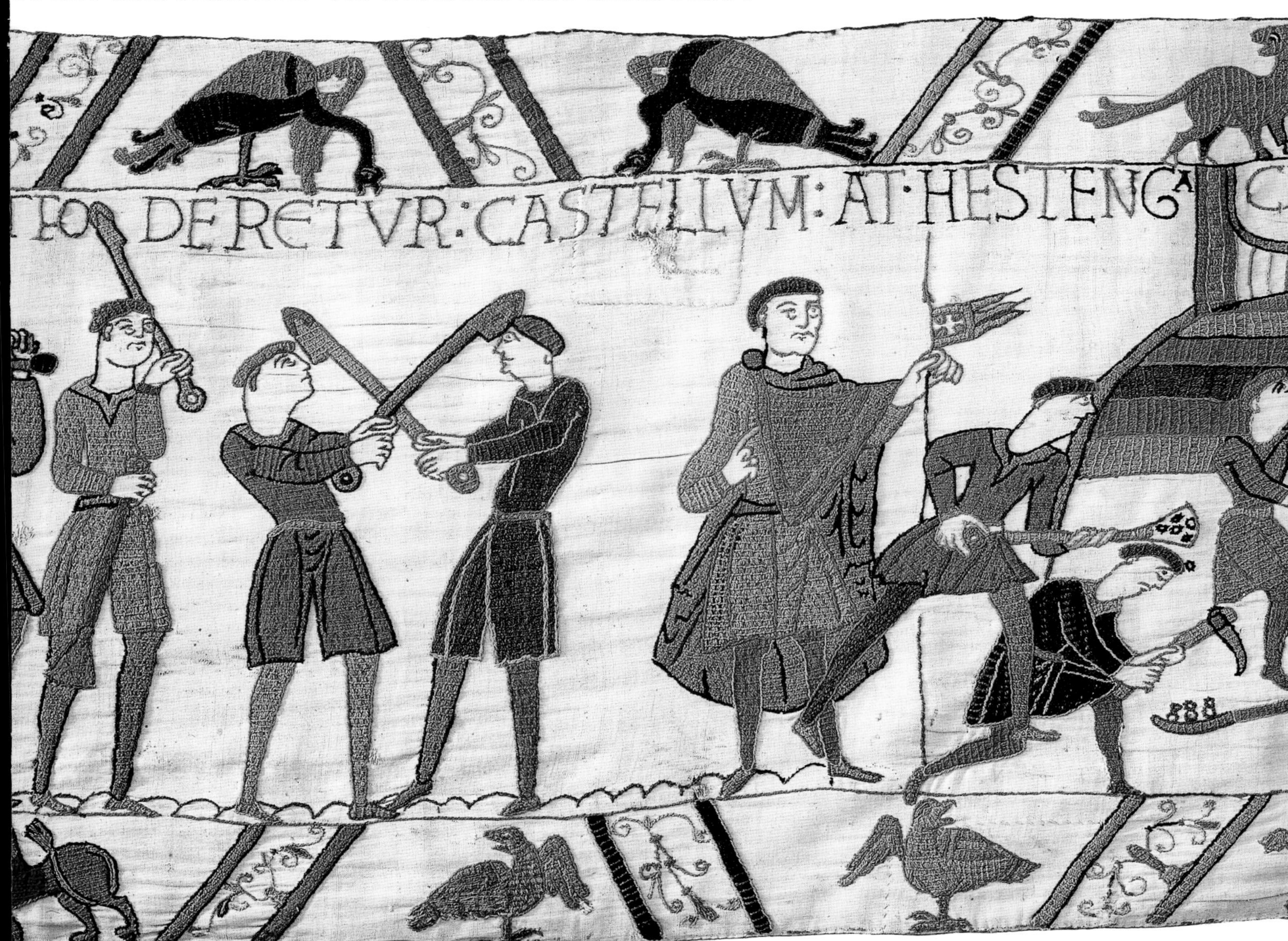

The latter ordered that a castle should be dug at Hastings.

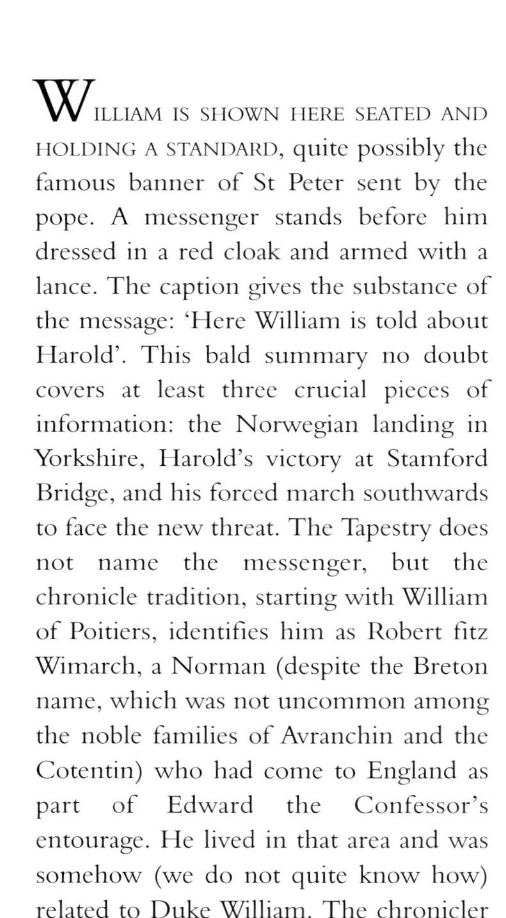

WILLIAM IS SHOWN HERE SEATED AND HOLDING A STANDARD, quite possibly the famous banner of St Peter sent by the pope. A messenger stands before him dressed in a red cloak and armed with a lance. The caption gives the substance of the message: 'Here William is told about Harold'. This bald summary no doubt covers at least three crucial pieces of information: the Norwegian landing in Yorkshire, Harold's victory at Stamford Bridge, and his forced march southwards to face the new threat. The Tapestry does not name the messenger, but the chronicle tradition, starting with William of Poitiers, identifies him as Robert fitz Wimarch, a Norman (despite the Breton name, which was not uncommon among the noble families of Avranchin and the Cotentin) who had come to England as part of Edward the Confessor's entourage. He lived in that area and was somehow (we do not quite know how) related to Duke William. The chronicler claims in addition that Robert advised the duke to sit tight within the defences he was erecting, but that William rejected this cautious counsel.[95]

Harold was still at York, clearing up after the defeat of the Norwegians and the death of his brother Tostig, when news of the Norman landing reached him on 1 October. The very next day he decided to head south by way of London. The astonishing speed of his forced march is legendary. Harold then spent five days in London (from 6 to 11 or 12 October), presumably raising further troops for his counter-attack against the Norman bridgehead. This information, derived from the *Anglo-Saxon Chronicle*, is crucial to explaining the course of the final battle. The core of his army was battle-hardened but also battle-weary: their two forced marches up and down England in a matter of weeks had been interrupted only by fierce fighting in which they had taken heavy losses. The larger part of Harold's army at Hastings was made up of men who were recalled to arms on his return to London. This did not bode well for the cohesion of his force on the battlefield, though this makes its actual performance on the day all the more remarkable.

Around Hastings William's workmen were clearing the ground to facilitate the manoeuvres of his knights. Here they are torching the two-storeyed house of a well-dressed English lady (her head is veiled and her gown has fashionably long sleeves) while she leads her son away

[95] William of Poitiers, ed. Foreville, p. 170 (Davis and Chibnall, pp. 116-17). On Robert fitz Wimarch see S. Keynes, 'Regenbald the Chancellor', *Anglo-Norman Studies* 10 (1987), pp. 185-222, at note 205. His son built a castle at Rayleigh in Essex towards the end of the eleventh century.

HIC NUNTIATUM EST

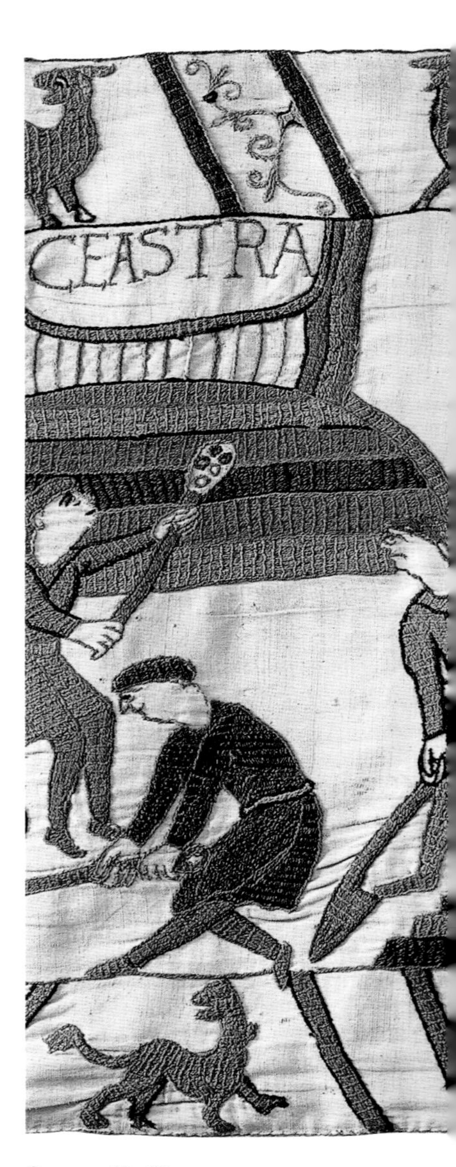

SCENES 46–47

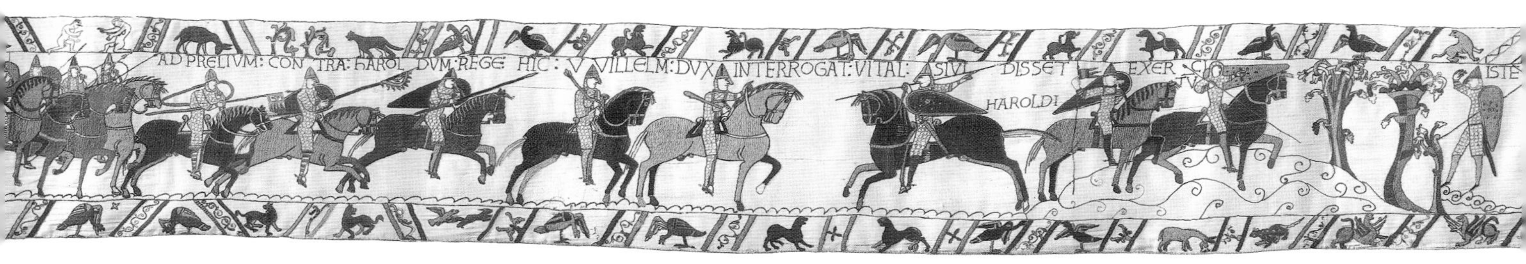

VILLELMO DE HAROLD. HIC DOMUS INCENDITUR.

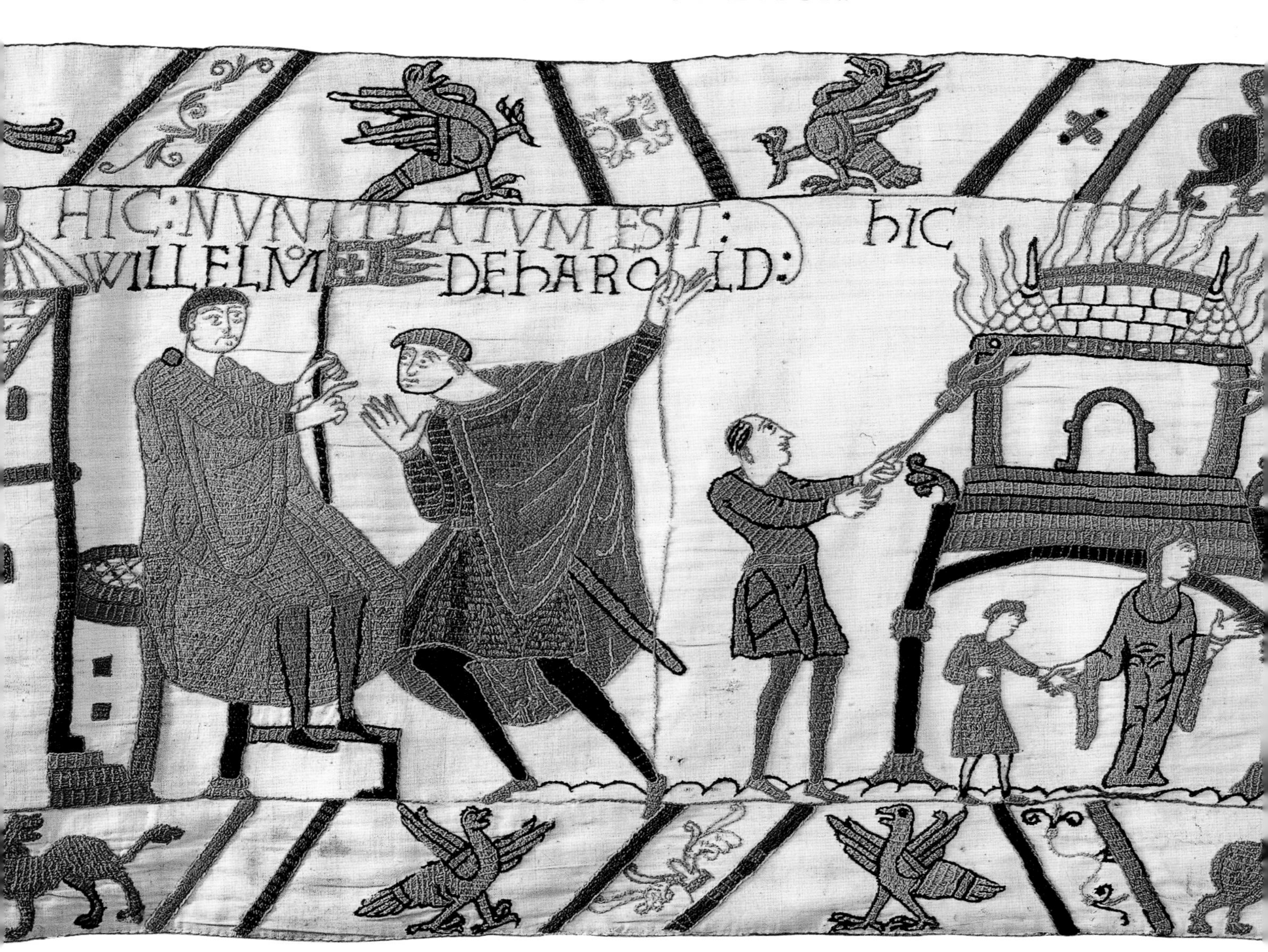

Here William is told about Harold. Here a house is burned.

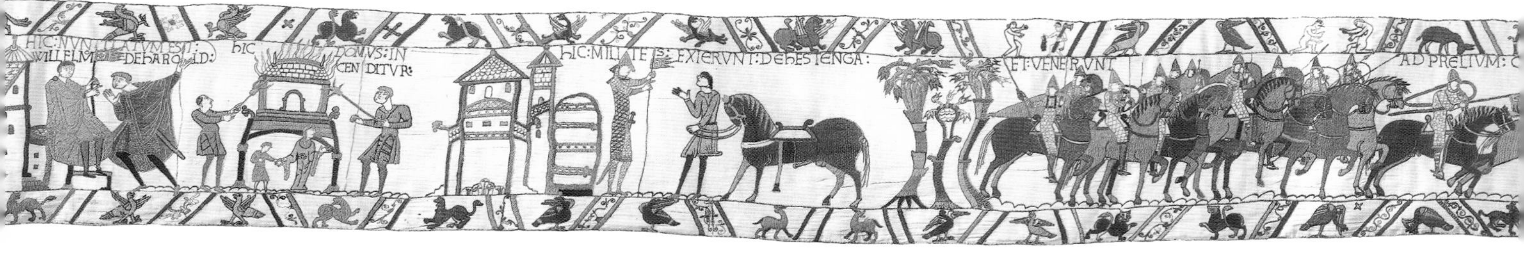

from the scene. The house has some curious decorations: the floral motifs at the upper corners of the ground floor.

The rather complex building to the right seems to stand for the entire town of Hastings, which is named in the ensuing caption. Consisting apparently of three floors, and flanked by a turret-staircase, it has an outsize door hung on metal strap-hinges. It seems to mark the transition between the aftermath of the landing and the prelude to the battle. From now on most of the figures who appear are armed for combat. The three stylised trees at the start of the next scene (p. 220) mark the complete change of subject and mood. Between the building and the trees a stable-lad presents a saddled and bridled mount to a tall, fully-armed knight. Since he seems to be holding the same banner as Duke William in scene 46 (p. 217), it is generally agreed that this is the duke himself.

SCENE 47

HIC MILITES EXIERU

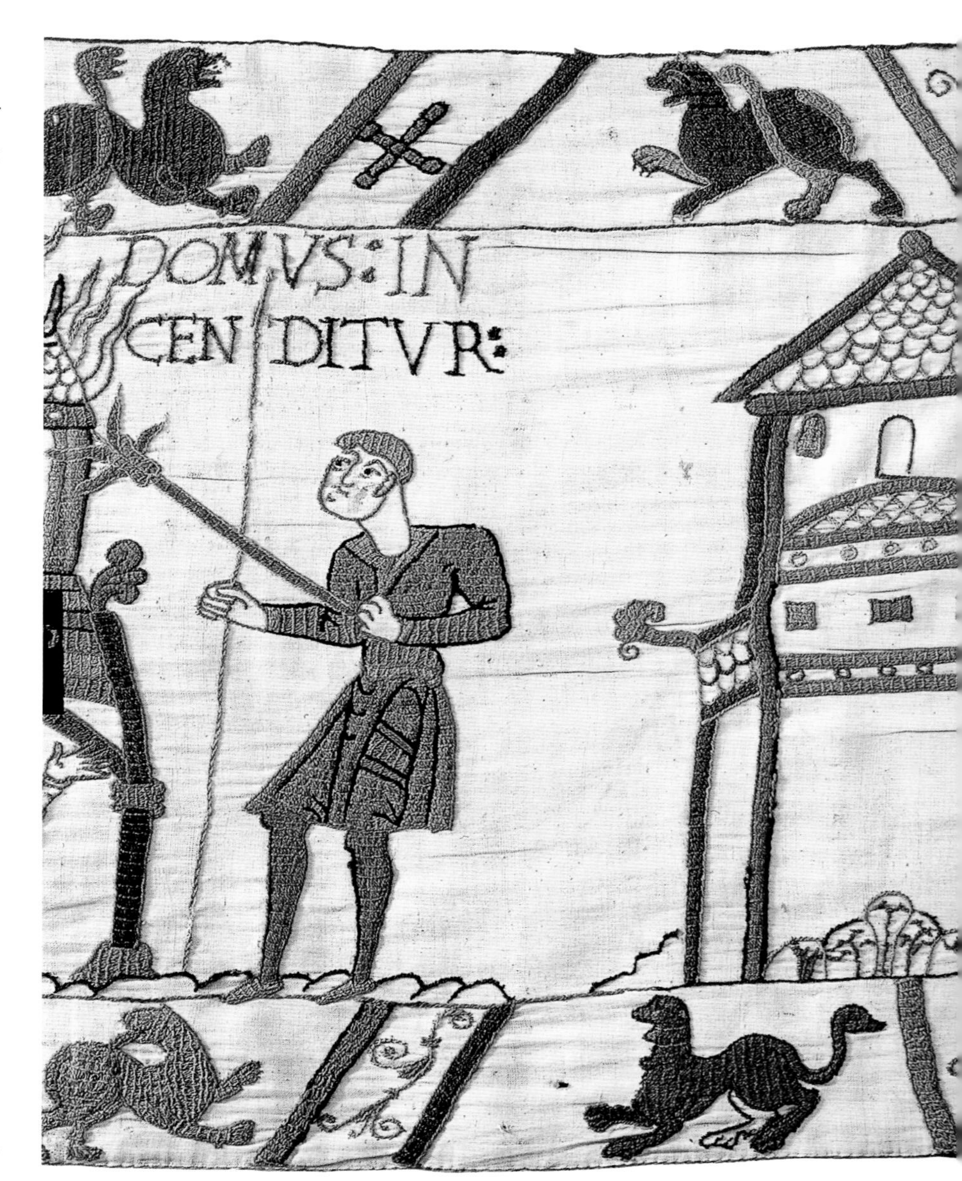

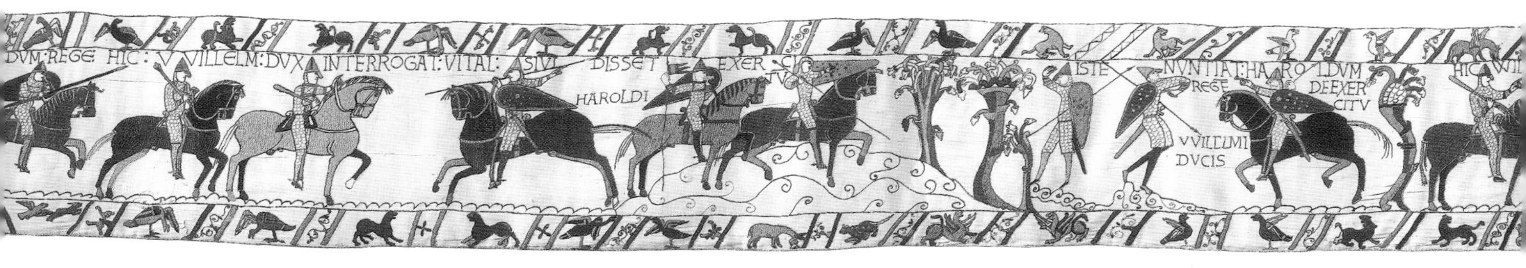

E HESTENGA…

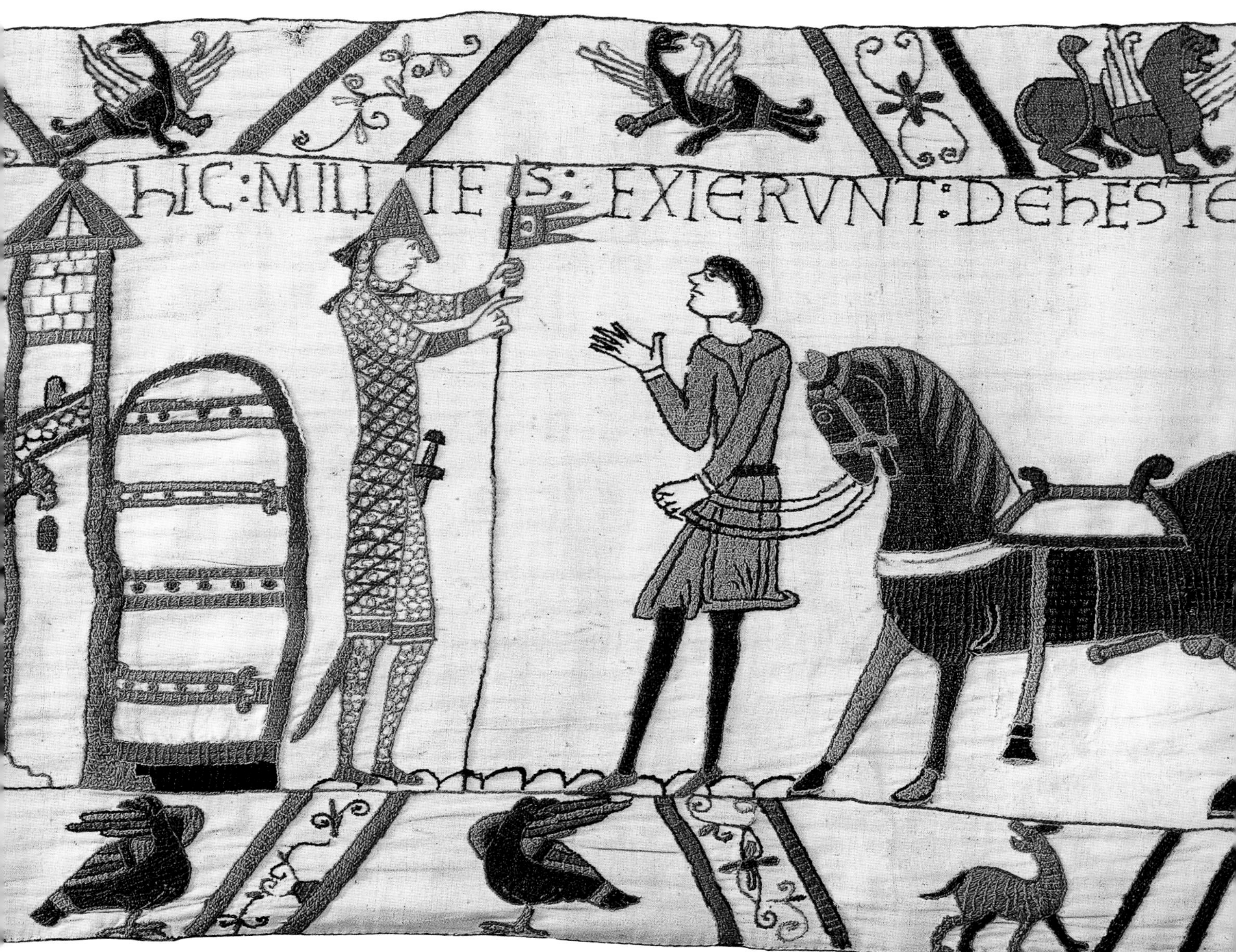

Here knights leave Hastings …

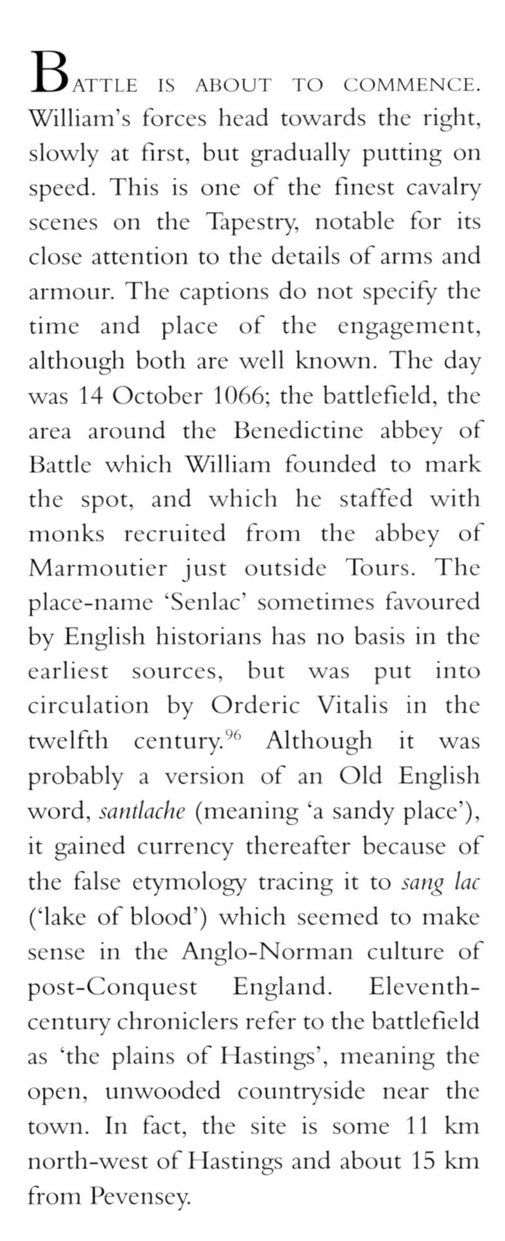

Battle is about to commence. William's forces head towards the right, slowly at first, but gradually putting on speed. This is one of the finest cavalry scenes on the Tapestry, notable for its close attention to the details of arms and armour. The captions do not specify the time and place of the engagement, although both are well known. The day was 14 October 1066; the battlefield, the area around the Benedictine abbey of Battle which William founded to mark the spot, and which he staffed with monks recruited from the abbey of Marmoutier just outside Tours. The place-name 'Senlac' sometimes favoured by English historians has no basis in the earliest sources, but was put into circulation by Orderic Vitalis in the twelfth century.[96] Although it was probably a version of an Old English word, *santlache* (meaning 'a sandy place'), it gained currency thereafter because of the false etymology tracing it to *sang lac* ('lake of blood') which seemed to make sense in the Anglo-Norman culture of post-Conquest England. Eleventh-century chroniclers refer to the battlefield as 'the plains of Hastings', meaning the open, unwooded countryside near the town. In fact, the site is some 11 km north-west of Hastings and about 15 km from Pevensey.

... ET VENERUNT AD PR

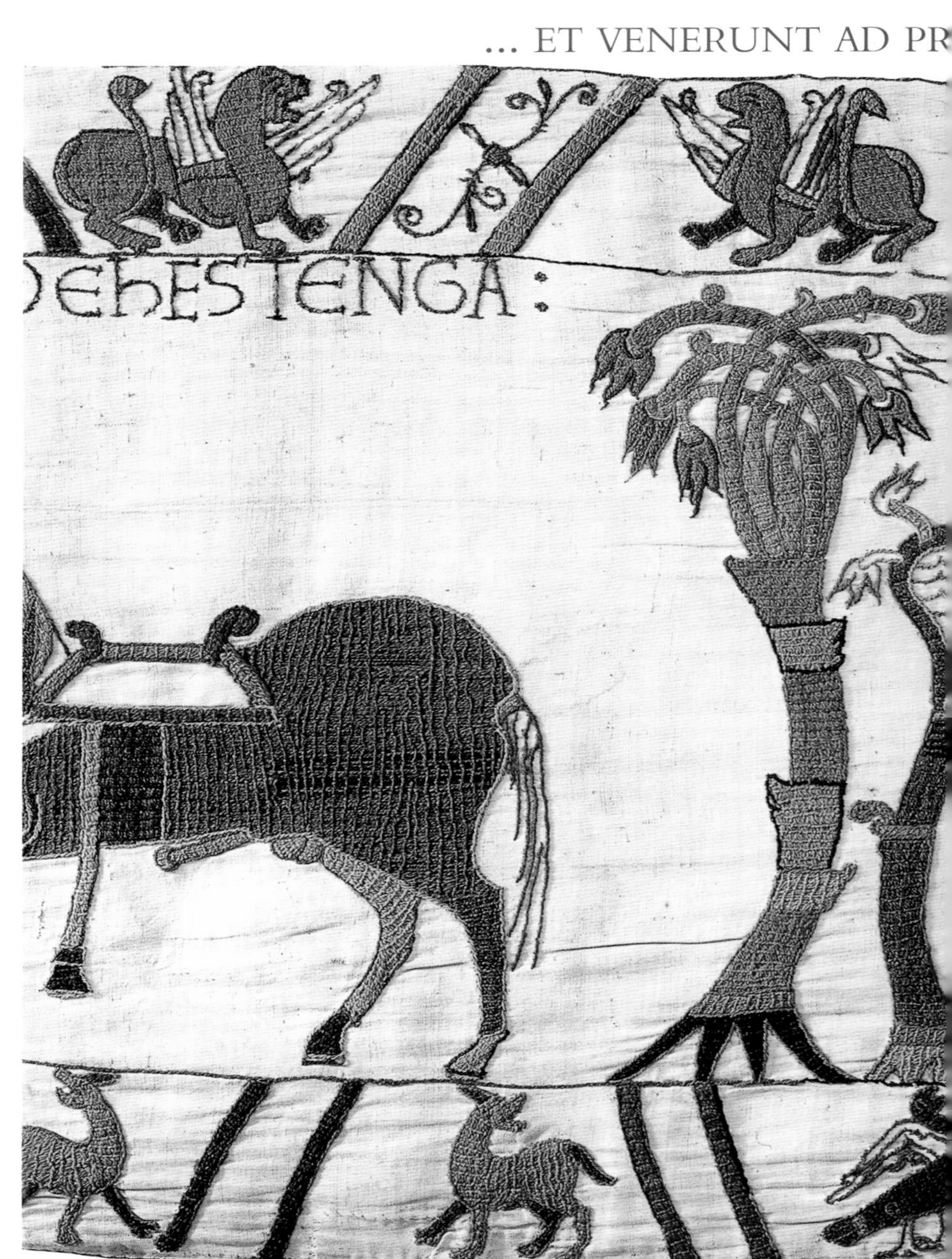

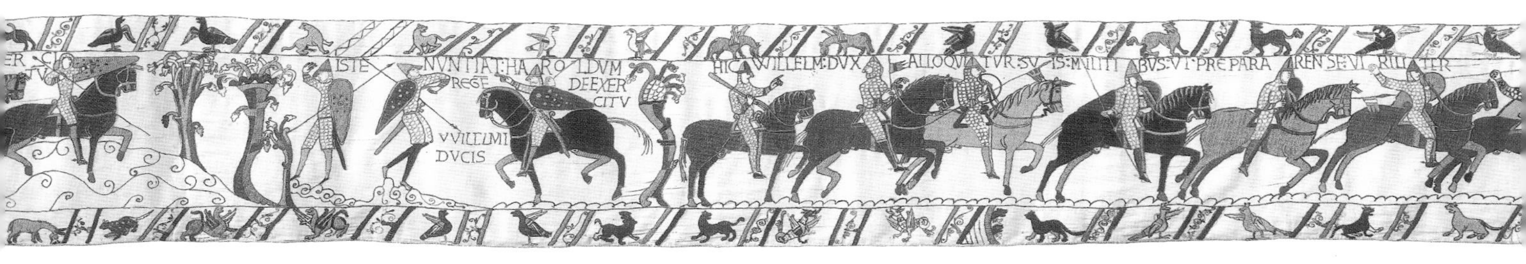

LIUM CONTRA HAROLDUM REGE(M).

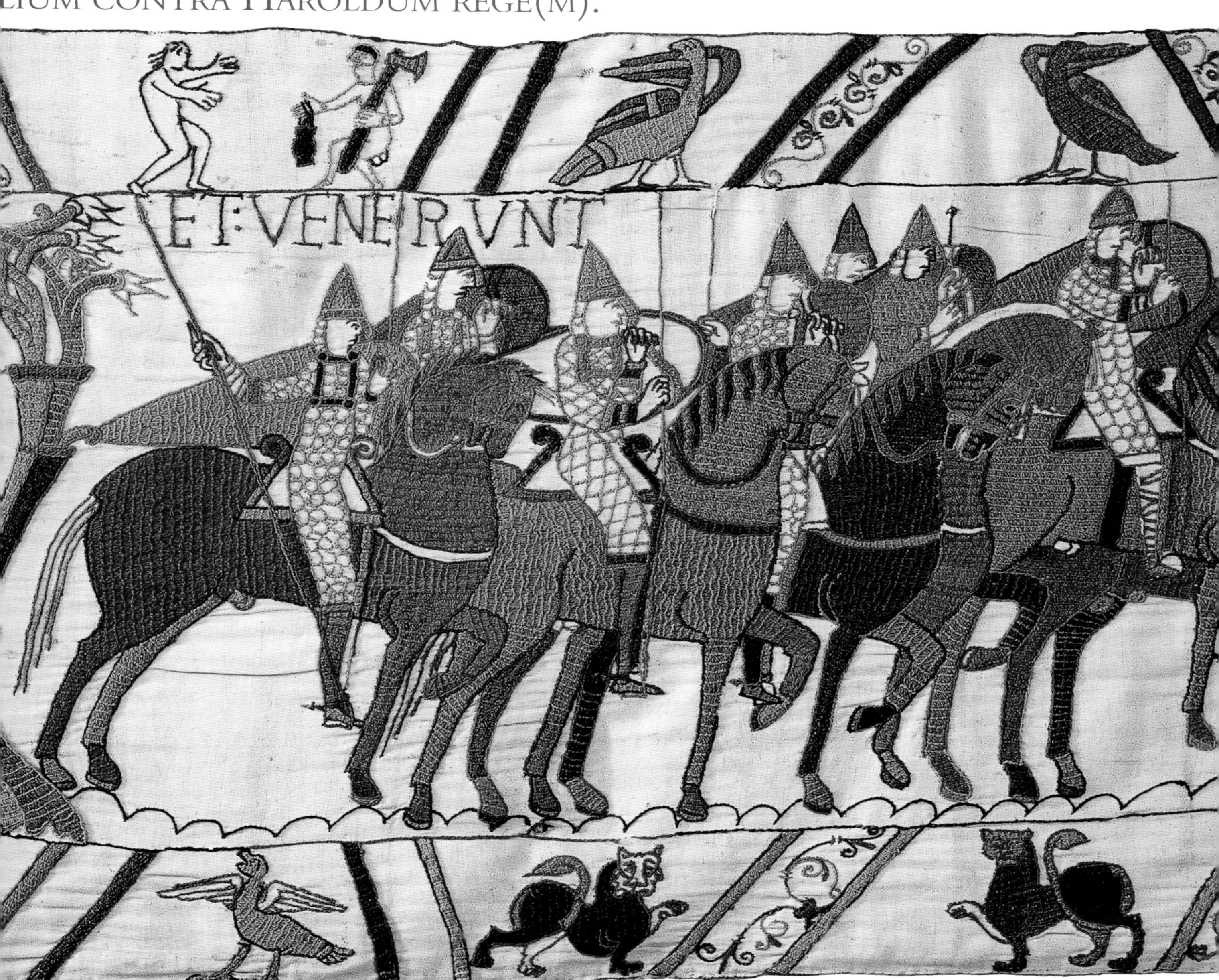

…and came to fight against King Harold.

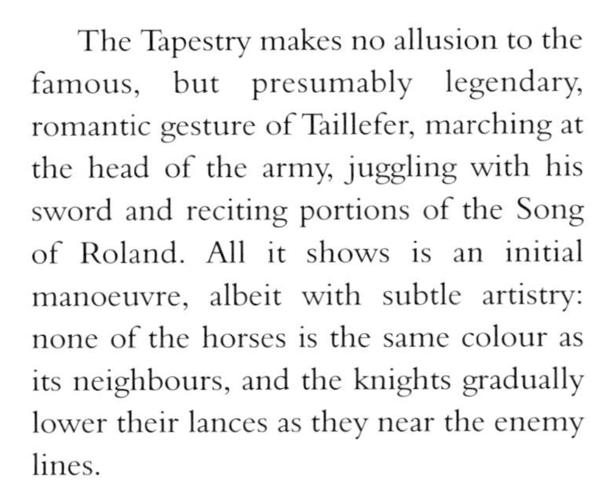

The Tapestry makes no allusion to the famous, but presumably legendary, romantic gesture of Taillefer, marching at the head of the army, juggling with his sword and reciting portions of the Song of Roland. All it shows is an initial manoeuvre, albeit with subtle artistry: none of the horses is the same colour as its neighbours, and the knights gradually lower their lances as they near the enemy lines.

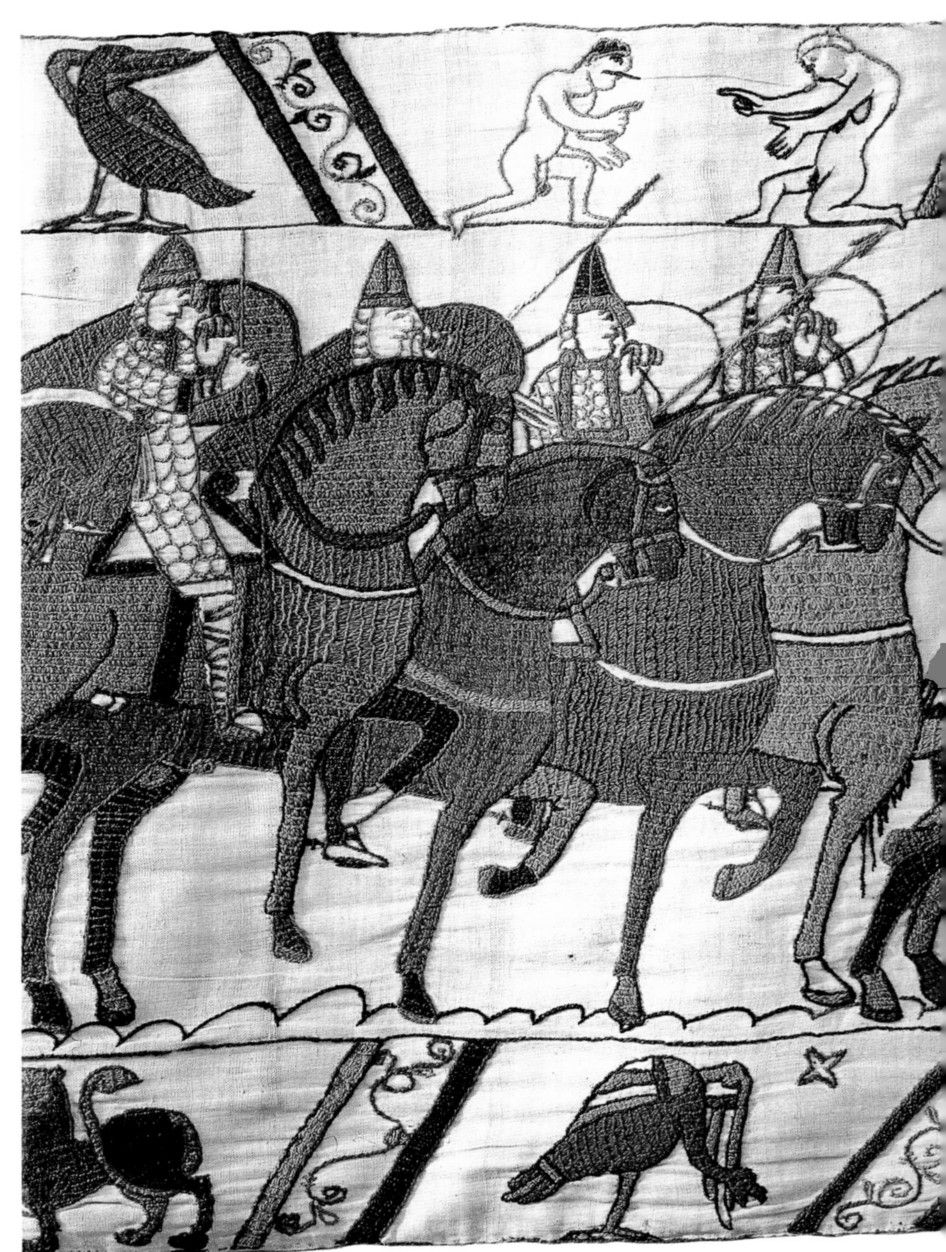

[96] Orderic Vitalis, ed. Chibnall, vol. 2, p. 172: 'ad locum qui Senlac antiquitus vocabatur'.

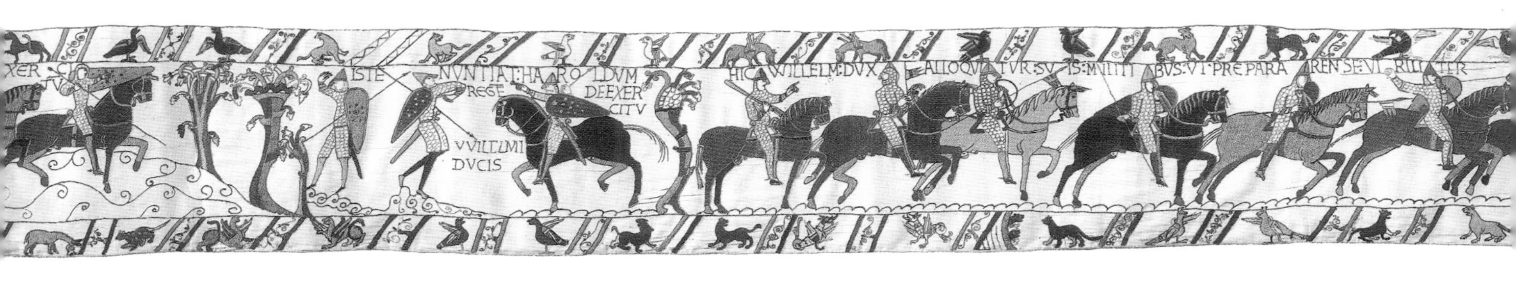

ISTE
NVNTIAT: HAROLDVM
REGE
DE EXER
CITV
VVILLEMI
DVCIS
HIC WILLELM: DVX
ALLOQVITVR: SVIS: MILITIBVS: VT PREPARARENT SE: VIRILITER

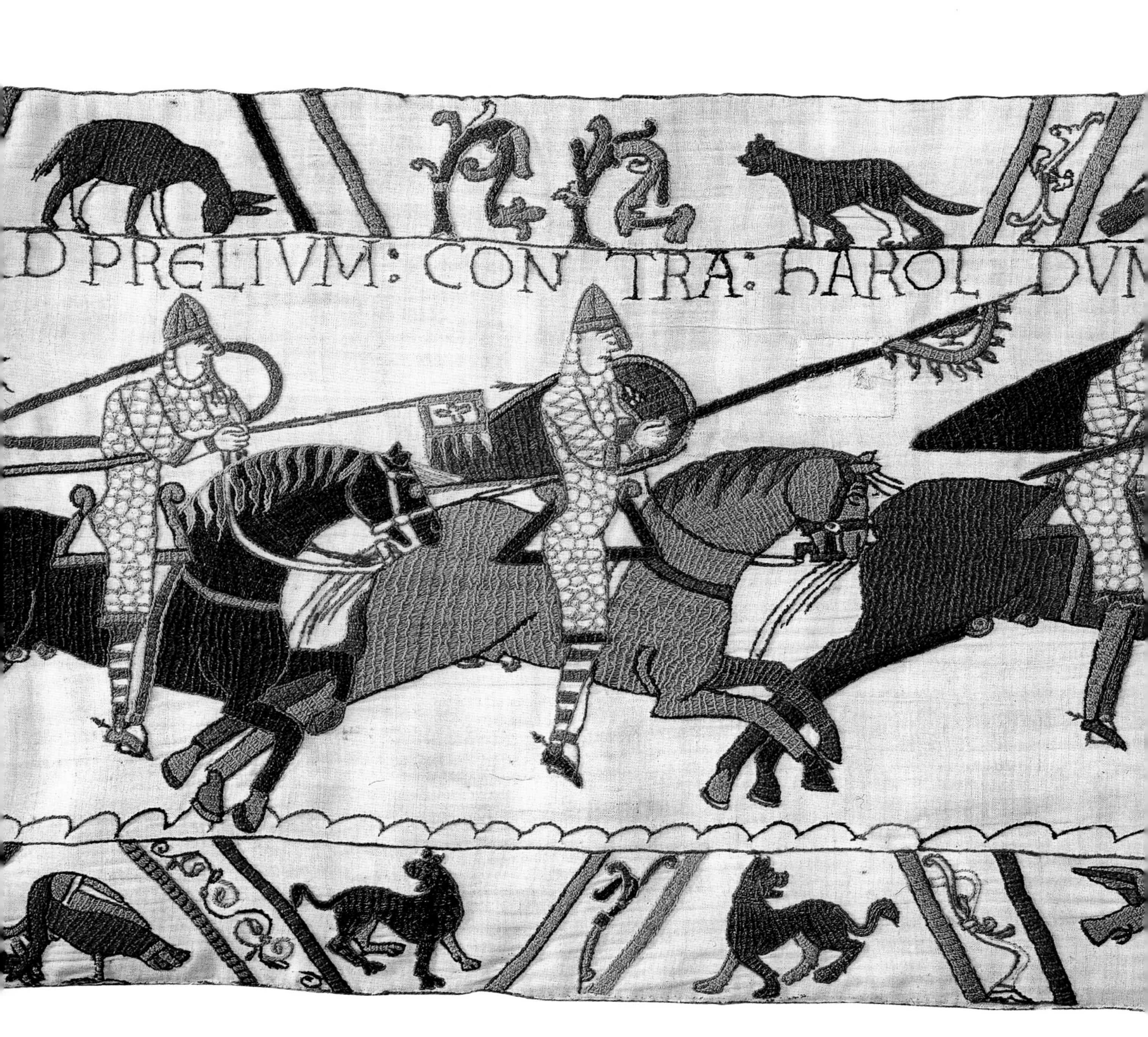

D PRELIVM: CON TRA: HAROL DVM

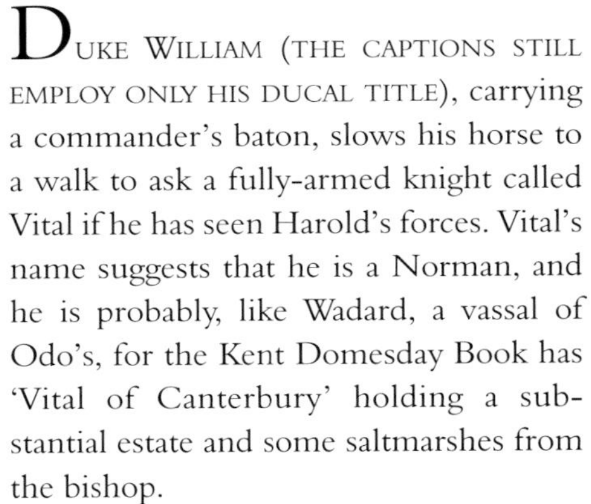

Duke William (the captions still employ only his ducal title), carrying a commander's baton, slows his horse to a walk to ask a fully-armed knight called Vital if he has seen Harold's forces. Vital's name suggests that he is a Norman, and he is probably, like Wadard, a vassal of Odo's, for the Kent Domesday Book has 'Vital of Canterbury' holding a substantial estate and some saltmarshes from the bishop.

A little further along the Tapestry are two knights, one of them without a helmet, taking up position on some rising ground, perhaps in order to provide cover for the duke (pp. 226–228). Three trees conceal them from English eyes. Vital is presumably pointing towards where the English are to be found. William now knows that the enemy is at hand.

Scene 49

Hic Willelm dux interrogat Vital si vid

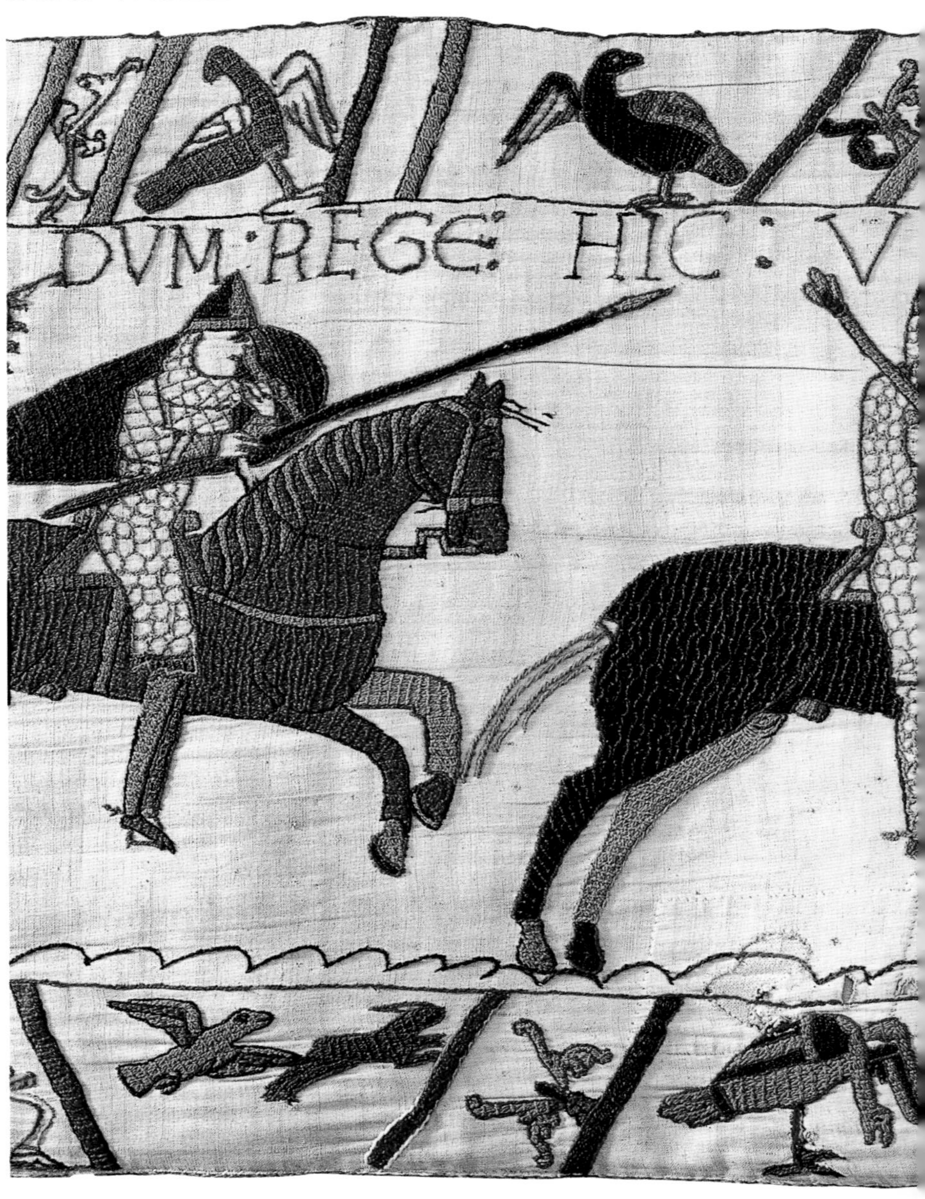

Here Duke William asks Vital if he had seen Harold's army.

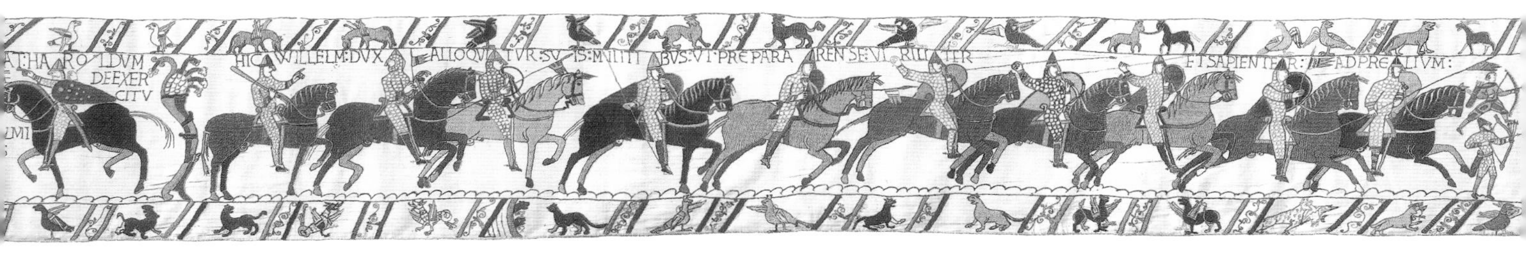

ET EXERCITUM HAROLDI.

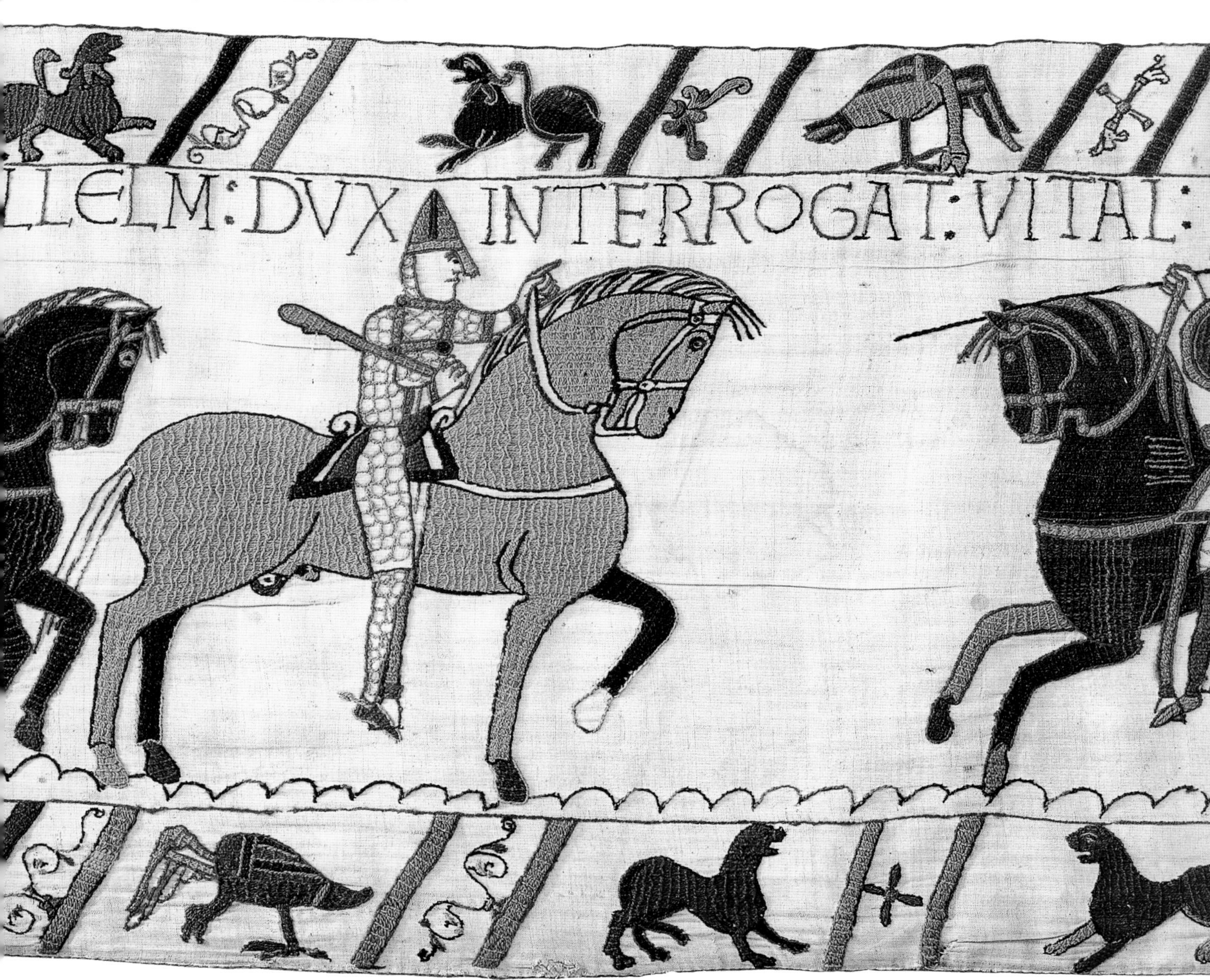

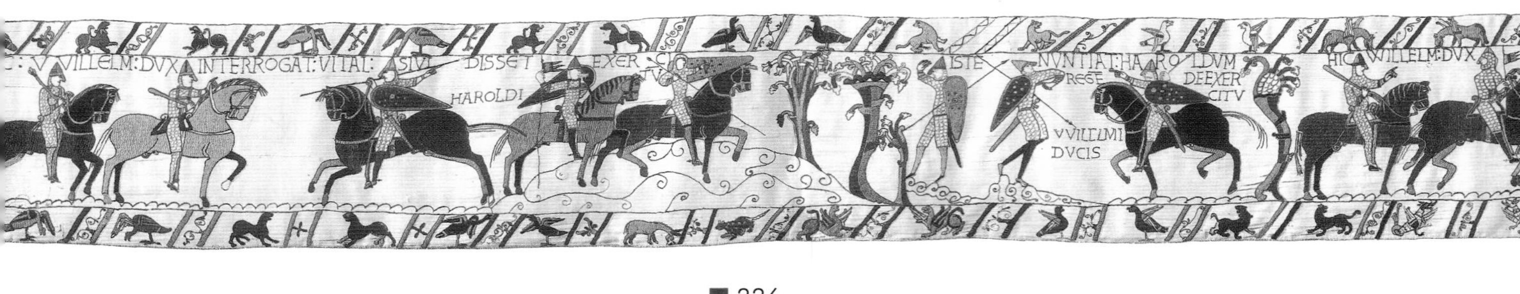
VVILLELM:DVX INTERROGAT:VITAL: ASIVI DISSET EXER CITV
HAROLDI
ISTE NVNTIAT:HAROLDVM REGE DEEXERCITV
VVILLELMI DVCIS
HIC WILLELM:DVX

226

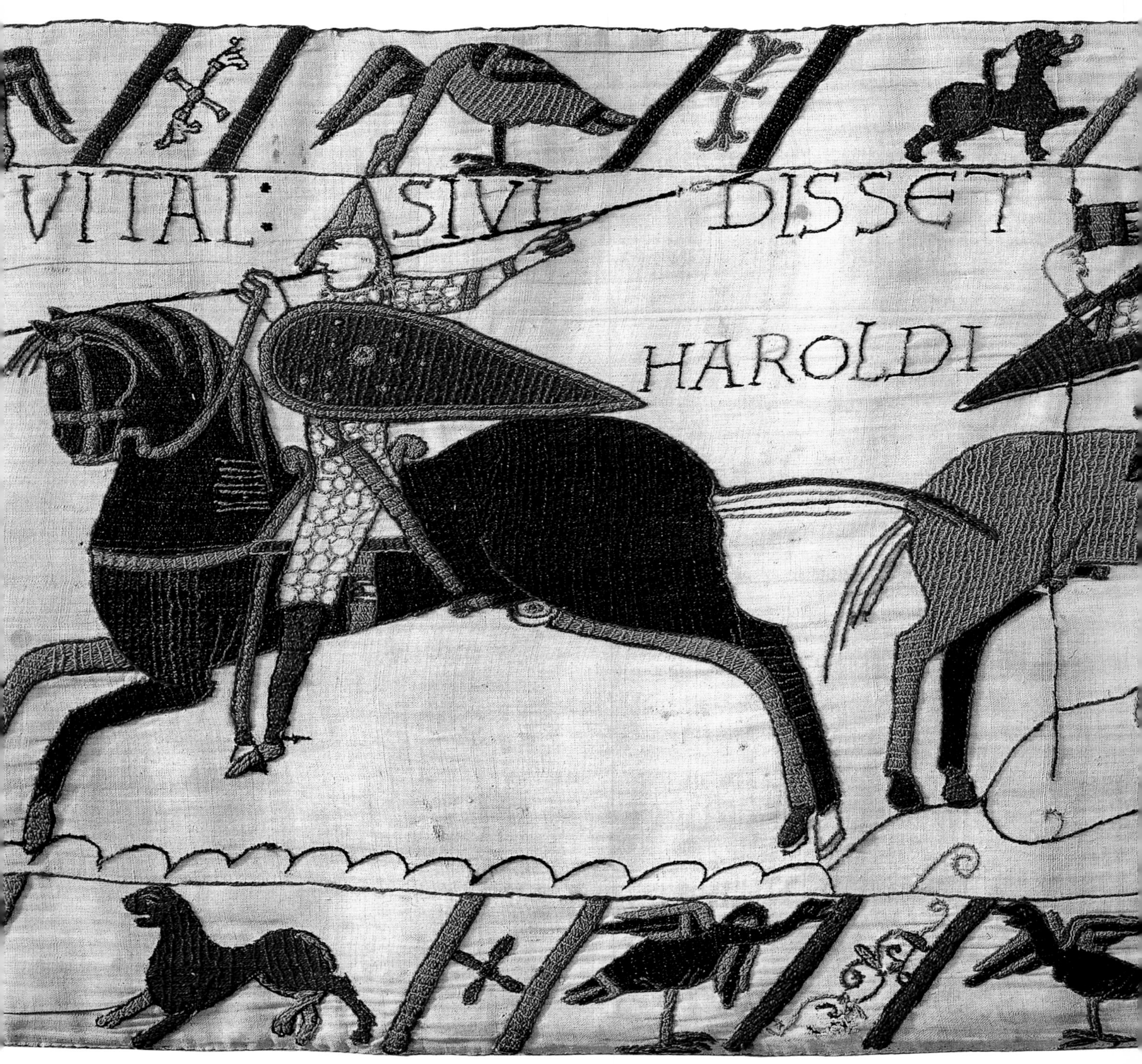
VITAL: SIVI DISSET
HAROLDI

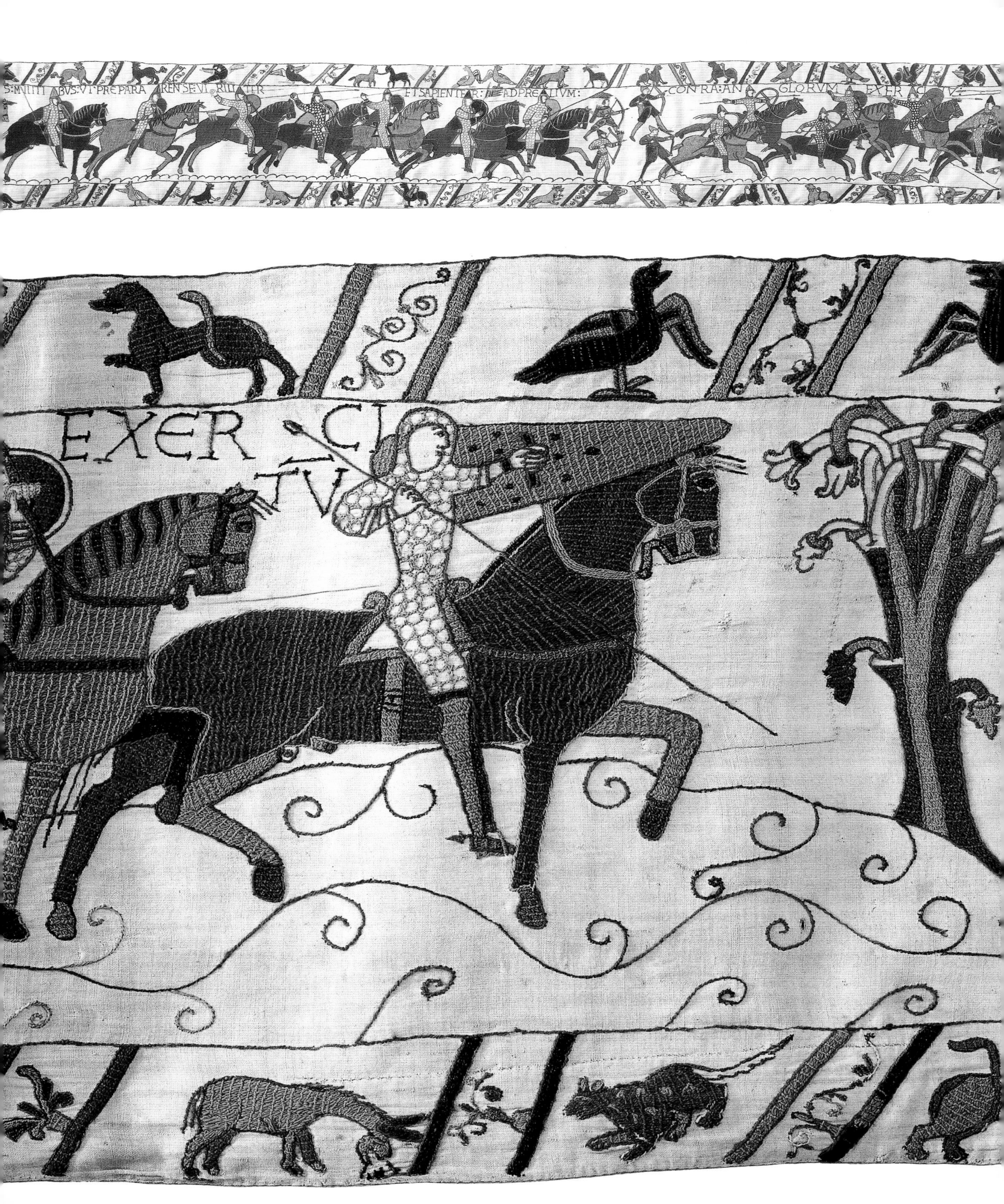
S:MILITIBUS:UT PREPARARENT SE VIRILITER ET SAPIENTER: AD PRELIUM: CONTRA: ANGLORUM EXERCITU:
EXER CI TU

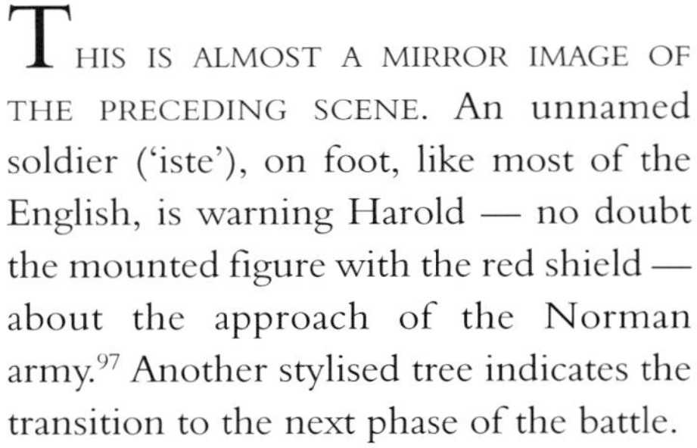

ISTE NUNTIAT HAROL

THIS IS ALMOST A MIRROR IMAGE OF THE PRECEDING SCENE. An unnamed soldier ('iste'), on foot, like most of the English, is warning Harold — no doubt the mounted figure with the red shield — about the approach of the Norman army.[97] Another stylised tree indicates the transition to the next phase of the battle.

The focus is once more on the duke and his knights. This is where William, still carrying his baton, delivered his famous speech to his men. The caption puts it rather well: 'Here Duke William tells his soldiers to prepare themselves manfully and wisely for the battle against the army of the English'. One of the knights is turning his head to hear better; the others are commencing a rapid advance towards the English lines, a manoeuvre which continues in the next scene.

There is a possibility that the little tree shown here is meant to represent the 'grey apple-tree' which, according to one recension of the *Anglo-Saxon Chronicle*, gave its name to the battlefield (although a case could also be made for the tree which appears later on the hillside in scene 54, p. 248). But there is no way of knowing, and the Norman sources are in any case silent on this detail.

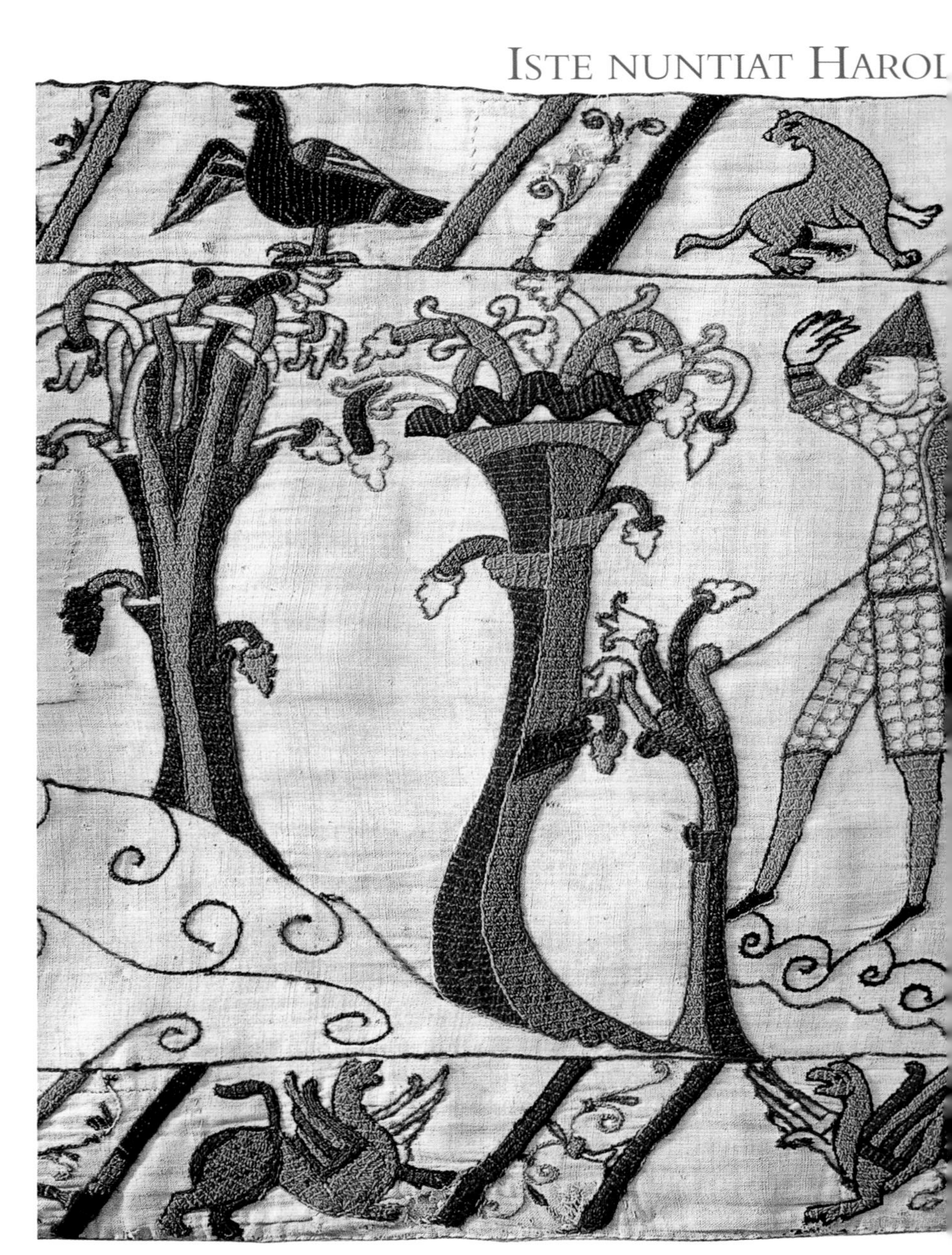

SCENE 50

[97] Harold's horse is shown in a position which conventionally indicated an amble, that is, with both right legs raised. See T. Witt, 'De forsvundne gangere', *Skalk* 1 (1978), pp. 18-27, at p. 21.

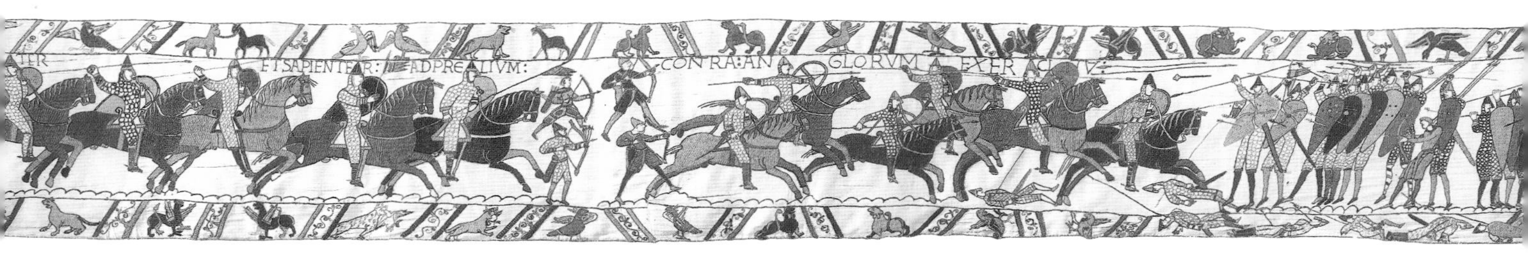

M DE EXERCITU WILLELMI DUCIS.

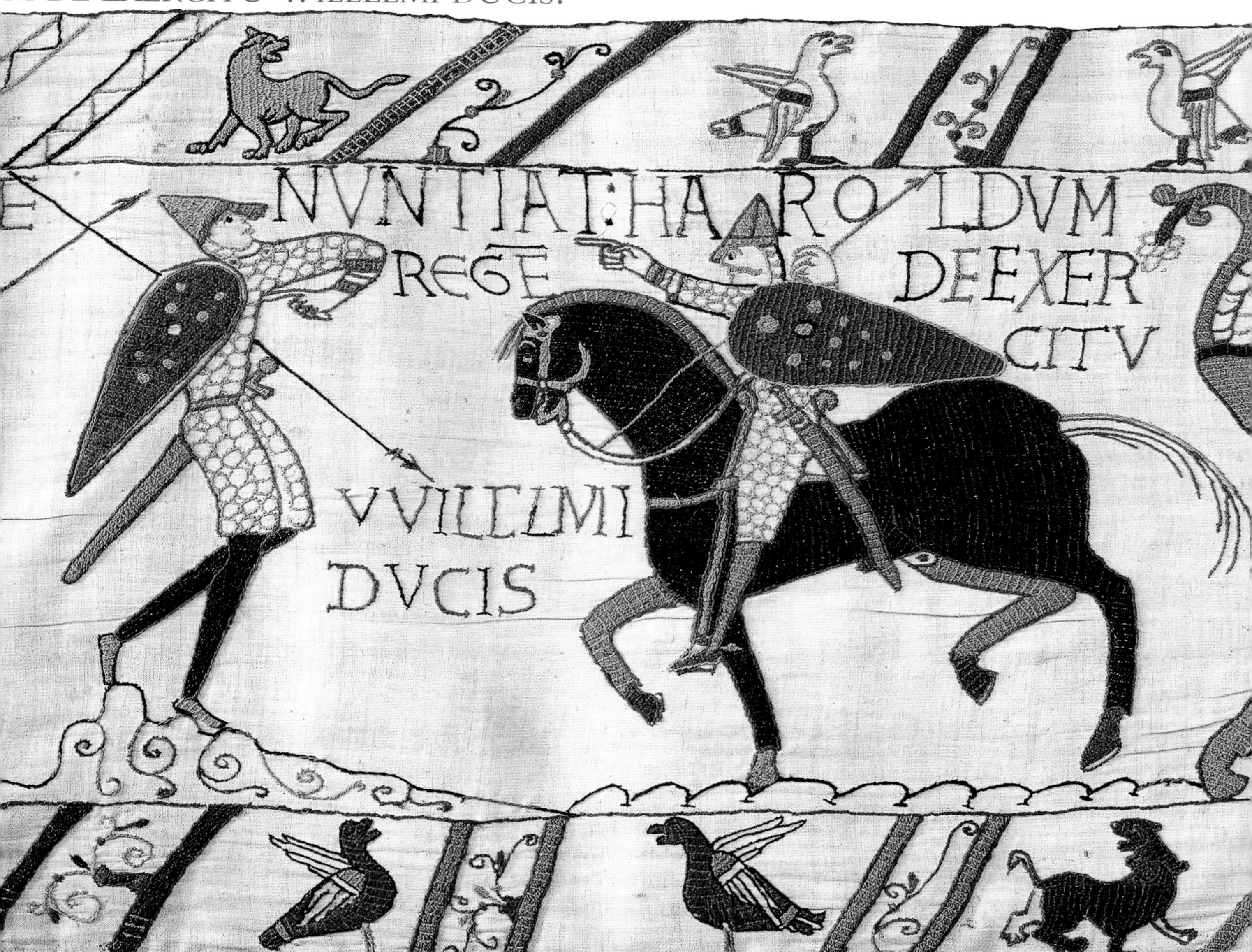

He tells Harold about Duke William's army.

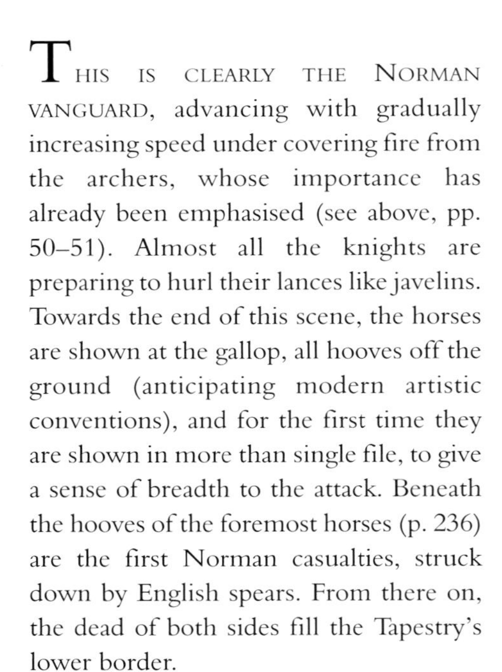

Hic Willelm dux al

This is clearly the Norman vanguard, advancing with gradually increasing speed under covering fire from the archers, whose importance has already been emphasised (see above, pp. 50–51). Almost all the knights are preparing to hurl their lances like javelins. Towards the end of this scene, the horses are shown at the gallop, all hooves off the ground (anticipating modern artistic conventions), and for the first time they are shown in more than single file, to give a sense of breadth to the attack. Beneath the hooves of the foremost horses (p. 236) are the first Norman casualties, struck down by English spears. From there on, the dead of both sides fill the Tapestry's lower border.

At this point the Norman cavalry engages with the serried ranks of English infantry, massed behind the shield wall and armed with spears and battle-axes. The Tapestry makes no attempt to distinguish the various elements of William's army, which according to the chronicles consisted of French and Flemings on the right, a Norman centre, and Bretons on the left, all charging up the hill towards the English positions at the top.

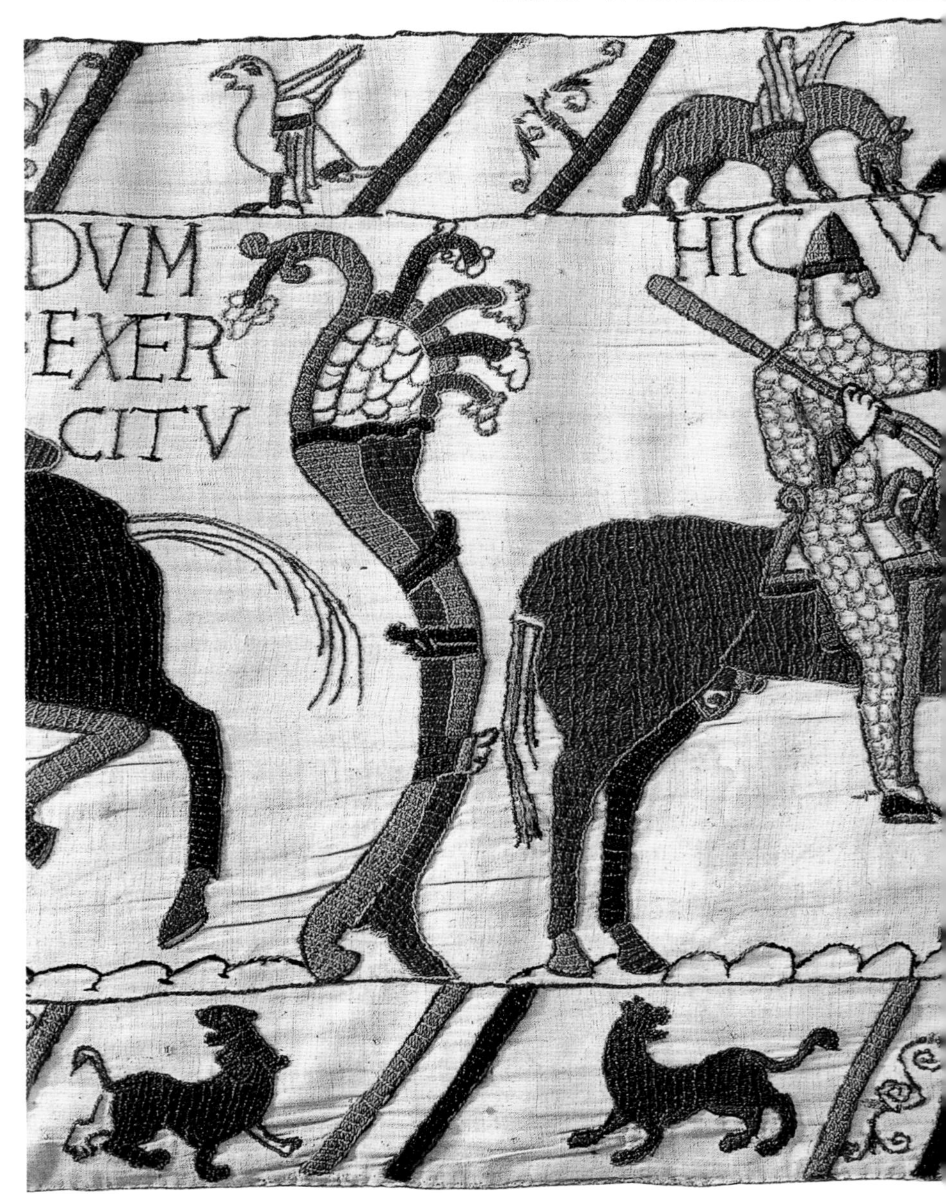

Scenes 50–51

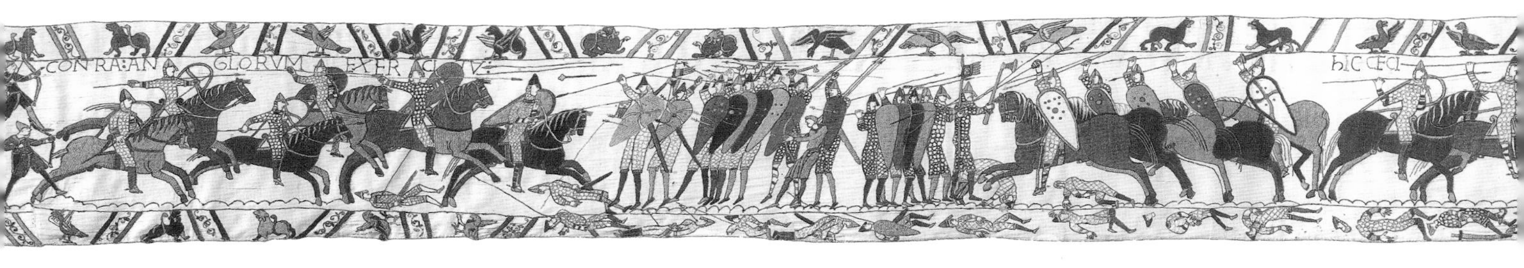

OQUITUR SUIS MILITIBUS...

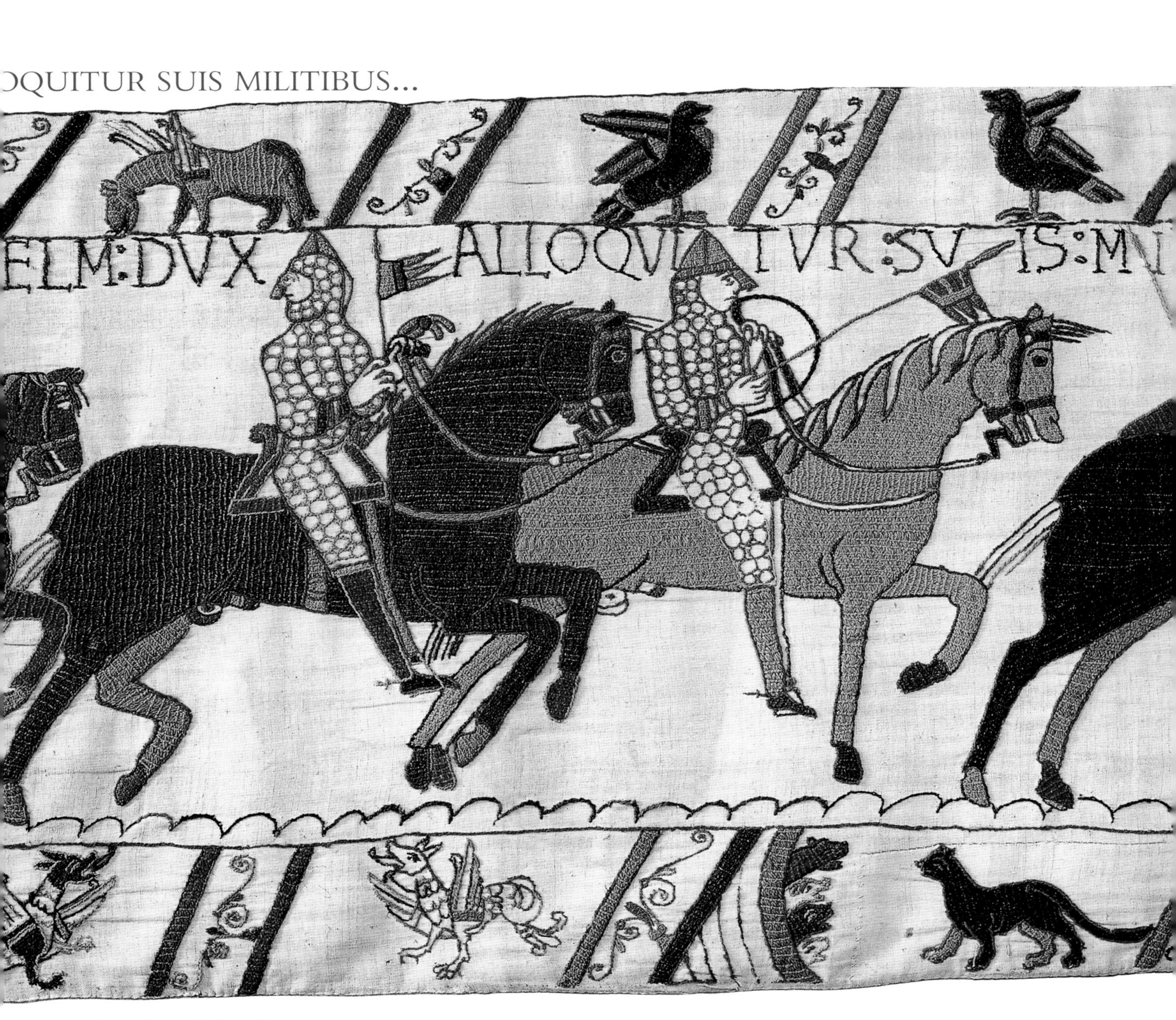

Here Duke William tells his soldiers …

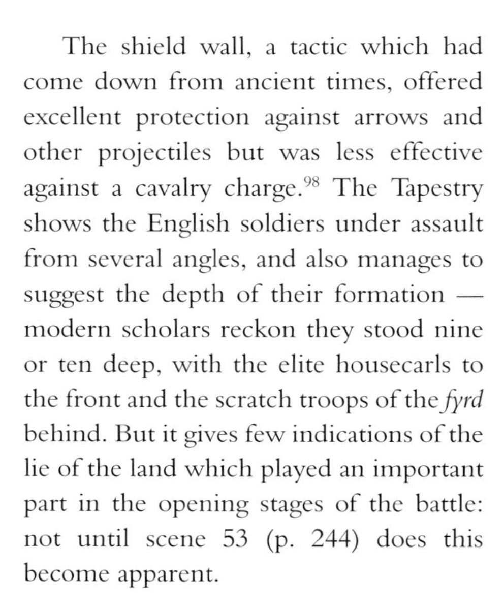

The shield wall, a tactic which had come down from ancient times, offered excellent protection against arrows and other projectiles but was less effective against a cavalry charge.[98] The Tapestry shows the English soldiers under assault from several angles, and also manages to suggest the depth of their formation — modern scholars reckon they stood nine or ten deep, with the elite housecarls to the front and the scratch troops of the *fyrd* behind. But it gives few indications of the lie of the land which played an important part in the opening stages of the battle: not until scene 53 (p. 244) does this become apparent.

UT PREPARARENT SE V

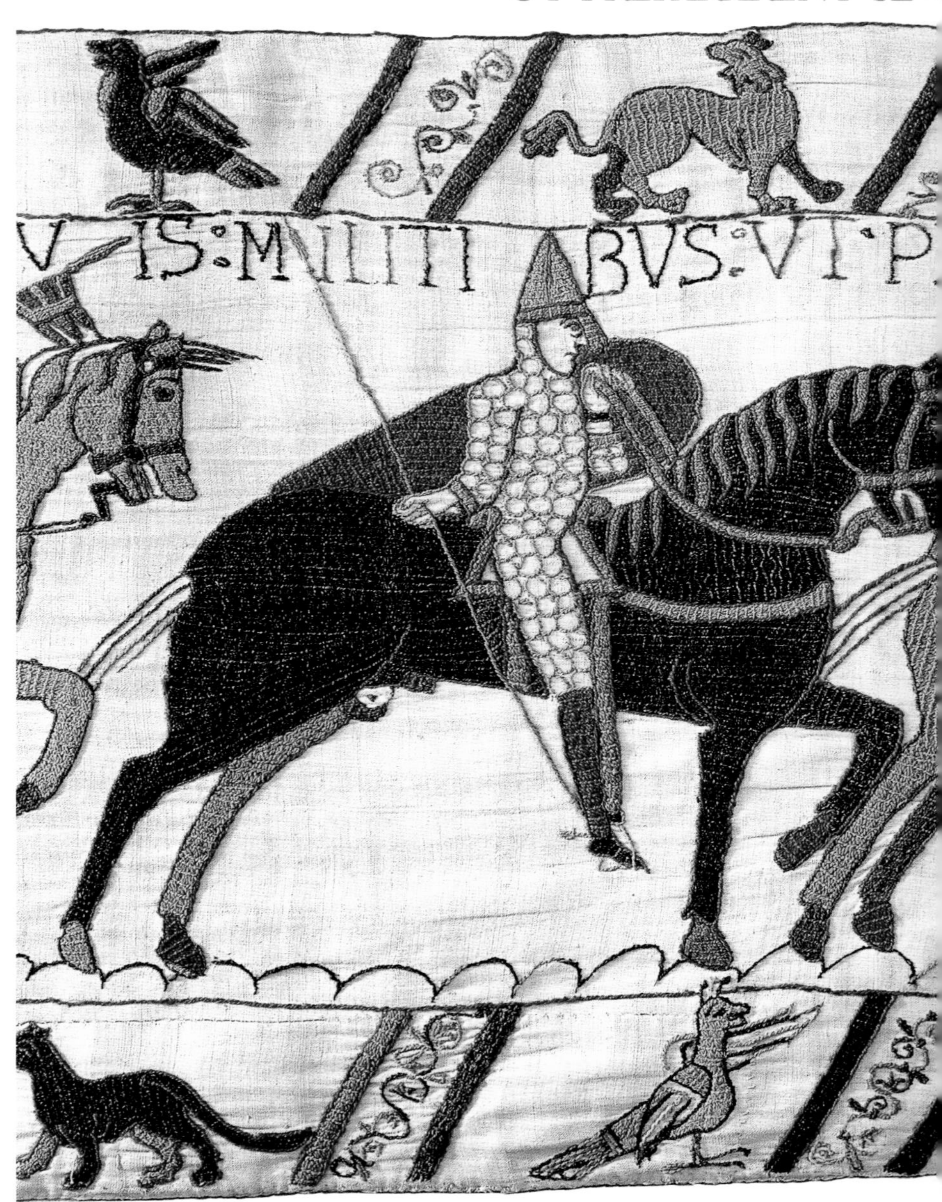

[98] The best modern accounts of the battle are those of C. H. Lemmon, *The Field of Hastings* (3rd edn. St Leonards, 1964); and 'The Campaign of 1066', in Whitelock, Douglas, Lemmon, Barlow, *The Norman Conquest* (London, 1966), with excellent plans and photographs of the battlefield.

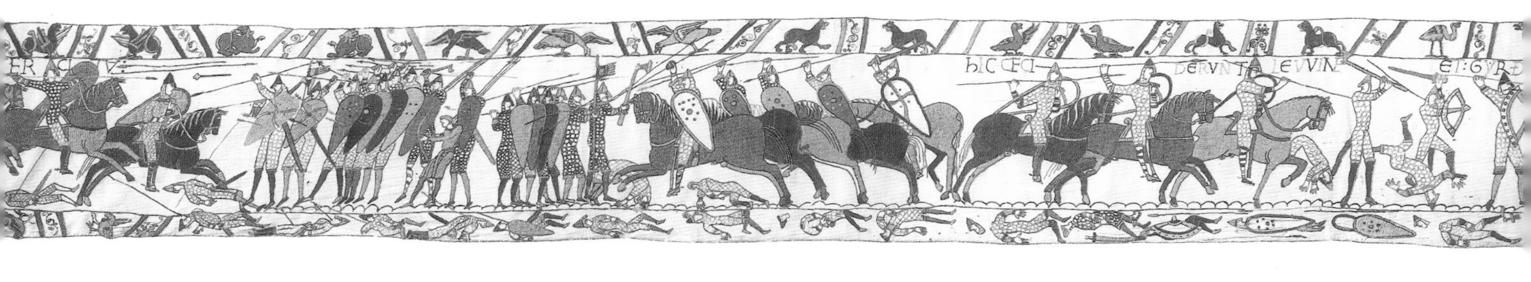

ILITER ET SAPIENTER...

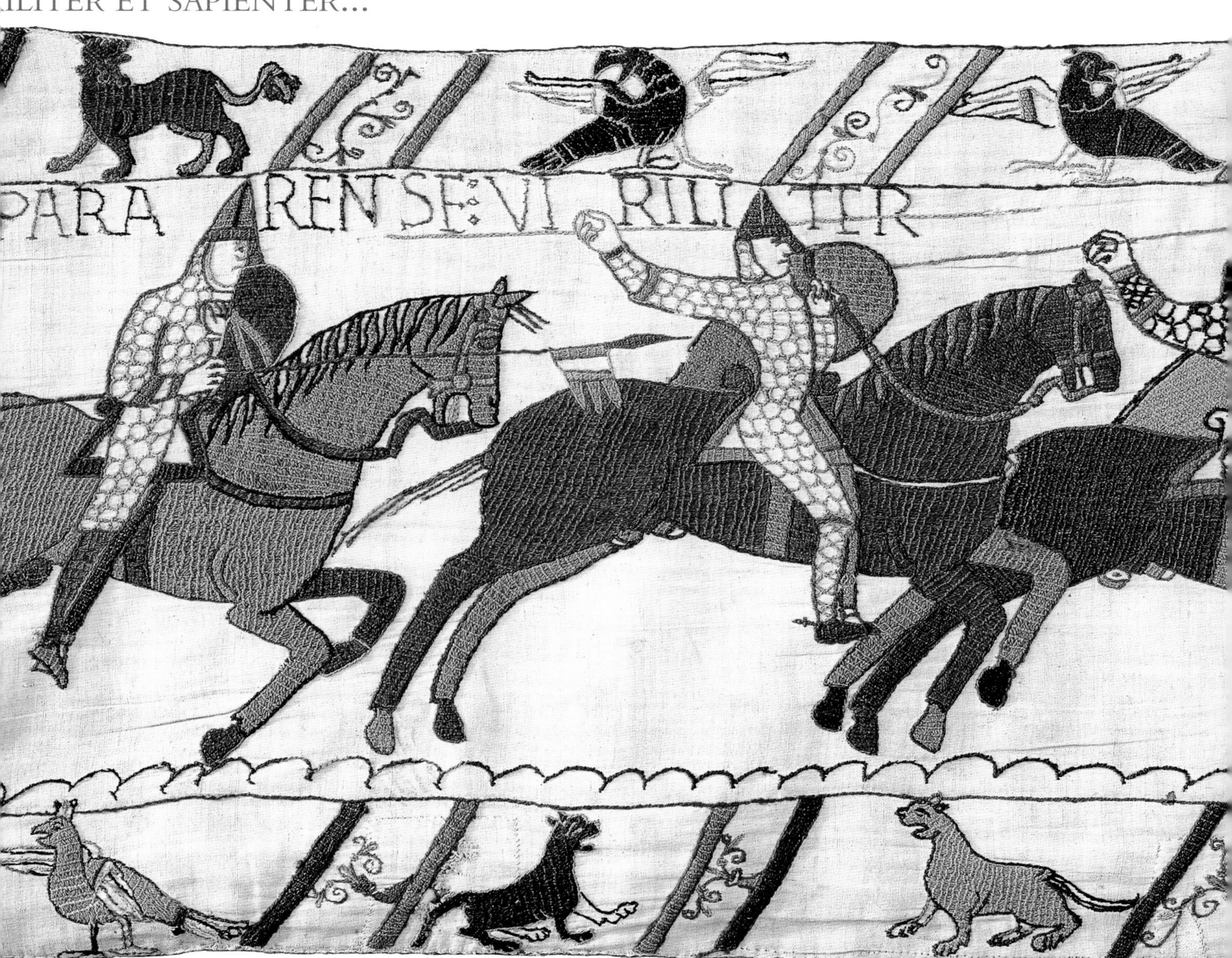

...to prepare themselves manfully and wisely ...

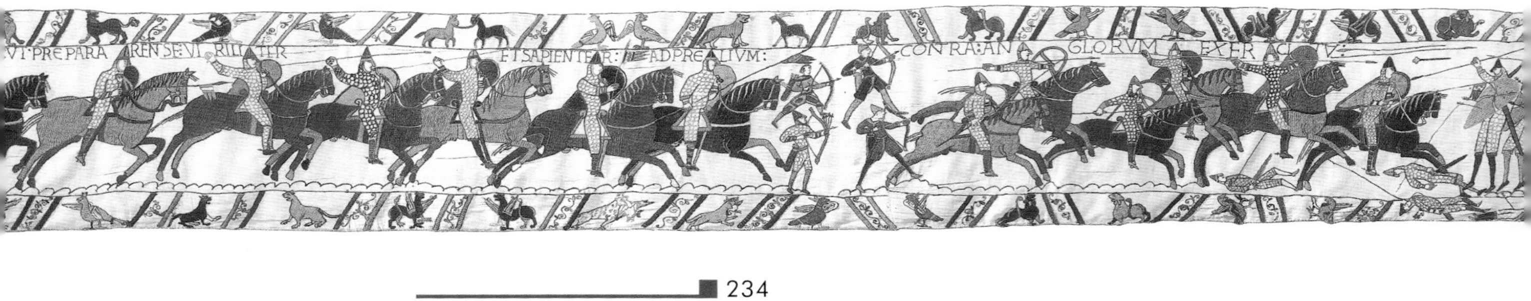

234

... AD PRELIUM CONTR

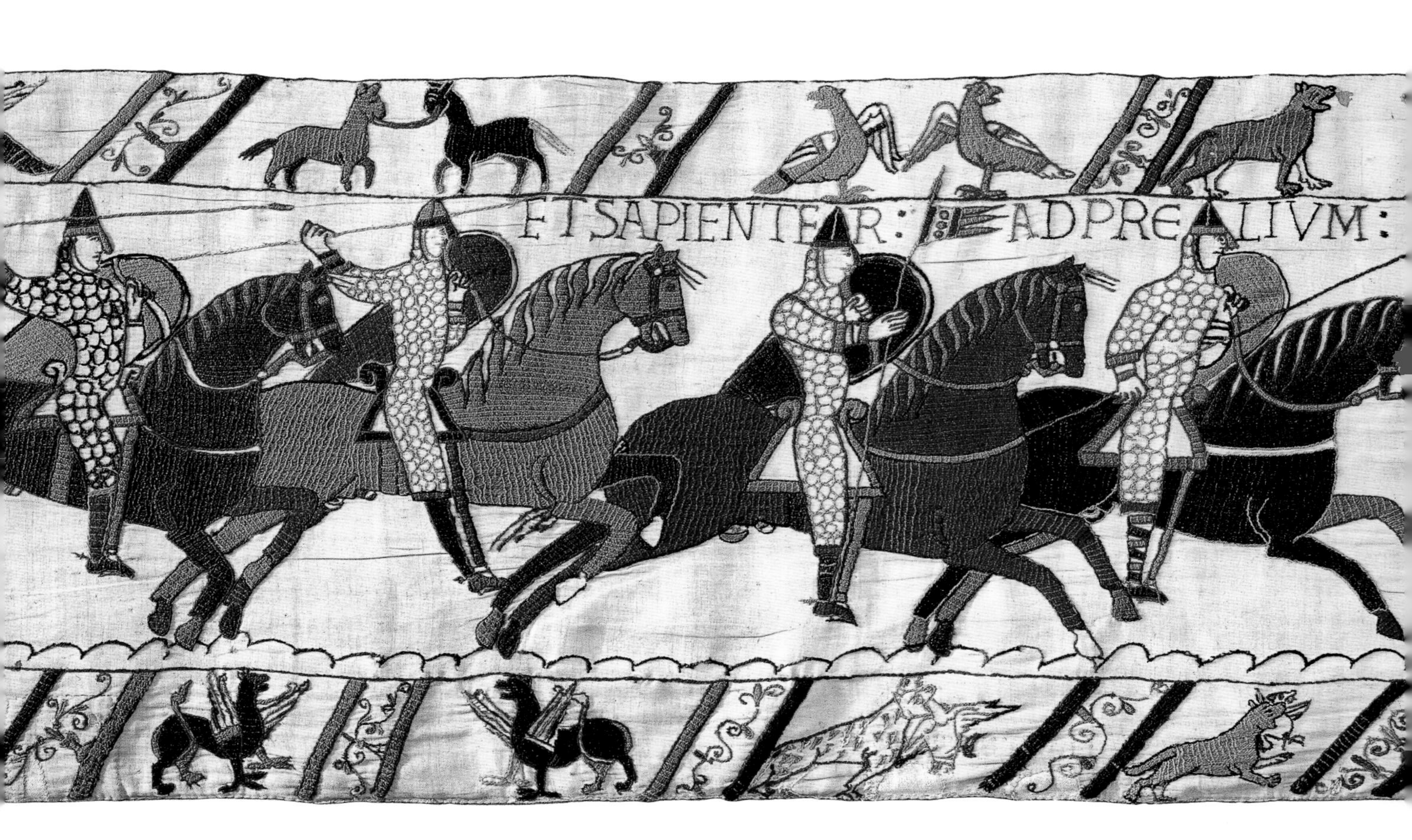

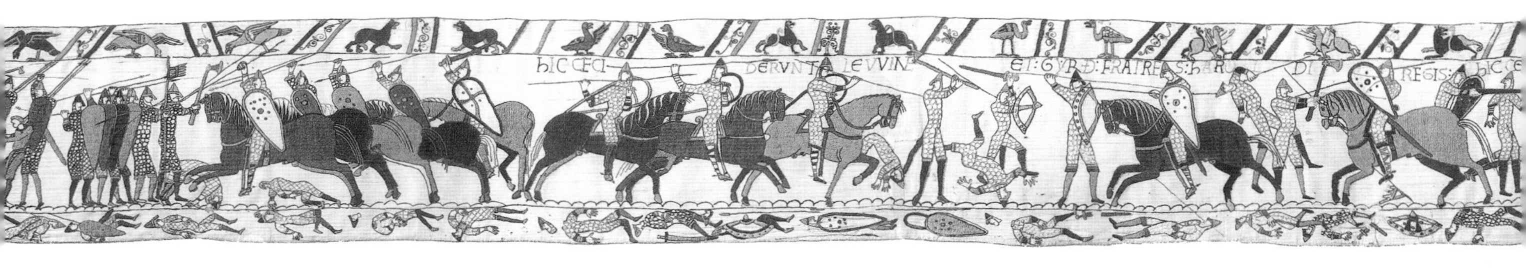

NGLORUM EXERCITUM.

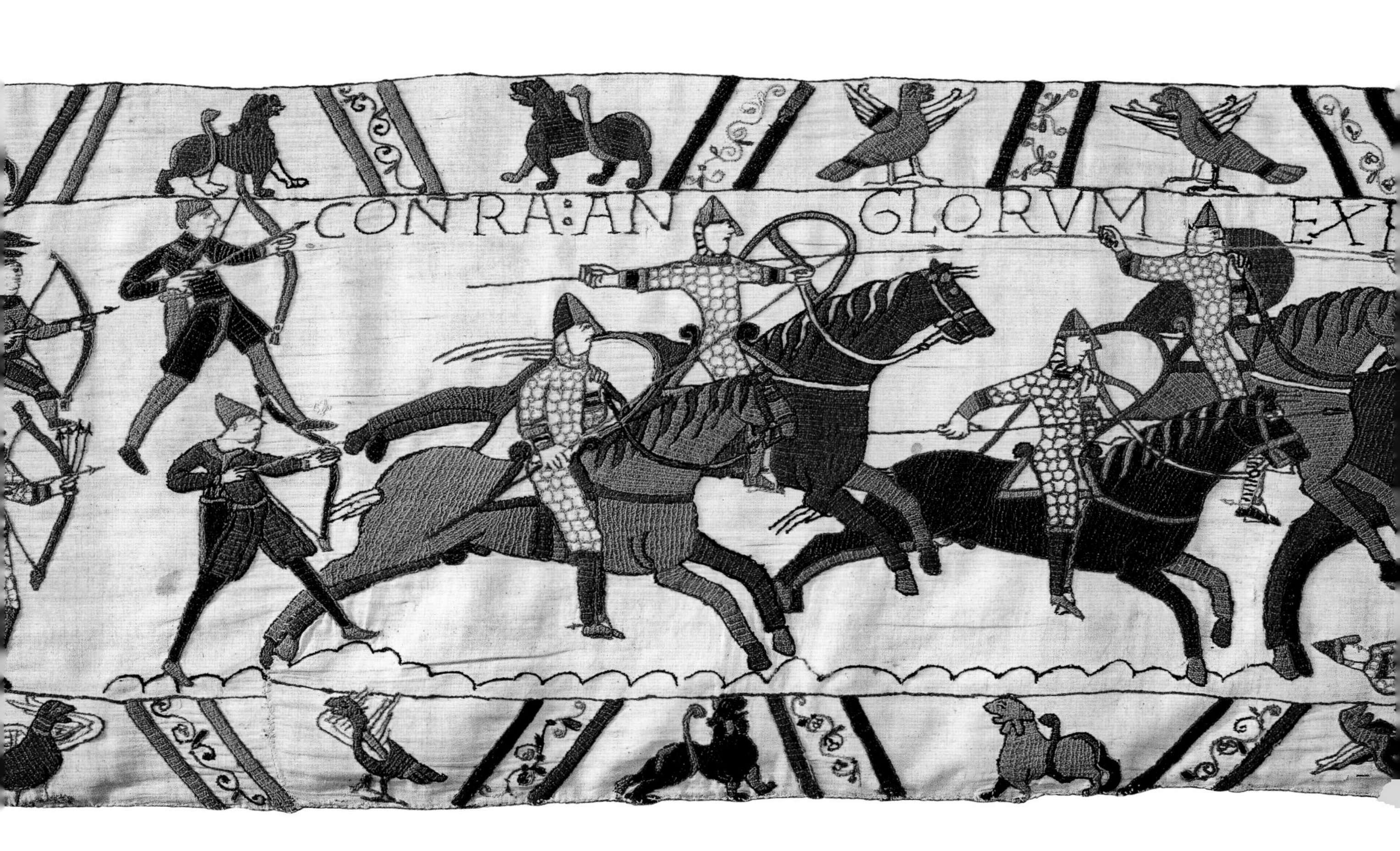

...for the battle against the army of the English.

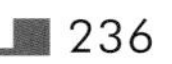
236

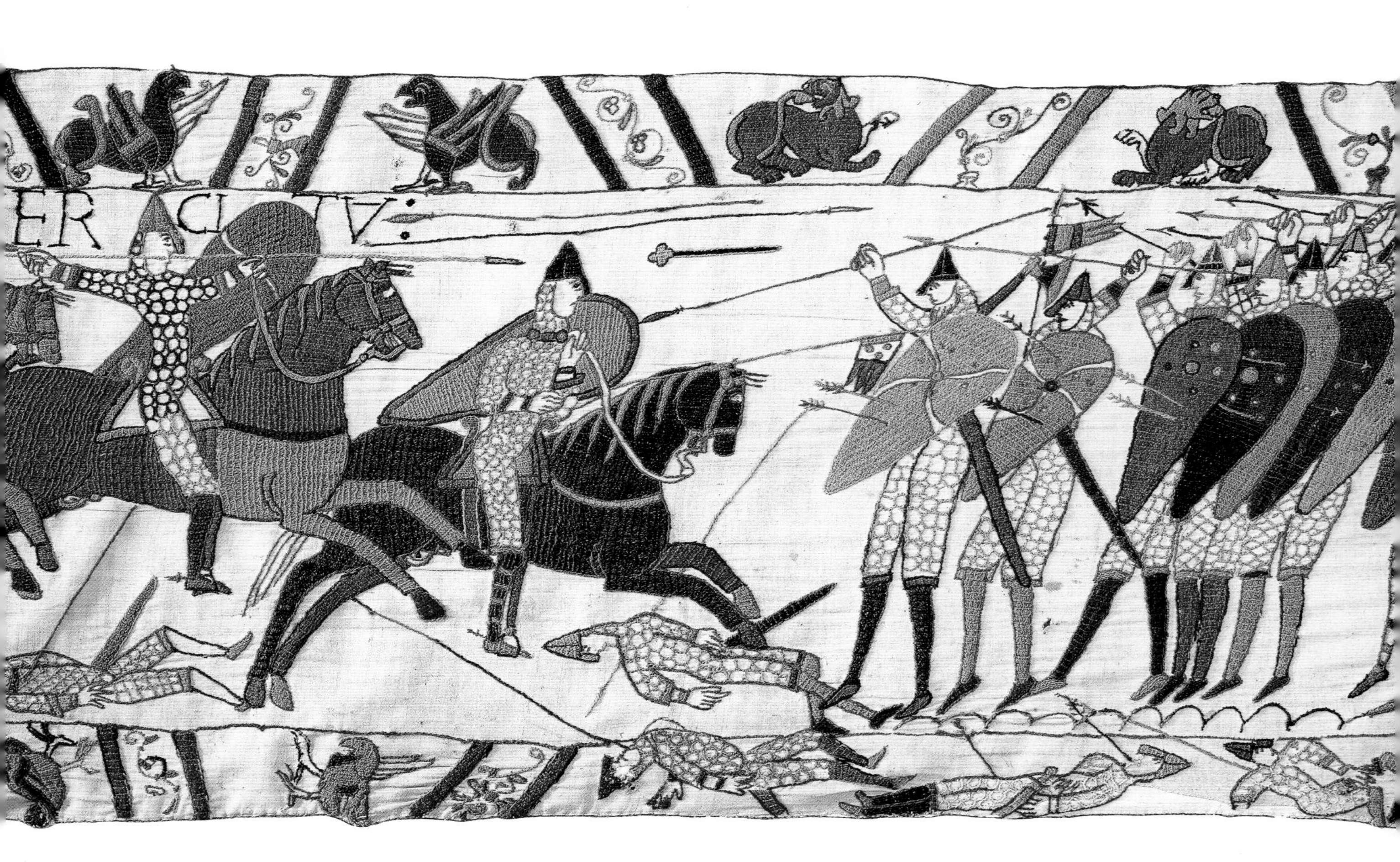

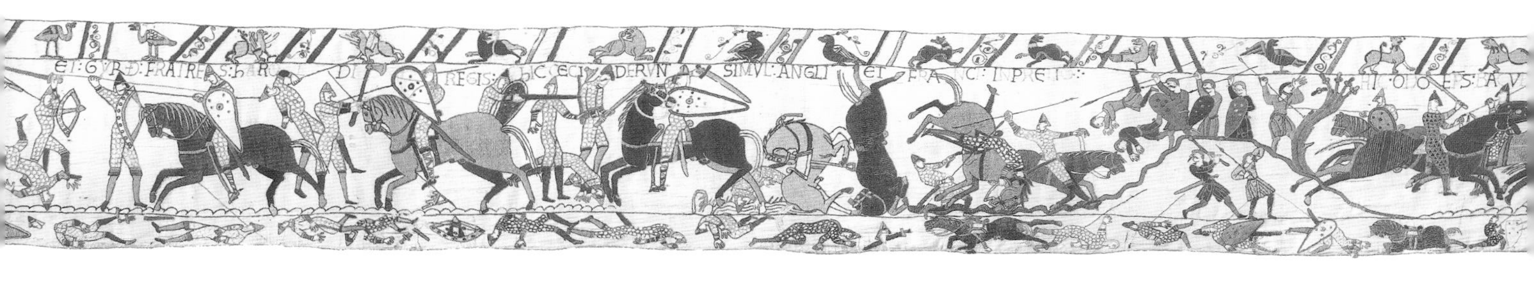

ET: GYRD: FRATRES:
REGIS:
SIMUL: ANGLI
ET

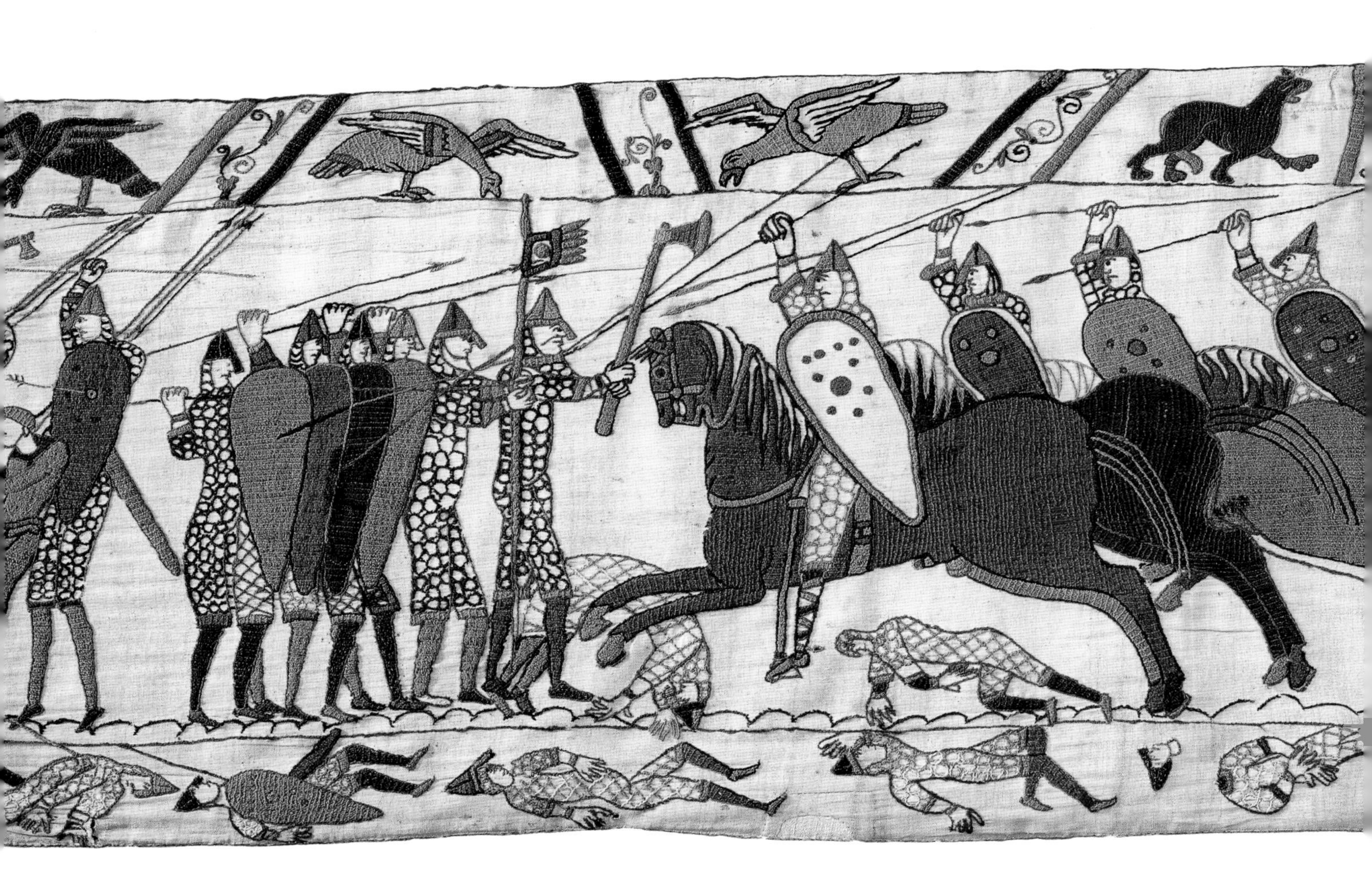

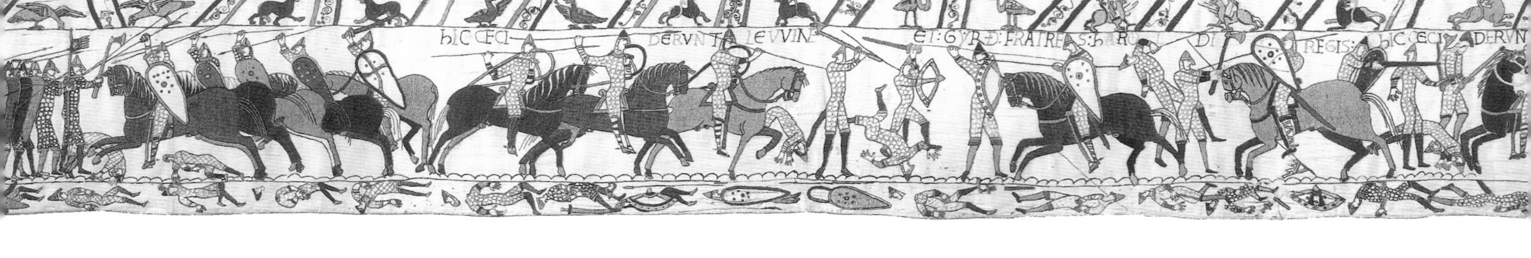

Hic ceciderunt Le[v]

The Tapestry pays particular attention to the death of Harold's two brothers, Leofwine and Gyrth, Godwin's fourth and fifth sons. Along with Harold himself they are the only casualties mentioned by name. Despite their high birth, they were not figures of especial political importance, and had not been endowed with their earldoms (both of them in south-east England) until late 1057. Domesday Book shows Odo in possession of several of Leofwine's former domains, and Leofwine's Kentish connections may help account for the prominence accorded him on a work of art created in Canterbury. But the chief reason for the emphasis on the fate of these two men is that, following the death of their elder brother Tostig at Stamford Bridge, they were next in line for the throne after Harold.

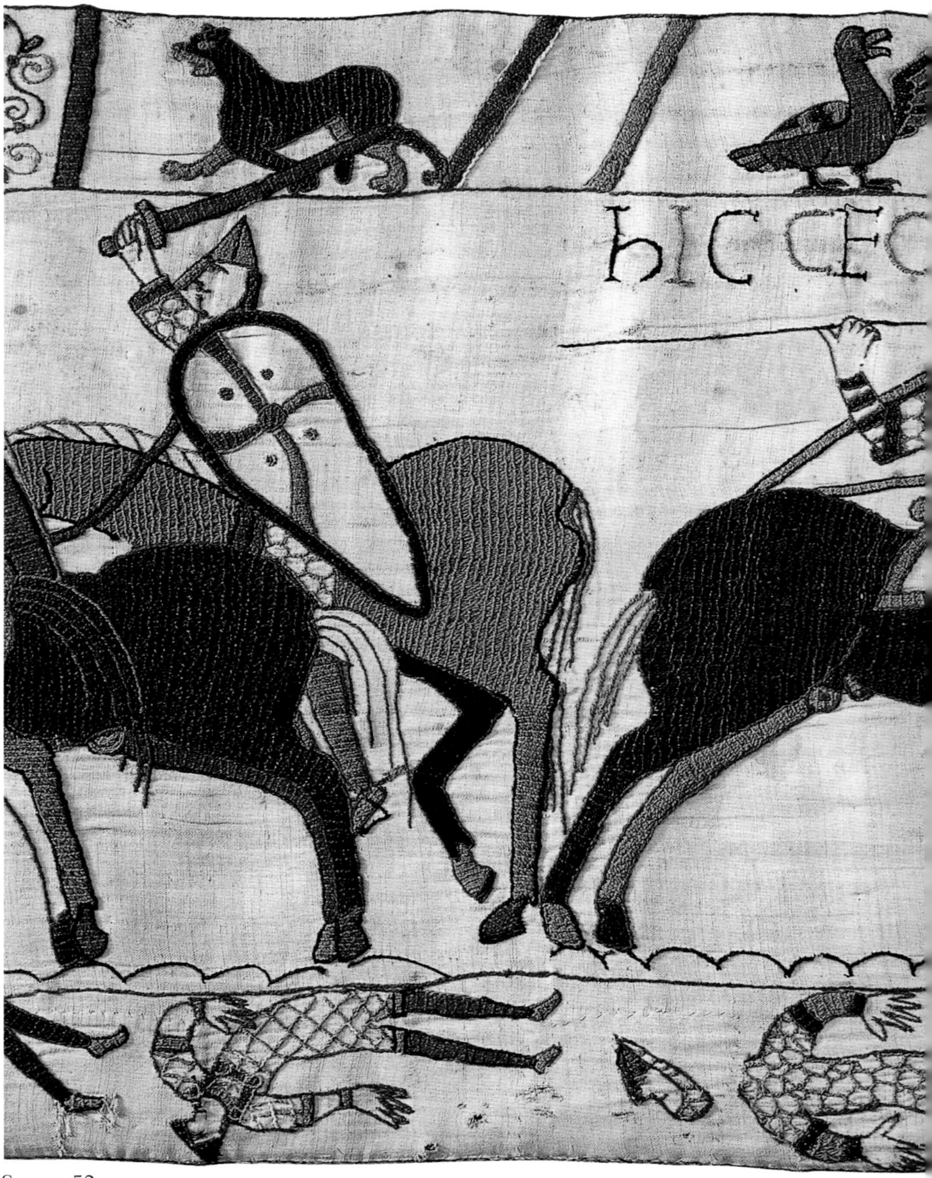

Scene 52

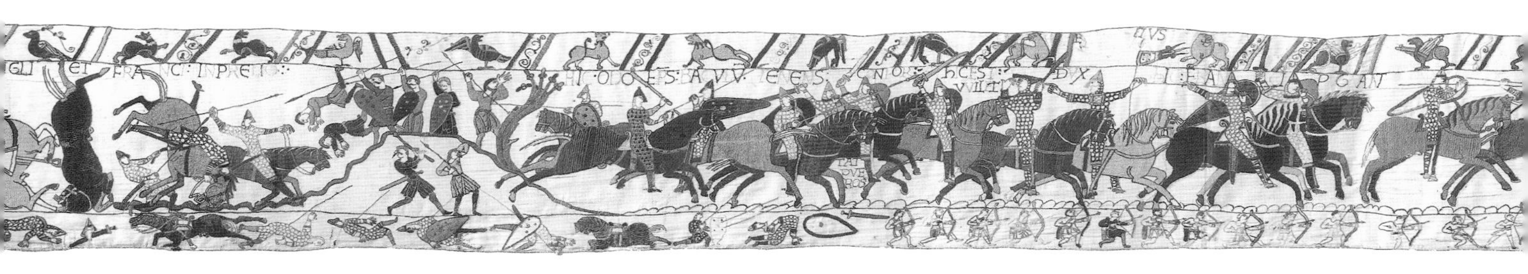

E…

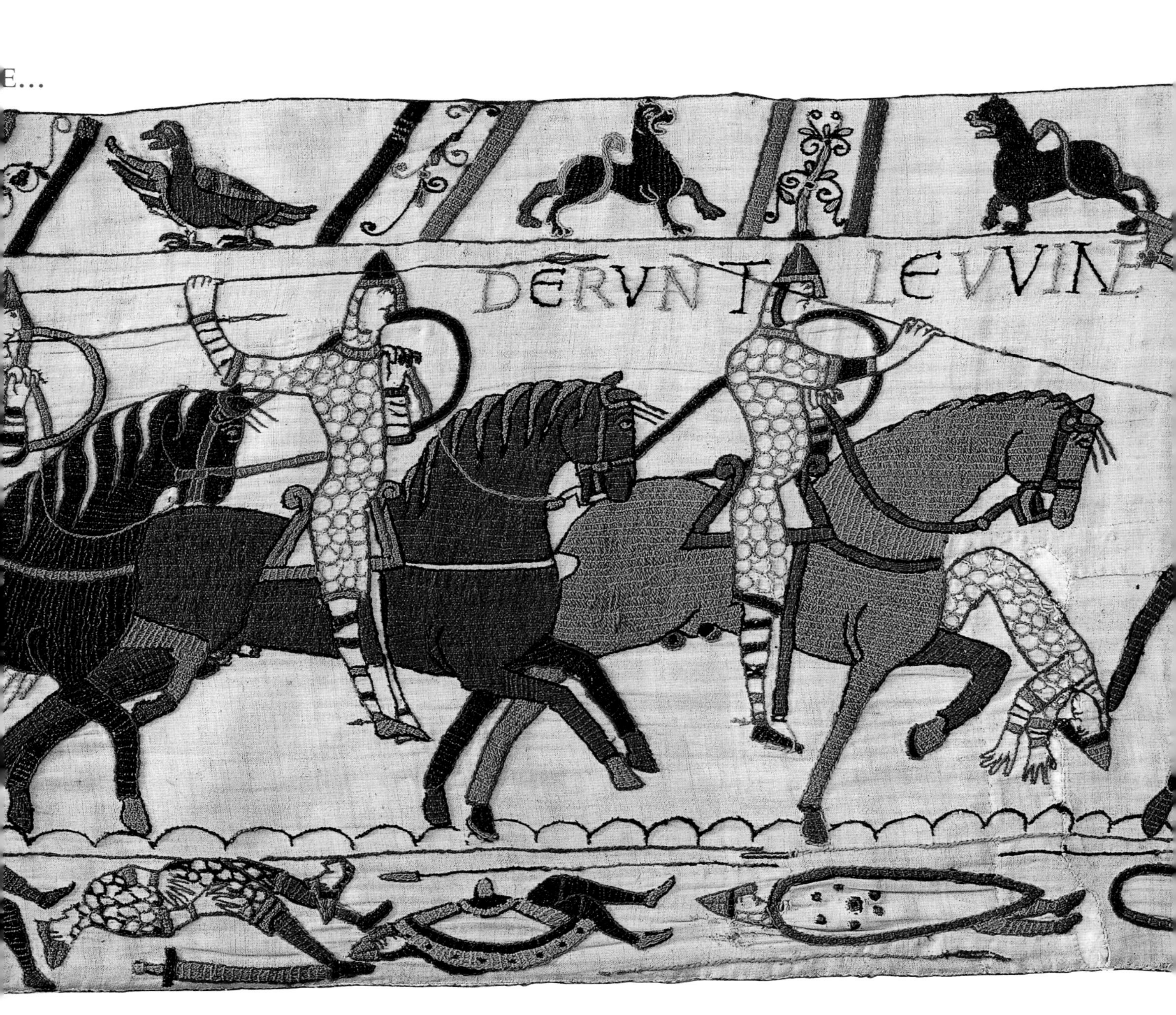

Here fell Leofwyne …

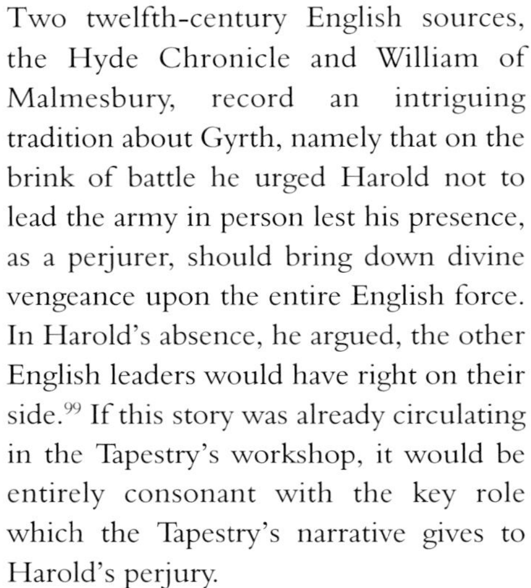

Two twelfth-century English sources, the Hyde Chronicle and William of Malmesbury, record an intriguing tradition about Gyrth, namely that on the brink of battle he urged Harold not to lead the army in person lest his presence, as a perjurer, should bring down divine vengeance upon the entire English force. In Harold's absence, he argued, the other English leaders would have right on their side.[99] If this story was already circulating in the Tapestry's workshop, it would be entirely consonant with the key role which the Tapestry's narrative gives to Harold's perjury.

The precise moment when Harold's brothers fell is not clear. Henry of Huntingdon and Wace put it in the closing stages of the battle, after Harold's own death, while the *Carmen de Hastingae proelio* has it near the start. The chronicles throw up many such puzzles. It is worth noting that the Tapestry shows no signs of the later tradition which had Gyrth slain by the hand of William himself.[100]

... ET GYRTH FRATRES

SCENE 52

[99] *Chronica monasterii de Hida*, in *Liber de monasterii de Hyda*, ed. E. Edwards (London: Rolls Series, 1866), pp. 283-321, at pp. 293-94; William of Malmesbury, *De Gestis Regum Anglorum*, ed. Stubbs, vol. 2, p. 301.

[100] As early as Wace, 'Guert' was being given a major role in the battle. Wace, ed. Holden, vol. 2, p. 214, lines 8819-28. Burgess and Van Houts, p. 190. *Carmen de Hastingae Proelio*, lines 471-80. Henry of Huntingdon, *Historia Anglorum*, ed. Greenway, pp. 394-95.

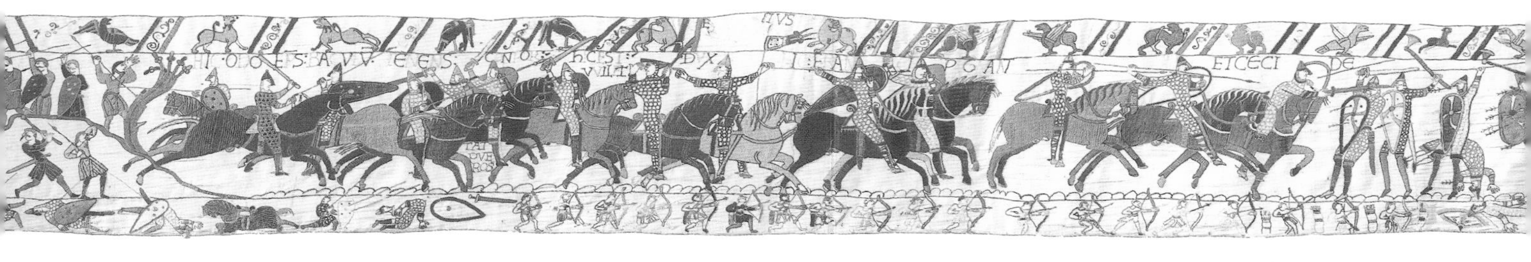

HAROLDI REGIS

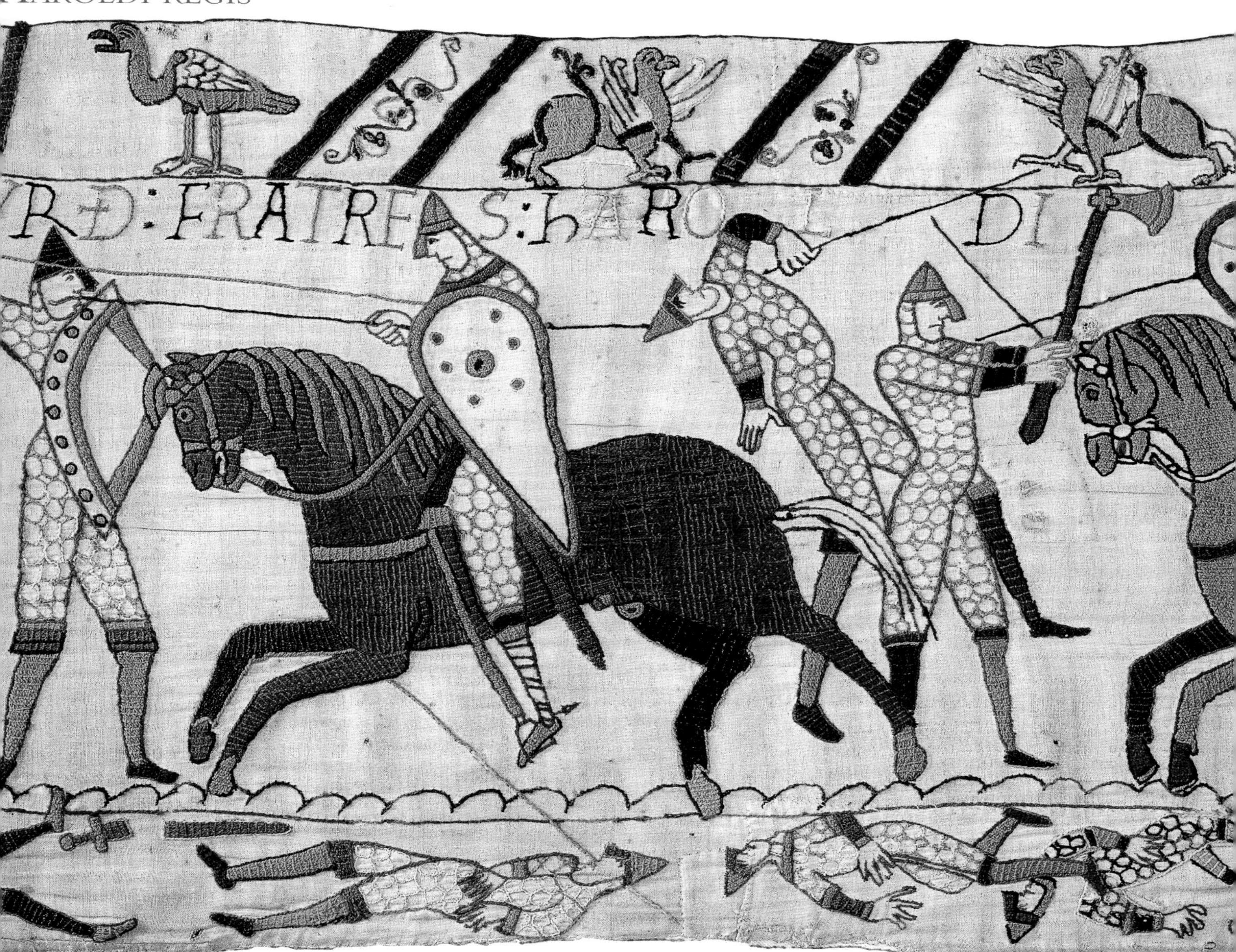

...and Gyrth, King Harold's brothers.

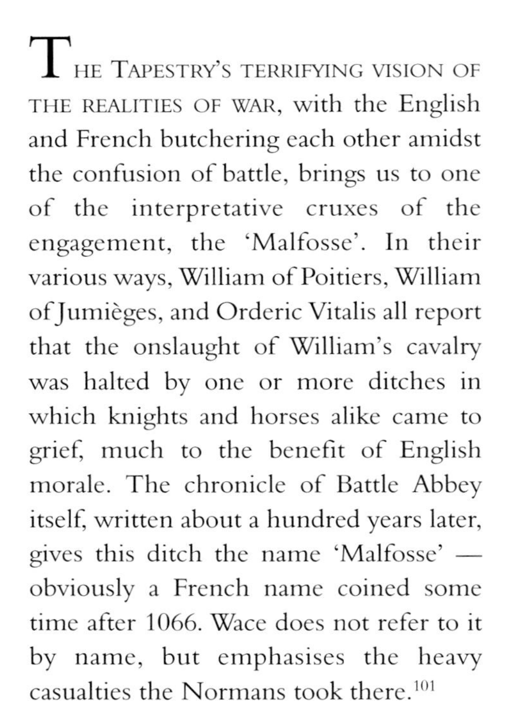

THE TAPESTRY'S TERRIFYING VISION OF THE REALITIES OF WAR, with the English and French butchering each other amidst the confusion of battle, brings us to one of the interpretative cruxes of the engagement, the 'Malfosse'. In their various ways, William of Poitiers, William of Jumièges, and Orderic Vitalis all report that the onslaught of William's cavalry was halted by one or more ditches in which knights and horses alike came to grief, much to the benefit of English morale. The chronicle of Battle Abbey itself, written about a hundred years later, gives this ditch the name 'Malfosse' — obviously a French name coined some time after 1066. Wace does not refer to it by name, but emphasises the heavy casualties the Normans took there.[101]

These accounts would seem to explain this scene, one of the most vivid on the Tapestry, which shows knights and their mounts falling head-first into a ditch at the foot of some rising ground held by English infantry. Unfortunately, though unsurprisingly, the chroniclers fail to agree on precisely when this episode took place: Wace makes it part of the main assault, while William of Jumièges and the Battle Abbey chronicle place it in the context of the final rout of the defeated English troops.

C. H. Lemmon concludes that two separate incidents are intended, though it could just be a matter of confused recollections of a single episode to which different chroniclers sought to give unwarranted precision. Studies of the battlefield itself have been unable to resolve the problem. If the 'Malfosse' disaster occurred during the final rout, then the ditch may correspond to a natural gully (today partly filled in) running about a kilometre beyond the abbey church. This gully is called 'Maufosse' (sometimes read as 'Manfosse') in a document of 1279.[102] But if it occurred during the main assault, as Wace suggests, then the ditch would have run at the foot of the hill on which the remains of the abbey still stand, an area known today as Asten Valley. Given the testimony of the Tapestry, I incline towards the latter interpretation.

It is a fearful scene. Horses and men fall and break their necks, dismembered bodies litter the ground (in the lower border), and riderless mounts mill around. But it is not clear whether this results from a natural obstacle more or less hidden from the Normans' view, or whether it was some kind of hastily improvised defensive feature. None of the documentary sources suggests a deliberate trap. They speak instead of ditches and slopes hidden from view by long grass.[103] But some scholars believe

(H)IC CECIDERUNT

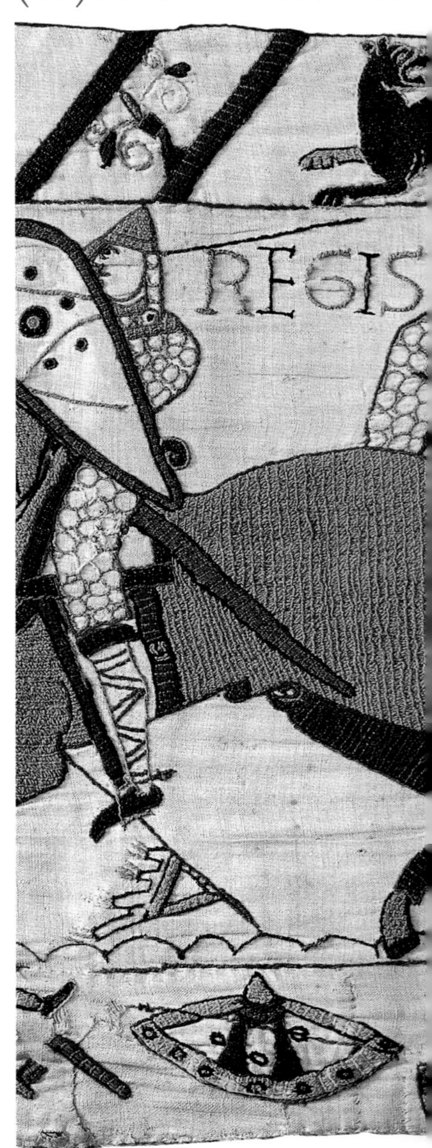

SCENE 53

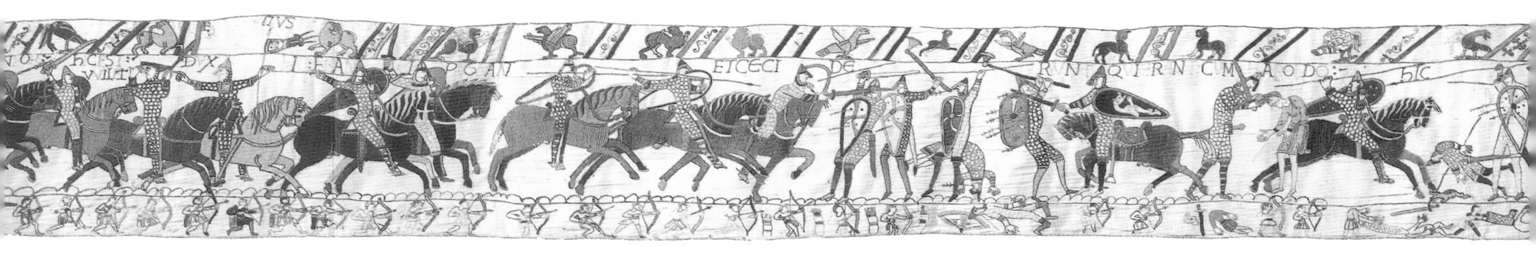

ul Angli et Franci in prelio.

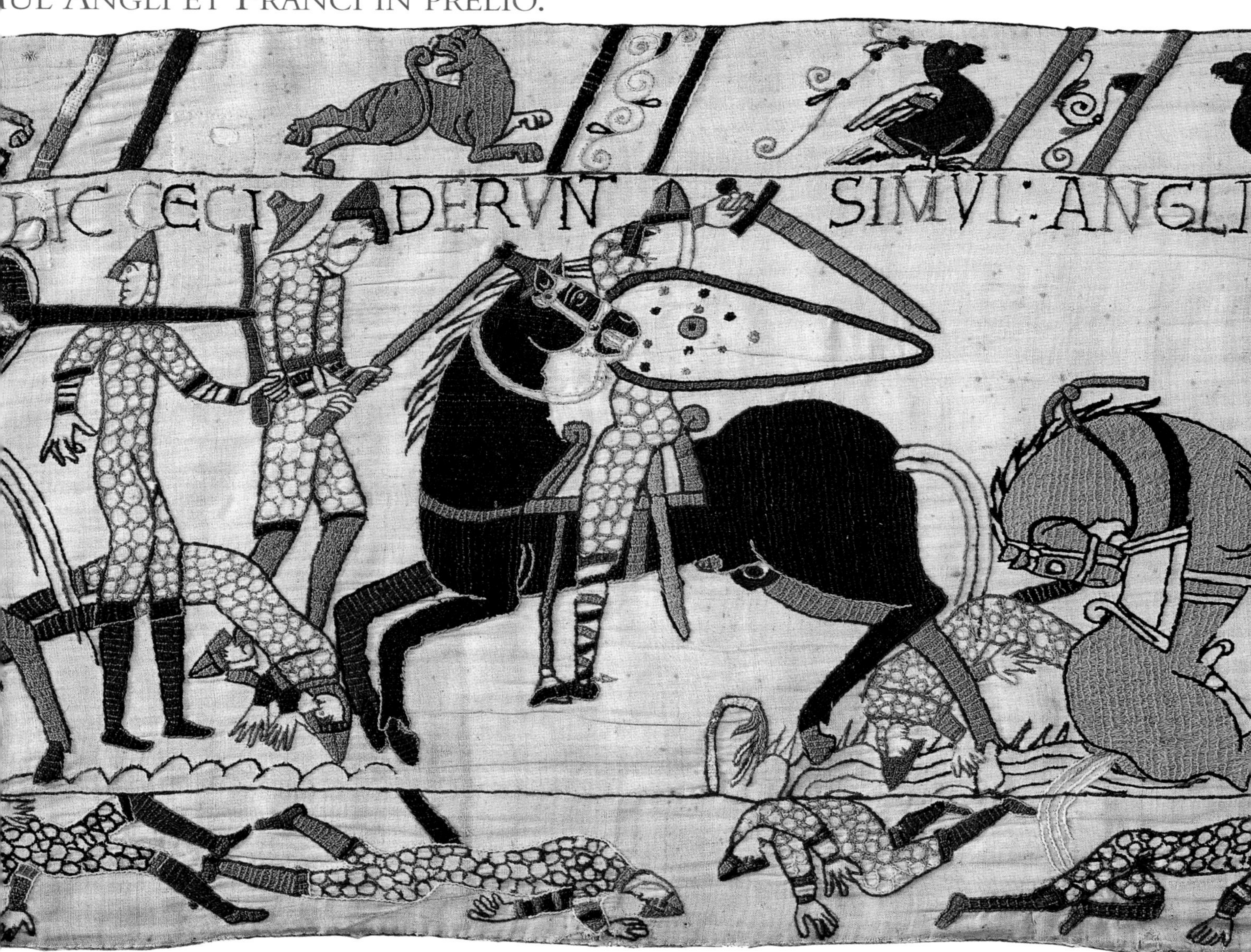

Here English and French fell together in the fight.

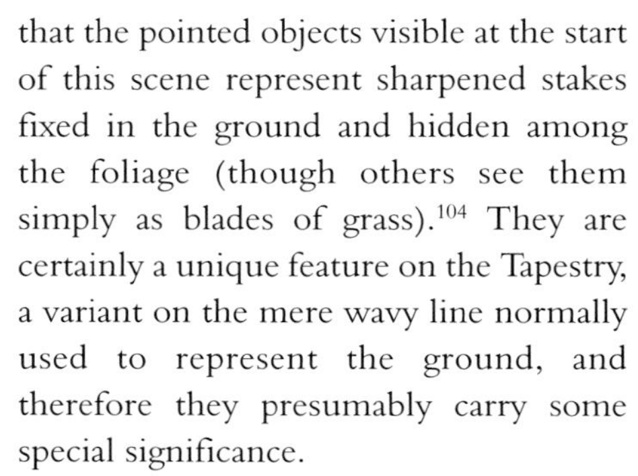

that the pointed objects visible at the start of this scene represent sharpened stakes fixed in the ground and hidden among the foliage (though others see them simply as blades of grass).[104] They are certainly a unique feature on the Tapestry, a variant on the mere wavy line normally used to represent the ground, and therefore they presumably carry some special significance.

The caption at this point deserves some comment: 'Here English and French fell together in the fight'. It seems purposefully impartial, judiciously refraining from praise or blame for either side.

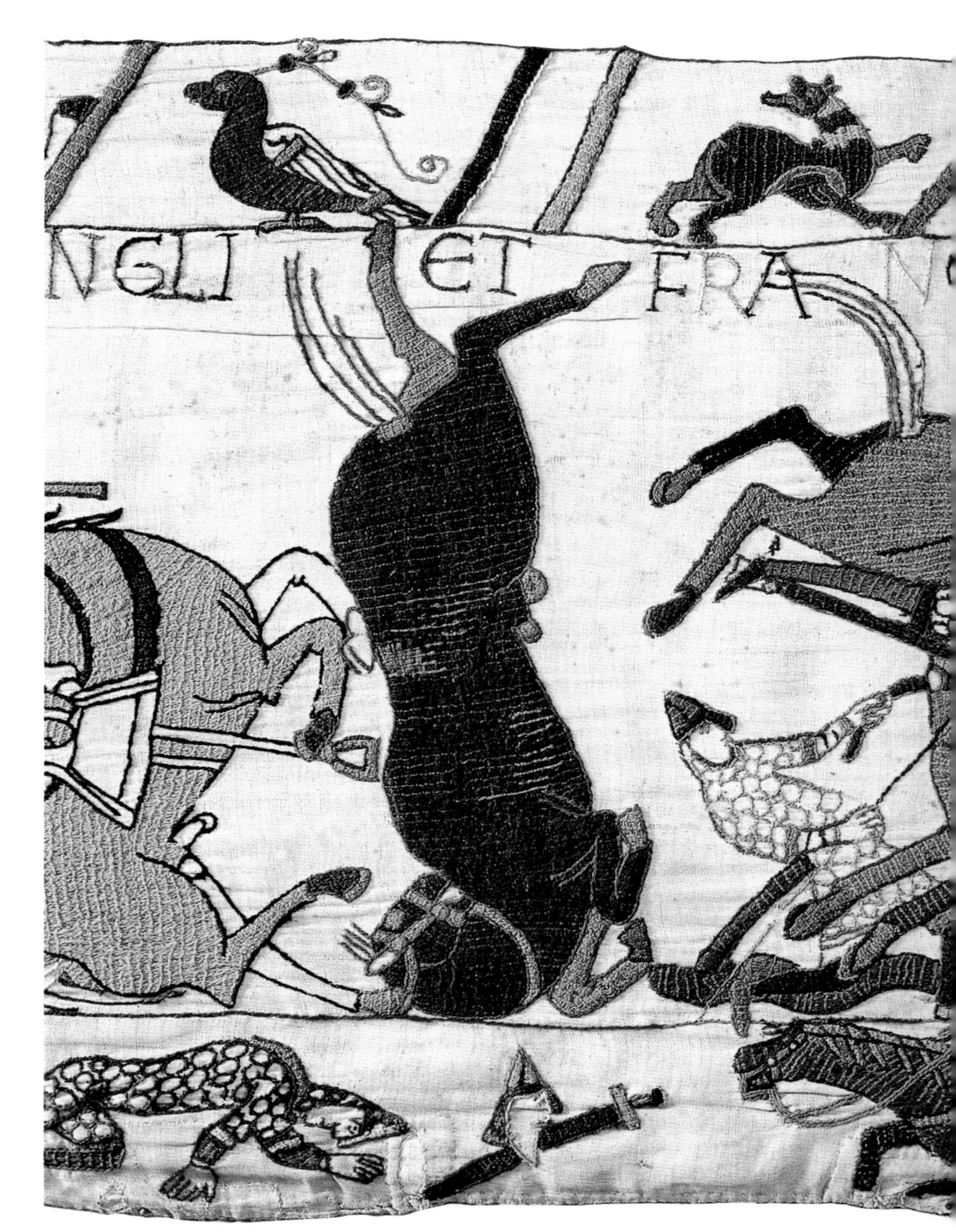

SCENES 53–54

[101] *The Chronicle of Battle Abbey*, ed. E. Searle (Oxford, 1980), p. 38. Wace, ed. Holden, vol. 2, pp. 185-86, lines 8079-8102 (Burgess and Van Houts, p. 182); William of Poitiers, ed. Foreville, p. 202 (Davis and Chibnall, pp. 138-39); William of Jumièges, ed. Van Houts, vol. 2, pp. 168-69; Orderic Vitalis, ed. Chibnall, vol. 2, pp. 176-77.

[102] W. H. Stevenson, 'Senlac and Malfosse', *English Historical Review* 28 (1913), pp. 292-303.

[103] The various texts are cited and analysed by Lemmon, *The Field of Hastings*, pp. 50-53.

[104] R. Drögereit argues for stakes in his review of the German translation of F. Stenton, *Der Wandteppich von Bayeux* (Cologne, 1957), in *Historische Zeitschrift* 188 (1959), pp. 352-58, at p. 357.

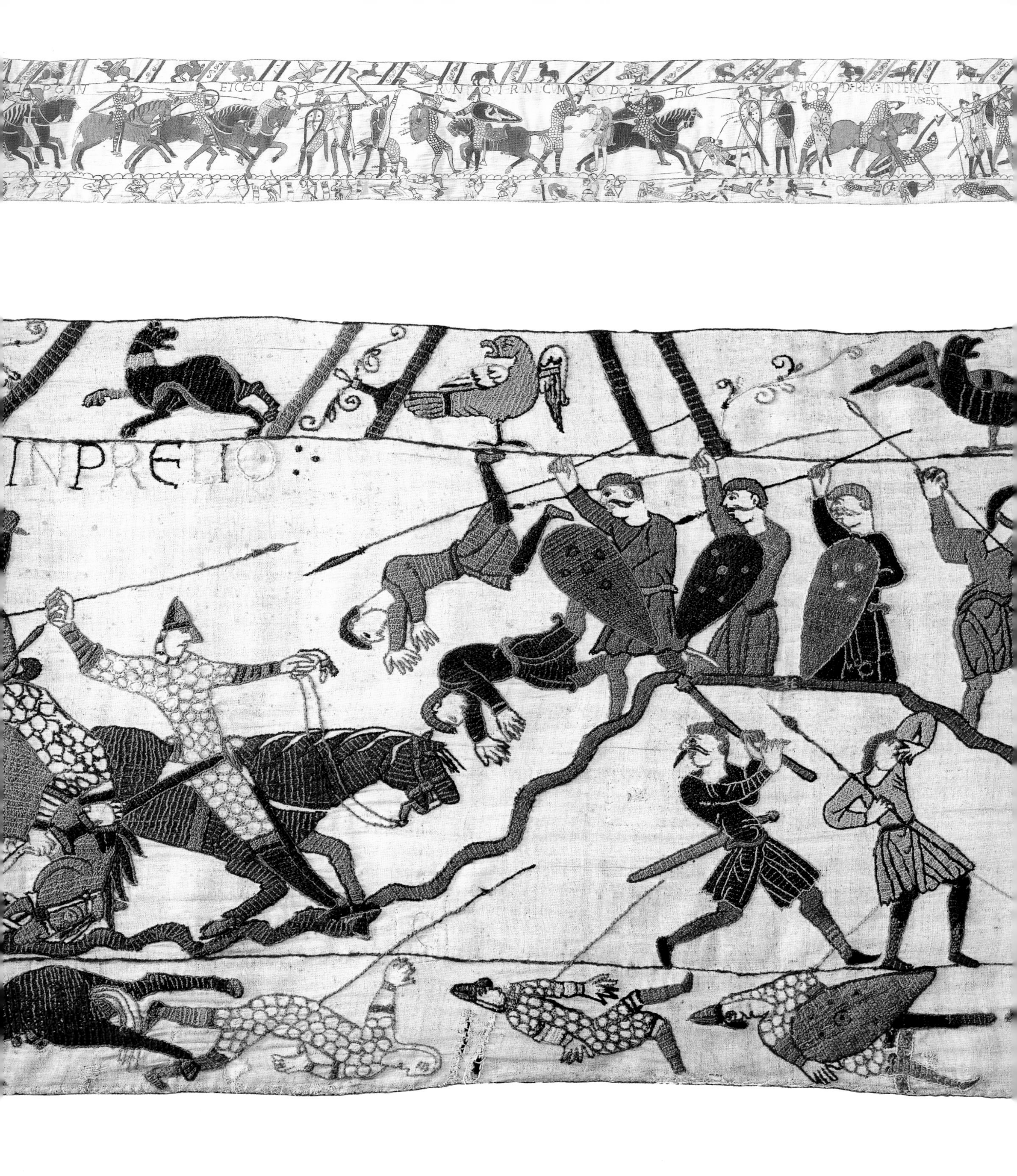
ET CECI DE
RUNT QUI ERANT CUM HAROLDO:
HIC
HAROLD REX INTERFEC
TUS EST
INPRELIO :

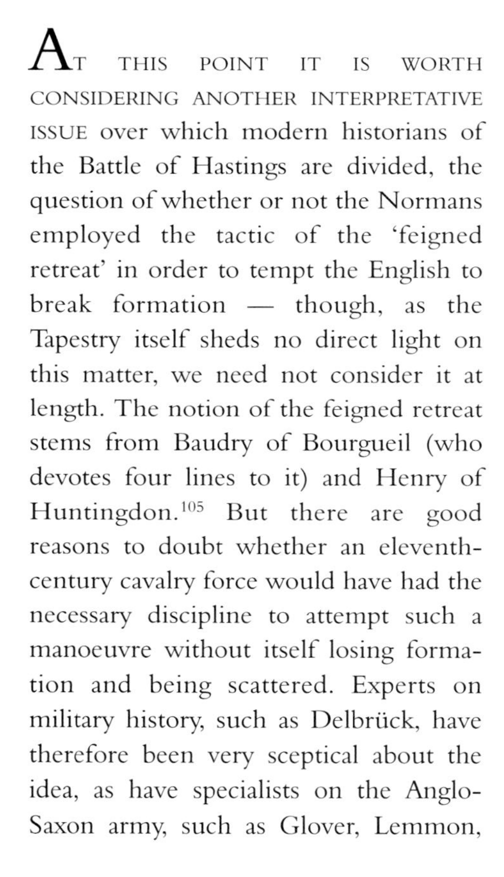

At this point it is worth considering another interpretative issue over which modern historians of the Battle of Hastings are divided, the question of whether or not the Normans employed the tactic of the 'feigned retreat' in order to tempt the English to break formation — though, as the Tapestry itself sheds no direct light on this matter, we need not consider it at length. The notion of the feigned retreat stems from Baudry of Bourgueil (who devotes four lines to it) and Henry of Huntingdon.[105] But there are good reasons to doubt whether an eleventh-century cavalry force would have had the necessary discipline to attempt such a manoeuvre without itself losing formation and being scattered. Experts on military history, such as Delbrück, have therefore been very sceptical about the idea, as have specialists on the Anglo-Saxon army, such as Glover, Lemmon, and Hollister.[106] Yet scholars such as Verbruggen have found it plausible, while Bachrach has even constructed an 'archaeology' of the tactic, detecting its origins in classical antiquity and tracing its development by various peoples involved in the 'barbarian invasions', above all those who emerged from the Steppes.[107] There can be no doubt that such a manoeuvre would have called for rigorous peacetime training and extraordinary battlefield discipline. If something of the kind did take place at Hastings, though, it may not have been quite so purposeful: when a retreat can be prevented from degenerating into a rout, it is always a good idea to portray it afterwards as a tactical withdrawal! In any case, no such thing is seen on the Tapestry. On the contrary, the ensuing scene bespeaks a degree of panic and confusion which hardly accords with the idea of such a manoeuvre.

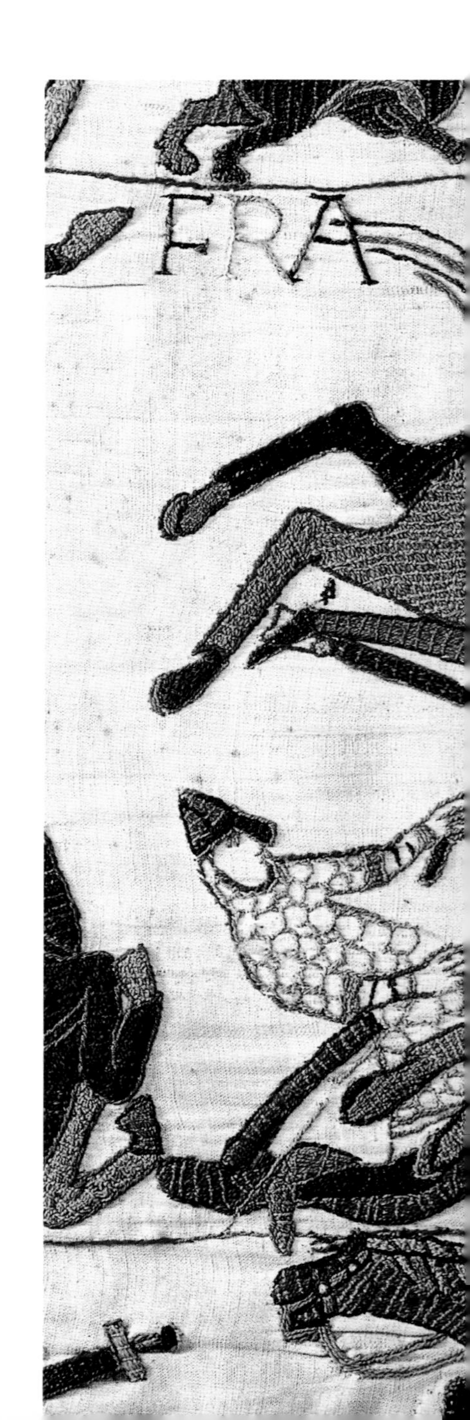

[105] Baudry, ed. Lauer, p. 49, lines 429-32; Henry of Huntingdon, *Historia Anglorum*, ed. Greenway, pp. 392-93.

[106] See in particular R. Glover, 'English Warfare in 1066', *English Historical Review* 57 (1959), pp. 1-18; and C. Warren Hollister, *Anglo-Saxon Military Institutions on the Eve of the Norman Conquest* (Oxford, 1962), p. 150, note 1. Hans Delbruck, *History of the Art of War*, tr. W. J. Renfroe Jr. (4 vols. Westport & London, 1975-85), vol. III, pp. 147-61.

[107] J. F. Verbruggen, 'La tactique militaire des armées de chevaliers', *Revue de Nord* 29 (1947), pp. 161-80, at p. 174; B. S. Bachrach, 'The Feigned Retreat at Hastings', *Mediaeval Studies* 33 (1971), pp. 344-47.

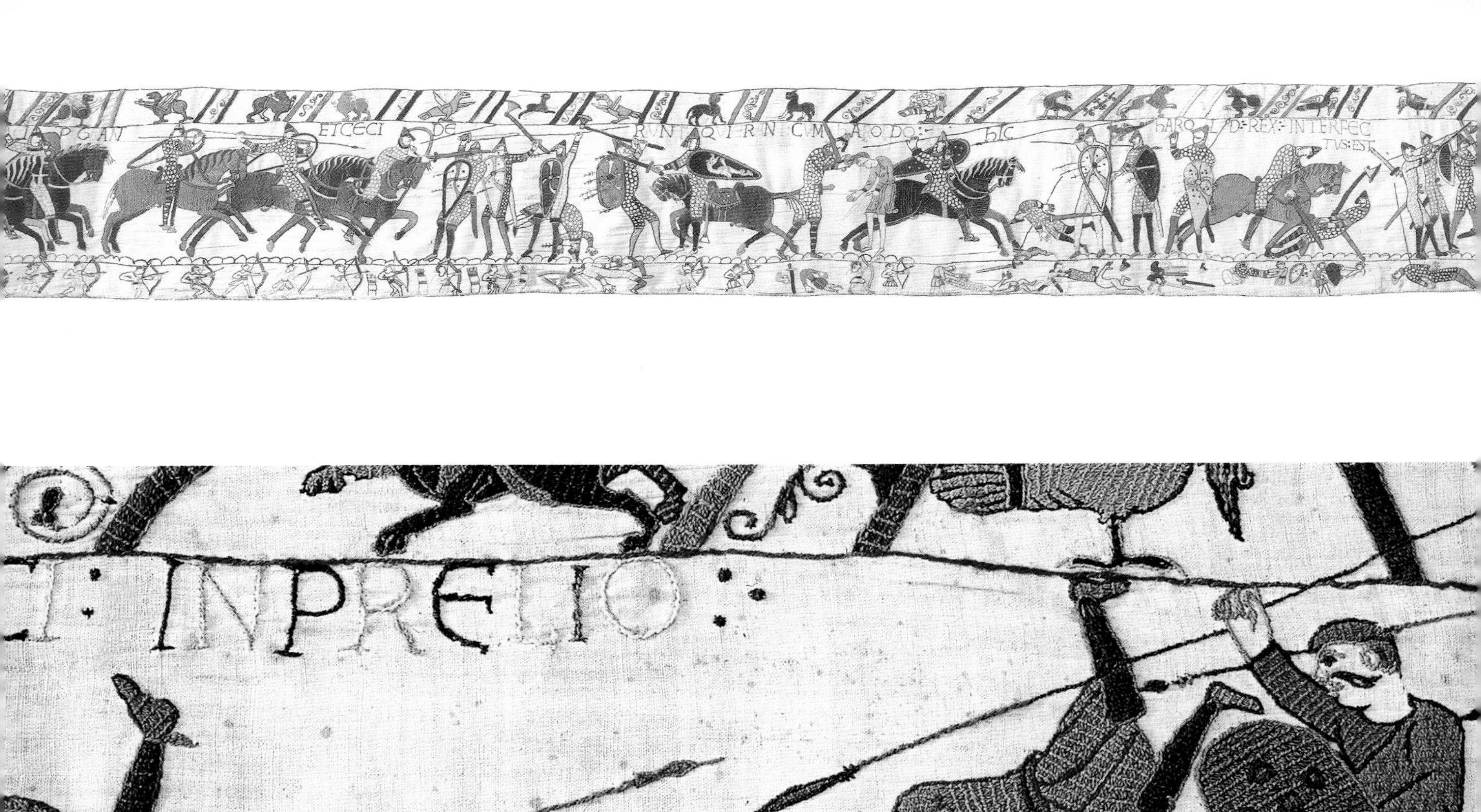
ET CECI DE
RUNT QUI ERANT CUM HAROLDO
HIC HAROLD REX INTERFEC
TUS EST

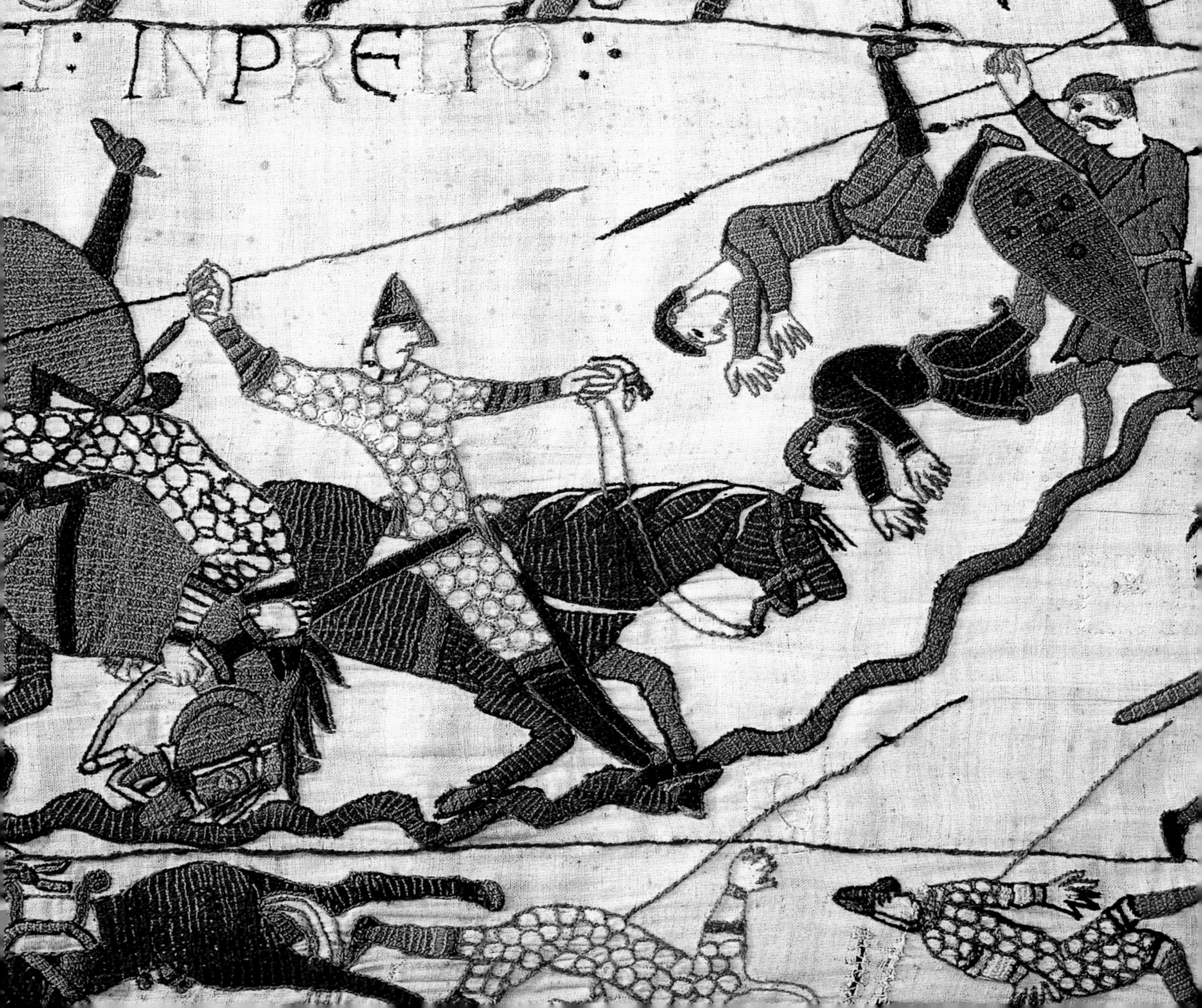
INPRELIO

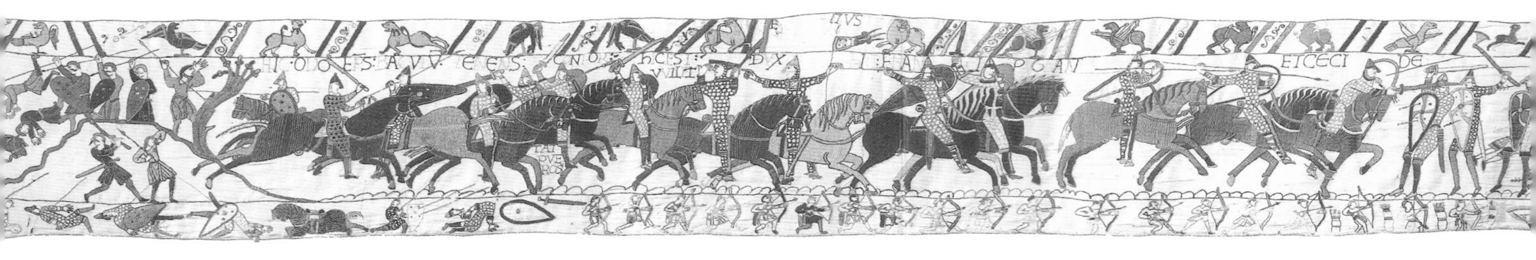

Hic Odo episcopus

The rising ground is still held by the English infantry — here, apparently, the *fyrd*, as the men have neither hauberks nor helmets — who successfully withstand a Norman assault. But, as the corpses pile up, a disaster threatens to undermine Norman morale. This is the turning-point of the battle.

The central figure of this scene is Bishop Odo, whose intervention is highlighted by the caption: 'Here Bishop Odo, holding his staff, encourages the lads'. A rumour was spreading that Duke William had been killed or seriously wounded. As the whole invasion had been undertaken to vindicate his claim to the English throne, his death would have rendered further fighting pointless. There would have been nothing for it but to negotiate with Harold for a withdrawal on the best terms possible, much as the Norwegians had done a fortnight or so earlier. But the rumour was false: in the next scene, William is shown removing his helmet to reassure his troops that he was still with them (p. 251).

Alongside William rides a figure who points him out with an eloquent finger, to underline the significance of the duke's gesture. This man's name is given in the margin above and, though most of the letters are now missing, it can be made out as *Eustatius*. He is therefore to be identified as Eustace II, Count of Boulogne, one of the leaders of William's army. Himself a brother-in-law of Edward the Confessor, having married Edward's sister Godgifu, Eustace was one of the principal actors in the drama of 1066, and he subsequently betrayed William in order to pursue his own ambitions in English politics. The pennant on his lance is perhaps the Tapestry's only example of authentic heraldry in the proper sense, for it shows a cross surrounded by four bezants, his actual armorial bearings.[108]

The figure of Odo has given rise to divergent interpretations. Like the other Normans he is on horseback and he wears a helmet. But, as Allen Brown observes, he does not seem to have a coat of mail. His predominantly red costume, perhaps made from some sort of quilted material, looks more like that which William himself was wearing back in scene 16 (p. 131), at the start of the Breton expedition. His staff, or *baculum* as the caption calls it, is also problematic. It is certainly not a bishop's crozier, but it might be a mace or club, or else simply a commander's baton of the kind carried by William in scenes 49-50 (pp. 225 and 230). If it was a weapon, then it would

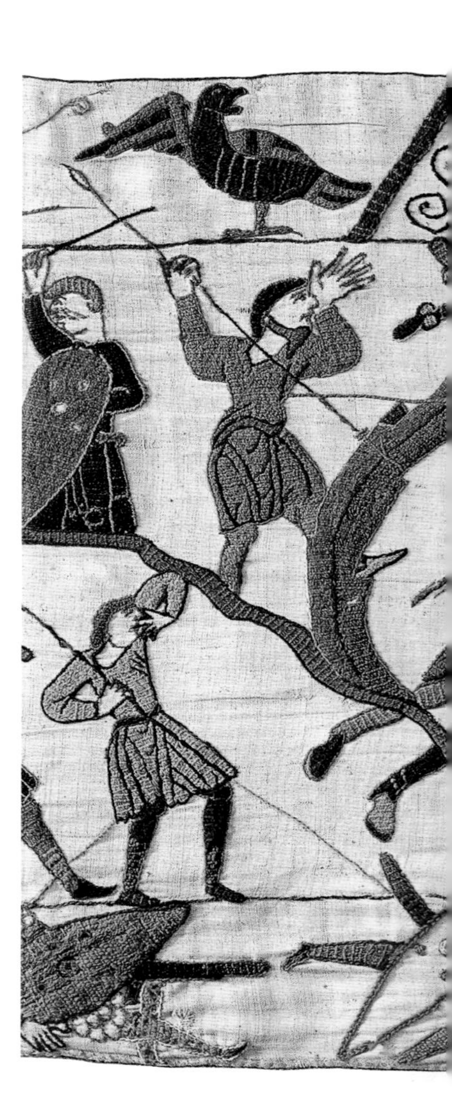

Scene 54

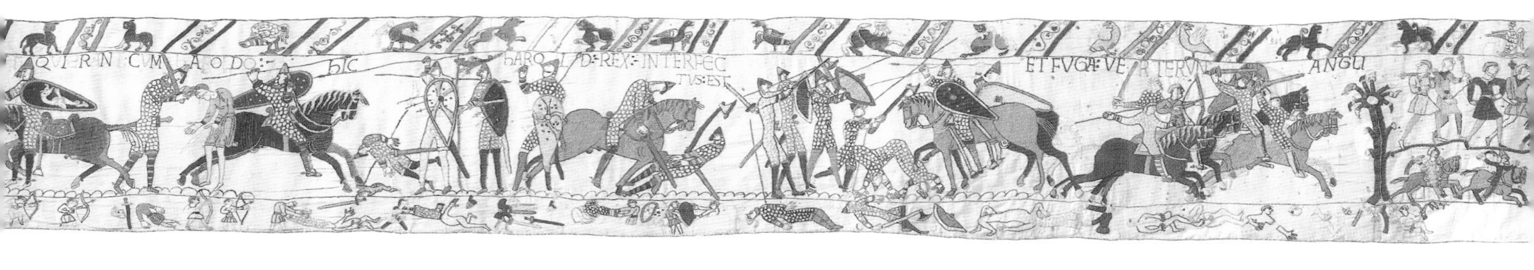

BACULUM TENENS CONFORTAT PUEROS.

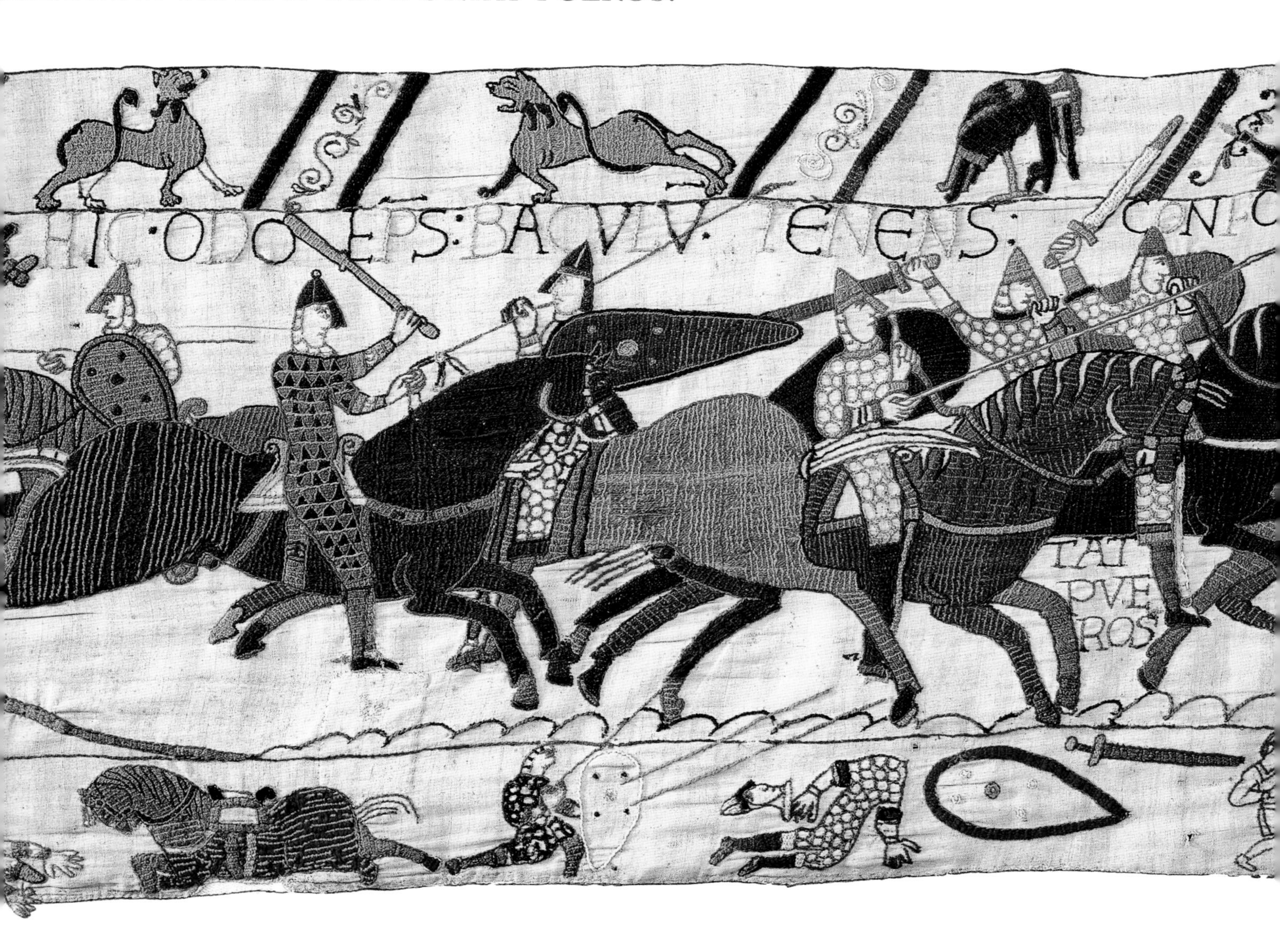

Here Bishop Odo, holding his staff, encourages the lads.

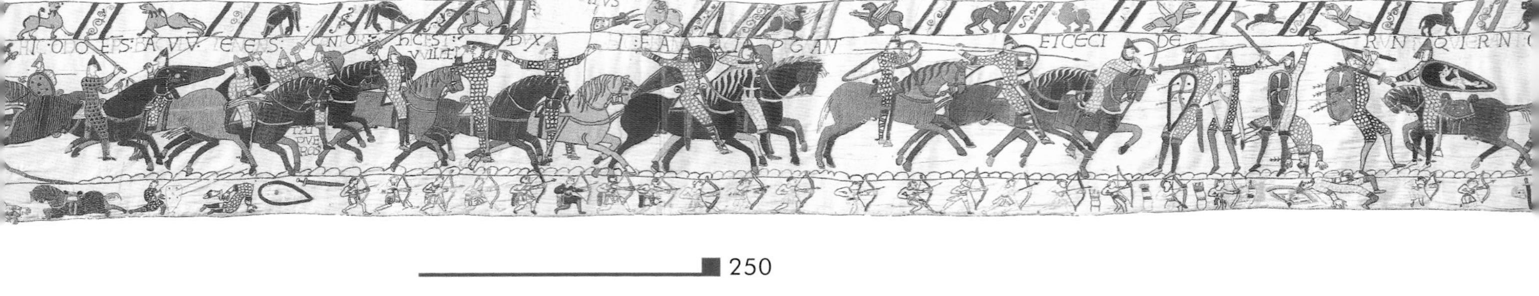

have been chosen to evade the canon law which forbade clergymen from shedding blood — a somewhat hypocritical expedient, though Catholic prelates are known to have resorted to it occasionally.[109] But it does not seem likely in this case. Wace speaks merely of a 'baton', and seems to mean an emblem of rank, used to communicate orders to the knights, a medieval counterpart of the later French marshal's baton.[110] Allen Brown concludes that Odo was no more a combatant at Hastings than was Bishop Geoffrey of Coutances. The question must remain open, though it would be bold indeed to argue that Odo's conduct conformed in every respect to the precepts of canon law. But Orderic Vitalis was probably about right when he reported of Hastings that 'There were present two bishops, Odo of Bayeux and Geoffrey of Coutances, with many monks and clerks, whose duty was to support the fight with their prayers and counsel'.[111]

William of Poitiers gives a prominent place to the story of how Duke William showed his face to his troops, embellishing it with the rhetorical flourishes and classical allusions he loved so much, but without any reference to Eustace of Boulogne.[112] This particular moment in the battle made a lasting impression on the Normans. It opened a new phase of the action: the Normans returned to the charge in good order, supported by a strong force of archers who are shown in the lower border. In the next scene, their arrows bristle in the shields of the English housecarls.

[108] This standard has also been taken at times for the banner of St Peter, but C. Morton, 'Pope Alexander II and the Norman Conquest', *Latomus* 34 (1975), p. 362-82, at p. 367, argues convincingly that these were the heraldic arms of the Counts of Boulogne. For Eustace's role on the Tapestry see S. A. Brown, 'The Bayeux Tapestry: Why Eustace, Odo and William?', *Anglo-Norman Studies* 12 (1989), pp. 7-28, which, despite numerous errors of detail, poses some interesting questions, such as whether Eustace's moustache was added later and whether the prominence given to Eustace reflects the events of 1075-77.

[109] From the time of St Augustine, for which see P. Brown, *Religion and Society in the Age of St Augustine* (London, 1972), pp. 336-37, to that of Bishop Ulrich of Augsburg in the 10th century, for which see L. W. Weinreich, 'Tradition und Individualität in den Quellen zur Lechfeldschlacht', *Deutsches Archiv* 27 (1971), p. 311.

[110] Wace, ed. Holden, vol. 2, p. 187, line 8123 (Burgess and Van Houts, p. 182, where it is rendered 'club'). But Wace has Odo riding a white horse; on the Tapestry it is black.

[111] R. Allen Brown, 'The Battle of Hastings', *Anglo-Norman Studies* 3 (1980), pp. 1-21 and notes, p. 196, note 15. Orderic Vitalis, ed. Chibnall, vol. 2, pp. 172-73.

[112] William of Poitiers, ed. Foreville, p. 190 (Davis and Chibnall, pp. 128-31).

HIC EST WILLELM DU

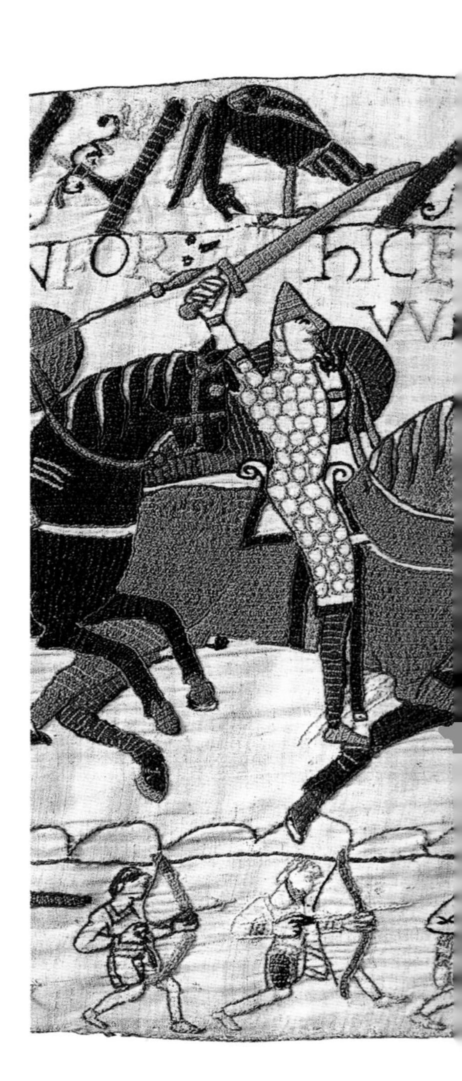

SCENE 55

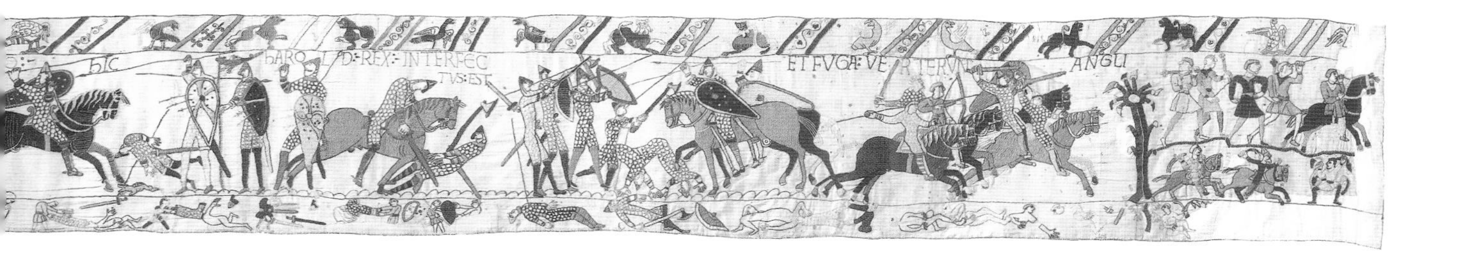

(USTA)TIUS.

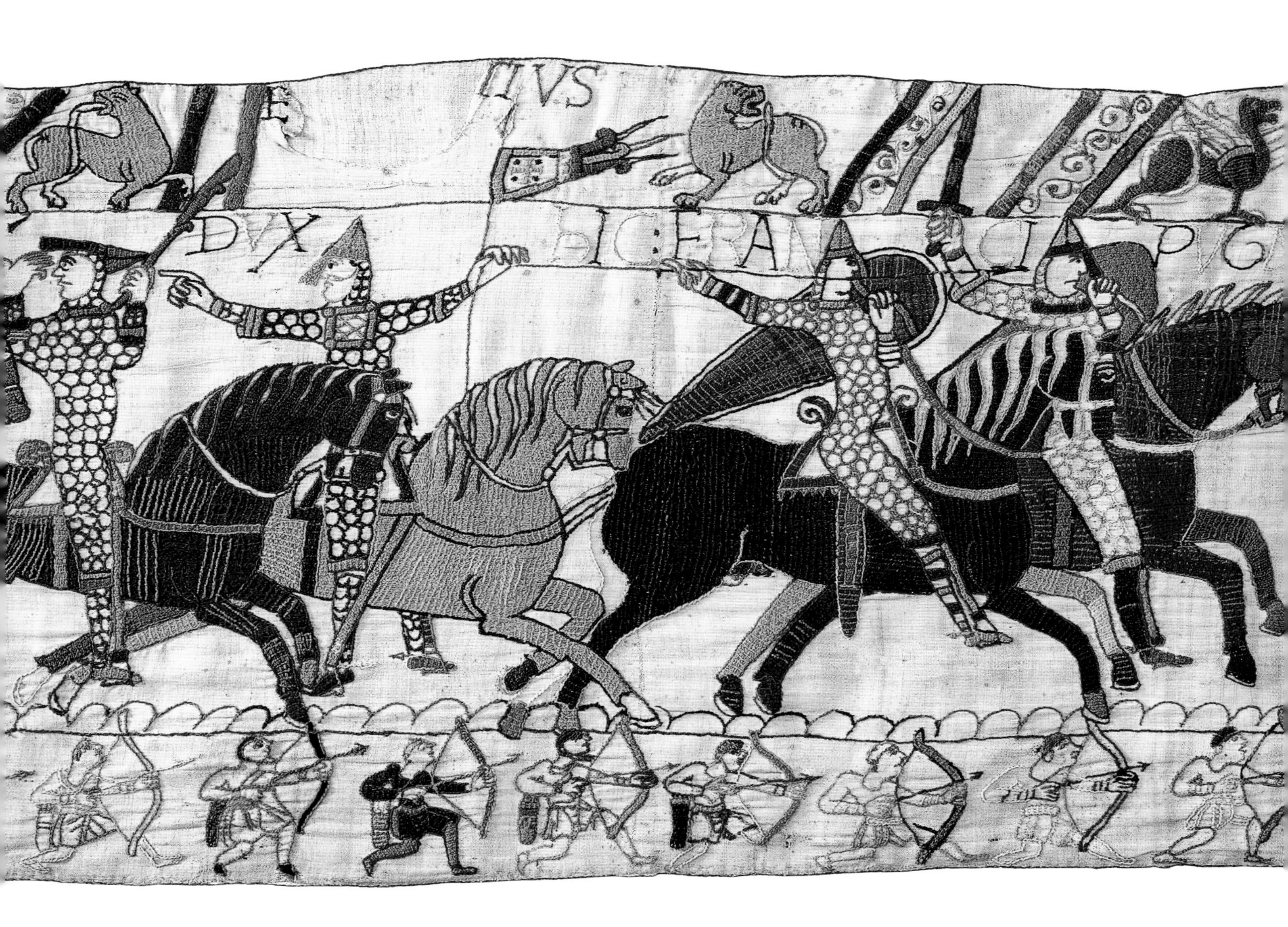

Here is Duke William. Eustace.

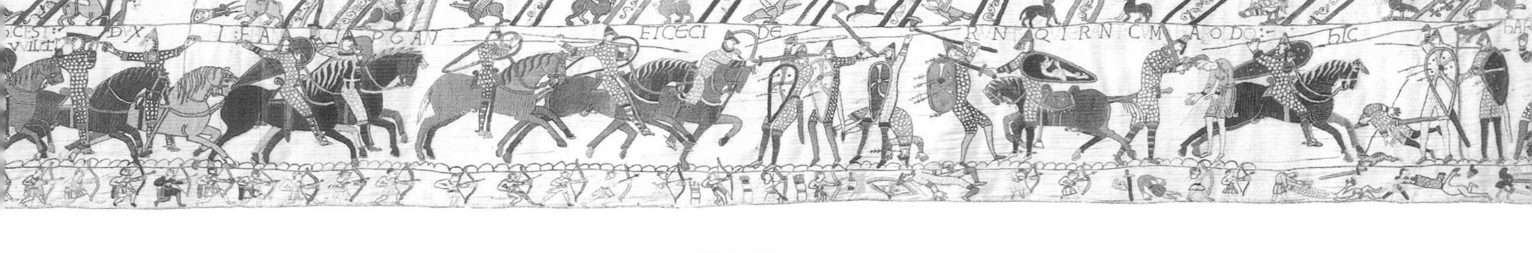

Hic Franci pugnant

For the second time William's cavalry hurls itself against the English ranks — this time the housecarls of Harold's bodyguard rather than, as in the previous scene, the men of the *fyrd*. The fight is as fierce as ever, but now the archers take on a decisive role, advancing in tight formation and with amply stocked quivers. 'Those who were with Harold fell', the caption reads, evidently, as the picture shows, under a hail of fire: one of the fallen has an arrow in the face. The Tapestry may be laying particular emphasis on the contribution of the archers precisely because the English force had relatively few of them.

The action still seems to be unfolding amidst considerable confusion. The English are facing in both directions, and the Normans attacking from both sides. The battle is losing all coherence, breaking up into a series of single combats. It ends in sheer massacre: dismembered bodies litter the ground, and an unarmed Englishman, held by the hair, abandons the struggle, resigned to his grisly fate.

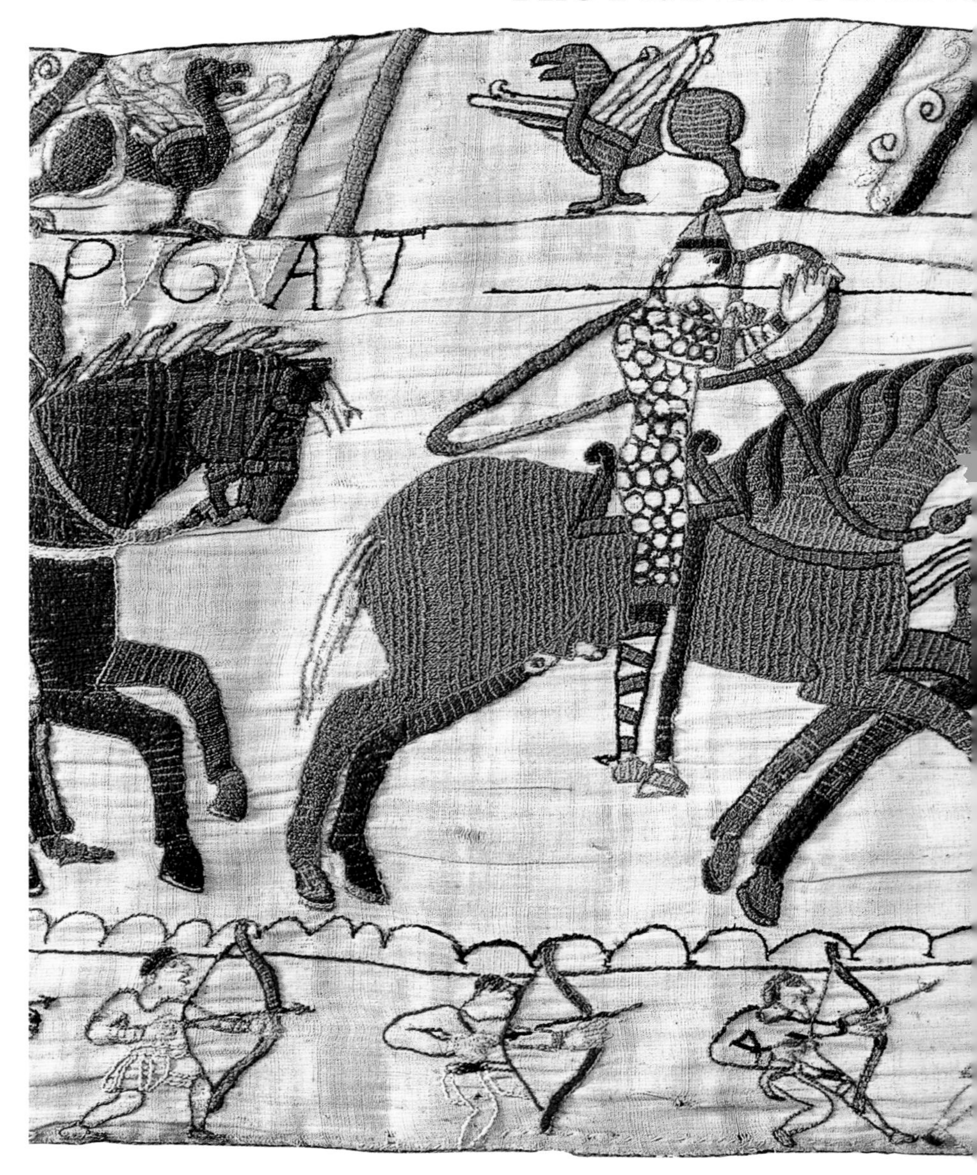

Scene 56

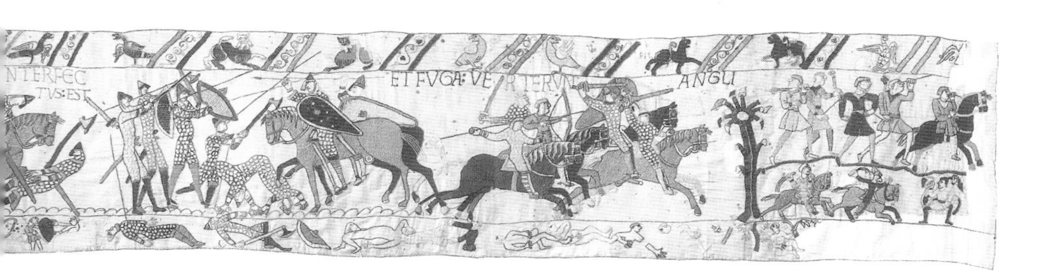

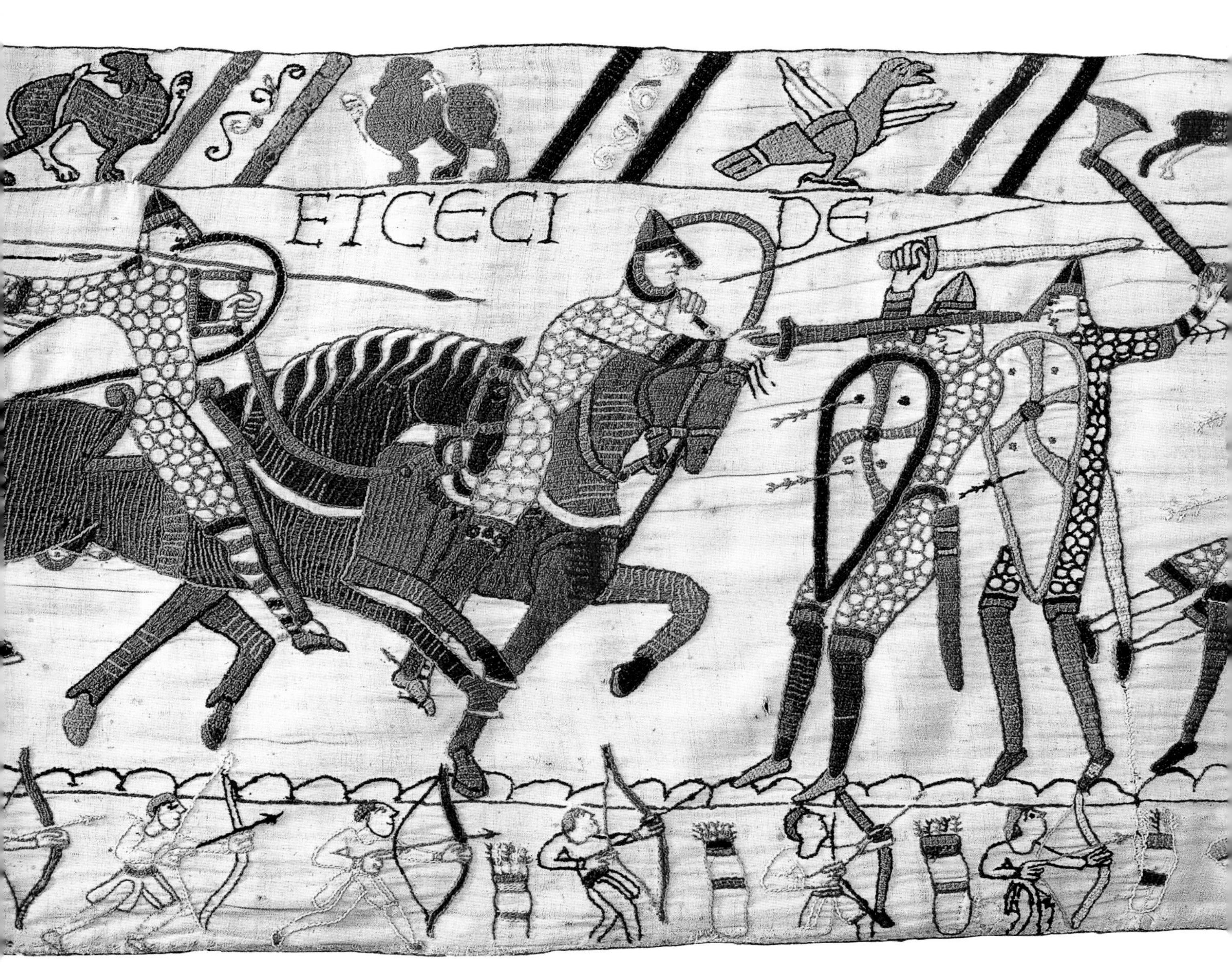

Here the French fight …

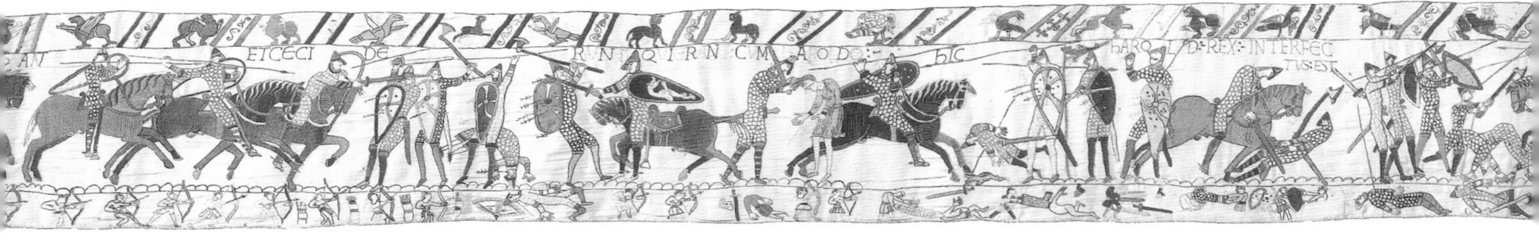

... ET CECIDERUNT QU

The most striking figure in this scene is the knight riding towards the left on a finely harnessed mount, his shield decorated with a splendid dragon. Neither the duke nor his brothers appear in these scenes of carnage, as if to absolve them from responsibility for the atrocities. There is also a slight oddity here, in that the man about to execute the unarmed Englishman seems to have two swords, one at his belt and the other in his hand. This could merely be a slip on the part of the seamstresses or the designer: perhaps the sword at his waist is meant to be a scabbard.

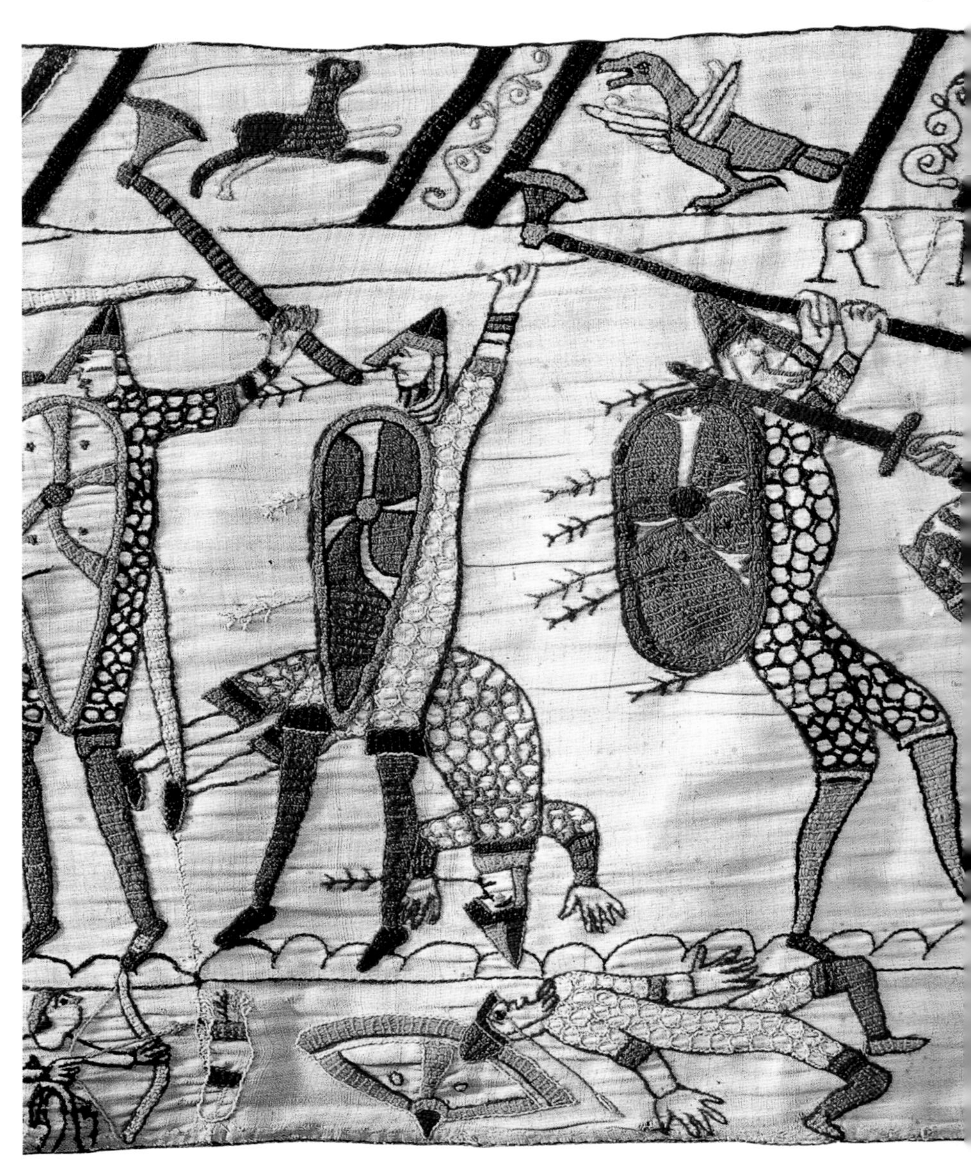

Scene 56

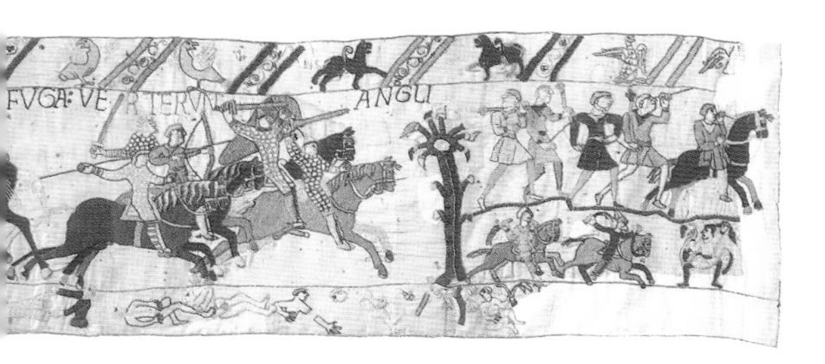

ERANT CUM HAROLDO.

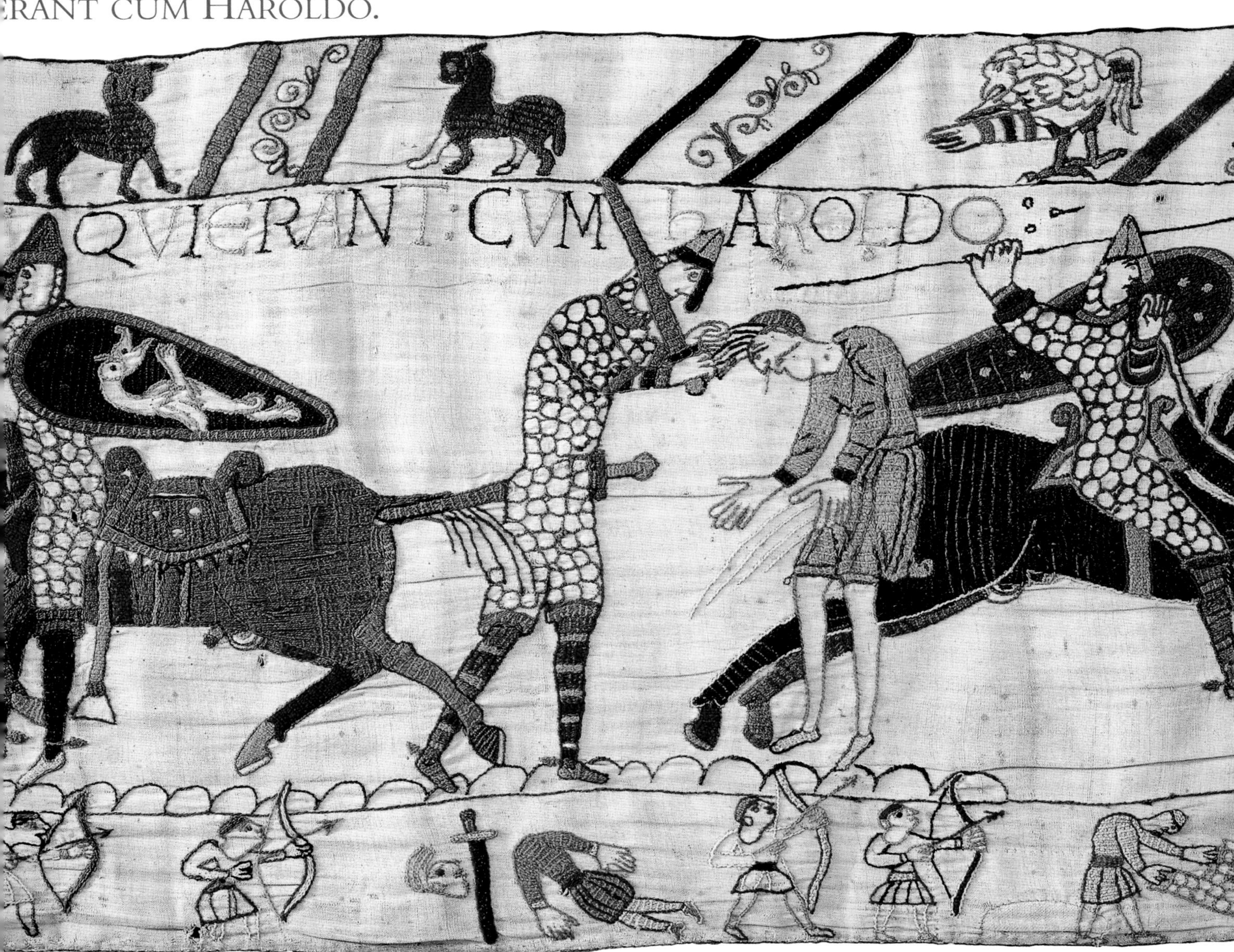

…and those who were with Harold fell.

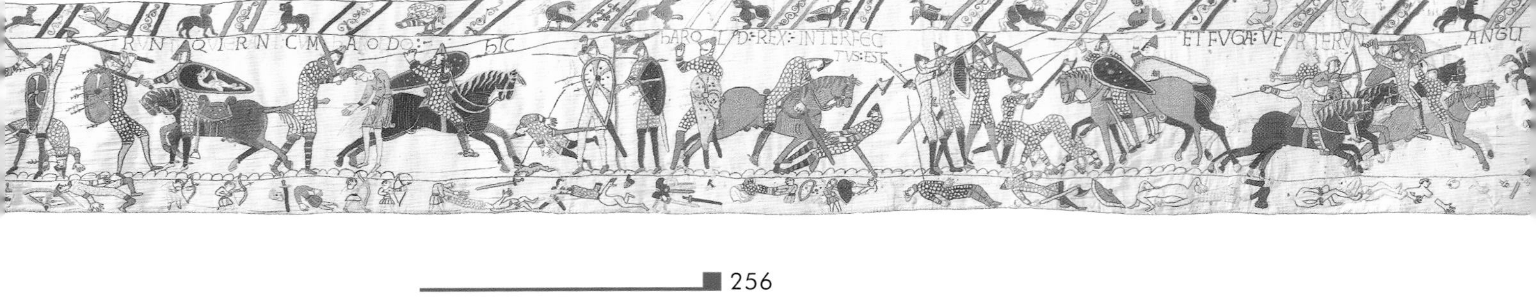

HIC HAROLD REX IN

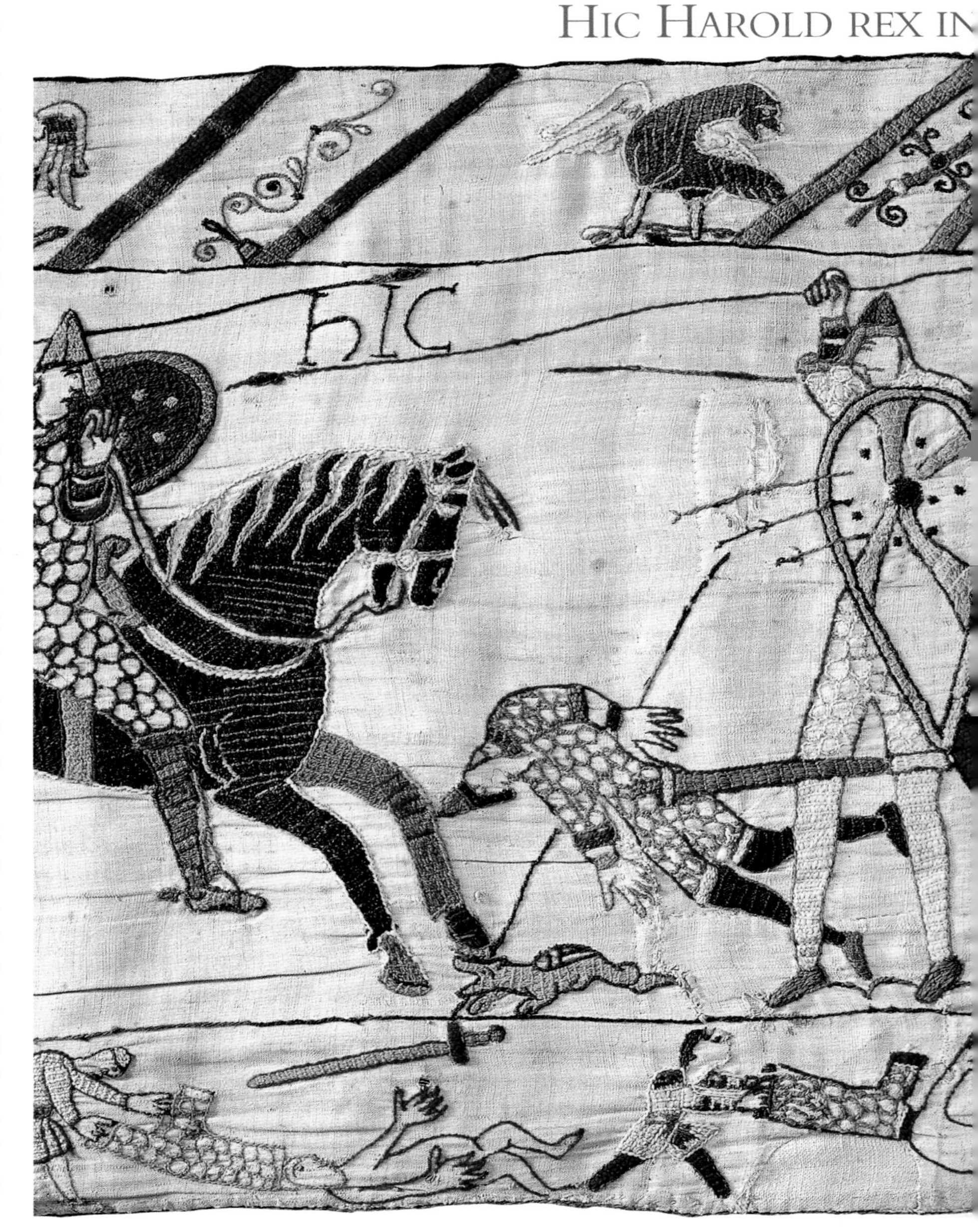

SCENE 57

'HERE KING HAROLD IS SLAIN.' Harold's death sets the seal on the English defeat, though the manner of his death and its depiction on the Tapestry are the subject of much debate. The Tapestry, evidently, implies that his death occurred in the closing stages of the battle, but Orderic Vitalis has the king dying in the first Norman assault.[113] This seems inherently unlikely, however, and William of Poitiers definitely endorses the Tapestry's version. But his chronicle brings together Harold's death with those of his brothers, emphasising that their bodies were found close together (*propius*) afterwards, while the Tapestry apparently separates them by a considerable interval (scenes 52 and 57, pp. 240 and 257).[114] It may be that the designer of the Tapestry has deliberately distorted the real chronology in order to bring out the significance of Harold's death as the logical conclusion of his moral tale.

The crucial question, though, is just how Harold died, and the Tapestry allows three possible answers, depending on which figure is taken to represent the king: the warrior standing directly beneath the name 'Harold', trying to pull an arrow out of his eye; the axe-wielding soldier on the right, cut down with a blow to the thigh by the mounted knight; or, least plausibly, the mounted soldier himself, slumping forward over his horse's neck underneath the word *rex*.

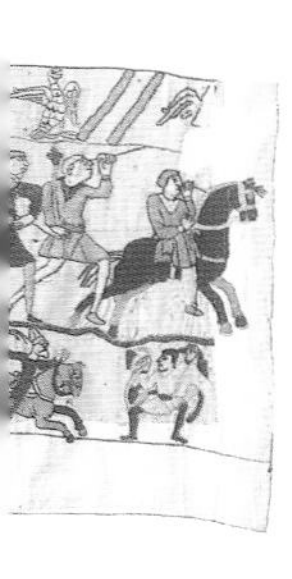

TERFECTUS EST.

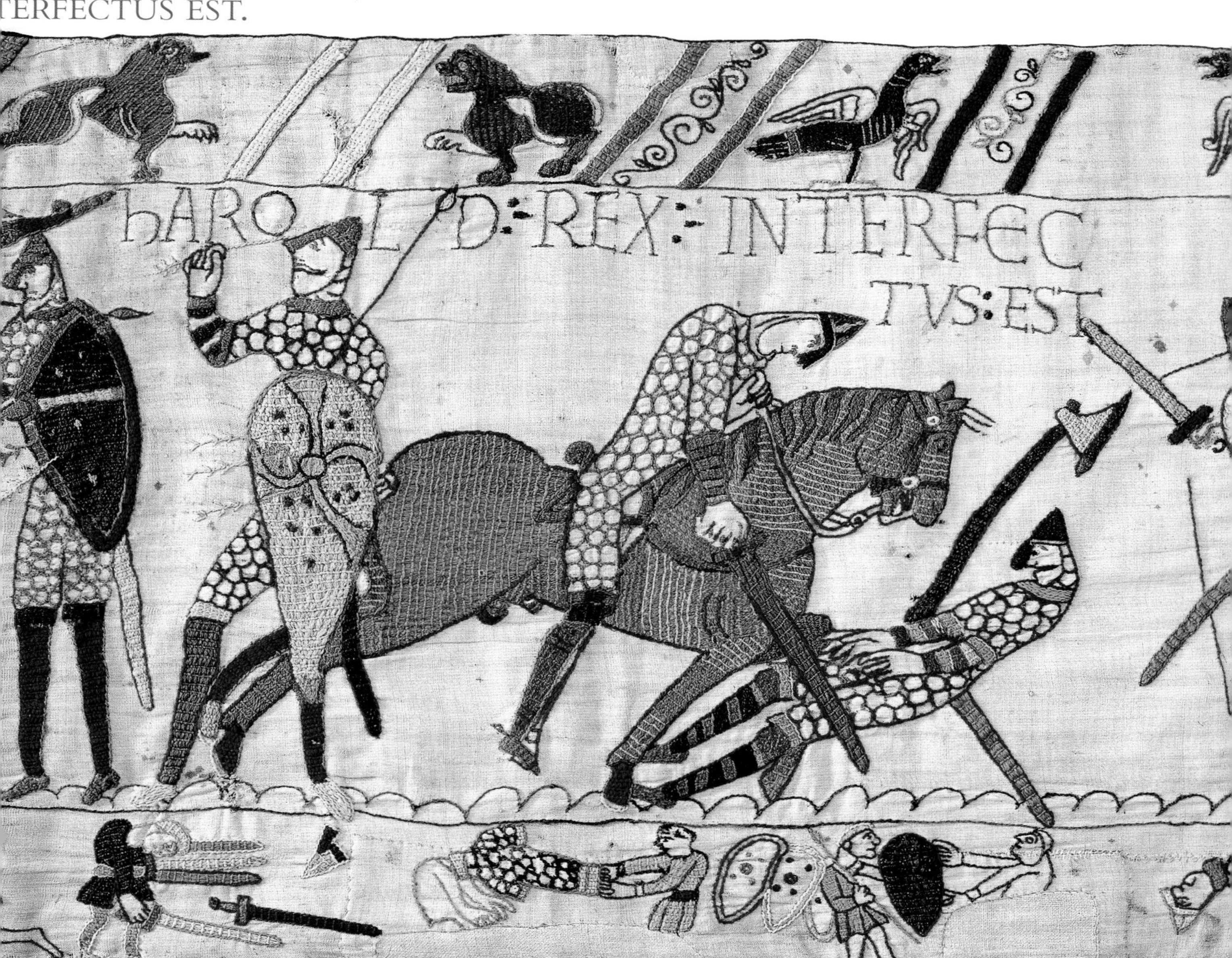

Here King Harold is slain.

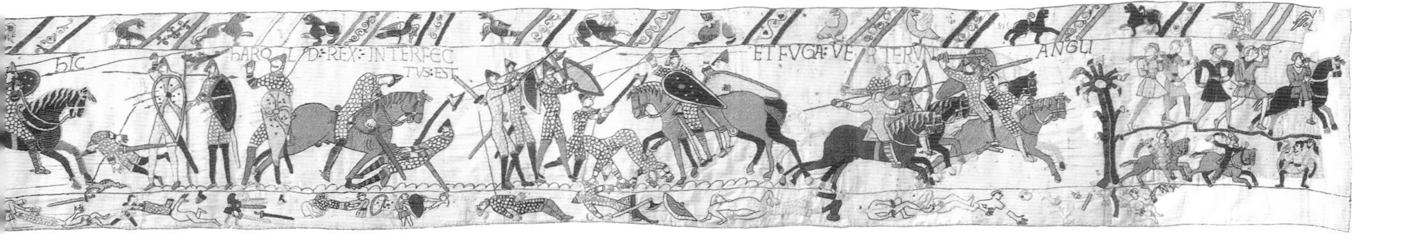

Each of these possibilities has its advocates. As to the first, it must be admitted that the arrow in the eye is without doubt a modern restoration. However, expert examination of the Tapestry at the time of its last move confirmed that the restored needlework is broadly authentic: the needle-holes prove that there was originally something there, though it could perhaps have been a lance. Moreover, an entire strand of the chronicle tradition — Baudry de Bourgueil, William of Malmesbury, Henry of Huntingdon, and Wace — agrees that an arrow in the eye was the cause of Harold's death.[115] But the same tradition adds that after he had been wounded, a knight struck him on the thigh with a sword. It could be that the Tapestry is trying to portray both events in succession: unless, as has also been argued, the chroniclers have conflated in Harold the fates of two distinct people. For the third possibility there is the fact that Harold was shown on horseback earlier in the battle (scene 50, p. 229).

[113] Orderic Vitalis, ed. Chibnall, vol. 2, p. 174: 'in primo militum congressu Haroldus rex peremptus est'.
[114] William of Poitiers, ed. Foreville, p. 204 (Davis and Chibnall, pp. 138-41).
[115] Baudry, ed. Lauer, p. 150, line 463; William of Malmesbury, *De Gestis Regum Anglorum*, ed. Stubbs, vol. 2, p. 303; Henry of Huntingdon, *Historia Anglorum*, ed. Greenway, pp. 394-95. Wace has the arrow strike him some time before his death: Wace, ed. Holden, vol. 2, p. 189, lines 3161-66 and p. 124, lines 8811-18 (Burgess and Van Houts, pp. 183 and 190).

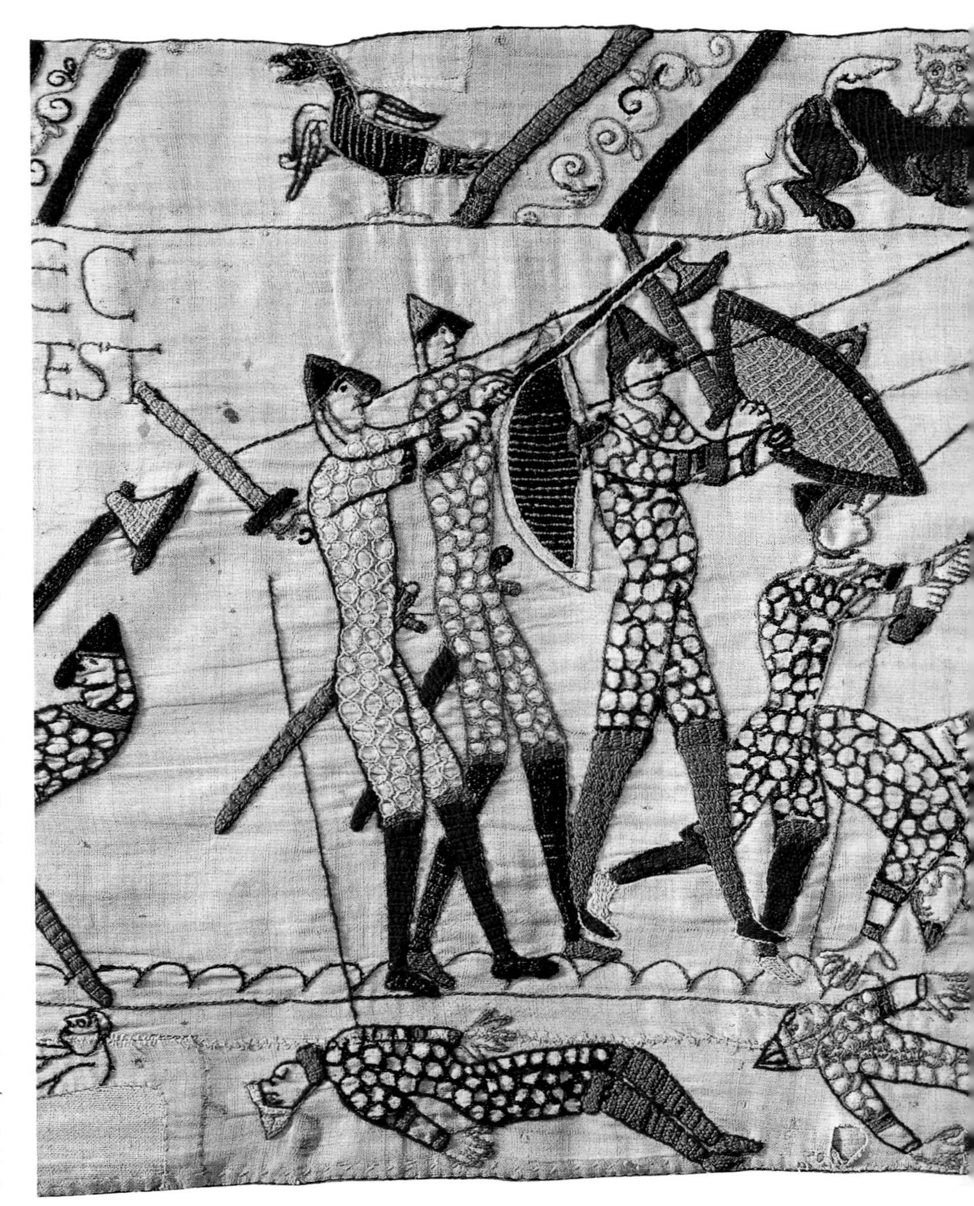

SCENE 57

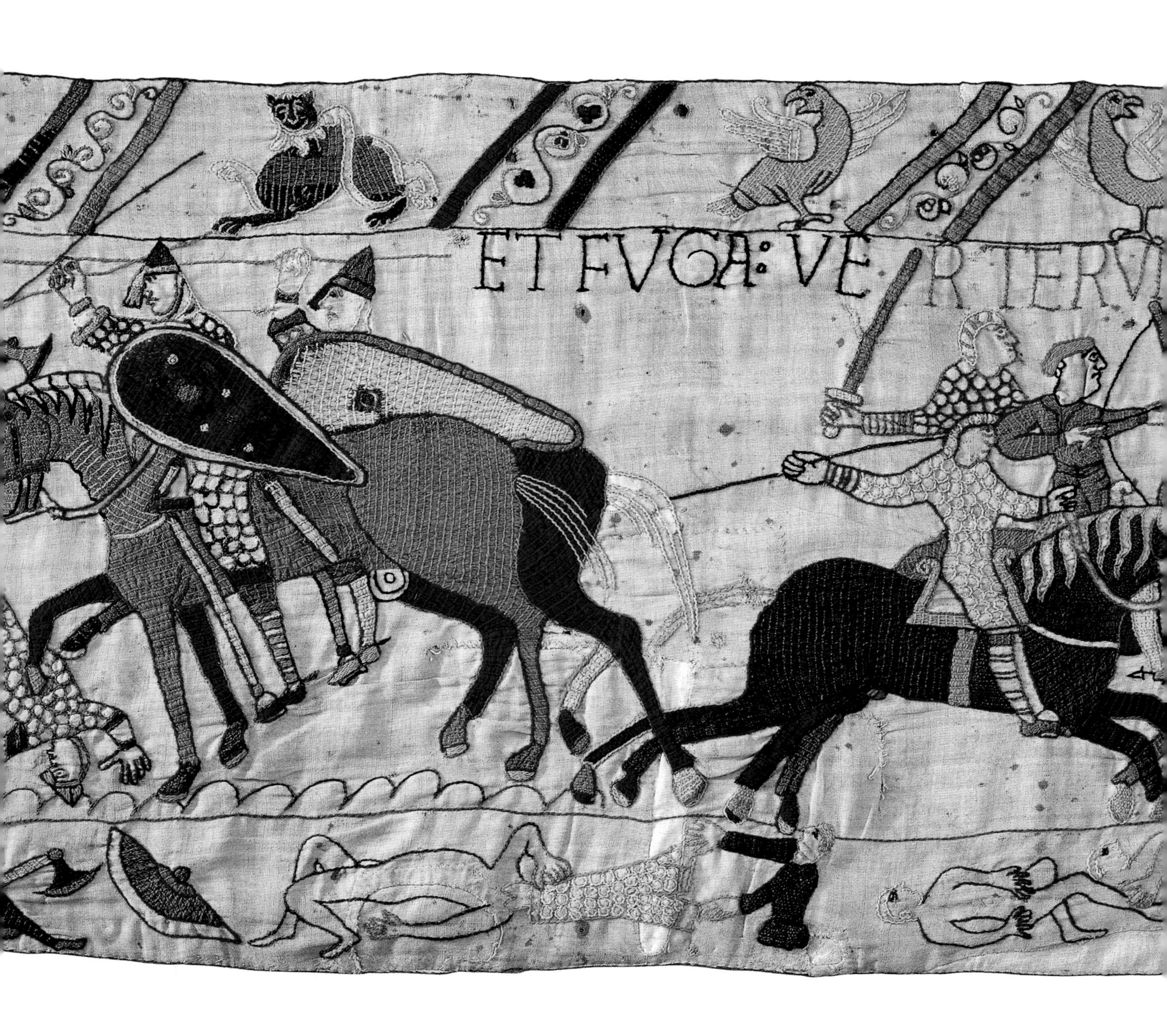
ET FVGA: VE RTERV

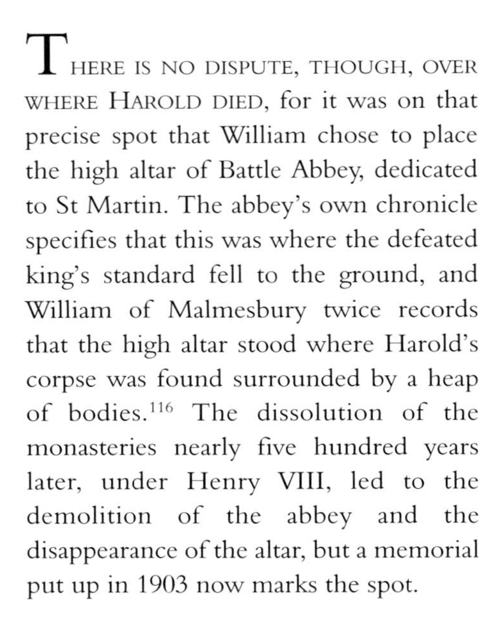

There is no dispute, though, over where Harold died, for it was on that precise spot that William chose to place the high altar of Battle Abbey, dedicated to St Martin. The abbey's own chronicle specifies that this was where the defeated king's standard fell to the ground, and William of Malmesbury twice records that the high altar stood where Harold's corpse was found surrounded by a heap of bodies.[116] The dissolution of the monasteries nearly five hundred years later, under Henry VIII, led to the demolition of the abbey and the disappearance of the altar, but a memorial put up in 1903 now marks the spot.

The figure of the housecarl acting as standard-bearer, right next to the king, is of particular interest. From the top of his lance flies the image of a red dragon. The dragon was frequently used as a battle standard in eleventh-century Scandinavia, usually in the form of an image cut from sheet bronze. Several of these still survive thanks to having later been turned into weathervanes for churches (see above, p. 54). But the chronicles contradict the Tapestry. According to William of Poitiers, Harold's standard was an armed man embroidered in gold thread (which would also imply that it was made from cloth), and William the Conqueror subsequently sent it as a trophy to the pope.[117] But it is doubtful that he had seen it himself. Wace confirms that Harold was next to his standard when he was cut down, but he does not describe it.[118]

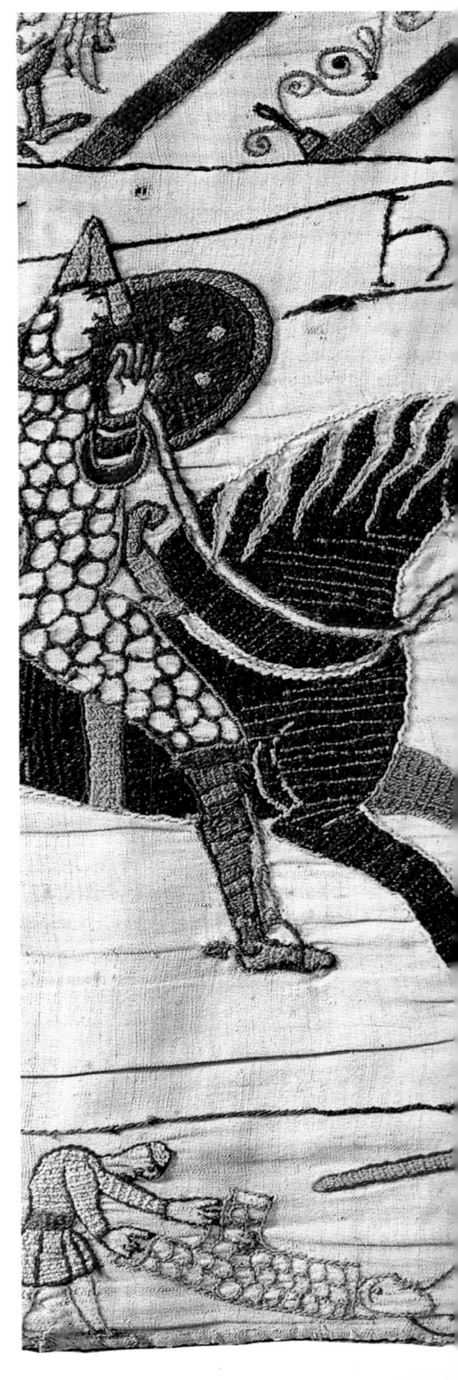

[116] *The Chronicle of Battle Abbey*, ed. E. Searle (Oxford, 1980), p. 44; William of Malmesbury, *Gesta regum*, ed. Stubbs, pp. 326-27, and *Gesta pontificum*, ed. Hamilton, p. 207.
[117] William of Poitiers, ed. Foreville, p. 224 (Davis and Chibnall, pp. 152-53).
[118] Wace, ed. Holden, vol. 2, p. 213, line 8805. Burgess and Van Houts, p. 190.

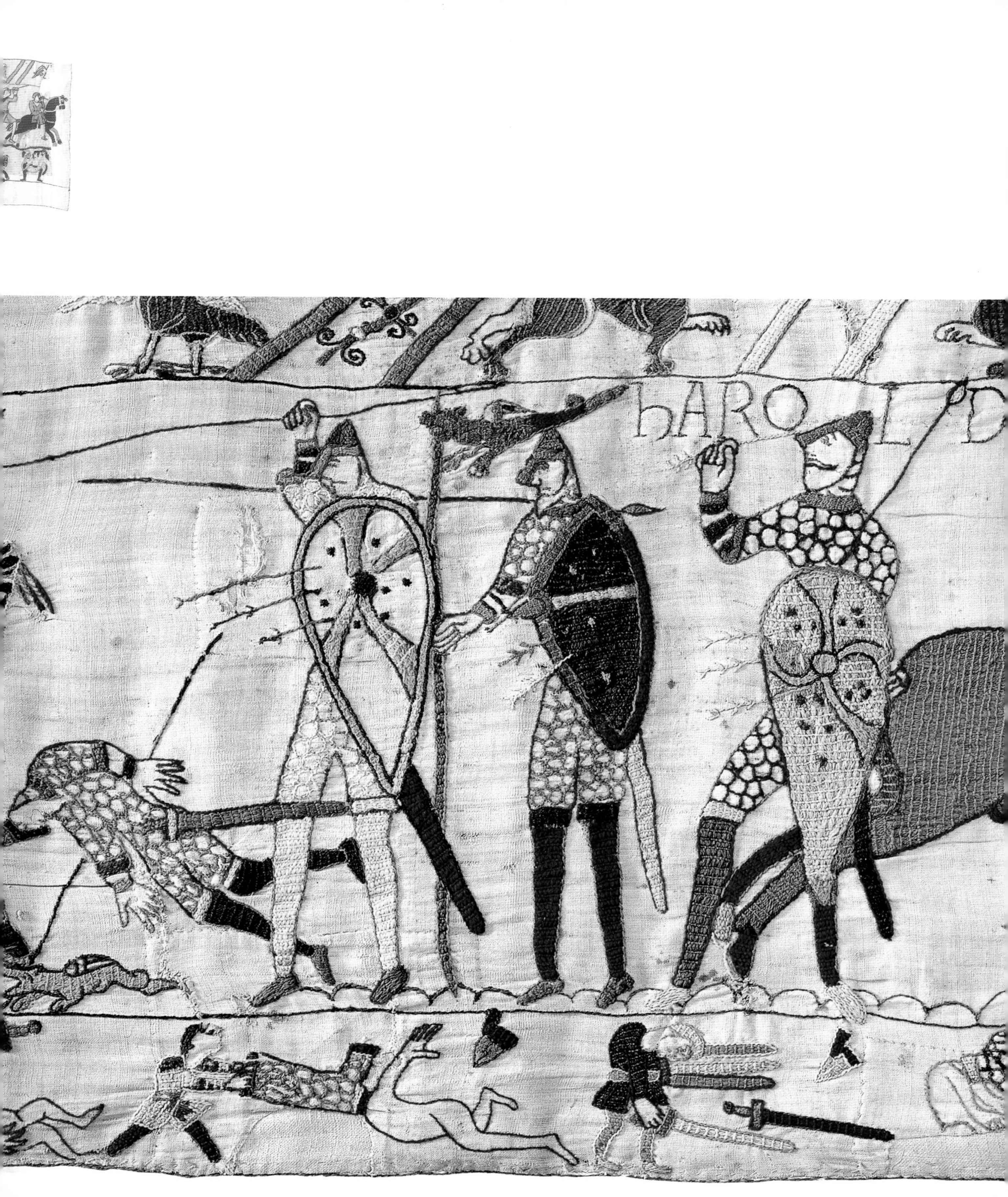
hAROLD

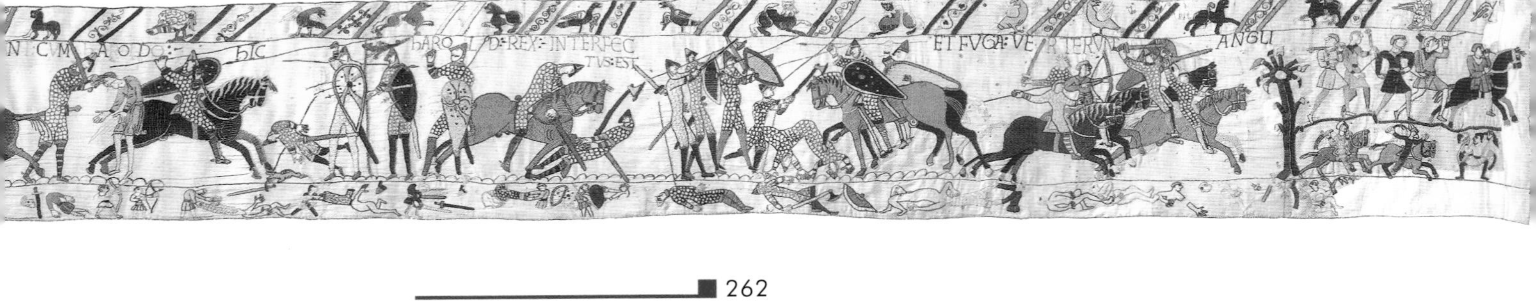

LEGENDS RAPIDLY GREW UP concerning the death and burial of King Harold. One of the strangest is found in the *Carmen de Hastingae proelio*, which says that on the orders of William the mutilated body of the king was wrapped in a purple shroud, taken down to the shore, and, despite the pleas of his mother, buried on a rocky outcrop. It adds that nevertheless an anonymous relative of Harold's, of mixed English and Norman stock, left an inscription there which read: 'By order of the duke you rest here, King Harold, to remain as guardian of the shore and the sea'. As for the rest of the English dead, they were left for the scavengers.[119] Not-withstanding the arguments of Morton and Muntz, who would like to see in this something akin to the pagan funeral rites of a Viking chief, and interpret the rocky outcrop (*rupes*) as a tumulus, the whole thing sounds deeply implausible. William of Poitiers states simply that the body of the king was taken back to William's camp and there entrusted for burial to a Norman lord of perhaps partly English ancestry, William Malet, of Graville-Sainte-Honorine (now part of Le Havre), later made Sheriff of York.[120]

More fanciful still are the legends which tell of the identification of Harold's body on the battlefield by his mistress Edith Swan-Neck (this was a twelfth-century invention), of his survival and subsequent career as a hermit or a pilgrim, or of the transfer of his remains to his own religious foundation at Waltham (later known as Waltham Abbey) in Essex, which from the twelfth century claimed to be the site of his tomb. There may be something in the story that Harold's mother pleaded to be given his body, but was rebuffed. Wace is already persuaded of Harold's burial at Waltham, though he admits on several occasions his ignorance of who it was that killed the king.[121] He also has a story of English noblewomen searching the battlefield for the corpses of husbands, sons, and fathers and then taking them home for burial in local churches.[122] We know that some of the dead Norman barons were taken home for burial, for example Robert Fils Erneis, Seigneur du Cinglais (just south of Caen), who 'on the orders of King William' was laid to rest in the Abbey of Saint-Étienne de Fontenay.[123] The Tapestry, however, provides no evidence for the careful recovery of bodies with a view to decent burial. Its lower borders show altogether less savoury but doubtless more realistic images of the brutal looting and desecration of the dead. Archaeologists have not found any tombs on the site.

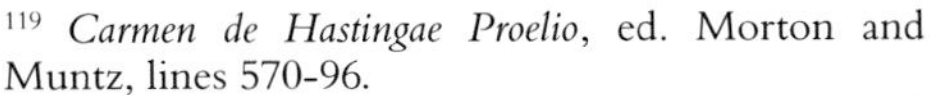

[119] *Carmen de Hastingae Proelio*, ed. Morton and Muntz, lines 570-96.
[120] *Carmen de Hastingae Proelio*, ed. Morton and Muntz, introduction, pp. XLIII-IV. The alleged inscription seems to have been inspired by a passage in William of Poitiers, ed. Foreville, p. 204 (Davis and Chibnall, pp. 140-41) which in context reads more like some mockery of the dead.
[121] Wace, ed. Holden, vol. 2, p. 219, lines 8966-67 (Burgess and Van Houts, p. 192).
[122] Wace, ed. Holden, vol. 2, p. 219, lines 8966-62 (Burgess and Van Houts, p. 192).
[123] According to charter D of Fontenay, drawn up in 1217. See *Gallia Christiana*, t. XI, *instr.* col. 333.

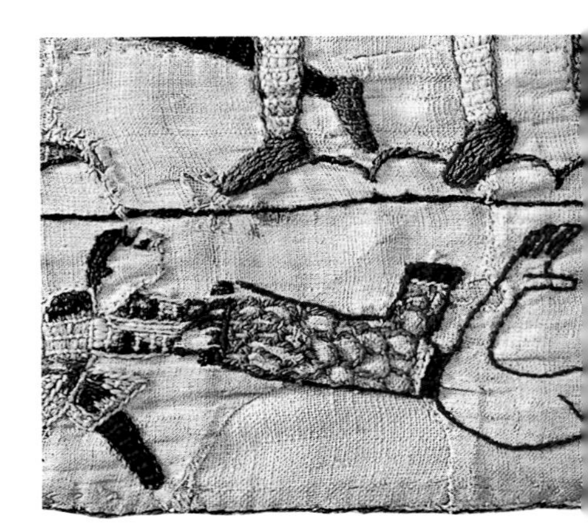

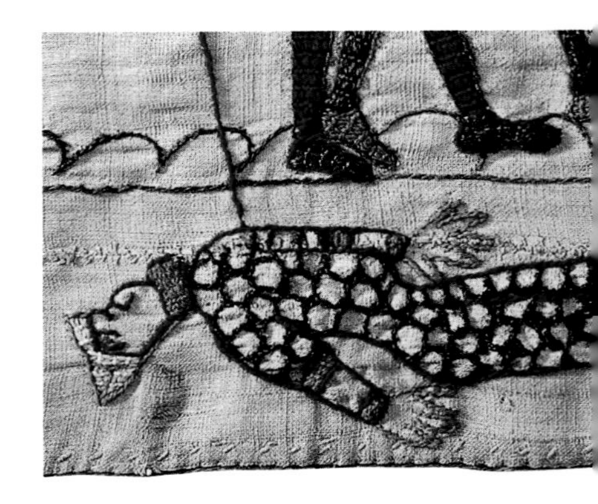

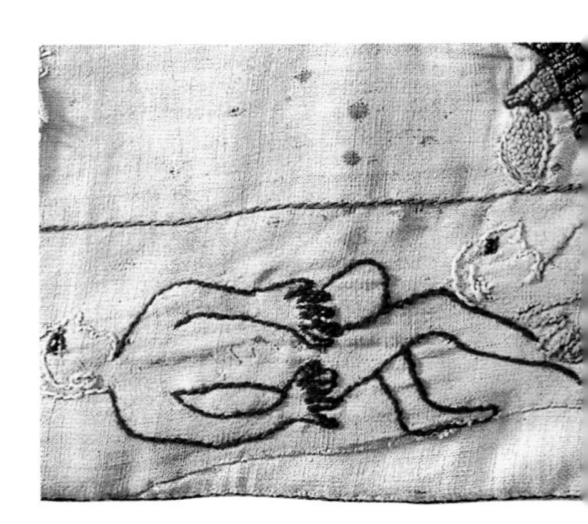

SCENE 57

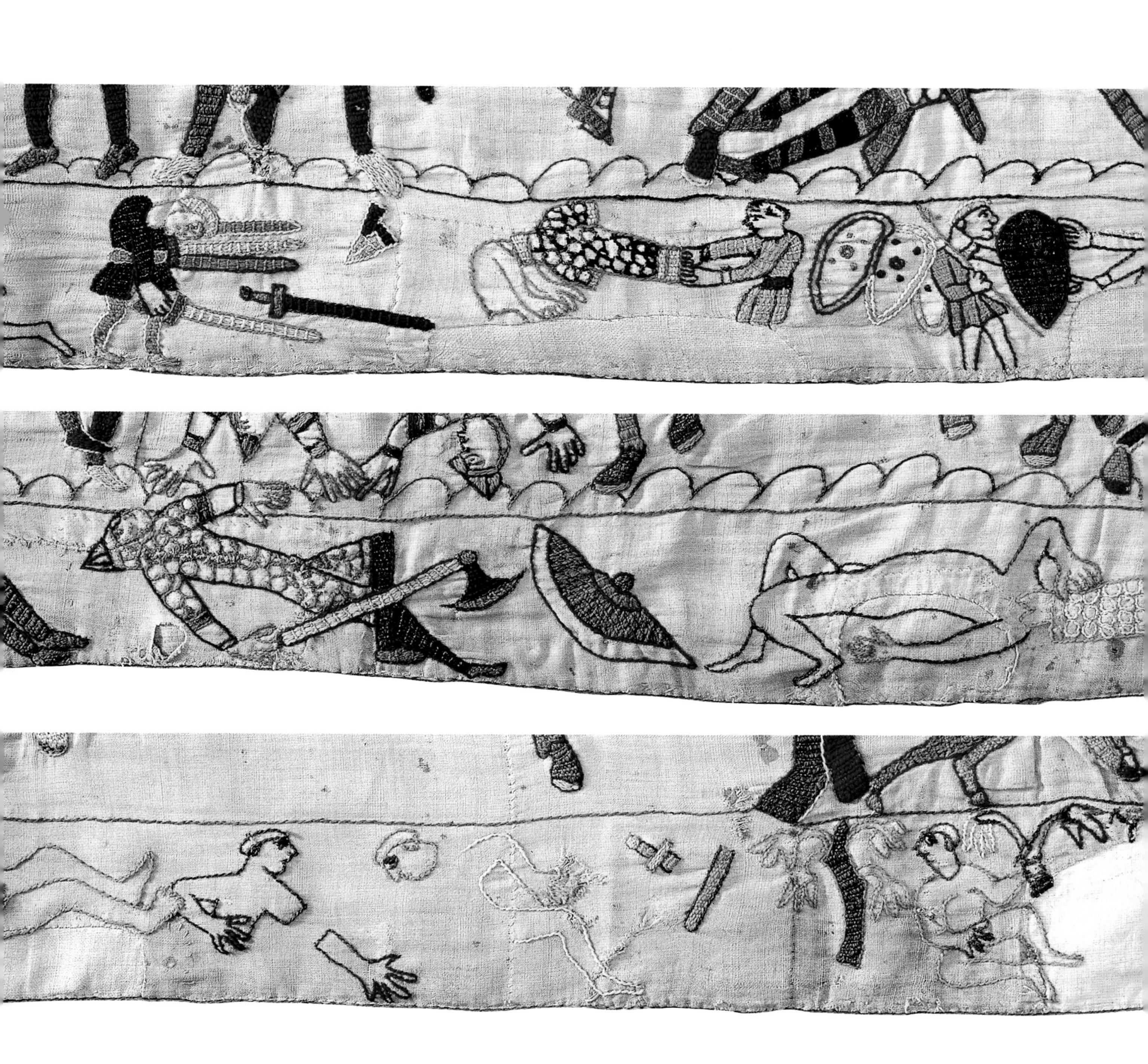

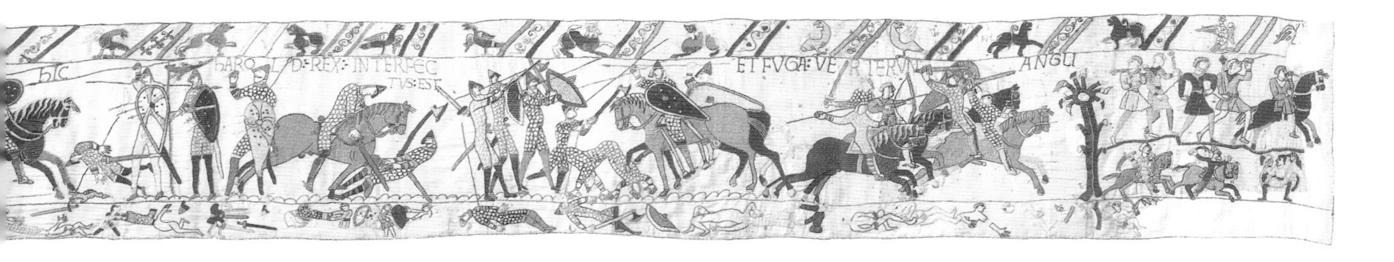

It is worth recapitulating some of the key facts about the battle which thus drew to its close. Experts reckon that the English army did not reach the battlefield until the evening of Friday 13 October, and that the Norman forces did not take up their positions until dawn the following day. Battle was joined at about 09.00, and the English put up fierce resistance until about 17.00. The subsequent butchery went on until nightfall. This was, therefore, a particularly long and bitter struggle, which must have cost thousands of lives. Norman losses are estimated at between a quarter and a third of those present, and English casualties must have been far heavier.

The Normans spent Sunday burying their dead, and then regrouped at Hastings before resuming their advance into England. William headed first for Dover and Canterbury, and then made for Winchester, bypassing but also cutting off London, which he entered by agreement on Christmas Eve. His coronation took place at Westminster on Christmas Day, a little less than a year after Edward's death.

As the battle scenes of the Tapestry likewise draw to a close, it is worth offering a few general observations on them. They lack the slightly exotic touch of the maritime scenes, but it has to be said that they provide some of the most striking images of the realities of war at the dawn of the 'age of chivalry': the realities of blood and butchery but also of almost epic heroism. Today, these images are continually being used to illustrate books on this period of Western European history. That they still manage to retain their freshness is a tribute to the artistic mastery of the Tapestry's creator.

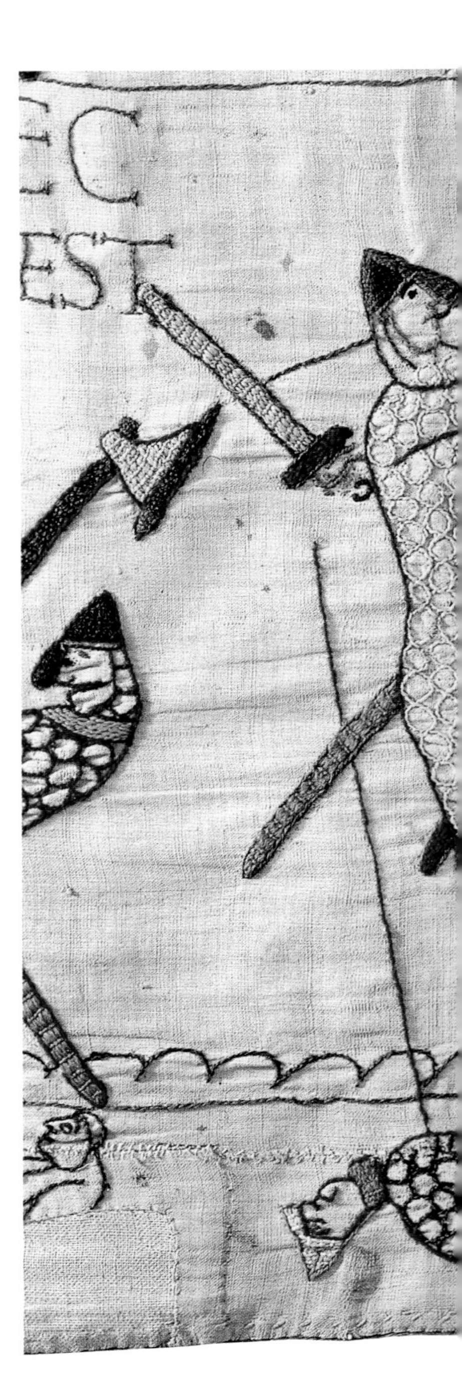

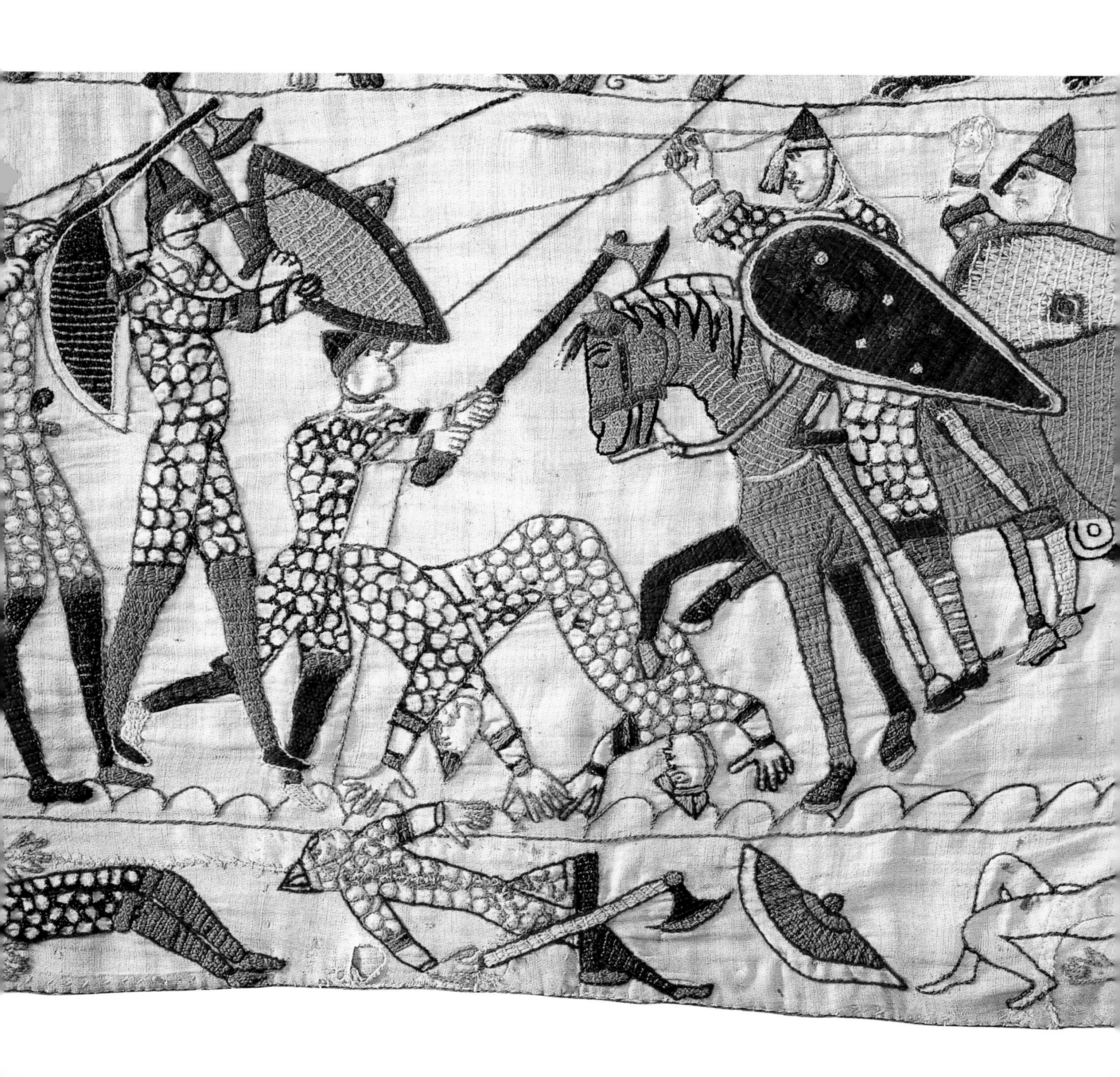

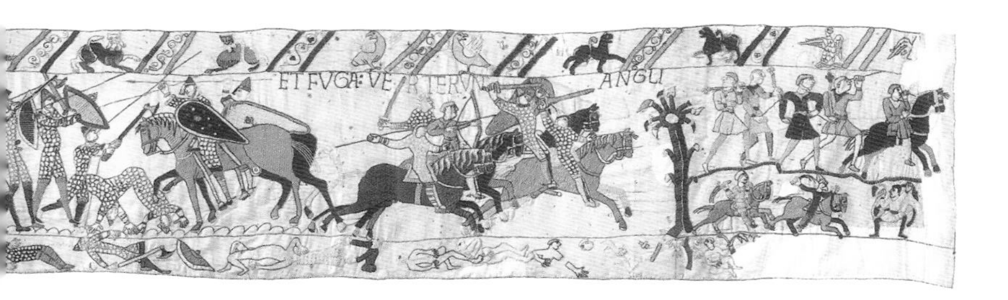

MUCH OF THIS FINAL SCENE OF ROUT is the product of heavy-handed nineteenth-century restoration. Its inscription ('Et fuga verterunt Angli') is entirely spurious, and the tree which separates the hunters from the hunted looks nothing like the rest of the trees on the Tapestry. The unprecedented image of an archer on horseback is somewhat surprising, but seems to be authentic. As for the fleeing Englishmen beyond the tree, scarcely a single detail can be trusted, from the curious headgear of the foremost of the horsemen to the whips with which they urge on their steeds (not to mention the bizarre figure just ahead of them).

The earliest surviving accounts of the Tapestry show that it was already heavily mutilated towards the end, but it is not clear how much has been lost. Montfaucon's eighteenth-century engraving shows it stopping at much the same point as today, though without the horseman right at the end and several of the images in the upper border, and with the other figures barely visible as outlines. The text at that time ended with the words 'interfectus est', and Ducarel explicitly observes that after these words 'the inscriptions are completely erased'.[124] There is no sign here of any such vertical border as is seen at the beginning (though that is itself essentially a modern restoration).

Personally, I doubt that there was much more on the original Tapestry. Harold's death, the just deserts of his perjury, is the logical end to the story. It has often been suggested that there should have been a final image of William seated in majesty on the throne of England.[125] This idea derives from a reading of the Tapestry's theme as essentially historical rather than religious, and rests on two main arguments. The first is from symmetry: an image of William crowned at the end would match that of Edward at the beginning. The second is from the rather questionable source that is Baudry de Bourgueil's account of the hangings in Countess Adela's chamber, which closes with a rather vague evocation of the coronation on 25 December 1066. But his narrative of events from Harold's death to the coronation is nothing but empty rhetoric. If indeed he did see the Bayeux Tapestry, he saw nothing notable on it beyond what we see today. And even if perhaps this one conjecture about a coronation scene were correct, we would still have lost nothing of great significance.

[124] Montfaucon, *Monumens de la Monarchie Françoise*, vol. 2, p. 6.
[125] This hypothesis was first canvassed by Montfaucon, *Monumens de la Monarchie Françoise*, vol. 2, p. 3.

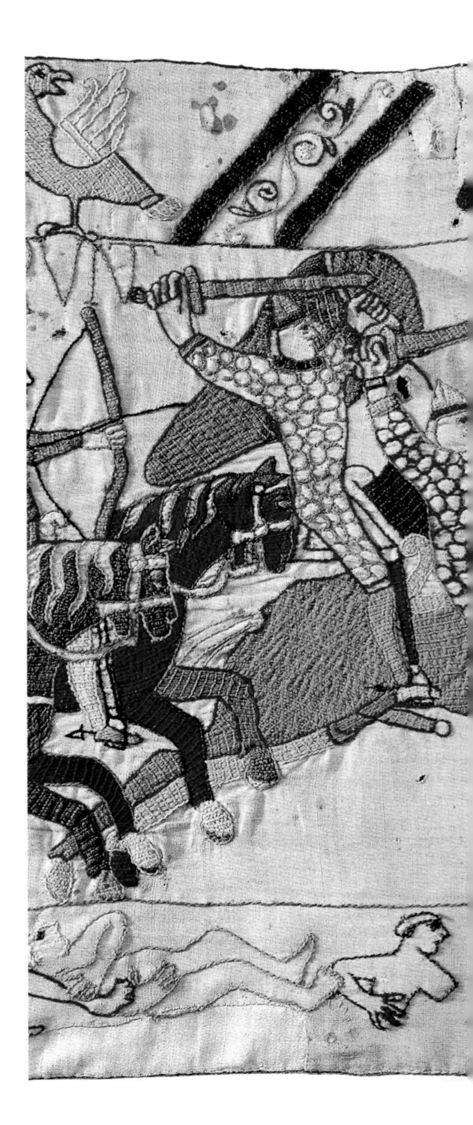

SCENE 58

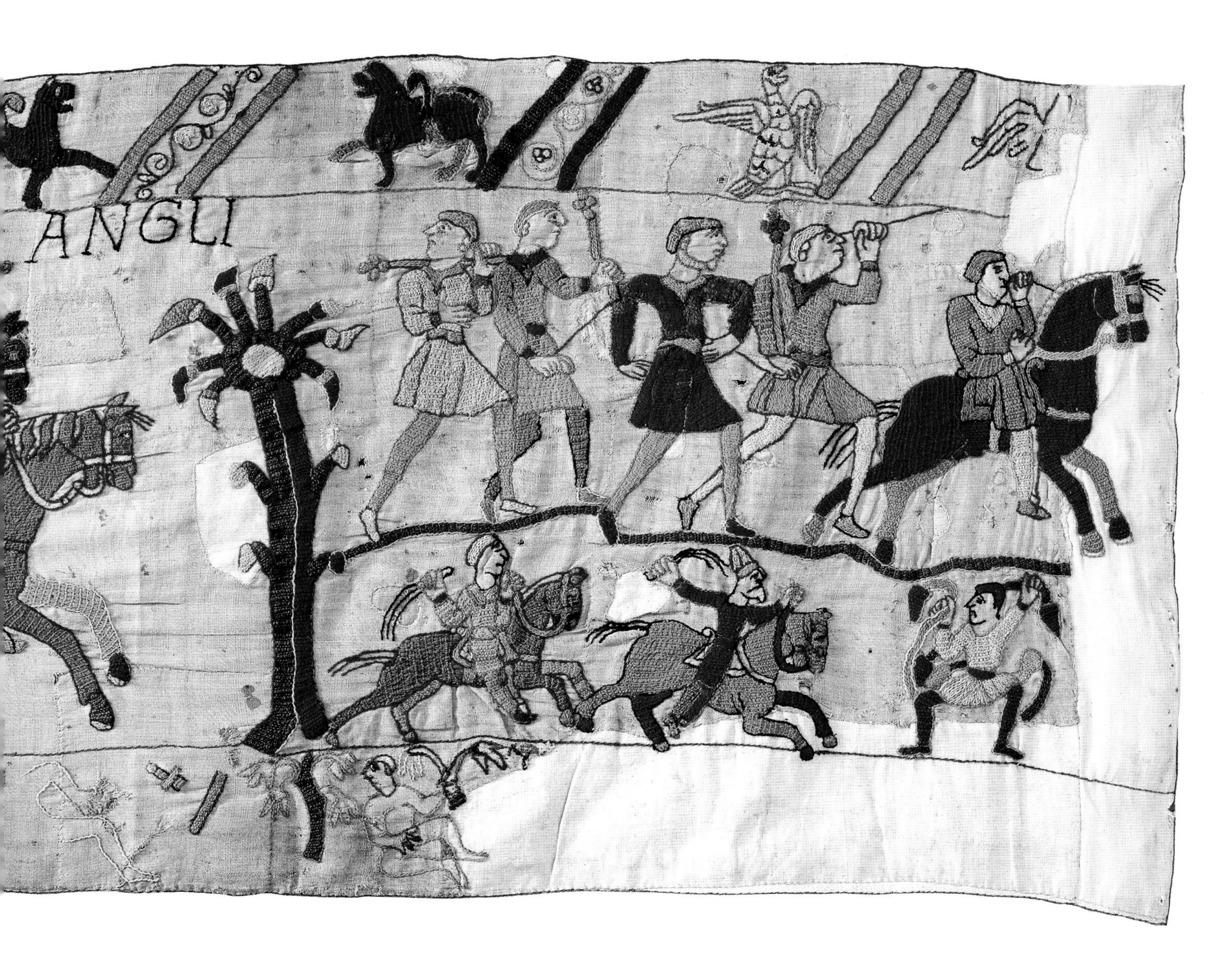
ANGLI

A. The Norman and English Dynasties

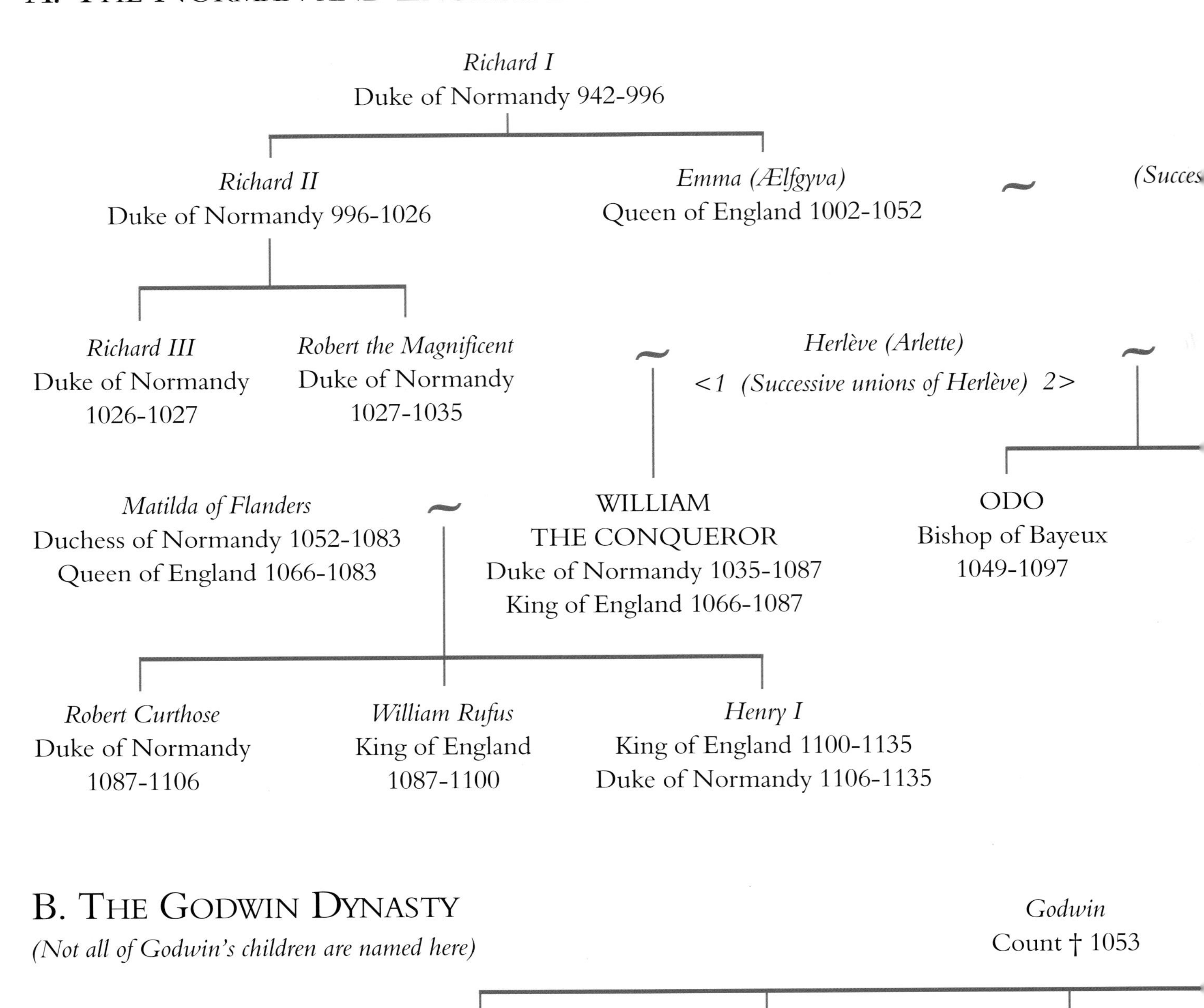

B. The Godwin Dynasty

(Not all of Godwin's children are named here)

Godwin
Count † 1053

EDWARD
THE CONFESSOR
King of England
1042-1066

~

Edith
Queen of England
1045-1075

HAROLD II
King of England 1066
(Count 1053-1066)

Tosti
Count of Northumbria
† 1066

GENEALOGICAL TABLES

Names in CAPITALS are of persons named in the captions of the Tapestry

Names in *italics* are those of their ancestors, descendants, or relatives not named on the Tapestry

The date-ranges represent regnal dates

~ : indicates a marriage or relationship

† : indicates a date of death

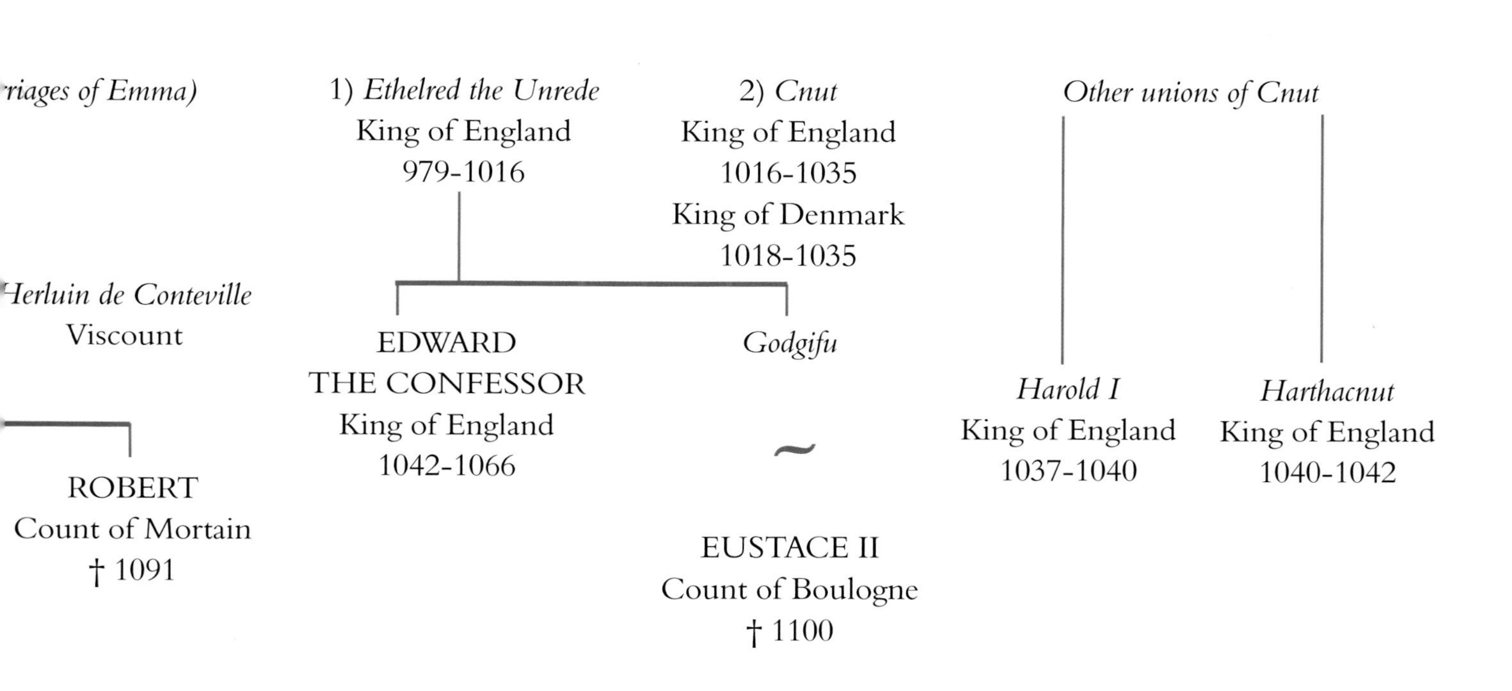

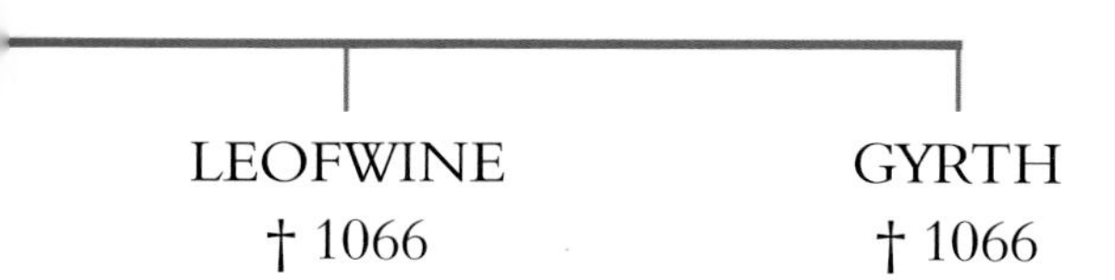

The Complete Text of the Captions

Eadwardus rex. (U)bi Harold dux Anglorum et sui milites equitant ad Bosham. Ecclesia. Hic Harold mare navigavit et velis vento plenis venit in terra Widonis comitis. Harold. Hic apprehendit Wido Haroldum et duxit eum ad Belrem et ibi eum tenuit. (U)bi Harold et Wido parabolant. Ubi nuntii Willelmi ducis venerunt ad Widonem. Turold. Nuntii Willelmi. + Hic venit nuntius ad Wilgelmum ducem. Hic Wido adduxit Haroldum ad Wilgelmum Normannorum ducem. Hic dux Wilgelm cum Haroldo venit ad palatium suum. Ubi unus clericus et Ælfgyva. Hic Willelm dux et exercitus ejus venerunt ad Montem Michaelis, et hic transierunt flumen Cosnonis et venerunt ad Dol. Hic Harold dux trahebat eos de arena. Et Conan fuga vertit. Rednes. Hic milites Willelmi ducis pugnant contra Dinantes et Cunan claves porrexit. Hic Willelm dedit Haroldo arma. Hie! Willelm venit Bagias. Ubi Harold sacramentum fecit Willelmo duci. Hic Harold dux reversus est ad Anglicam terram et venit ad Edwardum regem. Hic portatur corpus Eadwardi regis ad ecclesiam Sancti Petri apostoli. (Hic) Eadwardus rex in lecto alloquitur fideles, et hic defunctus est. Hic dederunt Haroldo coronam regis. Hic residet Harold rex Anglorum. Stigant archiepiscopus. Isti mirant stella(m). Harold. Hic navis anglica venit in terram Willelmi ducis. Hic Willelm dux jussit naves edificare. Hic trahunt naves ad mare. Isti portant armas ad naves et hic trahunt carrum cum vino et armis. + Hic Willelm dux in magno navigio mare transivit et venit ad Pevenesæ. Hic exeunt caballi de navibus. Et hic milites festinaverunt Hestinga ut cibum raperentur. Hic est Wadard. Hic coquitur caro et hic ministraverunt ministri. Hic fecerunt prandium et hic episcopus cibu(m) et potum benedicit. Odo episcopus. Willelm. Rotbert. Iste jussit ut foderetur castellum « at Hestenga ceastra ». Hic nuntiatum est Willelmo de Harold. Hic domus incenditur. Hic milites exierunt de Hestenga et venerunt ad prelium contra Haroldum rege(m). Hic Willelm dux interrogat Vital si vidisset exercitum Haroldi. Iste nuntiat Haroldum de exercitu Willelmi ducis. Hic Willelm dux alloquitur suis militibus ut prepararent se viriliter et sapienter ad prelium contra Anglorum exercitum. Hic ceciderunt Lewine et Gyrt fratres Haroldi regis. (H)ic ceciderunt simul Angli et Franci in prelio. Hic Odo episcopus baculum tenens confortat pueros. Hic est Willelm dux. E(usta)tius. Hic Franci pugnant et ceciderunt qui erant cum Haroldo. Hic Harold rex interf(ec)tus est.

King Edward. Where Harold, Duke of the English, and his knights ride to Bosham. The church. Here Harold sailed by sea and with wind-filled sails arrived in the land of Count Wido. Here Wido apprehended Harold and took him to Beaurain and held him there. Where Harold and Wido parlay. Where messengers of Duke William came to Wido. Turold. William's messengers. + Here a messenger comes to Duke William. Here Wido took Harold to William, Duke of the Normans. Here Duke William came with Harold to his palace. Where one cleric and Ælfgyva. Here Duke William and his army came to Mont (Saint) Michel, and here they crossed the River Couesnon and came to Dol. Here Duke Harold dragged them from the sand. And Conan turned and fled. Rennes. Here Duke William's knights fight against Dinan and Conan hands over the keys. Here William gave arms to Harold. Here William came to Bayeux. Where Harold took an oath to Duke William. Here Duke Harold returned to the English land and came to King Edward. Here the corpse of King Edward is borne to the church of the Apostle Saint Peter. Here King Edward speaks with his followers on his bed, and here he died. Here they gave the king's crown to Harold. Here sits Harold, King of the English. Archbishop Stigand. They wonder at the star. Harold. Here an English ship comes to the land of Duke William. Here Duke William ordered ships to be built. Here they drag the ships to the sea. These men carry weapons to the ships and here they drag a cart laden with wine and weapons. + Here Duke William crossed the sea in a great ship and came to Pevensey. Here the horses leave the ships. And here the knights hurried to Hastings to get food. Here is Wadard. Here meat is cooked and here servants serve it. Here they have a meal and here the bishop blesses the food and drink. Bishop Odo. William. Robert. The latter ordered that a castle should be dug at Hastings. Here William is told about Harold. Here a house is burned. Here knights leave Hastings and came to fight against King Harold. Here Duke William asks Vital if he had seen Harold's army. He tells Harold about Duke William's army. Here Duke William tells his soldiers to prepare themselves manfully and wisely for the battle against the army of the English. Here fell Leofwyne and Gyrth, King Harold's brothers. Here English and French fell together in the fight. Here Bishop Odo, holding his staff, encourages the lads. Here is Duke William. Eustace. Here the French fight and those who were with Harold fell. Here King Harold is slain.

Select Bibliography

It has been decided to list only a few essential titles, mainly post 1945. Other title information appears in the appropriate areas of the notes to the two sections.

I. EDITIONS

J. Verrier, *La broderie de Bayeux dite Tapisserie de la reine Mathilde,* Paris, 1946.

E. Maclagan, *The Bayeux Tapestry,* London, 1953 (paperback).

Sir Frank Stenton, ed., *The Bayeux Tapestry,* London, 1957; French translation, Paris n.d. (scholarly commentary).

S. Bertrand, *La Tapisserie de Bayeux et la manière de vivre au XIe siècle,* éditions Zodiaque, La Pierre-qui-Vire, 1968.

M. Parisse, *La Tapisserie de Bayeux, Un documentaire du XIe siècle,* Paris, 1983.

D.M. Wilson, ed., *The Bayeux Tapestry,* London, 1985, French translation, Paris, 1985 (scholarly edition).

II. STUDIES

A.Marignan, *La Tapisserie de Bayeux,* Paris, 1902.

A. Levé, *La Tapisserie de la reine Mathilde dite la la Tapisserie de Bayeux,* Paris, 1919.

R.N. Sauvage, 'La Tapisserie de la reine Mathilde à Bayeux', *Bibliothèque de l'École des Chartes,* LXXXII, 1921, pp. 157–165.

H. Prentout, 'La Conquête de l'Angleterre par les Normands. Les sources. I. La Tapisserie de Bayeux', *Revue des Cours et Conférences,* XXIII, 1922, 15 April, pp. 16–29.

R.S. Loomis, 'The origin and date of the Bayeux embroidery', *The Art Bulletin,* VI, September 1923.

H. Prentout, 'Essai d'identification des personnages inconnus de la Tapisserie de Bayeux', *Revue historique,* CLXXV, 1936, pp. 14–23.

L. Musset, 'Récentes contributions scandinaves à l'exégèse de la Tapisserie de Bayeux', *Bull. de la Soc. des Antiquaires de Normandie,* LI, 1948–1951, pp. 275-279.

F. Barlow, *Edward the Confessor and the Norman Conquest,* Hastings, Bexhill, 1966, 15 pp.

F. Barlow 'The Carmen de Hastingae proelio', *Studies in International History,* ed. K. Bourne and D.C. Watts, London, 1967, pp. 35–67.

N.P. Brooks and H.E. Walker, 'The authority and interpretation of the Bayeux Tapestry', *Battle,* I, 1978, pp. 1–34.

J.Y. Tilliette, 'La chambre de la comtesse Adèle…', *Romania,* CII, 1981, pp. 145–171.

S.A. Brown, *The Bayeux Tapestry: History and Bibliography,* Woodbridge, 1989.

R. Gameson, ed., *The Study of the Bayeux Tapestry,* Woodbridge,1997 (12 articles originally published between 1821 and 1994).

III. HISTORICAL BACKGROUND

Sir Frank Stenton, *Anglo-Saxon England, c. 550-1087,* Oxford, 1943 (3rd edition, 1971).

H.R.Loyn, *Anglo-Saxon England and the Norman Conquest,* London, 1962.

*D.C. Douglas, *William the Conqueror,* London, 1964.

J. Le Patourel, *Norman barons,* Hastings, Bexhill, 1966.

D. Whitelock, D.C. Douglas, Ch. M. Lemmon, F. Barlow, *The Norman Conquest. Its setting and impact,* London, 1966.

*F. Barlow, *Edward the Confessor,* London, 1970.

R. Allen Brown, 'The Battle of Hastings', *Battle* III, 1980, pp. 1–21.

J.L. Nelson, 'The rites of the Conqueror', *Battle,* IV, 1981, pp. 117–139.

*R .Allen Brown, *The Normans,* Woodbridge, 1984.

*M. de Boüard, *Guillaume le Conquérant,* Paris, 1984.

L. Musset, 'Prestige des siècles romans en Normandie', *Art de Basse-Normandie,* 1985, no. 92, pp. 5–14.

G. Garnett, 'Coronation and Propaganda. Some implications of the Norman claim to the throne of England in 1066', *Transactions of the Royal Historical Society,* 5th series, XXXVI, 1986, pp. 91–116.

S.T. Morillo, *Battle of Hastings: Sources and interpretation,* Woodbridge, 1996 (selection of annotated texts; debatable).

L. Musset, *Nordica et Normannica,* Paris, 1997 (collected studies on early Scandinavia and the formation of Normandy).

The Gesta Guillelmi of William of Poitiers, ed. and trans. by R.H.C. Davies and M. Chibnall, 'Oxford Medieval Texts', Oxford, 1998.

*Asterisked works are essential reading.

Sources of the illustrations

All photographs of the Tapestry belong to the Ville de Bayeux, except the following illustrations:

Antikvarisk-topograiska arkivet, The National Heritage Board, Stockholm: p. 59 (photographer Harald Faith, 1933).
The Bridgeman Art Library, Paris: pp. 29 and 30.
G. Dagli Orti, Paris: pp. 48, 52 top and bottom.
Scala, Florence: pp. 31 and 32.
Photothèque Zodiaque: pp. 22, 24–25, 27, 28 centre, 58 and 68.
Drawings by Brother Noël Deney, from documents supplied by the author: pp. 20, 21, 28 top and bottom, 54, 63, 70, 152–153 and 168.
Photoengraving, Edilog, Paris